THE PACIFIC SLOPE

A History

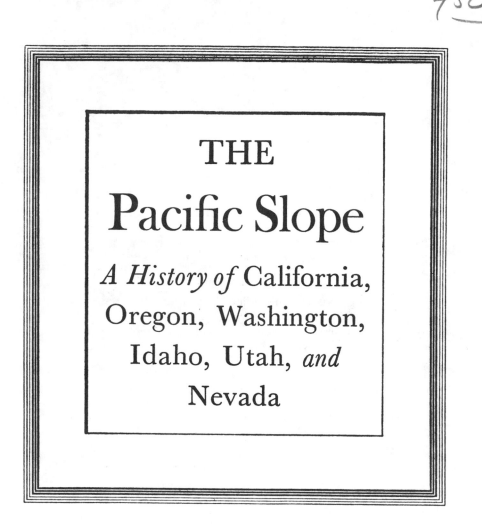

THE Pacific Slope

A History of California, Oregon, Washington, Idaho, Utah, *and* Nevada

by Earl Pomeroy

University of Nebraska Press
Lincoln and London

Manufactured in the United States of America

First Bison Book printing: 1991
Most recent printing indicated by the last digit below:
10 9 8 7 6 5 4 3 2 1

Library of Congress Cataloging-in-Publication Data
Pomeroy, Earl S. (Earl Spencer), 1915–
The Pacific slope: history of California, Oregon, Washington, Idaho, Utah, and Nevada / by Earl Pomeroy.
p. cm.
Reprint. Originally published: New York: Knopf, 1965.
Includes bibliographical references and index.
ISBN 0-8032-8729-1
1. Northwest, Pacific—History. 2. Southwest, New—History. I. Title.
F851.P57 1992
979—dc20
91-19101

Reprinted by arrangement with Earl Pomeroy

PREFACE

MANY HISTORIES of the Far West devote more space to explorers who came when almost no one else was there than to the Western society that men now living can remember, though memories still reach over most of the area's recorded history. The charm and significance of beginnings is undeniable, especially of beginnings that had ends, beginnings that began more than themselves. Yet conventional emphasis leaves a large part of the story untold, even the story of people who accept conventions. I have tried to focus on men and events that explain the West as a developing community, emphasizing traits and institutions. The early years need not lose meaning if we traverse them at more than the speed of an immigrant's oxcart, the later years at less than the speed of a jet-propelled aircraft.

Deciding what areas belong in a survey of the Pacific slope becomes difficult as soon as it reaches beyond one state. Congress paid little attention to Western geography or to Westerners when it divided the map. In some states, the people have had no more unity than the experience of living together under a common state government has given them. The metropolises of Idaho are Spokane and Salt Lake City; in Nevada you need say no more than "the city" when you mean San Francisco, except in Las Vegas, which is a recreational suburb of Los Angeles. Both Idaho and Nevada were accidents of Civil War politics and of overenthusiasm for an ephemeral industry; economically and socially they are adjuncts of their neighbors. Utah appears here partly because it has to appear somewhere, but with considerable justification: like San Francisco Bay, the Great Salt Lake lay beyond a belt of rugged wilderness, out of overland contact with organized American society at the beginning, and it figured intimately in the fur trade of the Columbia River country and in the overland migration to Oregon and California. The

Mormon state of Deseret claimed both "eastern California" (Utah and Nevada) and much of what became known as southern California; and until 1861 the territory of Utah extended to the Sierra Nevada. Idaho and California have more Mormons than Utah's other neighbors. Ogden is the Eastern outpost of the old Central Pacific Railroad empire, whose capital was San Francisco; Salt Lake City is a junction for several transportation systems whose rate structures dictate that Colorado trade with Chicago and St. Louis, Utah with San Francisco and Los Angeles. Congress has recognized Utah's economic connections with the coast by assigning it to the jurisdictions of the Federal Reserve, Land, and Immediate Credit banks based on San Francisco Bay. (On the other hand, both Idaho and Utah stand apart from the coast in much of their social and political behavior.) Arizona resembles the states to the west and north, especially now that Phoenix has become a kind of inland San Diego; but pioneer Arizona looked more to New Mexico than to the coast, and in becoming more like southern California it has found no great need for fellowship and traffic with it. Furthermore, any grouping has to stop somewhere, and I see no reason to duplicate Gene Hollon's account of *The Southwest: Old and New*;[1] he knows it far better than I do.

Within the area of six Far Western states—California, Idaho, Nevada, Oregon, Utah, and Washington—I emphasize the regions that have had the largest populations, both because I am writing history rather than physical geography and because they have left the fullest records. California looms large in any story of the Far West, however conceived: there have been many Californians (in 1964, as in 1860, the state had about three times as many inhabitants as had the other five states combined), and in California the West has come to focus. The history of California is the quintessence alike of romance and of prophecy. Whatever the neighboring states were, they were in large part beecause it served as catalyst, banker, and base of operations; and much of what it was depended on the tribute they paid. "What America is to Europe, what Western America is to Eastern," wrote Lord Bryce, "that California is to the other Western States."[2] As an apostatized Californian, I know how easy it is to dwell too much on the metropolis and also how much its history contains that I have not told, going back to what I first heard

[1] W. Eugene Hollon: *The Southwest: Old and New* (New York: Alfred A. Knopf; 1961).

[2] James Bryce: *The American Commonwealth* (London: Macmillan and Co.; 1889), Vol. II, p. 372.

from a neighbor who came with the Donner party and from relatives born there during the gold rush, including some of Mexican descent. All that can fit between two covers is a selection. In order to give as significant coverage as possible to an expanding field, and simply to keep from scattering my fire, I have slighted old friends in every period. When one approaches Western history from the point of view of the development of communities, traits, and institutions, farms, cities, political parties, and social ideas loom larger than trouble with Indians, who were never the barrier to settlement west of the Rockies that they were to the east. This is not to disparage romantic history, but merely to note that I have not written it.

I began work specifically on this book about ten years ago, but have been interrupted several times. *In Search of the Golden West: The Tourist in Western America* (New York: Alfred A. Knopf; 1957) was a by-product. I read, for background, all the travelers' accounts of the West within reach, and in them I found a theme.

For assistance, I wish to thank especially the personnel of the libraries of the University of Oregon and other universities in the region, the Henry E. Huntington Library, and the Bancroft Library; Martin Schmitt, who suggested illustrations and read my manuscript; Walter Johnson, who read drafts of several chapters; James E. Hendrickson, who checked footnotes; the estate of Miss Carrie Beekman, which by supporting my position at the University of Oregon from 1961 on gave me time to read and write after it seemed that I should never be able to; the John Simon Guggenheim Memorial Foundation and the University of Oregon, which financed a year's leave; and the Huntington Library, which gave me a summer fellowship. I am especially grateful to Alfred A. Knopf for his patience, encouragement, and constructive suggestions.

Earl Pomeroy

Eugene, Oregon

ADDENDUM, 1973

In preparing this reprint edition, I have left the text as it was. A list of Errata, which follows this Preface, corrects those mistakes that seem likely to mislead rather than simply to annoy. The "Notes on Further Reading" are new: I have added titles of books published since 1965 and also titles of older books that I did not cite in the footnotes, while omitting most titles that I did so cite, on the assumption that readers would find them there.

I began to write *The Pacific Slope* as one of eight regional histories of the United States that Alfred Knopf planned in 1954–5. Only two of the other projected volumes appeared: W. Eugene Hollon: *The Southwest: Old and New* (New York: Alfred A. Knopf; 1961) and Robert G. Athearn: *High Country Empire: The High Plains and Rockies* (New York: McGraw-Hill Book Company, Inc.; 1960). As Athearn, Hollon, and I and Walter Johnson as editor planned our part of the series in 1954–6, my volume sometimes appeared as "The West Coast" or as "The West Coast and the Rocky Mountains," with my eastern boundary at one point including Arizona and parts of Colorado and Montana and Hollon's and Athearn's western boundaries at other times including Utah. Ultimately Athearn kept all of Montana and Colorado, Hollon Arizona, and I Utah, which meant that our respective regions were about equal in area and that none looked like the victim of a gerrymander but that, of course, Hollon and I had many more people to deal with than Athearn—in 1960, I had three times as many; in 1860, the first census year when there were people to count on the high plains, Hollon had nearly four times as many. If we had divided the territory otherwise, I would have written on a different Pacific slope and rationalized the difference.

If I were writing another book covering the same ground now, or rewriting this one, I would change proportions and emphases as well as bibliography. I would, for instance, do more with minorities, including Indians, although I would be content to leave armed conflict between Indians and emigrants or settlers as a subordinate theme. I might do more with most topics, no longer having to compress to stay within a standard length set for a series. Obviously I would have to take Ronald Reagan from Malibu to Sacramento, and perhaps Richard Nixon from New York to Washington and San Clemente, instead of leaving him as the defeated candidate for the governorship of California, losing to Reagan's predecessor in 1962. But some of the most striking developments on the Western scene since the early 1960's, such as the turmoil on the college campuses and the new right-wing politics of California, are so much intertwined with national (and international) developments that we have not yet fully investigated and analyzed that any accounts of them now are likely to be more provisional than most accounts of recent events. The main departures from the proportions and interpretations of previous surveys of the Far West, as the emphases on cities and on this century, still seem valid, and of interest to students and others who want a general look at the region.

E. P.

Addendum to the Bison Book Edition, 1991

The genesis of this book goes back to 1954, when Alfred A. Knopf asked Robert G. Athearn of the University of Colorado and me to write two Far-Western volumes in a series of eight regional histories of the United States that Walter Johnson, then at the University of Chicago, was to edit. Since the contracts that Knopf sent to us and the next year to W. Eugene Hollon, then at the University of Oklahoma, who was to do a third, did not define our jurisdictions either clearly or workably, Walter left us to agree on how to interpret them. They gave both Bob and me the Rockies (respectively West Coast and Rocky Mountains and Plains and Rocky Mountains) while enumerating Colorado, Montana, Wyoming, the Dakotas, Nebraska, and Kansas for him; Arizona, Washington, Oregon, California, Arizona, Utah, Nevada, Idaho, "and overlap on Montana" for me; Oklahoma, Texas, and New Mexico for Gene. Bob proposed to emphasize the Plains, getting into the Rockies mainly for mining and then chiefly on the east slopes and leaving western Colorado to me, I to emphasize the Pacific coast. Walter suggested that Gene "do something with Utah and Arizona" and that Bob and I divide the other intermountain states, which would have made our jurisdictions somewhat less unequal. I first headed outlines The Pacific Coast and The Far West, intending to include Arizona but not much recognizing states other than the coastal three in subtopics. I also passed over Alaska and Hawaii except in the context of concerns with the Pacific basin but finally accepted responsibility for Utah, feeling at once unqualified for it and attracted by the possibilities that Leonard Arrington and others were developing. Since by that arrangement I still had much more than a third of the population of the seventeen states between the Missouri River and the Pacific Ocean—in 1960, three times as many people as Bob—I had no regrets about turning Arizona over to Gene.

Neither the regional series, for which Knopf had signed up seven authors by 1955, nor a chronological series came out as planned. Walter withdrew as editor in 1959, I understood after disagreements with

Knopf, who then said that he probably would publish separate volumes only. When Knopf and Bob disagreed to the point of displaying their correspondence at meetings, Bob took his manuscript to McGraw-Hill, which published it as *High Country Empire: The High Plains and Rockies* (1960). Knopf published Gene's volume, *The Southwest, Old and New* (1961), and four years later mine in similar format but without reference to a series.

Walter had read drafts of five of my chapters by 1958; Knopf did not replace him, instead relying on members of his staff. The editor who saw me through to publication in 1963–65 was Herbert Weinstock, biographer of Berlioz and other composers, who made quite general suggestions, mainly that I shorten the whole by thirty percent and change proportions to amplify parts on beginnings, reduce those on the twentieth century, and subordinate detail of what he called "economic sociology." Spending the academic year 1963–64 at Bologna, I had to revise without referring much to sources. That proved to be less of a handicap than I feared, in that while this was the only time when I had to work at any length away from a research library suited to my purposes, it was also the only time when I had a research assistant in the usual sense, and in that he was unusually competent and conscientious. James E. Hendrickson, who that fall accepted but had not yet moved to a position at the University of Victoria, was finishing his thesis at Eugene; he checked quotations and footnotes, answered many questions, and collected prints for illustrations that I had selected, generously putting aside his work for mine. Further, having less temptation than I should have had in this country to add to as well as substract from my manuscript, in shortening it I was able to concentrate on making it more readable and intelligible, although without help from others even in proofreading typescript. The Italian typist that I engaged turned my copy over to her mother, who, as I learned only after she had finished, knew no English. Later I also had less than optimum help from my copy-editor at Knopf's, some of whose preferences puzzled me until upon meeting her I found that her native language was Spanish.

Although after Walter left Knopf and I had discussed enlisting another reader, the only historian who read the entire manuscript draft was Martin Schmitt, curator of special collections at the University of Oregon Library, whom I had long depended on for such help, and the draft he read was an early one. Before the University of Washington Press reprinted the book in 1973 I asked authors of published reviews to give me further advice, as some did to my profit. Because it and later the University of Nebraska Press did not ask me to revise the original edition and I should not have wished to do that, wanting to concentrate on another project in which I approached some of the same times and events differently, nearly all the text remains as Knopf published it in 1965. I have made a few small changes, some of them to correct typographical errors, occasionally to get away from wording that is not clear. I have revised throughout only this addendum to the preface and the "Notes on Further Reading," the "Notes" to include titles of books published since 1965 and also titles of a few older books that I had not cited in footnotes.

If I were rewriting the whole or writing another history of the same six states, I should do much otherwise than I did in 1965, taking the opportunity to make approaches that I should not have made in 1965 and approaches that I might have made then but did not make simply because one book cannot incorporate all possible approaches. With or without the same boundary on the east, I should want to revise and reinterpret other boundaries, looking more north and south beyond boundaries with Canada and Mexico and extending the western boundary to encompass Alaska and Hawaii in more than peripheral vision beyond phases of early maritime contacts, and so to recognize how much, especially since the development of oil on the North Slope and tourist trade in the islands, they have moved in step with the contiguous coastal states. I also should want further to explore society within both old and new boundaries, considering Native Americans and immigrants from other countries and other parts of the United States more as components of western cultural mosaics and mixtures and as contributors to cultural change, less predominantly as objects of discrimination, acceptance, or esteem and as factors in production and evidences of economic change. As well as considering western cities as copies of eastern and as beachheads for immigration and occupation, I should put them more in the context of processes of reorganizing and redefining city, suburb, and hinterland that increasingly transcended old urban-rural distinctions. But most of what I did without benefit of such reconsideration still seems not yet become period piece, testimony to the biases of another time, and so here appears again essentially as it was.

Errata

page 19, lines 31–32: *for* practically did away with the menace of *read* killed about two-thirds of
page 20, line 15: *change to read* Astor's American Fur Company paid to crush his opposition, had the
page 22, line 27: *for* the natives *read* Mexican ranchers
page 22, line 23: *change to read* at low prices, the army's agents commonly paying in worthless drafts.[1]
page 46, line 23: *for* hose on a nozzle *read* hose and a nozzle
page 89, line 28: *for* feudal kinds of uses *read* precapitalist kinds of uses
page 95, lines 31–32: *for* by the following year *read* three years later
page 104, line 8: *change to read* On the average, northwestern farms were smaller than Californian
page 122, line 11: *for* Eastern fathers *read* eastern parents
page 128, line 16: *for* from the mouth of the bay *read* from the city
page 135, lines 10–11: *for* seemed the creation of its citizens *read* more unified in spirit
page 179, line 19: *for* a closed-shop city *read* almost a closed-shop city
page 185, line 15: *for* 1912 *read* 1911
page 185, lines 32–33: *for* native Americans *read* older Americans
page 193, line 1: *change to read* was convicted of taking bribes in land frauds. Perhaps the S. P. was
page 213, line 20: *for* excluding alien landowners *read* discriminating against aliens
page 219, line 7: *for* invested *read* investigated
page 248, line 16: *for* John H. Haynes *read* John R. Haynes
page 248, line 23: *for* monopoly *read* opposition
page 394, line 30: *for* though always on a limited scale *read* in early years on a limited scale
Index, page xv, s.v. sugar: *for* Utah, 122 *read* Utah, 112

CONTENTS

ILLUSTRATIONS

NOOTKA SOUND
Vancouver
FRASER R.
BRITISH COLUMBIA
KOOTENAY R.
CANADA
ALBERTA
Victoria
JUAN DE FUCA STRAIT
Bellingham
Fort Colville
OLYMPIC NATIONAL PARK
Seattle
CASCADES
COLUMBIA R.
GRAND COULEE DAM
Wenatchee
Coeur d'Alene
MONTANA
MISSOURI R.
Spokane
Tacoma
Olympia
MOUNT RAINIER NATIONAL PARK
WASHINGTON
BITTER ROOT
ROCKY MOUNTAINS
PALOUSE R.
Pullman
Astoria
Longview
Yakima
Waiilatpu
SNAKE R.
Lewiston
Vancouver
BONNEVILLE DAM
COLUMBIA R.
CLEARWATER R.
Pacific
Portland
Hood River
Pendleton
Oregon City
Salem
WILLAMETTE R.
DESCHUTES R.
WALLOWA LAKE
SALMON R.
CASCADES
Eugene
Bend
Ocean
WYOMING
Boise
OREGON
IDAHO
CRATER LAKE
Medford
OWYHEE R.
SNAKE R.
Pocatello
BEAR LAKE
GREEN R.
GREAT SALT LAKE
Logan
Fort Bridger
N
S
E
W

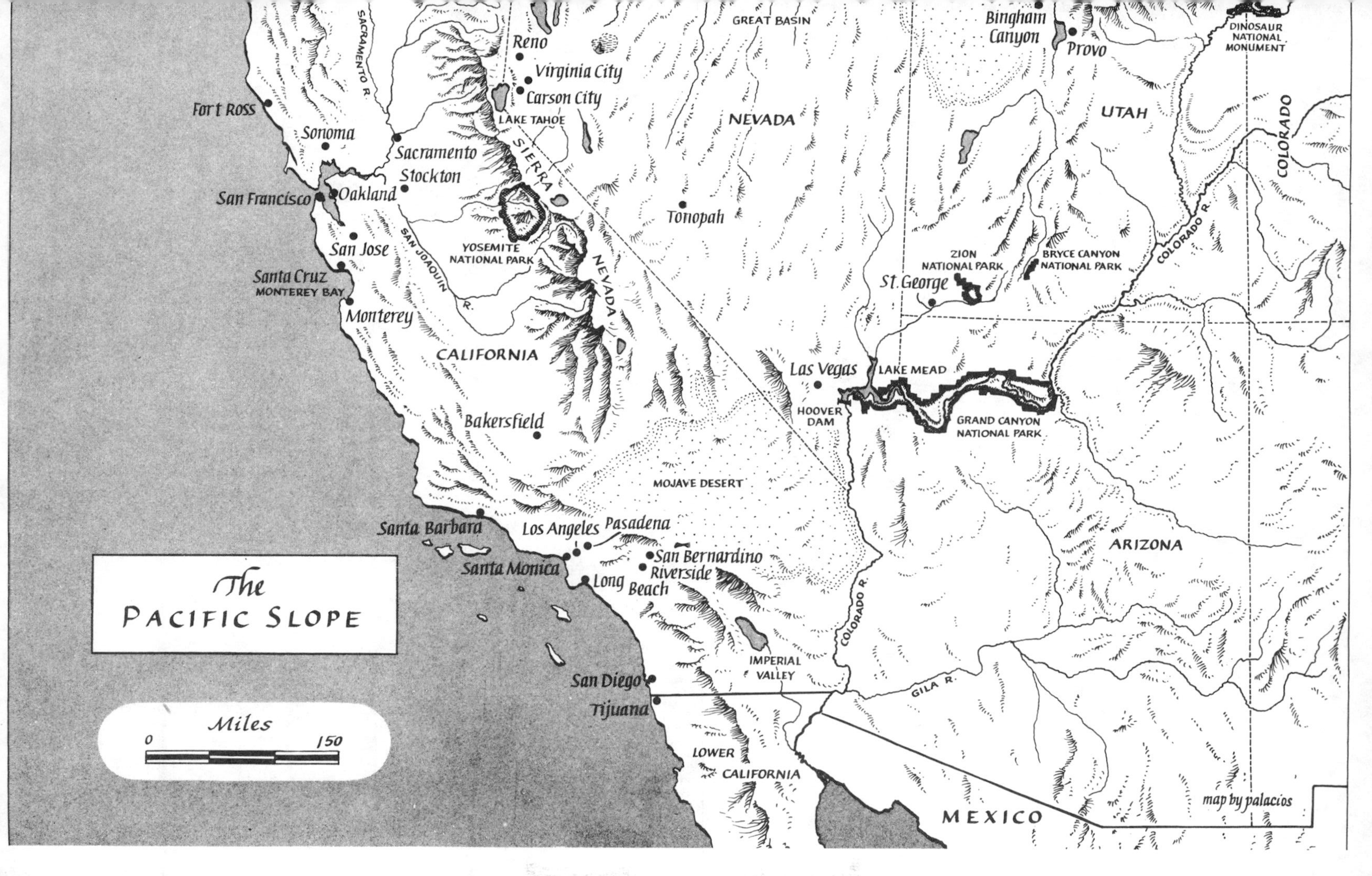
The
Pacific Slope
Miles
0
150
map by palacios
Fort Ross
Sonoma
Sacramento R.
Sacramento
Stockton
San Francisco
Oakland
San Jose
Santa Cruz
Monterey Bay
Monterey
San Joaquin R.
Yosemite National Park
California
Bakersfield
Santa Barbara
Santa Monica
Los Angeles
Pasadena
Long Beach
San Bernardino
Riverside
San Diego
Tijuana
Lower California
Imperial Valley
Colorado R.
Mojave Desert
Sierra Nevada
Reno
Virginia City
Carson City
Lake Tahoe
Great Basin
Nevada
Tonopah
Las Vegas
Hoover Dam
Lake Mead
Grand Canyon National Park
St. George
Zion National Park
Bryce Canyon National Park
Bingham Canyon
Provo
Utah
Dinosaur National Monument
Colorado
Colorado R.
Arizona
Gila R.
Mexico

THE PACIFIC SLOPE

A History

I

INTRODUCTION: NEW AND OLD IN THE FAR WEST

THE PACIFIC SLOPE is both the most Western and, after the East itself, the most Eastern part of America. No other section is more like the Atlantic seaboard and Western Europe; no part is more different; and no part has wished more to be both.

Some of the greatest differences between the states west of the Rocky Mountains and the rest of the United States follow on geography and especially on climate and the consequences of climate. Mountains, canyons, and deserts divide the habitable parts of the Far West from the Middle West and from each other. The Great Plains are dry enough—Americans have called them sometimes the Great American Desert and sometimes the Dust Bowl; but dust storms blow up only in country that is wet enough from time to time so that farmers have ventured to break the sod that tied down the land before they came. Driving west of the Missouri River, the summer traveler finds Nebraska drier than Iowa, and Colorado and Wyoming drier than Nebraska; yet Denver has more rain in June than in December and January. To the west—around Salt Lake City, Los Angeles, San Francisco, and even Portland and Seattle—summer is the dry season. Parts of the Pacific Northwest have the heaviest rainfalls in the country; the Coast Range and the Cascades are green with Douglas fir, rhododendron, and huckleberry all through the months when most of the California hillsides are yellow and brown, and the Columbia River normally reaches flood stage in May and June; but by August the forests may be so dry that the Forest Service has to forbid all logging. Sparks from the friction of a falling tree burst into flame near Tillamook (average annual rainfall, 93.5 inches) in western Oregon in August 1933, eventually destroying 310,000 acres of timber, and the Tillamook burn remains an ugly scar along the highway from Portland to the coast. Tourists are delighted to be able to camp under clear skies and then puzzled to learn that they must build fires only within stone-and-iron fireplaces or drop coins into electric stoves alongside an automatic electric hot-water heater.

Drought, distance, and their corollaries gave the Far West a distinctive pattern of development from the beginning, and fixed a high price on it. When a farmer moved from Wisconsin to Iowa in the 1840's, he might make the trip by easy stages in his own wagons, and without missing a growing season. But beyond the Missouri River, the best farmlands lay nearly two thousand miles away, in the Willamette Valley, past a gauntlet of desert that seemed too poor even for Indians and buffalo; the trip was long enough to consume one growing season and expensive enough to consume the profits of another. A man might walk the Oregon Trail alongside an oxcart, but the trip was neither pleasant nor economic; few tried it after "the cars" began to run, despite the high cost of early railroad travel. Well before the end of the nineteenth century, most Far Westerners had come by train or steamship, leaving the covered wagons to the Mississippi Valley pioneers and to the holiday pageants of their grandchildren.

The dry deserts between the Rockies and the Cascades exacted a heavy toll from the pioneer who had to cross them to reach the first land worth settling on, in one of the less-than-desert valleys beyond, along Great Salt Lake or along the Willamette, the Sacramento, or the San Joaquin; but still heavier tolls fell due after he arrived. The new West was expensive to reach and expensive to develop even after Middle Western hog-and-corn men had paid the price of learning how to grow oranges. Farming in dry country had to carry a high overhead, for land, for water rights and drainage, for machinery, for sprays and fertilizers, for labor. Even if a man was so lucky that he need not buy water, which was exceptional, he probably had to pay heavy charges for transportation and handling to reach markets that were distant in the West itself, as well as in the East.

The Western miner incurred similar penalties. He had to pay heavily for freight to move his machinery in and his ore out. When the bonanzas were richest, and the big gold and silver lodes lay close to the surface, freight charges were highest and so evened out the gains. Drought and distance raised the prices of water for washing ore and of timber for shoring up shafts and tunnels. In time freight became cheaper, but refractory ores demanded elaborate and expensive refining processes. The prospector was helpless without a chemist and a banker. The "honest miner" of Western political folklore either worked for a million-dollar corporation or wished he did.

Removed by barriers of rock and sagebrush desert from the habitable lands of the Mississippi Valley, and dedicated to a new and distinctive pattern of life based on drought and distance, the Far West nevertheless was closer to the East and to Europe than the earlier Wests had been. Passenger service became faster, more frequent, and more comfortable between New York and California than between Ohio or Kentucky and the Dakotas; it was beginning to be so even in the middle of the nineteenth century, when the trip from one coast to the other took three weeks by steamer rather than five or six hours by plane. So it was easier for New Yorkers and New Englanders to move to Portland and San Francisco than to Sioux Falls and Sioux City, and enough of them went to become dominant minorities. The steamer and airplane connections were both causes and results: while the sea was the natural highway between the two coasts, those who traveled it came not only because the ships were there but also because the new West offered opportunities to their kind of men. Before men changed it, the dry country was not much more like the East than it was like the Middle West, but it needed Eastern capital and Eastern skills and offered them the prospect of ample rewards. The percentage of Eastern emigrants to the Pacific coast states was higher in the 1850's than a century later, when General Electric and International Business Machines were recruiting engineers to move across the continent to an industrialized West, and when those who moved lost nothing in urban convenience and urban congestion.

The Easterners who went west led in building towns and cities; the cities they built drew other Easterners accustomed to city life, whereas in the countryside the count of Southerners and Middle Westerners ran higher. Earlier Wests had had their cities, too: the most rural-looking of Middle Western counties banked and bought and sold somewhere and sent away their surplus population, those who wanted a city job, those who had saved enough to retire on, and those who could go to college. But the Far West was more distinctively urban in its own way. San Francisco and Portland grew earlier, in comparison with their hinterlands, than Chicago and Detroit; they were the bridgeheads from which the East conquered the wilderness. And they were general headquarters as well, throughout the complex warfare of settlement and development. They collected and paid out the capital that the whole region needed—to water its dry land, to dig its mines, to build its railroads, to collect its ores and crops and ship them back to the East. Some of the emptiest-looking parts of the West, where the cowboy and prospector seemed to live the life that Frederic Remington and Charlie Russell painted, were most tributary to the city. Some of the irrigated country, where long before the New Deal the farmers were accustomed to electricity and telephones and the sight of their neighbors' city-type bungalows just beyond the next bus stop, was more independent economically, if more urbanized socially.

The urban-ness of the Far West persisted to a far greater extent than another distinctive quality of early pioneer days, its foreign-ness. Once the Pacific coast was Spanish and British and Russian more than it was American. Yet the original European substratum was extraordinarily thin and insubstantial. There are more Basque sheepherders in the deserts of Nevada and eastern Oregon today than ever there were Spaniards in all of Spanish California. San Francisco was more American—New York and Boston American—and less Latin under the rule of its first *alcalde* (1846–7) than it was later, when Latin Americans and Spaniards and Frenchmen poured in with the other gold seekers. The Spaniards who had been in California affected the country less in the long run by making it Spanish than by making it ready to become American, though nothing was more remote from their expectations. The Spanish and cosmopolitan aspects of the Pacific coast in the twentieth century owed less to the heritage of *padres* and *rancheros* than to the promoters of the current Western mythology and to the growth of an urbanized and industrialized economy that reached out for the commerce and the art and the labor of other nations.

Yet Far Western society was never simply a product of geography or a transplant from the East coast. The mark of history is deep on this newest part of the continental United States. The missionaries of Oregon, the miners of California, the Saints of Utah live in more than pageants and historical novels. If the West has synthesized the heritages of the older states, much of the synthesis has been on its own terms.

II

THE FAR FAR WEST OF THE 1830's AND 1840's

Americans knew and visited the Pacific coast for half a century before they thought seriously of going there to live. They held back not because Englishmen and Spaniards and Russians were there already—far more foreigners lived in Canada and Florida and Louisiana, which Americans were quite ready to take—but because it was so far away and because it offered so little to compensate for the distance from home. When a New England sea captain embarked for the Columbia River in the 1790's or early 1800's, he knew that he was not likely to see his family again until after forty thousand miles and three years under sail, when he would return by way of China and perhaps Hawaii. A few Americans saw the coast regularly, though they seldom ventured far off their own decks; for most the distance made it as unknowable as Honolulu, which, indeed, was Americanized before Monterey and Los Angeles. Most New England families knew Chinese tea and silks better than the hides and pelts of California and Oregon.

The foreigners had not done much better. When Captain Robert Gray of Boston first landed on the Oregon coast in 1788, there were no European settlements between Sitka and San Francisco, though Spanish and English navigators had been there from time to time for two centuries and more.

European settlement of any kind was extraordinarily late. The first wave of the Spanish advance had reached out as far as the Pacific within the generation after Columbus: Cortés had barely conquered Mexico (1519–21) when he was building ships on the west coast of New Spain, and one of them reached Lower California in 1533–4. An expedition that set out under Juan Rodríguez Cabrillo in 1542 touched at San Diego Bay and beyond along the coast; it may have gone as far as southern Oregon. The Spanish ships (galleons) that began making the long voyage from Manila to New Spain in 1566 followed the prevailing winds and currents across the north Pacific and south along the west coast of North America to Acapulco; Francis Drake had come in search of the galleons' treasures when he stopped in the vicinity of San Francisco Bay in 1579.[1] There may have been an English plan to establish a settlement in New Albion in 1581, six years before the first colony in Virginia; and the dual purpose of a Spanish expedition that went north along the coast under the command of Sebastián Vizcaíno in 1602 was to investigate the value of the pearl fishery off Lower California and to look into the problem of safeguarding vessels returning from the Far East. Vizcaíno recommended establishing a station at Monterey Bay, where the galleons could find shelter and refreshment without deviating much from the direct route, but a new viceroy felt that Monterey was too far from the settled parts of New Spain for adequate defense. Thereafter the Spanish turned in other directions, particularly toward South America and the mining provinces of New Spain. Monterey remained a half-forgotten proposal in the archives for over a century and a half; for more than half the time Europeans have

---

[1] Herbert E. Bolton and D. S. Watson: *Drake's Plate of Brass* (San Francisco: California Historical Society; 1938). Walter A. Starr: "Drake Landed in San Francisco Bay in 1579: The Testimony of the Plate of Brass," *California Historical Society Quarterly*, Vol. XLI (September 1962 supplement), pp. 1–29.

known the west coast of what is now the United States (1542–1769 and since 1769), none stopped except to look, take on water, or make repairs.

Perhaps the main reason for the long delay was that, despite the early conquests in Mexico and Peru, Spain was not rich and powerful enough to continue expanding along the vast peripheries of an empire that reached from the West Indies, Florida, and Mexico to Patagonia and the Philippines. As time passed, moreover, instead of gathering strength for a new wave of conquest and settlement, she lost both territory and commerce as foreigners probed into the Caribbean itself. But what little anyone knew of this distant frontier must have aroused only slight regret among Spanish treasure hunters, missionaries, and settlers alike. The first indications were that neither human nor geographical resources were worth the taking. None of the Indians approached the cultural level of the Aztecs and Incas; they had neither treasure nor efficient labor to offer to conquerors. None cultivated the soil, and the general aridity and the character of the natural crops—the great staple in California was acorns—gave the impression that the country was no more suitable for agriculture than for mining.

The aborigines whom Europeans first saw along the Pacific coast were, in fact, among the least impressive in the Western Hemisphere. Being food gatherers rather than food raisers, most of them moved about seasonally; their seminomadic habits and, in California, their division into many linguistically separate groups kept them at low levels of social organization. Most of the Californians had no better shelters than crude huts of sticks, reeds, and mud. The Paiutes and other desert peoples of the interior had to split into small bands and glean large areas for food, as the cattle of most of Nevada did in later times. Only the Northwesterners, whom the Spanish and English encountered late in the eighteenth century, lived much above the level of bare subsistence; the most prosperous were the maritime people of Puget Sound and the islands and coasts to the north, some of whom wove woolen blankets and built large plank houses and seagoing canoes. In the Northwestern interior, the Nez Percés had had horses for nearly a century when the first whites reached them in 1805.

The immediate occasion for Spain's advance into this remote and unpromising country was not that she had discovered new uses for it but that she feared others might take possession and, using it as a base, threaten the mines of New Spain to the south. A Russian expedition under Vitus Bering had sailed far enough to sight Mount St. Elias, in southern Alaska, in 1741, and though Bering died after his ship broke up on an island off the coast of Kamchatka, the skins of the sea otters that the castaways killed for food suggested a new interest in the new land. Soon the fur hunters were scouring the Aleutians for sea otters and seals, whose pelts commanded high prices in China and Europe. Although the Russians did not establish their first settlement in the new world, on Kodiak Island, until 1784, Spanish colonial administrators feared a further Russian—or perhaps English or French—advance on Monterey. The changes of territory in 1762–3 brought new responsibilities to Spain in the vast territories of Louisiana, and new concern about England, which took Canada as well as the Floridas. But in some respects the case for occupying Alta (Upper) California, as it became known, had weakened since Vizcaíno's time. Much of Spain's commerce with her own empire had slipped away, and the British had acquired in 1713 the monopoly of the slave trade and also the right to send goods to the Isthmus of Panama. The great commercial powers such as England became more concerned with the steady profit of such peacetime trade and less with Elizabethan dreams of capturing cargoes of precious metals and silk bound for Spain. Although the Manila galleon—which a British ship had captured in 1742—continued to sail off the coast of California until nearly the end of Spanish rule, after the Napoleonic wars its sailings became irregular, and it no longer carried rich treasure; after 1763, goods could go directly from the Philippines to Spain, instead of across the Pacific and then across Mexico to the Atlantic. This rerouting reduced California's importance in the defense of Spanish trade even as it reduced costs for the Philippines; and the weakness and impoverishment of the Spanish Empire under the system of regulations that Spain contrived to control its commerce were evident in Britain's capture of both Havana and Manila in 1762 and then in her decision to retain the Floridas instead.

Thus Spain had to divide already insufficient energies and resources among vastly larger responsibilities. Given further the unattractive appearance of California, the prospects for its occupation seemed discouraging. Gaspar de Portolá, governor of the Californias and commander of the occupying expeditions in 1769, observed that if the Russians wanted California, he would let them have it; and the Father Superior of the College that trained the Franciscan friars who came to found missions predicted failure.[2]

---

[2] Charles E. Chapman: *A History of California; The Spanish Period* (New York: The Macmillan Company; 1921), pp. 229–31, 246–7.

The beginnings were slow and meager. The occupying forces arrived at San Diego in 1769, exhausted and sick; most of one ship's company died of scurvy during a struggle against contrary winds for one hundred and ten days along the coast of Lower California. Governor Portolá pushed on past Monterey Bay, not recognizing it from overgenerous seventeenth-century descriptions, wandered around San Francisco Bay without enthusiasm, and returned south in discouragement. On a second trip he identified Monterey, and Father Junípero Serra and his five fellow Franciscan friars began founding the chain of missions that reached nine by the time of Serra's death in 1784, and eventually twenty-one. Lame and elderly (he was fifty-six when he reached California), this former professor of philosophy and his associates baptized over six thousand Indians and taught many of them how to raise crops, how to make sun-dried bricks from mud (adobe), and even how to decorate chapels, sing psalms, tell their beads, and say their *paternosters*. But it was not until 1774 that the first settlers began to arrive and not until 1781 that the government began to foster the growth of towns (*pueblos*) to provide food and horses for the garrisons. Soon thereafter, the Spanish government fell to less wise and energetic leadership and shortly Spain itself was in the maelstrom of the wars of the French Revolution, which eventually all but severed Spain's connections with America.

As Portolá had pointed out, the occupation or even the fortification of Monterey (which Spain never did undertake) would not safeguard California against the Russians, for there were other ports they might use if they wished to take it. In the same burst of energy that had led to the occupation, Spanish expeditions in 1773 and 1775 probed beyond California, making the first European landing on the northwest coast and taking possession of points as far north as 57°20′, well within Alaska. In 1788 and 1789 reports of Russian activity led others to Nootka Sound, on Vancouver Island, where a Spaniard, Pérez, had preceded Captain James Cook and the English; but the Spanish commander ended by fraternizing with the English he found there, and his government eventually conceded that they had a right to settle (1790). Spain never occupied or effectively claimed much beyond the coastal strip that Portolá had covered in 1769 in his search for Monterey. Searching for a new overland route to California, Father Silvestre Vélez de Escalante wandered from New Mexico as far as Utah Lake in 1776–7; this was the one manifestation of Spanish interest in the Great Basin. Control of the interior valleys of California hardly went beyond occasional forays into the San Joaquin to retrieve escaped Indians. Then the Russians came; they bought a tract of land from the Indians and established an agricultural settlement at Fort Ross, less than a hundred miles north of San Francisco Bay, as well as a fishing station on the Farallone Islands (1812). But Spain offered no resistance, because she was too weak or because Ross was so unimpressive. The presence of the Russians may have contributed to the founding of the last two missions—San Rafael (1817) and Sonoma (1823)—but neither antagonist had enough force in these distant outposts seriously to intimidate the other. By 1821 Spain had lost Mexico itself through revolution, the climax of a long process in national and imperial disintegration in which the homeland had bled itself in civil and international wars and the colonies had tasted virtual independence, if not self-government. Instead of grasping the opportunity afforded by the weakness of their neighbor, the Russians, who for twenty years had been trying to raise wheat on poor soil in the coastal fogs, now turned to a new site inland, on the Russian River, and then sold their property to a Swiss adventurer, John A. Sutter, in 1841.

Meanwhile Englishmen and Americans went less to California than to the Northwest coast, not merely because Spain excluded foreign traders but because for a generation the better trade was in the fur pelts of colder climates. When Captain James Cook explored the coast in 1778, his mission was to establish whether there was any basis for the rumors, which had circulated since the sixteenth century, of a Northwest passage—a strait connecting the Atlantic with the Pacific and so affording a short water route from Europe to the Far East. Although he failed to quash the idea despite what he considered ample proof, and though he found neither the Columbia River nor Puget Sound, Cook's men did stumble into the Cantonese market for Northwestern furs. The circumstances were somewhat like those of the opening of the Aleutian trade, in that the discovery followed Cook's death, as the earlier discovery followed Bering's; and the rush for pelts and profits was as eager. A Connecticut sailor, John Ledyard, told the story in his published journal in 1783: "We purchased [at Nootka Sound, on Vancouver Island] about 1500 beaver . . . having no thoughts at that time of using them to any other advantage than converting them to the purposes of cloathing, but it afterwards happened that skins which did not cost the purchaser sixpence sterling sold in China for 100 dollars."[3] By 1785 Englishmen had come to trade at Nootka, and Americans, who were already sailing to China, soon pressed in so energetically that they gathered the better part of the Northwestern fur harvest. Robert Gray not only had made the pioneering American voyage to the coast (1787–90) but also had built a ship there when he entered the Columbia River in 1792; his success in discovery matched American resourcefulness in commerce and seafaring generally.

All the early traders came by sea, so that for them the coast might as well have been an island as a part of the continent. Initially it was the British who were most interested in finding an overland route to the Northwest, and naturally enough, inasmuch as they had commanded the fur trade of the northern interior without serious question since they took Canada from France in 1763. The comfortable factories of the Hudson's Bay Company reached halfway across the continent; the posts of its rival, the North-West Company, went well beyond, to Lake Athabasca, in what later became northeastern Alberta. A partner of the North-West Company, Alexander Mackenzie, first found a way across in 1792–3. He portaged westward and southward from Fort Chipewyan, on Lake Athabasca, first ascended the Peace River, and finally descended the Bella Coola to the sea well to the north of Vancouver Island. He had discovered the first route across the continent north of Mexico, but it included so rugged a succession of portages and ice-cold rapids between steep canyons that only the prospect of intensified commercial rivalry justified developing it. In 1801, in his journals, he wrote that the profits of the coastal trade fell to American adventurers, who "would instantly disappear from before a well-regulated trade" anchored in posts connecting the Pacific Ocean with British establishments east of the continental divide.[4] It was not until 1808 that another party of North-Westers reached the mouth of the Fraser, and not till 1810 that the company determined to establish posts near the coast in answer to rumors that American traders were coming to establish themselves.

---

[3] John Ledyard: *A Journal of Captain Cook's Last Voyage to the Pacific Ocean, and in Quest of a North-West Passage* . . . (Hartford: Nathaniel Patten; 1783), p. 70.

[4] Alexander Mackenzie: *Voyage from Montreal . . . to the Frozen and Pacific Oceans in the Years 1789 and 1793* . . . (Toronto: Radisson Society of Canada, Ltd.; 1927), pp. 493–4.

Traders of both nations, in fact, used the sea route to the Northwest exclusively for over twenty years; on the American side, a landsman and no great friend of the maritime interests, Thomas Jefferson, was responsible for the first overland passage. As American minister to France in the 1780's, Jefferson had encouraged John Ledyard to cross the continent even before Mackenzie; and when he was secretary of state he had planned an expedition to the Pacific for the American Philosophical Society (1793). Perhaps because as President he had to be even more discreet than his normal taste for indirection prompted, or because he was not, in fact, interested in China, as Ledyard had been, when Jefferson planned the expedition that Meriwether Lewis and William Clark led to the Columbia in 1804–6, he did not reveal whether he hoped to strengthen the trans-Pacific trade or replace it with a transcontinental portage. In his secret message to Congress early in 1803 he began by discussing the conversion of Indian tribes east of the Mississippi to the sedentary habits of agriculture, which would entail the decline of the American fur trade unless new trapping fields to the west were available. He proposed to explore such possibilities by sending an expedition up the Missouri and "even to the Western ocean," and pointed out the competitive advantages of a route south of the British traders, "offering . . . a continued navigation [from the source of the Missouri], and possibly with a single portage, from the Western Ocean. . . ." "Should you reach the Pacific Ocean," he instructed Meriwether Lewis, "inform yourself of the circumstances which may decide whether the furs of those parts may not be collected as advantageously at the head of the Missouri (convenient as is supposed to the water of the Colorado & Oregon or Columbia) as at Nootka Sound or any other point of that coast; & that trade be consequently conducted through the Missouri & U.S. more beneficially than by circumnavigation now practised."[5] (He did not say whether he was thinking of abandoning the sale of furs in China or of shipping them there after bringing them from the Rockies through the Mississippi Valley—which Spain still controlled.)

On the other hand, Lewis and Clark took with them a copy of Mackenzie's book, in which he recommended a strong continental footing

[5] Ralph B. Guinness: "The Purpose of the Lewis and Clark Expedition," *Mississippi Valley Historical Review*, Vol. XX (June 1933), pp. 90–6. Thomas Jefferson: *Works*, ed. Paul L. Ford (New York: G. P. Putnam's Sons; 1904–5), Vol. I, pp. 103–4; Vol. IX, pp. 424, 428, 433.

for the direct overseas trade; and on returning from the Pacific in 1806, they speculated quite specifically about the possibilities of trade with China, about bringing the furs of the Missouri River country to Canton by way of the Columbia "earlier than the furs which are annually shiped from Montreal arrive in England." With adequate assistance from the government, Lewis predicted perhaps more optimistically than his own experience justified, the trade would develop so that "in the course of 10 or 12 Years a tour across the Continent by this rout will be undertaken with as little concern as a voyage across the Atlantic is at present."[6] Lewis and Clark's idea was to carry the fur harvest westward from the interior to the Columbia, as Mackenzie had proposed and as the Hudson's Bay Company later did. But Jefferson did not act on these suggestions or even make public the findings of the expedition. While he was President, the government gave no further assistance to the fur trade; it did not even exclude foreign traders from American territory. And within a few weeks of his conversations with the explorers, he proclaimed an embargo that almost completely shut down the Far Eastern trade and other branches of foreign commerce for the rest of his administration.

Lewis and Clark in any case found a route to the Pacific—"the most practicable communication which does exist across the continent," Lewis reported to the President—strengthened American claims to the Oregon country, and set records for efficient command in the field and for geographical discovery. By great prudence the expedition lost only one man in traveling nine thousand miles (Sergeant John Floyd, who died of "a Biliose Chorlick," possibly appendicitis, before they had reached the mountains); it arrived in better health and general condition than did many parties of emigrants that traveled by short stages through better-known country forty years later. It did less for the early and lasting development of American commerce with the Pacific coast, either by land or by sea. Though the expedition got along well with the Nez Percé and Flathead Indians, it left an ugly trail of enmity behind it in the Blackfoot country, and those who came afterwards in less force found the Blackfeet murderous as well as thievish. John Colter, the

[6] Meriwether Lewis to Jefferson, Sept. 23, 1806, and William Clark to George R. Clark, Sept. 24, 1806, in *Original Journals of the Lewis and Clark Expedition, 1804–1806*, ed. Reuben G. Thwaites (New York: Dodd, Mead & Co., 1904–5), Vol. VII, pp. 335–9. Lewis doubted that the transcontinental route could compete with the British route by way of the Cape of Good Hope except in "articles not bulky brittle nor of a perishable nature."

sole enlisted man in the expedition who chose a life of trapping rather than return to the states, and took his discharge at the Mandan villages, barely escaped from the Blackfeet in 1808, running naked six miles over a thorn-covered plain to hide under a raft of driftwood. The Missouri Fur Company, in which Clark joined, along with Manuel Lisa and others of the traders at St. Louis (1808), established the first American post west of the divide in 1809 but felt compelled to abandon it the following year.

On the Pacific side, John Jacob Astor, the New York merchant who established the first American trading post on the coast, at the mouth of the Columbia, in 1811, sent his overland party over much of the route that Lewis and Clark had used, but it would be difficult to demonstrate that he profited much by their example or significantly advanced American interests in the Pacific Northwest. Certainly he did not advance his own through what one of his employees accurately enough called "a commercial speculation." This venture, the best known of his long and enormously successful commercial career, was substantially his only failure. Astor was no novice in the Pacific: he had begun to send furs from New York to the Orient as early as 1800, and by 1809 he was instructing one of his captains to make a voyage embracing the Northwest coast, California, New Archangel or Sitka in Russian America, and Canton. He already had substantial connections at St. Petersburg, Canton, and Montreal, and he hoped to consolidate them into an international fur trust by which he would carry Russian and British as well as American pelts to China. At Astoria he was the victim of bad tactics, bad luck, and bad strategy. The most obvious blunders were those of the officers of his ship, the *Tonquin*, who carelessly permitted Indians to board and capture her, and those of the partners on land who embarked on the Snake River without having scouted the rapids below and the bleak desert high above its canyon. Sixty-five deaths were the measure of mismanagement. By the time the decimated parties assembled at Astoria, England and the United States had been at war for the better part of a year, and the best way to salvage something from a precarious investment seemed to be to sell to the North-West Company. But even with better luck, the whole venture on the Columbia would have been seriously unqualified either as a trading enterprise or as a step to American immigration and American control. It lacked strength in the rear, on the Missouri River and at St. Louis, where the American traders resented Astor as rival and intruder and distrusted him for collaborating with the merchants of Montreal, whom he had tried to draw into his Pacific Fur Company. Thus the settlement of Astoria was the weak link in an essentially maritime operation in the tradition of Ledyard and the New England traders to Canton, rather than an outlet for solid continental development.

Reports of Astor's plans (which, far from regarding as a secret, he hoped would induce the North-West Company to join him) may have prompted the North-Westers to dispatch David Thompson on an expedition down the Columbia in 1811; on arriving, he enjoyed the hospitality of Astor's Canadian employees. But the Nor'westers already were reaching for the Columbia from forts established west of the mountains in what is now British Columbia, on McLeod Lake in 1805, on Fraser and Stuart lakes in 1806, and on the Fraser River in 1807. When Astoria became Fort George in 1813, it rested on a dual system of British communications by sea and land, partly taken over from Astor's Pacific Fur Company, but stronger and more extensive. The American site itself had been unsatisfactory from the beginning, and soon after the Hudson's Bay Company absorbed the North-West Company (1821), it moved the headquarters on the Columbia upstream and to the north bank, opposite the mouth of the Willamette, where the Indians were better neighbors, the possibilities of agriculture greater, and the major trapping fields closer.

Here at Fort Vancouver the symbol and chief instrument of the enlarged Company's power was Dr. John McLoughlin, chief factor of the Columbia district from 1824 to 1846. Tall, stern-faced, and white-haired, he was a man of commanding presence as he dispensed justice among the Indians and dispatched couriers over his empire. Visitors found a precise and courtly, if at times somewhat incongruous, decorum at his table, roast grizzly bear and mountain trout served in proper sequence on fine china, the Indian wives of his officers dressed in the best imported silks and laces. (When American missionaries began coming in the 1830's, their wives wrote that it was a mistake to bring a great many goods overland: one could buy most household supplies at reasonable prices at the fort.) Within the stockade, over seven acres in area, McLoughlin's house, the quarters of his staff, a schoolhouse, and the barns filled with foodstuffs and furs seemed midway between a well-ordered military post and a prosperous country estate. Outside it were flourishing farms, eventually three thousand acres, chiefly in wheat, and herds of livestock. But the headquarters fort was only one element in a system that included sixteen posts in the interior, others on the northern coast, and ships. The Hudson's Bay Company inherited not only Astor's posts but in time also his traffic with the Russians in Alaska, which became a virtual monopoly by the terms of a contract with the Russian American Company in 1839.

However useful Astor's expedition may have been later in reinforcing American claims to the Oregon country and eventually in arousing popular American interest in it, for over twenty years Americans attempted no permanent establishments on the Northwest coast; for thirty years British fur traders dominated the whole region. Until 1842 there were, in fact, more British (Canadian) than American settlers in the Oregon country, and nearly as many even south of the Columbia, although before 1841 the Company did not encourage settlers to come out and a provision of the Company's charter (which Dr. McLoughlin construed liberally) required it to return all retired *engagés* to Montreal. Although the Company's vast experience and efficient organization entrenched it on the mainland, Yankee individualism and skill in shipbuilding gave the Boston merchants advantages in the lucrative trade with China, from which the British government excluded those of its own subjects not with the East India Company. Yet the profits of the American intercoastal trade reached their peak and then declined during the 1820's as overfishing depleted the herds of sea otters; Astor himself withdrew from China by about 1825.

West of the mountains, American trappers did little to occupy the country except insofar as some of them showed the way to the missionaries and farmers who came in the thirties and forties; the few who retired to the land as returns from trapping declined were conspicuously poor farmers, though one of these, Joe Meek, perhaps because of his utter failure in agriculture, had time to cut a colorful figure in frontier politics. Perhaps the trappers helped the cause of settlement also by importing diseases, such as the smallpox that practically did away with the menace of the Blackfeet in 1837. Their style of trading depended on free movement through the wilderness rather than on fortified posts, and the only noteworthy successor to the Pacific Fur Company's posts at Astoria and Fort Okanogan on the lower and upper Columbia, which the North-West Company had taken over in 1813, was Fort Hall (1834) on the Snake. However, this fort was of little use to its founders and remained American for only three years before the Hudson's Bay Company bought it. Even the itinerant American trappers who made their rendezvous in the Rockies seldom ventured farther west. By 1824 parties from St. Louis had crossed to the tributaries of the Columbia, but in the same year Sir George Simpson decided that the Hudson's Bay Company should forestall the Americans by stripping the beaver population from the Snake River and the entire region south of the Columbia. Four years later Jedediah Smith found so few furs in southern Oregon, and saw enough evidence of the Company's strength when he visited Fort Vancouver (1828), that he advised his associates to remain in the Rockies. When other Americans pushed well into the company's territory in 1827–8, it was not because prospects there had improved, but because they had had too much trouble with the Blackfeet and had found too few furs in the Snake River country, where their small parties were at a great disadvantage in comparison to the British. Their own cutthroat competition with each other, and especially the reckless prices Astor's Fur Company paid to crush his American opposition, had the effect of supporting the British policy of creating a "fur desert." By 1833, having achieved a virtual monopoly of the Missouri River trade, Astor agreed formally to stay out of Hudson's Bay territory. By that time the Northwestern beaver trade had reached its peak; when beaver hats went out of style in the middle thirties, the profits declined precipitately.[7]

While British subjects dominated the Oregon country, Americans began to penetrate Mexican California. Shortly after the Spanish monopoly disappeared with the last Spanish officials when Mexico became independent in 1821, Boston traders appeared openly at Monterey to tap the new market. Although a British firm anticipated them, contracting for the bulk of the missions' output of hides and tallow, by 1828 the New Englanders were dominant and rejoicing in a market with a larger potential than the Northwest. The catch of sea otters soon declined, as it had declined on the Oregon coast, after overfishing that dated from Spanish days, and the Americans turned to the hides of the half-wild long-horned native cattle. By the time the supply of hides dropped off in the 1840's, reflecting the economic breakdown of the missions and the confusion of civil war among the petty politicians of Mexican California, the Americans were rapidly becoming economic masters of the province, for whatever it was worth.

---

[7] John S. Galbraith: *The Hudson's Bay Company as an Imperial Factor, 1821–1869* (Berkeley: University of California Press; 1957), pp. 95–8. On Astor's withdrawal, see Kenneth W. Porter: *John Jacob Astor, Business Man* (Cambridge: Harvard University Press, 1931), Vol. II, pp. 777–8.

The California of the first American settlers has acquired the reputation of an idyllic pastoral society, a kind of social equilibrium in which no one wanted or sinned. "It seems to me that there never was a more peaceful or happy people on the face of the earth," wrote a member of an old California family nearly half a century later, "than the Spanish, Mexican, and Indian population of Alta California before the American conquest."[8] Actually California was changing rapidly at that time, and still greater turbulence soon followed.

Spanish California, in fact, was little more than a memory by the 1840's. There had been little enough to remember, for the bulk of the Spanish-speaking population had come on the eve of the American conquest. The missions that the Franciscan fathers had founded along the coast from San Diego to Sonoma had ruled rather than civilized their Indian neophytes, though under close tutelage the Indians cultivated vineyards and orchards with primitive tools and practiced simple crafts that delighted casual visitors, who also appreciated dining on fresh beef, vegetables, and fruit, with a bottle of wine, after a long trip by land or sea. "If one did not look too critically below the surface," Sir George Simpson recalled, "the contrast between the untamed savages and the half-civilized converts could hardly fail to complete, in the eyes of the hasty wayfarer, a kind of terrestrial paradise." By 1833, when the Mexican government restricted the friars to purely religious functions, they had accumulated over eight hundred thousand head of livestock and were at the height of their prosperity. Thereafter the Indians drifted away and the missions decayed. Several years later half of the Indians who remained died of smallpox; the death rate had long been so high that even before Spanish rule ended, the missions had begun to lose population, and for some time before that had maintained themselves more by the conversion of savages than by natural increase among the Christians. "The final outcome of [the missionaries'] work, therefore," according to Josiah Royce, "was . . . simply nothing; for, with their power, nearly every trace of their labors vanished from the world."[9] Soon the people of Monterey were stripping tiles from the mission at

---

[8] Guadalupe Vallejo: "Ranch and Mission Days in Alta California," *Century Magazine,* Vol. XLI (December 1890), p. 183.

[9] George Simpson: *Narrative of a Journey Round the World, during the Years 1841 and 1842* (London: Henry Colburn, Publisher; 1847), Vol. I, p. 333. Josiah Royce: *California, from the Conquest in 1846 to the Second Vigilance Committee in San Francisco; a Study of American Character* (first edition, 1886; New York: Alfred A. Knopf; 1948), p. 14.

Carmel to roof their own houses, exposing the adobe walls to rains that returned them to mud.

The heirs of the missionaries were the ranchers—typically, retired soldiers who had come from culturally backward areas of northwestern Mexico. The overwhelming majority were late arrivals. The Spanish authorities had made fewer than twenty grants of land (by 1821), whereas the Mexicans made several hundred in the thirteen years between the law of secularization in 1833 and the arrival of American military forces in 1846. The ranchers' ways were more colorful than those of the missionaries, whom they surpassed in extravagance while they fell behind them in the arts of agriculture and management. Yankee visitors such as Richard Henry Dana, who was there in 1835, found their incredible inefficiency as striking as their flamboyant costumes—gilt trimmings on hats and pantaloons, red sashes, lace mantillas, and sleeveless silk gowns—and their musical speech and elaborate courtesies. "The Californians," he wrote, "are an idle, thriftless people, and can make nothing for themselves." In an ideal climate for fruit, as the missionaries had shown, the ranchers bought wine made in Boston from the inferior grapes of New England and shoes made in Boston from the hides of their own cattle. In Spanish days the missionaries tended to blame the general backwardness of the settlers on the military system, which denied them goods to buy and requisitioned their crops at low prices.[1]

Mexicans replaced Spaniards (that is, Spanish missionaries) in controlling California's land, but Americans took command of its commerce. In this they replaced virtually no one, for the English had developed very little trade, and though the natives hungered after imported goods, they were not competent or interested in the process of importation and lacked capital and mercantile connections with which to undertake it. Left to themselves, they had lived on their own herds and gardens and cared nothing for the surplus. In the towns most of the shopkeepers were foreigners; they made large profits by gathering hides and tallow from the ranchers in exchange for Yankee goods. Dana saw men of this class at Monterey in 1835; and he himself had come as an employee of the Boston firm that, after first concentrating on the Northwest, had be-

[1] Richard Henry Dana: *Two Years before the Mast* (New York: Dodd, Mead & Co.; 1946), p. 62. Fray José Señán to Marqués de Branciforte, May 14, 1796, in *The Letters of José Señán, O.F.M., Mission San Buenaventura, 1796–1823*, ed. Lesley B. Simpson (San Francisco: John Howell—Books; 1962), pp. 2–4.

come the biggest shipper in California. By that time the trade in hides had passed its peak, and as secularization of the missions advanced, both the quality and the quantity of the hides declined because the ranchers killed the animals indiscriminately and would not bother with curing. But the decline in the market seemed to foster rather than retard American control. The Californians' tastes for imported luxuries grew according to what they saw rather than what they had, and increasingly they paid for American goods and services not merely with their income but with their capital—by mortgaging their land. The Americans, Simpson wrote in 1842, "not only from their numbers, but from their pushing and active habits, and forward character, have much influence, and may be said to give law to the country." Thomas O. Larkin, who became American consul at Monterey, had arrived in 1833, and shortly became well respected. He built the first two-story timbered house; its green shutters proclaim its New England antecedents, but native Californians imitated it so widely in the 1840's and 1850's that later generations supposed it to be Spanish.[2] Americans of small means sometimes married Mexican women (daughters of officials, perhaps, or of landowners) and professed to be good Roman Catholics. Larkin married the widow of another New Englander, however, and they sent their sons first to Honolulu, nearest outpost of New England, and then back to Boston for their education.

The early traders in California never were numerous; their influence and their resistance to assimilation testify to their energy rather than to their numbers. In 1840 there were fewer than four hundred Americans—of all kinds—in California, and they were a varied lot. As early as 1816 Yankee sailors were electing to remain, more often as craftsmen than as farmers; after 1826, when Jedediah Smith pressed westward from the Salt Lake country to the Mojave Desert and the San Gabriel Valley in search of beaver, the trappers began to drift in, shadowy figures who sometimes wandered about the interior for several years, hunting and stealing horses, before they moved on or settled down. None of the early overland immigrants, before 1841, brought his family, and none came directly as a settler, though some eventually became ranchers, like John Marsh, the eccentric New Englander who practiced

---

[2] Simpson to John H. Pelly, March 10, 1842, in "Letters of Sir George Simpson, 1841–1843," ed. Joseph Schafer, *American Historical Review*, Vol. XIV (October 1908), p. 89. Harold Kirker: *California's Architectural Frontier* (San Marino: Huntington Library; 1960), pp. 17, 19–21.

medicine at his rough ranch near Mount Diablo on the strength of his bachelor's diploma from Harvard College. The rancher best known to Americans in the 1840's was German-born John Sutter, who had lived briefly in the United States but was still a Swiss citizen when the Mexican governor of California gave him permission to settle in the Sacramento Valley in 1839; Sutter had gone to Oregon in 1838 and had reached California by way of Alaska and Hawaii.

In Oregon, meanwhile, a few former employees of the Hudson's Bay Company lived with their Indian wives on the lower Willamette River; in the 1830's some independent American trappers built homesteads, but the Canadians exceeded them in numbers and, for the most part, in industry. Ewing Young, one of the best-known of the trappers, came north from California, driving a herd of horses and later several hundred cattle. When he arrived, he had a hard time persuading John McLoughlin that he was not a horse thief. Even in 1840, the entire American population of Oregon, including missionaries, was less than two hundred.

Thus in the 1830's the prospects of American settlement and control along the Pacific coast were developing promisingly in Mexican California, though still on a small scale, whereas the Oregon country, where American claims were at least arguable, was more British in population and economy than it had been when the Astorians withdrew in 1813. But even as Astor was making his final capitulation in 1833, agreeing to stay east of the Rocky Mountains, Americans were preparing what became the first settlements of American families on the Pacific slope. For the next decade, under missionary auspices, Oregon seemed more promising and popular than California.

The Methodist mission that Jason Lee founded on the Williamette River in 1834 marked a revival of American interests in the Northwest coast along both novel and traditional lines. On the one hand, the missionaries came largely from the East, as the early traders had come, and some made the trip by sea. On the other hand, the first contingents planned to work among inland tribes, and those who went overland to the Far West showed that families could travel across the mountains. They soon fostered a new tide of immigration from the older Western states of the Mississippi Valley.

For some years indications had been that if American missionaries came to the Northwest they would settle on the coast. Much of the early discussion developed in Hawaii, which was the principal center of missionary activity in the Pacific in the 1820's and 1830's. As a way station for traders to the Northwest coast and California, which it had been since the earlier years when traders first came for sea-otter skins, Hawaii was the nearest outpost of New England. A committee of the American Board in 1827 suggested planting a coastal station as an extension of the missions that were already flourishing in the islands: "Thus may be sent forth another Plymouth colony." Accordingly, in 1829 the Reverend Jonathan S. Green explored the Northwest coast for the American Board and recommended establishing a mission and a colony in the vicinity of the Columbia, where climate and soil offered excellent prospects for growth. The Methodists had less of a tradition of interest in the Pacific than the New Englanders of the American Board churches, but when Ross Cox, one of the Astorians of 1811–13, published his memoirs in 1831, a reviewer in the *Methodist Magazine* discussed the region with enthusiasm and proposed founding without delay "an aboriginal mission at Astoria at the mouth of the Columbia river," which he said would "soon become a place of considerable traffic. . . ."[3]

By chance, or perhaps as a result of a long chain of events going back to Lewis and Clark and their successors, funds became available for missions in the northern Cascades rather than in western Oregon. The Nez Percé Indians had been interested in the white man's religion (that is, in his medicine, or power) ever since they had first seen his guns and trading goods. In 1831–2 a party of three, joined by a Flathead, visited St. Louis, where they talked to William Clark and others, probably without making themselves understood; two of the group died and were buried in a Roman Catholic cemetery. An account of this obscure episode in the Methodist *Christian Advocate and Journal* the next year transmuted it into an appeal from the Flatheads for Protestant instruction; the Flatheads allegedly were in special need of missionaries to persuade them to stop binding their children's heads in infancy. (Actually the name of the tribe was derived not from physiognomy or from cosmetic practice, but from Indian sign language.) The result was the sending of the first missionaries to the Northwest, though not their establishment among the mountain peoples. Jason Lee, who headed the Methodist mission to the Flatheads in 1834, decided

---

[3] *Missionary Herald,* Vol. XXIII (December 1827), p. 397; Vol. XXVI (April 1830), pp. 132–3; Vol. XXVII (April 1831), pp. 106–7. *Methodist Magazine,* Vol. XIV (July 1832), pp. 281, 312.

that they were poor prospects for conversion and that it would be better to work among the Indians west of the Cascades, who lived in a good agricultural country and might more easily accept civilization as a step to Christianization. Accordingly he settled instead on the Willamette River, near the farms of the retired fur traders.

The traffic of American settlers soon exceeded most expectations; the conversion of the Indians lagged from the beginning. "It is rather my opinion that it is easier converting a tribe of Indians at a *Missionary Meeting*," Lee reported, "than in the wilderness."[4] Just before the missionaries came, disease swept away large numbers of Indians—in John McLoughlin's estimate, perhaps ninety percent of those below the falls of the Columbia River. Most who remained proved unpromising pupils, as seafarers who knew the coast had long predicted they would. But at least they were in no position, few as they were and so close to Fort Vancouver, to make much trouble. The experiment of converting the horse-riding hunting Indians of the interior fell to agents of the American Board, including Dr. Marcus Whitman, who went west in 1835 to confirm the report that the Indians desired instruction and who established a mission among the Cayuse at Waiilatpu, near Walla Walla, in 1836. The new establishments already were proving prohibitively expensive in proportion to the spiritual returns, when the depression of 1837 compounded the problem of raising funds, and by 1844 the Methodists closed their Northwestern missions. The Whitmans were resisting similar decisions of the American Board (1842) when Dr. Whitman rode east in 1842–3 to argue in person that the mission should continue. The massacre of Whitman and his family in 1847 was the bloodiest and most tragic of a series of reversals. Ironically, perhaps the clearest evidence of Whitman's success as a missionary was that the Cayuse were unable to hold out in the desultory war (1848–50) that followed his death: they had learned enough farming so that they were unable to live as hunters. The only substantially successful missionaries were the Roman Catholics, who converted McLoughlin himself; in 1841 Father Pierre-Jean De Smet establisted a station among the Flatheads in the Bitter Root Valley, on the east side of the divide.

The tragedy of the Whitmans' deaths has helped their admirers to exaggerate their part in the settlement of Oregon, and exaggeration

[4] Cornelius J. Brosnan: *Jason Lee, Prophet of the New Oregon* (New York: The Macmillan Company; 1932), p. 62.

in turn has helped their critics to minimize it. Soon the surviving missionaries found their influence declining as newcomers outnumbered them, men who felt that they owed little to their predecessors, whether at Fort Vancouver or at the declining mission stations. Yet to the authorities of the Hudson's Bay Company—watching the growing stream of immigrants with both anxiety and sympathy, doling out supplies both out of charity and out of fear that the Americans might take them by force, or at least turn to rival merchants—Lee and Whitman and their associates were the catalysts of American settlement, and perhaps more. "It always seemed," McLoughlin wrote in 1847, trying to explain why the Americans came and so swiftly destroyed the Company's monopoly, "that the great influx of American Missionaries . . . [and] the statements of the Country these Missionaries sent to their friends circulated through the United States in the public papers [were] the remote cause. . . ." The immigrants had barely established themselves when they began to testify that they had not only survived but also had prospered, eating strawberries as well as wheat, and green peas picked on Christmas day. The missionaries offered physical assistance as well at stations in the Snake River Country, a good five hundred miles east of Fort Vancouver; and though some of the immigrants ungratefully charged that prices were extortionate, many of them might not have begun or completed their journeys but for the supplies and shelter and directions the missionaries offered them.[5]

Yet the missionaries were neither first nor alone in advertising the Oregon country. Hall J. Kelley, the eccentric New Englander and self-anointed apostle of the Oregon country, was sending letters and pamphlets to members of Congress as early as 1828. In turn he may have caught fire from Representative John Floyd, who was arguing in 1821 that Oregon might be settled, though to Floyd the most likely source of colonists was China. Misfortune seemed less to disillusion

---

[5] McLoughlin, enclosure in Peter S. Ogden and James Douglas to George Simpson, March 16, 1847, in *The Letters of John McLoughlin . . . Third Series, 1844–46*, ed. E. E. Rich (Toronto: Champlain Society, 1944), p. 295. It is commonplace to criticize the missionaries for worldliness because they established farms as well as churches. Yet the officers of the American Board, while instructing them to keep "all yr worldly and secular concerns" to a minimum, contemplated that the mission families should add to their scanty stipends by providing for most of their own needs—which meant establishing farms and mills—and the original proposals for Oregon missions contemplated sending surpluses of "timber, fish, and other necessaries" to the mission in Hawaii.

some of these early advocates than to direct their enthusiasm into new channels: the missionaries' inability to make Indians into good farmers and willing Christians freed them, in a sense, to urge white settlers to move into the Indians' lands; Kelley's quarrels with the Hudson Bay Company gave him a patriotic cause. Neither did the memory of his own failure in 1811–2 restrain John Jacob Astor from commissioning a tribute to his own vision along lines quite foreign to the original commercial enterprise. In writing *Astoria* (1836), Washington Irving glorified his patron as the architect of settlement on a large scale, "along the shores of the Pacific as . . . [along] the shores of the Atlantic," and emphasized the "mildness and equability of the climate": the seven months from March to October "serene and delightful," with scarcely any rain. If Astor had succeeded, he went on, "the country would have been explored and settled by industrious husbandmen; and the fertile valleys bordering its rivers, and shut up among its mountains, would have been made to pour forth their agricultural treasures to contribute to the general wealth." When Senator Lewis F. Linn of Missouri drew on Irving and others in reporting on Oregon in 1838, he had improved further on the climate—"it may almost be considered tropical"—and by the height of the Oregon controversy in the 1840's, Oregon abounded in all the products of the states except Indian corn. "Oranges, lemons, citrons, pomegranates and vegetables common to the warm climates can be cultivated here," said a writer in 1843. "The cotton plant is said to flourish well."[6]

Meanwhile California also had its literary advocates, who dwelt especially on climate and the contrast with the conditions of the overland passage, calling it the land of "eternal spring." John C. Frémont descended into the Sacramento Valley in March 1844 after an uncomfortable winter journey through the mountains of Oregon, to enjoy "green pastures with varied flowers . . . the warm green spring, to look at the rocky and snowy peaks where lately we had suffered so much." Lansford Hastings wrote in his *Emigrants' Guide* (1845) of oats eight feet high with stalks half an inch in diameter, "sufficiently

[6] *Annals of Congress*, 16 Cong., 2 Sess., January 25, 1821, pp. 956–7. Washington Irving: *Astoria; or, Anecdotes of an Enterprise beyond the Rocky Mountains* (New York: G. P. Putnam; 1861), *Works*, Vol. VIII, pp. 39, 333–4, 499–500. *Senate Reports*, 25 Cong., 2 Sess., no. 470 (June 6, 1838), p. 18. "Oregon," *United States Magazine, and Democratic Review*, Vol. XII (April 1843), pp. 343, 345.

large and strong, for walking sticks," and wheat yielding 120 bushels to the acre.[7] But this fairyland languished in the hands of members of a degenerate race who ignored their opportunities, wasted their substance, and harassed foreign visitors.

The Capitol at Washington become a sounding board for some of the most effective propaganda for Oregon and California in the early 1840's. Senator Thomas Hart Benton of Missouri, who at one time had felt that the United States could not incorporate states on the Pacific coast, contended in his memoirs that the government in the generation after the War of 1812 had served chiefly to endanger title to Oregon, prevent immigration, and incur the loss of the country, whereas the people had saved it. The news of Senator Linn's bill to donate land to settlers (which passed the Senate in 1843) and the reports of Frémont's explorations helped the people to know what they should save, "giving them encouragement," as Benton said, "from the apparent interest which the government took in their enterprise." As early as 1831 the Senate had incorporated in a published report a letter of the fur traders, Smith, Jackson, and Sublette, describing the route they had taken to the head of Wind River and asserting that "the wagons could easily have crossed the Rocky Mountains. . . ."[8]

By the time the politicians made issues of Oregon, California, and Texas in 1843–6, the immigrants were on their way, and Western senators found eager demand for copies of government reports and maps and of their own speeches about the Oregon question. The controversy with Great Britain over the Northwestern boundary that Polk and the Democrats warmed up for the campaigns of 1844 and 1846 gave Oregon the best publicity it had had, in no wise hampered by the impression that New England Whigs might be willing to give way on the Columbia River while pressing for San Francisco.[9] And a

---

[7] J. C. Frémont: *Report of the Exploring Expedition to . . . Oregon and North California in the Years 1843–44* (Washington: Gales & Seaton; 1845), p. 249. Lansford W. Hastings: *The Emigrants' Guide to Oregon and California . . .* (Cincinnati: George Conklin; 1845), pp. 87, 89.

[8] Thomas H. Benton: *Thirty Years' View; or, a History of the Working of the American Government for Thirty Years, from 1820 to 1850 . . .* (New York: D. Appleton & Co.; 1886), Vol. II, pp. 469, 477–8. *Senate Documents*, 21 Cong., 2 Sess., no. 39. *Message from the President of the United States . . .*, January 24, 1831 (1831), pp. 21–2.

[9] Edwin A. Miles: " 'Fifty-four Forty or Fight'—An American Political Legend," *Mississippi Valley Historical Review*, Vol. XLIV (September 1957), pp. 291–309, demonstrates that "Fifty-four Forty or Fight" was not a Democratic campaign slogan.

climactic advertisement, carried in newspapers of all political persuasions, came in the shape of the Mexican War, which brought American troops into control of California almost as the diplomats were agreeing to divide the Oregon country. Some of the biggest land booms in American history had ridden in the baggage trains of troops fighting earlier Western wars, glorious and inglorious; the conquest of California promised to sustain the tradition even before miners began to pan gold on the American River in 1848.

The war coincided with a third wave of migration to the Far West, later than the beginnings of Oregon and California and larger in its first stages: the Mormon occupation of Utah. Soon after the prophet Joseph Smith (1805–44) proclaimed the Church of Jesus Christ of Latter-day Saints in 1830, its members began to try to gather the faithful together on the frontier and considered moving even beyond the Rockies, perhaps to Oregon. Smith laid the cornerstone of Zion at Independence, Missouri, in 1831, and Saints later settled at another prophetically named Missouri town, Far West. But their unconverted neighbors drove them from Kirtland, Ohio, in 1837, the next year from Missouri, and finally from Illinois, where a mob killed Smith in 1844. In 1846 the refugees in Illinois crossed the Mississippi into Iowa, and their new leader, Brigham Young (1801–77), prepared to seek a new refuge in the unsettled country around Great Salt Lake. The area was not quite unknown, for fur traders had made rendezvous there four times between 1825 and 1828; Jedediah Smith had called it his mountain home; and John C. Frémont explored the lake itself in a rubber boat in 1843. The arrival of the party that Young led to Salt Lake in July 1847 had a quality of fulfillment that reminded Mormons of the Israelites' descent into the Land of Canaan after a pillar of cloud and fire; but their destination was clear enough before they started, so that members of a separate party, which Sam Brannan took by sea to San Francisco in 1846, had little difficulty in meeting them. The Mormons bought out their only competitor nearby, a Yankee wanderer named Miles Goodyear, who had a farm at the site of Ogden, and prepared to consolidate their empire. By the next year, 1848, there were nearly five thousand of them—about as many people as went to Oregon in the ten years after the first American settlement in 1834.

In later years the pioneers disagreed about why they had come, and several decades of patriotic oratory at old settlers' meetings did little to sharpen their memories or help them to distinguish cause from effect. Peter H. Burnett, who went from Missouri to Oregon in 1843, insisted when he wrote his memoirs that he had gone first of all to "assist in building up a great American community on the Pacific coast"—a motive fitting enough for a man who became the first governor of California. But he recalled also that he had become interested when he read a Congressional report on Oregon and learned that by the Linn bill he would be entitled to receive 1,600 acres of land for himself and his wife and six children; and the descriptions of the Oregon climate had appealed because Mrs. Burnett had been in poor health and suffered from the cold winters of Missouri. Times were hard in the Mississippi Valley in the early 1840's. The depression of 1837 had arrived late but lingered long. The market at New Orleans was glutted. And the burden of buying a farm in a harsh climate seemed heavy to men who read of free farms in the land of high wages and perpetual spring, all of this accessible, according to Frémont, by "an easy carriage road across our continent from the Western states to the Oregon." No "country in the world," Burnett wrote from the promised land in 1844, "affords so fair an opportunity to acquire a living as this. . . . As for the climate, it is the finest you ever saw:—Winter commences in December, and ends in February." Although the Linn bill had failed to come to a vote in the House, its passage in the Senate, recalled Senator Benton, greatly stimulated immigration. At Fort Vancouver, Dr. McLoughlin saw it mount: from about 875 in the fall of 1843 to about 1,400 in 1844 and nearly 3,000 in 1845. Not so many came the next year, but in 1845 the coast seemed an extension of the Mississippi Valley frontier. "Our people," the California correspondent of a Baltimore paper reported, "like a sure heavy and sullen tide, are overflowing the country. Among them, I can almost imagine myself in Indiana."[1]

Yet the migration to the coast differed both in size and in kind from that to other Wests. The teams and wagons of the immigrants converged on Independence and other outfitting points for the overland trails during several weeks each spring and made them look more crowded than they were, which was perfectly agreeable to promoters and to politicians committed to expansion. But the steady tide of migration

[1] Peter H. Burnett: *Recollections and Opinions of an Old Pioneer* (New York: D. Appleton & Co.; 1880), pp. 97—8, 192. Burnett letter, July 25, 1844, in *Niles' National Register,* Vol. LXVIII (November 2, 1844), p. 130; Vol. LXV (October 28, 1843), p. 139. Benton: *Thirty Years' View,* Vol. II, p. 477. *Baltimore Patriot,* quoted in *Niles' National Register,* Vol. LXIX (December 20, 1845), p. 244.

into the older territories and states was larger by far. The census of 1850 shows that the increase in population in any one Mississippi Valley state over the previous ten years had been larger than the total population of the United States west of the Rockies, including both the Mormons of 1847–50 and the gold hunters of 1848–50. Much the smallest state in the Mississippi Valley was Iowa, which added 149,102 persons to the 43,112 it had had in 1840, whereas Oregon, California, and Utah combined in 1850 had only 117,271 persons (or ten times the population of 1846). Wisconsin in the same years increased by 274,446, from a population of 30,945 in 1840.[2]

That more emigrants did not come to the coast is understandable enough in view of the cost and the difficulty of the journey, which were not entirely unknown in the East. And all published descriptions were not so favorable as those of Kelley, Irving, and Frémont. The earliest visitors to the Oregon country were fur traders and explorers who saw chiefly the coasts and rivers and sent back reports of heavy forests, incessant rain, and difficult and dangerous approaches by land or sea. Lewis and Clark spent a miserable winter along the lower Columbia in 1805–6, "cold and wet, our clothes and bedding rotten"; in a ten-day period there was no interval longer than two hours without rain. Likewise Thomas J. Farnham, who wrote in 1840 that Oregon was "in every respect . . . overrated," had had an unhappy experience with wet weather—by one account, he lost his way in the woods and spent a night up to his ankles in a mire. Frémont reported the gloominess of an Oregon winter in 1843. The most ambitious expedition of the 1830's, which Nathaniel Wyeth organized in 1832–3, was not only a commercial disaster for its leader but also a literary defeat for the Oregon country, which his nephew, John B. Wyeth, described in *Oregon, or a Short History of a Long Journey* (1833)—perhaps a book "of *little lies* told for gain," as the elder Wyeth called it, but of considerable influence. In a letter that a Congressional committee printed, John Wyeth described the land along the Columbia as "a mere collection of sand and rocks." Summarizing the most authoritative estimates in 1844, the librarian of the Department of State, who had presented the American claim for the Oregon country, painted a decidedly conservative picture

---

[2] Native Iowans resident in the state in 1850 numbered only 41,357, as compared with 129,574 born in other states and 20,969 born abroad. *Seventh Census of the United States: 1850* Washington: Robert Armstrong; 1853), p. 948 and *passim*.

of its prospects: whereas Oregon contained "lands in small detached portions, which may afford to the industrious cultivator the means of subsistence . . . it produces no precious metals, no opium, no cotton, no rice, no sugar, no coffee. . . . With regard to commerce, it offers no great advantages, present or immediately prospective."[3]

Negative reports meanwhile came even out of California, which seemed to have a singular capacity to turn a different face to every visitor. Lieutenant Charles Wilkes of the United States Exploring Expedition came in a dry year (1841), when the cattle were starving in the fields, and, like most visitors before the 1870's, he left with a most unfavorable impression of the future metropolis of San Francisco: dilapidated buildings, sand, rock, mud flats, and inclement winds that reminded his officers of Cape Horn.[4] Disappointed immigrants shuttled from California to Oregon to escape the drought, from Oregon to California to escape the rains, and back to the states to escape both; and they wrote letters that got into the press and gratified those who had been wise enough to stay at home. The only part of the Far West that generally proved better than first reports indicated was the Great Salt Lake country, which only a dedicated faith such as the Mormons' could make worth considering, and whose chief merit may have been that no one else would come there to bother a persecuted people.

In later years, when most of the coast had prospered more than anyone expected in pioneer days, and when the men and women who had decided to live there had more to say about themselves and why they had gone than others had to say about why they had remained in the older states, it was easy to build up a picture of a pioneer who was stronger, wiser, and more virtuous than most other Americans. At the time some competent observers had different impressions. Sir George Simpson, governor of the Hudson's Bay Company, distrusted

---

[3] *History of the Expedition under the Command of Captains Lewis and Clark . . .*, ed. Paul Allen (New York: New Amsterdam Book Co.; 1902), Vol. II, pp. 254–99. *Niles' National Register*, Vol. LVIII (June 20, 1840), p. 242. Charles Wilkes: *Narrative of the United States exploring Expedition . . .* (Philadelphia: Lee & Blanchard; 1845), Vol. IV, p. 362. J. C. Frémont: *Report of the Exploring Expedition to the Rocky Mountains in the Year 1842, and to Oregon and North California in the Years 1843–'44* (Washington: Gales & Seaton; 1845), pp. 191, 194–5. *Dictionary of American Biography*, Vol. XX, pp. 576–7. Wyeth to Cushing, Feb. 4, 1839, quoted in *House Reports*, 25 Cong., 3 Sess., no. 101, supplement, February 16, 1839, pp. 15–6. Robert Greenhow: *The History of Oregon and California . . .* (Boston: Charles C. Little & James Brown; 1844), p. 399.

[4] Wilkes: *Narrative of the United States Exploring Expedition.* Vol. V, pp. 152–4.

the Willamette Valley settlers as "men of desperate character and fortune," and instructed Dr. McLoughlin (1845) to withdraw to Fort Victoria on Vancouver Island, "so as to be as much as possible out of reach of the troublesome people by whom you are surrounded at present." The American settlers, an English naval officer observed, were "almost all from the Western Provinces and chiefly from the Missouri." Older American residents deplored the manners of the newcomers and their violence against McLoughlin. Watching and assisting the stream of settlers, Whitman wished that there might be more Easterners among them.[5]

Yet the truth about the pioneers may lie closer to their own rosy estimates of themselves. Much of the immigration of the forties came from Missouri, but much of it also came from the East. Nearly half of the adult white males in Oregon Territory in 1850 had been born in Atlantic-coast states, only about eleven percent of them west of the Mississippi River, and most of the Oregonians listed as natives of Missouri were children. The gold-rush immigrants dominate the census figures for California, but unofficial tabulations of those who came from year to year show that there also, through the 1840's, most immigrants came from the states east of the Mississippi, though New England had lost its old dominance and New Englanders thus had grounds for complaint. Moreover, those who went all the way to the coast were distinctly better educated than those who stopped in the western Mississippi Valley, and probably had been more prosperous as well. The rate of illiteracy in Oregon (1850) was less than a third the rate in Iowa, less than a fifth that in Missouri. "They brought large herds of cattle, and judging from their appearance," McLoughlin wrote of the migration of 1845, "they seem with few exceptions to have been in easy circumstances in their own Country." Peter Burnett had been a debtor in Missouri but also a fairly prosperous and successful lawyer.[6] The new Far Westerners were not seminary graduates, but neither were

---

[5] Frederick W. Merk: "The Oregon Pioneers and the Boundry," *American Historical Review,* Vol. XXIX (July 1924), pp. 691–3. Whitman to David Greene, April 8, 1845, and Greene to Whitman, April 14, 1845, in *Marcus Whitman, Crusader,* eds. Archer B. and Dorothy P. Hulbert, Part III, *1843 to 1847* (Denver: Stewart Commission of Colorado College and the Denver Public Library; 1941), *Overland to the Pacific,* Vol. VIII, pp. 132, 139–40, 252–3.

[6] Jesse S. Douglas: "Origins of the Population of Oregon in 1850," *Pacific Northwest Quarterly,* Vol. XLI (April 1950), pp. 95–108. McLoughlin to Governor *et al.,* Hudson's Bay Company, *McLoughlin Letters . . . , 1844–46,* p. 143. Burnett: *Recollections,* p. 98.

they border ruffians. They assumed a more respectable appearance when they had had time to clean up after the journey. Soon the immigrants of 1841–8 settled down to deplore the manners and morals of those who came in 1849, and then the pioneer societies incorporated both groups, to criticize those who came later still.

The settlers who went to the valley of Great Salt Lake in 1847 always have seemed more different from other Far Westerners than the successive waves of immigrants to the coast seemed different from each other. Senator Elbert Thomas liked to say that he came from the only state where the Jews were Gentiles and the Irish were Republicans; these are the least of a long series of novelties. When Brigham Young led in the first band of Mormon pioneers, the Salt Lake country was not yet Utah, but rather "eastern California" or "the Rocky Mountains" (which also referred to Oregon when the missionaries first went there); but no one confused either the land or the people. The Mormons alone had settled out of easy reach of the water route to the states. They alone not only brought their church with them but also came as a church, united to themselves and divided from the rest of the West in their heroic flight from persecution and in beliefs that other Americans thought at best fantastic. Suspicion mingled with the relief that the overland emigrants to Oregon and California felt on first glimpsing the glittering roofs and green orchards of Salt Lake City and with the pleasant expectations of profitable trading that the Mormon merchants felt when the emigrants stopped to refit for the journey beyond.

Yet the Mormons shared much with other Far Westerners when they came, and still more as they stayed. Although their last homes had been in Missouri and Illinois, they had come more from the East than from the Middle Western frontiers. The new Saints of the 1830's and 1840's were chiefly townspeople from well-established communities.[7] Their distaste for Missourians came not only from their experiences at Independence and Far West, where they had sought Zion in the 1830's, but also from their prejudices as Northerners and New Englanders. Some of the main statistical tests of the census-makers—literacy, birthplace, urban-rural ratios—set them apart from their neighbors in the Mississippi Valley. And they came by essentially the same route as the

---

[7] Samuel George Ellsworth: "A History of Mormon Missions in the United States and Canada, 1830–1860" (unpublished doctoral thesis, University of California at Berkeley; 1951), pp. 332–7.

California and Oregon immigrants, along the Platte River, and used the same reports and maps to guide them.

By the middle forties the coast had changed vastly since Americans first had known it in the 1780's, but it was still the most remote of American frontiers. It seemed no closer to American control than it had when Gray entered the Columbia. For half a century Oregon had been open, the *North American Review* observed early in 1846, and yet, until the preceding four or five years, its only tenants had been Indians, wolves, bears, and hunters. The *Review* was misinformed, but only in detail. For all the fanfare in Congress and in the press, those who had gone west of the Rockies by 1846 were fewer in number than those who had gone to a single county of the territory of Wisconsin. The chief frontier of settlement was still in the Mississippi Valley. "Eastern men," wrote P. L. Edwards, a Missourian (1842) who had spent four winters in Oregon and preferred his own state, "are more generally pleased with the country than those of the west."[8] Only a few hundred had come to see and then had liked it well enough to stay.

Through the 1830's the Americans who went to the coast were chiefly Easterners, seamen, traders, and missionaries. Most of them farmed only because they had to, and incidentally. In the forties, for several years, most of their successors came as farmers, and overland from the Mississippi Valley rather than by sea from the East. They were Baptists and Methodists rather than Congregationalists, insofar as they were anything—and to some of their predecessors they seemed little enough.

As it happened, the newcomers of the forties, and their ways, were not so new as they seemed. They were a blend of old stocks in new proportions rather than a simple transplantation from the Missouri frontier. Their backgrounds, the cost of the trip west, and the climate and situation of the new country conspired to distinguish the settlers who went west of the Rockies from those who remained in the interior. Then within three years, 1846–9, an international war and the discovery of gold on the American River made the Far West still closer to the older states, and at once more like and more unlike them than anyone had thought possible.

---

[8] *North American Review*, Vol. LXII (January 1846), p. 216. P. L. Edwards: *Sketch of the Oregon Territory or, Emigrants' Guide* (reprint of edition published at Liberty, Mo., 1842 [Kansas City: H. C. Revercomb; 1951]), p. 19.

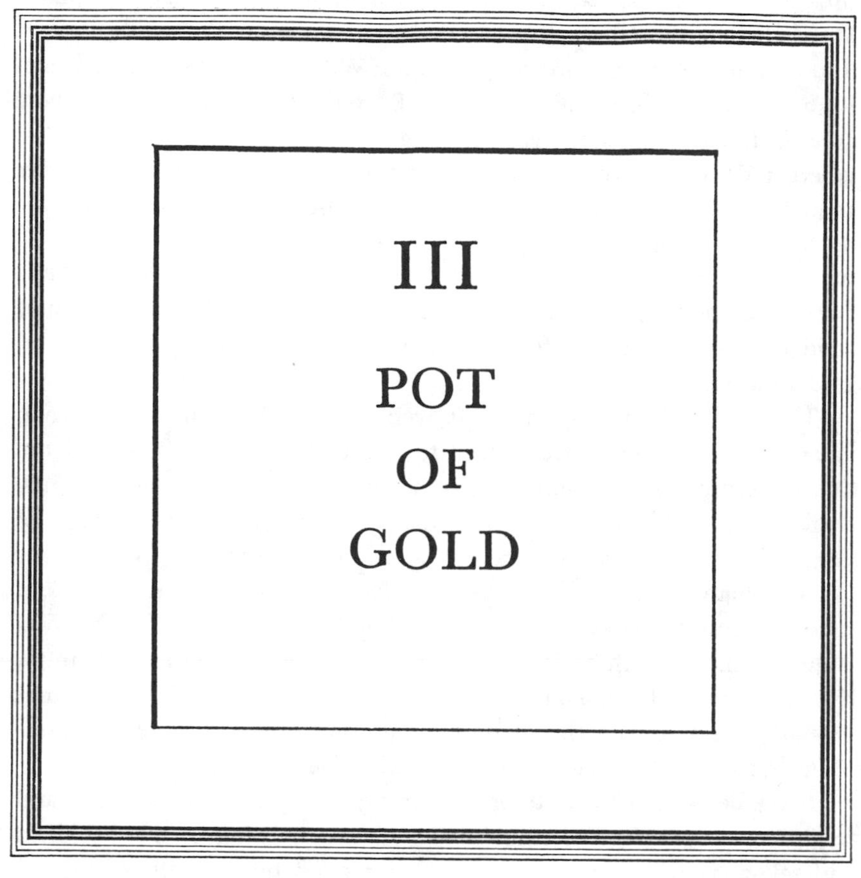

III

POT OF GOLD

In February 1848, Representative Truman Smith of Connecticut asked Commander Charles Wilkes, U. S. N., who had commanded the United States Exploring Expedition ten years earlier, to comment on the value of Upper California. Wilkes's reply was uniformly pessimistic, as Smith probably had expected it to be. The country had been badly overrated. Agriculture would have to struggle against alternate drought and flood. Having little to offer in exchange, California could support neither extensive commerce nor settlement for business purposes nor cities. "You may now be disposed to ask," he concluded, "for what is California fit? I answer, its good harbors are well adapted for our whaling fleet to recruit in, for a naval depot, and to ensure us the full command of the Pacific."[1] Five weeks earlier, on January 24, James Marshall had picked up the first flakes of gold on the south fork of the American River, and by the time Wilkes's words reached San Francisco, the male population of the Eastern states seemed on its way as well. It would be some years before an impartial observer could tell whether Wilkes or the forty-niners were more nearly right. It would be some years before there were any impartial observers of California.

Yet, as Wilkes himself suggested, interest in California was already running high; and it is almost as clear that Marshall would not have discovered gold but for the migration of 1847 as it is that there would have been no rush to California in 1849 if someone had not discovered gold in 1848.

Through 1848 more immigrants went to Oregon than to California; in 1847 and 1848 more went even to Utah. President Polk signed the treaty dividing the Oregon country at the forty-ninth parallel in June 1846, too late to have much effect that summer, but in the spring the largest emigration up to then left Missouri for the Far West, three times as many as had left the year before. Most were farm families, a solid and industrious-looking lot, and they headed chiefly for the Willamette Valley, which had the reputation of being the best farm country. Not until 1848 did Congress authorize a territorial government; not until 1850 did it pass the land bill that pioneers had expected since 1843; but the main uncertainties seemed to be over.

A smaller and a far different group went to California in 1847 and 1848; it was composed of single males rather than family men, soldiers and sailors rather than civilians, and it moved by sea rather than by land. The most conspicuous were the 950 New York volunteers, who made up half the immigration of 1847. Secretary of War Marcy had specified that they should be "as far as practicable of various pursuits, and such as would be likely to desire to remain, at the end of the war, either in Oregon or any other territory in that region of the globe which may be then a part of the United States." When they were mustered out in 1848, most of them were free to investigate the news from the American River.[2]

Meanwhile California saw more of commerce and speculation than

---

[1] Wilkes to Smith, Feb. 28, 1848, in *Congressional Globe,* 30 Cong., 1 Sess., Appendix, March 2, 1848, pp. 390–1.

[2] Hubert H. Bancroft: *History of California,* Vol. V (San Francisco: History Company; 1886), pp. 500, 554–5.

of agriculture. The military had had relatively little to do there during the war, so that some troops originally assigned to the coast remained in New Mexico, but the spending of military payrolls and the flow of military supplies gave San Francisco Bay its first substantial share of the traffic that American visitors for decades had been saying it ought to have. Many of the military had time for private business and speculation, especially at the rising city of Yerba Buena, which took the more widely known name of San Francisco in January 1847 to hold its advantage over a rival town-site enterprise farther inland. All around the bay the speculators were busy. Justice Stephen J. Field later recalled that his brother, David Dudley Field, who had studied the geography of the coast while preparing two articles on the Northwestern boundary, had advised him, when they were practicing law together in New York City in 1846, to enlist for service in California, pointing out the opportunities in San Francisco and offering funds to buy land. Field waited until 1849, but others came earlier. A Pennsylvanian, James Lick, accumulated $30,000 in South America and went on to San Francisco in 1847, investing heavily in town lots during the next year, while prices were still low. Land at Montgomery and Sutter streets, where he built the Lick House, cost him $300; when he died, it was worth $750,000.[3] A contemporary and competitor was Sam Brannan, the Mormon leader, who arrived by ship from the East in July 1846, crossed the mountains the next spring, and met Brigham Young on the Green River, but returned to San Francisco and made his fortune in real estate. Farming also was profitable but less exciting; there were still enough cattle to furnish plenty of cheap meat, though not enough to sustain the old hide trade. At Monterey, Larkin became full-time consul; some of his mercantile colleagues shifted base to San Francisco, where quarters were cramped but business was more active. Building supplies sold at a premium. The demand for lumber prompted John Sutter, the German-born lord of New Helvetia (near Sacramento), to begin building a mill on the western slope of the Sierra Nevada late in 1847. His partner, James Marshall, was inspecting the tailrace one morning when he saw something glitter in the mud.

According to legend, the California gold rush began in San Francisco

[3] Stephen J. Field: *Personal Reminiscences of Early Days in California* (n.p.: the author; 1893), pp. 1–2. John S. Hittell: *A History of the City of San Francisco and Incidentally of the State of California* (San Francisco: A. L. Bancroft & Co.; 1878), pp. 87, 117, 418.

in May 1848, when Sam Brannan shouted the news in the streets. It might have begun anyway, under other circumstances, but the setting was almost ideal: a rising city of promoters like Brannan; the war just over, and young men just out of the army; a subsidized steamship service scheduled to start that fall between New York and San Francisco by way of a portage across the Isthmus of Panama. By the time the *California* entered the Golden Gate in February with the first load of forty-niners from the East, San Francisco and the whole coast seemed to be taking their places like actors in a play. For a while almost anything would sell, at almost any distance, from Oregon City to Los Angeles, and everyone who had come West seemed justified. Soon even the Mormons at Salt Lake found gentiles rewarding instead of persecuting them, grateful for the opportunity to sell cheaply and buy dearly at this improbable oasis halfway between the Rockies and the Sierra.

If in retrospect the coast soon seemed to have been ready to find gold, and San Francisco and Sacramento seemed to have created the mines almost as truly as the mines created them, yet no one had seemed to expect the windfall to come as it did. The promoters had extended themselves to the point where failures were likely to follow wholesale, but they were slower to respond to Brannan's cry than Easterners were some months later, when word finally reached New York and Washington. The Californians, Walter Colton said, at first could not conceive of gold having lain so long undiscovered. "The idea seemed to convict them of stupidity."[4] There had never been anything in the American experience quite like the gold rush or any Western immigrants quite like the goldseekers. It was all so extraordinary that when the surviving forty-niners organized pioneer societies a few years later to commemorate what they knew was worth commemorating because it was unique, they sometimes found themselves imposing the patterns of other and different pioneering experiences and the standards of their sedate old age on what they themselves had done and seen, making the story racier or more respectable than the fact.

As a man in a census report, the forty-niner was a little more like a soldier than like the pioneer husband and father of early American frontiers. He was young: over half of all Californians in 1850 were in

[4] For a prediction of rich mineral discoveries in California, see L. W. Sloat: "The Mines of Upper California," *Merchants' Magazine*, Vol. XVI (April 1847), pp. 365–7. Walter Colton: *Three Years in California* (New York: A. S. Barnes & Co.; 1850), p. 246.

their twenties, and a man was old if, like Sutter, he had reached forty-five (only one out of thirty-three was as old as fifty). He was single and much bereft of female society: only one out of thirty Californians in their twenties was female, and children were as scarce in California as they were plentiful in Iowa and Missouri. Like the typical soldier of twentieth-century America, whose cities have many more hands to spare for military service than its farms do, he came from the Eastern seaboard rather than from the corn belt: one out of every six Americans who went to California was a native of New England.[5] And a lusty quality to the amusements of mining-camp towns and of San Francisco itself was more reminiscent of military leaves off-limits than of cracker-barrel society at a Middle Western crossroads trading center.

The miners of 1849 or 1850 lived somewhat in the spirit of later-day college boys on vacation, though the drudgery of months in the wet diggings was a far cry from a week's fishing in the Maine woods or packing into the Grand Tetons. At least they were there for a lark rather than for a career; hardly anyone expected to stay after he had "seen the elephant" (that is, the latest wonder) and saved enough gold dust to pay for his time and passage and perhaps to give him a start in business at home. In later years some of them became convinced that they had gone out as commonwealth-builders, but this came of listening to orations. "Five years was the longest period any one expected to stay," recalled the San Francisco poet, Prentice Mulford, who went slightly later. "Five years at most was to be given to rifling California of her treasures, and then that country was to be thrown aside like a used-up newspaper and the rich adventurers would spend the remainder of their days in wealth, peace, and prosperity at their Eastern homes. No one talked then of going out 'to build up the glorious State of California.' No one then ever took pride in the thought that he might be called a 'Californian.' So they went."[6]

There is less than prima facie evidence of low character or low social standing in some of the records of forty-niner history: the miners

---

[5] According to the census of 1850, of the 62,691 native Americans in California who were born in other states, 27,829 were born in states west of the Appalachians, 34,862 in Eastern states (including 11,736 in New England, 10,160 in New York, and 4,506 in Pennsylvania). As in Oregon, a high percentage of males fifteen years of age and older came from the East; many listed in the census as natives of Missouri had been born into families of Easterners on their way west.

[6] *Prentice Mulford's Story* (Oakland: Biobooks; 1953), pp. 2–3.

all liked to have their pictures taken, but the best-educated of them put on the roughest clothes for the occasion, preferring the "foppery of rags and undress" to the dandyism of shaven face and white shirts. At the photographer's, a British visitor reported, "men of a lower class wanted to be shown in . . . coat, waistcoat, white shirt and neckcloth; while gentlemen miners were anxious to appear in character, in the most ragged style of California dress."[7] The ample supply of surviving diaries and letters testifies to one of the highest rates of literacy in the country. The shooting scrapes they described were a kind of literary convention as well as an actuality. ("This place is getting so civilized that really I have nothing to write," a New Englander at Weaverville complained in 1860.[8])

The cost of transportation was not in itself a decisive selective factor, for more Americans went overland in 1849 than by Cape Horn or Panama, but a brisk demand kept one of the most unseaworthy fleets in history crowded with men glad to pay $500 and more for one-way passage from New York to San Francisco; and there was no route for the utterly destitute. The high level of wages for unskilled laborers in the first years of the gold rush probably attested as much to the cost of the trip as to the yield of the mines. "Transplanting oneself to California from any part of the world involved an outlay beyond the means of the bulk of the labouring classes," recalled a Welshman, J. D. Borthwick, who went out in 1851. "The consequence was that labourers' and mechanics' wages were ridiculously high; and, as a general thing, the lower the description of labour, or of service, required, the more extravagant in proportion were the wages paid."[9]

Whatever the miners had been at home, the mining country as a whole included samples of all varieties of human nature as well as of all of Satan's principal reagents for human metallurgy. Society throughout California was much in flux, and not merely because the creek beds of the Sierra lay open as a kind of national or international lottery. The temptation of unaccustomed and accidental wealth joined the cor-

---

[7] J. D. Borthwick: *Three Years in California* (Oakland: Biobooks; 1948), p. 166.

[8] Franklin Buck: *A Yankee Trader in Gold Rush*, comp. Katherine A. White (Boston: Houghton Mifflin Co.; 1930), p. 182.

[9] John H. Kemble: *The Panama Route, 1848–1869* (Berkeley: University of California Press; 1943), pp. 54–7. Borthwick: *Three Years in Californa,* p. 53. The rate of illiteracy in native white and free colored populations over twenty years of age in 1850 was 2.86 percent for California, 8.69 percent for Iowa, 10.35 percent for the United States, 13.49 percent for Missouri.

rosive experience of living adrift in a land where almost no one cared, and without the restraints and minor decencies conventional in more settled communities. Boys barely out of school, who might never have earned a normal wage or learned to face down the devil without parents and neighbors to stiffen their virtue, found themselves on the great adventure alone, or at least among men and boys they had never seen before and expected never to see again. "When the day of toil is over," a New Yorker wrote, "they have no home or social circle to enter. The tavern tent is the resort of all, here the cards are the only books that are to be found, or looked into."[1] Most of the time the miners lived frugally and quietly, but morality seemed as unstable as a camp's population. Men who literally starved themselves into scurvy, calculating carefully the cheapest diet they could find, forgot all prudence on holidays; and then Saturday night's champagne bottle served economically as candleholder, to save buying a lamp. There seemed no midpoint between weekday salt pork and weekend oysters. That in such surroundings many sinned conspicuously may be less significant than that some abstained privately.

In later years the pioneers set down affectionate vignettes of an idyllic stage of society in the mines, usually dated 1848 but sometimes 1849, when man's natural goodness prevailed and person and property were as safe as in the legendary days of good King Henry Beauclerc. A miner found that while he was away from camp someone had borrowed his scales and buckskin bag, but had carefully poured his gold dust into a dish; a group of men donated a rich stake to a young greenhorn; neighbors neglected their claims to tend the sick. The literary variants include the favorite theme of Bret Harte, who projected the era of goodness into more sophisticated times: the camp sinner with the heart of gold. Yet the reign of virtue was brief, ending perhaps as soon as foreigners arrived (were the stories argument for expelling Mexicans and Chinese and Australian convicts?) or when it was no longer so easy to find gold as it was to steal it.

Perhaps the time to believe in Eldorado was either in retrospect, after many years, or before a man left the East, where getting ahead depended more and more on the capital he could invest in goods and tools, and where at first only the best news came from the mines. Cali-

[1] J. D. Stevenson to James H. Brady, San Francisco, April, 1849, *California Emigrant Letters*, ed. Walker D. Wyman (New York: Bookman Associates, Publishers; 1952), p. 175.

fornia seemed the fulfillment of agrarian dreams of equality and opportunity at a time when industrial inequality was closing in rapidly over the older states.[2] And it seemed especially attractive in that a man need not exile himself permanently but could bring opportunity back to enjoy it at home. "We rejoice," the editor of the New York *Merchants' Magazine* wrote, "that the El Dorado was revealed not to adventurers . . . but to the hardy emigrant, who went out to make, not to find fortune, and whom fortune has found." It was doubly fortunate that the treasure was gold rather than silver, which ordinarily demands more expensive processing. "As it is, the laborer is now the capitalist in California," Bayard Taylor reported. "There is no room for the exclusiveness and monopoly of capital."[3]

It was so easy for Taylor to find what he had come to find that he returned from California to write a best seller, after four months of reporting for Horace Greeley, with his hands still clean and uncalloused. ("Don't be frightened at what I may say of Indians, grizzly bears, and the like," he had written from Monterey to his fiancée; "the greatest thing to be feared in this country is fleas. . . ."[4]) For most of the gold seekers, primitive virtue and trust in human nature and the first bloom of confidence in El Dorado itself evaporated before they arrived, perhaps in one of the crowded hulks between Panama and San Francisco or in an overland caravan. And at the diggings what order there was at first seemed curiously negative, the absence of restraint as well as of violence in a society that hardly anyone thought to organize because hardly anyone thought of himself apart from the society he had left, temporarily, in the East.

The worst consequences of placer mining in its early stages, from the social point of view, followed on the very circumstances that made it seem the fulfillment of democracy. The first reports were of gold so plentiful that one found it almost without looking for it: in the words

---

[2] "At home," wrote a young printer of West Chester, Pennsylvania, who went to California in 1849–50, "there is little chance for a mechanic without capital to rise very fast. I must therefore, if possible, make something to begin with before I return." Enos Christman: *One Man's Gold. The Letters & Journal of a Forty-Niner*, ed. Florence M. Christman (New York: Whittlesey House; 1930), pp. 225–6.

[3] *Merchants' Magazine*, Vol. XX (January 1849), p. 61. Bayard Taylor: *Eldorado, or Adventures in the Path of Empire* (New York: G. P. Putnam's Sons; 1894), p. 314.

[4] Sept. 23, 1849, Taylor to Mary Agnew, in *Life and Letters of Bayard Taylor*, ed. Marie Hansen-Taylor and Horace E. Scudder (Boston: Houghton, Mifflin & Co.; 1884), Vol. I, p. 157.

of Walter Colton, "a German . . . picking a hole . . . for a tent-pole, struck a piece of gold, weighing about three ounces"; "a little girl . . . picked up what she thought a curious stone, and brought it to her mother, who . . . found it a lump of pure gold, weighing between six and seven pounds." It was disturbing enough to the prudent and moral to reflect on how such unearned riches would undermine thrift and the doctrine of hard work. It was still more disturbing to those willing so to be corrupted to find, upon arriving, that most of the gold lay at least several feet under mud and rock, and that hardly any of it in the streams occurred in lumps or pockets large and compact enough to make a man rich overnight. Whoever found a promising deposit also found neighbors ready to share it with him: there was no keeping a secret in this open-air industry, and a successful prospector usually served others more than himself. The more ambitious or impatient turned to other and surer means of making a living, often means that levied toll on the miner and insured that he could keep little of what he earned. "When one hears of the return of men with large fortunes," John W. Audubon wrote in 1850, "ask if speculations in land or trade, bar-keeping or Monte dealing has not swollen the first few hundreds, dug and gained with hard labor, privation, or, in rare cases, wonderful luck."[5]

Most of the miners heard stories of the good luck of other miners but had none themselves. Their search for El Dorado was all the more monotonous because hope or desperation and the novelty of being free to make a change kept them working under conditions that they would have rebelled against in the East: feet in an icy mountain stream, head in the broiling sun; long hours, because they were their own bosses, and poor food, because they were their own cooks. Everything they did seemed to reflect the makeshift arrangements of a country where a man owned none of the land he worked and might at any moment decide to move on to the next diggings or return home.

But the camp on a creek bank did not survive much longer than the miner himself. Placer mining evolved rapidly from treasure hunt to engineering venture. Even in the summer of 1849 men were associating to divert streams from their channels, and the next year the first of the ditch and flume companies began to carry water to diggings that were

[5] Walter Colton: *Three Years in California*, pp. 291–2. *Audubon's Western Journal: 1849–1850 . . .*, ed. Frank H. Hodder (Cleveland: Arthur H. Clark Co.; 1906), pp. 205–6.

too dry rather than too wet. Gold dust in the deep gravels of prehistoric stream beds was ordinarily out of the reach of the lone man with a pickax.

Quartz or vein mining ultimately involved still more drastic changes and larger capitalization. Some of the earliest prospectors realized that the gold dust in stream beds was only the washings of larger deposits somewhere upstream and that if they knew where to look they might follow a vein of gold into the earth as easily as a vein of coal. When they did, mining became an industry, and though the operations of the 1850's were relatively simple, it was an industry with a rapidly increasing appetite for capital. Men still dug in the largest mines, but few men could independently shore up a tunnel, build a railroad, drain a shaft, crush heavy masses of quartz or "cement," and separate it from the metal.

Meanwhile technique advanced still more spectacularly among miners searching deeper and deeper for placer gold. Some of the richest deposits were in ancient river beds buried so far under accumulations of glacial debris that digging after them was both laborious and dangerous, though in the early fifties many miners were tunneling like animals into the banks of streams in the Sierra Nevada—coyoting, they called it. Shortly, ground-sluicing supplemented simple digging: water from a ditch or flume washed down the earth, enlarging a trench into a gully. By 1853 a hose on a nozzle had succeeded the simple flume, and hydraulic power was soon tearing down hillsides at enormous savings in time and labor and exposing the gold left hundreds of feet under the surface by the prehistoric Tertiary Yuba River. Eventually the volume of sand and gravel swept into river beds and lowlands did such great injury to navigation, to agriculture, and to the very safety of the river towns that the courts virtually prohibited hydraulic mining (1884). But for a generation water power mined the gold.[6]

The "honest miner" long continued a celebrated figure in Far Western politics and folklore, but gold mining quickly ceased to be democratic opportunity and became instead big business. "In 1848," Rodman Paul concludes, "it had offered to all the world the chance to be one's own master, and to all it had promised an equal opportunity for wealth.

---

[6] Robert L. Kelley: "Forgotten Giant: The Hydraulic Gold Mining Industry in California," *Pacific Historical Review*, Vol. XXIII (November 1954), pp. 343–56; Kelley: "The Mining Debris Controversy in the Sacramento Valley," *Pacific Historical Review*, Vol. XXV (November 1956), pp. 331–46.

In 1873 its attractions were only those of an eastern factory town. . . ."[7] Yet it was chronically hungry for capital, ample demonstration of the old maxim that "it takes a mine to work a mine," and chronically annoyed at the San Francisco bankers for their reluctance to take risks. Meanwhile the successors to the forty-niners became chiefly prospectors, who hoped to find the vein that would support a new advance of the industry, or marked time in a limbo between starvation and comfort, doing well enough to buy bacon from week to week but not well enough to buy a ticket home.

There was no doubt that forty-nine was a fraud: after all costs, the returns in the mines on the average were less than the forty-niners might have made by investing their time and capital closer to home. (Gold mining, a California mining engineer of a later generation has said, "is an unprofitable business in any country. Taking the world as a whole, the gold produced costs more than it sells for."[8]) There is no doubt, however, that the idea of yellow gold waiting in the earth, free for the taking, and the spectacle of mines that transcended the average and made men rich, spurred the development of the Far West incalculably.

The most visible responses to the stimulus of gold were in the cities that served the miners and in the urban services they were willing to pay for. The first of the forty-niners found their way precariously from San Francisco to Sacramento in a crazy miscellany of crude sloops and launches, crowded together on open decks. Bayard Taylor made the same trip a few weeks later on the steamer *Senator*, formerly on the Boston-Eastport run, with its "well-known bell," tables "set below in the same style as at home"; "I could scarcely believe that I was in California."[9] Not everything from Eastern cities could make the trip around the Horn so easily as ships, but importers of prefabricated buildings did a comfortable business. The fantastic and costly improvisations of San Francisco testified equally to the rate of economic growth: ships converted to hotels and to waterfront fill; sidewalks of surplus merchandise, coffee, cast-iron stoves, and plug tobacco; houses with calico partitions and Oriental rugs.

Large profits came to some who served the miners directly: cooks,

---

[7] Rodman W. Paul: *California Gold . . .* (Cambridge: Harvard University Press; 1947), pp. 332–3 and *passim.* See also, on this whole chapter, Paul: *Mining Frontiers of the Far West, 1848–1880* (New York: Holt, Rinehart & Winston; 1963).

[8] Herbert C. Hoover: *Memoirs, The Years of Adventure, 1874–1920* (New York: The Macmillan Company; 1951), p. 82.

[9] Taylor: *Eldorado* (1894 ed.), p. 293.

physicians, gamblers, stagecoach operators, and saloonkeepers in the mining towns. *Hunt's Merchants' Magazine* (1852) published a letter from a woman who sold $18,000 worth of pies: "$11,000 I baked in one little iron skillet, a considerable portion by a camp fire, without the shelter of a tree from the broiling sun."[1] Some storekeepers profited more (and most less) than their prices or the volume of their business would suggest, for they became involuntary partners to miners who could not buy groceries except on credit. The greater fortunes, however, came to merchants who depended ultimately on the gold rush but lived apart from it. The gold dust washed through the miners' sluices to the businessmen of Sacramento and San Francisco, but much of the merchants' original capital came directly from the East, and they put little of it into mining stocks as long as loans secured by city property paid from three to five percent a month. The organizers of the Central Pacific Railroad, a decade after the gold rush, were dealers in hardware, groceries, and jewelry in Sacramento who had neither mined nor invested in mines.

California had leaped overnight from a decadent pastoral economy, much inferior to that of the Mississippi Valley states, to an economy of industry, commerce, and services, and before long the countryside responded to the demands of the cities. In the earliest stages of the gold fever, agriculture declined as farmers rushed to the mines from all along the coast. Then the profits of farming and especially of selling fresh produce increased so spectacularly that they overcame prejudices against Californian soil and the dry Californian climate, and men gambled by planting peas or potatoes as they gambled by digging mines and ditches. In 1849 a German farmer near Sacramento made $30,000 from melons alone; in 1851 onions from two acres in the Napa Valley sold for $2,000. The declining California cattle industry, which had been no more than an undependable outlet for hides, quickly readjusted to a spectacular demand for beef, and the ranchers found both ready markets at the mines for their longhorn stock and the means of importing bulls to improve the breed. Outside California, agriculture fared variously. Some farmers from the Northwest simply stayed in California when they had had enough of the mines; even if they had the means of returning, crops grew faster, and they were closer to the best markets. (As an English financial editor put it, hardly anyone would "scratch

[1] *Hunt's Merchants' Magazine,* Vol. XXVI (June 1852), p. 777.

the sterile soil [of Vancouver Island] for a few oats and potatoes, when he can earn five times more by the same labor in cultivating the rich alluvial valleys of California, within six days' sail of your forbidding shores."[2]) But the Mormon farmers around Salt Lake, who barely had been able to feed themselves in 1847–8, thereafter carried on a lucrative trade in produce with overland parties, and exchanged wagons and livestock at favorable ratios. Oregon had seemed deserted in 1848; in the fifties, before newer orchards began to bear, farmers of the Willamette Valley received as much as a dollar a pound for apples, which sold for $1.50 each at the mines.[3]

Meanwhile the California gold rush further affected the rest of the Far West, first by drawing population on to the overland routes, then by suggesting that there might be other bonanzas in other mountains. As early as the spring of 1850 a party of Mormons on their way to California found gold on the eastern slope of the Sierra Nevada, in the western part of what Congress shortly called Utah Territory; and a few prospectors panned for gold in Gold Canyon through the 1850's, despite modest yields, a chronic shortage of water, and inconvenient distances from the main centers of supply across the mountains. In 1852 prospectors returning to Oregon from California thought that the dry, madrone- and oak-covered Siskiyous of the upper Rogue Valley looked so much like the Sierra Nevada that they also might be gold-bearing, as they were; and Jacksonville became for a time the second city of the Northwest, a respectable town where men brought their families and built homes and churches. No one got rich overnight; the returns were steady but modest. The first rushes substantially outside California came, almost perversely, in some of the most inaccessible parts of the West: a local rush on the upper Columbia River, near the old Hudson's Bay Company post at Fort Colville, in 1855, and then reports of a new California on the rugged Fraser River, just across the Canadian border, in 1858. That spring and summer, until the miners learned that they had been deceived, they reenacted the rush up the Sacramento under far more difficult conditions; in a few weeks perhaps 123,000 came from California, and an additional third overland. When they returned to San Francisco, they learned of gold in western Kansas, near

---

[2] Theodore H. Hittell: *History of California* (San Francisco: Pacific Press Publishing House; 1885–97), Vol. III, p. 866. *Bankers' Magazine* . . . , Vol. III (April 1849), pp. 690–7.

[3] Charles H. Carey: *History of Oregon* (Chicago: Pioneer Historical Publishing Co.; 1922), Vol. I, p. 800.

Pike's Peak, and then the next year, 1859, they heard of a strike two Irishmen made when they dug a water hole near Gold Canyon. Word soon spread that the Comstock Lode was impressively rich, in silver rather than gold, but in a form that required remarkably little processing —crushing and amalgamation rather than smelting. As soon as parties from California could cross the mountains in 1860, Virginia City became the center of a frenzy of speculation.[4]

The Comstock broke effectively through California's monopoly of Far Western mining, even though western Utah was essentially tributary to San Francisco rather than to Salt Lake City. Strikes followed in the Humboldt Mountains and the Esmeralda Mountains (1860), east of the Sierra; the population seemed so likely to stay that Congress created the territory of Nevada in 1861. The next rushes were to eastern Washington, which by 1863 was Idaho: in 1860–1 at Pierce City, on the Clearwater; in 1861 at Florence, on the Salmon River; in 1862 around the Boise River; in 1863 at Silver City, on the Owyhee. Despite the short duration of the mining season in the high mountains and the difficulties of reaching them through rugged Indian country, most of the early mining towns of Idaho passed quickly from strike to boom and then fell to the Chinese, who were patient enough to glean what the white men scorned.[5] The miners of Idaho were in large part Californians, as miners everywhere seemed to be, but the districts they organized east of the Cascades were too far away for the California merchants to dominate, as well as, perhaps, too ephemeral to justify setting up the machinery of domination at a time when steadier prospects were close at hand. Idaho looked to Salt Lake City and Portland; Portland in its relation to the interior became a kind of Northwestern San Francisco. In turn there were strikes on the way, in eastern Oregon, and Oregonians developed Lewiston, on the Snake, as an outfitting point for the Salmon River country. The mines of northern Idaho were remote enough so that much of their traffic from the East came through Utah or the upper Missouri River country rather than by way of the Columbia, and in 1863 and 1864 prospectors on their way west to the Salmon River made strikes

[4] The standard account of the Comstock, and the liveliest, is Eliot Lord: *Comstock Mining and Miners* (Washington: Government Printing Office; 1883), United States Geological Survey Monographs, Vol. IV. But see also Grant H. Smith: *The History of the Comstock Lode, 1850–1920*, University of Nevada Bulletin, Vol. XXXVII, no. 3, Geology and Mining Series, no. 37 (Reno, 1943).

[5] Merle W. Wells: *Rush to Idaho*, Idaho Bureau of Mines and Geology, Bulletin no. 19 ([Moscow: 1962]), pp. 2–13, 23–25a.

in what Congress called Montana Territory, in the northern Rockies.

Although silver drew attention away from the placers of California, capitalists in San Francisco, Portland, and the East were increasingly to control the newer mines of Nevada and the Northwest. This was partly because the San Franciscans caught the speculative fever in the 1860's and 1870's, in contrast to the prudent bankers and merchants of the earlier years, who had preferred to leave grubstaking and speculation to those on the scene. More fundamentally, it was because by degrees the processes of extraction became too complex for local technology and local capital. Hydraulicking per se required nothing new in either metallurgical processes or scale, but to work the deep gravels of Nevada and Butte counties in northeastern California most efficiently called eventually for enormous complexes of canals, ditches, flumes, reservoirs, and dredges as well as for machinery and large expanses of land. Gold quartz and the silver of the Comstock also were relatively simple to refine, but a major lode or vein required lawyers to defend it, shafts and tunnels on a new scale to reach it, and with them systems of ventilators, hoists, drains, and railroads. In time one of the richest men who came out of the Comstock was Adolph Sutro, builder of the nearly four-mile-long tunnel that drained water from the lower levels of the mines, though he made most of his fortune by shifting his investments to San Francisco real estate before others realized that the tunnel had come too late to be profitable.[6] Sutro's successes at speculation and his failures at mining made it ironically appropriate that he become a popular hero of the Comstock, a champion of the interests of the common miners against those of the bankers and operators who opposed his tunnel. Eventually he was Populist mayor of San Francisco, where he opened his gardens to the people for their pleasure.

There was further irony in the fact that both the Comstock (before Congress took western Utah to make Nevada Territory in 1861) and the first of the copper and lead-silver mines, which required more complex and expensive processing, were in the region the Mormons had set aside for their return to the pastoral simplicity of Biblical times. Before the Emma mine (1869), southeast of Great Salt Lake, became a scandal in international finance, its success attracted the merchants of Salt Lake

[6] Paul: *Mining Frontiers*, pp. 56–108. Robert E. Stewart, Jr., and Mary F. Stewart: *Adolph Sutro . . .* (Berkeley: Howell-North; 1962). W. Turrentine Jackson: *Treasure Hill: Portrait of a Silver Mining Camp* (Tucson: University of Arizona Press; 1963) describes the role of British capital in the White Pine region of Nevada, 1868–9.

City to other and metallurgically more difficult deposits. Eventually Utah's greatest mines, and for a time her greatest industry, were situated at Bingham Canyon, where the soldiers sent from California to watch the Saints during the Civil War had aroused their contempt and their concern—and contributed at once to Zion's economic salvation and to its spiritual unrest—by prospecting for gold; but the gigantic operations of the Utah Copper Company were not to take place until the following century (1903). Idaho meanwhile stagnated for a decade after the Civil War, complaining about the "gougers" who, by taking the best ore, made subsequent work difficult, and about the Chinese, whose increase there as elsewhere was a sign of returns too scanty to hold the interest of other miners. In the later seventies southern Idaho experienced a revival, though in lead-silver deposits that, like those of Montana in the same years, were most profitable to capitalists in San Francisco, Portland, New York, and London, and to smelters in Utah. Discoveries of gold in the Coeur d'Alene Valley of northern Idaho in 1882 proved to be precursors of a more enduring but also more thoroughly capitalized development; the new Northern Pacific Railroad (1883) brought in a flood of Argonauts who came in greater comfort than those of forty-nine, only to take their places in the West's most bitter industrial warfare.[7]

Mining rushes continued in other new areas of the West through the century and beyond—in 1862 in western New Mexico, which became Arizona; in 1875–6 in the Black Hills of Dakota; in 1897 on the Yukon, east of the Alaskan panhandle; in 1900 at Tonopah, Nevada. But within fifteen years after 1849 the rushes had done their main work in opening up the Pacific slope. The gold and silver lay as if scattered for some Gargantuan treasure hunt. By the time the prospectors had sought out the main deposits, they had made the states and territories of the Pacific slope known and inhabited as agricultural penetration probably would not have made them known for another generation.

The mining rushes, moreover, confirmed distinctive characteristics of the West that had seemed close to eclipse in the 1840's. This was not altogether clear at the time. The early overland parties especially seemed to leave the nineteenth century behind once they crossed the Mississippi River. The needs of mules and oxen dictated their routes

---

[7] Paul: *Mining Frontiers,* pp. 149–55, 143–5. Dale L. Morgan: *The Great Salt Lake* (Indianapolis: The Bobbs-Merrill Co.; 1947), pp. 286–9, 391–3. Merrill D. Beal and Merle W. Wells: *History of Idaho* (New York: Lewis Historical Publishing Co.; 1959), Vol. I, pp. 417–21.

and their timing, and the daily routine of the camp was easiest for the boys who had had to haul water, make fires, and graze livestock on the farm. In the primitive life of the diggings, the miners developed, if they had not carried with them, a kind of mining-camp agrarianism: they stood firm against monopoly when they seemed interested in standing for or against little else. And they felt a hostility toward the city that recalls the suspicions of Western farmers. All of this suggested that the respectable merchants of pastoral California and the Hudson's Bay Company traders and missionaries of Oregon were giving way to a further inundation of frontiersmen who were closer to the mountain men and the hunters from Tennessee and the drifters from Missouri who were coming west in the middle forties.

On the whole, such impressions were illusory. The miners were more civilized than their imaginations and their physical circumstances made them seem. Perhaps some sensed that this was their last and best chance for adventure outdoors, but they came less as refugees from advancing urbanism than as its exponents. Many of them were financed by the surplus of a commercial and industrial society, and most of them hoped to find the means to establish themselves in trade or industry in one of the older states.

The mining West was itself heavily urbanized, or soon became so, drawing so much on its own mineral wealth and on the savings of Eastern investors that it was able to vault almost directly from a pre-agricultural to an industrial and commercial economy. Given its scanty population, it was already remarkably urbanized before 1848, and perhaps necessarily so. Whereas earlier Western states had tended to develop from urban jumping-off points and supply centers outside their own boundaries (so that Pittsburgh, Cincinnati, and St. Louis successively fed Wests just beyond them), the Pacific coast was too far away, too far even from Honolulu, which it depended on for a while. Thus perhaps some Western Portlands and San Franciscos and Salt Lake Cities would have had to arise even without Yankee traders, missionaries, and Mormon immigrants to found them. At all events, mining became unmistakably an industry rather than a treasure hunt; and even before the quartz-mill operators and the hydraulickers assembled their huge factories, the miners lived about as urban a life as the times and their circumstances permitted, taking their holidays or their winters in San Francisco when they could and importing the refinements and the vices of the city when they could not.

Gold was both symbol and cause of the Eastern-ness of the early Far West. Once found, it attracted Eastern capital and steamships and furnishings, as well as a population so committed to Eastern ways that it wanted a fortune rather than a livelihood, and preferred the most negotiable kind of Western wealth to the kind that would require it to live in the West. The great merit of gold to them was precisely that it had no locus: it was not a new California banknote, but the universal currency.

At the same time the people whom the gold attracted were those most likely to find it; there was more than superstition in the idea of some of the old Californians that God must have wanted the Yankees to find gold, having withheld it until California was theirs. The Americans already at hand in 1848 were typical of those who shortly came west specifically to go to the mines: city people, speculators, alert and ambitious. San Francisco was a would-be metropolis without an empire, almost entirely American, largely Eastern, and much on the make. It had drawn so many drafts on the future and as yet had so little else to justify its hopes that it was glad to shut up shop and take passage when the news came from the American River. It was attuned to gold before it knew that gold was there.

The gold rush started so much else that it soon submerged itself; soon those who had seen but left the mines far exceeded those who stayed to dig. Yet few events have so well epitomized the history of a region or so greatly influenced it. The forty-niners reinforced the Eastern and urban element that had come to the coast in more than normal strength in earlier years and that seemed, in California at least, misled in its hopes, ahead of its time. In their imprudence, their enthusiasm, their success, the forty-niners justified improbability and anticipated the shape and tenor of the coast in the century to come.

IV

POLITICAL TIES

ONE OF THE ENDURING PIECES of apocrypha in Far Western history is the story that when Sam Brannan and his shipload of Mormon colonists sailed into San Francisco Bay in the *Brooklyn* on the last day of July 1846, having left New York nearly six months earlier, when Mexico and the United States were still at peace, Sam exclaimed: "There's that damned flag again!" The odds are that he said no such thing, or even thought it, but the legend illustrates the speed of events on a coast where for many years change had been both infrequent and unlikely. Less than two years before, the United States had governed no farther west than Iowa, not yet a state; within a month it divided Oregon and seized California, which slightly over three years later was electing senators of its own and was ready to help organize its neighbors.

Months before the Civil War ended, by election day 1864, there were three states and four territories west of the Rockies, a total of five states and nine territories west of the Missouri River, and more on the way.

Yet the political definition of the Far West was a prolonged process that sometimes seems not yet over. Even on a formal level, the decisions dragged over the better part of a century, from the discussions of the Oregon question with Great Britain after the War of 1812 to the admission of Utah in 1896. Oregonians, proud that they had become a minor issue in the presidential campaign of 1844, had no territorial government until 1849.

For over half a century, title to the Oregon country had been one of the less pressing problems of American diplomacy. If Robert Gray established American title when he entered the Columbia River on May 11, 1792, he seems to have been no more aware of it at the time than the British, who never had made much of Francis Drake's landing on the California coast in 1579, nearly two centuries before the Spanish occupation. The log kept by John Boit, the seventeen-year-old fifth mate of the *Columbia*, contains the terse entry: "I landed abrest the Ship with Capt. Gray to view the Country and take possession." The last three words are in a later hand, however, apparently that of someone who realized that the great river of the West might have more than commercial possibilities.[1] For a generation no one asserted whatever American title may have followed on Gray's landing or on the explorations of Lewis and Clark; and when Oregon finally did appear on American diplomatic instructions, the problem was negative, to postpone rather than to conclude a settlement. American diplomats cautiously excluded the Northwest coast from discussions with Great Britain and Russia before the War of 1812, and at the peace conference refused to make any agreement that would disturb the American title. The Treaty of Ghent (1814) deferred the issue, requiring each party to restore territory taken during the war, which meant that the British must permit the American flag to return to Astoria (Fort George), as it did in 1817. By the Convention of 1818 the United States and Great Britain postponed deciding sovereignty for ten years, leaving Americans and Englishmen on an equal basis within the disputed area. Before the ten years had expired, in 1827, the two powers indefinitely extended this principle of amicable

[1] *Voyages of the "Columbia" to the Northwest Coast 1787–1790 and 1790–1793*, ed. Frederic W. Howay (Boston: The Massachusetts Historical Society; 1941), *Collections*, Vol. LXXIX, p. 398.

disagreement, sometimes inaccurately called joint occupation, even though what made it practicable was dearth of settlement and absence of genuine government.

By 1818, Secretary of State John Quincy Adams had begun to work quietly and stubbornly to establish title to both banks of the Columbia River and to the Puget Sound country as well. In the Transcontinental (Adams-Onís) Treaty of 1819 with Spain, Adams traded a vague tissue of claims to Texas for title to Florida and secured in the bargain whatever rights Spain had to the Northwest coast north of forty-two degrees, later to be the northern boundary of California and Nevada. Thus the competitors for the Oregon country dropped from four to three, the United States, Great Britain, and Russia; and the American case rested not only on the explorations of Gray and Lewis and Clark and on Astor's short-lived enterprise, but also on Spanish voyages made, or alleged to have been made, since the sixteenth century.

Adams, as secretary of state in 1818 and President in 1826–7, offered the British government the boundary of the forty-ninth parallel, which they eventually accepted in 1846, but the possibility of establishing it then seemed remote. What aroused the government was more the spirit of nationalism that burst out in the Monroe Doctrine—warning European colonizers away from American shores—than any serious thought of incorporating this distant territory into the republic. Even Jefferson, who expected that Cuba would fall naturally to the United States, and who watched with excitement the settlement at Astoria, confined his visions of the Pacific coast, as he described them to Astor on the eve of the War of 1812, to settlements of "free and independent Americans, unconnected with us but by the ties of blood and interest, and employing like us the rights of self-government." Thomas Hart Benton and most of the Congressional advocates of Oregon went no further in the 1820's. President Monroe himself in 1824 considered publicly opposing the settlement of Oregon, arguing that settlements on the Pacific "would necessarily soon separate from this Union"[2]—this only three months after he sent his Doctrine to Congress and only one month before Russia agreed to withdraw its claims northward to the parallel of fifty-four degrees forty minutes, which became the southern limit of the Alaskan

[2] Jefferson to Astor, May 24, 1812, in *Works*, ed. Ford, Vol. XI, p. 244, cited by Frederick Merk: *Albert Gallatin and the Oregon Problem: A Study in Anglo-American Diplomacy* (Cambridge: Harvard University Press; 1950), p. 12. *Memoir of John Quincy Adams*, ed. Charles Francis Adams, Vol. VI (Philadelphia: J. B. Lippincott & Co.; 1875), March 9, 1824, pp. 250–1.

panhandle. Only fanatics such as Hall Kelley publicly contended that the United States might some day send as many colonists to the Columbia River as lived under the protection of the Hudson's Bay Company, which dominated Oregon and most of British North America almost as the East India Company dominated India.

In the early forties, American settlement on a limited scale was a fact and was crowding the British so badly that in 1845 the Hudson's Bay Company withdrew its headquarters two hundred fifty miles northward from Fort Vancouver on the Columbia to Vancouver Island. Paradoxically, the American government considered renouncing Oregon north of the Columbia in 1843 and 1844 more seriously than it had twenty years earlier: Secretary of State Daniel Webster developed an elaborate plan to trade, in effect, the country east of the Olympic peninsula for northern California. The Bay of San Francisco had become more interesting to American maritime interests than either Puget Sound—a harbor without a hinterland—or the Columbia itself, which commanded the only parts of Oregon where Americans had settled, but was difficult to enter. However, the Democratic Party committed itself in the election of 1844 to a dual program of annexation designed to appeal to its twin bases of support in South and West: the whole of both Texas and Oregon. Although President Polk in 1846 preferred fighting Mexico for more than all of Texas to fighting Great Britain for all of Oregon, he did achieve, in the treaty of June 15, 1846, the boundary of forty-nine degrees that Adams had proposed in 1818, a compromise not only between British and American claims but also between factions in American sectional politics. The boundary was a victory for those who sympathized with the settlements in the Willamette Valley and also for those who thought less of the Oregon country than of continued peace with Great Britain. Until the United States had California as well, some of the staunchest friends of westward expansion could not envision a sovereignty extending to the Pacific. John Quincy Adams told the House: "I want the [Oregon] country for our western pioneers . . . for them to go out to make a great nation that is to arise there, and which must come from us as a fountain comes from its source, of free, independent, sovereign republics. . . ."[3] This was in February, two and a half months before the fighting began along the Rio Grande.

Before the settlers on the Pacific coast learned that American control

[3] *Congressional Globe*, 29 Cong., 1 Sess., February 9, 1846, p. 342.

had become complete between the forty-second and forty-ninth parallels, it already extended farther south. On May 31 Congress announced a state of war with Mexico, and on July 7 Commodore John D. Sloat of the Pacific Squadron took Monterey, beginning the occupation of California. President Polk had been watching the course of revolution and disorder in California, whose ties to Mexico seemed so precarious that it might fall without bloodshed into American hands. Texas agreed to be annexed in July 1845. That summer and fall Polk sent instructions to Commodore Sloat to seize San Francisco if Mexico declared war on the United States, and to Consul Thomas O. Larkin at Monterey to co-operate with the revolutionists if they succeeded; and he dispatched a special agent to Mexico with an offer to purchase California and New Mexico in the course of a general settlement of differences. The preparations were so thorough that by August 1846, three months after Congress declared that war had begun "by the act of the Republic of Mexico" on the Texan boundary, the American occupation of California and the Southwest seemed complete, and the American commanders were consolidating a regime that, although technically merely military occupation, frankly looked forward to annexation. Two years later, in August 1848, almost anticlimactically amid the uproar of the gold rush, word arrived at San Francisco that the American government had agreed to ratify the Treaty of Guadalupe Hidalgo, establishing its title over both California and New Mexico.

Definition of American sovereignty on the coast sometimes followed, sometimes preceded the beginning of American government. In the Oregon country there could be no general government operating over both British and American settlers before 1845: the Hudson's Bay Company governed only British subjects, practically all of whom were its own employees or pensioners. Although the Methodists chose a justice of the peace and a constable as early as 1838, no official had any kind of general jurisdiction until the Reverend Elijah White arrived in the Willamette Valley in September 1842 with a commission as United States sub-Indian agent, empowered to supervise relations between the Indian tribes and the citizens of the United States. White remained for three years, hoping in vain that the Americans would authorize him to act as a chief civil magistrate as well, but handicapped by having been a party to differences among the missionaries. Assorted problems—the administration of the estate of a pioneer who died intestate, attacks on livestock by wild animals, and perhaps jealousy of Dr. McLoughlin for his land claims at Oregon City—turned the minds of the settlers to plans for a provisional government, and they met from time to time between 1841 and 1843. Finally, in May 1843, a group at Champoeg agreed by a narrow margin to establish a rudimentary government, which began operations the following year on the basis of the laws of Iowa Territory. By the summer of 1844 it had established the office of governor and a legislature and courts. The government thus constituted was a voluntary compact of those who agreed to submit to it and lacked any connection with either the British or the American government; but when the officers of the Hudson's Bay Company, fearing the consequences of remaining outside, agreed in 1845 to pay taxes to it and to comply with its laws, it approached general jurisdiction. However uncertain of status and crude in form, it was the government of Oregon until Governor Joseph Lane, commissioned under the territorial act of August 14, 1848, arrived at Oregon City in March 1849.

In California, inasmuch as the United States was the occupying rather than the sovereign power while the war lasted, the first American government was military in form. Yet in substance it differed little from the preliminary stages of government that Congress had established over newly organized territories in the Mississippi Valley earlier in the century. Before war came, the President had sketched out a policy not only of watchfulness and intrigue, but also of friendship and conciliation. Consul Larkin was to warn the people of California against European dominion and to prepare to cooperate with "distinguished and influential" Californians in the event that they moved peacefully toward independence and union with the United States; Commodore Sloat was to avoid violence if possible and to "conciliate the confidence of the people in California . . . towards the government of the United States," encouraging them to "neutrality, self-government, and friendship" and promoting their "attachment" to the United States "without any strife" in the event that California separated itself from "our enemy, the central Mexican government."[4]

The policy of conciliation suffered a rude interruption when a group of American settlers on the northern frontier of California, encouraged by Lieutenant John C. Frémont, took possession of the town of Sonoma on June 14, 1846, before anyone in California knew that Mexico and

---

[4] *House Executive Documents,* 29 Cong., 2 Sess., no. 19, quoted in Josiah Royce: *California: . . . A Study of American Character* (New York: Alfred A. Knopf; 1948), pp. 99–100.

the United States were at war, and made a prisoner of General Mariano Guadalupe Vallejo, who had neither hostile intentions nor military force and was one of the most actively pro-American of native Californian leaders. The local collaborators in this adventure, which they subsequently called the founding of the Bear Flag Republic, were chiefly of the class of trappers and ne'er-do-wells who had been drifting from Tennessee and Missouri over the Western mountains, men of no standing in the American colony at large. Frémont, whose personal ambitions depended chiefly on his family connections, was never able to produce the instructions he claimed he had received from Washington. In time Frémont returned east under orders, to stand trial for insubordination, and there was a fair continuity or consistency of policy at the top even when the facts of conquest and military occupation succeeded the earlier hopes of annexation by consent or by request. When the war ended in 1848, Colonel Richard B. Mason, who served as governor and commander-in-chief of United States forces in California from 1847 to 1849, called for local elections to fill vacancies and let it be known that he favored forming a provisional government on the spot if Congress failed to establish one. Brigadier General Bennett Riley, who succeeded Mason as governor in April 1849, shortly called elections to establish a provisional civil government[5] and to draw up a state constitution. By October 13 the delegates sitting at Monterey signed the constitution; a month later the people ratified it; on December 20, Riley gave up his authority, and Peter Burnett became governor of the state of California, which Congress did not recognize until the following September. Seldom had the military been so eager to abdicate.

The Mormons at Salt Lake City meanwhile lived unto themselves more than the Californians did. They had had no war to fight, no Mexican authority to supersede, and therefore no American military government. A battalion of five hundred Mormons had joined the force that Brigadier General Stephen Watts Kearny marched overland to New Mexico and California in 1846; their enlistment helped to assure Polk that they would not threaten the long American lines of communication, and their military pay helped to assure Brigham Young that the Church would have the financial means to make the move west. But for years neither the American government nor the Church felt much confidence

[5] William E. Franklin: "Peter H. Burnett and the Provisional Government Movement," *California Historical Society Quarterly*, Vol. XL (June 1961), pp. 123–36.

in the other. Mormons were obsessed with the idea that Missourians were still after them, perhaps poisoning springs on the trail. Parties of migrants to the coast stirred with rumors that the Saints might seek vengeance for what they had suffered in the states, and found grounds for suspicion both in the fact that Young had settled where no one else wanted to live and in the possibility that he might want to move somewhere else. The Saints themselves were far less sure of their destiny than in later years they felt they had been; Young himself gave an inconclusive answer to Sam Brannan, who urged him to continue beyond the Sierra Nevada: "The camp will not go to the west coast or to your place at present; we have not the means."[6] Only gradually did the people give up thoughts of returning to their former headquarters in Missouri or of extending their dominion southwestward to the coast at San Pedro, and in fact they maintained a chain of settlements to San Bernardino until 1857.

Having no one else to govern for them, the Mormons had to improvise. When they adopted a constitution for the state of Deseret in March 1849,[7] they did little more, essentially, than the Californians did later that same year or than the Oregonians had done in 1843–5; there was a long tradition of spontaneous political arrangements in the West. Deseret differed from the provisional governments other frontier communities had established in that it continued the rule of Brigham Young as governor that he had taken up in 1847 as president of the Church, which in any location assumed broader social responsibilities than most American religious groups. Thus it impressed gentiles as a powerful theocracy rather than simply an economical means of covering political needs until Congress made other provisions. It offended further in that it claimed boundaries reaching to the Rio Grande and the Gila River and to the port of San Diego, though there were good arguments for taking in southern California, most of which was more akin geographically to the Salt Lake country than to San Francisco Bay and the northern coastal strip. The whole Southwest had so few people that President Taylor himself proposed establishing one state, California, to include all the newly acquired territory west of New Mexico. Instead, Congress created the territory of Utah on the same day (September 9, 1850) that

[6] Paul Bailey: *Sam Brannan and the California Mormons* (Los Angeles: Westernlore Press; 1953), p. 100.

[7] Dale L. Morgan: "The State of Deseret," *Utah Historical Quarterly*, Vol. VIII (April–July–October 1940), pp. 67–155.

it admitted the state of California. As President Fillmore appointed Brigham Young territorial governor, which he remained until 1857, there was substantial continuity from the old regime, but government in Utah was an arena for controversy between Mormon and gentile until statehood in 1896.

Congress redefined the map of the Far West by stages over the twenty years from 1848 to 1868, beginning with the act establishing Oregon Territory in the region between the British holdings at the forty-ninth parallel and the former Mexican boundary at the forty-second, and eastward to the continental watershed in the Rockies. To the south, by common usage in the states, California had extended inland as far as New Mexico, though their meeting was a matter of general indifference; under Mexico, practically no one had lived between the settlements along the Rio Grande and those along the Pacific Ocean. The legislation of September 1850 arbitrarily sliced the former Mexican holdings into three parts, corresponding roughly to the three main centers of population along the coast, the Great Salt Lake, and the upper Rio Grande, but following parallels and meridians rather than mountains and river basins. The state of California did not include the parts of the eastern side of the Sierra Nevada system that shortly became tributary both economically and socially to San Francisco: the Comstock Lode country. It included, on the other hand, the desert east of Los Angeles. New Mexico included parts of two diverse drainage systems, that of the Rio Grande, leading to the Gulf of Mexico, and that of the Colorado, leading to the Gulf of California. Utah omitted the natural outlet to the sea south of Los Angeles—the Mormons' great desire; the boundary ran far east of the mountains. But it included parts of the Sierra Nevada to the north that were less accessible from Salt Lake, and also the country across the Wasatch Mountains to the east and as far as the crest of the Rockies.

Later changes in boundaries served chiefly to bring government closer to developing settlements and to reduce oversized territories to units of less unwieldy size, preliminary to statehood. Washington Territory (1853) cut off from Oregon south of the Columbia both the Puget Sound country and the principal interior settlements, from the fur-trading post of Fort Hall, on the Snake River, just north of Salt Lake, to the missions in the Nez Percé country. Colorado Territory (1861), to oblige the miners of western Kansas, reduced Utah from the crest of the Rockies, leaving her on the Green River. A few weeks later the first of three successive slices of western Utah went to form the territory of Nevada, to afford a government for the Comstock Lode; in 1863, following another series of mining strikes, the Territory of Idaho brought under one ungainly jurisdiction a miscellany of geographical leftovers that socially and economically still look about as much to Washington, Oregon, and Utah as to each other.[8] Finally Montana (1864) appeared astride the northern Rockies, incorporating parts of Idaho and Dakota; and then Wyoming (1868) to the south, carved out of Utah, Idaho, and Montana.

The Far West was so large and its society at once so primitive and so far advanced beyond the usual level of the frontier that its early politics were more local than territorial or statewide, more urban than rural. The miners especially violated custom by being both richer (or at least temporarily possessed of more negotiable riches) and more unstable in their habits and expectations than conventional Western homesteaders; they had unusual need for government, and especially for police protection, but they seemed slow to recognize their stakes and obligations in the community. Of the major settlements west of the Rockies, perhaps only Salt Lake City proceeded from wilderness to order without passing through an agony of anarchy, though even Salt Lake had its troubles before the Mormons proved themselves eligible for statehood by developing conventional diversity in politics and conventional unity in matrimony.

Some of the more sober pioneers throughout the Far West hoped that they might emulate the order, if not of Zion or the world to come, at least of the older states. "Society is fast improving," wrote the wife of a sea captain from Maine who went to Portland in 1850, "& soon this immense forest . . . will be inhabited by a people enjoying all the privileges and blessings of a New England life. . . . For the first time since I left my much loved home, [I] have found the society and customs correspond with those of our happy land."[9] Even Salt Lake City and the Mormon villages recalled New England more than accidentally: their architecture blended Eastern forms with adobe materials; the village economy seemed to spring from the Bible communities of Massachusetts

---

[8] B. E. Thomas: "Boundaries and Internal Problems of Idaho," *Geographical Review,* Vol. XXXIX (January 1949), pp. 99–109.

[9] Mrs. Zachariah C. Norton, March 7, 1850, "Voyage of the Sequin, 1849," *Oregon Historical Quarterly,* Vol. XXXIV (September 1933), p. 257.

and Connecticut as well as from the Book of Mormon. Similarly, one could see the shape of New England in Monterey, where Consul Larkin lived in an adobe house with green shutters, and in the very hulls of abandoned Yankee ships that formed part of San Francisco's water-wront section in gold-rush days. "*Here* is *our* Colony," the Reverend Timothy D. Hunt said to the New England Society of San Francisco in 1852. "No higher ambition could urge us to noble deeds than, on the basis of the colony of Plymouth, to make CALIFORNIA THE MASSACHUSETTS OF THE PACIFIC."[1]

At one time such hopes had seemed within easy reach, when sober New England merchants dominated the port towns and most of the riffraff stayed in the interior to farm and hunt and paid unwilling tribute to their betters. Then the war and the gold rush cast down some visions and raised others. By the summer of 1847, the streets of San Francisco were full of raucous and drunken idlers waiting for the fortunes everyone said they would make. The following spring and summer, after the news came from the American River, the town emptied itself into the Sacramento Valley as if in the first deceptive stages of a tidal wave, when the waters flee from the land; fewer than three hundred of its eight hundred inhabitants remained. "Three-fourths of the houses . . . are deserted," Larkin wrote. "Houses are sold at the price of the ground lots."[2] That winter, when some of those who had had enough of the mines returned, San Francisco had become a city of tents and shanties straggling over the sand hills. As its architecture became more temporary and disreputable in appearance, shacks of scrap lumber outnumbering the few adobe buildings left over from Mexican days, the price of real estate rose to Eastern levels: a lot reputedly traded for a barrel of whiskey sold for $18,000 two years later. Yet hardly anyone wanted to live in San Francisco, and only a fraction of the people who slept there considered themselves residents. Estimates of the population in the fall of 1849 range from eight thousand to thirty thousand. If the local speculators were right, it would soon be much more, but the advocates of

---

[1] Hunt: *Address delivered before the New England Society of San Francisco . . .* (San Francisco: Cooke, Kenny & Co., Publishers; 1853), p. 20, cited by William Hanchett: "The Question of Religion and the Taming of California, 1849–1854," Part II, *California Historical Society Quarterly*, Vol. XXXII (June 1953), p. 136.

[2] Larkin to Buchanan, June 28, 1848, quoted in Joseph W. Revere: *Naval Duty in California* (Oakland: Biobooks; 1947), p. 201.

rival towns might be right instead: Benicia, Richmond, Port Chicago, or New York of the Pacific, all of which were closer to the mines and to the overland routes.

The shifting fortunes and population of San Francisco in gold-rush days seemed as unsubstantial foundations for orderly government as the sand hills and fill that supported its tents and green-lumber shacks. The majority were only passing through, and too busy to bother with politics. "Hitherto, in California," a committee of Whigs said in 1852, "we have been too much disposed to regard ourselves as mere sojourners having but little permanent interest in the permanent welfare of the State; hence the general distaste to mingle or take part in public affairs."[3] The result of such political aloofness, an editor at San Francisco noted, was California's inefficient and mismanaged government: intelligent and honest men "came here for the most part to make money only, and were quite indifferent. . . ."[4]

By the summer of 1849, the merchants of San Francisco were beginning to learn that attending to business could be the ruin of it, and of more besides; that aloofness from the untidy politics of the West sacrificed the political heritage of the East. In March a popular legislative assembly substituted a police magistrate for the alcalde, although General Riley soon told its members that they were premature and restored the Mexican system of government, such as it was. In July the arrogance of a gang of hoodlums who called themselves The Hounds evoked a vigilance committee that tried and expelled them publicly and with full public support. The members of the committee unmistakably operated outside the law, and had usurped governmental powers from the regular, though ineffectual, organs of authority; but they copied the forms of a legal trial and emulated authorities that seemed more legal to them than Mexican alcaldes and ayuntamiento. They reserved their most eloquent apostrophes for the Anglo-Saxon traditions of due process. The cure for crime and the compromise between respect and disrespect for law were all too facile; other newcomers had to learn the same lessons; and in 1851 and 1856 San Franciscans again resorted to vigilante justice, in a considerably less idealistic spirit. But civil disorder was giving way to civic conscience, or at least to conventional and reasonably effective municipal government. So-

---

[3] San Francisco *Daily Evening Picayune,* February 19, 1852, p. 1, col. 4.
[4] Ibid., p. 2, cols. 1, 4.

journers had begun to become citizens, first as vigilantes or as volunteers in neighborhood fire and police patrols, finally as voters and candidates.[5]

In the towns closer to the diggings, and at the diggings themselves, civil institutions were more rudimentary. The Mexican title of alcalde, or mayor, sometimes denoted the head of municipal government even in towns founded well after Mexican authority had collapsed in 1846. Settlers at Stockton, at the head of navigation on the San Joaquin River, elected an alcalde in the autumn of 1848. John Sutter was already technically alcalde over the Sacramento River country by Mexican appointment, but the early settlers of Sacramento elected a magistrate and recorder the following winter. Stockton and Sacramento were outfitting and transfer points essentially, somewhat apart from the excitement, riches, and temptations of the seaports and the mines. The main problems of government were those common to most municipalities: how to record deeds to lots, put out fires, and repress disorder. A visitor to Sacramento in 1851 found the police "a tolerably well organized body chiefly employed in watching the streets in the night, and the storehouses of the merchants by whose contribution they are chiefly maintained." At Hudson Gulch or Rough and Ready Camp or Indian Bar, the inhabitants themselves were the government at first; they met to agree on a few simple rules and reconvened to deal with transgressors. The archives might repose behind the counter of a saloon where the miners spent their leisure hours; the officers might be only the judge and prosecutor whom the miners chose *ad hoc* to try a case.[6]

In the camps everyone was so busy that no one had time to practice government for its own sake; the miners commonly began by trying to get along without any government at all except the authority of their own agreement on the principles of establishing their claims: how many feet a man might dig and how he might mark them as his. "We needed no law," a pioneer recalled, "until the lawyers came."[7] If it was unlikely that the Argonauts would remain in San Francisco, it was unthinkable

---

[5] Bernard Moses: *The Establishment of Municipal Government in San Francisco* (Baltimore: Johns Hopkins University; 1889), pp. 37–46. Earl Pomeroy: "The Trial of the Hounds . . . ," *California Historical Society Quarterly,* Vol. XXIX (June 1950), pp. 161–5. Charles L. Heiser to Christopher Heiser, San Francisco, June 30, 1851, January 14, 1853, Heiser Papers, New-York Historical Society.

[6] *The Wanderings of Edward Ely; A Mid-19th Century Seafarer's Diary,* ed. Anthony and Allison Sirna (New York: Hastings House; 1954), p. 158. Charles H. Shinn: *Mining Camps, a Study in American Frontier Government* (New York: Alfred A. Knopf; 1948), p. 145.

[7] Shinn: *Mining Camps,* p. 113.

that they would remain in the diggings; hardly anyone developed civic pride or political ambition or accumulated much of the kind of property likely to be most valuable in the city: buildings and lots. But the very fluidity of society and (sometimes) the lack of ordinary doors, locks, and walls meant that other more portable kinds of property were unusually vulnerable and precious, that the community had to recognize that it was a community and organize for the common protection of gold, tools, horses, and food. Local government proliferated, therefore, and it developed a crude efficiency, which it expressed ordinarily with the lash or the noose. Eventually the camps that promised to become towns chose first alcaldes, sheriffs, recorders, and justices of the peace, then mayors and town councils, and when state government found its way into the hills it had only to lend its sanction to machinery already in operation.

Order and government grew out of the miners' crude compacts not only in the ravines of the tributaries of the Sacramento and San Joaquin rivers, but also in Nevada and the Northwest. Alcaldes ruled according to the neo-Californian tradition during the early 1850's in the Rogue River mines of southwestern Oregon, far beyond the reach of Spanish and Mexican jurisdictions and populations and completely disregarding Spanish law and practice. In the northern Cascades and Rockies and on the eastern slopes of the Sierra Nevada, mining-camp government developed further along Californian lines than in California itself, perhaps in part because San Francisco and Sacramento were too far away for a man to retreat to them in winter, in part because the deep veins of the Comstock Lode and the Coeur d'Alene greatly exceeded the scrapings and pannings of the placer miners. In western Utah and in eastern Washington (which became Nevada, Idaho, and Montana), the main centers of population and eventually of government were inland and adjacent to the mines rather than at ocean and river ports miles removed from them, as they were in California, Oregon, and Washington. Camps became cities and so in a sense formed territories and states as well as the mining regulations that territorial and state governments recognized.

However, the dominant spirits in most Western cities, including those, like Sacramento and Boise, that flourished as markets for the mines, were merchants and lawyers rather than miners, mature men with a shrewdly calculating sense of the abstract realities of economic and political interest and capital gains rather than youths with a romantic vision of tangible gold who moved across whole states and territories upon reports of new strikes or merely upon changes in the seasons. The miners and their experiences in the diggings had less lasting influence in determining the form of government (and most matters other than its location) than the grocers, bankers, and professional politicians who came after them, though they had more influence than the Spaniards and Mexicans who had come before. "In those days," an Idaho pioneer recalled, referring to the beginnings of the territory shortly after the first gold rushes (1864), "the people, as a rule, paid but little attention to legislation, but attended strictly to their work, except lawyers and office-holders."[8] It was the purpose of these more influential men—influential because they had more wealth and experience, and also more opportunity to make themselves known—to reduce the variables where they could, in government and in business. The Western states and territories accepted the proceedings of miners' meetings in their courts, as the United States did,[9] but in so doing concerned themselves with mineral rights and, in time, water rights, rather than with larger frames of social organization. The Argonaut may be most important for his achievements as "an organizer of society," in the words of Charles Howard Shinn, historian of the mining camp.[1] Yet merely as a miner he scarcely qualified for this role, except insofar as in a rudimentary way he cast his vote for order rather than disorder.

Government developed in the hands of influential men who knew what it was about and in the framework of relations with the main part of the nation east of the Mississippi River. This was so not merely because exiles thought of themselves more as Americans than as Californians, Oregonians, Nevadans, or because their material interests led them to look to national authority and Congressional appropriations, but also because Congress shortly imposed political systems on all new communities.

Aside from California, which after four years of technically military government became a state in the full sense of the word, all of the Far West lived under territorial governments that Congress established by

[8] John Hailey: *The History of Idaho* (Boise: Press of Syms-York Co., Inc.; 1910), p. 91.

[9] California in 1851, Nevada in 1861, Idaho in 1864, Oregon in 1867, the United States in 1866 and 1872.

[1] Shinn: *Mining Camps* (1948 ed.), pp. 266–71, 127.

stages between 1848 and 1868 and that lasted from three and a half years (Nevada, 1861–4) to sixty-two years (New Mexico and Arizona, 1850–1912). By tradition and general understanding, the purpose of the territorial system was to extend to new settlements such main features of state government as were consistent with their limited means and dependent status. Each territory had a governor and other executive officers, a bicameral legislature, and a judiciary, much as in the states. The chief legal difference between territorial and state government was that Congress had complete municipal authority over the whole territorial system and thus might intervene in it at will. The chief practical differences were that the President of the United States, rather than the people, chose the territorial governor and judges, who until the 1880's were likely to be nonresidents, that the United States paid the basic costs of government, and that the people chose neither presidential electors nor members of Congress (aside from a territorial delegate, who had a voice but no vote). Because the territorial condition was temporary, ending in admission to the Union on a basis of full equality with the older states, the West on the whole complained little about its shortcomings, and Congress did little to correct them.

The relative satisfaction of most Westerners with territorial government, or at least their failure to protest more loudly against it, contrasts significantly with their eagerness for physical change. When James Bryce, in company with Henry Villard, addressed the legislators of Washington Territory (1881), he expressed what to a Scot, aware of the parallels between constitutional changes in the British Empire and in the United States, seemed "trite and obvious." But it was surprising, he recalled, "to hear several members who afterwards conversed with me remark that the political point of view—the fact that they were the founders of new commonwealths, and responsible to posterity for the foundations they laid . . . had not crossed their minds." To Bryce, their attitude signified absorption in material development. "The arrangements of his government lie in the dim background of the picture which fills the Western eye. The foreground is filled by ploughs and sawmills, ore-crushers and railway locomotives. These so absorb his thoughts as to leave little time for constitutions and legislation. . . ."[2] Yet there was a substantial difference between the development of a British dominion out of a crown colony and the development of an American state out

[2] James Bryce: *The American Commonwealth* (London: Macmillan and Co.; 1889), Vol. II, p. 689.

of a territory. If the people of Washington Territory prized a railroad more than a state government, that may have indicated not only that they placed excessive value on material conditions and speculative profits but also that they were already one political community with their fellow Americans, though they were not yet one economic and physical community. The territorial government they had was much like the state government they knew they eventually would have; and they knew that admission to the Union would surely follow on the railroad.

West of the Rockies, the people were so much better educated, so much more prosperous, so much more Eastern in background than the people of most of the Mississippi Valley frontier that they might have seemed to qualify more promptly for statehood. Congress moved sooner than it has on the average in admitting California in 1850, Oregon in 1859 (after ten years of territorial government), and Nevada in 1864 (after three years of separate territorial government), despite the instability of mining populations and the objections of Southerners to California's entering as a free state and of Northerners to Oregon's entering with a constitution that suggested sympathy for slavery. Political expediency prompted the admission of Nevada in 1864—not only with fewer inhabitants than a state should have, but also with good prospects of losing those it had—to confirm the Republican Party's control of the presidency.[3] Thereafter the prospects for further admissions dimmed, while Republicans and Democrats in Congress, in effect, vetoed each other's nominees for statehood, agreeing only in opposing Utah. After Nevada, only Nebraska (1867) and Colorado (1876) became states until the deadlock broke in a compromise by which Congress admitted six new states within eight months (1889–90): North Dakota and South Dakota, Montana, Washington, Idaho, and Wyoming. Utah had to wait six years longer, although five states had smaller populations.

To Western politicians eager for statehood, and possibly for the right to run for office, territorial government seemed to withhold more than it conferred. Still, political processes always were active within the territories, and the fact that they were subject to authority in Wash-

[3] Henry H. Simms: "The Controversy Over the Admission of the State of Oregon," *Mississippi Valley Historical Review*, Vol. XXXII (December 1945), pp. 355–74. Earl Pomeroy: "Lincoln, the Thirteenth Amendment, and the Admission of Nevada," *Pacific Historical Review*, Vol. XII (December 1943), pp. 362–8.

ington helped to relate them to national political organizations and practices. Appointed governors sometimes were lame ducks or carpetbaggers, as their opponents liked to call them, but usually they were also experienced politicians. If they could, they led party organizations and, whether to advance themselves or to advance the territories, justified the East to the West as well as the West to the East. If they failed as leaders, the very grievance of their failure might consolidate the political opposition, bringing it into sharper focus against the national leaders of the party that had sent them. By popularity or influence, a governor might go to Congress: three of the delegates from Idaho had been territorial governors or secretaries, and nine of the senators and representatives that the five new states (excluding California) selected had served as appointed territorial officers.

Utah may seem to be an exception to this hypothesis of political acculturation; the territorial system became more autocratic there while it was becoming more liberal elsewhere. Impatient at the persistence of polygamy and aroused by appeals from the gentile minority, Congress authorized a Commission (1882) to manage registration of voters and elections, and through the Edmunds-Tucker anti-polygamy law (1887) moved drastically against the Church in its secular capacities, treating the territory almost as a conquered province. Yet this heavy-handed intervention was preliminary to a fuller assimilation and heralded an end to Utah's long political subservience. Between 1890 and 1893, whether because the Church's retreat from polygamy in the Woodruff Manifesto (1890) had destroyed the most inflammatory issue between Mormons and gentiles or because in a bid for statehood the leaders of the Church felt it wise to become less distinctive politically as well as maritally, the people of Utah abandoned the People's (Mormon) and Liberal (gentile) parties and organized as Republicans and Democrats. The Republican and Democratic parties had figured importantly in only one territorial election (1894), when they had chosen nominees for the new state government that took office in January 1896. Thereafter Utah soon became one of the most orthodox states politically, differing from its neighbors chiefly in its history, in the strength of the Mormon Church, and in the intensity of the personal morality and social idealism associated with Mormon teachings. When the specter of theocracy next attracted national attention—for the last time—it was at the initiative of members of the gentile clergy, who protested that one of the Twelve Apostles could not serve as a United States senator in Congress without violating the constitutional separation of church and state; the Apostle was Reed Smoot, who for a generation (1903–33) defended Republican protectionist principles in the Senate, until another Apostle, a New Dealer, defeated him.[4]

Throughout the West, the national political parties effectively linked the new territories and states with the old. They flourished not only on the loyalties and antagonisms that officers appointed from Washington aroused, but also on the habits of political behavior that immigrants from the older states brought with them and that time and distance sometimes intensified. And both interest and experience seemed to attach Westerners to the national government more than turn them against it.

Except in Utah, the parties organized early. In Oregon, patronage and the personal popularity of Joseph Lane helped to keep both him and the Democrats in office. In California the Democrats likewise made an early start, by virtue of appointments during the military government and of the influence of men such as Colonel Frémont, Mayor John Geary of San Francisco, Colonel Jonathan D. Stevenson of the New York Volunteers and Senator David C. Broderick (both members of the Tammany organization in New York City), and Senator William M. Gwin, formerly a representative from Mississippi. "It was curious," Bayard Taylor wrote when he returned from the state constitutional convention to find that a Democratic convention had organized at San Francisco in 1849, "how soon the American passion for politics, forgotten during the first stages of the state organization, revived and emulated the excitement of an election in the older states."[5] Party leaders imported the techniques they had known in the East, and much of the rhetoric. "When President Taylor was elected in 1848," the New York *Herald* said several years later, somewhat oversimplifying the case, "all the democratic politicians in the United States were thrown out of employment; and gold being discovered simultaneously in California, they went off there. . . . They introduced the New York system

[4] Nels Anderson: *Desert Saints: The Mormon Frontier in Utah* (Chicago: University of Chicago Press; 1942), pp. 312, 318–19, 326–9. Thomas F. O'Dea: *The Mormons* (Chicago: University of Chicago Press; 1957), pp. 172–3, 253–5.

[5] Robert W. Johannsen: *Frontier Politics and the Sectional Conflict: The Pacific Northwest on the Eve of the Civil War* (Seattle: University of Washington Press; 1955), pp. 59–60. William Henry Ellison: *A Self-governing Dominion: California, 1849–1860* (Berkeley: University of California Press; 1950), pp. 269–81. Bayard Taylor: *Eldorado, or Adventures in the Path of Empire* (New York: G. P. Putnam's Sons; 1894), pp. 207–8.

of politics into San Franscisco. . . ."[6] The coast not only imported national labels and techniques but also contributed two candidates for national office: Frémont on the Republican ticket in 1856 and Lane on the Democratic ticket in 1860.

Yet the fervor of the campaigns and the exigencies of personal and sectional politics obscured differences in interest and in prevailing sentiment that sometimes seemed as great as the physical distances between the coasts. Far Westerners often were more loyal to party labels and to the stands the parties had taken in earlier years than they were conversant with the national issues that became dominant after they left the older states. The delegates from the Pacific-coast states at the Democratic national convention at Charleston in May 1860 followed pro-slavery Southern leadership because of Senator Joseph Lane's sympathies and ambitions and because of understandings with the Buchanan administration respecting the California patronage, not because of any general attachment to the Southern cause on the eve of secession. Insofar as Oregon Democrats voted for Breckinridge and Lane, they did so to a large extent with Oregon's favorite son in mind, and with the thought that Breckinridge would preserve the union. The Douglas Democrats were at least equally out of step with Eastern interpretations of the party's issues: Senator Douglas's principle of popular sovereignty had appealed in the Pacific Northwest largely on its face value, that is, as a bid for more self-government in the territories. It had been in the interest of most factions on the coast to avoid the national debate over slavery; both the institution and Negroes were unpopular in communities that had been drawn largely from the North and West, where there had been strong reaction against the use of Negroes in the mines. According to Captain Sutter, Southerners at the California constitutional convention at Monterey had deferred to local prejudices by keeping "very quiet" when the question came up, "as they wanted office."[7] The Know-Nothing Party of California dodged even the anti-foreign and religious issues, nominating a Roman Catholic for governor in 1854.[8]

---

[6] New York *Herald,* quoted in San Francisco *Daily Alta California,* July 16, 1856, p. 1, col. 1.

[7] Johannsen: *Frontier Politics,* pp. 24–6, 68–9, 103–4, 150–3. Roy F. Nichols: *The Disruption of American Democracy* (New York: The Macmillan Company; 1948), pp. 295, 546. San Francisco *Daily Evening Bulletin,* July 26, 1860, p. 2, col. 2. James A. B. Scherer: *"The Lion of the Vigilantes": William T. Coleman . . .* (Indianapolis: The Bobbs-Merrill Co.; 1939), p. 89.

[8] Peyton Hurt: "The Rise and Fall of the 'Know Nothings' in California," *California Historical Society Quarterly,* Vol. IX (March 1930), pp. 28–9.

Throughout the 1850's, Western politicians tried to keep on good terms with all sides and particularly with the Southerners, who dominated the government. As California counted her chances for admission, she found it expedient on the one hand to leave the Negro question out of the state constitution and on the other hand possibly to elect officers acceptable to the pro-slavery factions in Washington.[9]

The admission of California and Oregon (1850 and 1859) satisfied their people's first desires. But even with the leverage of votes in Congress and in the electoral college, the new states remained politically apart. Their new senators and representatives, all Democrats, asked for favors that the national leaders of the party were unwilling to grant. Bills concerning land were probably the most numerous; bills to subsidize transcontinental railroads were the most urgent. The new Republican Party, organized in 1854, tried to monopolize the railroad issue, scoffing at "Buck and the Dromedary Line"—the camel corps the Buchanan administration sent out to Los Angeles as an experiment in transportation across the desert. Still, everyone on the coast promised a railroad, ignoring national platforms and decrying the "sectional issues" of the older states. "The railroad is of more value to us," the San Francisco *Alta California* commented in 1856, "than the election of forty Presidents."[1]

As the Civil War approached, the coast continued out of the main stream of national politics. Lincoln carried Oregon and California, as he later said, by the "closest political bookkeeping that I know of."[2] The Republican vote had greatly increased in both states—in California from about a tenth of those voting in 1859 to almost a third in 1860—but the party's appeal was moderate in kind as well as in extent. One of the most useful advocates of Republicanism in California, the San Francisco *Daily Evening Bulletin,* rested much of its case on corruption among Democratic officeholders, and so on need for change rather than on Republican principles, which it did not bother to defend. The pro-Southern delegates from California to the Democratic convention of-

---

[9] *Memoirs of Elisha Oscar Crosby: Reminiscences of California and Guatemala from 1849 to 1864,* ed. Charles A. Barker (San Marino: Huntington Library; 1945), pp. 41, 62–3.

[1] Ellison: *A Self-governing Dominion,* pp. 105–8, 130. Sacramento *Daily Union,* August 28, 1856, p. 2, col. 3. San Francisco *Daily Evening Bulletin,* September 30, 1856, p. 2, col. 1. San Francisco Daily *Alta California,* August 7, 1856, p. 2, col. 1.

[2] Milton H. Shutes: "Colonel E. D. Baker," *California Historical Society Quarterly,* Vol. XVII (December 1938), p. 316.

fended simply in being irrelevant, in involving themselves "in a local quarrel [slavery] that does not concern them!"[3] In California the Republicans had been moderate on the slavery question from the beginning; they specified at the state convention of 1856 that they opposed interference with slavery in the states, but they adopted no resolution on the extension of slavery. In the Northwest they identified themselves more closely with the Douglas Democrats than with their colleagues in the older states, and affirmed the "Kansas-Nebraska doctrine of popular sovereignty" in a party that had begun in the Middle West as a protest against the Kansas-Nebraska Act.[4]

For a few months after South Carolina seceded, Far Westerners talked coolly of the possibility of a division between East and West as well as between North and South. The idea of secession lacked power to shock men who had heard even Thomas Hart Benton and Zachary Taylor suggest that the Pacific states might have to separate, or who themselves for over a decade had mingled appeals for a Pacific railroad with warnings that the alternative was a Pacific republic. In California the governor as well as the senators predicted that the Far West would also secede.[5]

Such utterances and sentiments shortly subsided, although the fervor with which Westerners eventually attacked "secesh" newspapers and leaders suggests a sense of guilt or of danger. Most of them sympathized with the Union from the beginning, but they were so well accustomed to regarding both the Republican and the pro-slavery Democratic doctrines as sectional, their own aloofness as national, that it seemed possible that they might slip from nationalist neutrality into defiance along with the border states. Even Lincoln's friend from Illinois, Colonel Edward D. Baker, the "Grey Eagle of Republicanism," whose oratory had swept Oregon into the Republican columns and himself into the Senate in 1860, and who shortly died "cheering on his command" at the battle of Ball's Bluff, differed from most of his colleagues from other states by endorsing compromise for the sake of peace and union. He

[3] San Francisco *Daily Evening Bulletin,* May 5, 1860, p. 2, col. 1; May 25, 1860, p. 2, col. 1; July 16, 1860, p. 2, col. 1.

[4] Johannsen: *Frontier Politics,* pp. 76–7.

[5] Smith: *Virgin Land,* p. 26. Joseph Ellison: *California and the Nation, 1850–1869, A Study of the Relations of a Frontier Community With the Federal Government* (Berkeley: University of California Press; 1927), pp. 142, 143, 152, 155, 181. Joseph Ellison: "Designs for a Pacific Republic, 1843–62," *Oregon Historical Quarterly,* Vol. XXXI (December 1930), pp. 319–42. Johannsen: *Frontier Politics,* pp. 163–5.

freely admitted that the proposal of the Washington Peace Conference of 1861 might vary from the Republican platform. "Suppose it does," he told the Senate. "I stand today, as I believe, at least, in the presence of peace and war; and if it were true that I did violate the Chicago platform, the Chicago platform is not a Constitution of the United States to me. . . . When I was called upon to read that chapter in the platform . . . which declares that Congress has not the power to establish slavery in the Territories . . . I cannot for my life see, if Congress had the constitutional power to prohibit, why it had not the same constitutional right to establish; and therefore I read that in a very faint tone of voice, and got off the subject as soon as I could. [Laughter] . . ."[6]

During the war the Lincoln administration treated the Far West as tactfully as it had treated the border states early in 1861. The President never applied the draft west of Iowa and Kansas, apparently considering that it was not expedient to draw more men from the coast than had volunteered. The army feared it would waste its strength tracking draft-dodgers and deserters through the back country, and Western businessmen repeatedly expressed fear of secessionist uprisings. Some of these protests may have indicated little more than hysteria and the desire of merchants and boardinghouse keepers for military business, but there was no doubt that some forces were necessary to protect the overland mail routes, repel the Confederate forces that General H. H. Sibley led from Texas into New Mexico late in 1861, and watch the Indians (though the Indian uprisings of the 1860's had more to do with trespasses by miners than with sympathy for the Confederacy). Meanwhile the government deferred to the main political demands and prejudices of the Far West, organizing new territories and states, offering subsidies of public lands to both railroads and settlers, and hoping that the legislatures of California, Oregon, and Nevada would accept legal tender notes as well as the gold coin that most of the people preferred.[7]

---

[6] *Congressional Globe,* 36 Cong., 2 Sess., March 1, 1861, p. 1315; March 2, 1861, p. 1385. Johannsen: *Frontier Politics,* pp. 177–8.

[7] Edwin M. Stanton to Schuyler Colfax, Feb. 27, 1865, *Official Records,* Series III, Vol. IV, p. 1201. J. S. Mason *to J. B. Fry, Sept. 2, 1864, Official Records,* Series I, Vol. L, part 2, p. 967. G. E. Scott to J. B. Fry, March 17, 1866, *Official Records,* Series III, Vol. V, p. 715. Ellison: *California and the Nation,* pp. 186–230. Fred A. Shannon: *The Organization and Administration of the Union Army, 1861–1865* (Cleveland: Arthur H. Clark Co.; 1928), Vol. II, pp. 112–3. Glenn Thomas Edwards, Jr.: "Oregon Regiments in the Civil War Years: Duty on the Indian Frontier" (unpublished master's thesis, University of Oregon; 1960).

There was a strong prospect after the war that the end of the Unionist coalition of Republicans and Douglas Democrats would throw the West back into Democratic control and thus out of step with the national government. It was common knowledge that men of military age had filled the mining camps, to the extent that the governor of Iowa had called for guards along the Missouri River to intercept draft-dodgers on their way west. Even during the war, when Republicans ran on Union tickets (sometimes with Andrew Jackson's picture alongside Lincoln's, to gather in the Democratic vote), the Republican-Unionist ascendancy was incomplete. Lincoln drew smaller percentages of the total votes in 1864 than the leading Republicans had drawn in the previous general elections in both California and Oregon; in the territories, which as creatures of Congress had incentives to follow the party in power, Democratic delegates for a time predominated, representing Utah solidly from 1863 to 1873 and Idaho from 1865 to 1875. Draft-dodgers and Missouri Democrats were especially conspicuous in rural areas; the larger cities continued predominantly Eastern and Northern. An Oregonian explained that "'the left wing of Price's army' was still encamped in [the eastern] part of Oregon, and that the Oregon democracy generally were only a step removed from Gov. Price[8] and Jefferson Davis."[9] Oregon attracted attention by returning to the Democrats in the Congressional election of 1868.[1] In the next twenty years California elected twenty-nine Democratic United States senators and representatives to thirty Republicans; Oregon, eight to eleven. During the same period the territories of Idaho, Utah, and Washington together elected Democratic delegates eighteen times, Republicans fifteen.

Yet the political transformation of the West had been impressive, particularly in view of the close balance of the parties in the national government, which the Republicans did not completely control for any four-year period from 1873 to 1899, and in view of the transformation of the Republican Party itself from a Western, radical, agrarian organ to an Eastern, conservative, industrial and financial organ. It may have followed in part on gratitude for favors received, although both rail-

[8] Former Governor Sterling Price of Missouri, who raised a guerrilla force in 1861, joined the Confederate army, and fought from Missouri to Texas.

[9] Shannon: *Organization and Administration,* Vol. II, pp. 188–9. James F. Rusling: *Across America: or, The Great West and The Pacific Coast* (New York: Sheldon & Co.; 1875), pp. 240–1, 267–8.

[1] *Diary of Gideon Welles . . . ,* ed. John T. Morse, Jr. (Boston: Houghton Mifflin Co.; 1911), Vol. III, p. 375.

roads and land grants became grievances as well as boons; or on the wholesale migration of veterans westward, although the new immigration as a whole was more Western and Southern, less Northeastern than the old. If the Republican Party appealed by being nationalistic, it must have done so on sentimental rather than practical bases—the nationalism of the veteran of the war, of the pageants of the Grand Army of the Republic. Only in the twentieth century did Westerners look to Washington for irrigation and electric power.

The new political complexion of the West may have drawn something from old traditions of conservatism, corresponding to the backgrounds and fortunes of its leaders. Conservative principles had been strong on the earlier Western frontiers, among the Federalists of the early plantation Southwest and the Whigs of the Mississippi Valley. The Democratic Party had appealed to the Pacific coast both as the party of manifest destiny and as the party of respect for order and property, including property in slaves. Robert Johannsen sees conservatism as the key to the strength of the pro-slavery and neutralist Democrats of the Northwest in the 1850's, of the Republicans thereafter. In resorting to arms, the Confederacy not only attacked Kentucky and the other border states, but assailed the foundations of society. It was true, an army officer in Nevada wrote in 1864, that many Southerners had come west, including the noisiest of the local secessionists. But, he said, "some of the largest property holders in the Territory are [also] from the South, and their interests require them to do all they can to prevent an outbreak and to assist in sustaining the Federal Authority."[2] After the war the Republican Party may have continued strong not so much because Westerners remembered what it had been as because they knew what it had become. Although the Democratic Party of Tilden and Cleveland was no less devoted to conservative principles, it suffered in the West, as it did nationally, from a reputation for irresponsibility that the Republicans kept alive by pointing to the memory of insurrection and the threat of free trade.

The changes in the reputations of the parties coincided with changes in Western society, which became more prosperous and more stable as it developed beyond the mining rushes. The census recorded advances in wealth, income, and education as well as in immigration from tradi-

[2] Johannsen: *Frontier Politics,* pp. 205, 218–19, and *passim.* Major Charles McDermit to Colonel R. C. Drum, April 11, 1864, *Official Records,* Series I, Vol. L, part 2, p. 813.

tionally Democratic sections. Nowhere was the change more striking than in Utah, where settlers arrived on foot in the 1850's, pulling their possessions in handcarts. They were slow at first to forget the Democratic backgrounds of their forebears, including Joseph Smith himself, a candidate for the Democratic nomination for the presidency in 1844; tradition seemed to harden when Republicans denounced slavery and polygamy as twin relics of barbarism, and Democrats compared the South under the reconstruction acts with Utah under the anti-polygamy legislation of 1862 and 1882. The indignities the Saints suffered in the Mormon war at the hands of the Buchanan administration, which sent troops upon rumors of civil resistance in Utah (1857) but hesitated to meet actual military insurrection in South Carolina, seemed to react against the United States government rather than against the Democratic Party. The Mormons "make scant pretense of patriotism," reported one of the more objective witnesses, Richard Burton, who visited Utah in 1860–1 and described their "silent contempt" for the Fourth of July. "They regard the States pretty much as the States regarded England after the War of Independence. . . ."[3] On the eve of statehood, after the Church renounced polygamy in the Woodruff Manifesto (1890), the members were still so predominantly Democratic that their leaders allegedly had to advise some of them to become Republicans in order to show Congress that the old order had changed. Yet Reed Smoot and George Sutherland and other Mormon Republican leaders did not have to dissemble. Persecuted as they were, even the first generation of Mormons had deeply venerated American institutions: the Constitution, Brigham Young said, was "dictated by the revelations of Jesus Christ." Eventually Lincoln appeared posthumously as a friend of Utah and God's instrument for serving the Constitution and the Union; Mormon writers accepted a picturesque story of how Lincoln had outlined his policy toward the Mormons, recalling that he had plowed around logs that were too hard to split, too wet to burn, too heavy to move. By the nineties, moreover, the anti-polygamy crusade had ceased to be a Republican monopoly—a Democratic administration had taken the severest steps, in pursuance of the Edmunds-Tucker Act of 1887. Then polygamy ceased to be a national issue, and the in-

[3] Richard F. Burton: *The City of the Saints* . . . (London: Longman, Green, Longman, & Roberts; 1861), p. 304.

Hydraulic mining near Idaho City, about 1880.

Hydraulicking originated in California in 1853 when placer miners discovered that the gold dust they panned came from the bed of an ancient river into which geologically modern streams had cut. To maintain a flow of water under sufficient pressure (in a stream from six to eight inches across and reaching several hundred feet) required enormous investments in dams and flumes.

Tonopah, Nevada, about 1901–4.

Mining rushes seemed to bring entire territories and states forward in time, the miners themselves backward, as these views of twentieth-century mining towns suggest. For a time, before the railroad came (1904), the freight wagons brought even the water supply.

Bingham, Utah, about 1910.

United States soldiers panned gold in Bingham Canyon in 1863; lead and silver followed in the 1880's and 1890's, and finally copper. Bingham had been much like Virginia City and Reno; under the Utah Copper Company, which since 1904 has dug away the mountain on which the town clings, it became like Butte or Anaconda.

Skid Road.

This type of logging prevailed in western Washington and Oregon from the 1850's through the 1880's.

Wells Fargo: Virginia City, about 1866.

Mail, passengers, and sooner or later nearly everything and everyone came to the express office.

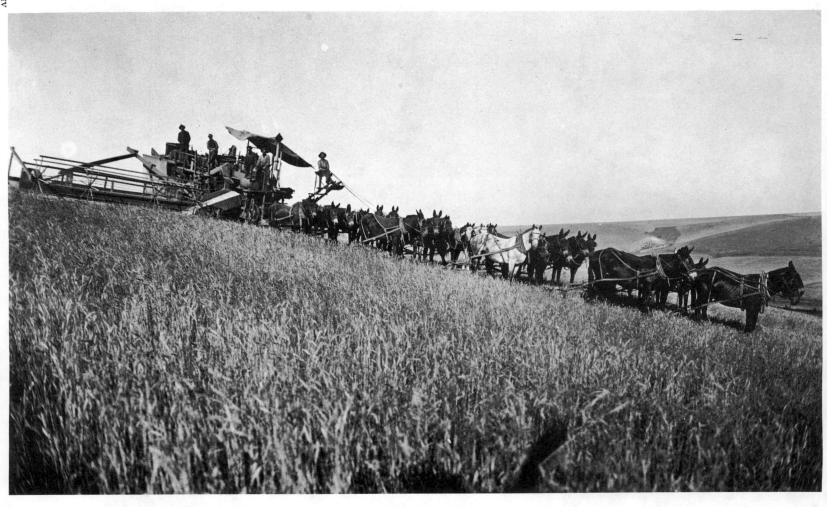

Harvesting in eastern Oregon, about 1900.

Loading lumber at Port Blakely, 1900.

These ships loading at Port Blakely, Washington, in 1900, were destined for ports in California, Hawaii, Chile, Japan, Australia, England, and Germany.

James J. Hill speaking at Bend, Oregon, 1911.

The completion of the Great Northern Railway's line to Bend was the occasion for an enthusiastic celebration. James J. Hill, founder of the railway, drove the final spike and addressed the crowd.

Farm demonstration train at Quincy, Washington, 1910.

The railroads' traveling exhibits promoted settlement and also offered instruction in better farming.

San Francisco, 1856 or 1857.

Within a decade of the discovery of gold, and following a series of six major fires by 1851, San Francisco had developed from a village to a city and from a city of cloth to one of stone. The large building at the left is the City Hall, built in 1851–2 as the Jenny Lind Theater.

Salt Lake City, 1872.

The large building is the Salt Lake Theater, which Brigham Young built in 1861–2 with nails from the wagons of the United States Army. Note the Gentile influences, right foreground. The ties are for a mule-car line.

creasing preoccupation of leaders of the Church and the Republican Party with economic orthodoxy began to bring the two together.[4]

The transformation of Mormon politics and society had followed on a growing intimacy of contact between the whole Pacific slope and the older states. The telegraph and the railroad brought news and ideas from East to West; they also brought a new kind of settler and the means for further novelties in condition. The new immigration of the era of the railroad, beginning with the 1860's, sampled the whole nation less than the immigration of the era of the automobile to come, half a century later, but sampled it much more than the immigration that had preceded it. The new immigration was older and richer, and included for the first time many who had achieved comfort in their old homes and expected it in their new. It was also poorer; it included the contract laborers who built the railroads or raised the crops and dug the ore that railroads carried away.

Politically the expanding population of the Far West brought a large part of it into statehood soon after the railroads and their passengers arrived: the growth of Montana, and still more of Washington, which attracted more new settlers than California in the 1880's, made territorial government so patently anachronistic that the politicians had to swallow their fears and take the risks of a new balance of power. By 1896, when Utah followed the new states of 1889–90, the political map of continental United States was complete except for Oklahoma, New Mexico, Arizona, and finally Alaska, which before the Klondike-Yukon gold rush of 1897 seemed more remote than Hawaii and just as insular.

The processes of political assimilation and political change continued after the nineties, though on a less exclusively political plane. Most Westerners had not felt unfree under territorial government, but statehood gave them a kind of freedom to innovate and disagree that new economic issues shortly made more valuable and that they had

---

[4] Anderson: *Desert Saints,* pp. 327–8. Howard Stansbury: *An Expedition in the Valley of the Great Salt Lake . . .* (Philadelphia: Lippincott, Grambo & Co.; 1855), p. 145. William A. Linn: *The Story of the Mormons . . .* (New York: The Macmillan Company; 1902), p. 544. George V. Hubbard: "Abraham Lincoln as Seen by the Mormons," *Utah Historical Quarterly,* Vol. XXXI (Spring 1963), pp. 91–108. Ray B. West, Jr.: *Kingdom of the Saints . . .* (New York: Viking Press; 1957), pp. 283. O'Dea: *The Mormons,* pp. 172–3, 215–6.

been too busy or too timid or too youthful to demand in the new state constitutions that they submitted for approval by the national government.[5] Increasingly, the Far West took the lead not only in devices of democratic control, which spread from Oregon, California, and Arizona to other progressive states, but also in systems of land and water use, of social control. By sheer weight of larger population and wealth, a region that was by nature much in need of government came to have more of it and to have more influence in national politics, to contribute ideas and candidates almost regularly. And it made more lasting contributions to politics after it had passed the spectacular eras of the discoverers and the Argonauts, after it had ceased to be a region of mining camps and had become one of solid, balanced agricultural and industrial development and metropolitan concentration.

[5] John D. Hicks: *The Constitutions of the Northwest States,* University Studies, Vol. XXIII, nos. 1–2 (Lincoln: University of Nebraska; 1923), pp. 45–6 and *passim.*

V

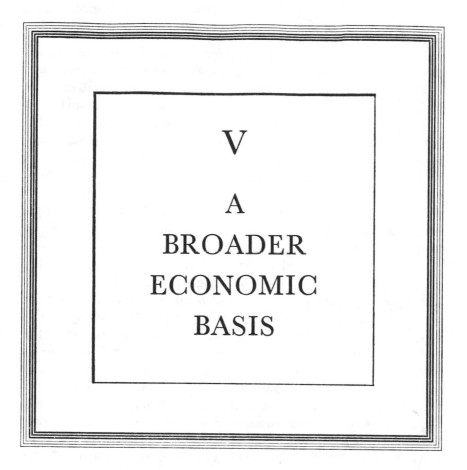

A BROADER ECONOMIC BASIS

THE ECONOMIC ADVANCE of the Pacific slope to something like the condition of the East was no less striking than its advances in population and government, though more complex than the process of admission to statehood. California in 1849–50 was still a mining camp; much of its economy was as ephemeral in appearance as Nevada's was to be in fact a few years later. It was not so much behind the East in the manner of the new agricultural territories and states of the Mississippi Valley as it was committed to a different kind of development. Its economy was basically colonial and rested on the extraction of nature's bounty, which seemed likely to flow eastward along with those who extracted it. In comparison to most new settlements, it is true that unusually large numbers of its people lived in cities and had the kinds of jobs that are likely to be more common in a mature rather than a pioneer community—as waiters, barbers, laundresses, entertainers, and journalists rather than as farmers or manual laborers. Yet many of them in the beginning were essentially camp followers, come to fatten on the miners as transient gamblers and saloonkeepers fatten on soldiers in wartime. Then the miners and most of the mining camps dwindled, but cities and employees in the urban service trades increased. California's agricultural riches became unparalleled, but California and the coast as a whole did not go through the predominantly agricultural, rural phase that has been the beginning of most parts of the West. Since 1860, date of the first reliable census in the Far West, California has been more urban than the rest of the nation; and its occupational patterns have ranked it with the older states of the East rather than with its contemporaries in the Mississippi Valley.

Even in Utah, where Brigham Young scorned gold mining and at first discouraged commerce in favor of a subsistence agriculture reminiscent both of the patriarchy of Abraham and of the ideal eighteenth-century American yeomanry of Thomas Jefferson, a substantial part of society soon became non-agricultural. Utah was significantly urban from the beginning, despite the spectacular successes of the Mormon bishops in converting immigrant artisans to the ways of a novel agriculture, for managing migration and settlement and maintaining Old Testament simplicity and virtue in Zion demanded something more than Old Testament rural social organization. In more than one sense Mormonism was, as Emerson said, an "after-clap of Puritanism." The practice of the Mormon religion drew the faithful into the close social contacts of the Church's wards and stakes, as the practice of Congregationalism had held their ancestors together in the towns of western New England. By the 1860's and 1870's, moreover, despite earlier hopes, Utah was becoming at least as commercial as the upper Connecticut Valley and western New York had been in their first generations. Like the Jeffersonian Republicans half a century earlier, the Mormons had had to foster their own trade and industry in order to avoid the vices of a larger commercial and industrial society. It was not enough to rely on the gifts that the Lord sent in care of the miners who lightened their wagons on their way to California in 1849 or of the soldiers returning to the states in 1860–1. By 1868–9 the Church was not merely opposing gentile merchants, who in early years served a useful but unpopular role comparable to that of Jewish moneylenders in medieval Europe, but was also advancing its own efficient commercial apparatus, Zion's Cooperative Mercantile Institution. The history of Utah became the history of Salt Lake City and of its larger offshoots rather than of the Mormon agricultural villages. In 1860 a fifth of the population was urban, well above the levels of gentile territories in the Mississippi Valley; by 1900 the fraction was nearly two fifths.[1] Utah has been the most urban and commercial of the interior territories and states of the Far West, more akin to the coastal states in distribution of population than to any of its closer neighbors.

The apparently anachronistic doctrines and organization of the Saints thus proved peculiarly adaptable to the bustling economic climate of the West and to the arid plains of Utah. President Young and his hierarchy soon built canals more reminiscent of the theocratic irrigation states of Biblical times than of anything in the modern American experience, and also an iron works, a railroad, and a telegraph. Their system at once rejected and successfully emulated nineteenth-century capitalism. Within a generation, thanks to the devotion of their followers and their consequent ability thereby to command (as the state of Israel could a century later) the savings of co-religionists in communities more representative of their time, the Saints seemed to move from the centralized economy of the patriarchs to that of the bankers without passing through the more typically American experience of small businessmen and independent yeoman farmers.

The patterns of employment in all the Pacific states came to reflect the unusual Western demand for capital and, moreover, the unusual availability of capital. It was not enough that Salt Lake City and Los Angeles wanted more water, Portland and Sacramento less; that the Northwest needed railroads to carry its wheat and red-cedar shingles, and labor-saving machinery to help it pay for freight and still compete with producers closer to market. Nature has made other lands as distant and as dry. But few new settlements have been able to invest so quickly in their own futures, and so much to control the funds that came in from other parts of the world. If the Western economy sometimes

---

[1] Leon L. Watters: *The Pioneer Jews of Utah* (New York: American Jewish Historical Society; 1952), pp. 42–58. "Measures of Economic Changes in Utah, 1847–1947," *Utah Economic and Business Review*, Vol. VII (December 1947), p. 13.

seemed colonial, some of its greatest monopolies were home-grown. Montgomery Street gave orders far more than it took them, even when San Francisco was still young.

The United States occupied the coast during a brief interlude of slack business and general economic deterioration. The Franciscan mission system of Upper California began to fall apart in the early 1830's; the Russian American Fur Company sold its fogbound outpost at Fort Ross in 1841; and the Hudson's Bay Company, which had passed by an opportunity to take over the Russian properties, withdrew from Yerba Buena in 1843. "The sooner we break off all communication, either directly or indirectly with California, the better," Sir George Simpson wrote after looking over the ground in 1842.[2] At Fort Vancouver, Dr. McLoughlin was preparing to liquidate a fur-trading empire that was inherently incompatible with any substantial economic advance, though for a generation it had represented most of what law, order, and civilization there had been in the Columbia River country. On the Sacramento River, John Sutter built himself within Mexican territory a satrapy that no fully sovereign government would have tolerated, and he imagined that the growing stream of American settlers, pouring indiscriminately over the valleys in complete indifference to the claims of the native ranchers, would spare his ranch because he was not a native Mexican. On the coast, Consul Larkin saw the future of San Francisco in the decay of Monterey.

There was, nevertheless, no time after the breakdown of the European monopolies when the Pacific slope as a whole lived as a simple agrarian democracy. Even on the trip West, few could forget organized economic power. Travelers sometimes joined temporarily for protection in an immigrant company, or paid toll to a steamship company, perhaps one of those that Congress had subsidized to carry the mails from New York to San Francisco. Immigrants who in the 1830's and early 1840's might have sought the hospitality and credit of the Hudson's Bay Company at Fort Hall or Fort Vancouver, after 1847 often looked to the Latter-day Saints at Salt Lake City, and it was a rare gentile merchant who competed successfully with the Mormons save in the protected market of an army camp.

The Mormons were better businessmen than Sutter, whose enterprises also seemed to bridge the pastoral and capitalist eras. Before

[2] Simpson to John McLoughlin, March 1, 1842, in *The Letters of John McLoughlin from Fort Vancouver . . .*, second series, 1839–44, Vol. VI, p. 268.

the gold rush, he seemed the precursor as well as the benefactor of the new American immigrants whom he welcomed at his "fort" on the Sacramento River, and their associate in establishing American control. Afterwards, when hordes of prospectors and squatters swept over his land, he was as gullible and helpless as the Mexicans whom he had tried to supersede. He looked forward first to the successes of speculations that included a town site with substantial natural advantages over its neighbors as well as the mill where James Marshall discovered gold in 1848, then backward to the glories of a feudal principality. Within twenty years the Sacramento Valley passed from Sutter's monopoly to that of the managers of the Central Pacific Railroad, and the Argonauts who consumed Sutter's cattle and his crops had forgotten their debts to him more completely than he had forgotten what he owed to the merchants and ranchers who had given him his start.

Sutter was not alone in miscalculating the shape of Western opportunity. He was only the most visible of failures in the early days when property was so vulnerable and prospects were so shifting that a man might be fortunate in not being "on the ground floor." Gold mining itself was seldom the bonanza the miners expected it to be. Comparing the miners' costs and the value of their labor with returns, the *Louisville Journal* estimated that between 1849 and 1854 they had lost over $180,000,000.[3] Sometimes it seemed that gold had developed extravagant tastes for imported luxuries rather than solid productive capital. "The seven or eight hundred millions of dollars which we have exported, have gone we know not where, and for we know not what," a San Franciscan declared in 1857. "They have left no trace behind, except the record of our own folly in receiving and paying for the world's surplus in a ten-fold ratio to our actual wants."[4] John Ross Browne, who surveyed Western mineral resources for the United States government after the Civil War, observed that more fortunes had come lately from farms in Illinois than from mines in California.[5]

Trade sometimes was no less speculative than mining, especially in the early days when demand was so brisk that the whole world hastened

---

[3] *Hunt's Merchants' Magazine*, Vol. XXXII (March 1855), p. 354.

[4] *Report of the First Industrial Exhibition of the Mechanics' Institute of the City of San Francisco* . . . [September 7–26, 1857] (San Francisco: Printed at the Franklin Office; 1858), p. xxiv.

[5] J. Ross Browne and James W. Taylor: *Reports upon the Mineral Resources of the United States* (Washington: Government Printing Office; 1867), p. 69.

to satisfy it, and when the market was so small that one shipload might flood it; those who tried too greedily to increase their capital sometimes lost all of it. But in the long run trade paid well, and the leading capitalists made their first stakes as merchants rather than as miners or speculators in land. William Sharon kept store in Sacramento before he sold real estate in San Francisco; James C. Flood and William S. O'Brien were saloonkeepers in San Francisco; John W. Mackay sold lumber in Virginia City; Henry Miller was a butcher in San Francisco; of the men who created and controlled the Central Pacific empire, Mark Hopkins and Collis P. Huntington dealt in hardware, Leland Stanford in groceries, Charles Crocker in dry goods.

The success of the merchant class testified to the great advantages of local residence and limited risks in a mercurial though expanding market. In the early years no one could be sure of the future of the coast: a man who put his capital into town-site speculation, or farmlands, or mining, might easily lose it there. ("Why, when I came to California," John C. Frémont said in 1865, reviewing his investments, "I was worth nothing, and now I owe two millions of dollars."[6]) The man who invested in assorted goods for sale could move them to another town at the worst if the mines played out where he was. The merchants of Salt Lake, Portland, San Francisco, and Sacramento levied toll over territories so large and varied that they could watch with some detachment the efforts of others who were discovering at great expense where the gold was, how to refine the ore, what varieties of grapes could make the best wine, and how to drain swamplands and dig irrigation ditches.

Even while outside capital flowed into the country through more glamorous channels—through the sluices of gold mines and later the ditches of irrigation companies—these petty resident capitalists accumulated and controlled substantial funds that eventually supported widespread economic development. They helped to create a system that may not have been democratic but was not colonial in the sense of the absentee capitalism that prevailed in most new and far-off lands. For some time it was not consolidated under either Eastern or Western control, for the storekeeper-capitalists and bankers of San Francisco and Portland were reluctant to invest in enterprises too far out of town for them to watch: in the 1850's the miners complained not so much that

[6] Samuel Bowles: *Across the Continent: A Summer's Journey to the Rocky Mountains, the Mormons, and the Pacific States, with Speaker Colfax* (Springfield: Samuel Bowles & Co.; 1865), p. 312.

city men extracted hard terms as that they offered no terms at all. The burden of developing the mines rested primarily on the miners themselves, on their friends and relatives at home, and on the local businessmen who had begun by selling beans and bacon on credit. In the 1860's San Franciscans became interested in the mines of Virginia City and reaped for Nob Hill the richest harvest of the Comstock, which became virtually the foreclosed property of the Bank of California; but in the long run Nevada went to San Francisco rather than San Francisco to Nevada. The leaders of the Bank of California were careful to milk as much as possible from local sources, and persuaded counties and independent mining companies to subscribe funds for the railroad they needed to serve their own holdings. And the flow of Eastern and foreign capital into the mines continued; it contributed to payrolls and profits all over the coast, even if not to the dividends of distant stockholders.[7] Meanwhile there were Western funds for agriculture, lumbering, fisheries, enterprises in transportation, and manufacturing, to such an extent that development often began on a large scale, in the pattern of monopoly capitalism, and the West at least shared control with the East.

Perhaps the economic transformation of the coast was most striking in the farmlands of California, whose owners during the Mexican regime had neither plowed nor fenced, but had left the native grasses and timber essentially intact. The rancheros knew nothing of capital, interest, appreciation, amortization, or even of the exact extent of their holdings. Yet they left to the next century a heritage that included more than romantic tradition; rancher and ladies and courtly festivity and hospitality soon passed, but many of the ranches themselves persisted as large units of land that became subject to the most intensive and capitalistic rather than the most extensive and feudal kinds of uses or occupation.

Early Western speculators found four major sources of agricultural lands at bargain prices: United States government land, state land, railroad land, and (in California) Mexican ranches. Some of the ranchers sold outright. General Edward Fitzgerald Beale in later years liked to tell how he had to persuade the Mexican owners of the Tejón ranch that they had title and could sell their land to him; he paid five cents an acre for much of a tract of nearly 200,000 acres. Other ranchers bor-

[7] Rodman W. Paul: *California Gold . . .* (Cambridge: Harvard University Press; 1947), pp. 168–9. C. B. Glasscock: *The Big Bonanza; the Story of the Comstock Lode* (Indianapolis: The Bobbs-Merrill Co.; 1931), pp. 152-6, 161, 171–8. W. Turrentine Jackson: "British Capital in Northwest Mines," *Pacific Northwest Quarterly,* Vol. XLVII (July 1956), pp. 75–85.

rowed at ruinous interest rates to pay lawyers' fees incurred in establishing their titles or to buy more American store goods, and thus were forced to live on their capital. One owner of several thousand acres near Los Angeles reputedly borrowed two hundred dollars at interest charges of 12½ percent a week; the lender foreclosed when the debt reached $22,000. Another borrowed $3445.37 in 1861 at a monthly interest of 3 percent; the mortgagee foreclosed eight years later and received the Rancho San Rafael, over 36,000 acres, which later became the site of the city of Glendale. The downfall of many of the old California ranchers was the drought of 1862–3, which took heavier toll of native cattle than of the crossbred stock lately introduced by the newcomers: already badly pressed by the competition of the newer breeds, they were unable to restock their ranges.[8] Some Americans, like Henry Miller, found a way to cut the price of ranch land still further by buying the interest of one member of a family, which by custom gave the purchasers unlimited grazing rights and thus the opportunity to acquire the whole on their own terms.

Probably the greatest bargains were available from the state of California itself, which disposed of over two million acres of "swamp and overflowed land" in the central valleys in tracts as large as 98,120 acres, at prices of a dollar an acre or less on credit, or even gave them away on proof of expenditures for reclamation. Among the richest lands in the West, easily drained and watered, by the 1880's they were worth at the least one hundred dollars an acre.[9]

One of the major ironies of Western history is that such cheap lands shortly reached prices so high that their owners felt unable to use any but the cheapest farm labor: land values became capitalized on the basis

---

[8] Stephen Bonsal: *Edward Fitzgerald Beale, a Pioneer in the Path of Empire, 1822–1903* (New York: G. P. Putnam's Sons; 1912), pp. 278–9. Harris Newmark: *Sixty Years in Southern California, 1853–1913* (New York: Knickerbocker Press; 1916), p. 130. W. W. Robinson: *Ranchos Become Cities* (Pasadena: San Pasqual Press; 1939), pp. 41–8. Levi V. Fuller: "The Supply of Agricultural Labor as a Factor in the Evolution of Farm Organization in California" (unpublished doctoral thesis, University of California at Berkeley; 1939), pp. 77–8. Levi T. Burcham: "Historical Geography of the Range Livestock Industry of California" (unpublished doctoral thesis, University of California at Berkeley; 1956), pp. 244–5.

[9] Marsden Manson: "The Swamp and Marsh Lands of California," Technical Society of the Pacific Coast, *Transactions,* Vol. V (December 1888), pp. 84–99. Charles Nordhoff: *Northern California, Oregon, and the Sandwich Islands* (New York: Harper & Brothers; 1874), p. 128. W. W. Robinson: *Land in California: The Story of Mission Lands, Ranchos, Squatters, Mining Claims, Railroad Grants, Land Scrip, Homesteads* (Berkeley: University of California Press; 1948), pp. 191–3.

of Chinese coolie wages. If the land was dry, it responded gratefully to water; and drought itself could be an advantage, sparing farmers the threat of storms at harvest time. The pioneers throughout the irrigation country, like the Mormon Pioneers of 1847, at first merely cut into adjacent streams to flood their fields. The gradients along Bear River and in the Boise and the California valleys were gratifyingly slight, and there were few trees to clear. The climate of the Sacramento Valley, Charles Nordhoff wrote in 1874, "with its long dry summer, is very favorable to the drying and curing of every fruit; no expensive houses, no ovens or other machinery are needed."[1] Yet the land had been cheap not merely because there was so much of it compared to the number of immigrants interested in living in a far-off land, or because titles were uncertain and markets remote, but because few at first knew how to use it. Those who learned to irrigate often found that even at high prices for land the first costs were the lowest.

The empire of Miller and Lux illustrates both the availability of a great deal of land at low cost and the new uses of capital. When Henry Miller (1827–1916) became a rancher in the San Joaquin Valley in 1857, he was a butcher expanding into cattle raising. He began buying land on a large scale in the drought of 1862–3, when rental charges for grazing sometimes exceeded selling prices, and when the price of land in turn sometimes exceeded the value of the cattle on it. By the seventies, he had acquired substantial acreage in swamplands and was in the water business as well: he used the riparian rights that his land brought him to exact favorable terms from the San Joaquin and Kings River Canal and Irrigation Company and, when the company overextended itself, took control of it and made substantial profits on the losses of the original investors. In Nevada and Oregon, Miller also singled out swamplands and springs as the keys to affiliated empires, which he increased during dry years, when others were willing to sell. Perhaps no one can ever tell how much land he controlled, for he bought land in the name of salaried employees, of settlers whom he had financed, and of fictitious persons. His ranches in Nevada, amounting to about 70,000 acres, may have commanded more than 200,000 square miles by virtue of their water supplies.[2]

---

[1] Nordhoff: *Northern California,* p. 118.

[2] Edward F. Treadwell: *The Cattle King, a Dramatized Biography* (New York: The Macmillan Company; 1931), pp. 65–115, 124–47, 201. William D. Lawrence: "Henry Miller and the San Joaquin Valley" (unpublished master's thesis, University of California at Berkeley; 1933), pp. 45, 57–8.

Miller lived well into the era of twentieth-century corporate farming, of the great latifundia that the banks and canneries learned to operate as vast agricultural assembly lines. He had begun when Far Westerners first were venturing beyond production for subsistence, when cattle and wheat ranching represented intensive agriculture in comparison with what had preceded it. At first some of the richest land seemed the most sterile. Nathaniel Wyeth reported (1839) that around Walla Walla agriculture must be limited to the needs of pastoral people; there was "little prospect for the tiller of the soil." The story of Jim Bridger's offering a thousand dollars for a bushel of the corn raised near Great Salt Lake is one of the most enduring and compelling legends among the Mormons, who feel that they demonstrated the power of revelation and faith as well as hard work in proving him wrong; but if he underrated their prospects, he was probably not alone. To the forty-niners, most of California looked little better than Utah. The interior valleys seemed adapted by nature for grazing rather than for agriculture, though there was little wild clover or rich natural grass; the climate was unhealthful, the land arid and infertile. Chaplain Walter Colton interspersed his cheerful accounts of rich deposits of gold with the gloomiest prognostications for agriculture east of the Coast Range. "Take California as a whole," he said, "she is not the country which agriculturists would select."[3]

In Utah, the Mormons learned, a generation or two before most of their neighbors, the arts of irrigation and dry farming, and so succeeded in feeding both themselves and travelers on the trails to California and Oregon. Still, their economy continued to be fundamentally pastoral, as it seemed likely to be when President Young and the members of the Pioneer Party of 1847 first looked down on the rich meadows of the Salt Lake basin. "It is obvious to the most casual observer," Young said in 1853, "that the natural wealth of this country consists in stock raising, and grazing."[4] Despite the apparently providential descent of sea gulls on locusts that threatened to consume the crops, desperately lean years continued as late as 1856. "The harvests have been light," a former

[3] Wyeth to Caleb Cushing, Feb. 4, 1839, in *House Reports,* 25 Cong., 3 Sess., Supplemental Reports, no. 101, pp. 15–16. Theodore T. Johnson: *Sights in the Gold Region and Scenes by the Way* (New York: Baker & Scribner; 1849), pp. 218–20. Colton: Three Years in California, pp. 370–1.

[4] Annual message of December 13, 1853, quoted in Andrew L. Neff: *History of Utah,* 1847–1849, ed. Leland H. Creer (Salt Lake City: Deseret News Press; 1940), p. 270.

resident wrote in 1857, "and many starving persons were compelled to subsist on wild roots during the winter. . . ."[5] During the 1850's, cattle increased less than population, though the Mormon herds were of good stock, with a proportion of dairy cows vastly higher than among the bony longhorns of California.

In Oregon and Washington also, most of the early settlers were stock raisers and grain growers, though under more favorable circumstances in the valleys of the Willamette, Umpqua, and Rogue and in the environs of Walla Walla and of Puget Sound than in the Great Basin. With population slightly more than half again as large as Utah's in 1860, the Northwest had over five times as many cattle and over twice as many sheep; the wheat crop in Oregon was nearly sixteen bushels per capita as against about nine and a half in Utah. The problem was surpluses rather than shortages, save during a few profitable years, as in 1849–53, when the miners consumed the output at high prices and Northwestern flour and fruit were in great demand in San Francisco. A pioneer in the Walla Walla country, George France, later told how lucrative farming had been when produce sold for more per pound at the mines than the government asked for an acre of land; then prices collapsed with the mining rushes, and the cost of river freight consumed all the profits of stock raising.[6] Lacking dependable markets and cheap transportation to tidewater, most farmers cultivated relatively small acreages.

In California the gold rush both stimulated and retarded the arts of husbandry. The miners paid high prices for farm produce—so high that sound agricultural practice seemed unnecessary—but hoped for still higher returns in the diggings; few were willing to work as farm hands. Most of them saw little of the state except the mining regions, parched brown hills and canyons, many of which yielded no regular return until the tourists began to flock there a century later. When placer mining declined after 1853 and some of the miners moved on, as most of them had expected to do when they came west, they took away impressions of drought, sand, and rock, impressions far less favorable than visitors to the missions along the coast had formed early in the century. They took also the most lucrative, though unpredictable, market for agricultural products. The hazards of agriculture in California, the presi-

---

[5] John Hyde: *Mormonism, Its Leaders and Designs* (New York: W. P. Fetridge & Co.; 1857), pp. 42–4.

[6] George W. France: *The Struggles for Life and Home in the North-West By a Pioneer Homebuilder. Life, 1865–1889* (New York: L. Goldmann; 1890), pp. 127–8.

dent of the State Agricultural Society observed in 1856, "are greater than the hazards of mining."[7] When the city council of San Francisco adopted a new system of street grades in 1853, it assumed that ships would continue to require rock as ballast, for lack of export cargoes. Only a "comparative small proportion" of the area of the state could be cultivated, former Governor Downey said in 1860. "Our commercial position on the continent, our vast mineral resources, and our unsurpassed climate will always guarantee to California a respectably numerous, but we need never hope for a dense population, such as will swarm the great northwest, 'where every rood of land will maintain its man.' "[8]

In fact, the agricultural output of the state increased enormously as placer mining declined, but it did not absorb the placer miners themselves or fulfill the hopes of those who envisioned California as a community of yeoman farmers living in the style of their Eastern forebears. The interior valleys and the southern plains became a vast livestock range, supporting, according to the census of 1860, 1,180,142 cattle and 1,088,002 sheep, respectively almost four and sixty times as many as ten years earlier. Despite its size, the livestock industry was already sick, victim of the high prices of mining-rush days, which had tempted the ranchers to increase their herds and their debts without regard for the capacity of their ranges and the quality of the stock itself.

Then a series of dry years, 1862–5, substantially destroyed the open-range cattle industry and the remnants of the society that had prospered on it. At the following census, in 1870, when new stock had come in and herds had greatly increased, there were still only 631,398 head of cattle. The drought took what the moneylenders had not already taken, and the land passed to speculators, wheat farmers, and a more prudent class of stockmen.[9] In 1860 the wheat crop was 5,928,470 bushels, or nearly five times the production of the rest of the United States west of the Rockies; by 1870 it was 16,676,702 bushels.

These large crops were profitable exports. The hot, rainless summers

---

[7] Titus F. Cronise: *The Agricultural and Other Resources of California* (San Francisco: A. Roman & Co.; 1870), pp. 5, 9. *Official Report of the California State Agricultural Society's Third Annual Agricultural Fair . . .* (San Francisco: California Farmer Office; 1856), p. 24.

[8] John S. Hittell: *A History of the City of San Francisco . . .* (San Francisco: A. L. Bancroft & Co.; 1878), p. 437. *Agriculture of the United States in 1860 . . . 8th Census* (Washington, 1864), p. clxxi.

[9] Robert G. Cleland: *The Cattle on a Thousand Hills; Southern California, 1850–1880* (San Marino: Huntington Library; 1951), pp. 106–37. My figures are those of the census reports, which differ from Cleland's.

made the wheat so dry and hard that it stood the long voyage around Cape Horn, and the increase in production coincided with heavy demand in the Eastern states and in Europe. Yet the wheat fields did not absorb the displaced placer miner: there had been far too many miners, and farming here was too different from farming in the older states. The census figures indicate that the increase in persons engaged in agriculture in California in the 1860's amounted to considerably less than a fifth of the number who left the mines; total population grew by nearly a half in the same years. The grain ranches of the Salinas, Sacramento, and San Joaquin valleys were nearer in size to the Mexican cattle ranches they replaced than to the 80- and 160-acre farms that Congress offered by the terms of the Homestead Act of 1862.

That Far Western agriculture developed more as a branch of commerce than as a way of life has no simple explanation. A major fact in the early growth of the bonanza grain ranches of California was the difficulty of transporting the crop to market—that is, to dockside. Small farmers did not want land even at low prices unless they could reach a railroad. Stockmen and speculators bought it instead and had it when the railroad began to extend into the best wheatlands in the later 1860's and early 1870's. Some of the great land barons undertook to develop their own systems of transportation: for example, Dr. Hugh Glenn, who by 1880 owned 66,000 acres of wheatland along the Sacramento River, chartered twelve ships to carry his crop to Liverpool.[1] But more wheat moved by rail than by ship. Henry Miller received rebates from the Southern Pacific on carload and trainload lots. His neighbors were less likely to command such favors and felt the full weight of monopoly in transportation as in land.

The West's systems of transportation had long been a major factor in its economy. The traffic from the mines had brought the great express companies west: Adams and Company, of Boston, had an office in San Francisco by October 1849; the Wells Fargo Company, by the following year. Their traffic was so large that even the United States government got its figures on mineral output from Wells Fargo. In handling the West's gold, they did the West's banking, and by 1866 they controlled the principal stagecoach lines. Freighting was highly profitable also, though on a more regional scale. By 1854 the traffic on the Sacramento

---

[1] Reynold M. Wik: *Steam Power on the American Farm* (Philadelphia: University of Pennsylvania Press; 1954), pp. 54–6.

River was a monopoly of the California Steam Navigation Company, which paid dividends of 21½ percent; by 1863 the traffic on the Columbia belonged to the Oregon Steam Navigation Company, which shortly expanded into the Snake and beyond.[2] Control of the route from Salt Lake to southern California had fallen by the middle fifties to Phineas Banning, who had started freighting from the Wilmington docks to Los Angeles. Few local enterprises were as large and as powerful as those that carried their goods.

The power of the railroad companies was nevertheless a new fact in Western life, in kind and in degree. Although the railroads shortly engulfed their predecessors and competitors—steamship lines, express companies, and perhaps their patrons as well—most of the great Western railroads were railroads from the beginning, created and endowed as such by Congress. They owed much to the United States government, which extended its credit and the bounty of the public lands; most of them drew heavily on local capital and local leadership as well. The richest and most powerful of them, in fact, unlike the largest of the express and stagecoach companies, was a strictly Far Western enterprise, conceived in Sacramento and managed from San Francisco. The Central Pacific–Southern Pacific system received a great deal from the United States: over eleven and a half million acres of land in California, nearly eleven million in Nevada, Utah, and Oregon; a loan of over twenty-seven million in six-percent government bonds; and free access to building materials on the public lands. It also received funds and land from Western states, cities, and counties amounting to another million dollars by 1869. Its leaders—Stanford, Crocker, Huntington, and Hopkins—were cautious investors, accustomed to receiving full value for their money when they dealt in groceries and hardware. With their associates they put $159,000 into the Central Pacific, which reached a capitalization of $139,000,000 under their management. The people of Los Angeles granted them $602,000, nearly four times as much as their own investment, to insure that the road would go through their city, as Congress already had required. Merely the profits of building the Central Pacific have been estimated at five or six hundred per-

[2] Joseph A. McGowan: "Freighting to the Mines in California 1849–1859" (unpublished doctoral thesis, University of California at Berkeley; 1949), pp. iv, 158–61, 426. Dorothy O. Johansen: "The Oregon Steam Navigation Company: An Example of Capitalism on the Frontier," *Pacific Historical Review*, Vol. X (June 1941), pp. 179–88.

cent over a six-year period, or well over two hundred million dollars, which went to the insiders rather than to the railroad itself.[3]

With its affiliates and subsidiaries, notably the Southern Pacific Railroad Company, which eventually absorbed its parent, the Central Pacific came to dominate the whole region south of the Columbia River and west of the Colorado and Great Salt Lake. It reached out swiftly to forestall rivals, who entered Los Angeles only in 1885 and San Francisco only in 1900. No one else ran trains eastward from San Francisco until 1910 or northward from San Francisco until 1931. Its leaders planned a grand strategy by which they first fortified their positions at points that an enemy would have to take—passes, harbors, river crossings—and then digested their conquests at leisure. They received about five hundred acres of the Oakland waterfront and refused entrance there to all others for nearly forty years, until the courts denied their sovereignty. Perhaps their power was greatest early in the twentieth century; by then they had achieved some measure of control over all the railroad lines and all but one of the steamship lines between the East and California. In 1901 a potential competitor planned a line from Los Angeles to Salt Lake; the monopoly's partner, the Union Pacific, annexed it in 1902, three years before completion. A local competitor appeared in 1895, the San Francisco and San Joaquin Valley Railway, the "people's railroad," which aroused the farmers' hopes and commanded their support as the Southern Pacific itself had twenty years earlier. By 1897 the Valley line ran from deep water at Stockton to the head of the valley at Bakersfield. The following year it sold out to the Santa Fe Railway. In 1905 the monopoly made peace with the Santa Fe and had two directors on its board. "One octopus has absorbed the other," Frank Norris had said, "and the last state is worse than the first."[4]

Steel tentacles rested not much more lightly on the Pacific Northwest, which the Southern Pacific entered (1887) after two other lines,

---

[3] Robert S. Henry: "The Railroad Land Grant Legend . . . ," *Mississippi Valley Historical Review*, Vol. XXXII (September 1945), p. 194. Stuart Daggett: *Chapters on the History of the Southern Pacific* (New York: Ronald Press Co.; 1922), pp. 26, 81. John R. Robinson: *The Octopus; a History of the Construction, Conspiracies, Extortions, Robberies, and Villainous Acts of the Central Pacific . . .* (San Francisco, 1894), pp. 9–11.

[4] Daggett: *Chapters on the History of the Southern Pacific*, pp. 317–46. Nelson Trottman: *History of the Union Pacific . . .* (New York: Ronald Press Co.; 1923), pp. 324, 327–30. Frank Norris to Mrs. Lille Lewis Parks, Nov. 9, 1899, in *The Letters of Frank Norris*, ed. Franklin Walker (San Francisco: Book Club of California; 1956), p. 45.

the Northern Pacific (1883) and the Union Pacific (1884). For a generation the monopoly in the Northwest had been of steamboats rather than of railroads, despite early projects to run a transcontinental line along the Columbia. The Oregon Steam Navigation Company was organized (1860) for the specific purpose of bringing order out of the competition of its predecessors on the lower and middle Columbia, which had benefited no one except the people who lived on either bank. In 1863 it bought and discontinued service on the Oregon Portage Railroad, which had begun to look dangerous when it replaced mule power with steam. Local capital at first controlled transportation in Oregon as in California, but unlike the rulers of the Central Pacific, the principal capitalists of Oregon were not interested in a railroad connection with the East, and the properties of the Oregon Steam Navigation Company were not at the disposal of any railroad interests (aside from a brief period of control by the Northern Pacific, 1872–3) until an outsider, Henry Villard, acquired control in 1879.[5]

In Villard's hands the Oregon Railway and Navigation Company, successor to the O. S. N. Company, became Oregon's principal outlet to the East and the Western outlet of a new transportation empire. In 1880 Frederick Billings of the Northern Pacific Railway arranged to use the O. R. & N.'s tracks along the south bank of the Columbia on condition that the N. P. should not build along the north bank; when Billings decided instead to lay his own tracks to Portland, Tacoma, and Seattle, Villard bought control of the Northern Pacific.[6] After 1884 the O. R. & N. had also the traffic of the Oregon Short Line, which leased it in 1887.

Meanwhile James J. Hill completed the Great Northern (1893) and acquired controlling interests in the Northern Pacific and the Burlington, thus dominating the Far West north of the Columbia as E. H. Harriman and the Union Pacific and Southern Pacific (both of which he controlled after 1901) dominated the territory to the south. Hill was never able to win away much traffic south of the Columbia. When he announced plans to build into Oregon (1905) and laid tracks along the

---

[5] Frank B. Gill: "Oregon's First Railway: The Oregon Portage Railroad . . . ," *Oregon Historical Quarterly*, Vol. XXV (September 1924), pp. 171–235. James B. Hedges: *Henry Villard and the Railways of the Northwest* (New Haven: Yale University Press; 1930), pp. 54–60. Johansen: "The Oregon Steam Navigation Company," *Pacific Historical Review*, Vol. X, pp. 179–88.

[6] Thomas C. Cochran: *Railroad Leaders, 1845–1890: The Business Mind in Action* (Cambridge: Harvard University Press; 1953), pp. 50–51.

north bank to Portland (1908), Harriman countered effectively by threatening to build to Puget Sound; the result was an agreement for joint use of the Northern Pacific tracks between Portland and Seattle. In 1909 construction crews of the Hill and Harriman lines were driving south from the Columbia, up the Deschutes River, in scenes reminiscent of the battles of the Santa Fe and the Rio Grande for the Royal Gorge of the Arkansas River in the 1870's. In six months the two sides had come to a compromise,[7] the first of a series, and the Deschutes line of the Great Northern delayed connection with San Francisco Bay until 1931, as if respecting the "Harriman fence" around central Oregon. The fourth of the northern American transcontinental lines, the Milwaukee Road, did not reach Seattle till 1909, badly weakened by the strain of building, and like the Western Pacific (part of the Gould system), which entered Oakland in 1910, it tapped only one major port area and lacked the laterals that turned the most profitable traffic to the older lines. The extension of these newer transcontinental systems did not so much challenge the power of the others as testify to it. Their rivals, by denying them traffic, compelled them to build farther westward.

Within their jurisdictions, the lords of the rails ruled as probably only the Du Ponts have ruled in Delaware or the copper magnates in Montana. "On the plains and in the mountains," Charles Nordhoff wrote in 1882, "the railroad will seem to you the great fact. Man seems but an accessory; he appears to exist only that the road may be worked. . . . Whatever you notice by the way that is the handiwork of man, appears to be there mainly for your convenience or safety who are passing over the road."[8] To the resident the dominance of track over countryside meant much more than the means of serving his needs as a traveler. He had invested himself and his savings in a country whose development depended on the kind of transportation that only railroads could supply, and it seemed sometimes that the managers of the railroads were collecting all the dividends. He found small reassurance in reflecting that extraordinary profits had followed on extraordinary risks, that great power naturally followed on great responsibility and on the

---

[7] Portland *Oregonian*, January 23, 1910, p. 1, col. 1. Cf. Randall V. Mills: "Early Electric Interurbans in Oregon," *Oregon Historical Quarterly*, Vol. XLIV (March 1943), pp. 83–7; and Jonas A. Jonasson: "They Rode the Trains: Railroad Passenger Traffic and Regional Reaction," *Pacific Northwest Quarterly*, Vol. LII (April 1961), pp. 41–9.

[8] Charles Nordhoff: *California for Health, Pleasure and Residence . . .* (New York: Harper & Brothers; 1882), pp. 24–5.

privileges that governments and communities had extended to induce private capital to undertake ventures that were both socially useful and economically uncertain.

It was in large part because Westerners had hoped for so much from the railroad—almost expecting that by connecting them with the East it would solve the problems they had inherited when they came west—that the name Southern Pacific became anathema to most of the people of California, Nevada, and Oregon. But their hopes, while exaggerated, were not altogether misplaced. On the basis of the difference between the cost of freight carried by wagon in Tulare County (California) in 1870 and the lower tariffs that a railroad would charge, an advocate of subsidies estimated that the people were paying "the sum of $77,780 per annum, for the privilege of being without a railroad."[9] Actually, traffic and the use of the land did not remain what they had been. Land that had found no buyers at a fraction of the government's minimum of $1.25 an acre commanded several hundred times $1.25 in the boom that followed the roads into southern California. Values of farms in Tulare County, which had neither orange groves nor winter resorts, more than quadrupled in the decade after the railroad came.

The rule of the lords of transportation was both onerous and, according to their lights, benevolent. They were all enthusiastic boosters, some of them as residents, all of them as investors so heavily committed to the territory they served that they had to underwrite it broadly to safeguard their own profits. Their subsidiaries and satrapies seemed to multiply endlessly. Tacoma in the 1880's was a company town of the Northern Pacific, which operated it through the Tacoma Land and Improvement Company; railroad executives controlled the Tacoma Light and Water Company, the gas works, and the streetcar company.[1] The Southern Pacific undertook to increase its total return in the San Francisco Bay area by operating a local transportation system that, taken separately, may have lost money: its objective was more to build up the suburban areas, especially on the east side of the bay, where the company's stakes were large, than to register profits on ferry and passenger train service. Similarly, Henry E. Huntington used the Pacific

---

[9] J. Ross Browne: *The Policy of Extending Local Aid to Railroads, with Special Reference to the Proposed Line Through the San Joaquin Valley . . .* (San Francisco: Alta California Printing House; 1870), pp. 9–10.

[1] William I. Davisson: "Public Utilities in a Frontier City . . . ," *Pacific Northwest Quarterly,* Vol. XLVI (April 1955), pp. 40–5.

Electric Company, which linked the principal suburbs of Los Angeles—and largely created them—as an adjunct to his interest in real estate and main-line freight traffic; and the Northwestern lines eventually built competing electric lines up the Willamette Valley, one of the most thinly populated commuting areas in the nation, probably chiefly as advertising ventures. On Monterey Bay the Southern Pacific operated vacation resorts for various social strata—the Hotel del Monte and later Carmel and Pebble Beach for wealthy San Franciscans and Easterners, Santa Cruz and Capitola for the white-collar class, Pacific Grove (which it acquired from a Methodist group) for the religious. Accounts in the hotel, land, and traffic departments balanced each other.

By the end of the century, the railroads and their owners had assumed large responsibilities, extending from advertisement to social and intellectual improvement. The Southern Pacific began publishing *Sunset Magazine* (1898) essentially as publicity for railroad lands; the Northern Pacific subsidized *The Northwest.* All the lines distributed bales of independently published Western magazines, such as Charles F. Lummis's *Land of Sunshine,* reports of state and territorial governors, and their own immigration propaganda. Railroad agents sought out immigrants in Europe and shepherded them across the United States in special low-fare sleeping cars equipped with basic cooking facilities rather than with a buffet. Once the immigrants had settled, the railroad sent out agents of what amounted to its private agricultural extension service to teach them to grow better crops. Railroad money may have purged the faculty at the Leland Stanford Jr. University; railroad money also had built the university: railroad architects designed the Romanesque sandstone colonnades as they had designed the Hotel del Monte and other properties a few years earlier. James J. Hill and Henry Villard especially enjoyed the role of benevolent despot. Hill introduced seeds, nursery stock, blooded cattle, lumber mills, banks, and churches where he thought they were needed, admonishing the settlers meanwhile to learn to help themselves; Villard endowed the University of Oregon. The rule of the railroads was undemocratic and in some respects both economically and politically oppressive. But in the long run the companies' interests were in the country's favor much more than against it, and materially the railroads built more than they smothered or destroyed.

Westerners sometimes complained that the railroads stifled Western industry by making westbound rates too low and oppressed Western agriculture by making eastbound rates too high. Yet it was in large part because of the railroads—because of their existence and their policies—that the Far West emerged from a colonial to a mature and more balanced economy. The lines needed a great volume and a diversity of eastbound freight bulkier than gold and more valuable than hides or buffalo bones; they needed people to demand goods shipped by railroad from the East. And they had rich farmland to sell, suited to new crops; sites for industrial and commercial enterprises along their rights of way; capital with which to advertise the West to the East or to develop it themselves if Easterners would not; and enormous power to increase their capital by levying on governments and private investors.

In time the best-known agricultural products of the Far West became its fruits and vegetables, especially those shipped fresh, canned, or frozen, but in the last third of the nineteenth century the most valuable were still cereals and meat. The largest agricultural expansion occurred in the grain, cattle and sheep country, where the principal new railroad construction took place. Even in California, extensive crops such as forage and cereals accounted for most of the value of agricultural production—96.1 percent in 1879, 56.7 percent in 1899; the proportions were higher and remained more constant in the Northwest and east of the Sierra Nevada. In California, cereals declined in proportion to other crops in the 1880's and 1890's, but the census of 1890 reported the largest wheat harvest in California's history, worth almost three times the output of gold, and second only to Minnesota's in the country.[2]

Californians long had predicted that agricultural development would follow on a transcontinental railroad, which would open new markets directly in Utah and the "middle regions" and indirectly in the whole Pacific basin: the China clippers would bring silk and tea to the railhead at San Fancisco Bay and exchange them for outbound cargoes of crops. They did not realize such hopes literally—the Oriental market remained a will-o'-the-wisp and did not regain the place in the American economy that it had in the half century after the American Revolution. But in the long run they realized their hopes substantially, especially as the feeder lines branched out and as the later transcontinentals built into land more productive than the Nevada desert and less productive

[2] Paul S. Taylor and Tom Vasey: "Historical Background of California Farm Labor," *Rural Sociology*, Vol. I (September 1936), pp. 284–6. Osgood Hardy: "Agricultural Changes in California, 1860–1900," American Historical Association, Pacific Coast Branch, *Proceedings*, 1929 (Washington: Government Printing Office; 1930), pp. 221–2.

than the small farms in the environs of San Francisco. The Southern Pacific chose to reach Los Angeles by an inland route because the best lands along the coast already were privately owned. Thereby the San Joaquin Valley, which had seemed singularly unpromising to the first Americans who crossed it, became one of the most productive and rapidly changing parts of the West. The completion of the line in 1876 coincided with the peak of California's wool clip; but the railroad meant the end of the open range, and wool production declined sharply —by nearly half in the next decade[3]—as sheep gave way to cereals and then, more slowly, cereals to fruit. The Valley and southern California had more than their share of traffic, promotion, and development, in part because monopoly was incomplete: the Santa Fe competed for business at Los Angeles and shortly in the Valley as well. Moreover, development followed no less on monopoly than on competition: the Southern Pacific promoted transcontinental traffic through Los Angeles not only to meet the challenge of the Santa Fe but also because it was the largest owner of arable land in the territory that the two lines served and because the traffic that it carried east by the southern route rode a greater distance over the company's rails (to New Orleans) than traffic originating nearer to San Francisco (to Ogden only).

In the Northwest the railroads also stimulated development in the same years. Between 1883 and 1893, Oregon and Washington, whose combined populations in 1880 were less than the population of the city of San Francisco, got three direct transcontinental rail connections, as compared with one for northern California and two for southern California (whose population had been still smaller—less than a tenth of San Francisco's). The greatest influx of population on the coast after the gold rushes followed the lines that came to Washington Territory on the eve of statehood. The largest growth was in the urban counties, in the cities of Seattle, Tacoma, and Spokane, but in the same years Washington realized its agricultural possibilities. In western Washington, foodstuffs imported from California had been so cheap that agriculture had seemed less attractive than lumbering and mining; then the growing populations of Tacoma and Seattle afforded a larger market, and the railroads opened the wheat country east of the Cascades. Farmers had planted the rich rolling hills of the Palouse country

[3] Frank C. Doty: "The History and Development of Pacific Coast Manufacturing" (unpublished manuscript, University of California; [Palo Alto, 1896]), pp. 17–20.

in the 1860's, but the high costs of river transportation held back the Inland Empire. As long as the Oregon Railway and Navigation Company received as much for Walla Walla wheat in Portland as the farmer did, California and the western counties of the Northwest held an advantage; actually, though the wheat crop in Washington more than tripled in the 1880's, at the end of the decade the Willamette Valley still produced more,[4] and California produced more than six times as much. On the average, however, the Northwestern farms were smaller, more nearly homesteads than corporate estates, and they drew a larger immigration. During the 1880's nearly two and a half times as many newcomers reached Washington from other territories and states as reached California.[5] The larger gains in total population in California came from natural increase rather than from immigration, despite the aroma of orange blossoms.

The increase in cereal crops represented not merely a movement of agriculture into rich interior valleys and into uplands such as the Palouse country of Washington, but also its fuller mechanization. For years the California wheat farmers had operated as if they expected to remain only a season, spending little on houses, outbuildings, equipment, or even the processes of planting and harvesting, trusting to the crop to seed itself and to the weather to allow them to gather it at leisure. But the smoothness of the terrain and the dryness of the harvest season soon prompted the use of machinery over large tracts of land: horse-drawn gang plows and, as early as 1854 in the Santa Clara Valley, combine harvesters. Eventually, in the 1890's, traction engines suitable only for the Far West came into use.[6] By the 1880's, eastern Washington and central California supported the most mechanized agriculture in the nation.

---

[4] *Appleton's Annual Cyclopedia, 1879*, p. 710. Donald W. Meinig: "Wheat Sacks Out to Sea," *Pacific Northwest Quarterly*, Vol. XLV (January 1954), pp. 13–18. David S. Halbakken: "A History of Wheatgrowing in Oregon during the Nineteenth Century" (unpublished master's thesis, University of Oregon; 1948), pp. 101, 105–6.

[5] The number of residents who had been born in other states or territories increased in the 1880's from 27,955 to 165,104 in Washington; from 65,308 to 120,158 in California. The net migration to California in the 1880's was 214,200; to the Northwest, 350,900 (Washington, 205,400; Oregon, 85,900; Idaho, 44,600). Everett S. Lee: *Population Redistribution and Economic Growth, United States, 1870–1950*, Vol. I (Philadelphia: American Philosophical Society; 1957 [Memoirs, Vol. XLV]), pp. 114, 132, 194, 219.

[6] Leo Rogin: *The Introduction of Farm Machinery in Its Relation to the Productivity of Labor . . .* (Berkeley: University of California Press; 1931), pp. 42–4. Wik: *Steam Power on the American Farm*, pp. 53, 86, 88, 94–5.

The movement of the wheat farmers, who themselves were advancing toward richer lands but also were retreating before a more intensive agriculture in the irrigable lands, prompted a movement of the stockmen. Sheep were grazing on the eastern ranges even before the railroads came, and soon increased there massively: in 1870 eastern Oregon had a fourth of the state's 318,123 sheep; in 1877, nearly two thirds of its 1,963,556. Having already discovered the pastures on the mountains on either side of the Sacramento and San Joaquin valleys and along the coasts of northern California and Oregon, in the early 1880's the stockmen moved wholesale from Oregon and Washington into Idaho and Montana. They drove their herds into the hills to continue an older way of life and found themselves forced to undertake winter feeding and to protect the animals from cold, disease, and predators, though the boosters still told of "self-raising livestock."[7]

Eventually the most radical changes in Far Western agriculture concerned not so much the opening of new lands for grain and livestock, traditionally the major staples of new states, as the development of entirely new markets for fruits and vegetables, which farmers throughout most of the earlier West had grown only for their own use. Since the 1840's, there had been a local market for truck and orchard produce, larger and more free-spending than the markets of most pioneer rural and agricultural communities. Henderson Lewelling had planted the first orchards of grafted fruit on the coast in 1847, bringing a wagonload of nursery stock from Salem, Iowa, to Milwaukie, Oregon, in time to profit by the prices miners were willing to pay for fresh fruit. Soon California offered a metropolitan market on San Fancisco Bay, steadier, though less spectacular, than the mercurial demand of the lode country. Situated downstream from the Santa Clara, Sacramento, and San Joaquin valleys, it enjoyed easy transportation by sea from the richest farm country of western Oregon and southern California as well. Sacramento and Alameda counties as early as 1860 were among the thirty-three richest in the United States in value of market garden produce, almost all of it consumed in the bay cities. "It is safe to say," a writer on *The Golden State* reported in 1872, three years after the overland

[7] J. Orin Oliphant: "The Cattle Trade from the Far Northwest to Montana," *Agricultural History,* Vol. VI (April 1932), pp. 69–83. Oliphant: "Encroachments of Cattlemen on Indian Reservations in the Pacific Northwest, 1870–1890," *Agricultural History,* Vol. XXIV (January 1950), pp. 42–58. Dexter K. Strong: "Beef Cattle Industry in Oregon, 1890–1938," *Oregon Historical Quarterly,* Vol. XLI (September 1940), pp. 262–3.

railroad opened, "that nine-tenths of all the fruit raised in the State seeks San Francisco for a market. . . ."[8]

A large part of the fruit crop seemed quite unsuitable for export, given the cost and quality of transportation available into the 1880's. Apples predominated among orchard fruits until close to the end of the century, but the early Western apples were far inferior in flavor to the crisp, juicy Eastern varieties. Even shipments of citrus fruits were small. "The [California] orange is at a disadvantage," John S. Hittell wrote in 1879, "in being unfit for drying, as grapes and figs are, or for pickling, like olives." Its chief advantage was in the local market, where it arrived in better condition than fruit from the Hawaiian and Society islands.[9] The supply of deciduous fruits often far outran the demand, and the fruit rotted in the fields. Low prices, however, gave opportunity to the driers and canners, and between 1875 and 1880 shipments of canned fruit from California by rail increased nearly nine times (to 6,707,650 pounds), while shipments of fresh—in the trade, green—fruit increased less than one twentieth (to 3,141,500 pounds).[1]

Although shipments of fruit from Sacramento far exceeded those from Los Angeles, the most famous of the horticultural booms developed in southern California, around the orange groves. "This golden sphere is the very touchstone of the boomers of choice acres," a promoter reported in 1887, observing that northern Californians talked in vain of strawberries and asparagus in December, until they, too, staged their citrus fairs, and then the land sold.[2] As a tropical fruit, the orange symbolized the gentleness of the Southwestern climate to travelers in flight from Eastern winters; the glossy green leaves were welcome contrast to the dusty deserts they had crossed and suggested the possibility of living more as country squires than as Kansas wheat farmers or Dakota cattlemen. Citrus prices at San Francisco still were high enough so that a year's profits might pay off the cost of an orchard.

---

[8] W. P. Duruz: "Notes on the Early History of Horticulture in Oregon . . . , *Agricultural History,* Vol. XV (April 1941), pp. 84–97. R. Guy McClellan: *The Golden State: A History of the Region West of the Rocky Mountains* . . . (Philadelphia: W. Flint & Co.; 1872), p. 328.

[9] John S. Hittell: *The Resources of California* . . . , seventh edition (San Francisco: A. L. Bancroft & Co.; 1879), pp. 262–3.

[1] U. S. Treasury: *Report on the Internal Commerce of the United States for the Year 1890,* 51 Cong., 2 Sess., House Executive Document no. 6, part 2, p. 314.

[2] Ben C. Truman in *The New York Times,* April 24, 1887, p. 4, col. 5.

The result was a series of orange-grove settlements in the wake of Riverside, which planted its first trees in 1871, and Pasadena, which began in 1875. At Riverside the first navel orange trees fruited in 1878 (two to a tree), setting off a new wave of enthusiasm. The first carload of three hundred boxes of California oranges had gone east in 1877 and had taken a month in transit to St. Louis, at a cost of $500. The new plantings of navel oranges were just coming into production and threatened to glut the market, despite the best efforts of a pestilence of scale insects, when the Southern Pacific recognized the possibilities of a profitable citrus traffic and cut freight rates nearly in half in 1881.[3] The arrival of the Santa Fe Railway at Los Angeles four years later added leverage to the boom as two lines competed for the traffic of an area that had hardly enough population for one line. The rate war of 1886–7 reduced passenger fares from the Missouri River to $25 and less and brought in a flood of visitors, promoters, and settlers, all entranced by visions of a future as improbable and as glamorous as that which southern California shortly realized.

The new migration into southern California differed in many respects from any that had yet come to the coast, but it shared a general disposition to prefer, in the traditions of the states from which it came, neighbors to isolation, trees, shrubs, and flowers to dry fields, orchards to wheat fields and cattle ranges. At its crest, the speculation of the mid-1880's concerned residential lots rather than orchard tracts, and prices rose fantastically beyond mere agricultural returns; the immigrants were, or aspired to be, city people rather than farmers. Yet most aspired to live among the orange blossoms and to gather as well as consume the harvests in the new Elysium. In general they were a prosperous and an ambitious lot, well able to bear the risks of an experimental economy. When real-estate prices collapsed in 1888, the orchards remained, as did most of the immigrants and their savings. Almost providentially, the Department of Agriculture succeeded in controlling scale infestation with another insect, the Australian ladybug, and a second boom in oranges succeeded the boom in town lots. The value of farm land in southern California increased more than four times in

[3] John S. Hittell: *The Commerce and Industries of the Pacific Coast of North America* . . . (San Francisco: A. L. Bancroft & Co.; 1882), p. 235. *The Citrus Industry,* ed. Herbert J. Webber and Leon D. Batchelor (Berkeley: University of California Press; 1943), Vol. I, pp. 36, 39, 531. Minnie Tibbets Mills: "Luther Calvin Tibbets . . . ," Historical Society of Southern California, *Quarterly,* Vol. XXV (December 1943), pp. 149, 151.

a decade (1880–90); population and the value of farm production, nearly twice. "The beauty of the groves," the Los Angeles editor and promoter, Charles F. Lummis, recalled, "made the orange almost as epidemic a fever as gold had been," and the orange had done "far more for the permanent development of the State than gold or other mining ever did."[4]

The orchards of the Pacific Northwest developed more slowly than those to the south, despite early beginnings in the Willamette Valley. The high fruit prices of the 1850's had led in the 1860's to overproduction, which turned interest to other crops; Portland never became the market that San Francisco was, and San Francisco was much too close to competing producers in northern California. Until the Northern Pacific was ready for traffic, Jay Cooke's efforts to promote agriculture along its route brought forth little more than slurs at "Cooke's Banana Belt": California had a monopoly of railroad transportation and the lion's share of immigrants with enough capital to buy nursery stock and water rights and to wait several years for a crop. Then "the cars" began running to the Columbia River as well; and though the most fertile parts of the Northwest offered neither perpetual summer nor suburban living nor the glamour of the orange blossom, a new immigrant with new prospects was moving in. "It was left to the present generation," Governor Semple of Washington wrote in 1887, "and to the comparatively wealthy class of settlers, who come in these years of security and of railways, to invest time and money in obtaining the more delicate harvests of this region."[5]

The arrival of the Oregon Short Line (Union Pacific) had a comparable effect in Idaho, where, Governor Bunn observed in 1884: "The business of fruit-growing is [now] reduced to a science based upon the great American principle, 'Make it pay.'"[6] Between 1879 and 1899 the value of orchard products in Idaho increased nearly fifteen times, in Washington nearly seven times. The Northwest both followed and consciously imitated California, as it had in mining-rush days. Wash-

[4] *The New York Times,* December 28, 1890, p. 20, cols. 1–2. *Encyclopedia Britannica,* tenth edition (London: 1902), Vol. II, p. 503.

[5] *Report of the Secretary of the Interior,* 50 Cong., 1 Sess., House Executive Document no. 1, part 5, Vol. I (1887), p. 939.

[6] Governor William M. Bunn, October 18, 1884, in *Report of the Secretary of the Interior,* 48 Cong., 2 Sess., House Executive Document no. 1, part 5, Vol. II (1884), p. 550.

ingtonians were proud to boast (1888) that a Californian vintner had bought land in the Yakima Valley to grow champagne grapes.[7]

In both Southwest and Northwest, the new agriculture depended on improved transportation and artificial water supplies. By 1890, more than a fourth of the farms in California, nearly two thirds of those in Idaho, and more than nine tenths of those in Utah and Nevada were irrigated. The beginnings of irrigation were early—in the 1830's in eastern Washington, where Marcus Whitman had located at Waiilatpu in part because it was easy to divert water to the mission's gardens there; but railroads opened the markets that irrigated crops on the commercial scale needed. They also offered the assistance and encouragement of railroad engineers, whose surveys impressed investors with the sanction of the wealth and shrewd business sense behind them. The Northern Pacific Railroad contributed both advice and capital to the Yakima Canal and Land Company (1889), which became the largest irrigation enterprise in the Northwest; James J. Hill assisted in early irrigation at Wenatchee.[8]

In California, as in the interior Northwest, some of the earliest irrigation companies had begun by carrying water to the mines (which thus bore the initial burden of financing) and then gradually had added agricultural clients. When orchards first began to displace wheat fields in the central valleys, they tapped simple gravity ditches near the rivers. The citrus-grove colonists of the 1870's and 1880's in southern California relied largely on local water supplies that required neither elaborate engineering works nor great outlays of capital. Yet the expense soon outran individual or even cooperative resources. As early as 1871, an irrigation company that drew on the capital of some of the richest men of California, including Henry Miller of Miller and Lux and William Chapman Ralston of the Bank of California, learned from its engineer that the project was too large for merely private enterprise. The California Development Company more dramatically demonstrated the dangers of venturing beyond one's means and engineering compe-

---

[7] *Report of the Secretary of the Interior*, 50 Cong., 2 Sess., House Executive Document no. 1, part 5, Vol. III (1888), p. 910.

[8] Rose M. Boening: "History of Irrigation in the State of Washington," *Washington Historical Quarterly*, Vol. IX (October 1918), pp. 259–76; Vol. X (January 1919), pp. 21–45. Emmett K. Vendevere: "History of Irrigation in Washington" (unpublished doctoral thesis, University of Washington; 1948), p. 36.

tence when it diverted water from the Colorado River to the desert area just north of the Mexican border that it called the Imperial Valley. All went well until, during a series of disastrous floods, the river itself broke into their canal, creating an inland sea. As a result the Southern Pacific, to which President Theodore Roosevelt appealed, returned the river to its channel in a long and costly battle and, in 1905, took control of the company.[9]

The new fruit and vegetable ranches required connections with irrigation canals and railroads and progressive sophistication of technique extending from field to market. When the first Far Western produce went east on the new Pacific railroad in 1869—thirty-three tons of pears, apples, grapes, and plums—it rode in ventilated cars, and the heat of the journey, even after summer was over, made spoilage prohibitive for any but fruit grown in foothill country, with a relatively high sugar content and a low water content. In the middle 1880's refrigerator cars operated successfully east of the Mississippi, and in June 1888 a carload of refrigerated apricots and cherries went without reicing from Suisun, near San Francisco, to New York. Proof that it was possible to ship valley and irrigated fruits in summer weather eventually revolutionized shipping practices, and life in rural California. Shipments of fresh fruit, which had increased by less than five percent between 1875 and 1880, increased nearly fifteen times between 1880 and 1885, exceeding shipments of canned fruit by weight. A traveler reported in 1887 that the daily express on the overland route consisted of "two sleeping cars, two or three passenger cars, and twenty cars loaded with green fruit," and complained that the railroad took more care with the fruit than with the passengers.[1] By 1892 California fruit was moving to London via New York. The new technique was ready just in time to serve the orange groves planted in the boom of the

---

[9] R. M. Brereton: "The Dawn of National Irrigation in the United States," *Bonville's Western Monthly,* Vol. IV (October 1909), pp. 315–18. In 1916 the Southern Pacific sold the system to an irrigation district. Paul L. Kleinsorge: *The Boulder Canyon Project: Historical and Economic Aspects* (Stanford: Stanford University Press; 1941), pp. 21–5. Albert N. Williams: *The Water and the Power Development of the Five Great Rivers of the West* (New York: Duell, Sloan & Pearce; 1951), pp. 57–61.

[1] William A. Taylor: "The Influence of Refrigeration on the Fruit Industry," U. S. Department of Agriculture, *Yearbook, 1900* (Washington: Government Printing Office; 1901), pp. 574, 576, 579. U. S. Treasury: *Report on the Internal Commerce of the United States for the Year 1890,* 51 Cong., 2 Sess., House Executive Document no. 6, part 2, p. 314. *The New York Times,* September 5, 1887, p. 5, col. 5.

1880's: in 1886 shipments increased to 1,000 carloads; in 1890 to 4,000; in 1900 to 25,000.[2] The new costs of water and of shipping in turn had had further corollaries. Irrigation demanded drainage, which had been a problem at first chiefly in the swamplands of the San Joaquin and along the banks of the Sacramento. Truck farmers began building dikes as early as 1869 along the Sacramento, whose channel filled up as debris poured down from the hydraulic mines upstream. Ditching, diking, and cultivating (to reduce loss of moisture through evaporation) in turn called for machinery, so that even as the great steam combine grain harvesters retreated out of the valleys to the uplands and to the Inland Empire of the Pacific Northwest, other and more specialized equipment came into use.[3] To assure that the produce would arrive in condition to compete with crops of Eastern states, it had to be sprayed, gassed, washed, and packed as it had never had to be on the other coast.

By the end of the century, the people of the Pacific coast had succeeded in raising crops that resembled those of the older states, but by vastly different processes. Over large areas from southern California into the Northwest, they were perfecting forms of intensive agriculture that in some respects—in use of machinery, in specialization, in emphasis on quality, in dependence on national rather than local markets—were more sophisticated than the industries of Western cities.

Manufacturers meanwhile were slower in finding any lasting opportunities, despite the proximity of a local market as hungry for industrial as for agricultural products, and despite the predisposition of much of the early population of the West to live in cities. Ultimately they succeeded. Manufacturers in the twentieth century gave a solid underpinning to urban populations that in the first years after the gold rush had seemed to sustain themselves by some miracle of economic levitation. For two or three generations the issue was in doubt: Far Western industry lagged or even deteriorated while Far Western agriculture advanced in technique and prospered.

The Mormons may justifiably claim to have been the first industrialists of the region as well as the first irrigationists, though theirs were also the first industrial failures. Brigham Young described how

---

[2] Oscar E. Anderson, Jr.: *Refrigeration in America, a History of a New Technology and Its Impact* (Princeton: Princeton University Press; 1953), pp. 52, 153–6.

[3] Robert C. Nesbit and Charles M. Gates: "Agriculture in Eastern Washington, 1890–1910," *Pacific Northwest Quarterly*, Vol. XXXVII (October 1946), pp. 279–302.

Utah in five years, though without gold, had "her mills and manufactories, her roads and her bridges, raising her own bread and beef, besides exporting considerable quantities. . . ."[4] In fact, her most successful export may have been her faith; the Church encouraged immigrant converts to bring goods beyond their personal needs. "They were as merchant trains of matchless worth," recalls a Mormon historian, E. W. Tullidge.[5] The first paper mill, the first ironworks, and the first sugar refinery west of the Rockies all appeared in Utah in the 1850's; but all of them eventually expired. The pioneer Mormon manufacturers learned their techniques in the hardest ways, generally without benefit of expert advice, but their major burden, as well as the principal justification for their enterprises, was the high cost of transportation from the states, at rates of from fourteen to thirty cents a pound. The authorities therefore had to balance freight charges on manufactured goods against freight charges on the machinery to make them, and both against other demands on their precariously small reserves of specie. In building up sources of necessities, they calculated, as nicely as any eighteenth-century mercantilists, what they could concede to their people's taste for comforts and luxuries. Their technology, however, often lagged behind their social engineering. The Deseret Manufacturing Company went bankrupt hauling heavy British sugar-refining machinery across the plains in forty wagons, only to find that vital parts were missing. The completion of the Union Pacific Railroad in 1869 would have facilitated such efforts but also made them useless; iron production immediately ceased.[6] Thus the Mormons anticipated much of the economic history of their neighbors: Western manufacturers could not compete with the mass production of the older states, except in goods that had to be custom-made or cost too much to ship, and each new railroad therefore brought death to infant industry.

---

[4] William Mulder: *Homeward to Zion: The Mormon Migration from Scandinavia* (Minneapolis: University of Minnesota Press; 1957), p. 71.

[5] P. A. M. Taylor and L. J. Arrington: "Religion and Planning in the Far West: The First Generation of Mormons in Utah," *Economic History Review,* second series, Vol. XI (August 1958), p. 75.

[6] Claude Adams: "History of Papermaking in the Pacific Northwest: I," *Oregon Historical Quarterly,* Vol. LII (March 1951), p. 22. Milton R. Hunter: *Utah, The Story of Her People, 1540–1947* . . . (Salt Lake City: Deseret News Press; 1946), pp. 373–7. Richard F. Burton: *The City of the Saints* . . . (New York: Harper & Brothers; 1862), pp. 316, 320. Fred G. Taylor: *A Saga of Sugar* . . . (Salt Lake City: Utah-Idaho Sugar Co.; 1944), pp. 30–60.

On the coast, manufacturing had to develop without the encouragement of the Mormon Church, which husbanded the resources of its members to build a permanent and self-sufficient community in the years when most other Far Westerners considered themselves sojourners, or at most exiles, rather than residents and lacked the Mormons' staunch loyalty to local enterprise. The frenetic economies of the mining camps and the ports that served them supported selling more readily than producing. The businessmen of San Francisco and Portland were content to put their capital into the finished goods that came from the East. The cost of ocean freight and the mark-ups of the Eastern commission merchants seemed less than the inflated interest charges and wages that would have to go into local manufactures.

Yet the beginnings were many, particularly at San Francisco, where a substantial market fretted at delays in filling orders from the East. A decade after the discovery of gold, the Mechanics' Institute awarded prizes to manufacturers of farm machinery, steam engines, quartz stamps, furniture, bricks, musical instruments, carriages and wagons, boots, clothing, guns, surgical instruments, iron and tin work, chemicals, and sewing machines, as well as illuminating gas, soap, sugar, and flour. Production increased as freight charges mounted during the Civil War; an impressive industrial community developed in time to suffer from the resumption of normal seaborne commerce when the war ended. "Contrast the present," a speaker before the Mechanics' Institute said in 1865, "with the time . . . when our onions and potatoes came from the Sandwich Islands, our soiled linen [was] washed in China, our eggs and butter [were] brought from Boston, our lumber from Australia, and our bricks from New York."[7] Californians long had lamented the imbalance in an economy that shipped treasure to the East in exchange for food and building material that the coast itself might have produced; but in the common eagerness for rapid communication, they seemed to expect that the railroad would bring the stimulus of a larger market rather than the blight of competition. It might bring Utah and the interior West into direct competition with California farmers in the mining country east of the Sierra, but it would also turn a vast trans-

---

[7] San Francisco Mechanics' Institute: *Report of the Second Industrial Exhibition of the Mechanics' Institute of the City of San Francisco . . .* [September 2–26, 1858] (San Francisco: Frank Eastman, Printer; 1859), pp. 43–127. *Report of the Fifth Industrial Exhibition of the Mechanics' Institute of San Francisco . . .* (San Francisco: Mining and Scientific Press Book and Job Printing Office; 1865), p. 21.

Pacific commerce through San Francisco, and so open new opportunities for Far Western Manchesters, Lynns, and Lowells that might sell throughout Asia, the Americas, and the South Seas and draw on China for cheap labor.[8]

Chinese laborers did work in some California factories, but the San Francisco merchants foresaw neither the development of mass production in Eastern factories on a scale far beyond the ability of local industry to compete with nor the convenience of the new Suez Canal as a cheap route from the East coast to the Far East. "The manufactures of California," John S. Hittell reported frankly in 1874, "are mostly of a coarse class, requiring little labor, relatively, and much raw material, and of classes costing much, relatively, for importation. . . . We produce no manufactures for exportation. . . ."[9] Looking forward to the completion of the transcontinental line in 1868, Henry George had seemed to foresee some of these disappointments: "The locomotive is a great centralizer. It kills little towns and builds up great cities, and in the same way kills little businesses and builds up great ones."[1] The Californians had to learn that the locomotive might advance Eastern over Western businesses as well as the business of San Francisco over that of Portland or Los Angeles.

In Oregon and the Northwest, beginnings were slower than in California, though Salem produced woolen goods by machine in 1857, the first on the Pacific coast. Most of the Portland merchants preferred to invest in consumer goods available at San Francisco, while the proprietors of the Willamette Woolen Mills struggled against the low prices of Eastern yard goods and the high prices of Western capital, which in 1858 was costing them two percent a month. Yet here also there were hopes for the railroads to puncture. Near Portland, at Oswego, Simeon G. Reed of the Oregon Railway and Navigation Company induced Henry Villard to join him in the Oregon Iron and Steel Company (1882), which they supposed could sell profitably to their own railroad

---

[8] *Report of the Sixth Industrial Exhibition of the Merchanics' Institute of San Francisco* . . . (San Francisco: Women's Co-operative Union Print; 1868), pp. 18–19. Henry Robinson: "Our Manufacturing Era," *Overland Monthly*, Vol. II (March 1869), pp. 281–2.

[9] Margaret S. Gordon: *Employment Expansion and Population Growth: The California Experience, 1900–1950* (Berkeley: University of California Press; 1954), p. 36. Hittell: *Resources of California*, pp. 182–3, 445.

[1] Henry George: "What the Railroad Will Bring Us," *Overland Monthly*, Vol. I (October 1868), p. 303.

and others then building along the Columbia and the Willamette. And near Seattle, on Lake Washington, an English ironmaster who had found a local market for steel rails planned a still larger enterprise, the Great Western Iron and Steel Company. The Oswego company survived the arrival of the Northern Pacific by eleven years[2] and then fell victim both to the depression of 1893 and to the competition of larger and more efficient Eastern mills, whose products by this time were arriving in the Northwest on four railroad systems at competitive rates. The Great Western failed before it could open.

Even manufacturers of bulkier goods in the Northwest suffered from Eastern competition in the 1880's and 1890's while journalist prophets of a new era exhorted businessmen to greater risks. The main problem, the *Oregonian* observed in surveying the decline of manufactures after the railroad entered in 1883, was typical Oregon conservatism: the unwillingness of "mossback" capitalists to invest their own money or to make way for others, as in developing waterpower at Oregon City. A more fundamental difficulty was the lack of a market large enough to justify production along specialized and therefore efficient lines. By the end of the century, Northwestern wagon factories had become "practically only repair shops." "The Eastern men had the world before them," a pioneer Portland furniture manufacturer concluded, "and we had it behind us, and our limited market could not sustain the factory."[3]

Yet, despite serious disappointments, the Pacific slope as a whole continued to advance industrially. During the last twenty years of the nineteenth century, both the industrial product and the numbers of wage earners in manufacturing and mechanical pursuits increased absolutely as well as relative to the total numbers of employed persons in the six states. The shift of population from other occupations to manufacturing proceeded, in fact, more rapidly in the Far West than in the nation as a whole. In 1880, less than one of ten employed persons in the six states was in manufacturing, as compared with nearly one in six in the nation; by 1900 the respective ratios were better than one in eight as compared with about one in five and a half. It is true that California

[2] Alfred L. Lomax: "Pioneer Woolen Mills in Oregon," *Oregon Historical Quarterly*, Vol. XXX (June, September, December 1929), pp. 147–60, 238–58, 339–43. Dorothy O. Johansen: "Organization and Finance of the Oregon Iron and Steel Company, 1880–1895," *Pacific Northwest Quarterly*, Vol. XXXI (April 1940), pp. 123–59.

[3] Portland *Oregonian*, January 1, 1885, p. 3, col. 1; September 22, 1890, p. 10, col. 1; December 29, 1884, p. 4, col. 2; November 8, 1901, p. 8, col. 1; May 16, 1894, p. 8, col. 2.

exceeded its neighbors and that Oregon actually dropped behind in ratio of working population devoted to manufactures over one ten-year period, 1890 to 1900 (from better than one in eight to less than one in ten). Still, no area was entirely without hope, and the development of new raw materials from Western mines and forests and new sources of power encouraged the advocates of an industrial economy.

The steadier and more promising mineral industries of the coast in the eighties and nineties yielded fuel for local consumption and, as in pioneer days, gold and silver; the relatively simple processes of extraction continued to be dominant over fabrication. Although the bituminous deposits near Lake Washington never quite justified the hopes of those who hastened to build railroad connections from mines to deep water, Seattle began shipping coal to San Francisco in the sixties; Newcastle was a promising colliery town until fire destroyed the mine in 1894. Coal mining eventually declined not so much because of the competition of other states to the East as because of the competition of fuel oil from California. The early oil wells on the coast, the first of which broke through in Humboldt County in 1865, were too small to threaten either Western coal miners or Eastern oilmen; but by 1886, oil from wells in Pico Canyon was reaching the San Francisco market through a pipeline from Newhall to Ventura, and a revolutionary transformation of the economies of southern California and the coast followed a spectacular series of strikes in new fields over the decade 1892–1901. Edward L. Doheny brought in the first well in the Los Angeles basin in 1892; others followed in Santa Barbara County and in Kern County, at the upper end of the San Joaquin Valley. Oil fuel began to replace coal on Western railroads in 1895. The prospects were bright enough by 1900 to attract Standard Oil of New Jersey, which built a refinery at Point Richmond, on San Francisco Bay, in 1901–2 and began serving it by pipeline from Bakersfield in 1903.[4]

In the Cascades meanwhile, and in the basins and ranges beyond,

[4] Marilyn Tharp: "Story of Coal at Newcastle," *Pacific Northwest Quarterly*, Vol. XLVIII (October 1957), pp. 120–126. F. E. Melder: "History of the Discoveries and Physical Development of the Coal Industry in the State of Washington," *Pacific Northwest Quarterly*, Vol. XXIX (April 1938), pp. 151–65. Frank J. Taylor and Earl M. Welty: *Black Bonanza . . .* (New York: Whittlesey House; 1950), pp. 52–68. John Ise: *The United States Oil Policy* (New Haven: Yale University Press; 1926), pp. 87–91. Ralph W. and Muriel E. Hidy: *Pioneering in Big Business, 1882–1911; History of Standard Oil Company* (New Jersey), Vol. I (New York: Harper & Brothers; 1955), pp. 343–52, 358.

industrial mining developed less conspicuously than the oil boom, though more solidly than either the placer operations that preceded it or the hydraulickers of the Sierra Nevada. Even when, through the anti-debris legislation of the eighties, hydraulic mining became illegal in the only forms that had made it profitable, capitalists from the coast and still more from the East began to take over the mines of Idaho. The result was a spectacular rise in output, by about four times in the 1880's; by the end of the century, Idaho's production had passed Nevada's, which depended more exclusively on the precious metals. Yet the economy of northern Idaho continued fundamentally extractive: population increased less than mineral production; class consciousness, radical unionism, and violent labor disputes developed more than cities. (The one exception was Spokane, which drew some of its strength from the traffic of the mines across the state line.) Idahoans liked to talk of the more romantic days of the 1860's and of the discovery of the "Jackass Mine" in 1885 in the Coeur d'Alene, but there was never any question of reviving placer mining and the kind of society it attracted. Not only was the mining industry so heavily capitalized that it had to pay large returns to investors in distant areas—which was true to a smaller extent of much of the oil industry as well—but also its product was essentially inert, economically speaking, and had none of the catalytic effect on the economy that may follow on the development of a major source of power or fuel. Most of Idaho's gold, silver, and copper went directly east, as ingots. Most of California's oil and all of her gas and waterpower stayed on the coast.

The lumber industry of the coastal states meanwhile continued to produce largely for the Far Western and Pacific markets, but it was already well capitalized before the end of the century and increasingly under outside control. Although California continued into the 1880's to be the largest producer west of the Mississippi, chiefly on the basis of the redwood forests of the Santa Cruz and Humboldt areas, the local demand for lumber was so large that it drew on piling from Puget Sound as early as 1850. San Francisco capital soon moved heavily into Northwestern mills. The Northern Pacific Railroad saw in the lumber industry both a market for the land it had received from the United States government and a source of freight. By 1887–9 it succeeded in attracting a Minnesota firm to Washington Territory and thus initiated the first large-scale movement of capital from the upper Mississippi

Valley pine country, which still remained the most productive region at the end of the century, but was fast exhausting its reserves. Reduction of freight rates by the three main competing railroad lines brought a further movement of the industry in the 1890's, culminating in 1900 in the Northern Pacific's sale of 900,000 acres to Frederick Weyerhaeuser, neighbor and friend of James J. Hill.[5]

The newcomers greatly expanded production, which increased ten times in Oregon and Washington between 1880 and 1905; they also revamped the methods used in the industry. They had no choice but to introduce more efficient techniques on the coast than they had used along the Mississippi and the Great Lakes. The days of loading green logs directly on schooners from San Francisco were long past. By the 1880's, logging railroads were pushing into the interior, and high-line logging soon followed. Heavy outlays for land and transportation required rapid cutting and still more mechanization, to save on labor.[6] The greatest growth of the lumber industry on the coast lay ahead, but Oregon was proud to show the new Forestry Building at the Lewis and Clark Exposition in 1905 as a symbol of its economy.

The same years saw a great expansion of the salmon-canning industry in the Northwest, which had moved north from California after hydraulic mining had ruined the streams for fish in the 1860's. Competition led to consolidation in the industry in the 1880's and 1890's and to new techniques, which in turn brought larger catches and packs. Fish wheels appeared on the Columbia by 1879; gasoline-powered boats on Puget Sound by 1898. The pack in Oregon, Washington, and California continued to increase, but the runs in home waters no longer were enough. The canners had begun to reach out from the coast to

---

[5] Edwin T. Coman, Jr., and Helen M. Gibbs: *Time, Tide, and Timber, A Century of Pope and Talbot* (Stanford: Stanford University Press; 1949), pp. 33–48, 55. John H. Cox: "Organization of the Lumber Industry in the Pacific Northwest, 1889–1914" (unpublished doctoral thesis, University of California at Berkeley; 1937), pp. 2, 4–5. Cox: "Trade Associations in the Lumber Industry of the Pacific Northwest, 1899–1914," *Pacific Northwest Quarterly,* Vol. XLI (October 1950), pp. 285–311. Roy E. Appleman: "Timber Empire from the Public Domain," *Mississippi Valley Historical Review,* Vol. XXVI (September 1939), pp. 193–208.

[6] Howard B. Melendy: "One Hundred Years of the Redwood Lumber Industry, 1850–1950" (unpublished doctoral thesis, Stanford University; 1952), pp. 44–50. Edmund S. Meany, Jr.: "The History of the Lumber Industry in the Pacific Northwest to 1917" (unpublished doctoral thesis, Harvard University; 1935), pp. 260–4. Vernon H. Jensen: *Lumber and Labor* (New York: Farrar & Rinehart; 1945), pp. 100–1.

operate in Alaska as early as 1877, and by 1892 Alaska salmon accounted for the greater part of the American pack.[7]

By the end of the century, the Pacific slope had achieved a more solid and more diversified economic base than gold mining had provided, and was capable of supporting a larger population. When the United States first moved to assume control in 1846, the area still had been an economic outpost, less interesting as a loading station for furs and hides than it had been, and less certain of an agricultural future than any of the new territories of the Mississippi Valley. Two generations later, wheat, cattle, and sheep ranches had developed and were rapidly retreating east of the main mountain systems to make room for a more intensive agriculture. The mines had long since ceased to be treasure trove and had become factories; industry and commerce in the larger cities were increasingly capable of standing up to Eastern competition. Economic control, moreover, in significant areas had shifted from Easterners to Westerners, from outsiders to residents.

Yet economic life was still more colonial than Westerners liked to see it; the coast was much more devoted to the extractive industries, to extensive agriculture, to mining and logging than to manufacturing. And the centralization of economic control at San Francisco and Portland was no satisfaction to Westerners, who resented Montgomery Street no less than Wall Street. There was no doubt about the richness and the diverse material promise of the Far West, but the returns from them varied greatly.

---

[7] Mary de Sales McLellan: "William Hume, 1830–1902," *Oregon Historical Quarterly*, Vol. XXXV (September 1934), pp. 269–78. *Pygmy Monopolist: The Life and Doings of R. D. Hume . . .*, ed. Gordon B. Dodds (Madison: State Historical Society of Wisconsin; 1961). Daniel B. De Loach: *The Salmon Canning Industry* (Corvallis: Oregon State College; 1939), pp. 15–16. Clark P. Spurlock: "A History of the Salmon Industry in the Pacific Northwest" (unpublished master's thesis, University of Oregon; 1940), pp. 52–3, 61–4, 91–2, 129–38. John N. Cobb: *Pacific Salmon Fisheries*, third edition (Washington: Government Printing Office; 1921), Bureau of Fisheries Document no. 902, pp. 152–3, 168.

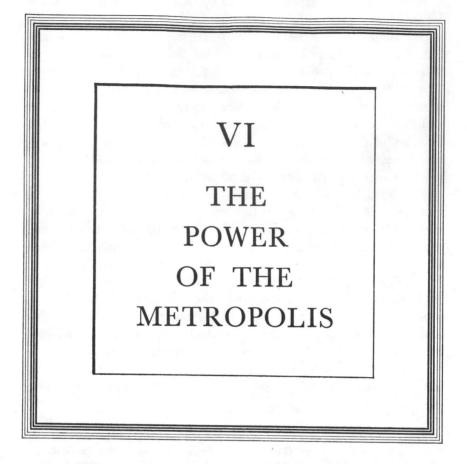

VI THE POWER OF THE METROPOLIS

FROM THE TIME of the first American settlements, the Pacific slope was significantly urban. Even those Far Westerners who did not live in cities (most did not until after 1900) looked to them to an unusual degree; even in states and areas where population was sparse, society was remarkably urbanized. The prospective settler headed for Salt Lake City, San Francisco, Portland, or one of their later rivals; if he did not work in the city, he visited it often, and it dominated his life. Economically and culturally, the most significant divisions were not state boundaries but the watersheds of urban allegiance and control: Spokane and Salt Lake City, rather than Boise, were the foci of Idaho; San Francisco and (in later years) Los Angeles, rather than Reno, those of Nevada.

VI · *The Power of the Metropolis*

The first cities of the coast were, of course, Boston and New York, and after them, with less certain authority, Honolulu. They served California and Oregon much as Seattle and San Francisco served Alaska a century later. The discovery of gold drew adventurers and commerce from all sections, but even in 1849, less than one of eight American vessels bound for California cleared from Southern and Gulf ports, which were closer to the Isthmus.[1] The early American traders of the 1820's and 1830's made home port in the East; it was only by degrees that they moved their merchandise from ship to shore, stayed the year rather than the season, brought out their wives, and sent their children to school in Monterey rather than in Honolulu or Boston. Even after statehood, some of the principal bankers and merchants of San Francisco were agents or associates of firms based in Boston and New York, as well as St. Louis; and it was long the habit of the San Francisco merchants to draw frequently on wholesalers in New York rather than to keep large stocks on hand. But distance from the East demanded subsidiary centers or forward staging areas even before the gold rush. In older Wests, the cities of adjacent older states served as outfitting points and trading centers until the new farmlands supported their own metropolis; but no state was adjacent to California, and the city had to come first. On the one hand, the United States government became interested in acquiring the coast to a large extent because of the prospects of its principal ports at the Columbia River and San Francisco Bay as way stations to the Orient;[2] on the other hand, when homesteaders and miners began to move into Oregon and California, they needed ports to handle their supplies and their commerce.

Cities grew in the new settlements both because distance required them and geography invited them and because the settlers wanted them. The commercial and speculative opportunities of the new country, the advantages of travel by sea rather than by land, and the high cost of any form of travel conspired to draw immigrants from the Eastern and urban rather than the Western and rural parts of the United States, in the 1840's and for a generation after. New Yorkers and New Englanders predominated in California, Oregon, and Utah through 1870. Their in-

---

[1] *The Merchants' Magazine,* Vol. XXII (February 1850), p. 208. John S. Hittell: *A History of the City of San Francisco* . . . (San Francisco: A. L. Bancroft & Co.; 1878), pp. 210–12.

[2] This is the thesis of Norman A. Graebner: *Empire on the Pacific: A Study in American Continental Expansion* (New York: Ronald Press Co.; 1955).

fluence, moreover, considerably outran their number: Easterners made up a larger fraction of the adult males, the voters, the officeholders, the leaders in business and in the professions, than of the population at large. Of a group of 136 successful lawyers in San Francisco in 1851, 55 were from New York, 24 from other Eastern states, and only 18 from the Middle West, including two from Missouri. In the San Francisco public schools in 1860, children born in New York and New England far outnumbered those born in all other states, including California. And though the census showed a large representation from Missouri in the population at large, many of the natives of Missouri who came to the coast were minor children of Eastern fathers.[3]

The nature of the pioneer economy, which had attracted settlers of urban orientation, confirmed their influence and that of the cities where they lived. Society during the gold rush was particularly careless of cost and dependent on imports. "If they had been deprived of what they obtained from abroad," according to Hittell, "the Californians could scarcely have lived for a day."[4] They bought through importers at San Francisco not only vast quantities of foodstuffs that in other states normally were products of the community that consumed them, but also bricks and prefabricated buildings of wood, stone, and iron, from as far as China and England. About six hundred houses, some framed, some of galvanized iron, had arrived in San Francisco by the fall of 1849; carpenters in New York City were building the Astor House, which was to have three and a half stories and a hundred rooms. Eastern traders began by sending their most decrepit hulks and unwanted merchandise —derelict fashions and rusty pork—to California, but shortly devised and employed the finest clipper ships for a market willing to pay a premium for fast service in luxury goods. Over three fifths of the businessmen of San Francisco in 1850 called themselves commission

---

[3] Doris M. Wright: "The Making of Cosmopolitan California; An Analysis of Immigration, 1848–1870," *California Historical Society Quarterly*, Vol. XIX (December 1940), pp. 323–42, Vol. XX (March 1941), pp. 65–79. Commonwealth Club of California: *The Population of California* . . . (San Francisco: Parker Printing Co.; 1946). *A "Pile", or, A Glance at the Wealth of the Monied Men of San Francisco and Sacramento City* . . . (San Francisco: Cooke & Lecourt; 1851), pp. 13–15. John S. Hittell: *The Resources of California* . . . (1866 ed.), p. 361. Jesse S. Douglas: "Origins of the Population of Oregon in 1850," *Pacific Northwest Quarterly*, Vol. XLI (April 1950), pp. 95–108.

[4] Hittell: *A History of the City of San Francisco*, p. 215.

merchants and importers. The San Franciscans burned illuminating gas produced from Australian coal (at from thirty-six to forty dollars a ton even in 1854); they cooled their drinks with ice from Alaska.[5]

The extraordinary commercial profits of the gold rushes and the urban habits and ambitions of much of the population led to the growth of cities and to plans for cities far beyond the dimensions of townsite developments on other Western frontiers that, on the basis of their agricultural hinterlands, apparently had more solid prospects. San Francisco was far too large for the population of California, a forty-niner complained: "to be upheld in its present overweening pretensions [1852], [it] would require a thriving population [in the state] of at least a couple of millions."[6] The wealthy and the ambitious put their savings more into city lots than into mining in the early years, at higher prices than income from rentals could justify. Much of this kind of speculation had, in fact, considerably preceded the discovery of gold and reflected shrewd calculation of commercial possibilities on a coast that seemed to have sites for only three major seaports and that might soon have a transcontinental railroad at one of them. Beach and water lots, some of them thirty feet under water, sold for from $100 to $700 at auction in 1847. By January 1850, water lots sold at nearly $1,500 each, and in 1853 at from $8,000 to $27,000 on the basis of tenure for ninety-nine years.[7]

Cities grew to a great extent out of the free-spending habits of gold miners and the imagination of real-estate speculators, but they continued growing after a more balanced economy had developed. Until after the railroads came, nearly all trade with the interior passed through San Francisco and Portland; and though they diverted much commerce

---

[5] *Littel's Living Age*, Vol. XXIII (December 8, 1849), pp. 450–1. Harris Newmark: *Sixty Years in Southern California, 1853–1913* (New York: Knickerbocker Press; 1916), p. 120. *Bogardus' Business Directory, for San Francisco and Sacramento City, for May, 1850* (San Francisco: William B. Cooke & Co's Bookstore; 1850). Charles M. Coleman: *P. G. and E. of California: The Centennial Story of Pacific Gas and Electric Company* . . . (New York: McGraw-Hill Book Co.; 1952), pp. 12, 15.

[6] William Kelly: *A Stroll through the Diggings of California* (Oakland: Biobooks; 1950), p. 159.

[7] Chester S. Lyman: *Around the Horn to the Sandwich Islands and California, 1845–1850* . . . , ed. Frederick J. Taggart (New Haven: Yale University Press; 1924), pp. 214, 226. A *"Pile"* . . . (1851). *Coleville's San Francisco Directory* . . . (San Francisco: Monson, Valentine & Co.; 1856), p. xviii. Frank Soule *et. al.: The Annals of San Francisco* . . . (New York: D. Appleton & Co.; 1855), pp. 182, 482, 500.

and industry from the principal ports, old habits persisted. "As San Francisco commands so much capital," a resident commented in 1876, "and all the large importers and wholesale dealers are here, these difficulties have adjusted themselves, and she still remains 'queen of the Pacific.'"[8] Rate schedules, established under pressure from the merchants of San Francisco, protected the cities from the competition of interior towns along the line. The power of Western capital insured that Westerners should not easily forget habits established during the free-spending days of the gold rushes, that San Francisco and Portland and Salt Lake City should maintain their power.

Neither did the growth of agriculture adulterate the urban character of the West. Except in Mormon country, most early farmers lived too far apart to form effective rural communities. The Donation Land Act of 1850 dispersed the agricultural population of Oregon, in the words of the Portland editor Harvey Scott, by opening a "banquet at which each guest was encouraged to swallow more than he could digest";[9] in California the original availability to speculators of land in large tracts and its relative unavailability to settlers, and later the high capitalization of dry farming and irrigation, tended to keep many owners from contact with each other and with the land itself. "There is by far too much of a disposition to farm in the San Joaquin Valley and live in San Francisco," a visitor from Illinois observed in 1877; "or, in other words, there is too much of the old ways of the planters of the Gulf States in *ante bellum* times. . . ."[1] Whether resident or nonresident, the California farmer tended increasingly to think of himself as a businessman supplying an urban market, dependent on distant processors, shippers, and financiers, and committed to mass-production methods, resting on the arts of the chemist and the mechanic.

Of the Far Western city-states, San Francsico was first in time and for long first in power. At its height it overshadowed Alaska, British Columbia, Arizona and western New Mexico, much of the west coast of Mexico, and Hawaii. "Not a settler in all the Pacific States and

---

[8] B. E. Lloyd: *Lights and Shades in San Francisco* (San Francisco: A. L. Bancroft & Co.; 1876), pp. 28–9.

[9] Portland *Oregonian,* June 16, 1899, quoted in Harvey W. Scott: *History of the Oregon Country,* compiled by Leslie M. Scott (Cambridge: Riverside Press; 1924), Vol. I, p. 260. Robert C. Clark: *History of the Willamette Valley, Oregon* (Chicago: S. J. Clarke Publishing Co.; 1927), Vol. I, p. 408.

[1] David L. Phillips: *Letters from California . . .* (Springfield: Illinois State Journal Co.; 1877), p. 140.

Territories but must pay San Francisco tribute," Henry George wrote in 1868; "not an ounce of gold dug, a pound of ore smelted, a field gleaned, or a tree felled in all their thousands of square miles, but must . . . add to her wealth. . . ."[2] The railroad disturbed and modified the power of the metropolis, as George had predicted, without destroying it. "San Francisco dwarfs the other cities," Lord Bryce wrote twenty years later, "and is a commercial and intellectual centre, and source of influence for the surrounding regions, more powerful over them than is any Eastern city over its neighborhood. It is a New York which has got no Boston on one side of it, and no shrewd and orderly rural population on the other, to keep it in order."[3] It became (1880) by far the largest city west of Chicago; larger in population than Washington and Oregon combined; seven times as large as its next largest rival in the Far West, which was Oakland, its own bedroom and railroad yard; thirteen times as large as Portland. It was "the city" even in Los Angeles well into the next century, when Los Angeles had assured its own imperium.

The development of the hinterland for many years advanced rather than weakened San Francisco, giving it wider economic and social jurisdiction. The Comstock Lode supported a thriving population on the side of Mount Washington, but Virginia City was "half colony and half suburb," as Mark Twain said, rather than serious aspirant to its own riches. There was never any question of rivalry with the metropolis, or of where those who struck it rich would take their money and themselves, if, indeed, the riches they dug were their own rather than the property of the bankers and the railroad kings. Surveying the deserts to the east and south, Hittell noted that the greater part of the West was so poor in resources for enjoyment that "most of the luxury of the slope has collected in and about San Francisco. The people from the wide region between the British and Mexican lines west of the Rocky mountains have come hither for twenty years to seek compensation for the toils and privations of frontier life. . . ."[4]

The miners' gold had supported fine restaurants and expensive

---

[2] John S. Hittell: *The Resources of California* (1863 ed.), pp. 327–30. Henry George: "What the Railroad Will Bring Us," *Overland Monthly,* Vol. I (October 1868), p. 300.

[3] James Bryce: *The American Commonwealth* (Chicago: Charles H. Sergel & Co.; 1891), Vol. II, p. 388.

[4] Samuel L. Clemens: *Roughing It* (New York: Harper & Brothers; 1913), Vol. II, p. 76. Hittell, *History of San Francisco,* pp. 462, 443.

shops even in the early fifties, and hotels more comfortable than seemed likely in a city that allowed itself to be burned six times in much less than two years (1849–1851). It was not yet a beautiful city: no one applies the word "architecture" to the pine and brick boxes that were the first advance over adobe and canvas, and ocean breezes brought dust and sand as well as the characteristic fog, which demanded long acquaintance before it could command affection. Still, San Francisco had energy and an interesting nexus of cosmopolitanism and of wealth, all of it spent with spirit and some of it with taste.

By the sixties, seventies, and eighties the city's face was catching up with its ambitions; the hotels no longer were bachelors' barracks and boardinghouses, but imitations of the best of both sides of the Atlantic. James Lick, eccentric owner of a mahogany-paneled gristmill at San Jose, had built the Lick House (1862), first of the Western luxury hotels, where visitors marveled at the high cost of decorations—until others surpassed it. Then William C. Ralston sank his fortune in the Palace Hotel (1875), twice as high as the Lick, a vast, colonnaded extravagance of apartments opening from a central court in the Viennese style and facing outward through large bay windows, reached by elevators, soon lighted by arc lamps, and equipped with shops, laundries, and all the paraphernalia of a young city. The Palace was so fashionable that many San Franciscans took rooms there, continuing a tradition of hotel living that had begun as an economy in days of scarce housing but then became display. Great private residences were rising, the most exotic and expensive of them the castles that the railroad magnates Crocker, Stanford, and Hopkins built on Nob Hill, which Stanford made accessible by the California Street Cable Railroad Company.[5]

The city thus became a showpiece, much of whose delight was its variety, extending from the dives of the Barbary Coast to the family picnic grounds of Woodward's Gardens, the view of sea and seals from the Cliff House, and the fine shops on Kearny Street. Oscar Wilde called Chinatown "the most artistic town I have ever come across" (1883); more conventional tourists gaped and shrank and imagined that they had seen Oriental depravity in the bowels of the earth. San

[5] Major William L. Cole: *California: Its Scenery, Climate, Production and Inhabitants* . . . (New York: Irish-American Office; 1871), p. 40. Edgar M. Kahn: *Cable Car Days in San Francisco,* revised edition (Stanford University: Stanford University Press; 1944), pp. 43–53.

Francisco added the graces of a cosmpolitan and sophisticated society to the uninhibited vigor and power of a Chicago. It presented at a a glance the economy of a region: the tribute of the countryside in the flower stands and at the fruiterers', the fragrance and bustle of the docks and railroad terminals, the excitement of the Stock Exchange, which Robert Louis Stevenson called (1882) "the heart of San Francisco; a great pump we might call it, continually pumping up the savings of the lower quarters into the pockets of the millionaires upon the hill,"[6] and the great mansions themselves. A large part of its attraction was in the surprising emergence of unity out of heterogeneity, creativity out of brute power, distinction out of extravagance. The new city hall seemed to a foreign visitor (1881) "an awkward pile of red bricks, with a huge tower somewhere, the whole caravansary having somewhat the appearance of those gigantic breweries to be found in the great cities of the Northwest." Yet the same critic found San Francisco's architecture ahead of the East's: "There is evidently more imagination, more originality of conception west of the Sierras than on the Atlantic coast."[7]

A generation after the gold rush, San Francisco society was fast achieving a reputation for gentility as young pioneers became family men, recalled ancestral traditions or learned to simulate them, and above all learned to spend their money. "San Franciscans are beginning to have artistocratic notions," a visitor observed in 1881. "They hint at pedigree, 'old stock,' and talk exclusiveness." Alongside "awkward matrons with powdered red faces and uncomfortable avoirdupois" reminiscent of days behind the bar or the washboard, their daughters were at once refreshingly unconventional, as they could afford to be in a community still predominantly male, and diligent students of Eastern and European styles.[8] "Fashion is the only tyrant," Lady Duffus Hardy commented, "for if a San Francisco lady is not in the fashion she is nowhere. . . . The girls all wonder how their dresses will look in print, and to that end select them."[9]

---

[6] Oscar Wilde: *Impressions of America*, ed. Stuart Mason (Sunderland: Keystone Press; 1906), p. 29. Stevenson: *Works* (1906), Vol. II, p. 194.

[7] A. E. D. DeRupert: *Californians and Mormons* (New York: John Wurtele Lovell; 1881), pp. 21–22.

[8] *Ibid.*, pp. 58, 95, 97.

[9] Lady Duffus Hardy: *Through Cities and Prairie Lands: Sketches of an American Tour* (London: Chapman and Hall, Ltd.; 1881), pp. 156, 164.

Like its prototypes on the East coast and in Europe, the metropolis developed focal points and also suburbs and retreats. Limited to the end of a narrow peninsula, San Francisco itself after the first explosive years grew far less rapidly than the state, and in the twentieth century became almost static, whereas "the peninsula" to the south and the "east bay district" were so unmistakably adjuncts that they failed for many years to develop shopping and entertainment districts commensurate with their size. The peninsular settlements at first were estates of the wealthy, where members of the Burlingame Country Club lived in "punctiliously conventional" style and enjoyed, in the words of an Englishman resident in California, "all the advantages of country life in France or England"; then middle-class residential communities developed along the stations on the railroad to San Jose. When railroad service along the narrow-gauge route extended into the Santa Cruz Mountains (1877), even the little mill town of Los Gatos, fifty miles from the mouth of the bay, developed rapidly as a suburb, though with a flavor of its own because of its climate and the nearby mineral springs; in the nineties it had a Keeley sanitarium,[1] which justified the nickname "Jagtown."

The communities across the bay to east and north made similar pretensions. (Berkeley, site of the new state university in 1868, liked to think of itself as a Western Newport or Long Branch.) Railroads transformed them, as Oakland acquired first the terminal of the transcontinental railroad late in 1869, and then, in the 1890's and early 1900's, rapid interurban service by railroad and ferry. Most of the railroad builders were landholders who built their lines to augment the value of their lands: F. M. ("Borax") Smith had made twenty million dollars and put most of it into a vast real-estate and transit speculation, beginning with thirteen thousand acres in and near Oakland that he proposed to subdivide. Smith's syndicate came to control all the electric lines on the east side of the bay, in Alameda and Contra Costa counties, and built the "Key Route" ferries and electric trains (1903) as the first phase of a system intended to extend southwestward to San Jose and Los Gatos and eastward into the San Joaquin Valley. It was Smith who established a trans-bay fare of ten cents a ride or three dollars for a monthly commutation ticket, and whose enterprise inspired the Southern Pacific, also a large landholder, to refurbish and electrify its suburban

[1] Horace A. Vachell: *Life and Sport on the Pacific Slope* (New York: Dodd, Mead & Co.; 1901), pp. 154–6.

lines in 1908–11. Each system eventually withdrew from passenger service after it had developed its properties and after commuters had turned to automobiles in the 1930's and 1940's; but Oakland and its neighbors grew enormously. Oakland also developed industrially, so that far from all of its working population entrained each day for San Francisco: the scrap iron that arrived from Europe as ballast in the wheat ships of the 1880's and 1890's went into foundries and machine shops that shortly promised to justify its claim to be the Glasgow of the United States, the Marseille of the Pacific.[2]

Across the Sierra Nevada, at the eastern end of the Central Pacific Railroad, the Mormon cities on and near Great Salt Lake were the second largest urban concentration in the Far West just after the Civil War. Salt Lake City was the unquestioned metropolis of what the Mormons sometimes called "the second Pacific State" and of a far larger region that they settled from Idaho into southern California. No other American city excepting El Paso is so isolated, so far from other major cities; no other city has so distinctive and dominant an influence over so large a territory.[3] Even early gentile travelers crossing Utah to Oregon or California who stopped in Salt Lake City only because it offered the surcease of food and drink or the spectacle of "the Mormon Chamber of Horrors" (or "the Principle," as the Saints sometimes primly referred to it) sensed that the city was more than an oasis, more than a refuge for polygamists. For Utah was primarily a religious colony, as thoroughly churched as early California was unchurched, and moreover one whose Biblical principles demanded an elaborate urban organization of society as foreign to the days of the patriarchs as to the nineteenth century, though determined to realize the ideals of both.

Zion, as the Saints tried to build it, brought rural ways into the city and gave an urban shape to agriculture. The urban character of Salt Lake City never was in doubt; freighters and emigrants converged on it from the beginning, and generations of travelers testified to its prosperity and to the relief of descending from the mountains into its broad streets, "regularly and handsomely laid out, with many fine buildings,"

---

[2] *Golden Era,* Vol. XXXV (July 1886), p. 423. *Oakland 1852–1938 . . . ,* ed. Edgar J. Hinkel and William E. McCann (Oakland: Oakland Public Library; 1939), pp. 14–50, 828, 876–7, 886.

[3] *Western Galaxy,* Vol. I (March 1888), p. 138. Chauncy D. Harris: "Salt Lake City, A Regional Capital" (unpublished doctoral thesis, University of Chicago; 1940), pp. iii, 3, and *passim.*

as Samuel Bowles recalled, "and filled with thick gardens of trees and flowers, that gave it a fairy-land aspect. . . ." Albert D. Richardson, who was there in 1865, called it "the natural metropolis of all Utah and portions of Nevada, Idaho, Montana and Colorado. It contains nearly twenty thousand people, and bids fair to continue the largest city between St. Louis and San Francisco."[4] Yet there was a curiously rural quality to the city—not only in the first years, when everyone cultivated his own land, no one put out a tradesman's sign, and a boy collected the family cows each morning, driving them through the city streets to pasture, but also later in the century, when city lots were still large (house lots were originally eight to a ten-acre block) and most yards still were orchards. "Salt Lake City by no means fulfils our ideas of a city," an English visitor of 1855–6 observed, "but is rather a gigantic village, or a collection of suburbs."[5] It seemed more permanent than the cities of the coast in the 1850's, despite this anticipation of twentieth-century suburbanization and despite the oddity of adobe construction, which most visitors took as a makeshift, to be superseded by fired brick and frame, rather than as precursor of a new Western architecture.

The Mormons' distinctive social order prevailed longer in the smaller cities and in the villages, which remained more generally agricultural; the people continued to go out to the fields each day while residing within the close ecclesiastical associations of ward and stake. The farmlands proper typically lay in concentric belts beyond the residential area, scrupulously divided so that no one suffered discrimination in distance from home and water or in quality of soil. It has been said that the Mormon villages resembled the gentile mining towns in compactness, though not in virtue.[6] They resembled much more closely the towns of interior New England from which the ancestors of many of the early Saints had come, as their smaller tabernacles resembled New England

---

[4] Samuel Bowles: *Across the Continent: a Summer's Journey to the Rocky Mountains, the Mormons, and the Pacific States, with Speaker Colfax* (Springfield: S. Bowles & Co.; 1865), p. 82. Albert D. Richardson: *Beyond the Mississippi* . . . (San Francisco: A. Roman & Co.; 1873), p. 351. Edward W. Tullidge: *The History of Salt Lake City* . . . (Salt Lake City: Star Printing Co.; 1886), pp. 664–5.

[5] William Chandless: *A Visit to Salt Lake* . . . (London: Smith, Elder, & Co.; 1857), p. 154.

[6] Nels Anderson: *Desert Saints: The Mormon Frontier in Utah* (Chicago: University of Chicago Press; 1942), pp. 428–9. Lowry Nelson: *The Mormon Village* . . . (Salt Lake City: University of Utah Press; 1952). Joseph E. Spencer: "The Development of Agricultural Villages in Southern Utah," *Agricultural History*, Vol. XIV (October 1940), pp. 183–4.

Congregational steepled meeting houses, and their social and religious doctrines the Old Testament rigor and majesty of early colonial Puritanism.

Commerce and the arts of the city strongly conditioned the Mormon community from the beginning, despite Brigham Young's early resolution not "to have any trade or commerce with the gentile world."[7] Although few except the pioneers of 1847 ate imported food within the decade when Californians were buying New York butter and Westphalian hams, still at first this was less because agriculture flourished than because the Saints were disciplined and poor enough to do without. Even so, they probably could not have survived without regular freight service from St. Louis and San Francisco, the leavings of gentile transients, and the contributions of converts in the East and Europe. Such windfalls helped to balance freight charges of thirty cents a pound and a generally unfavorable balance of trade with the states. The community had to enforce the most rigorous self-denial and an elaborate mercantilism that restricted some importations in order to apply dollar exchange to others and encouraged production both for use and for lucrative sale (for instance, of wine, which orthodox Mormons denied to themselves). Gentiles even gossiped of whiskey-distilling under respectable auspices.[8]

The Mormon community repeatedly struggled with tensions among its various principles, as between loyalty to the United States and the idea of a special covenant and a separate community, but probably at no time did it face problems as frustrating as those that followed on its attempts to preserve its agrarian ideal in the face of the gentile industrial world that pressed on it from the 1860's on. The Saints preferred agriculture to mining and the industrial and commercial arts because agriculture recalled the pastoral Israelites of Biblical times as against the Ninevites and Babylonians and because it seemed to stand for orderly, lasting development as against the erratic social influences of gold fever that they saw the forty-niners carrying through Utah on their way to California. Their concern revived traditional American anxieties; Brigham Young saw industrialism and urbanism undermining virtuous Mor-

[7] Norton Jacob: *Diary,* July 28, 1847, quoted in Harris: "Salt Lake City, A Regional Capital," pp. 54–5.

[8] Jules Rémy and Julius Brenchley: *A Journal to Great-Salt-Lake City . . .* (London: W. Jeffs; 1861), Vol. I, p. 270. *Frank Roney, Irish Rebel and California Labor Leader; an Autobiography,* ed. Ira B. Cross (Berkeley; University of California Press; 1931), pp. 249–51.

monism, much as Jefferson had seen them undermining virtuous republicanism; gentile miners and merchants gathering the wealth of the territory to themselves and setting examples of profligacy and inequality; gentile railroads importing "bummers, gamblers, saloon and hurdy-gurdy keepers, border ruffians, and desperados generally. . . ."[9] The gentile problem was as shocking to the Mormons as the Mormon problem (that is, polygamy) was to the gentiles, and far more imminent. It had been easier to resist force when Brigadier-General Albert Sidney Johnston moved into Utah with United States troops in 1857–8 than it was to resist Mammon when the Pacific railroad arrived a decade later. To resist Mammon was especially difficult because the Mormons aspired to material progress, among other American and Biblical goods, and lived close to substantial mineral deposits and astride the main roads across the continent.

The first merchants had appeared in the 1850's, all of them gentiles and most of them not only indifferent to the Church's purposes but also more prosperous in their wickedness than the Saints were in their virtue. Anxiety led to organized persecution and boycotts and then to comprehensive social engineering. The School of the Prophets (1867), which appeared as the central planning agency, encouraged and established manufactures for local use and for export (recommending reductions in wages to meet Eastern competition), planned the construction of local and branch railroads, and channeled imports through one trading organization, Zion's Cooperative Mercantile Institution (1869). Cooperatives were not new, but previously their purpose had been to initiate productive enterprises and social services (such as the Deseret Telegraph) for which individual capital was not available, rather than to wage economic warfare. The success of the School of the Prophets, according to Leonard Arrington, is evident in Utah's resistance to Eastern capitalists, whose control shortly extended over Montana, Wyoming, Arizona, and other territories and states of comparable physical resources.[1]

---

[9] O'Dea: *The Mormons*, pp. 169 and *passim*. Leonard J. Arrington: "The Transcontinental Railroad and Mormon Economic Policy," *Pacific Historical Review*, Vol. XX (May 1951), pp. 143–57.

[1] Leon L. Watters: *The Pioneer Jews of Utah* (New York: American Jewish Historical Society; 1952), pp. 42, 47–53, 55–8. Arrington in *Pacific Historical Review*, Vol. XX, pp. 148–57. Arrington: "The Deseret Telegraph—A Church-owned Public Utility," *Journal of Economic History*, Vol. XI (Spring 1951), pp. 137–9.

Yet the price of victory over the outsider seemed to include a considerable departure from the Mormon social ideal, or at least from that part of the Mormon social ideal that emphasized the virtues of village life. The drift to the city all over Utah accelerated; during the seventies Salt Lake City grew nearly as fast as Los Angeles, and by 1880 it was nearly twice as large; a survey of income in Utah over the years when the United States collected an income tax, 1862–72, shows that 85 percent of income-tax payments were made by residents of Salt Lake City and that the distribution of income, which had been more equal in Utah than in the nation as a whole before 1869, rapidly approximated national inequality. Small numbers of shareholders owned the larger cooperatives, such as Z.C.M.I., and ownership increasingly became concentrated. William Jennings, superintendent of Z.C.M.I. and president of the Utah Southern Railroad, left an estate of $838,000 in 1886.[2] Eventually Mormons thought of Z.C.M.I. as "America's first department store" rather than as a bastion against the gentile way of life.

Toward the end of his life, in 1874, President Young announced that he wished the people to enter the United Order or the Order of Enoch, the earthly fulfillment of Mormon social doctrine, by which families used even common kitchens and dining tables, and for several years some of the faithful lived thus at St. George and other outlying settlements, sharing and working together as during the flight from Nauvoo to Salt Lake thirty years earlier. Young said that his purpose was "to get the people into the same unity in all things temporal, that we find ourselves in with regard to things spiritual."[3] Yet the United Order proved to be only an Indian summer of primitive Mormonism. Most of the land then thought to be irrigable was already under cultivation, and the most promising economic opportunities for Mormons, as for gentiles, were industrial, commercial, financial, and capitalistic rather than agricultural and cooperative. The Order of Enoch did not enter Salt Lake City and expired soon after Young's death (1877); Young himself never joined it. More typical of the new era was Zion's Board of Trade (1879–84), whose principal purpose was to encourage manufacturing. "The Mormons are eminently a manufacturing community,"

[2] Arrington: "Taxable Income in Utah, 1862–1872," *Utah Historical Quarterly,* Vol. XXIV (January 1956), pp. 26–32, 42–5.

[3] Edward J. Allen: *The Second United Order Among the Mormons,* Columbia University Studies in History, Economics, and Public Law, no. 419 (New York: Columbia University Press; 1936), pp. 49–59.

observed the editor of *Tullidge's Magazine*, who applauded its efforts. "Natively they are a manufacturing people rather than an agricultural, and our Territory very much resembles Great Britain in its resources of iron and coal and that class of industries which properly belongs to her."[4]

By the seventies and eighties, Salt Lake City was rapidly approximating the shape of other Western centers. The influence of the Church remained paramount; and it continued temporally active, investing the fruits of tithings in business as well as in charity and mobilizing its resources and commanding the patronage of its members to such an extent that outsiders sometimes charged conspiracy. "The hopelessness of contending in a business way with this autocrat must be perfectly apparent to your minds," Senator Thomas Kearns told the Senate in 1905, charging that President Smith conducted "railways, streetcar lines, power and light companies, coal mines, salt works, sugar factories, shoe factories, mercantile houses, drug stores, newspapers, magazines, theaters, and almost every conceivable kind of business. . . . ." Still, the gentile community grew and prospered (Kearns himself with it, as mine owner and politician), while the Mormons insisted less on the uniqueness of their own ways and increasingly welcomed gentile co-operation and approval; it seemed a long time since Brigham Young had warned the Saints against the temptations of the gold mines: "Go and be damned!" Frank Roney, a labor leader who found the speculative spirit in the valley of the mountains as on the coast, recalled that in the early 1870's "Utah was a large mining camp and Salt Lake City was its main street."[5] The president of the Salt Lake Chamber of Commerce reported with pleasure the advance in the price of real estate (1888), in which the city promised to approximate its Western neighbors: "The present extraordinary prosperity and development of Denver, Los Angeles, Omaha and Kansas City had their origin in real estate speculation. The one almost necessarily succeeds the other, as prices of land can be sustained in times of speculative excitement only by the building up of manufacturing and mercantile industries, to

---

[4] Arrington: "Zion's Board of Trade: A Third United Order," *Western Humanities Review*, Vol. V (Winter 1950–1), pp. 1–20. *Tullidge's Quarterly Magazine*, Vol. I (April 1881), p. 420.

[5] *Conditions in Utah. Speech of Hon. Thomas Kearns, of Utah, in the Senate of the United States, Tuesday, February 28, 1905* (Washington, 1905), p. 6. *Frank Roney's Autobiography*, p. 258.

which the speculator himself is often driven for self-protection." Although the Chamber of Commerce was originally non-Mormon in leadership, its purpose was in large part to carry on the work of the Church-sponsored Board of Trade, and Mormons were cooperating actively before the end of the century.[6]

If Salt Lake City blended the vision of the Saints into the practical details both of the desert underfoot and of the gentile world around, and if the distinctive shape and flavor of San Francisco comprised strains at once proletarian and patrician, spendthrift and prudent, earthy and cultured, Portland by comparison seemed the creation of its citizens. The chief founders of Portland were traders, including the Maine merchant (agent for a New York firm) who gave the city its name and the Newburyport sea captain who made it the terminus of his shipping and mercantile business in 1846. Rival ports hoped to inherit the future along the Willamette and the Columbia as on San Francisco Bay. ("Nearly every man in Oregon has a City of his own," Medorum Crawford reported in 1850, "and it is impossible to tell what point on the Columbia will take the preference."[7]) But the merchants of Portland had a choice anchorage and the advantages of their own skill and financial resources over the former missionaries at Oregon City, the Missourians at Linnton, and the miscellaneous small speculators who lived "by skining travilers [sic] on their way up and down."[8]

Established just in time to respond to the great stimulus of California gold, and near enough to the gold fields to undertake a profitable provisioning trade, Portland was further from the personal and economic immoralities of San Francisco than San Francisco was from the extreme risks and uncertainties of the mining camps. Its leaders were prudent men; and prudence being dependably profitable, they remained prudent despite large advances in fortune. During Henry W. Corbett's first residence as a merchant in Portland in 1851–2, he cleared

---

[6] "Salt Lake Chamber of Commerce," *The Western Galaxy*, Vol. I (March 1888), p. 62. Arrington in *Western Humanities Review*, Vol. V, pp. 19–20.

[7] Crawford to Father, Oregon City, Jan. 24, 1850 (Crawford papers, University of Oregon).

[8] "Report of Lieutenant Neil M. Howison on Oregon, 1846," *Oregon Historical Quarterly*, Vol. XIV (March 1913), p. 43. Works Progress Administration: *History of Portland, Oregon* (Portland, 1940), pp. 8–9.

$20,000 on capital that a New York firm advanced; when he returned the next year, he began plowing his profits into transportation, telegraph, real-estate, and banking enterprises; eventually he built Portland's finest hotel and bought its leading newspaper. Another New Englander, William S. Ladd, began as a clerk in a grocery store; nine years later he founded the city's first bank, which increased its capital twenty times in the next seven years.[9] Such gains were satisfying rather than exhilarating; typically, Portland's capitalists and civic leaders scorned mere speculative profits and any temptation to exceed their destiny, in a spirit that evoked complaints of "mossbackism" in boom times and praise for Oregon's "soundness" when California and Nevada suffered deflation. Portland would "never be the centre of fashion, speculation or thought," Judge Matthew P. Deady warned (1868). "Do what it will, it will be comparatively a provincial place . . . but it will be worth more dollars per head than either London or New York, and its good citizens will sleep sounder and live longer than the San Franciscans."[1]

So it became; so they did. The Eastern visitor to Portland, Ray Stannard Baker remarked in 1903, expects a "new, crude Western town; what he really sees is a fine old city, a bit, as it might be, of central New York—a square with the post-office in the center, tree-shaded streets, comfortable homes, and plenty of churches and clubs, the signs of conservatism and solid respectability. . . ."[2] Portland had seemed old even when it was young, respectable when it was still crude, before it had what Baker called "the momentum of stored riches." "In many ways life here . . . was more primitive than it was in the early times in Illinois and Missouri," recalled the publisher Harvey W. Scott, who arrived in 1852. "But in others it was far more advanced. . . . We could get the world's commodities here which could not be had, then, or scarcely at all, in the interior of Illinois or Missouri." Almost from the beginning it was past beginnings; from

---

[9] Arthur L. Throckmorton: "The Role of the Merchant on the Oregon Frontier: The Early Business Career of Henry W. Corbett, 1851–1869," *Journal of Economic History,* Vol. XVI (December 1956), pp. 539–50. Throckmorton: *Oregon Argonauts; Merchant Adventurers on the Western Frontier* (Portland: Oregon Historical Society; 1961).

[1] Deady: "Portland-on-Wallamet," *Overland,* Vol. I (July 1868), p. 43.

[2] Baker: "The Great Northwest," *Century,* Vol. LXV (March 1903), pp. 658–9.

pioneer days, travelers from New England often found it more familiar than any place they had seen since they had left home.[3]

In time, Portlanders permitted themselves un-Puritan display in residential architecture, but they never approached the riotous extravagance of the bonanza kings of San Francisco: the houses themselves might have come from contemporary New England or New York, as their designs often had. Under the influence of the firm of McKim, Mead and White, the Portland Hotel resembled the Queen-Anne-style Casino of Newport, Rhode Island, and the Portland Public Library was a reduced version of the neo-Renaissance Boston Public Library. "Invoke the spirit of the lamp and transport a resident of some Eastern city," the illustrated magazine *West Shore* boasted, "and put him down in the streets of Portland, and he would observe little difference between his new surroundings and those he beheld but a moment before in his native city."[4] The rich men of Portland lived at home, whereas those of San Francisco went abroad; and for the most part they lived quietly, solidly; the new rich of the mining states moved rather to San Francisco or the suburbs of Los Angeles. Senator John Mitchell, agent of the Oregon railroad interests, bought a fine house in Portland—and paintings in dozen lots to furnish it—but not the respect of Portland society, which laughed at his taste and at his wife's malapropisms, as when she confused the scavenger with the caterer. Though the city was younger than many of its first citizens, in some Northwestern communities people spoke of it as old and as substantial as Rome.[5]

Portland's reputation sprang from influence as well as respect-

---

[3] Scott: "Habits of Oregon in the Early Time," *Oregon Historical Quarterly*, Vol. XVIII (December 1917), pp. 247–8. Mrs. Zachariah C. Norton, March 7, 1850, in "Voyage of the Sequin, 1849," *Oregon Historical Quarterly*, Vol. XXXIV (September 1933), p. 257. Hubert H. Bancroft: *Retrospection, Political and Personal* (New York: Bancroft Company; 1912), p. 305. Olive Rand: *A Vacation Excursion, From Massachusetts Bay to Puget Sound* (Manchester, N. H.: Press of John B. Clarke; 1884), p. 132.

[4] Marion D. Ross: "Architecture in Oregon, 1845–1895," *Oregon Historical Quarterly*, Vol. LVII (March 1956), pp. 61–3. *West Shore*, Vol. XII (January 1886), p. 11.

[5] Joaquin Miller: "The Great Emerald Land," *Overland*, new series, Vol. XXVIII (December 1896), p. 643. O. Muiriel Fuller: *John Muir of Wall Street* . . . (New York: The Knickerbocker Press; 1927), p. 143. *Harper's Weekly*, Vol. LVI (February 17, 1912), p. 11. Frank A. Marriott, "The City of Portland," *Overland*, new series, Vol. XLV (May 1905), p. 437. *World's Work*, Vol. X (August 1905), p. 6501.

ability, and especially from its economic dominion over the Pacific Northwest, which seemed almost the gift of nature and Providence rather than the consequence of mere enterprise. For two generations or so, it was the principal commercial headquarters of the region; warehouses along Front Street contributed, according to a visitor of the early 1880's, "a metropolitan appearance unlooked for in a place of its size."[6] The committee in charge of defining regions and headquarters for federal reserve districts in 1913–14 found that Portland's financial preeminence persisted even while the city lagged behind Seattle in population; a writer in the *Bankers Magazine* (1913) reported that Portland commanded "a territory greater in extent than Germany."[7]

In the early eighties, as the railroad builders converged on the lower Columbia, the hopes of Portlanders for further influence had risen along with the hopes of the tributary population for liberation from Portland's domination. "That San Francisco must suffer a serious relapse . . . nothing can be more true," *West Shore* observed in 1881, noting that Portland and its domain would soon have not only rails to the East, but also more railroads than San Francisco. But the new railroads seemed to import disappointment for both the Portland businessmen and their customers. Outcries arose against the "mossbackism" of leading citizens, who preferred waiting to leading and who scorned the undignified promotional efforts of rival cities on Puget Sound.[8]

In time Portland also learned to promote itself. It staged an exposition celebrating the hundredth anniversary of the Lewis and Clark expedition—more in the spirit of bustling California than in the traditional spirit of Oregon. Yet much of the old complacency survived and claimed justification. When the Northern Pacific ran its mainline traffic west from Pasco over the Cascades to Puget Sound, reaching Portland by a spur to Kalama rather than through the water-level route of the Columbia Gorge, Portland waited more in sorrow than in despair, assuring itself that Seattle and Tacoma never could rely on more than local business or the vagaries of the Alaskan trade, that in time the railroad would have to come. And eventually the Northern Pacific

---

[6] Rand: *Vacation Excursion*, p. 133.

[7] C. H. Williams: "Portland—A City of Remarkable Growth," *Bankers Magazine*, Vol. LXXXVI (April 1913), p. 505.

[8] *West Shore*, Vol. VII (February 1881), p. 53. Portland *Oregonian*, January 1, 1885, p. 4, col. 1. *West Shore*, Vol. XI (March 1885), p. 61; Vol. XIII (January 1887), p. 103.

came, when Hill built the North Bank line. The *Oregonian* observed that this was only the inevitable: "All roads led to Rome in the old days, and all railroads lead to Portland . . . in the twentieth century."[9] The boom in Portland and in eastern Oregon in the decade after the Exposition of 1905 seemed to justify both those who bustled and those who waited; Portland became in consequence more like her neighbors and yet retained much of her old self. "The Columbia River has made the spirit of Portland," a member of an old family remarked in later years. "Portland people were toll takers at the gate. In time, they became conservative, took fewer chances and relied upon the geographic position of their tollgate. . . . Maybe too much sitting at the tollgate."[1]

At another extremity from Portland stood southern California and its metropolis, Los Angeles, as different in spirit as it was in climate and situation. Los Angeles was, in every sense but the most literal, one of the youngest of the major cities of the Pacific coast: old in that it had begun as a Spanish pueblo in 1781, when only Indians had discovered Salt Lake, the Columbia River, and Puget Sound, and anything worthy of the name of commerce on San Francisco Bay was still over sixty years in the future; young in that it began unmistakably to anticipate its future only in the 1870's and did not grow larger than Portland and Salt Lake City until the 1880's. Only Seattle has seemed so much the product of the twentieth century, of the automobile, the airplane, the assembly line, and the advertising agency.

For ninety years or so the pueblo bore the burden of a reputation for roughness without glamour or success. Americans controlled most of the trade, including the traffic with the mines in the mountains to the east, but it was a small prize; life moved slowly along the dusty streets. The chief justification for a city half a day's journey from the coast and a hundred and fifty miles from a good harbor was the cattle industry, which collapsed during the disastrous droughts of 1862–4. Taxes became delinquent on at least five sixths of the property in the county;[2] the chief hindrance to general foreclosure was that almost

---

[9] F. A. Marriott: "A Conspicuous Success," *Overland*, Vol. XLV (June 1905), p. 553. Major Alfred F. Sears, C. E., in Portland *Oregonian*, November 4, 1900, p. 8, col. 3.

[1] Leslie Scott: "Early Portland Contrasts," *Oregon Historical Quarterly*, Vol. XXXII (December 1931), p. 313.

[2] Robert G. Cleland: *The Cattle on a Thousand Hills: Southern California, 1850–1880* (San Marino: The Huntington Library; 1951), p. 136.

no one wanted the land. Ranchers and townspeople grasped frantically after a substitute for cattle, which in the next several years some thought they had found in castor beans or silk or wool or the Australian eucalyptus tree.

When the collapse in land values eventually gave way to general economic revival and the first southern Californian real-estate boom in 1868–9, the availability of land coincided with new demand and with new financial and civic leadership. The first major subdivider in 1865 was former Governor John G. Downey, a local merchant with large resources and connections, who also established (1868) the first bank in Los Angeles, in association with a San Francisco capitalist, and was interested in the Los Angeles City Water Company and the Los Angeles and San Pedro Railroad. The largest promotion was that of the Robinson Trust, in which a group of San Francisco investors associated themselves to acquire 177,797 acres in the vicinity of Los Angeles and San Bernardino from Abel Stearns, who once had been the wealthiest man in California, but who like most old residents and ranchers had contracted debts far beyond his ability to pay.[3]

Meanwhile the prospects of Los Angeles were feeding on rumors of a transcontinental railroad connection, which businessmen and landholders hoped to attract by subsidizing a line to the coast at San Pedro (1868–9). Three years later (1872), the city and county voted, over strong rural opposition, a larger subsidy to the Southern Pacific Railroad, then building south from San Francisco Bay through the San Joaquin Valley, to persuade it to run its tracks through Los Angeles rather than behind the mountains to the east. Completion of the Southern Pacific line to Los Angeles in 1876, and its extension eastward to meet the Texas and Pacific east of El Paso in 1881, gave Los Angeles direct access to New Orleans as well as to San Francisco. Although the expected boom did not develop, and in fact the new railroads seem to import instead the nationwide depression of the seventies, capital continued to flow in. A San Francisco group had organized to "develop" the San Fernando Valley in 1869; Senator John P. Jones, the Nevada silver millionaire, built a local line (1874–5) and pro-

[3] Remi A. Nadeau: *City Makers: The Men Who Transformed Los Angeles to Metropolis during the First Great Boom, 1868–76* (New York: Doubleday & Co.; 1948), pp. 44–8. Cleland: *Cattle on a Thousand Hills*, pp. 172–6, 198–207.

moted the town of Santa Monica as his seaport; and Leland Stanford, president of the Southern Pacific, provided funds to develop the San Fernando Valley further in 1874. The most spectacular of the new investors was another San Franciscan, E. J. ("Lucky") Baldwin, who withdrew five million dollars from his Comstock holdings in 1875, just before values collapsed, and bought heavily in the San Gabriel Valley, where he built his Santa Anita ranch as a personal indulgence and as an attraction to buyers.[4]

Los Angeles may seem to have found the formula for its eventual success in the late 1860's and early 1870's: vigorous promotion, including rapturous advertising; attraction of outsiders with capital; heavy spending to overcome the area's natural handicaps in transportation. But success was not yet at hand. The metropolis of the region was still San Francisco, which consumed its agricultural surplus and provided most of the goods that Los Angeles conveyed into the back country. The subdividers, like those of later generations, were interested in developing new and semi-rural settlements rather than in planning a central city, and, indeed, the best prospects of the area still seemed agricultural. Thus Los Angeles had suburbs such as Compton (1869) and Pasadena (1875), before it was a city in any but the legal sense. David Starr Jordan, who was there in 1879, recalled it as "still a mere village,—mostly Mexican . . . and the country round was practically a desert of cactus and sagebrush."[5]

When the boom came, in 1886–8, it represented an extraordinary combination of effort and enthusiasm. The Southern Pacific had more at stake than the county, which had subsidized it: it was a new and expensive transcontinental line, which reached the coast in the vicinity of vast landholdings that it hoped to sell, but which as yet had little population or patronage except traffic passing through to San Francisco. Then came a competitor, the Santa Fe, which had its own tracks by 1887, and an aggressive disposition that shortly drove fares down to as little as five dollars from the Mississippi River. The first to guess

---

[4] Nadeau: *City Makers*, pp. 24–30, 191–8. John S. McGroarty: *Los Angeles from the Mountains to the Sea* (Chicago: American Historical Society; 1921), Vol. I, p. 109. C. B. Glasscock: *Lucky Baldwin, the Story of an Unconventional Success* (Indianapolis: The Bobbs-Merrill Co.; 1933), pp. 175–8.

[5] David Starr Jordan: *The Days of a Man . . .* (Yonkers: World Book Co.; 1922), Vol. I, p. 202.

what railroads might do for the real-estate market were the local subdividers. Mayor Workman, for example, had built a streetcar line to serve one of his own subdivisions, had gone into politics to assure its water supply, and had worked to bring in the Santa Fe and a line from Salt Lake. Another subdivider donated land to the Southern Pacific for a new railroad station in a tract that he hoped to "develop." But the growth of the market exceeded the rosiest local expectations. It developed to a large extent under the ministrations of professional "boomers" from the Middle West, who arrived along with the crowds of tourists, colonists, and curiosity-seekers taking advantage of bargain railroad fares. Social and commercial uncertainties abounded. "The man with whom you were doing business every day might be an ex-convict," the president of the Historical Society of Southern California recalled (1890), "or he might be one whom the stripes were destined to ornament some time in the future."[6] The newspapers announced new "developments," where the prices of lots would advance at specified hours—and did, purchasers standing in line to beat the deadlines; all in an atmosphere of brass bands and processions, circus animals and sideshow freaks on the street to draw attention, free lunches and auctions in circus tents. In one day in 1887 real-estate sales reached nearly three times the amount of the subsidy paid to the Southern Pacific fourteen years before; over the year they were third only to sales in New York and Chicago.[7]

The collapse of the boom in 1888 left the town deflated as only a community that has lived chiefly by and for increasing real-estate values can be, with bunting in shreds, temporary buildings abandoned, and permanent buildings unfinished. Population dropped by about three eighths in two years. With the streets no longer filled with buyers just arrived from the East, it was easier to see that most of them were unpaved. Assessed valuations, which had increased nearly five times be-

---

[6] Boyle Workman: *The City That Grew,* ed. Caroline Walker (Los Angeles: Southland Publishing Co.; 1935), pp. 182–3, 230–1, 237–8. J. M. Guinn: "The Great Real Estate Boom of 1887," Historical Society of Southern California, *Publications,* Vol. I (1890), pp. 15, 19.

[7] Charles D. Willard: *The Herald's History of Los Angeles City* (Los Angeles: Kingsley-Barnes & Neuner Co.; 1901), p. 340. Harris Newmark: *Sixty Years in Southern California, 1853–1913,* third edition (Boston: Houghton Mifflin Co.; 1930), pp. 57–84. Glenn S. Dumke: *The Boom of the Eighties in Southern California* (San Marino: Huntington Library; 1944).

tween 1880 and 1888, slumped by only about one third in the following two years;[8] in the decade, the population increased nearly four times, and during the 1890's, Los Angeles exceeded any other city west of the Rockies except San Francisco in size, any except Seattle in rate of growth.

Despite the slump, the town still had its principal assets—climate, space, and "big men" determined that it should continue to grow along with its rapidly developing agricultural hinterland. In October 1888, while the most reckless of the speculators nursed their wounds, Harrison Gray Otis, publisher of the *Los Angeles Times,* proposed the establishment of the Los Angeles Chamber of Commerce, which set about developing manufactures, finding fuel, raw materials, and markets, and attracting "practical farmers." The Chamber was ever ready with stationary and traveling exhibits and personal advice and solicitation; it mailed out copies of local newspapers, magazines such as the flamboyant *Land of Sunshine* (financed by its secretary and edited by the former city editor of the *Times*), and its own pamphlets; it sent delegations far afield to promote commerce and the tourist trade; it arranged tours for influential visitors, such as Eastern editors, and even provided accounts of their trips and of southern Californian weather for them to send back home. In 1894, when trade was slack, businessmen introduced the "Fiesta de Los Angeles," advertising their products and those of the region. The street railways continued to figure importantly in the growth of the city; by 1898 Henry E. Huntington and a San Francisco syndicate had organized the Los Angeles Railway Company as part of an enormous complex of electric railway lines and urban development. He became known as the "greatest single landowner in Southern California."[9]

Ever since the boom of the eighties, the growth of Los Angeles has been inseparable from the growth of its neighbors, though at first the

---

[8] Newmark: *Sixty Years,* pp. 582–4. Dumke: *Boom of the Eighties,* pp. 46, 55. Charles D. Willard: *History of the Chamber of Commerce of Los Angeles* . . . (Los Angeles: Press of Kingsley-Barnes & Neuner Co.; 1899), pp. 21, 35, 37, 39.

[9] Willard: *Herald's History,* pp. 62–70. Edwin R. Bingham: *Charles F. Lummis; Editor of the Southwest* (San Marino: Huntington Library; 1955), pp. 37–47. Willard: *History of the Chamber of Commerce,* pp. 318 and *passim.* Glenn S. Dumke: "Early Interurban Transportation in the Los Angeles Area," Historical Society of Southern California, *Quarterly,* Vol. XX (December 1940), pp. 136–8.

city was not large enough to impose its will on them. The Chamber of Commerce spoke for the county and even for the southern half of the state. One of its principal projects, if not its chief project, was to develop a harbor that would confer on the Los Angeles area the kind of commercial and industrial advantage that San Francisco Bay had in northern California; by 1905 the Chamber was beating the drums for the first of the vast water-supply projects that were the key to the growth of metropolitan Los Angeles in the twentieth century. The Huntington electric railway system (reorganized as the Pacific Electric in 1911) reached out its tracks by 1913 to envelop forty-two incorporated cities within a radius of thirty-five miles, and others beyond. "The arterial system that holds them together," a reporter wrote, "is the double trackage of the interurban electric road." Life came to focus where the tracks intersected in enormous terminals on Main Street, but Huntington and his colleagues were concerned with townsites as well as with commuters. "At first lines were built for towns; then towns were built for lines."[1]

Most of the early neighboring towns had begun, not as San Francisco's suburbs had—to afford easy access to space and climate and other residential advantages not available within the city limits—but in the hope of more independent destinies. Typically, their first residents had been in Los Angeles only to change trains or to confer with real-estate agents. Some were offshoots of Eastern or Middle Western rather than Californian cities. Following the examples of Anaheim (1857) and Riverside (1870), which were essentially agricultural colonies and pioneers in the economic and social possibilities of citrus raising on small irrigated plots, the sponsors of the San Gabriel Orange Grove Association (1874) offered fifteen acres to the holder of each $250 share, and Pasadena began as a community of gentlemen farmers. "It is a singular fact," an early member and local historian recalled, "that there was not a professional and hardly a practical horticulturist or farmer among them."[2] Orchards and gardens soon grew up among the oak trees; Charlotte Perkins Stetson Gilman, who arrived in 1888, found "calm sublimity of contour, richness of color, profusion of flowers, fruit and foliage, and

---

[1] Rufus Steele: "The Red Car of Empire," *Sunset, The Pacific Monthly*, Vol. XXXI (October 1913), pp. 711, 713.

[2] Joseph M. Guinn: *Historical and Biographical Record of Southern California* . . . (Chicago: Chapman Publishing Co.; 1902), p. 140.

the steady peace of its climate. . . . Everywhere there was beauty, and the nerve-rest of steady windless weather." When direct railroad connections with the East effectively opened the tourist business in 1881, the owners of the leading Boston travel agency selected Pasadena rather than Los Angeles as the stopping place for their patrons. The palatial Raymond Hotel shortly began to attract new residents from Eastern cities, who rode to hounds after jackrabbits, coyotes, and wildcats where the long-horned Spanish cattle had grazed a few years earlier.[3]

Most of the other towns were "colonies" only in the sense that their promoters saw fit to concentrate their efforts on specific groups of prospects, but some soon developed identifiable traditions and clienteles. Compton (1869) attracted Methodists and teetotalers; Long Beach (founded in 1878 as Willmore City, and later known as "Capital of Iowa"), retired Middle Westerners; Whittier (1887), Quakers; Claremont (1887), New Englanders; La Verne (1891), Dunkers. The subdividers found that whereas speculators had been willing to bid recklessly on canyons and swamplands during the boom, those who paid and remained were the steady and the prosperous; it was good business to outlaw the saloon and to build schools, churches, and libraries, and perhaps to identify the city with some respectable group that might recruit colonists or give them a sense of community in a strange land. In a day when the offerings far exceeded the takers—half a million lots in sixty new towns with a total population (1889) of 2,351; thirty-six towns between Los Angeles and the San Bernardino county line, just thirty-six miles away[4]—the social prospects were as important as the geographical prospects. Thus homogeneity developed with dispersion, the occasional unity of the suburb along with the disunity of the budding metropolis.

Although perhaps no part of the United States has changed more drastically and more improbably in landscape—and atmosphere—than southern California in the last century, the later urban development of the Pacific Northwest diverged almost as much from the early tendencies of the region. Before the Northwestern railroads came,

---

[3] Gilman: *The Living of Charlotte Perkins Gilman* (New York: D. Appleton-Century Co.; 1935), p. 107; Charles F. Holder: *All about Pasadena and its Vicinity* . . . (Boston: Lee & Shepard Publishers; 1889), pp. 81–2, 90–6.

[4] Richard Bigger and James D. Kitchen: *How the Cities Grew* . . . , *Metropolitan Los Angeles* . . . , Vol. II (Los Angeles: Bureau of Governmental Research, University of California; 1952), p. 16; Dumke: *Boom of the Eighties,* p. 60. Guinn: *Historical and Biographical Record,* p. 142.

and with them the promoters, it was easy to equate the Northwest with Portland and with Portland's phlegmatic temperament, and California with a more ambitious and energetic spirit, whether that of the young merchants and financiers who poured from the commuter trains toward the canyons of Montgomery Street each morning or that of the orators who praised southern California on boulevards already named but not yet carved from pastureland. The contrast seemed almost inborn. The people of the Northwest, John Murphy, a British traveler, wrote in 1879, "are much more cold and sedate than those of California, and also lack their electrical buoyancy. This frigidity must be the result of climate, as both classes are composed of the same material; yet while those of the more southern region are easily aroused and prompt to undertake any financial scheme that promises the most shadowy results, their northern kindred rarely yield to excitement, and indulge in no speculations that do not give an emphatic indication of success."[5]

But Portland's neighbors to the north, subjected to essentially the same physical climate, soon became as fast-growing as Los Angeles, as buoyantly speculative in spirit. The very lateness of their growth seemed to spur ambition. They took hope from the examples of others and drew heavily, like Los Angeles, on the prosperous Pullman-car migration that followed the coming of the railroads, though the brisk Northwestern climate attracted a younger, less sedentary population than southern California.

Seattle had begun as a mill town looking toward the markets of San Francisco. It differed from Portland and the Willamette Valley towns in that at first it had neither a hinterland to trade with nor missionaries to restrain it and in that its speculative horizons were larger almost from the beginning. Agricultural opportunity was further away on the gravelly banks of Puget Sound and on the Willamette, but the commerce of Japan and Alaska seemed closer, and Douglas-fir timber stood next to deep water. The timber trade attracted outside capital, particularly from San Francisco, and so supported mechanized mills on a vastly larger scale than the modest operations in Oregon, which often were only adjuncts to gristmills. The very lack of the kind of steady, reliable traffic with the farmers of the Columbia Basin that

[5] John M. Murphy: *Rambles in North-western America, from the Pacific Ocean to the Rocky Mountains . . .* (London: Chapman & Hall; 1879), p. 47.

seemed to justify the conservatism of the Portlanders left Seattle men free in their imaginations to seek after new visions of fortune overseas, it also directed them psychologically toward each other in their efforts to improve themselves by developing and advertising their city, while at the same time it prompted them to seek outside capital almost on its own terms. "You could not expect us to develop our soil or our mines," a Washingtonian told a visitor in the early 1890's, "when we could buy a town lot on one day, and four days afterwards could sell it for fifty dollars more a front foot than we gave for it."[6]

The citizens of Seattle, like those of Los Angeles, were not content to take in each others' mortgages. They donated a site and buildings for a university (1862) before the territorial legislature, which had not altogether expected anyone to take it seriously, could change its mind about the location and several years before there were students prepared for university work. They raised funds for a terminal for the Northern Pacific Railroad and, when the company chose to develop a company town at Tacoma, organized two railroads of their own (1873 and 1885). They may have been less in command of events than they thought they were—it was Jim Hill who selected Seattle as terminus for the Great Northern, not Seattle that selected Hill—but at least they worked confidently toward the future. When the city burned (1889), they rebuilt it finer than before and took special pride in the Denny (Washington) Hotel on Denny Hill as a symbol of recovery—and then removed the hill in the course of regrading that lowered streets by one hundred feet and more.[7] They dug a canal from Puget Sound to Lake Washington (1885–1917), thus opening a great fresh-water harbor; and they used the excavations from the canal and from regrading to fill thirty-five square miles of tideflats and create a new waterfront district. They undertook some of the largest of these public-works projects during the depression of 1893; they planned a great exposition during the panic of 1907.

There was something of the exuberance of the frontier in what residents liked to call "the 'Seattle spirit,' the willingness of the citizens

[6] Julian Ralph: *Our Great West . . .* (New York: Harper & Brothers; 1893), p. 307.

[7] Robert C. Nesbit: *He Built Seattle: A Biography of Judge Thomas Burke* (Seattle: University of Washington Press; 1961), p. xvi. Arthur H. Dimock: "Preparing the Groundwork for a City: The Regrading of Seattle, Washington," American Society of Civil Engineers, *Transactions,* Vol. XCII (1928), pp. 717–34.

to pay their money to help the town";[8] it recalled log raisings and pioneer townsite speculation. When gold arrived from Alaska in 1897 and Seattle became chief outfitting port for the Yukon, as San Francisco had been for the Sierra Nevada in 1849, much of the roughness and speculative excitement of the miners came to the waterfront, and much of it remained for a long time. Yet Seattle, like San Francisco half a century earlier, was ready for its most colorful experience, ready to believe in the mines themselves and in Seattle's preeminent qualifications to supply them. Its success was a triumph for generations of frontier optimists who had dreamed of a thriving city rising out of the wilderness to traffic in silk and gold as well as in salmon and lumber; it was also a triumph for a Chamber of Commerce (1882) and speculators and expert city-planners who knew how to promote their dreams. Seattle owed much to leaders like Reginald H. Thomson, the Indiana-born engineer who moved from California in the declining years of hydraulic mining, who turned the techniques of the hydraulickers to the problem of regrading Seattle's hills, and whose work on the problems of bringing water twenty-eight miles from a mountain stream, of extending the waterfront, and of routing rail and highway transportation recalls the experiences of communities in southern California. The city's leaders in the fast-moving years around the turn of the century were, like those of early San Francisco, predominantly Easterners—nearly three fifths from states east of the Mississippi and north of the Ohio—and, because they lacked the capital that San Francisco had, they were eager to import investments and investors. It was significant of the status and influence of outside capital that the first governor of the state, a former territorial governor and Seattle banker, was attorney for the Northern Pacific, and that a territorial chief justice, Seattle's leading real-estate broker, was attorney for the Great Northern.[9]

Thirty miles south of Seattle, on Commencement Bay, Tacoma began (1868) essentially as a townsite speculation of a Californian who had laid out the city of Sacramento for the Sutters; it developed as an

---

[8] R. S. Baker in *Century*, Vol. LXV, p. 660.

[9] *That Man Thomson*, ed. Grant H. Redford (Seattle: University of Washington Press; 1950), pp. 9, 60. Norbert McDonald: "The Business Leaders of Seattle, 1880–1910," *Pacific Northwest Quarterly*, Vol. L (January 1959), p. 4. W. H. P.: "The Larger Coast Cities," *World's Work*, Vol. X (August 1905), p. 6494. McDonald shows that New England contributed 4.7 percent of the population (1900) but 11.5 percent of the leaders; the Pacific states, 20.1 percent and 3.5 percent.

adjunct of the Northern Pacific. The railroad was no less speculation in land than it was a transportation system. Jay Cooke had counted heavily on real-estate investments in Duluth, which he developed as his Eastern terminus in preference to the older city of Superior, and when he selected Tacoma rather than Seattle for his Western terminus in 1873, he was hard pressed for cash to cover the cost of construction along the Sound.[1]

The city mushroomed out of the forest in a series of booms. The first extended over the five months from its selection until the completion of the first railroad line from the Columbia River (which the crew, not having been paid, began tearing up after the last-spike ceremony). The second took off from the connection with the East (1883); the third from the completion of the Northern Pacific's own line from Pasco (1887). The Tacoma Land Company, operating for the Northern Pacific in Tacoma as a subsidiary of the Southern Pacific operated on the Monterey Peninsula, built a fine hotel and stipulated good construction on its lots, which contrasted strangely with the surrounding charred stumps, brakes, and brambles. "The town was thrown like a broken set of dominoes over all," wrote Rudyard Kipling, who was there in 1889; "hotels with Turkish mosque trinketry on their shameless tops, and the pine stumps at their very doors . . . houses built in imitation of the ones on Nob Hill, San Francisco—after the Dutch fashion. . . ."[2] Boosters compared it with Rome, London, Babylon, and Tyre, and suggested that the financial center of the nation ought to move from New York and Chicago to Tacoma, which was nearer the center of American holdings and interests. Visitors who saw ships loaded to circle the globe "at the back door of the world, which is putting up porches in expectation of becoming the front door," in the words of a writer in *World's Work,* felt half persuaded.[3]

Then the bubble burst. The Great Northern Railway, completed on the eve of the depression of 1893, located its main terminal at Seattle,

---

[1] Thomas W. Prosch: *McCarver and Tacoma* (Seattle: Lowman & Harford Stationery and Printing Co.; 1906), p. 54. Ellis P. Oberholtzer: *Jay Cooke, Financier of the Civil War* (Philadelphia: George W. Jacobs & Co.; 1907), Vol. II, p. 341.

[2] Archie Binns: *Northwest Gateway, The Story of the Port of Seattle* (New York: Doubleday, Doran & Co.; 1941), pp. 210–12. Rudyard Kipling: *From Sea to Sea* (1899), Vol. II, pp. 115–6.

[3] Charles Andrews: *Tacoma and "Destiny"* (Tacoma: Puget Sound Printing Co.; 1891), pp. 36–40. W. H. P. in *World's Work,* Vol. X, p. 6500.

where regrading had opened new yards and docks equal to its rival's. During the nineties, Tacoma grew hardly at all while both Portland and Seattle nearly doubled—sober, prudent Portland more so than Seattle. Thereafter, the two cities on the Sound remained unmistakably first and second in size, in a ratio of about three to one. Sheer numbers—the preponderance of the population of Seattle—eventually settled the burning question of what to call the mountain after which Tacoma called itself, and which Seattle called Mount Rainier. But Tacoma, while boasting more of its fine homes than of its commercial influence, less of the future than of the past that it enshrined at old Fort Nisqually and at the museum of the State Historical Society, continued proud and ambitious. After the nineties, it grew about as rapidly, on the average, as its larger neighbors to north and south; its civic pride was no less than theirs. It had never been a company town in any submissive sense, for the role of the Northern Pacific had been largely to focus the speculative energy of a region; shortly the railroad subsidiaries began to sell out, and Tacoma became an exemplar of municipal enterprise, boasting of its cheap electric power and calling itself the "Electric City."

In the interior Northwest the speculators had been ready from 1873 at Spokane Falls, where three Oregonians formed a townsite firm in hope that the Northern Pacific would come that way. When Jay Cooke's failure that fall left no immediate prospects of construction east from Puget Sound or west from Dakota Territory, most of the promoters lost interest; the new city was little more than a sawmill and a general store until the railroad arrived in 1881. Then it reawakened and flourished as other railroads came. While dividing their favors on the west coast, the Northern Pacific, the Union Pacific, the Great Northern, and the Milwaukee all came to Spokane, making it the outfitting point for the northern Idaho mines and their smelter and sawmill as well.[4]

The story of Spokane suggests both the dominance of urban ways and the limitations of some cities of second rank in the Far West. Spokane was large for the thinly settled region it served—the mining, grazing, wheat-raising country between the Rockies and the Cascades; in less than forty years it passed both Tacoma (which remained behind) and Salt Lake City (which thereafter moved well ahead). Although railroads made Spokane, it continued to gain when railroad transporta-

---

[4] *West Shore,* Vol. X (April 1884), p. 118. Lucile F. Fargo: *Spokane Story* (New York: Columbia University Press; 1950), pp. 97–102, 146–60.

tion became less important. It became four times as large (1960) as any other American city north of the Salt Lake Valley, east of the Willamette River, and west of Nebraska; its radio stations and its leading newspaper serve Idaho as well as western Washington. Yet the commercial and cultural watersheds of Seattle and Portland ran well east of the Cascades, enclosing the Yakima Valley and the upper Columbia.[5] Yakima and Lewiston and Ellensburg cared little for Spokane's battle with the seaport terminals for parity in freight rates; the rural hinterlands had their own grievances; and most of the intermountain region eventually took substantial pride in the larger cities of the coastal strip.

Throughout the Far West, lesser aspirants after the urban imperium gathered hope and excitement. San Diego hoped more, or longer, than the others: it was the oldest European settlement in California when the first American speculators planned a townsite nearby in 1850, built a wharf, and persuaded the army to add a depot and barracks. Other booms followed in 1856, 1867–70, and 1872, chiefly on the prospect that the harbor—second only to San Francisco's, south of Puget Sound—would attract a railroad. The Santa Fe received a handsome subsidy from San Diego and National City, totaling eight times what Los Angeles had paid the Southern Pacific, for running to San Diego in 1885, and the first large influx of population came with it. Still, the speculators seemed to have miscalculated badly: the Santa Fe shifted its favors to Los Angeles; San Diego all but stopped growing in the 1890's and had less than 40,000 inhabitants in 1910. Its destiny came not from commerce, but from climate, which began to attract wealthy vacationers in the late 1880's. In 1875, San Diegans were hoping to salvage something from earlier booms by selling land at five dollars an acre for Indian reservations;[6] by 1888, John D. Spreckels, the sugar magnate, had bought the Coronado Beach Hotel and was turning his millions into programs of improvement and promotion that eventually helped to bring a naval coaling station (1907), an exposition (1915–7), another railroad (1919), a naval training station (1923), and hosts of families of naval personnel and retired naval officers.

---

[5] Robert R. Martin: "The Inland Empire of the Pacific Northwest . . ." (unpublished doctoral thesis, University of Washington; 1935), pp. 140–2, 174.

[6] Andrew F. Rolle: *An American in California; the Biography of William Heath Davis, 1822–1909* (San Marino: Huntington Library; 1956), pp. 90–104. David L. Phillips: *Letters from California* (Springfield: Illinois State Journal Co.; 1877), pp. 98–100.

The mining rushes bred ghost towns, but also a number of stabler settlements: Stockton, which had begun as Tuleburg (1847); Bellingham (1903), which first prospered during the Fraser River rush of 1857, but learned to can fish by the 1890's; Walla Walla, which served the Idaho mines at Orofino (1861). Most of the settlements that survived had main-line railroads to reinforce them; those with no more than a spur connection declined, as Virginia City did until the tourist industry discovered it. The railroads created at least as many towns as they saved, along their routes and at their terminals: Reno began (1868) with a land auction sponsored by the Central Pacific; Pocatello (1882) with the junction of the Oregon Short Line (Union Pacific) and the Utah Northern. The Oregon and California established Medford (1883) in opposition to both Central Point and Jacksonville, which had been the metropolis of southern Oregon but never recovered from being left off the line; the Northern Pacific forced most of Yakima to move to the railroad's site at North Yakima (1884).

Most Far Western cities seemed more distinct from each other in the turbulence of youth than after the middle of the twentieth century, when a sociologist observed that a city block lifted from one Pacific-coast city to another would attract little attention.[7] Yet in comparison with other American cities, the cities of the Far West even in pioneer times were much alike in basic stock, cultural patterns, and influences.

The principal coastal cities resembled each other in population and commercial spirit—and particularly in their elite population, in their leadership—long before the First World War. New Englanders, New Yorkers, and Pennsylvanians comprised significantly large fractions of the adults, of heads of families, of city dwellers, and of community leaders. Commerce and finance dominated the cities and attracted residents from older commercial and financial centers. In later years the proportion of Easterners decreased more than their influence. In stock and in commercial orientation, San Francisco seemed more like the Northwestern cities than did Los Angeles; yet commercial instincts and antecedents were strong in southern California, some of whose principal promoters had acquired capital and experience in the Bay

[7] Carle C. Zimmerman and Richard E. DuWors: *Graphic Rural Sociology* (Cambridge: The Phillips Book Store; 1952), pp. 127–9.

region. Montgomery Street might give San Francisco the better image of Wall Street, but in Los Angeles, Spring Street was no less alert to speculative opportunity; not all the owners of mansions along West Adams Street or Orange Grove Avenue had come there to retire. Seattle and Los Angeles were far less different in aspiration and promotional energy than in landscape and climate; probably no two cities owed more to their chambers of commerce, their railroad builders, and the city engineers who planned their water supplies. Even Salt Lake City developed a commercial and financial atmosphere consistent with the background of much of its population, if not with the pastoral ideals of its early leaders.

The cultural levels of the cities testified further to the quality of the stock. From the beginning, the Pacific slope was unusually literate and well educated (hence the fullness of written testimony to roughness and crudity and nostalgia for better things left behind): in 1870 it was only 7.1 percent illiterate, as compared with 20 percent for the nation; in 1900, only 4.2 percent, as against 10.7 percent. The distribution of illiteracy within the region, moreover, varied significantly from the national pattern: whereas in the cities of the Northeast and the older Middle West, illiteracy was either greater than in rural and small-town areas or only slightly less, on the Pacific slope the urban rate was substantially lower (in 1900, 2.96 percent, as against 4.84 percent). And urban illiteracy was owing in large part to Oriental and Mexican immigrants,[8] who, unlike immigrants on the East coast, had little effect on dominant patterns of behavior. The ignorance and sloth that Clarence King had complained of when he saw, or at least described, the Newtys of Pike in the San Joaquin valley, tended to remain in the country, if they remained anywhere.

If most Western cities were wicked places—at least by the standards of fundamentalist evangelists, who exhorted them to greater virtue—even in their wickedness they were seldom altogether uncultivated. The first theaters in California in the 1850's, as later in the Rocky Mountain mining territories, were adjuncts of saloons, but interest in the drama soon became independent of alcohol, and often

[8] Stanford Winston: *Illiteracy in the United States* (Chapel Hill: University of North Carolina Press; 1930), pp. 9–13, 15, 17, 49–53. U. S. Bureau of the Census: *Illiteracy in the United States*, Bulletin 26 (Washington: Government Printing Office; 1905), pp. 18, 31, 38, 41.

was discriminating. Theatrical entertainment catered to several levels of taste and appetite, but pioneer San Francisco sat through most of Shakespeare and shortly found the posturings of Lola Montez and others who capitalized on the scarcity of their sex more ludicrous than dramatic. Audiences in the West Coast soon developed a reputation for independent judgment that sometimes seemed out of step with new Eastern standards; they also demanded and obtained the best talent long before the railroads came. Junius Booth the elder made his last major appearances in San Francisco in 1852, when his son "June" already was managing a company that included Edwin Booth.[9]

In the interior the inconveniences of stagecoach travel limited the field to less celebrated talent, but the Mormons, who had staged campfire entertainments on their way west in 1847, shortly developed flourishing dramatic and musical traditions. Brigham Young built the Salt Lake Theater in 1861–2, using nails from wagons that General Johnston's troops had abandoned; it had a capacity of 1,500. By 1869, Salt Lake City heard opera in the Theater as well as choral music in the Tabernacle, where the great organ was ready in 1867. San Francisco in the 1870's began taking light and grand opera along with refreshments at the Tivoli, which had begun as a beer garden; here it first heard Luisa Tetrazzini in *Martha,* when she came for her American debut (1904). The extension of railroad lines—and especially, by 1887, of lines encircling the whole coast—opened new dimensions of traveling entertainment. It was then that the Orpheum Theater opened in San Francsico and John Cort's Standard Theater in Seattle—both cities that had owed much of their early influence to the superior quality of the ribald entertainment they offered along, respectively, the Barbary Coast and Skid Road. More decorously, Spokane boasted that its opera house was the finest theater west of the Mississippi River and also that it was closed on Sundays. Within the next few years, variety theater fully emerged from the Western saloon into respectable family entertainment, operating over circuits that extended from San Francisco to Butte and finally to New York, until in the 1930's and 1940's it retreated into nightclubs and into the gambling establishments of Las Vegas. Meanwhile San Francisco learned to listen to serious music in more

---

[9] George R. MacMinn: *The Theater of the Golden Era in California* (Caldwell: Caxton Printers, Ltd.; 1941), pp. 21–6, 28–30. Edmond M. Gagey: *The San Francisco Stage, A History . . .* (New York: Columbia University Press; 1950), pp. 28–31, 52–3.

conventional settings; and when the new Tivoli opened in 1913 to recapture the audiences it had lost in the fire of 1906, the response was so slight that it gave its last opera in its first season.[1]

Although the press moved along with the theater into national orbits, drawing increasingly on the standardized offerings of the syndicates and deferring to styles set primarily in the East, it had a more distinctively regional flavor, even in the early years when the written word moved across the continent far more easily than performers and stage scenery. Westerners seemed to seek diversion, escape, and familiar entertainment on the stage; controversy in their newspapers. Well into the twentieth century, Far Western journalism was known rather for fervor and vehement partisanship than for concern with the possibilities of acculturation and solid civic improvement, apart from promotional causes. The "Oregon style" of editorial invective was distinctive, if at all, only in degree; sometimes it seemed that most Far Western editors invited libel suits, if not armed attack, and dared not relax their customary style lest they lose the public that followed them in hope of bloodshed. Scandalmongering and insults may have amused more than they deceived, for they became customary, almost automatic. "The venality of the Western Press does not make for immorality," Horace Vachell observed, "because (like a drunkard reeling through the streets) it is seen, and serves as a warning."[2]

Yet there was almost infinite variety in journalism, corresponding to the varied tastes of Westerners and to the differing competitive atmospheres of their cities. In Portland after the Civil War, the leading paper was the *Oregonian,* which corresponded in the Pacific Northwest to the Denver *Rocky Mountain News* and the Chicago *Inter-Ocean* in their areas, or perhaps to the Portland banks; it achieved the largest circulation west of Minneapolis and north of San Francisco on the strength of honest reporting and the respectable, Portland-like policies

[1] George D. Pyper: *The Romance of an Old Playhouse* (Salt Lake City: Seagull Press; 1928), pp. 69–85, 307–8. William J. McNiff: *Heaven on Earth; a Planned Mormon Society* (Oxford: Mississippi Valley Press; 1940), pp. 174, 182. Gagey: *San Francisco Stage, Its History,* pp. 177–8. Eugene C. Elliott: *A History of Variety-Vaudeville in Seattle From the Beginning to 1914* (Seattle: University of Washington Press; 1944), pp. 18–22, 45–54, 58–61. Julian Ralph: "Washington—the Evergreen State," *Harper's New Monthly Magazine,* Vol. LXXXV (September 1892), p. 597. James Stevens: "The Natural History of Seattle," *American Mercury,* Vol. XXVII (December 1932), pp. 402–9.

[2] Vachell: *Life and Sport on the Pacific Slope,* p. 216.

and vigorously independent Republican opinions of its editor and publisher, Harvey Scott. The *Oregonian* dominated both directly and by controlling Associated Press dispatches and influencing smaller newspapers. In Salt Lake City the *Deseret News* spoke for the Mormon Church while the Salt Lake *Tribune* and a succession of lesser papers specialized in advancing gentile politicians and deploring the horrors of polygamy and theocracy. Nevada supported an extraordinarily vigorous and competitive press; two Virginia City papers published separate daily stenographic reports of the state constitutional convention in 1863. The more prosperous mining communities expected skilled reporting as well as a vein of burlesque merging into satire that became conventional enough so that it may persuade an unwary twentieth-century reader of the Nevada and California press of the 1850's and 1860's that he has discovered some hitherto lost work of Mark Twain.[3]

In San Francisco the shooting of three editors within thirty years attests to a tradition of journalistic sensationalism antedating the birth of its best-known exponent. When William Randolph Hearst assumed control of the *Examiner* in 1887, he did not need to teach his reporters that news was whatever made a reader say "gee whiz"; he recruited them, already trained, from the offices of his competitors and liberally paid their expenses, including the costs of libel suits. The style of journalism in San Francisco, wrote W. L. MacGregor, a Scottish visitor, in 1876, when the city had thirty-five papers but not one above serious reproach, was "not calculated to elevate, but rather to lower the tone of public feeling. Certainly the press does not strive to lead or educate the latter, but rather to follow it, and follow it down to a low depth."[4]

Yet the press, and the San Francisco press in particular, reflected the better taste as well as the worst taste of the public and the energy of a highly competitive urban society, even when, in the words of

---

[3] Frank L. Mott: *American Journalism: A History of Newspapers in the United States . . .*, revised edition (New York: The Macmillan Company; 1950), pp. 475–6. E. V. Smalley: "Features of the New Northwest," *Century Magazine*, Vol. XXV (February 1883), p. 532. Ralph E. Dyar: *News for an Empire, the Story of the Spokesman-Review of Spokane, Washington . . .* (Caldwell: Caxton Printers, Ltd.; 1952), pp. 35–6. Wendell J. Ashton: *Voice in the West; Biography of a Pioneer Newspaper* (New York: Duell, Sloan & Pearce; 1950). *Mark Twain of the Enterprise . . .*, ed. Henry Nash Smith (Berkeley: University of California Press; 1957), pp. 10–11.

[4] Franklin Walker: *San Francisco's Literary Frontier* (New York: Alfred Knopf; 1939). William L. MacGregor: *San Francisco, California, in 1876* (Edinburgh: Thomas Laurie; 1876), pp. 37–8.

T. A. Rickard, the engineer and editor (1908), "the newspapers of San Francisco [were] owned by men without character and edited by men without principle." The pressure of competition yielded some of the best writing as well as some of the lowest ethics. The *Argonaut,* which reformers denounced (1911) as "the brazen, painted woman of the town, flaunting the silk and jewels bought by the sale of her honor"[5]—a creature of the Southern Pacific Railroad—carried the work of Ambrose Bierce, Charles Howard Shinn, Charles L. Stoddard, Frank Norris, and Jack London in its literary columns. It is significant of the climate of the community that the *Chronicle,* which prospered in the seventies by dwelling on sex and crime, and which many years later became for a time one of the best newspapers in the West—before it reverted to type—began (1865–8) as the *Dramatic Chronicle,* one of several free theater-program sheets that had to compete with the theater pages of the more conventional daily press.[6] Practically all papers had literary columns, which appeared alongside the editorials rather than among the household hints; satire merged into blackmail, but also into philosophy and social criticism.

The newspapers at either end of the coast likewise seemed to represent the tone and history of their rising communities; appropriately enough, the principal papers of Seattle, which fed on its hope for a railroad, were those that James J. Hill financed—the *Times* and the *Post-Intelligencer*—and much of the history of Los Angeles is the history of the *Los Angeles Times.* Probably no one profited more over the years from the fantastic appreciation in real-estate values in southern California than General Harrison Gray Otis, owner of the *Times* from 1883 until his death in 1917 and founder of the Los Angeles Chamber of Commerce. The newspaper, the city itself, its imperium, and the fortunes of Otis and his associates increased together, and in much the same spirit. "I have lived in Southern California four years," Upton Sinclair wrote in 1919, "and it is literally a fact that I have yet to meet a single person who does not despise and hate his '*Times.*' "[7] One was no more likely to meet a person who did not read

---

[5] T. A. Rickard: *Retrospect, an Autobiography* (New York: Whittlesey House; 1937), p. 104. *Pacific Outlook,* Vol. X (January 21, 1911), p. 3.

[6] Mott: *American Journalism,* pp. 473–4.

[7] Clarence Bagley: *History of Seattle from Earlier Settlements to the Present Time* (Chicago: S. J. Clarke Publishing Co. 1916), Vol. I, pp. 194–5. Upton Sinclair: *The Brass Check, A Study of American Journalism* (Pasadena, 1920), pp. 202, 243–4.

the *Times* or one of its imitators or subsidiaries; an area that lacked both political and social coherence joined at least in a kind of journalistic community. No newspaper in Los Angeles County effectively dissented from the *Times*'s social doctrines, journalistic standards, and ambitions for Los Angeles. The owner of the *Express* collaborated with Otis on one of his major real-estate speculations; Hearst's *Examiner*, which appeared in response to the appeals of unions for a pro-labor press, soon confined most of its differences to national issues; and the *Record* was one of the weaker members of the Scripps system.[8]

The level of urban culture appeared perhaps more clearly in the literary papers, which Mark Twain called sure signs, after crowded police-court dockets, "that trade is brisk and money plenty." They flourished in San Francisco from the early fifties, to such an extent that A. Roman, a bookseller and publisher who had watched the source and the demand, felt ready by 1868 to launch a full-sized monthly magazine that drew entirely on local talent. *Overland Monthly* lasted only eight years in its first form, but for most of its life it was both an economic and a literary success whose editors were able to apply national standards to local material; it failed as a result of the depression that struck California in 1875 and because it had done so well that its writers had gained recognition and found employment elsewhere. Henry George had looked ahead, in the first issue of *Overland*, to a San Francisco that would someday reward its writers adequately instead of driving them away or forcing them to "make a living by digging sand, peddling vegetables, or washing dishes in restaurants";[9] he was one of many writers who deplored the neglect of the arts—in publications whose existence and prosperity at least weakened their arguments. The poet Edward Rowland Sill complained of his "terrible isolation . . . out here in heathendom"—"no culture, no thought, no art"[1]—and then found the East no better and returned to spend the rest of his life on the Bay, teaching at the University of California. The complaint of shabby treatment became general after the depression, when Bret Harte exiled himself in Europe, and yet no other American city supported so many newspapers and writers in proportion to the total population or prized

---

[8] Carey McWilliams: *Southern California Country* . . . (New York: Duell, Sloan & Pearce; 1946), pp. 129, 187.

[9] Samuel L. Clemens: *Roughing It* (New York: Harper & Brothers; 1913), Vol. II, p. 96, *Overland Monthly*, Vol. I (October 1868), p. 304.

[1] William B. Parker: *Edward Rowland Sill; His Life and Work* (Boston: Houghton Mifflin Co.; 1915), pp. 52–3.

so much its associations with the arts and artists. No part of California was able, before well along in the twentieth century, to draw established authors from other sections for more than a visit or a health cure. That San Francisco could not hold all the talent it had meant not that the public failed to appreciate cultural values, but that the writers themselves aspired to be received at older literary courts and that Easterners and Europeans were ready to receive them. Meanwhile the rich men of San Francisco were glad to buy literary reputations for themselves and rub elbows with impecunious artists by joining the Bohemian Club, which had grown out of informal Sunday breakfasts at a newspaperman's home (1872).[2]

Elsewhere along the coast, San Francisco had no significant competitors in book and magazine publishing or in literary production. The Portland Library Association (1864), the Portland Art Association (1892), and the Portland Art Museum (1905) were only a few years behind their counterparts in San Francisco, though San Francisco's art exhibitions and private galleries dated from the 1850's and 1860's. But the magazine *West Shore* (Portland, 1875–91) devoted itself chiefly to laudatory descriptions of Northwestern communities and engravings of the respectable buildings in which their leading citizens lived and banked; and its successor, the *Pacific Monthly* (1898–1911), whose chief distinction lay in the contributions of its editor, Charles Erskine Scott Wood, eccentric corporation lawyer, poet, freethinker, and radical, filled only three feet of shelf space before *Sunset* (San Francisco, 1898–) absorbed it. In Los Angeles, Charles F. Lummis's *Land of Sunshine* (1894–1901; 1902–10, *Out West*) became for a time the leading literary journal of the coast, but it was never the equal of the old *Overland*, and a stridently promotional tone dominated its columns. Although (or because) *Land of Sunshine* began as the unofficial organ of the Los Angeles Chamber of Commerce, its focus was regional rather than urban; Lummis's extraordinary energy and enthusiasm ran to the past and future of the whole Southwest, and probably his ablest contributors lived out of town, even in New Mexico, San Francisco, or the East. Salt Lake City supported publications that did credit to a city of its size, pressing needs, and relative isolation: in the 1880's these included two short-lived magazines concerned chiefly

[2] Miller: "Our Prophets in Their Land," *Golden Era*, Vol. XXXV (August 1886), p. 510. Edward Bosqui: *Memoirs* ([San Francisco: 1904]), pp. 213–14.

with the overpowering history and mystique of the Mormon community. Sometimes they presented word pictures of local landscapes that conveyed the atmosphere of inland seas and desert retreats rather than of the literary salon and the brisk promise of economic development. Later the Church's Mutual Improvement Associations and its gentile critics dominated the periodical press.[3]

The influence of the larger Western cities appeared clearly in the deference that practically all parts of the region paid them. Even the clergy managed to find virtue in a saving balance with vice, and not only Episcopalian William Kip—who found that San Francisco in 1857 reminded him pleasantly of Paris, with its lively freedom from conventionality and its "Continental" Sundays, with theaters and saloons open and churches well attended—but also Congregationalist Horace Bushnell—who in 1856, year of the second vigilance committee, recommended founding a college nearby. "There is . . . more real virtue and more of good influence in the city, with all its vices," Bushnell concluded, "than anywhere else—a more elevating and conserving power of society."[4] The successful miner came to the city to live, enshrining his dreams and his success in architectural gingerbread; the unsuccessful walked wistfully rather than resentfully below the mansions of Nob Hill, "like castles that we read about," in the words of one of them, perhaps wondering which he had helped to build.[5] The greater part of the farm population lived close to the metropolis, eventually much of it along interurban electric railways; it received metropolitan morning newspapers at the gate and went to town to shop or to the theater. In some of the more remote farming districts, which grew wheat rather than truck-garden vegetables, steam and, later, gasoline harvesters and pumps became commonplace, so that the farm boy grew familiar with machinery and became an engineer on a tractor before his city cousin was a passenger on a cable car. Thus urban-rural conflicts, though sometimes bitter enough, were seldom clear-cut on

---

[3] Bingham: *Charles F. Lummis, Editor of the Southwest.* Franklin Walker: *A Literary History of Southern California* (Berkeley: University of California Press; 1950), pp. 137–44. Mott: *A History of American Magazines, 1885–1905* (Cambridge: Harvard University Press; 1957), Vol. IV, pp. 104, 297.

[4] William J. Kip: *The Early Days of My Episcopate* (New York: Thomas Whittaker; 1892), pp. 73, 78. Horace Bushnell: *California: Its Characteristics and Prospects* (San Francisco: Whitton, Towne & Co.; 1858), p. 398.

[5] *A Yankee Trader in the Gold Rush: The Letters of Franklin A. Buck,* ed. Katherine A. White (Boston: Houghton Mifflin Co.; 1930), p. 280.

the coast: the city was so well integrated with the country that it was not a wholly external force; San Mateo and Fresno counties sometimes knew more of San Francisco than of themselves.

From the beginning, and well into the twentieth century, the urbanized shape of Far Western society seemed abnormal, out of step with the rest of the nation, suggesting overoptimistic readiness to live on tomorrow's capital, immoral reluctance to undertake the more traditional occupations of the soil. The distribution of population seemed precariously Micawberish, justifiable only in the sense that a beach-head depot is justifiable in wartime, or perhaps as a speculation to be reduced, relative to the whole region, as farming increased. Not only were the early cities much too large relative to the countryside and the rural population, but also the social and occupational structure of the cities overemphasized distribution and service at the expense of production: too many hairdressers, lawyers, and clerks and not enough factory workers. "In New York there is one physician to every 610 inhabitants," the *Scientific American* reported in 1858; "in Ohio, one to every 465, in Maine, one to every 884; and in California one to every 147. We can envy Maine and pity California, for some must swallow physic at a frightful rate in the Golden State." Some did and continued to do so for many years; eventually economists explained that the occupational pattern on the coast followed naturally on high income, the high percentage of adults, the large volume of imports from Eastern states, and the high mobility of population.[6] But it was difficult for people accustomed to urban-rural ratios in the Mississippi Valley in the nineteenth century to regard the size and rate of growth of the coastal metropolises as other than a species of economic levitation sustained by remittances from the East, unjust exploitation of the interior West, or an overindulgent Providence, which supplied the Yukon to save Seattle, oil to save Los Angeles, and the United States navy to save San Diego.

It was easiest to accept San Francisco, Portland, and eventually Seattle, which at least looked somewhat like Eastern cities, with wharves and warehouses along side the masts of ocean liners, palatial downtown hotels, and the sober temples of finance. The purpose of the

---

[6] *Scientific American*, Vol. XIV (November 20, 1858), p. 88. Margaret S. Gordon: *Employment Expansion and Population Growth: The California Experience: 1900–1950* (Berkeley: University of California Press; 1954), p. 31.

early promoters appears in the fact that they gave the name of New York to early settlements on both San Francisco Bay and Puget Sound. San Francisco went home by ferry across the Bay to its suburbs in Staten Island, Long Island, and New Jersey, where the overland railroads had their terminals, or by train to Westchester or Connecticut along the Peninsula, or took a long weekend on Cape Cod or in Asbury Park or Ocean Grove, which were close neighbors on Monterey Bay. Seattle was comprehensible, once it demonstrated that it had a hinterland, and one might as well accept Salt Lake City if one accepted Salt Lake and the Mormons themselves and considered where else they might live and trade.

But Los Angeles seemed to defy all the laws of municipal gravity and growth, even when it was known for "chemically pure" morality rather than for the sordid violence that was inexhaustibly catalogued in its police files. Until 1905 it was a railroad stop rather than, in the full sense, a terminal; until 1906 it had no coastline or harbor and then had only an unfinished breakwater on the open sea; until 1913 it had no dependable water supply. If San Francisco had no architecture of its own, but rather (as Gelett Burgess put it) was built of "imitations which even if genuine would be inappropriate," Los Angeles seemed to have almost no architecture at all—"simply a Spanish mud village," Charles L. Brace, one of the early tourists, called it in 1868. From the beginning, residents hastened to escort visitors out of the central district into the suburbs. Upton Sinclair, who moved to southern California in 1916, reacted to it not only with the bias of a socialist, but also with that of an American accustomed to nineteenth-century American cities: "The country has been settled by retired elderly people, whose health has broken down, and who have come here to live on their income. They have no organic connection with one another; each is an individual, desiring to live his own little life, and to be protected in his own little privileges. The community is thus a parasite upon the great industrial centers of other parts of America."[7]

But Los Angeles belonged to a new century and a new calculus of urban development by which the most vital part of the city was not the center but the periphery; by which the consolidated channels of

---

[7] Gelett Burgess: "San Francisco the Joyous," *Smart Set*, Vol. XXXVIII (September 1912), p. 103. Charles L. Brace: *The New West; or, California in 1867–1868* (New York: G. P. Putnam & Son; 1869), p. 278. Sinclair: *Brass Check*, p. 197.

water and steam-railroad transportation influenced the distribution of population less than did the diffused mercurial flow of the electric trolley car and then the automobile; by which people came not only to work in factories, but also because of the climate and other amenities. The people of Los Angeles themselves did not altogether understand what they were doing and so dreamed of subways and skyscrapers while Easterners called them "Iowa on the loose." Or they resorted to supernatural guidance and justification ("Astrology Proves Los Angeles Logical West Coast Metropolis," ran a headline in 1912[8]).

Although San Francisco technically was younger than Los Angeles, it had taken shape earlier, in the era when waterways still dictated the location of a city, and in some respects it retained its nineteenth-century character. The ocean and the bay, on three sides, confined the city proper within a small area. It grew chiefly by moving the hills into the shallow edges of the bay; and the people, many of whom came from Eastern and European cities that had developed within the radii of horsecar transportation, learned to like flats built on lots twenty-five feet wide. For thirty or forty years San Franciscans had a reputation for living in hotels and for having no children, or one child at most. The bay and the spine of hills along the peninsula kept the main commuting area near the line of a single steam railroad. Despite the Willamette and Columbia rivers, Great Salt Lake, and the Wasatch Mountains, Portland and Salt Lake City had more space to grow in. Los Angeles lacked both waterways to make it a major city before the era of railroads and natural boundaries of any kind to confine the electric-railroad and automobile highways on which its growth came to depend. In absorbing neighboring communities, it was a little behind New York, which combined the five boroughs in 1900; it seemed further behind in that it had not consolidated itself before it encompassed others. But in all the Far Western metropolitan areas—in Los Angeles, it happened earlier and to a greater extent than in the others—the people came to expect to live in separate houses with gardens, even if they had to commute to Santa Monica or Oakland or Mercer Island to do it; well before 1914 they took for granted a suburban pattern of life that many New Yorkers seemed to become aware of only after 1945.

Decentralization never went far enough: the leaders of business and city government who planned the central districts seldom realized

---

[8] *West Coast Magazine*, Vol. XII (May 1912), pp. 214–5.

that they were building their cities differently as well as faster. For this reason, and simply because the suburbs grew so much that they continued to add to the absolute amount of traffic at the center as well as to draw away larger parts of the whole, downtown congestion was, if anything, eventually worse on the west coast than on the east coast. Political centralization increased with social and economic dispersion: people who moved into new suburban communities had to drive farther to do business at city hall as the metropolis annexed them. The political genius of the West turned more to agglomeration—adding neighboring municipalities to metropolitan water and sewerage districts—than to systems of decentralizing governmental business into boroughs or other regional units. Nevertheless, there was stagnation as well as congestion at the center, in West as in East; some streets in downtown Los Angeles in the twentieth century suggested the dinginess of the Chicago loop without the elevated lines. Even the ruthlessness of the builders of the freeways in the 1940's and 1950's left many downtown business buildings that looked as old as the boom of the 1880's. On the Pacific as well as on the Atlantic coast, downtown theaters became warehouses. All cities on the coast had skid roads; the name came from the logging industry of Seattle. Thus even the newest cities, which against their will skipped the stage of tightly packed urban concentrations through which the older sections had normally passed, eventually became rotten at the center and seemed to have overbuilt. But the main fact was that they had skipped this stage.

The cities of the coast, then, on the whole were ready for later developments on the eve of the First World War: for the automobile and the revolution it brought in urban living; for the patterns of employment that define a prosperous and mature urbanized civilization. When Seattle prepared to move the state university to the fairgrounds it had opened far northeast of the city on Lake Washington in 1909, when Los Angeles tapped the water of the Owens River Valley in 1913, they were making ready for an influx of population in the next generation. They were also ready for some of the harsher aspects of twentieth-century American life, for disappointment and conflict that extended from the countryside into the metropolis.

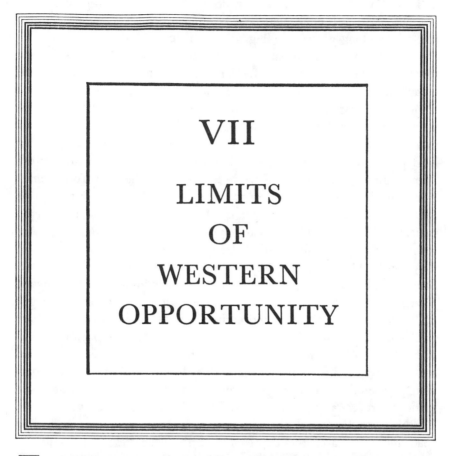

VII

LIMITS OF WESTERN OPPORTUNITY

EVERY WESTERN FRONTIER yielded both fulfillment and disappointment, but none attracted, rewarded, and punished those who came to it so much as the farthest continental frontier of all, that west of the Rocky Mountains. Both in the cities and in the countryside there were new social nobility, new opportunity, greater decency, comfort, and prosperity for the majority; and yet many pioneers failed utterly. The ordinary emigrant who refreshed himself at Salt Lake City did not see the families that met an early winter as they pulled their handcarts to Zion in 1856, though they lived in Mormon martyrology; most marginal homesteads hid beyond marginal roads and minimal tourist traffic; and the bindle stiffs of the Northwestern woods and the Joads and the *braceros* of the Southwestern truck gardens and orchards never attained the dignity and visibility of tenement dwellers. First nature and then man tempted and struck down the unwary in regions where the climate is both benevolent and tyrannical, where economic concentration was long as outstanding as economic opportunity.

From the beginning of substantial American settlement in the 1840's, the Pacific slope seemed to offer large opportunities to men of small means, at a cost only of hard work and separation from home and friends. The missionaries had emphasized this in writing of Oregon; for a generation after 1848, California's best-known attraction was not merely gold, but the idea that anyone might have access to it or at least profit by the high wages and prices that gold rushes supported. "Never in the world's history," wrote a member of the New York Volunteers who had gone to the mines when he received his discharge in 1848, "was there a better opportunity for a great, free, and republican nation like ours to offer to the oppressed and down-trodden of the whole world an asylum, and a place where by honest industry . . . they can build themselves happy homes and live like freemen."[1] California should be the most democratic country in the world, Bayard Taylor told the readers of *Harper's,* citing washmen who received eight dollars a dozen for laundry and earned double the wages of members of Congress. "To sum up all in three words, Labor is respectable. . . ." Although relatively few miners were still there by the sixties and seventies, wages did in fact remain higher than in the East and workingmen prospered as nowhere else and enjoyed their own houses and gardens. Travelers regularly reported the absence of poverty and caste. The best statistical evidence confirms such casual testimony well after 1849 and even after the depression of the seventies. A government investigator reported that saleswomen in San Francisco in 1887 received about twice as much as Eastern wages, though the cost of living was no higher than in New York.[2]

In the 1870's, when railroad construction opened new lands and the possibilities of new markets, the coast again excited the hopes of small farmers, as it had in the several years before the mining rushes.

---

[1] "Our Own Oregon," *Littell's Living Age,* Vol. X (July 1846), p. 189. E. Gould Buffum: *Six Months in the Gold Mines; from a Journal of 3 Years' Residence in Upper and Lower California, 1847–8–9* (Philadelphia: Lea & Blanchard; 1850), p. 106.

[2] Taylor: *Eldorado* (1949 ed.), pp. 223, 236. Lee Meriwether: *The Tramp at Home* (New York: Harper & Brothers; 1889), pp. 167–9.

The vision of agricultural opportunity even borrowed a new aura from the legends of forty-nine; on the lips of the prophets and promoters, the land of golden nuggets easily became the land of golden fruit almost ready for the taking. Judge John W. North described (1870) the social advantages of ten-acre irrigated farms at from $2.50 to $20 an acre east of Los Angeles, with "all the advantage of city life." Within six years Riverside was "a neat, clean Yankee-living village" of two-and-a-half-acre residential lots surrounded by farms worth from ten to a hundred times the original cost,[3] and the idea of rural opportunity for a class of small landed proprietors began to spread northward.

The extension of the Southern Pacific through the San Joaquin Valley, and later of the Northern Pacific and the Oregon Short Line through the Palouse country, moreover, coincided with and contributed to expansion and then to the collapse that brought down some of the larger landowners and threatened to break up their estates, as the drought of the 1860's had done for their predecessors. "This makes room for a new class of moderate means . . . ," a Californian wrote in 1880, "and will greatly tend to magnify the country population. . . ."[4] Impressed by the misfortunes of the great stock and grain farmers and by the relatively small revenues in freight that they sustained, the railroads' agents promoted intensive agriculture. They quoted approvingly from Charles Nordhoff, who proclaimed that "California was made for small farmers," and they contrasted the failures of the owners of great estates who lived in San Francisco with the bright prospects of "men willing to work on [the] land," especially in the great interior valleys. A writer for the Santa Fe described "apple orchards, six years planted, laden with fruit, [and] vineyards in full bearing . . . where on my first visit I was told it was hazardous to run one sheep over a dozen acres."[5]

The most enthusiastic hopes for Western agriculture revolved about California, much of which was almost immune to the effects of rains, which damaged crops in summer or leached away fertility in winter. California promised to become a land of small farms and gardens of ten and twenty acres, where the boys and girls of the family could

---

[3] John W. North: *Southern California Colony* (San Francisco, 1870).

[4] Phillips: *Letters from California*, pp. 111, 113. E. D. Holton: *Travels with Jottings From Midlands to the Pacific* . . . (Milwaukee: Trayser Brothers, Printers; 1880), p. 92.

[5] Charles Nordhoff: *California for Health, Pleasure, and Residence* . . . , new edition (New York: Harper & Brothers; 1882), pp. 11, 147–50, 167. Atchison, Topeka and Santa Fe Railway: *Southern California* (1890?).

do most of the work during vacations. Southern California appealed especially to people who had never farmed and who responded to the orange both because it symbolized the amenities of the Southern and Southwestern resort country and because the promoters told them that raising citrus trees called for specialization such that business experience was "a bigger asset than an equipment of outlived and exploded farming traditions."[6] But soon the irrigationists noted "the blessings of aridity" all over the Far West. "The great cities of the western valleys will not be cities in the old sense," wrote William E. Smythe, the apostle of the new agriculture, "but a long series of beautiful villages, connected by lines of electric motors, which will move their products and people from place to place. In this scene of intensely cultivated land . . . it will be difficult . . . to say where the town ends and the country begins." John S. McGroarty, journalist, poet, and promoter of Los Angeles, wrote (1908) of "The Greatest Story Ever Told . . . The Miracle of the Waters," and of a Westerner who was entirely different "from the proverbial farmer of the East that we have seen featured in the funny papers. . . ." No one lived more independently or more easily: he had "a fine home, he has money in the bank, his daughter has a piano, and his son owns an automobile." Even while coastal Washington was filling up with Scandinavians seeking a moist climate like that of northern Europe, other Northwesterners revived Jay Cooke's promise of a banana belt and noted that the interior Northwest had much in common with the Southwest. A writer in the Portland *Oregonian* compared southeastern Washington and northeastern Oregon to the Santa Clara, Sacramento, and San Joaquin valleys: it was really one valley, "more than equal to the whole three of the California valleys in extent and climate and in its marvellous fertility of soil."[7] And General John Gibbon extolled the possibilities of the Snake River desert, which had been a horror to visitors since the early fur traders: "It needs only water to enable it to blossom as the rose

---

[6] Charles D. Warner: *Our Italy* (New York: Harper & Brothers; 1891), pp. 107–8. "The Business Man as a Farmer," in Forrest Crissey: *Where Opportunity Knocks Twice* (Chicago: Reilly & Britton Co.; 1914), pp. 177–9.

[7] William E. Smythe: *The Conquest of Arid America,* new edition (New York: The Macmillan Company; 1905), pp. 31, 46. John S. McGroarty: " 'The Greatest Story Ever Told,' The Wonderful Work of the Reclamation Service—the Miracle of the Waters," *West Coast Magazine,* Vol. V (October 1908), p. 353. Portland *Oregonian,* December 1, 1887, p. 3, col. 2.

and produce the finest crops of grain, for sagebrush land produces the best of wheat. . . ."[8] By 1910, when the Oregon Trunk Line built southward from the Columbia River east of the Cascades, from Wishram to Bend, the Northwest was aflame with hope that the Deschutes Valley might be another Yakima or Imperial.

But disappointment came as often as success to the farmer who held such hopes, as it had come to the miner. Outside Utah, most farms were of the wrong size for the best use that soil and climate dictated (more often they were too large rather than too small); land and the means of using it were too costly, and the farmers themselves were slow to learn new techniques and to adjust to the new life. The traditional one-hundred-and-sixty-acre homestead of the older public-land states was never typical of the Far West, most of which could not efficiently use that much or that little land. In the Willamette Valley, one of the few parts of the Northwest where one hundred and sixty acres approximated optimum size for agriculture, Congress supposed that the Donation Land Act of 1850 would "get the Territory settled" by means of the extraordinary attraction of allotments two or four times homestead size. The effect of the Act, however, was to scatter the settlers and thus inflict on them the dual burden of isolation and high road taxes. Their holdings were large enough to leave them content with relatively inefficient uses of some of the potentially most productive land in the United States (much of which still was notoriously underdeveloped a century later), though not large enough to induce speculators to subdivide the land wholesale.[9] During the formative years in California, all factors seemed to conspire in the interest of extensive use of land by capitalists rather than intensive use by bona fide small farmers: the princely extents of Mexican ranches and railroad grants; prolonged uncertainty of land titles; extreme seasonal fluctuations in prices; the high costs of moving west and subsisting until the first harvest; charges for drainage, irrigation, and machinery. Even the generally high level of wages during most of the second half of the nineteenth century hampered the small farmer more than it did the larger landholder,

[8] *Report . . . on the Irrigation and Reclamation of Arid Lands,* 51 Cong., 1 Sess., Senate Report 928 (1890), part 2, Vol. I, pp. 303–4.

[9] *Congressional Globe,* 31 Cong., 1 Sess., September 17, 1850, p. 1841. Edward Higbee: *The American Oasis* (New York: Alfred A. Knopf; 1957), pp. 108–10. Robert C. Clark: *History of the Willamette Valley, Oregon* (Chicago: S. J. Clarke; 1927), Vol. I, pp. 406–9.

who could more easily afford to turn to machinery or to import cheap contract labor from the Orient. "It is ridiculous to try and make a fortune here without plenty of money to start with," wrote a young English farm wife north of San Francisco Bay in 1886: "fruit costs so much to put in, and one man could not look after a large orchard without assistance, and labour is the most expensive item of all."[1]

That a few ranches and corporations held much land that later lent itself to irrigation and to farming in small units meant not so much that they deprived small settlers of it in the early years as that they set examples of extensive use—mainly in stock raising at first, later in grain culture—of land that seemed dismally unpromising in Eastern and Midwestern eyes. "All the Sacramento Valley is good for in my opinion," a young Vermonter commented in 1864, "is to raise mosquitoes and fever ague."[2] Even John S. Hittell, author of the best-known handbook of the *Resources of California,* estimated (1863) that three fourths of the arable land was too dry for any crops but small grain, and that no more than one fourth could be farmed within the century. Floods, drought, and lack of trees made some of the best land unattractive to settlers, who thereby were all the more disposed to defer to men who regarded a farm as an outdoor assembly line rather than as a home. And public authority was slow to help men of small means to use new techniques.[3]

When these techniques were available and it was clear that some of the driest and some of the swampiest land in the West could also be the most productive, land previously undesirable for agriculture quickly gained value. Costs increased as unclaimed water supplies diminished and as irrigationists discovered the high costs of building pipes and ditches that wasted no more than they delivered and of carrying water away from the land as well as onto it. Instead of simply diverting streams into unimproved fields, and thus imitating the natural flooding of the bottom lands, farmers shaped the contours of the land, dug furrows for the water, and sometimes built wooden flumes or laid pipes underground, all at high expense, and all on top of the higher

---

[1] E. M. H.: *Ranch Life in California* . . . (London: W. H. Allen & Co.; 1886), pp. 166–7.

[2] Rollin C. Smith: *Postmarked Vermont and California, 1862–1864,* ed. Fannie S. Spurling (Rutland: Tuttle Publishing Co.; 1940), p. 162.

[3] John S. Hittell: *The Resources of California* . . . (San Francisco: A. Roman & Co.; 1863), pp. 151–2. Vincent P. Carosso: *The California Wine Industry, 1830–1895; A Study of the Formative Years* (Berkeley: University of California Press; 1951), p. 56.

prices of land and of water at the gate. By 1886, the Riverside Land Company was selling unimproved land with water rights for from $250 to $450 an acre; in 1889, land with oranges was worth from $750 to $2500 an acre. In Washington the average first cost of irrigation per acre increased from $4.03 to $34.47 between 1890 and 1910.[4]

Simple appreciation of land values was a pleasant experience for those who had bought early, but along with other costs it tended to exclude the poor or to shunt them onto the unimprovable desert land that was available for homesteading. Nearly all the newcomers were "of a superior class of settlers," the governor of Washington Territory reported in 1887, "for few that undertake to remove to a part of the country as distant as this will do so without ample means for the vicissitudes of at least two seasons."[5] Whereas in the earliest years the high levels of wages, prices, and interest seemed likely to operate to the advantage of the homesteader or squatter who thriftily worked his own fields and ate only what he raised, in practice the small farmer had to pay higher charges for a loan and for freight and for the land itself than his neighbor who had larger holdings did, and the small farmer also had to forego the economies of machinery to harvest his crop and of storage facilities to hold it for the best prices. The idyllic picture of farms that virtually ran themselves—dry summers protecting the mature crops, mild winters saving the costs of both fodder and barns—gave way to the costly reality of sprays, packing houses, and refrigeration. By 1916 the editor of the *Pacific Rural Press* estimated that under average conditions a farmer in California needed capital and credit of at least $20,000.[6]

In consequence, the owner of even a small successful farm had to be far more prosperous at the outset than most newcomers could be, and few successful farms were small. Outside the Willamette and Santa Clara valleys and the Mormon country, many men who called themselves ranchers or orchardists operated through agents, dealing in crops and the land itself from a distance so that their wives might

---

[4] Alvin H. Thompson: "Aspects of the Social History of California Agriculture, 1885–1902" (unpublished doctoral thesis, University of California at Berkeley; 1953), p. 326. *Report . . . on the Irrigation and Reclamation of Arid Lands,* 51 Cong., 1 Sess., Senate Report 928 (1890), part 2, Vol. I, p. 342. Nesbit and Gates in *Pacific Northwest Quarterly,* Vol. XXXVII, p. 287.

[5] *Report of the Secretary of the Interior . . . ,* Vol. I, *House Executive Documents,* 50 Cong., 1 Sess., no. 1, part 5, Vol. I (1887), p. 935.

[6] R. E. Hodges, E. J. Wickson, and W. C. Tesche: *Farming in California* (San Francisco: Californians, Inc.; 1927), p. 66.

have neighbors and their children attend city schools: thus the distances between bona fide farmhouses were often much greater even than the distances across farms. "There are very few real farmers in California," a wheat grower testified in 1876. "Our people have got to be simply men who . . . plunder the soil, cultivate crops a few years simply, by machinery, sow the wheat and by machinery gather it, and by machinery send it off on railroads. . . ."[7] "You go through miles and miles of wheat fields, you see the fertility of the land and the beauty of the scenery," a visitor wrote to *The New York Times* in 1887, "but where are the hundreds of farm houses . . . that you would see in Ohio or Iowa? In short . . . the present California is a feudal State. . . . When you point out this evil to the people, they tell you that the land is going to be cut up." Yet concentration increased despite repeated hopes that drought or depression or improved transportation would lead to subdivision, that water would wash away the sin of incorporation. In 1900, nearly two thirds of all farmland in the state was in farms of a thousand acres or more. The percentage of farm laborers (as compared with all persons engaged in agriculture) in California rose in each decade but one from 1860 to 1910; by 1890 it was larger than in the United States, by 1920 larger than in Mississippi. According to the California Commission on Immigration (1917), consolidation in ownership of land in southern California had continued from Mexican times. No more than two hundred and fifty men held title to half the non-public and non-railroad rural land of eight southern counties. "The great mass of the land is held by an insignificant few . . ." reported the Commission, "and the ideal of a rural society composed of many small-unit owners, each a tiller of the soil—the ideal of socially-minded men in all times—is one . . . for which there is not the slightest present basis of hope."[8]

Monopoly in land had gone further in California than anywhere else, so that even in the 1870's many immigrants chose to move on to the Northwest. But if the country east of the Cascades offered more space

---

[7] Paul S. Taylor: "Foundations of California Rural Society," *California Historical Society Quarterly*, Vol. XXIV (September 1945), p. 216. Phillips: *Letters from California*, pp. 125, 140.

[8] Letter by J. S. Moore, New York, Sept. 3, 1887, in *The New York Times*, Sept. 5, 1887, p. 5, col. 5. Thompson: "Aspects of the Social History of California Agriculture, 1885–1902," p. 338. Taylor and Vasey in *Rural Sociology*, Vol. I, p. 288. California Commission on Immigration and Housing: *A Report on Large Landholdings in Southern California with Recommendations* (Sacramento: California State Printing Office; 1919), pp. 13–14, 31.

and land that seemed to resemble that east of Los Angeles, it also had alkaline soils and early frosts, and the distance between the railroads was so great that in the boom country of central Oregon the ox-drawn freight wagon lasted well into the era of the automobile. Throughout the Far West, only in Utah, where the Church had allotted lands according to need, did farms average smaller than in the United States as a whole, and even in Utah the size increased four times between 1860 and 1890 (from 25 to 126 acres); only there and in Idaho, the only state where the Carey Act (1894) proved at all effective in promoting irrigation on small tracts, did the size of farms remain close to the traditional 160 acres.[9]

The social experience of the great masses of Western farmers varied greatly from that of the fortunate at Riverside and from the promoters' accounts. Low density of population might mean "elbow room" and "prices regulated by a sparse rural population," as the railroads claimed; it might also mean terrible isolation. "No one who has not actually seen it," recalled a woman who came to eastern Washington in 1905, "can have even the faintest idea of what the loneliness of one of those isolated homesteads is like."[1] Illness might be a disaster; given time, mild derangement was almost normal. Friendships among families under such conditions might be close, corresponding to their mutual dependence, but the burdens of maintaining and of supporting elementary communication with the outside world were heavy. If the valleys near San Francisco and Portland recalled the orchards and dairies of upstate New York, and the Mormon settlements along Salt Lake recalled the land of Canaan, much of the interior tested and broke the human spirit as mercilessly as the Great Plains.[2]

The worst hardships were probably those of the irrigation country, or what people called irrigation country. "It would be difficult to convey to people whose pioneering had been done in the wooded lands east of the Mississippi the complete helplessness of the individual in the arid West," wrote Mary Austin, whose family had settled on the Tejón ranch

---

[9] A. E. D. DeRupert: *Californians and Mormons* (New York: J. W. Lovell; 1881), pp. 102–3. *Census of 1890, Statistics of Agriculture,* p. 108.

[1] A. J. Wells: *California for the Settler . . .* (San Francisco: Passenger Department, Southern Pacific; 1910), p. 7. Mrs. Hugh Fraser and Hugh C. Fraser: *Seven Years on the Pacific Slope* (New York: Dodd, Mead & Co.; 1914), pp. 42–3, 48.

[2] Annie Pike Greenwood: *We Sagebrush Folks* (New York: D. Appleton-Century Co.; 1934). Isaiah Bowman: *The Pioneer Fringe* (New York: American Geographical Society; 1931).

in 1888. "Many of the people about us in the Southern San Joaquin Valley were in a state of supposing that, wherever there were enough people who wanted to farm, an irrigating ditch would simply appear." The Nevada desert deceived few except the prospectors, who never expected to grow their own food; most of this land was so patently untillable that even the stockmen were slow to interest themselves in it until their herds, grazing on the way from Oregon to the shipping points at Elko and Winnemucca, showed them the possibilities. But immigrants who had seen the orange groves at Pasadena and Riverside and the melon fields in the Imperial Valley were eager to invest their lives in land in the other states that looked no worse to them in its natural condition. The entire measure of their sacrifice and disappointment in the ordeal by heat, sand, and alkali that they inherited did not appear in the changing statistics of settlement, as many refused to acknowledge defeat or had no other place to go; yet many gave up, leaving the sight of their sun-warped shacks and dusty ditches and the burden of their taxes to invite their neighbors to follow them. Kern County, in the southern San Joaquin Valley, lost 62 percent of its school children between 1880 and 1886. Six counties in eastern Oregon had more children enrolled in school in the 1890's or early 1900's than a generation later, despite the state-wide tendency to larger and longer attendance. Sometimes population both declined and changed greatly, as owners gave way to tenants and laborers. In Franklin County, Washington, where the cost of water made small farms impracticable, there was almost a complete turnover in four years, 1910–14.[3] Over and over, at different times and locations, homesteaders learned that the sum of desert and water was not always Riverside or Hood River; that the total economic and social costs ran beyond those in older, more familiar regions where nature furnished more rain than wind. But always, as inducement to stay on or try again, there were stories of families that had waited, worked, and won.

From time to time, as in the older states, farmers organized to improve themselves. In California and Oregon, the Grange (1873) emphasized systems of cooperative marketing, warehousing, and shipping, and for nearly two years put Grange steamers on the Willamette

---

[3] Mary Austin: *Earth Horizon: Autobiography* (New York: Houghton Mifflin Co.; 1932), p. 199. *Report . . . on the Irrigation and Reclamation of Arid Lands,* 51 Cong., 1 Sess., Senate Report 928 (1890), part 2, Vol. I, p. 398. *Twentieth Biennal Report of the Superintendent of Public Instruction* . . . (Salem, 1913), p. 4. *Twenty-ninth Biennial Report* . . . (Salem, 1931), p. 78. Nesbit and Gates in *Pacific Northwest Quarterly,* Vol. XXXVII, pp. 285–6.

River in competition with the Oregon Steam Navigation Company. As individual voters, many Grangers probably supported the short-lived independent parties that controlled about one third of the legislatures of California and Oregon in 1873 and 1874 and elected Governor Newton Booth of California as United States senator on the Anti-Monopoly ticket. Some went into Denis Kearney's Workingmen's Party (1877) and pressed for the establishment of a railroad commission in the new California state constitution of 1879.[4] Neither the California nor the Oregon legislature carried out a Grange program along the lines of the states in the western Mississippi Valley, and much of the animus against monopolists came from urban areas; still, it was significant of rural discontent that California—only about a fifth of whose population lived on farms (about half the national rate)—entered even intermittently the paths of agrarian insurgency.

By the nineties, Populist and silverite candidates won impressive victories all over the Pacific slope. Yet the patterns of insurgent strength and policy differed considerably from those on the high plains then and earlier. The Far Western farmers were less interested in the problems of wheat, more in foreign trade, immigration, monopoly in land, and canning and processing. One of the leaders of the California Grange in the seventies had commented that low prices of wheat might "be in the end a blessing rather than a calamity." Small diversified farms, he predicted, would surpass the great ranches, "and California will more and more resemble the belt of fruit-growing States on the Atlantic Coast."[5] Although complaints of excessive freight rates were chronic, antagonism against the railroads was not so general and sustained as it was east of the Rockies, perhaps because most of the Far Western lines came late, perhaps because some of their officers, like Jim Hill of the Great Northern, shared the farmers' hopes for more intensive agricultural development and larger markets. The directors of the Central Pacific eventually realized that bonanza farming limited the railroad's revenues as well as the rural population; in the eighties (1884 and 1885) they lowered freight rates on fruit, and Collis P. Huntington came

[4] Ezra S. Carr: *The Patrons of Husbandry of the Pacific Coast* (San Francisco: A. L. Bancroft & Co.; 1875), p. 75 and *passim.* Edna A. Scott: "The Grange Movement in Oregon, 1873–1900" (unpublished master's thesis, University of Oregon; 1923), pp. 6–12, 24–6, 43–50. Irene L. Poppleton: "Oregon's First Monopoly—The O. S. N. Co.," *Oregon Historical Quarterly,* Vol. IX (September 1908), pp. 295–6. Solon J. Buck in *Essays in American History Dedicated to Frederick Jackson Turner* (New York: Henry Holt & Co.; 1910), pp. 153–4, 159, 161.

[5] Carr: *Patrons of Husbandry,* pp. 68, 83–4.

to favor excluding the Chinese, saying that "monopoly of land was keeping back the progress of the State"; the Southern Pacific's land agent favored a law limiting inheritance in land.[6] By the early 1900's, many farmers joined insurgents in the towns in concentrating on the offenses the railroads committed in their capacities as political bosses: in Oregon the most significant heritage of Populism was the movement for electoral reform that came to a climax in the adoption of the initiative and referendum and the direct election of senators, and whose chief exponents were William S. U'Ren and Jonathan Bourne, lawyers from Oregon City and Portland. Throughout the Pacific slope, Populism became distinctively strong in the more densely populated areas, whereas in the older states the cities defeated it. Some of this urban support followed on the mining industry and its investors; the issue of free silver was far more prominent throughout most of the Far West than it was in the Middle West and in the South. In California, which was less interested in silver than the others (and gave less than a tenth of its popular vote to the Populist presidential ticket in 1892), the farmers' alliances had drawn on the membership of Nationalist clubs, followers of Edward Bellamy, the Utopian novelist. In Washington, insurgency originated in the eastern wheat counties; the alliances took three years to move west of the Cascades (1891). But in Oregon Populism grew out a mixture of reform movements, primarily in the western counties, in which Prohibitionists and Knights of Labor at first greatly outnumbered members of farm organizations.[7]

The most substantial and enduring responses to the economic problems of the farmers were the producers' cooperatives, which for the most part developed quite outside politics. (In Utah, the Deseret

---

[6] Thompson: *"Aspects of the Social History of California Agriculture,"* pp. 193, 208–9, 244.

[7] Donald E. Walters: "The Feud Between California Populist T. V. Cator and Democrats James Maguire and James Barry," *Pacific Historical Review*, Vol. XXVII (August 1958), pp. 282–4. Fred R. Yoder: "The Farmers' Alliances in Washington—Prelude to Populism," State College of Washington, *Research Studies*, Vol. XVI (September–December 1948), pp. 126, 131. Marion Harrington: *The Populist Movement in Oregon, 1889–96* (master's thesis, University of Oregon; 1935, 1940), pp. 9, 45. In 1896, when Idaho, Nevada, Utah, and Washington were among the ten states that Bryan carried outside the South, he drew substantial support in the urban counties of the Far West, carrying King (Seattle), Pierce (Tacoma), Spokane, and Snohomish (Everett) counties in Washington, and Lane (Eugene) and Coos (North Bend–Marshfield) in Oregon; he had large minorities, well beyond those in more rural counties, in Benton (Corvallis), Clackamas (Oregon City), and Marion (Salem), and in San Francisco and Sacramento, while his majority in Salt Lake ran much above his majority in Utah.

Palace Hotel, San Francisco, as it was in 1875–1900.

The Palace, wrote an English visitor in 1884, "reminded me of the Louvre and the Grand Hôtel in Paris, having a vast courtyard, around which the 750 rooms are built, the whole occupying two acres and a half of land."

Stanford and Hopkins mansions, San Francisco, 1880.

Leland Stanford promoted the building of the California street cable line (1878) to serve the residents of Nob Hill, where he and Mark Hopkins had built their homes in 1875. "They cost a great deal of money," a young architect observed, "and whatever harsh criticism may fall upon them, they cannot be robbed of that prestige."

Los Angeles, 1885.

As the real-estate boom started, central Los Angeles still retained the flavor of slower-moving times. This is Spring Street, looking toward the site of the present city hall.

Regrading of Seattle.

Lowering Seattle's hills (1898–1910) involved moving more than sixteen million yards of earth and rock. The new grade of Denny Hill was 141 feet 6 inches under the floor of the Washington Hotel, which was the symbol of Seattle's recovery after the fire of 1889.

Los Angeles Times building, October 1, 1910.

"Unionist Bombs Wreck the Times," ran the banner in the *Los Angeles Times*, which called the explosion "The Crime of the Century." Twenty persons were killed.

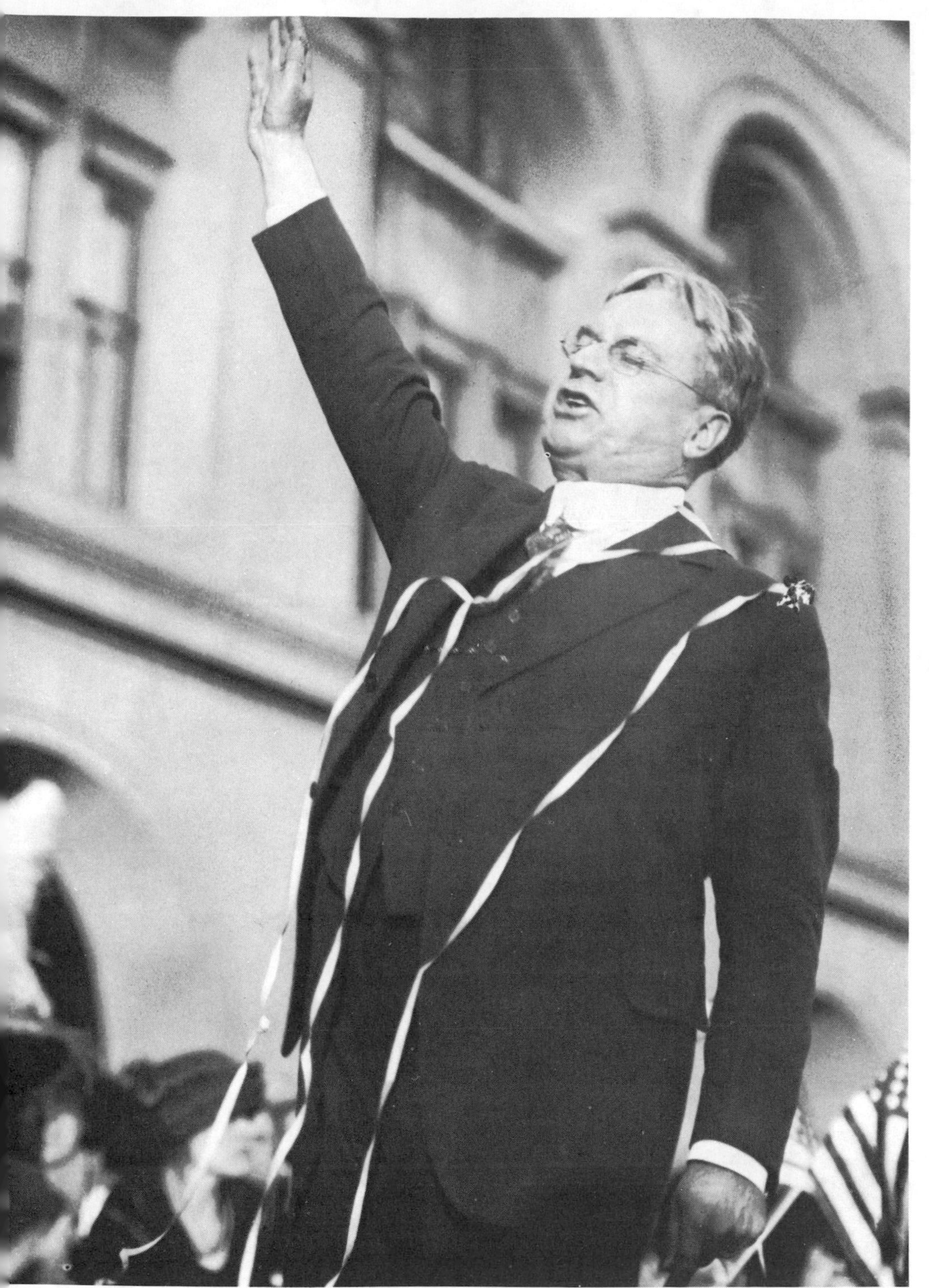

Hiram Johnson campaigning.

Preparedness Day Parade, San Francisco, 1916.

Vic Meyers, candidate for mayor of Seattle, 1932.

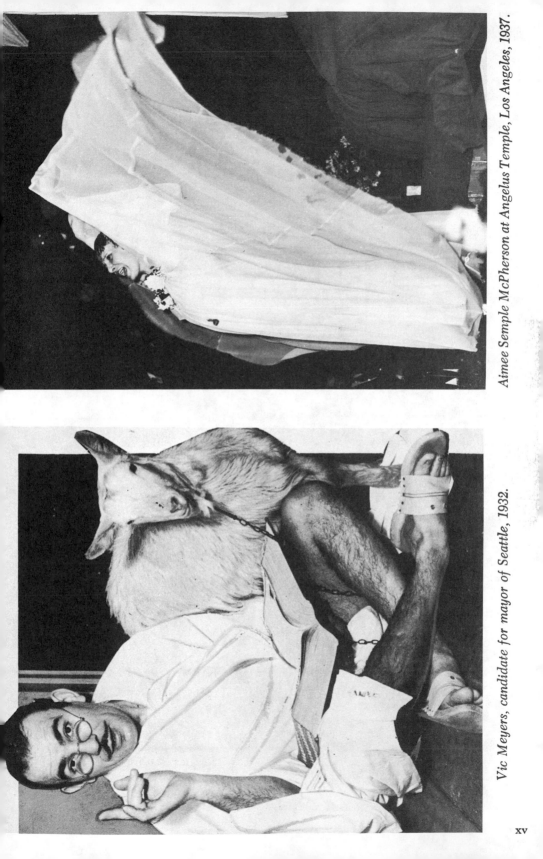

Aimee Semple McPherson at Angelus Temple, Los Angeles, 1937.

Chinese construction workers, about 1866.

Gangs of Chinese laborers graded the Central Pacific Railroad, hauling dirt in wheel-

Agricultural and Manufacturing Society, incorporated in 1856, acted for both church and state in planning agricultural production.) The Mormons pioneered in organizing the first marketing agency, the Utah Produce Company (1866), and in establishing cooperative herds of sheep (1869). For many years the farmers farther west seemed to lack the discipline to work together, railroads levied Draconian charges, and packers and commission merchants took care to protect themselves first in distant markets that were at best disorganized and erratic. By the early 1900's, farmers in a few counties had specialized enough in some crops, and the surviving growers had learned well enough the penalties of independence, so that effective agreements were possible. The growers of citrus fruit pioneered, organizing the Southern California Fruit Exchange (1895), which became the California Fruit Growers Exchange (1905); it sold fruit, supervised grading and packing, and coordinated buying. Similar associations appeared in the almond (1910), walnut, and raisin (1912) industries; the California Associated Raisin Company shortly made Sun Maid raisins as well known as Sunkist oranges. Aaron Sapiro, a California lawyer, came to specialize in agricultural cooperative law and organization and eventually carried the new gospel all over the country. The railroads themselves, which the cooperatives forced to grant more equitable terms, came to respect their effectiveness in expediting shipments and sales; the Southern Pacific matched funds with the Fruit Growers in an experimental high-presure campaign to advertise oranges in Iowa (1907). The Yakima Valley Fruit Growers' Association (1910), among others, modeled its methods after those of the Californians; Sapiro later showed the way to cooperative marketing in Northwestern wheat (1920).[8]

Labor was slower to begin solving its problems. Whereas the rail·

---

[8] Leonard J. Arrington: *Great Basin Kingdom: An Economic History of the Latter-day Saints, 1830–1900* (Cambridge: Harvard University Press; 1958), pp. 226–7, 296, 310. A. Schoendorf: *Beginnings of Cooperation in the Marketing of California Fresh Deciduous Fruits and History of the California Fruit Exchange* (Sacramento: Inland Press; 1947), p. 2. Erich Kraemer and H. E. Erdman: *History of Cooperation in the Marketing of California Fresh Deciduous Fruits,* University of California Agricultural Experiment Station, Bulletin 557 (Berkeley, 1933), pp. 119–20. Carl C. Taylor: *The Farmers' Movement, 1620–1920* (New York: American Book Co.; 1953), pp. 483–8. H. E. Erdman: "The Development and Significance of California Cooperatives, 1900–1915," *Agricultural History,* Vol. XXXII (July 1958), pp. 181–2. Herman Steen: *Coöperative Marketing: The Golden Rule in Agriculture* (New York: Doubleday, Page & Co.; 1923), pp. 6–7, 55, 215, and *passim.*

roads brought to the farmer at least the prospects of larger markets along with the burden of high freight rates (which, of course, were usually lower than rates for wagon freight had been) and monopolies in land and politics, to the laborer they meant new competition for both his job and his product. Moreover, the spirit of charity tended to lag, whether because communities were new and mobile or because the successful saw that Western wages were higher than Eastern wages and did not see that the difference was decreasing. Although the workingman in the West continued to earn more than his Eastern fellow, the family that had come west in response to rosy reports of last year's wage rates sometimes had to live and recoup the costs of moving on rates that drifted downward as more immigrants arrived. And the farmer, who on the coast was much more an employer and less a fellow toiler than in the older states, soon persuaded himself that he needed cheap labor, including contract labor from the Orient, to counter the high costs of land and freight, even while he applauded the rhetoric of nation-wide reform movements that strove to bring farmer and laborer together. The California Farmers Union resolved (1873) to consider using convict labor to produce sacks to sell to farmers at cost.[9]

The erosion of the laborer's original good fortune became especially severe in the first years of the Pacific railroad, perhaps because the railroads and other dominant employers were becoming larger, more powerful, and more impersonal than the small masters of pioneer days, perhaps simply because the railroad brought new competitors into the labor market, including the Chinese and the Irish who had built it. In 1873–5, when the depression of 1873 had not yet spread to the coast, immigration became greater than it had been since the gold rush. Then the eight-hour day gave way to the ten-hour day; shortly the first tramps were collecting at the freight yards and knocking at back doors. "It would seem to an outsider," Pendarves Vivian, an English visitor, observed in 1879, "as if the capital and labour question was destined to give more trouble here than in any other part of the world."[1]

---

[9] LaWanda F. Cox: "The American Agricultural Wage Earner; 1865–1900 . . . ," *Agricultural History*, Vol. XXII (April 1948), pp. 101–3. Carr: *Patrons of Husbandry*, p. 96.

[1] Ira B. Cross: *A History of the Labor Movement in California*, University of California Publications in Economics, Vol. XIV (Berkeley: University of California Press; 1935), pp. 54–5, 69, 71. A. Pendarves Vivian: *Wanderings in the Western Land* (London: S. Low, Marston, Searle & Rivington; 1879), pp. 346–7.

When the economy as a whole recovered in the early 1880's, the supply of labor more than kept up with the demand as the railroads cut transcontinental fares, and prospective farmers who faced speculative prices for land crowded into the cities. "Given the extent of land monopoly through large holdings and speculative syndicate purchases," wrote an agent of the Department of the Interior who surveyed labor conditions in the West, "and the condition of California can be told without further data. . . . Thus it is that, even in . . . the land of plenty . . . there are poverty and misery, and strikes against low wages."[2]

The fortunes of labor varied greatly over the West, and from year to year. For many years the history of organized labor in California centered in San Francisco, "that common sink," as an unemployed workman called it in 1887, "whither, sooner or later, all men on the Pacific slope must come for awhile, drawn by the magnetic influence of a great city."[3] The laborers of San Francisco had organized so effectively in the sixties that they had established the closed shop in several trades and the eight-hour day was state law. By the beginning of the twentieth century, San Francisco was a closed-shop city, as it was henceforth except after the First World War, and for the most part by general assent. The Building Trades Council, and the teamsters in particular, perfected a form of "business unionism" that enlisted employers in the task of unionization in the city and throughout the state and made labor's most successful leaders elder statesmen of the community.[4]

In San Francisco, too, antagonism between labor and capital led to unusual bitterness and violence and to attempts by opportunistic politicians to appeal to the grievances of labor. The depression of the 1870's brought forth Denis Kearney, the orator of the sandlot riots against the Chinese. Though the Workingmen's Party of California, which he formed in the fall of 1877, lasted only three years, it elected mayors of both San Francisco and Sacramento and a third of the dele-

[2] Meriwether: *The Tramp at Home,* pp. 196, 199.

[3] Morley Roberts: *The Western Avernus; or, Toil and Travel in Further North America* (London: Smith, Elder & Co.; 1887), p. 247.

[4] Cross: *History,* pp. 229, 249. Frederick L. Ryan: *Industrial Relations in the San Francisco Building Trades* (Norman: University of Oklahoma Press; 1935), pp. 32–60, 103–56. R. M. Robinson: "A History of the Teamsters in the San Francisco Bay Area, 1850–1950" (unpublished doctoral thesis, University of California at Berkeley; 1951), pp. 27–34, 43–85.

gates to the state convention that wrote the Constitution of 1879, which seemed a portent of anarchy. And the efforts of the San Francisco Employers' Association to break the unions in 1901 led to the formation of the Union Labor Party, which controlled San Francisco almost continuously from 1902 to 1911. Embittered by the predatory practices of crimps and masters, which were driving the American sailor from the sea despite the traditionally favorable differential between Pacific and Atlantic wages, and thrown together in the comparative isolation of the coastal market, the maritime workers in particular developed a strong sense of common grievance and organized under strongly socialist influences in the eighties. The very countenance of Andrew Furuseth, secretary of the Coast Seamen's Union and of its successor, the Sailors' Union of the Pacific (1891), was a reminder of hard fare. Under his crusading leadership, the sailors in the Pacific coastwise trade led American maritime labor and for a time set an example in Europe as well. Although Furuseth always distrusted longshoremen and landsmen and spurned socialism and most of the legislative remedies that appealed to labor ashore, the presence and the spirit of his sailors helped to develop solidarity against capital in the larger laboring community. San Francisco strongly sympathized with the Pullman strikers of 1894, despite the relatively harmonious labor relations of the Southern Pacific.[5]

In Los Angeles, meanwhile, labor was slower to organize effectively, whether because health-seekers and pensioners were willing to work under substandard conditions or because the *Los Angeles Times* crusaded against effective unionism and (in the words of the slogan in its masthead) "For Liberty and Law and Equal Rights and Industrial Freedom." "The open shop," the secretary of the Los Angeles Merchants' and Manufacturers' Association testified in 1914, "is Los Angeles' greatest asset as a creator of a high and consistent level of prosperity."[6] The M. and M. had organized (1893) partly to support General Harrison Gray Otis, who had imported non-union printers to enforce a lockout

[5] Cross: *History*, pp. 93–127, 241–6, 219–20. Ralph Kauer: "The Workingmen's Party of California," *Pacific Historical Review*, Vol. XIII (September 1944), pp. 278–91. Walton Bean: *Boss Ruef's San Francisco . . .* (Berkeley: University of California Press; 1952). Paul S. Taylor: *The Sailors' Union of the Pacific* (New York: Ronald Press Co.; 1923), pp. 9–10, 40–98. Hyman Weintraub: *Andrew Furuseth, Emancipator of the Seamen* (Berkeley: University of California Press; 1959). *Literary Digest*, Vol. IX (July 21, 1894), pp. 335–6.

[6] Los Angeles Merchants' and Manufacturers' Association: *Report* (Los Angeles, 1946), p. 28.

on the *Times* in 1890; by 1903 it had frankly dedicated itself, as a kind of West-coast Holy Alliance, to supporting any of its members against the unions. Much of the initiative in the southern-Californian labor movement correspondingly came from the unions and the employers of San Francisco, which came to see intervention as a safeguard against the spread of the open shop northward and the competition of goods produced at lower cost.[7]

Yet though the southern Californian workingmen were slow to organize effectively, they were far from content; if General Otis and his associates were more determined to maintain the open shop than were their counterparts in San Francisco, the unionists were unusually disposed to follow socialist and millennial programs that looked toward social reconstruction rather than to changes in the terms of employment in the immediate future. There was, as Grace Stimson points out, a distinctively semi-political, reformist quality in labor's leaders, an enthusiasm that seems to anticipate some other southern-Californian movements and crazes of later generations. Some of the more striking eccentrics and excesses of the Los Angeles labor movement were imported: Carl Browne, who believed that he and Jacob S. Coxey were a joint reincarnation of Jesus Christ, had been Denis Kearney's aide in San Francisco before he moved to Los Angeles; and both enemies and friends of labor blamed agents of San Francisco unions for the strife that broke out in 1910.[8] It was nevertheless in Los Angeles that extreme men and ideas found fullest expression and acceptance.

The tensions in southern Californian labor manifested themselves most sensationally when, in 1910–11, Los Angeles became the scene of violence without precedent on the coast and a Socialist was nearly elected mayor. Following strikes in street railways and breweries, the employers in the metals trades had met demands from their unions, first by beginning a lockout, then by persuading the City Council to pass an ordinance against picketing (July 16, 1910). The metal workers stayed out for four months while, according to Frederick Palmer, who reported on "Otistown of the Open Shop" in *Hampton's Magazine*, "as in every

[7] Grace H. Stimson: *Rise of the Labor Movement in Los Angeles* (Berkeley: University of California Press; 1955), pp. 104–22, 151, 255–6, 316–17. Cross: *History*, p. 282. See also Louis B. Perry: *A History of the Los Angeles Labor Movement, 1911–1941* (Berkeley: University of California Press; 1963).

[8] Stimson: *Rise of the Labor Movement*, pp. 154–5, 194, 362–407. Louis Adamic: *My America, 1928–1938* (New York: Harper & Brothers; 1938), pp. 16–18, 22–3.

strike of the last fifteen years in Los Angeles, organized labor looked beyond the employers to the *Times* as the real foeman." Unrest ran so high that when an explosion destroyed the *Times* building (October 1), many persons professed to believe that the owners of the *Times* themselves had conspired to set the dynamite or at least had callously neglected leaking gas. Sympathy for the union leaders who were arrested for the bombing—the brothers NcNamara—contributed to popular support for one of the union attorneys, Job Harriman, who became Socialist nominee for mayor and received nearly half the votes in the primary. When the NcNamaras dramatically pleaded guilty four days before the election, they destroyed his prospects and set off interminable recrimination both against and within the labor movement and the Socialist Party.[9]

Although in no other major urban center did labor succeed or fail so spectacularly as in San Francisco and Los Angeles, over much of the rest of the Pacific slope its aspirations, its grievances, and its sense of separateness contrasted with those of labor in the West of the cattle and wheat country east of the Rockies. The Mormon country stood apart, the Church maintaining peace and equity among the various parts of its family; and until late in the century the cities of the Northwest were too small to support much of a distinct laboring community, aside from the drifters on waterfront skid roads. In Portland during the early years, workmen felt the more secure because they could turn to cultivating the unoccupied marshy tracts scattered in and around the city.[1] In general, and in the long run, the cities and industrialized mining camps of the Far West, with their backgrounds of monopoly in land and transportation, were predisposed to discontent and class-consciousness; and railroads and steamships imported from the older states the disputes and the surpluses of labor that precipitated conflict.

Effective miners' unions had appeared in the 1870's in California and Nevada, testifying to the transmutation of an adventure into an industry in the preceding generation. They came still more quickly to the new northern mines. The Coeur d'Alene Executive Miners' Union, the first federation of hard-rock unions, was organized (1889) only six

---

[9] Frederick Palmer: "Otistown on the Open Shop: The Story of Los Angeles . . . ," *Hampton's Magazine,* Vol. XXVI (January 1911), p. 30. Cross: *History,* p. 282.

[1] Meriwether: *The Tramp at Home,* p. 291.

years after the first show of dust and nuggets; when the owners posted a wage cut in 1892, the union was ready, and in less than three months virtual warfare had broken out. The Western Federation of Miners, which was organized the next year, looked initially to northern Idaho for its leadership; and it was there, at Wardner in 1899, that miners dynamited and destroyed the Bunker Hill mine, and Governor Frank Steunenberg, by calling for troops, aroused hatred that led to his murder in 1905. The W. F. M. and the larger organization it helped to inspire and for a few months joined, the Industrial Workers of the World (1905), later acquired romantic reputations for frontier individualism that they do not wholly deserve. Their members were not so much (as they described themselves) "formerly self-employed prospectors and former mine-owners who had become 'wage slaves' of mining corporations rather recently acquired by back-east absentee ownership"[2] as they were veterans of industrial conflict in Michigan, Pennsylvania, and northern Europe, and their demands varied from elementary decency to anarchy and to the privilege of stealing ("high-grading") company property. But the passions that the Wobblies represented and aroused were real enough and spared no Far Western state, not even Utah, where Joe Hill (Hillstrom), their legendary bard, was executed for murder at Bingham in 1915. In later years members of the radical wing of the I. W. W. looked back to the Goldfield, Nevada, of 1906–7 as a kind of golden age, recalling how they refused to send committees to employers, but instead simply posted wage scales on a bulletin board outside the union hall, "and it was the LAW. The employers were forced to come and see the union committees."[3]

The discontent and social instability that the I. W. W. drew on be-

---

[2] Rodman W. Paul: *California Gold . . .* (Cambridge: Harvard University Press; 1947), pp. 326–33. Vernon H. Jensen: *Heritage of Conflict: Labor Relations in the Nonferrous Metals Industry up to 1930* (Ithaca: Cornell University Press; 1950), pp. 28–37, 197. *Bill Haywood's Book; The Autobiography of William D. Haywood* (New York: International Publishers; 1929), p. 63. Fred Thompson: *The I. W. W., Its First Fifty Years, 1905–1955 . . .* (Chicago: Industrial Workers of the World; 1955), p. 9. The words quoted are from Thompson.

[3] Robert L. Tyler: "The I. W. W. and the West," *American Quarterly*, Vol. XII (Summer 1960), pp. 175–87. Russell R. Elliott: "Labor Temples in the Mining Camp at Goldfield, Nevada, 1906–1908," *Pacific Historical Review*, Vol. XIX (November 1950), pp. 369–84. Robert L. Tyler: "Rebels of the Woods and Fields: a Study of the I. W. W. in the Pacific Northwest (unpublished doctoral thesis, University of Oregon; 1953). Paul F. Brissenden: *The I. W. W., A Study of American Syndicalism* (New York: Russell & Russell; 1957), p. 201. Brissenden quotes from Vincent St. John, general secretary-treasurer of the I. W. W.

came especially notorious in the lumber camps and towns of western Washington and Oregon, some of which eventually rivaled McKees Rocks, Lawrence, and Paterson for violence in labor disputes. Organization came late to the lumber industry; it was retarded by the persistence of scattered small-scale operations and by the tendency of some of the loggers to regard their jobs as no more than grubstakes for farming. The shingle weavers, who had organized in 1890, suffered repeated failures that reflected both the power of the operators and the inability or unwillingness of the weavers to stay with the union through strikes and bad times. Itinerant loggers and lumberworkers found a particular congeniality in the rough comradeship of the Wobblies' halls in the skid-road districts of the cities to which they drifted between jobs and in the sense of fraternity with which they greeted fellow anarchists in freight cars and hobo jungles. In their fireside philosophizing and in their rejection of central organization in labor as well as in business and government, they seemed the most anarchist wing of the most anarchist of American movements; their Eastern colleagues came greatly to admire the "Overall Brigades" from the Northwest as "genuine rebels —the red-blooded working stiffs."[4] They were probably fewer than they seemed, and certainly they were both fewer and less of a threat to orthodoxy than were the Socialists and the members of the W. F. M., whom they came to despise after the briefest of honeymoons.

The Far Western Socialists were a numerous and to a large extent a radical group, despite the Wobblies' contempt for them; in the six states, they cast a larger fraction of the presidential vote in 1912 than did the Socialists of the Northeastern states. The party in Washington was the strongest in the country in proportion to population, and it had been there and in Idaho that Eugene Debs hoped to establish socialist colonies in 1897–8. The Northwesterners were so revolutionary in leadership, so contemptuous of law, political action, and casual respectability that they indulged in doctrinaire eccentricities that caused comment even within the party. The delegates from Oregon at the convention of 1912 refused to eat at a restaurant that used tablecloths; the secretary removed cuspidors from state headquarters because they suggested bourgeois weakness. Paradoxically California, and particularly southern California, where the destruction of the *Times* building gave Socialists

[4] Vernon H. Jensen: *Lumber and Labor* (New York: Farrar & Rinehart; 1945). Brissenden: *I. W. W.*, pp. 221–4, 231–3.

a reputation for extremism, was under right-wing control in 1910, as was Washington. Job Harriman himself forbade Debs and Bill Haywood to appear before Socialist locals, and Harriman ran for mayor in 1911 with the support of the American Federation of Labor, which was anathema to the Northwesterners, and on a platform much of which corresponded to the purposes of the Los Angeles Chamber of Commerce, emphasizing the development of a municipal seaport and a municipal water supply. The pioneer Socialist candidate in California, Gaylord Wilshire, who published the most popular Socialist journal in the country, built up a circulation by offering, as premiums for subscriptions, orange groves and also advertising stock in a socialist gold mine; he financed his radical activities by real-estate speculations. As Ira Kipnis points out, the successful Socialist campaigns in California were contests between reformers and bosses. Much of the support for Reverend J. Stitt Wilson for mayor of Berkeley in 1912 came from respectable elements of the community (including those of the wealthy residential districts) that had turned against the machine, and he gave them an efficient administration like Milwaukee's.[5]

In the countryside, discontent also was chronic. Despite a climate that made rural life potentially more comfortable than throughout most of the nation east of the Rockies, the American ideal of the family farm was as remote as it was in the plantation country of the South, and it was receding year by year. The drift was toward farms on which expensive machines did the work and on which hired laborers outnumbered proprietors (as they did in California by 1900, amounting to 44 percent of the entire farm population there as compared with 27 percent in the nation). Before the First World War, machines had not yet opened up opportunity for the logger, but they were rapidly helping to price it out of reach of the farm laborer: the legendary agricultural ladder to tenancy and fee simple served relatively few other than immigrants from Asia and southeastern Europe, who thriftily allotted themselves less comfort and pleasure than most native Americans. Observing the economic and social wastefulness of much large-scale farming, agricultural economists particularly deplored its effects

[5] David A. Shannon: *The Socialist Party of America, A History* (New York: The Macmillan Company; 1955), pp. 37–40. Ira Kipnis: *The American Socialist Movement, 1897–1912* (New York: Columbia University Press; 1952), pp. 55–6, 303, 305, 342–3, 347, 373–4. Howard H. Quint: "Gaylord Wilshire and Socialism's First Congressional Campaign," *Pacific Historical Review*, Vol. XXVI (November 1957), pp. 327–40.

on rural society and on the migratory field hands who took their entire families into the fields from dawn to dark in the summer and drifted into the cities after the harvests without savings or prospects of further employment.

Yet, as union organizers discovered, most white farm laborers were so prone to think of their jobs as temporary and as second choice that they had little interest in advancing the common lot. Near Wheatland, California, in the eastern Sacramento Valley in 1913 one of the bonanza farmers knowingly recruited more hop-pickers than he needed, failed to provide even drinking water in the desert-like heat for those whom he hired at starvation wages (instead, he sold lemonade made of citric acid), and then called for sheriff's deputies when he feared that the consequences of his own inhumanity might get out of hand. The confused violence that ensued was an almost spontaneous explosion of resentment and fear; Wobbly agitators made themselves spokesmen for the laborers and spoke of a strike. Yet there was little sense of proletarian community even in the face of systematic exploitation. Professor Carleton H. Parker, whom the governor sent to Wheatland to investigate, reported that many of the families in the labor force were of the middle class and had "been in the habit of using the hop and fruit seasons to get their 'country vacations.'"[6] Most were not, but the typical itinerant laborers in the bonanza grain and fruit country were altogether different from the hired men and harvest hands of the Middle West and were not much more likely to organize in their collective interest than to crowd into the farmer's kitchen to feast on the best that his wife and daughters could serve them.

Although much of the agricultural West thus fell far short of the traditional American image of rural equality, fortune in the towns sometimes seemed no closer than on the farms or in the early mining camps. The majority of settlers who by 1910 lived in town had guessed right insofar as they had anticipated the predominantly urban trend of development in the Far West. But the rapid growth of the popula-

---

[6] Carl C. Taylor: *Trends in the Tenure Status of Farm Workers in the United States since 1880* (Washington: Bureau of Agricultural Economics; 1948), pp. 25–34. Stuart M. Jamieson: "Labor Unionism in American Agriculture" (unpublished doctoral thesis, University of California at Berkeley; 1943), pp. 154–5. Woodrow C. Whitten: "The Wheatland Episode," *Pacific Historical Review*, Vol. XVII (February 1948), pp. 37–42. Carleton H. Parker: *The Casual Laborer and Other Essays* (New York: Harcourt, Brace & Howe; 1920), p. 174.

tion, which greatly rewarded those who foresaw the specific locus of opportunity—that Portland and San Francisco would surpass Oregon City and New York-of-the-Pacific—correspondingly penalized those who had guessed wrong and tried to hedge their bets by waiting.

The precise shape of urban opportunity appeared slowly and along a path of great losses and disappointments. The distance from one coast to the other established a kind of leverage by which costs, profits, and risks all tended to be much greater in the newer than in the older states: the cost of transportation loomed so large in any enterprise that a slight shift in the price of the product might spell fortune or disaster, and the time that news and goods took to move made for extreme shortages and surpluses. Further, the cost and speed of transportation themselves shifted suddenly, as during the brief interludes of competition and especially when the expanding railroad systems replaced ships and wagon trains. Trade repeatedly went through crises reminiscent of those of gold-rush days in San Francisco, when merchants hastening to import scarce goods found that others had had the same idea and that the most obliging of customers "couldn't or wouldn't wear two pairs of boots, or four pairs of trousers, or three shirts, all at one time, however cheap these articles might be."[7] Yet, in general, trade was more profitable than manufacturing, which repeatedly succumbed to competition from Eastern and foreign producers with lower costs, and which repeatedly tempted new investors impressed by the apparent disparities between the wealth and number of Western consumers and the volume of Western production. Westerners were slow to realize that the unusually high number of persons occupied in the service trades rather than in industry meant not that the economy was on the threshold of a boom in manufacturing, but that society had skipped a few of the usual steps in approximating the shape of the East.

Speculative opportunity meant that some men rose and others fell so suddenly as to suggest a kind of gamblers' democracy; it also made the disparities between success and failure wider than in most new communities. Nowhere else had there been so much precedent for exploiting the public—the public as government extending subsidies or as consumer paying extortionate prices. Legitimate premiums for risks easily and even innocently became illegitimate. In the early years

---

[7] Ernest Seyd: *California and Its Resources* . . . (London: Trübner & Co.; 1858), p. 80.

of American control, distance from old homes and from supplies and markets both increased costs and invited a kind of hit-and-run economy in which wholesalers and agents thousands of miles away rigged prices sharply in their own favor, and in which businessmen on the scene often looked to current profits rather than to solid growth. This was probably truest in the 1850's, when many of the people seemed, as Horace Bushnell put it, passengers only, "adventurers, not emigrants," and California the Ireland of a new American empire. Later, exploitative habits continued in new forms as ranches and businesses became so large that they supported a ruthless kind of resident absenteeism, all the stronger because people had not expected it. Monopolistic control was infinitely more potent in the West than in the East around the turn of the century, Gifford Pinchot recalled. "We had come to regard the West as a place where 'men were men' and everybody was free, in spite of the fact that the big fellow had control of the little fellow to an infinitely greater extent west of the Father of Waters than east of it."[8] And the use of power often suggested neither vision nor generosity. A New England clergyman wrote in 1890 that the ruling sentiment was material aggrandizement. "The dominant passion is not to create wealth, indeed, but to make money, which is a very different thing."[9]

In its most prosperous and supposedly most cultured centers, the coast often seemed dominated by a harsh, narrow materialism. An Emperor Norton might live on the generosity of San Francisco—a derelict who had lost his mind with his money, and whose madness and the deference paid to him amused the tourists—but great and systematic benefactions were few and late and sometimes were popularly regarded as indications of eccentricity, as when James Lick donated an astronomical observatory and Adolph Sutro a garden and museum, or even when Leland and Jane Stanford endowed a university. In general the Californians, who were the richest of the Far Westerners, spent ostentatiously rather than freely or generously; they despised poverty and deferred to wealth with all the vanity of self-made men who like to flatter themselves by their estimates of others.[1] "It is, indeed," wrote

---

[8] Horace Bushnell: *Society and Religion: A Sermon . . .* (San Francisco: Sterett & Co.; 1856), pp. 25–6. Gifford Pinchot: "How Conservation Began in the United States," *Agricultural History* Vol. XI (October 1937), p. 264.

[9] Reverend A. W. Jackson: "New England and California," *New England Magazine,* new series, Vol. I (February 1890), p. 693.

[1] Walter M. Fisher: *The Californians* (London: Macmillan and Company; 1876), pp. 71–2.

a businessman from Illinois who visited California in the 1870's, "hardly an exaggeration to say that the general temper of Western society tends to make its poorer members not only unfortunate but infamous."[2]

Moreover, cultural causes lagged in comparison to the community's means, despite picturesque traditions of San Francisco's devotion to actresses and opera singers, and Salt Lake City's to the drama and choral music. In Utah the Church opposed free public education until it began to fear inroads by gentile missionaries who had opened private schools. The new rich of San Francisco, The *Californian* complained, patronized the arts by buying prodigally to decorate their homes, thus subsidizing "incompetent upstarts"; though they crowded into the operas (as then performed, often a kind of variety show)—and the bar—at the Tivoli, they ignored more serious music. "As for the general public," *The Californian* commented after concerts of the Mendelssohn Quintet Club of Boston in 1881, "in spite of the boasted cosmopolitanism of San Francisco, it is now generally conceded that for music without beer they have no taste."[3] "We live well enough, we summer in Yosemite, we see the *Exposition Internationale* . . . we bet high on the winning horse, we drink more than any people of our size and blow more than any people of our wind," *Overland* concluded (1872), "but our university buildings lie dormant in the quarry, and our Academy of Sciences is hid away in an attic."[4]

Yet relative opportunity, general prosperity, and cultural advance were facts, however short they fell of what many Westerners expected and experienced, however great the range that averages disguised. Success was a major factor in the callousness with which many Westerners regarded failure. In the chaos of nineteenth- and twentieth-century wage scales, Western rates characteristically dipped to or below Eastern rates in bad times and rose above them in good, but the Far Western workingman, urban or rural, generally fared better than his counterparts in other sections. The real incomes of factory workers in the six states, for example, fell within the range of the upper ten or twelve states between 1899 and 1914; the wages of farm laborers within the range of the upper eight in 1910—from $32 to $37 a month with board

---

[2] David L. Phillips: *Letters from California* (Springfield: Illinois State Journal Co.; 1877), p. 139.

[3] C. Merrill Hough: "Two School Systems in Conflict: 1867–1890," *Utah Historical Quarterly*, Vol. XXVIII (April 1960), pp. 113–28. *The Californian*, Vol. III (May, June 1881), pp. 474–5, 571–2.

[4] *Overland Monthly*, Vol. IX (October 1872), p. 375.

when the range in the North Atlantic states was from $18.75 to $25.[5] The community as a whole prospered, even while the general prosperity was almost an affront to those who planted the wrong crops, spent all their savings on railroad fare and worthless land, or worked for a tycoon who had stored up more money than magnanimity as he rose to power.

Along with easy wealth, the West developed at least a tradition of liberality of spirit, perhaps a heritage of the earliest gold-rush days when everyone was young and no one knew who his neighbor had been or might become. "This portion of the world has steep hills," Hittell observed, writing of San Francisco, "and a man on the down track moves very rapidly." Against the disposition of the newly rich to insist on their new status washed the erosion of high wages, migratory habits, and bachelor society, still young and free enough to laugh and hope. In the smaller and stabler communities, it was impossible to forget humble origins even if one would.[6] "Democracy is the ruling social principle," a British visitor to Portland commented in 1879, "on the very natural ground that the most exalted there have risen from obscurity by their own efforts, and, being known to all the old inhabitants, any assumption of stilted pretence would make them target for ridicule."[7]

Out of the jokes fortune played on Westerners in the two or three generations after the gold rush, moreover, a basis for reform eventually emerged. Men who had moved from Beacon Hill to Hardscrabble Farm, or from the saloon to the salon, hoped that their children might go to the museums, theaters, and schools they had known or missed. Vulgarity yearned for culture and acclaim. In the hurly-burly of the frontier it had been easier to learn coarseness than to acquire good breeding, but men who brought out their wives and built homes began to look to their manners and their consciences.

---

[5] Paul F. Brissenden: *Earnings of Factory Workers, 1899 to 1927 . . .*, Census Monographs, Vol. X (Washington: Government Printing Office; 1929), pp. 140–2. *History of Wages in the United States from Colonial Times to 1928*, Bureau of Labor Statistics Bulletin no. 604 (Washington: Government Printing Office; 1934), pp. 228–9 and *passim*. Rates for California are most commonly available.

[6] John S. Hittell: *The Resources of California . . .* (San Francisco: A. L. Bancroft & Co.; 1863), pp. 362–4. A. H. Tevis: *Beyond the Sierras; or, Observations on the Pacific Coast* (Philadelphia: J. B. Lippincott & Co.; 1877), p. 21.

[7] John M. Murphy: *Rambles in North-western America, from the Pacific Ocean to the Rocky Mountains* (London: Chapman & Hall; 1879), p. 47.

VIII

THE PROGRESSIVE MOVEMENT

If abuse provokes political reform, the Far West became ripe for change as early as any part of the country. Touring the West in the eighties, Lord Bryce saw the seeds of future political ills in the prevalent absorption in material development, the "feverish eagerness for quick and showy results." The evil as he saw it was far worse than that railroads abused the public trust: they did so openly, in perfect confidence that no one would challenge them effectively. In San Francisco, where an ex-convict turned preacher was elected mayor because he seemed the underdog in a feud with the publishers of a sensational newspaper that had exposed him, the reformer and social philosopher C. T. Hopkins lamented that businessmen had abandoned politics to the professionals: "We have here no leisure class—men of means and culture, who own allegiance to no other country, and are anxious to benefit the public by their studies, writings, and active participation in public affairs."[1] California's constitution of 1879 was a dead letter in part because Grangers and Workingmen had not known how to anticipate conservative judges; but Bryce's informants told him that instead of asking the courts to curb the powers of the new state Railroad Commission, the railroad magnates had found it cheaper to control the members. A Republican legislature sent President Leland Stanford of the Central Pacific and Southern Pacific to Washington as United States senator; a saloonkeeper, "Chris" Buckley, controlled the Democratic Party and the city of San Francisco in the railroad's interests. In Seattle, businessmen had gone so far in condoning corruption that they feared a change: to attack liquor, gambling, and prostitution was to threaten the whole financial community.[2] In Oregon, recalled Allen H. Eaton, who was a reformer as well as historian of reform, "fraud and force and cunning were for so many years features of . . . politics that they came to be accepted, not only as a part of the game, but by many as the attractive features of the game."[3]

The railroads may have made their hegemony too complete, so that people thought them responsible even for economic and political conditions that were beyond their control—for surpluses of wheat in Europe and for the peccadillos of every city-hall clerk. As William F. Herrin, chief counsel and political adviser for the Southern Pacific, told Lincoln Steffens: "We have to let these little skates get theirs; we have to sit by and see them run riot and take risks that risk our interests, too."[4] Probably the railroad erred in permitting its men in the California legislature to elect Stanford to the Senate; he was both too well known in the company and too unskilled in politics. The railroad's reputation suffered also when Senator John H. Mitchell, one of four members of the law firm that represented the railroad's interests in Oregon, offended the silverites by shifting from silver to gold and then

---

[1] James Bryce: *The American Commonwealth* (London: The Macmillan Company; 1889), Vol. II, pp. 372, 388, 689–90. C. T. Hopkins: "The Present Crisis in San Francisco," *The Californian*, Vol. I (May 1880), p. 411.

[2] Alexander Callow, Jr.: "San Francisco's Blind Boss," *Pacific Historical Review*, Vol. XXV (August 1956), pp. 261–79. Robert C. Nesbit: *"He Built Seattle." A Biography of Judge Thomas Burke* (Seattle: University of Washington Press; 1961), pp. 364–5.

[3] Allen H. Eaton: *The Oregon System . . .* (Chicago: A. C. McClurg & Co.; 1912), p. 3.

[4] *The Autobiography of Lincoln Steffens* (New York: Harcourt, Brace & Co.; 1931), Vol. II, p. 567.

was convicted of taking bribes in land frauds. Perhaps the S. P. was destined to suffer for supporting one of the rival coastal towns as the seaport of Los Angeles, which had never quite forgiven the railroad for accepting the subsidy that brought it there and made the city.

While becoming general scapegoats, the railroads especially aroused men who disliked paying high fares and high freight charges for poor service and seeing privilege subvert decency and popular control in government. Claus Spreckels, the sugar-beet refiner, fought the sugar trust and fought the railroad, financing two competitive lines; he fought the San Francisco Gas and Electric Company, which corrupt politicians associated with the railroad had helped to entrench. His sons too contributed heavily to the movement to drive the Southern Pacific out of politics in California on essentially moral grounds.

In the early years of the new century, when distaste for the methods and morals of machine politics ran high all over the country, few states were ahead of those on the Pacific slope in conditions that historians of the progressive movement have cited as predisposing electorates to interest in reform. The six states as a group were substantially more urban and less agricultural than the nation; even in the more rural states, settlement was concentrated, to an unusual degree, within easy reach of urban centers, as in the Willamette Valley, whose one hundred and twenty miles contained most of the people of Oregon. Although the average density of population in the Far West was still low, the traveler along the thirteen-hundred-mile route from Seattle to Los Angeles passed through five of the thirty-two largest cities in the United States. There were far fewer slums, urban or rural, in the West than in the East, Middle West, or South; the ratios of unskilled labor to skilled and of employment in industry to employment in the service trades and professions were unusually low. The occupational patterns were those of a mature and prosperous society, even though the economy was still rapidly expanding and had yet to tap some of its major opportunities. Not only was there less ignorance for demagogues to prey on than one might have expected from the large number of foreign born unskilled workers—the rates of illiteracy were lower than in any other six states put together—but educational achievement and cultural activity were unusually high. The typical Far Westerner lived within the delivery area of a daily newspaper; his children went to high school and could go to college by riding for no more than a few minutes on an interurban railway.

An electorate drawn from such a population—relatively independent economically, literate, and within easy reach of itself and of information and ideas—was not likely to tolerate indefinitely the political dominion of monopolists and grafters who catered to the newly rich and the ignorant poor. Throughout much of the Far West the social classes at either extreme of the scale seemed to have fared better than those in the middle—disproportionate rewards went to men who soiled their hands or their consciences. In the mines, on the ranches, and in the transportation systems, newly emerged capitalists and speculators edged aside the prudent small investors; C. Wright Mills concluded that the West stood out as the only section of the United States in which the business elite was drawn more from the lower classes than from the upper classes who were born there. It must have been hard for those Westerners who represented the upper cultural strata to see at supposedly select gatherings persons who (in the words of a New Englander who published an exposé of the fashionable set in San Francisco) "in New England would be considered unfit for decent society,"[5] to watch former saloonkeepers on Nob Hill or in city hall. Yet the reformers, when they eventually emerged, were men who personally had fared well, and their spirit was fundamentally optimistic.

The Western towns supplied the spurs to inquiry and to conscience familiar in the Northeastern and Middle Western communities from which most of their leaders had come. Chautauqua assemblies appeared in the 1880's and soon associated themselves with the colleges more than with the churches. Although the Far Western universities were notoriously conventional in curricula, some members of their faculties actively examined and questioned the social order. These included, at the University of Washington, Dean J. Allen Smith, whom a Populist president appointed (1897) after he lost his job in Ohio for supporting Bryan in 1896, whose *Spirit of American Government* (1907) anticipated the arguments of Charles A. Beard, and whom Harold Laski later called the only twentieth-century American political scientist whose works were seriously relevant to the contemporary scene; at the University of Oregon, Dean Frederic G. Young, founder of the *Oregon Historical Quarterly* (editor, 1900–28) and of the annual Com-

[5] C. Wright Mills: "The American Business Elite: A Collective Portrait," *Journal of Economic History*, supplement V (December 1945), pp. 25, 41. Addison Awes: *Why a Rich Yankee Did Not Settle in California* (Boston: Cubery & Co.; 1900), p. 12.

monwealth Conferences (1909) for the examination of public questions;[6] at Stanford, more briefly, until they trespassed too far on orthodoxy and on the inclinations of some trustees toward a vocational school rather than a university, Edward A. Ross (1866–1951), who worked there on *Social Control* (1901), and Thorstein Veblen (1857–1929),[7] author of *The Theory of the Leisure Class* (1902) and *The Theory of Business Enterprise* (1904).

By most fiscal criteria, education enjoyed fuller public support than in most states, new or old. In 1910 five of the six Far Western states ranked within the first seven of the nation in per capita expenses for education. Teachers' salaries tended to be high: of twelve American cities where elementary teachers averaged over $1,000 a year in 1912–13, seven were in California, and one each was in Oregon and Washington.[8] Expenditures did not guarantee results, but they indicated faith, comparable perhaps to the faith that led Westerners to irrigate desert farmlands. The colleges developed and prospered more unevenly, though again support was relatively generous: on the whole, it is more remarkable that they grew as much and as well as they did than that they sometimes grew in questionable directions.

On a map, Far Western political insurgency coincided closely with the incidence of interest in educational advance, of prior movements for social reform, and of New England conscience and religion. (Utah was an exception in these as in other matters: persisting tensions between Mormon and gentile and the hardships of finding a living in the desert had blighted early hopes for education; the University of Utah was one of the weakest as well as the earliest [1850] of the state universities west of the Missouri River. By the early 1900's, Utah was

[6] Eric F. Goldman: "J. Allen Smith; the Reformer and His Dilemma," *Pacific Northwest Quarterly*, Vol. XXXV (July 1944), pp. 195–214. Howard E. Dean: "J. Allen Smith: Jeffersonian Critic of the Federalist State," *American Political Science Review*, Vol. L (December 1956), pp. 1093–1104. Thomas C. McClintock: "J. Allen Smith, A Pacific Northwest Progressive," *Pacific Northwest Quarterly*, Vol. LIII (April 1962), pp. 49–59. George Frykman: "Frederic G. Young, Regionalist and Historian," *Pacific Northwest Quarterly*, Vol. XLVIII (April 1957), pp. 33–8.

[7] Ross and Veblen were at Stanford respectively from 1893 to 1900 and from 1906 to 1909.

[8] Mabel Newcomer: *Financial Statistics of Public Education in the United States, 1910–1920* . . . (New York: The Macmillan Company; 1924), p. 48. *A Comparative Study of the Salaries of Teachers and School Officers*, U. S. Bureau of Education, *Bulletin*, 1915, no. 31 (Washington: Government Printing Office; 1915), pp. 110–2.

staunchly orthodox in politics in relation to her neighbors, although she joined them in giving votes to women and in suppressing the liquor traffic.[9]) Utah, Washington, and Idaho were the only states in the country where either major party ventured to declare for prohibition before its adoption. In Oregon the local option had appealed as a means of cleaning up municipal politics more than as a step toward prohibition, but by 1910 the People's Progressive Government League favored state-wide prohibition. In California, where the wine-producing and Latin counties held the prohibitionists off until the passage of the eighteenth amendment, they were strong in the staunchly Protestant southern-Californian communities, including Los Angeles, which drew their populations from prohibitionist states[1] and "came out" also for political reform.

The most obvious continuity betwen nineteenth- and twentieth-century reform movements probably appeared in Oregon, where William S. U'Ren led first the Populist Party and then the Republican Party as the most promising vehicles for electoral reforms. Religious mystic, single taxer, and prohibitionist, U'Ren moved over a wide range of ethical enthusiasms without disengaging himself from the priorities of practical politics;[2] the development of the "Oregon system" paralleled his tireless efforts at political propaganda and political manipulation. But the link between old and new causes was not just one man: the farmers of Oregon found a strong appeal in the idea of direct legislation, either because they remembered the direct democracy of the New England states from which many of them came or because congregational ties were strong in the rural districts. Oregon farmers were at once more rural than the absentee owners of the bonanza farms of California—and so more prone to resent the power of metropolitan wealth in business and politics—and more urban than the corn and wheat farmers of the western Mississippi Valley, and thus naturally conversant with

[9] Idaho and Utah were, in fact, the first two of the six to adopt woman suffrage (1896), well before Washington (1910), California (1911), Oregon (1912), and Nevada (1914); but in Mormon country suffrage had been, from the gentile point of view, a bulwark of polygamy rather than a step toward progressivism. Prohibition came late to Utah, in 1918.

[1] John E. Caswell: "The Prohibition Movement in Oregon . . . ," *Oregon Historical Quarterly*, Vol. XL (March 1939), pp. 65, 75. E. P. Clarke: "Prohibition in Southern California," *Overland Monthly*, second series, Vol. XV (April 1890), p. 377.

[2] Robert C. Woodward: "W. S. U'Ren and the Single Tax in Oregon," *Oregon Historical Quarterly*, Vol. LXI (March 1960), pp. 46–63. Woodward: "William S. U'Ren, A Progressive Era Personality," *Idaho Yesterdays*, Vol. IV (Summer 1960), pp. 4–10.

ideas and movements in the valley towns. For a large part of the population of the state, in fact, conditions were similar to those of the socially critical mass in the urbanized rural community or the small city, which was literate enough and of sufficient size to generate activity, but small enough to concentrate activity in groups that could debate issues among themselves. Portland was large enough to stimulate and arouse its neighbors, but not large enough to stifle them or siphon off their residents as mere commuters. Although some of the chief spokesmen for reform were or had been members of the alliances and the People's Party, most of them lived near Portland, like U'Ren himself, or his partners, the Lewellings (who were not ordinary farmers but nurserymen, well known as hybridizers), or the members of the large Swiss colony in Milwaukie, who knew of direct legislation in the old country. Oregonians had used the referendum for limited purposes, chiefly within the towns and counties, since statehood; and one of the leaders of the Direct Legislation League had proposed it on a broader basis in the constitutional convention of 1857. The farmers' interest in the new devices of popular control followed on suspicions of elected officers that their grandfathers had written into the state constitution in 1857, suspicions that seemed justified when in the 1890's and early 1900's both state and national legislators showed themselves to be unworthy. Dissatisfaction with elected officers and restlessness under party discipline were endemic; factions of the Republican Party sometimes supported the Democratic opposition, so that Republicans held the governorship for only eight years out of twenty-eight (1887–1915), and no Republican governor succeeded himself before 1919, whereas during the same years a Democratic presidential candidate carried the state only once, in 1912, when the Republicans had split.

When the reporters from national magazines interviewed U'Ren at his modest home at Oregon City and asked him about the movement for direct legislation, he always denied that the credit was chiefly his. Perhaps he was maintaining a useful illusion, for he gained most by quietly persuading rather than by seeking publicity and office for himself, though publicity he had, and both admirers and enemies quoted the jibe of Harvey Scott, publisher of the *Oregonian,* that Oregon had two governments, one in Salem and one under U'Ren's hat. Perhaps he recognized the multiple origins of a movement that owed much, as William Allen White later recalled, to little Roosevelts and little La Follettes all over the land. By the 1890's, Oregonians of widely varying sentiments had lost faith in established legislative processes and in the established organs of the Republican, Democratic, and Populist parties, as the politics of electing United States senators increasingly interfered with ordinary legislative business. Jonathan Bourne, a wealthy attorney and mineowner, became conspicuous as a supporter of John H. Mitchell, one of the most notorious of the railroad senators.[3] When Mitchell rejected the cause of free silver, Bourne turned against him and, lacking enough votes to elect himself or some other candidate, kept the legislature of 1897 from organizing; for weeks he provided food and lodging for members whose absence prevented a quorum. U'Ren then demonstrated his characteristic versatility by allying himself with Bourne, the "prince of hold-ups," who opened his purse to the cause of superseding the machinery he had manipulated. The reformers sponsored a constitutional amendment for the initiative and referendum, which the voters approved in 1902.[4]

Once the legislature's monopoly on legislation was gone, further reforms followed in increasing volume. Some of the best-known and most distinctive were procedural, including the direct primary and an ingenious device by which the constitutional process of electing United States senators in the state legislature became little more than a ceremonial ratification of the people's choice. In 1906 Bourne himself ran for the Senate as a Republican; he conducted an "educational" campaign in which he addressed himself by mail to the voters, first explaining the new procedure and then appealing for their support against the candidate of the party machine. He won despite strong opposition from the old guard, and became known as the first senator elected by the people. Thus the legislature both lost and gained power: it became free of a responsibility, largely irrelevant to its other functions, that had corrupted and monopolized entire sessions, and it was encouraged to carry out the will of the people rather than of the railroads and the other interests that had dominated it. Meanwhile the stream of reform had broadened to include substantial social and economic legislation, such as the two measures that Louis D. Brandeis defended as Oregon's

---

[3] Mitchell (senator in 1873–9, 1885–97, 1901–5) and his partner, Joseph N. Dolph (senator in 1883–95), had been railroad lawyers from the 1860's. Dolph failed of reelection in 1895, when Bourne opposed him. In 1905 Mitchell was convicted of receiving fees for expediting land claims. Both often supported liberal measures; Mitchell approved the Oregon system.

[4] Albert H. Pike, Jr.: "Jonathan Bourne, Jr., Progressive" (unpublished doctoral thesis, University of Oregon; 1957).

representative before the Supreme Court of the United States in 1908 and 1914: the limitation of the working day for women to ten hours (1903) and the establishment of a state Industrial Welfare Commission with power to set minimum wages for women (1913). The second followed a survey of working conditions by a young social worker from Chicago, Caroline Gleason (later Sister Miriam Theresa, professor of sociology at Marylhurst College). Voting directly on a total of one hundred and seven measures in six elections, the people provided for regulation of the liquor traffic by local option (1904), prohibited the issue of free passes on railroads, established taxes on various utility companies (1906), regulated freight rates (1912), and established an Industrial Accident Commission (1913).

Much of this great outpouring of legislation may have been ill conceived and poorly drafted; occasionally, dishonest men wrested from the people, Allen Eaton admitted, "the tools which we so laboriously fashioned to protect ourselves." Yet a new spirit had entered the commonwealth. To Frederick C. Howe, who in *Hampton's Magazine* described Oregon as "the most complete democracy in the world," its most impressive feature was the dedication with which the people took up their responsibilities, studied their voters' pamphlets and decided on issues and candidates on the basis of objective evidence. "For two months," he wrote, "Oregon is turned into a university, where every whole community is being trained to a knowledge of politics." A study of the distribution of votes on progressive measures showed remarkable consensus between rich and poor, country and city.[5] Although the voters had seemed at the outset to do U'Ren's bidding like automatons, they demonstrated their independence by rejecting repeatedly the single tax, for whose sake he had become interested in direct legislation. In 1908 they chose a Republican legislature but a progressive Democratic senator, Governor George Chamberlain, defeating the Republican candidate whom U'Ren had supported in the primary, and the legislature obediently went through the form of electing Chamberlain. In 1910 they elected as governor another progressive Democrat, Oswald West, an ardent moralist and advocate of penal reform and of conservation.

---

[5] Eaton: *Oregon System,* p. 159. Frederick C. Howe: "Oregon, the Most Complete Democracy in the World," *Hampton's Magazine,* Vol. XXVI (April 1911), p. 467. William F. Ogburn and Delvin Patterson: "Political Thought of Social Classes," *Political Science Quarterly,* Vol. XXXI (June 1916), pp 300–17.

And in 1912 they retired Bourne himself from the Senate. "There has been a vitality, a genuineness in Oregon politics," George H. Haynes wrote in the *Political Science Quarterly* (1911), "sharply in contrast with the state campaigns in many of the eastern states."[6]

By that time California seemed to be awakening in the same spirit, politically speaking. The Southern Pacific Railroad was the great corporate antagonist; the Republican Party was the principal vehicle of reform; the principal instruments again became devices for popular participation in government that tended to destroy party discipline and responsibility. And one man dominated the movement: Hiram W. Johnson, a lawyer who became governor in 1911.

The origins of the progressive movement in California corresponded closely to the shape and strains of a rapidly growing urban society. Most of its leaders were men of substantial income and education who rebelled at the political and economic consequences of irresponsible corporate power. Dr. John R. Haynes of Los Angeles, who founded the Direct Legislation League (1895) to challenge the railroad's municipal machine, was a physician, a millionaire, a director in several corporations. The two reform mayors of San Francisco in the 1890's—a Populist and a Democrat—also were millionaires: Adolph Sutro, who had built the tunnel draining the Comstock Lode, and James D. Phelan, banker and heir to a great banking fortune. William Kent, who became probably the most progressive member of Congress from the Far West, had made his fortune in real estate in Chicago. Haynes, Phelan, and Rudolph Spreckels, another San Francisco banker and capitalist, contributed heavily to the costs of the progressives' battles for reform in their respective cities.

Such men as these, both wealthy and sensitive to the opportunities and obligations of wealth, may not have suffered much from personal frustrations, economic or social. But neither they nor the men of more moderate means who dominated the progressive movement could ignore the excesses of big business and labor and the strains between them. Progressives in Los Angeles opposed Harrison Gray Otis and the *Los Angeles Times* and also shared some of Otis's fears of organized labor. In San Francisco, labor developed a powerful distrust of reformers when Mayor Phelan's policemen rode with strike-breaking teamsters

[6] Randall R. Howard: "The Governor's Honor Men," *Outlook*, Vol. CI (July 27, 1912), pp. 716–24. Haynes: "People's Rule in Oregon, 1910," *Political Science Quarterly*, Vol. XXVI (March 1911), p. 62.

in 1901. Then the reformers in turn rebelled against Abe Ruef, boss of the Union Labor Party, who installed Eugene Schmitz, a handsome orchestra leader, as mayor to succeed Phelan and who openly collaborated with the Southern Pacific machine. Their most persuasive exhibit was a widely published photograph, captioned "The Shame of California," of the leaders at the Republican state convention at Santa Cruz in 1906: the railroad's choice for the governorship, Representative James N. Gillett, stood in the center with his hand resting on the shoulder of Ruef, who had received $14,000 for supporting him.[7]

The convention that carried out the railroad's orders had hardly adjourned before the scope of misgovernment in San Francisco began to become generally visible, whether because disorders following the earthquake and fire of the preceding April had uncovered it or merely because the appetites of Ruef's minions had extended it. Just after the elections that November, a grand jury filed the first indictments against Ruef and Schmitz. And during the following winter, investigations of graft at San Francisco vied for headlines with the flagrant thievery of the machine's agents and collaborators at Sacramento in the legislature of 1907. The graft trials produced two colorful figures who dramatized the issues of reform: Francis J. Heney, the deputy district attorney, who had already made a reputation by prosecuting Senator Mitchell and others for fraud in Oregon, and Hiram W. Johnson, who became special prosecutor in November 1908, when an ex-convict shot and nearly killed Heney in the courtroom. The trials also produced a victory for the reformers in the municipal election of 1907, at a time when a seven-month-long streetcar strike, one of the most violent in American labor history, aroused labor against one of the corporations with which Ruef and the Union Labor administration had been cooperating. Full of confidence, Heney went on to turn his attention to the bribe-givers, who included President Patrick Calhoun of the United Railroads.[8]

The prosecutors were too effective to achieve lasting reform in San Francisco. A substantial part of the labor movement had been reluctant from the beginning to accept the charges against Schmitz, perhaps because it feared that employers might make larger uses of the trials or perhaps because it admired the handsome mayor and rejoiced in his rise from the ranks; the Building Trades Council had denounced the

---

[7] George E. Mowry: *The California Progressives* (Berkeley: University of California Press; 1951), pp. 59–60.

[8] Bean: *Boss Ruef's San Francisco,* pp. 240–3, 256–99.

prosecution in 1906. (At Stanford, Thorstein Veblen told a colleague that he was not interested in the trials, "that they were a move of the middle class directed against the workers.")[9] Labor's attitude changed for a time as Heney accumulated irrefutable evidence, and union leaders pointed out correctly enough that the Union Labor Party was misnamed, that it had no connection with the Labor Council or its member unions. Then their doubts revived. And when the continuation of the trials became the main issue in the municipal elections of 1909, Heney as candidate of the Good Government League for district attorney lost disastrously to the anti-prosecution candidate of the Union Labor and Republican parties, Charles Fickert, and the successful Union Labor candidate for mayor, P. H. McCarthy, promised a "tolerant" administration that would restore the "get-together spirit" and make San Francisco "the Paris of America." "In San Francisco," Chester Rowell, progressive editor and politician, wrote later, "our class got possession of the government and then the lower class proceeded to combine with the upper class against the middle class in order to take the government from them again." In his view, the collectivists in labor understood the collectivism of capital better than they understood the individualism of reform; perhaps they remembered more clearly than their betters how recently some of their fellows had moved from south of Market Street to Nob Hill and the rich men's clubs.[1] In a state that only a few years earlier, during the gold rush, had seemed to reenact the social contract and approach an ideal democracy, civic virtue seemed limited to the hope that partners in crime would not stand together—not that the classes at the extremes of society would reform, but that government might fall to the one class that cherished the welfare of the commonwealth.

Yet insurgency had tapped broad streams of sentiment and support that converged between 1906 and 1910, in and out of San Francisco. Resistance to the railroad never had quite disappeared since the 1870's; it became formidable in the 1890's, extending into both major parties. Anti-railroad Democratic candidates almost won the governorship twice—in 1902 and again in 1906, when many Republicans resented the methods used in nominating Gillett. That same year, disclosures of the machine's arrogance in Los Angeles prompted a group of business and

[9] Joseph Dorfman: *Thorstein Veblen and His America* (New York: Viking Press; 1934), p. 273.

[1] Frederick Palmer: "San Francisco of the Closed Shop," *Hampton's Magazine,* Vol. XXVI (February 1911), pp. 223–7. Rowell in *Pacific Outlook,* Vol. X (January 7, 1911), p. 9.

professional men to present a non-partisan slate in the city election; having elected two thirds of their candidates, they prepared to elect a Good Government candidate as mayor in 1909. When a League of Lincoln-Roosevelt Republican Clubs (generally known as the Lincoln-Roosevelt League) organized at Oakland in August 1907, it drew on leaders of municipal insurgency in both San Francisco and Los Angeles, including some who had supported the Democratic candidate, Bell, against Gillett in 1906. In San Francisco, leaders of the League backed the Democratic candidate for mayor in 1907 and 1909. And though McCarthy and Fickert turned away from reform locally, the Lincoln-Roosevelt League captured the state Republican organization and found its leader for state-wide reform in the graft trials: it nominated Hiram Johnson for the governorship in 1910. Campaigning throughout the state in a red roadster with a brass bell to draw the crowds at crossroad stops, he attacked the Southern Pacific and its allies as vigorously as he had prosecuted Ruef and Schmitz, and with much broader consequences. His victory that fall changed the course of California politics for half a century or more.

For a time some progressives feared that, having had principles, but uneven success in selling them to the voters, they had found a leader who would not know where to take them. In the campaign, Johnson dwelt on his promise to "kick the Southern Pacific Railroad out of politics" and on the corrupting influences of two newspaper publishers, Otis and William Randolph Hearst, almost to the exclusion of platform promises that leaders of the Lincoln-Roosevelt had written pledging direct legislation, regulation of public utilities, employers' liability for industrial accidents, and protection for the rights of collective bargaining, among other progressive measures. There was little in his record to go on, since he had not held state office. "If you are going to write about me," he once told a reporter, "you won't have to go back of 1910."[2]

Actually, even Johnson's chief supporters, the leaders of the League, had had few occasions to show their hand. Most of them were outsiders denouncing the morals of insiders, and moreover, they were newcomers to politics; those who had served in the legislature had seemed concerned chiefly with ethical and procedural issues, and much of the initiative for the program of economic and social reform in the spirit

[2] Mowry: *California Progressives*, pp. 45–52, 124–33. Edward G. Lowry: *Washington Close-ups; Intimate Views of Some Public Figures* (Boston: Houghton Mifflin Co.; 1921), p. 55.

of Theodore Roosevelt's New Nationalism came from pressure groups such as the State Federation of Labor and from officers of state agencies. Recalling Phelan's strikebreakers in San Francisco and the anti-picketing legislation of Los Angeles, labor could not know what to expect from reformers in Sacramento, though Johnson himself had had congenial enough relations with labor in his private legal practice, serving as counsel for several unions. His attacks on the publishers from the stump were at the least confusing, for to most laboring men Hearst seemed almost as friendly as Otis seemed hostile. Further, Johnson had found his strongest support in southern California, where the leading reformers placed little trust in organized labor. During the campaign, which coincided with the height of the drive for the union shop in southern California, the Los Angeles City Council, elected on a Good Government ticket in 1909, adopted an extreme anti-picketing ordinance; five weeks before election, tension increased with the bombing of the *Times* building. Fear of violence and fear of a Socialist victory in the municipal election of 1911 prompted the Good Government group to cooperate with men who were anathema to labor and even hostile to reform itself.[3]

But if the California progressives seemed intent above all on purifying politics by checking combinations at the extremes of society that threatened to displace government's legal constituency, nevertheless the progressive regime that took power in 1911 soon also took up the larger tasks of the New Nationalism. Meyer Lissner, chairman of the Republican state central committee, had so feared that the new administration would have no program that he appointed committees to plan the work of the legislature. But soon he and other southern Californian progressives were opposing a bill to limit the working day for women to eight hours, which Johnson signed along with bills for a strengthened railroad commission, employers' liability, free textbooks for public schools, conservation, local option, and other measures that Theodore Roosevelt called "the most comprehensive program of constructive legislation ever passed at a single session of any American legislature."[4]

---

[3] Mowry: *California Progressives*, pp. 42–52. Gerald D. Nash: "Bureaucracy and Economic Reform: The Experience of California, 1899–1911," *Western Political Quarterly*, Vol. XIII (September 1960), pp. 678–91. Grace H. Stimson: *Rise of the Labor Movement in Los Angeles* (Berkeley: University of California Press; 1955), pp. 322–3, 343, 346.

[4] Mowry: *California Progressives*, pp. 135–57. *San Francisco Chronicle*, August 7, 1945, p. 10, col. 4.

Constitutional amendments included provisions for the regulation of public utilities, the initiative, referendum, and recall, and woman suffrage. The legislature of 1913 went still further; it established commissions with jurisdiction over conservation, industrial accidents, industrial welfare, and immigration and housing. In 1915 there followed legislation to encourage cooperative marketing and to establish a commission on colonization and rural credits. No other large state had accepted so boldly, Herbert Croly said in 1914, the whole progressive program of political and economic reform.[5]

In the state of Washington, the Republican Party was again the principal vehicle of progressive reform, though farm and labor organizations contributed more support than in California. The heavy-handed influence of railroads evoked both regulatory measures and a movement for direct legislation. The railroads had succeeded in confining the Populist governor, John R. Rogers (1897–1901), to reforms no more dangerous than support of public schools and economy in state government. When Rogers's successor, Governor Henry McBride, persuaded the state Republican convention of 1902 to promise a railroad commission, the railroads first defeated the bill in the legislature and then defeated McBride himself for renomination at the next convention. But they had gone too far. The new legislature went ahead to establish a commission (1905), and a Direct Primary League led the State Grange and State Federation of Labor in a vigorous fight for a primary law, adopted in 1907.[6]

Like San Francisco and Los Angeles, Seattle blew hot and cold on reform. The city had adopted Reginald Thomson's municipal water and power project in 1895 with the support of the Populists and against the opposition of the Seattle Power Company; it went so far as to authorize municipal ownership of the transit system (1896) and the recall of elected officials (1906). In 1904 the people elected a reform mayor, Richard A. Ballinger. But six years later Hiram C. Gill was mayor,

[5] Frances Cahn and Valeska Bary: *Welfare Activities of Federal, State, and Local Governments in California, 1850–1934* (Berkeley: University of California Press; 1936), pp. xiv–xix. Grace Larsen: "A Progressive in Agriculture: Harris Weinstock," *Agricultural History*, Vol. XXXII (July 1958), pp. 187–93. Herbert Croly to Chester Rowell, Sept. 10, 1914 (Rowell papers, Bancroft Library).

[6] Keith Murray: "Republican Party Politics in Washington during the Progressive Era" (unpublished doctoral thesis, University of Washington; 1946). Winston B. Thorson: "Washington State Nominating Conventions," *Pacific Northwest Quarterly*, Vol. XXXV (April 1944), pp. 111–6, 118.

victor on a platform that frankly promised to wink at graft and prostitution; he shortly became known (in the words of the *Pacific Monthly*) as "the most active public servant of private monopoly and vice entrenched city government," having established a "restricted district" and named a new superintendent for the city electric-light plant from the ranks of the company. Within months the voters recalled him (February 1911).[7]

By that time the state as a whole was in an actively progressive mood. A special legislative session in 1909 investigated irregularities in state government. In 1910, progressive candidates carried both the Republican primaries and the general election outside of Seattle, which returned the one "System Congressman" of the delegation; and a conference of farmers, trade unionists, and progressives formed the Direct Legislation League, enlisting the help of U'Ren and Bourne from Oregon. Under such pressure the legislature of 1911 proposed the initiative and referendum, which the people adopted the next year, and passed substantial bills for workmen's compensation and the eight-hour day for women.[8]

The states in the interior never developed comparable progressive movements and programs, although they did not lack social and political tension. Utah had been the first Far Western state to adopt the initiative and referendum (1900), but thereafter it stood apart, perhaps because its politics were still both conservative and respectable. "Utah is satisfied to let well enough alone," *Sunset* observed in 1914. Neither did William E. Borah, whose posture in the United States Senate eventually coupled him in the national news with Hiram Johnson and Robert M. La Follette, play the role in Idaho that they played in California and Wisconsin. He had bolted the party to support Bryan in 1896, but strictly on the issue of free silver, which most Republicans in Idaho favored. When, in consequence of this irregularity, he failed to get a senatorship from the legislature of 1903, he resorted to the party conventions rather than to Oregon's system of approximating direct election of senators. He campaigned for the Senate on the issues of prosperity and law and order

---

[7] Robert C. Nesbit: *He Built Seattle: A Biography of Judge Thomas Burke* (Seattle: University of Washington Press; 1961), pp. 374–6, 377–80. *Pacific Monthly*, Vol. XXVI (July, August 1911), pp. 2–3, 117–30.

[8] Keith A. Murray: "The Aberdeen Convention of 1912," *Pacific Northwest Quarterly*, Vol. XXXVIII (April 1947), p. 100. *La Follette's Weekly Magazine*, Vol. II (November 19, 1910), p. 7. Claudius O. Johnson: "The Adoption of the Initiative and Referendum in Washington," *Pacific Northwest Quarterly*, Vol. XXXV (October 1944), pp. 291–303.

and served after his election in 1906 as special prosecutor in the trial of William D. Haywood of the Western Federation of Miners (1907); he was himself a prosperous corporation lawyer and disappointing to most progressives on issues of conservation and seemed so respectable that Senator Aldrich and the conservatives were glad to give him important assignments to committees.[9] Shortly Borah began to make a different kind of record nationally, but in the presidential election of 1912, when progressive Republicans dominated Washington and California and a progressive Democrat served as governor of Oregon, Taft ran ahead of Roosevelt in Idaho as well as in Utah (which with Vermont, Brigham Young's birthplace, gave Taft his only electoral votes).[1]

Well before 1912, the Western progressives had begun to transfer their interests from state to nation. On the whole, they first looked eastward less because they had exhausted the competence of state legislatures in specific reforms than because the spectacle of progressivism already at work in the national government had quickened their hopes for similar reform at home and kindled the personal ambitions of their leaders for national office. Their principal steps to regulate railroads in the states followed rather than preceded the first effective national regulation of freight rates through the Hepburn and Elkins acts (1906, 1910). Further, although Oregon, Washington, Idaho, Utah, and Nevada had prohibited the sale of liquor (1914–8) before the adoption of the eighteenth amendment, they did so after the peaks of their progressive movements, and the largest popular majority for prohibition was in Utah, the most conservative of the Far Western states; California remained wet until Congress acted. (The California progressives thought it expedient in 1910 to give the nomination for lieutenant governor to Albert J. Wallace, president of the Anti-Saloon League of California and a Methodist minister, who had a loyal following in the southern counties, but Hiram Johnson thought him a bore and a drag in the campaign;

---

[9] *Sunset*, Vol. XXXIII (November 1914), p. 864. Claudius O. Johnson: "When William E. Borah Was Defeated for the United States Senate," *Pacific Historical Review*, Vol. XII (June 1943), pp. 125–38; and "William E. Borah: the People's Choice," *Pacific Northwest Quarterly*, Vol. XLIV (January 1953), pp. 15–22. David H. Grover: "Borah and the Haywood Trial," *Pacific Historical Review*, Vol. XXXII (February 1963), pp. 65–77. Merle W. Wells: "Fred T. Dubois and the Idaho Progressives, 1900–1914," *Idaho Yesterdays*, Vol. IV (Summer 1960), pp. 24–31.

[1] The percentages of popular votes cast for Roosevelt in 1912 were: California, 42.09%; Idaho, 24.14%; Nevada, 27.94%; Oregon, 27.44%; Utah, 21.51%; and Washington, 35.22%.

Chester Rowell called him "a very good man of the Sunday School type."[2])

The Californians had shown their interest in national politics when they organized in 1907 as the Lincoln-Roosevelt League and called for the nomination either of Roosevelt himself for a third term or of a candidate pledged to his policies. That was before they had gained control of even one city or indicated what they proposed to do in the government of the state except to free it from the control of the railroad. Progressive candidates for Congress displaced conservatives in California, Idaho, Oregon, and Washington in 1910, when California and Washington were just joining Oregon in progressive state government. Among the fifty signers of the announcement of the National Progressive Republican League in 1911, seven, including Jonathan Bourne, its president, were from the coast. The Far Westerners were among the most advanced in the national movement, at once zealous for the nomination of Roosevelt or La Follette and indisposed to truckle to them. C. E. S. Wood of Portland, for example, wrote that "Roosevelt owes his strength to the rebellion of the masses of the American people. The movement does not owe its strength to him."[3] When the new Progressive Party nominated Hiram Johnson for the vice presidency the next year, it was in fitting recognition of Johnson's leadership at Chicago—it was he among prominent progressives who first called for a new party and he who addressed the delegates who were preparing to form it—and also of the advanced positions of Johnson and the Californians in general.

Already the drift of the leaders to Congress had begun. Bourne had become well known as a progressive in Oregon only when he conducted his "educational compaign" to teach the voters the intricacies of the Oregon system and specifically the means for instructing the legislature to elect him to the Senate in 1906. Mrs. Hiram Johnson had consented to her husband's running for governor in 1910 only when friends had persuaded her that Sacramento was a way station to Washington. None who went to Congress succeeded in maintaining thereafter the kind of organization in his state that the La Follettes maintained in Wisconsin for two generations: Borah held his following without reference to affairs at Boise; Bourne innocently or carelessly neglected to

---

[2] Gilman M. Ostrander: *The Prohibition Movement in California, 1848–1933* (Berkeley: University of California Press; 1957), pp. 106, 115.

[3] *La Follette's Weekly Magazine,* Vol. II (November 12, 1910), pp. 5, 6; Vol. III (February 4, 1911), pp. 8–9. *Pacific Monthly,* Vol. XXV (January 1911), p. 106.

organize at all, and so lost his seat after one term and did not return either to Congress or to Oregon; Johnson trained the voters to reelect him regularly, but not his friends at home.

Yet few Westerners went to Congress with much of a program to advance. Eventually Bourne catered to the farmers' demands for help in reaching markets by pressing for the parcel-post law of 1912 and, after his term expired, for a federal road-building program. While he was in the Senate, he made himself the national exponent of the Oregon system of popular government, but probably did most to advance it by persuading the legislatures of Oregon and other states to adopt the presidential primary system: in this respect he spoke from Congress rather than acted through it. In his enthusiasm for applying "business principles to the conduct of the government,"[4] he probably appealed as much to old-guard conservative as to progressive interests. Both Bourne and Borah were sharply critical of national bureaucratic power; and because they went to Washington after free silver had ceased to be an issue, neither was able in the Senate to advance the monetary ideas that had preoccupied them in Oregon and Idaho.

During the administrations of Roosevelt and Taft, the Western progressives in Congress found the issues of the tariff and conservation particularly embarrassing. Bourne and Borah, among other Westerners, supported the Payne-Aldrich Tariff of 1909, apparently in exchange for favors that the conservatives extended to Western products, such as lumber. In the main, the progressives of the coastal states were conservationists. Johnson in California, West in Oregon, and Poindexter in Washington appealed to supporters of Roosevelt's and Pinchot's policies; progressive legislation in both California and Oregon established conservation commissions, and the first secretary of the California Commission was Louis R. Glavis, hero (to the conservationists) of the Ballinger-Pinchot controversy. But the conservationists and their helpers and critics were both progressive and conservative: the Southern Pacific had helped in the enlargement of Yosemite National Park through the influence of John Muir, a friend of E. H. Harriman; in the Northwest the establishment of parks at both Mount Hood and Mount Rainier smacked of conspiracy by private claimants and speculators, including the Northern Pacific Railroad.

---

[4] Editorial, *Saturday Evening Post,* Vol. CLXXXIV (April 13, 1912), p. 26. Bourne: "How to Spend a Billion Dollars," *Outlook,* Vol. XCIII (October 9, 1909), pp. 297–302.

Further, conservationists differed on what they should conserve, especially when conservation threatened economic growth. Some of the principal pressures for the establishment of forest reserves came from groups interested in developing urban water supplies, but they sometimes clashed with the irrigationists and the wilderness-lovers. Although the disastrous forest fires of September 1902 and August 1910 helped to reinforce the arguments for forest management, the *Oregonian* spoke for much of the West when it demanded that government stop delaying the construction of power plants that the region needed: "We want our country developed; we desire the conversion of its natural resources to some use rather than let them run wild, as heretofore; we wish the Government to part with the lands and allow them to be utilized. . . ."[5] Similarly, Borah defended the administration in the Ballinger-Pinchot controversy of 1909–10 and criticized the Forest Service for withholding lands from settlers.[6] In the irrigation country, public opinion swung behind governmental action as promotional companies, users' associations, and even railroads found their resources inadequate. But new divisions troubled the politicians: San Francisco, for instance, welcomed a municipal water supply (with federal cooperation), but resisted Congress's attempt to reserve electric power for public distribution; the central valleys of California asked for irrigation, but could not agree on the limit of 160 acres (in the reclamation act of 1912) on farms benefitted by federal projects; southern California was torn by advocates of the several claimants for water within the state and by its own people who had interests across the borders in Mexico and Arizona.

The choices for progressive politicians became no simpler during the presidency of Woodrow Wilson, when more of them were in Congress and the issues on which Congressmen might divide had multi-

---

[5] Richardson: *The Politics of Conservation; Crusades and Controversies, 1897–1913* (Berkeley: University of California Press; 1962), pp. 48, 117, 124–9. Holway R. Jones: "History of the Sierra Club, 1892–1926" (unpublished master's thesis, University of California at Berkeley; 1957), pp. 62–5. Lawrence Rakestraw: "Urban Influences on Forest Conservation," *Pacific Northwest Quarterly*, Vol. XLVI (October 1955), pp. 108–13; "Uncle Sam's Forest Reserves," *Pacific Northwest Quarterly*, Vol. XLIV (October 1953), pp. 145–51. Louise Peffer: *The Closing of the Public Domain: Disposal and Reservation Policies, 1900–50* (Stanford: Stanford University Press; 1951), pp. 52–8, 116. Portland *Oregonian*, January 2, 1910, Sec. III, p. 8, col. 3; January 8, 1910, p. 8, col. 1.

[6] Claudius Johnson: *Borah of Idaho* (New York: Longmans, Green & Co.; 1936), pp. 97–106.

plied. Within the states, many of the progressives had placed a low valuation on loyalty to party, both in the early idealistic stages of municipal reform, when Republicans and Democrats joined against the bosses, and later, when statewide primaries destroyed the discipline of party organization. When Wilson toured California in 1911, he remarked that party lines were so obscure that he did not know where he was: "I can't, for the life of me, in this place be certain that I can tell a Democrat from a Republican."[7] Nonpartisanship went back both to the silver politics of the nineties, when Populist, fusion, and silver Republican tickets constituted bridges from one major party to the other, and also to the cynically nonpartisan practices of the railroads themselves, which used whatever parties might serve them. Democrat J. D. Farrell of the Great Northern bossed Republican conventions in Washington, and Democrat William F. Herrin of the Southern Pacific shifted his support from the Republican Party to the Union Labor Party in San Francisco; so it was less surprising that Francis J. Heney could run on the Democratic ticket in 1909, on the Republican in 1912, on the Progressive in 1914, and on the Democratic in 1916. And it was not difficult for the voters of California in 1916 simultaneously to elect Woodrow Wilson as president on the Democratic ticket and Hiram Johnson as senator on the Republican ticket, only four months after Johnson had announced, in effect, that he was leaving the Progressive Party. They might have preferred Wilson to Charles Evans Hughes even if the right-wing Republicans had not taken charge of Hughes during his tour of the state and so contrived to make him seem to share their distaste for Johnson. Only Easterners and those Westerners who had opposed Johnson and progressive ways from the beginning found it necessary to believe that he had won by taking his revenge, trading votes with the Democrats.[8] But progressive irregularity did not easily survive the move to Washington.

The maverick in Congress, a body whose procedures assumed the party system, had seemed somewhat out of place even when he was a part of a Republican majority under a Republican president. As a practical politician, Theodore Roosevelt, who looked to insurgency to bring him and his principles back to power, never had quite accepted

---

[7] *California Outlook*, Vol. X (May 20, 1911), p. 7.

[8] Spencer C. Olin, Jr.: "Hiram Johnson, the California Progressives, and the Hughes Campaign of 1916," *Pacific Historical Review*, Vol. XXXI (November 1962), pp. 403–12.

it: "The insurgents in Congress," he told William Allen White in 1914, "were good for nothing except to insurge. Some of them, like Bourne, were on the whole, below the average rather than above the average of their fellows."[9] But even Bourne, whom Chauncey Depew called the plumed knight of the Senate Salvation Army, and who was one of the first to propose bolting the party in 1912, moved into a staunchly partisan position after 1915 as president of the Republican Publicity Association, denouncing Wilson and his works. And Johnson, entering the Senate when most Republicans were closing ranks because they had become a minority and because the nation was about to go to war, soon joined the club. "I really enjoy the Senate," he wrote to a friend in 1917. "I feared when first I came all sorts of things, none of which has transpired."[1] The papers soon noted that he was on excellent terms with Philander Knox, formerly Taft's secretary of state, who was his neighbor. "He does not carry a chip on his shoulder, a la La Follette," the conservative Seattle *Post Intelligencer* observed,[2] and Johnson himself privately deplored La Follette's inconoclastic stand on the war and his consequent loss of usefulness.[3]

The war made strange bedfellows and, as Johnson explained, left "no time . . . to develop differences and animosities upon domestic problem." "That which has been so intimate a part of our lives in California," he told Rowell, "could not now get the slightest hearing."[4] Even while he was still governor, in 1916, Johnson had become a charter member of the League to Enforce Peace, along with both progressives and antagonists as extreme as Harrison Gray Otis of the *Los Angeles Times* and Representative Joseph R. Knowland, who said that it was better to elect a Democrat than to have Johnson as senator.[5] After the war, the League of Nations further divided progressives and realigned them with conservatives, within the state as well as in the Senate. The effect was to loosen the progressive ties generally and to

---

[9] Roosevelt to White, Nov. 7, 1914, in *The Letters of Theodore Roosevelt,* ed. Elting E. Morison and John M. Blum (Cambridge: Harvard University Press; 1951–4), Vol. VIII, p. 835.

[1] *Independent,* Vol. LXX (June 29, 1911), p. 1411. William Allen White: *Autobiography* . . . (New York: The Macmillan Company; 1946), p. 453. Johnson to Arthur Arlett, June 23, 1917 (Arlett papers, Bancroft Library).

[2] *California Outlook,* Vol. XXI (October 1917), p. 155; (July 1917), pp. 75–6.

[3] Johnson to Chester Rowell, Sept. 17, 1917 (Rowell papers, Bancroft Library).

[4] Johnson to Arlett, June 23, 1917 (Arlett papers). Johnson to Rowell, April 10, 1917 (Rowell papers).

[5] Lyman Grimes to Rowell, April 12, 1916 (Rowell papers). Mowry: *California Progressives,* p. 254.

perpetuate neglect of domestic issues. The very nonpartisanship that had strengthened the progressives when they were attacking the established party organizations weakened them when they paused to reconsider their purposes.

Nationally, some of the leading Western progressives continued in Congress and continued to be influential. Borah served in the Senate until he died in 1940, Johnson until 1945; from Oregon, Charles L. McNary, who took his seat in 1917, served until 1944. McNary twice persuaded Congress to pass his plan for disposing of agricultural surpluses and raising agricultural prices, only to meet presidential vetoes in 1924 and 1928. After a struggle of nearly seven years and substantial compromises, Johnson put through his bill for a dam and irrigation and power facilities on the Colorado River (1928), which became the Hoover or Boulder dam project.

Within the states, progressivism seemed to have lost its momentum even as some of its leaders went on to national responsibilities. Some of the state projects for reclamation and settlement had expanded into marginal lands when postwar inflation and deflation hit them. By 1923 most of the old progressives were out of office. Many of those who remained were concerned more with excluding alien landowners, radicals, and imported goods, or simply with staying in office, than with advancing popular government and social welfare. William S. U'Ren lived on quietly in Portland until 1949, half forgotten. "I am wondering," wrote John F. Neylan (1921), one of Johnson's old associates, "if we will ever see again in our time another movement like the old progressive movement. . . . Of course, the progressive movement in California has developed into a collection of jobs."[6]

Actually the movement and its legacy never quite died out even when there were no longer Roosevelts, La Follettes, and Wilsons to encourage them nationally. Eventually it merged with local counterparts of the New Deal and later impulses to reform. The habit of ignoring party labels persisted: Oregon elected an independent as governor on a write-in vote in 1930; Washington adopted in 1935 a "blanket primary system" that permitted moving from one party's slate to another as often as one wished on a single ballot;[7] and California Democrats nominated the Republican incumbent for governor in 1946. Electorates con-

[6] J. F. Neylan to Arthur Arlett, Sept. 6, 1921 (Arlett papers).

[7] Daniel M. Ogden, Jr.: "The Blanket Primary and Party Regularity in Washington," *Pacific Northwest Quarterly*, Vol. XXXIX (January 1948), pp. 33–8.

tinued to wrestle with long lists of measures and candidates and regularly to decide questions as detailed as the level of a tax, the curriculum of a school system, and the location of a public library. And corruption and reaction never ceased to serve as invitations to vigilance and reform.

IX

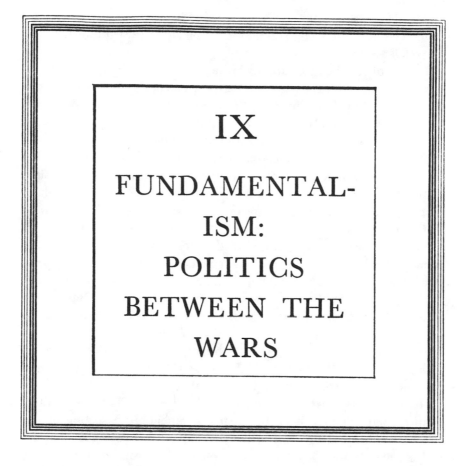

FUNDAMENTALISM: POLITICS BETWEEN THE WARS

At his inauguration as governor of New Jersey in 1911, Woodrow Wilson looked west for a model: the laws of Oregon, he said, seemed "to point the direction which we must also take." Later that year, he again paid tribute to Oregon in a speech at Portland: "In the East I am counted intensely progressive. In Oregon, I am not so sure." Wilson, La Follette, and Roosevelt sought the approval of U'Ren and other progressive leaders of the coast;[1] and if few Easterners shared the opinion of the California historian H. H. Bancroft that Theodore Roosevelt was to Hiram Johnson what St. John the Baptist had been to Jesus Christ, at least Roosevelt was more confident that he wanted Johnson

[1] Robert C. Woodward: "William S. U'Ren, A Progressive Era Personality," *Idaho Yesterdays,* Vol. IV (Summer 1960), pp. 7–8.

as his vice-presidential candidate in 1912 than Johnson and his associates were that Roosevelt had moved far enough forward to merit their unqualified support.[2]

As rapidly as the coast and its leaders built their reputation for progressivism, they lost it. Oregon by 1922 was one of the most conspicuous strongholds of the Ku Klux Klan. "Ten years ago," mused a reporter for *The Outlook* (1923), "no one . . . would have believed it possible"; and most surprising of all, it was "not the bad people of the State, but the good people—the *very* good people"—who had been "largely responsible for the transformation of the Oregon commonwealth into an invisible empire." And Oregon was not alone. "Contrary to what one hears sometimes about the free atmosphere of the Pacific coast," E. Haldeman-Julius, the Kansas Socialist publisher, observed several years later, California and Washington were two of the most reactionary states in the country. The Far West became less famous for reform than for repression as the people used direct legislation to discriminate against religious, racial, and political minorities. Meanwhile, Idaho and Utah, which at best had lagged in their progressivism, turned away from even the forms of direct legislation: the legislature of Idaho repealed the direct primary law of 1909 in 1919, and Utah ignored the initiative and referendum of 1917 until the people of Salt Lake City used it to vote down a proposal for municipal light and power in 1933.[3]

Insofar as the coast had changed, the First World War and its aftermath figured importantly in the changes. Probably no section of the country went through more drastic readjustments between 1916 and the early 1920's. It was no accident that one out of four representatives from the six states had voted against war in 1917 (one out of nine in the rest of the country) or that the representatives who had opposed the President on the war came from districts that had switched from their normally Republican and recently Progressive habits to support him for reelection in 1916, five months earlier. These districts included the progressive counties of eastern Washington and of California south

---

[2] Hubert H. Bancroft: *Retrospection, Political and Personal* (New York: The Bancroft Co.; 1912), p. 496. Mowry: *The California Progressives 1900–1920* (Berkeley: University of California Press; 1951), pp. 167–8, 186–7.

[3] Waldo Roberts: "The Ku Kluxing of Oregon," *Outlook*, Vol. CXXXIII (March 14, 1923), p. 491. E. Haldeman-Julius: *The Big American Parade* (Boston: Stanford Co.; 1929), p. 269. Boyd A. Martin: *The Direct Primary in Idaho* (Stanford: Stanford University Press; 1947), p. 70. *Time*, Vol. XXII (November 20, 1933), p. 15.

of San Francisco, which gave still larger majorities to Poindexter and Johnson for the Senate than to Wilson for the presidency. Although progressive and conservative Republicans in California accused each other of letting personal and factional feeling undermine the campaign for the national ticket, there and in most of the Far West the issues of peace and progressivism went far to explain Wilson's success against Hughes and beyond the other Democratic candidates. The women turned out in unusual force; the minor-party vote, which had been large, dropped off sharply; and both the women and the Socialists apparently favored Wilson as the man who had "kept us out of war"—with Germany and with Mexico. In Oregon, which was (with South Dakota) one of the two states west of the Missouri River that went solidly Republican, peace seemed the decisive issue in a somewhat different way: the German-Americans apparently voted almost as a bloc for Hughes. The outcome as a whole surprised the national Republican organization, which had expected Western women, as advanced suffragettes, to resent Wilson's failure to endorse equal suffrage. Instead the women's successes in getting the vote at home had helped turn their minds from the woes of their unfranchised sisters in the East to issues that would affect them and their families, such as neutrality.[4]

Having clung to peace and neutrality, Westerners were quick to demand proof of loyalty and support for the war, once the country entered it. Their changing temper stood out sharply in the wartime and postwar controversies over Thomas J. Mooney, the I. W. W., and criminal syndicalism.

The sponsors of the preparedness parade of July 22, 1916, in San Francisco had faced strong local criticism. As conservative a magazine as *Sunset* grumbled at "the red vapors of the Preparedness hysteria" for diverting attention from "the many important measures in which the West is vitally interested. . . ." But the parade and the explosion that killed ten spectators on the sidewalk along the line of march aroused controversy more because they were all too relevant to the tensions with which San Franciscans had lived since the days of Ruef and Schmitz. Prominent among the sponsors of the parade were the leaders of the "Law and Order Committee" formed a few days earlier to break the city's labor unions, and prominent among those who had met just before the parade to denounce it were leaders of labor and assorted progres-

[4] *The New York Times,* Nov. 12, 1916, p. 6, cols. 1–3. Mowry: *California Progressives,* pp. 275–6.

sive and radical causes. During the investigations and trials that followed, the principal antagonists became District Attorney Charles M. Fickert, who, as the candidate of the United Railroads, had defeated Francis Heney in 1909, and Fremont Older, friend of labor and editor of the *Bulletin,* who had exposed Ruef and then fought to free him. The organizer and grand marshal of the parade, who promptly accused Rudolph Spreckels of inciting the bombing, was an officer of the United Railroads who had been indicted during the graft trials in 1907 for bribing supervisors of the city and county of San Francisco. Organized labor looked on the parade as a demonstration for the open shop, whereas many of the opponents of the unions accepted the judgment of the president of the San Francisco Chamber of Commerce and chairman of the Law and Order Committee that the explosion "is another expression of that disease our . . . Committee has started out to combat."[5] To the conservative press, still outraged at the interlude of the Union Labor Party, it seemed that the bombing awoke San Francisco to the danger of government by organized labor, with "no opposition worth mentioning for many years."[6]

Mooney had been a minor figure in San Francisco and in labor, one of those unionists who diverged from the cautious conservatism of the leaders of the American Federation of Labor while remaining nominally within the ranks. A left-wing Socialist, he had acquired passing local notoriety by being arrested for a dynamite plot against the Pacific Gas and Electric Company and later by joining Emma Goldman and Alexander Berkman in editing an obscure radical paper, *The Blast,* which preached class warfare and opposition to all other wars. He became better known when he undertook to organize the streetcarmen of San Francisco in 1916 and the United Railroads posted its car barns with warnings to shun him. He was conspicuous enough so that even Fremont Older guessed after the explosion that Mooney had planned it. Fickert promptly brought into the district attorney's office the private detective who had been following Mooney for the United Railroads and directed him to put together a case against Mooney and his associates. On trial and summarily convicted (1917) on the basis of testi-

[5] *Sunset,* Vol. XXXVII (July 1916), p. 29. Sara B. Field: "San Francisco and the Bomb," *The Masses,* Vol. VIII (October 1916), p. 16. Robert L. Duffus: "Mooney and San Francisco," *New Republic,* Vol. XIV (March 16, 1918), p. 204.

[6] *Sunset,* Vol. XXXVII (September 1916), p. 40.

mony that probably was perjured, Mooney became an international figure as a victim of the class struggle. After mobs had demonstrated before the American embassy at Petrograd, the nation as a whole became conscious of him, and President Wilson asked Governor Stephens to commute his sentence from death to life imprisonment. "The basic motive underlying all the acts of the prosecution," reported the chief agent of the Department of Labor who invested the case at Wilson's order, "springs from a determination on the part of certain employer interests in the city of San Francisco to conduct their various business enterprises upon the principle of the open shop. There has been no other motive worth talking about."[7]

Whatever the purposes of the enemies of labor had been, Mooney soon came to symbolize martyrdom and labor's distress on the one hand, anarchy and treason on the other. The one image was stronger nationally and internationally; the other locally, within the state. Neither satisfactorily resembled the man, whose quarrelsome egotism was as great as his faith in himself and in his defense. ("He had no great or engaging qualities," *The New York Times* commented when he died, free and half forgotten, in 1942. "He just happened to be innocent.") Those who contributed to Mooney's defense came to include many who had had no knowledge whatever of him; but those who applauded or acquiesced in his conviction probably were far more numerous than those who had opposed labor and had favored preparedness in 1916. In a state where isolationism and pacifism had been widespread, and in a community where labor had long held at least the balance of power, to defend Mooney was to risk being called a German spy or a Sinn Feiner or a bomber. "Even the masses," the *Socialist Call* recalled in 1939, when at last one of the six governors of California who reviewed evidence of perjury freed the prisoners, "fell for anti-Socialist propaganda which was tied up with the war mongers' deliberate campaign to plunge the country into war." By that time the Communists had converted Mooney's cause to their own uses, whereas the conservative unions of San Francisco had never seen a way to answer the charges of disloyalty that the prosecution and the conservative press made against Mooney and militant labor.[8]

---

[7] R. L. Duffus: *The Tower of Jewels: Memories of San Francisco* (New York: W. W. Norton & Co.; 1960), pp. 139–43, 150–2, 156–60. *House Document* 157, 66 Cong., 1 Sess., p. 15.

[8] *The New York Times*, March 7, 1942, p. 16, col. 3. Evelyn Wells: *Fre-*

But although to those who believed in him Mooney personified the degradation of labor on the coast, and although Market Street, where labor had paraded its power so often, beheld labor's humiliation instead, San Francisco was not alone. The Industrial Workers of the World was in a more precarious situation than most of American labor in 1914, and was more vulnerable to the events that followed. Its fame had been increasing more than its power, especially in the West, where demonstrations for free speech were no substitute for the victories that Eastern Wobblies won in steel and textiles. The Westerners developed effective techniques of organizing migratory workers, particularly in lumber and agriculture. Rather than harangue mass meetings of the unemployed (though they did that also), they concentrated on recruiting members on the railroad freight cars that converged on the fields and camps; thus they increased collections of dues and initiation fees and improved their control of the labor supply. The typical Wobbly was not a family man on the picket line, but a homeless itinerant "riding the rods" between jobs that often lasted no longer than his immediate needs. At the hop ranch at Wheatland, California, in 1913, one of the Wobbly organizers had held a sick baby in his arms and said: "It's for the life of the kids that we're doing this," but at Wheatland barbarous treatment had made protest almost spontaneous, and no more than one in thirty of the pickers and their children was a member.[9] In Western agriculture generally, the family group did not displace the unmarried worker until the 1920's and 1930's, when cheap automobiles enabled families to follow the harvests.

The war brought both opportunity and catastrophe for the I. W. W. and its clientele. Improved economic conditions and the absorption of the unemployed into the wartime economy and into the armed forces encouraged strikes. By June and July 1917, if the I. W. W. lumber workers had not struck in Washington and Idaho, the A. F. of L. would have taken the lead, so general was the discontent at living and working conditions. The loggers "are—or, rather, have been made," the President's mediation commission reported the following year, "disintegrat-

---

mont Older (New York: D. Appleton-Century Co.; 1936), p. 322. *Socialist Call,* Vol. V (January 21, 1939), p. 4, col. 1. *The Masses,* Vol. IX (September 1917), p. 6. Governor E. G. Brown pardoned Warren K. Billings, Mooney's associate, on December 21, 1961.

[9] Carleton H. Parker: "The California Casual and his Revolt," *Quarterly Journal of Economics,* Vol. XXX (November 1915), pp. 110–26. Woodrow C. Whitten: "The Wheatland Episode," *Pacific Historical Review,* Vol. XVII (February 1948), pp. 37–42.

ing forces in society." The hostility of the operators toward any labor organization had "reaped for them an organization of destructive rather than constructive radicalism."[1] But whereas representatives of national and state government recognized the validity of the strikers' grievances, and historians ultimately credited the Wobblies with much of the spectacular improvement that followed, the I. W. W. became a casualty of the war and of its own successes.

Even before the United States entered the war, many employers had resolved to combat radicalism and to establish the open shop. In California, the Farmers' Protective League (1914) opposed both progressive legislation on labor's behalf and unionization in the fields. In Everett, Washington, in 1916, members of the Commercial Club assaulted Wobblies who were organizing the shingle weavers and later a shipload of members who had arrived for a free-speech meeting. Meanwhile, the outspoken opposition of the I. W. W. to wars and patriotism made it increasingly vulnerable to criticism as American neutrality itself became untenable. Actually the membership concentrated, in 1917 and 1918, on economic objectives, but the convention of 1916 had proclaimed "antimilitaristic propaganda in time of peace . . . and, in time of war, the general strike, in all industries"; these and other phrases lent themselves to quotation. More than anywhere else in the country, newspapers in the West during the war came to refer to Wobblies as international saboteurs, dynamiters, probably in the service of Germany—"Imperial Wilhelm's Warriors."[2]

Hostility to the I. W. W. was particularly strong in the Pacific Northwest because it threatened production in the lumber industry, which had become essential to the conduct of the war and was profitable beyond normal expectations. And both the Wobblies and the Timber Workers (A. F. of L.) furnished propaganda for the operators, who seized the opportunity to undermine all unionism. The Timber Workers tried to appeal to the public by contrasting their own loyalty and reasonableness with disloyalty in the I. W. W.; the operators rejected the first argument and accepted the second, refusing to negotiate with either

---

[1] Robert L. Tyler: "I. W. W. in the Pacific N. W.: Rebels of the Woods," *Oregon Historical Quarterly*, Vol. LV (March 1954), pp. 17–25. *Report of President's Mediation Commission* (Washington: Government Printing Office; 1918), p. 14.

[2] Mowry: *California Progressives*, pp. 200–4. Eldridge F. Dowell: *A History of Criminal Syndicalism Legislation in the United States* (Baltimore: Johns Hopkins Press, 1939), pp. 23, 33–4, 41, 74.

organization and insisting that the two were in fact collaborators and equally disloyal. The I. W. W. local at Spokane seemed to confirm their charges by threatening a general strike throughout the state if all "class war prisoners" did not go free at once. The consequences in the long run were disastrous to the I. W. W. and the union and less than satisfactory to the operators. Because in this atmosphere the mediators could find no basis for mediation, the War Department, which needed Western spruce for aircraft, sponsored a "patriotic association" embracing both employer and employee, the Loyal Legion of Loggers and Lumbermen, or Four L's (November 1917). The Spruce Production Division assigned soldiers to jobs in the woods to meet shortages in labor and perhaps also to emphasize the idea that production "was not inferior soldiering." As they received the going wage and the army demanded that bunk and board meet military standards, their presence also prompted drastic changes in the logging camps. Working through the Legion, the government both stopped strikes and persuaded the operators to concede most of labor's specific demands affecting hours and working conditions, thus expediting production as never before. It also established a new basis and a new medium for hostility toward the I.W.W. and radicalism in labor. The leaders of the Legion had no doubts about who was at fault in incidents like the one at the I. W. W. Hall in Centralia, Washington, in 1919, where there was ample reason to believe that parading veterans rather than Wobblies were the aggressors. "The red must go!" insisted the *Four L News*. "Out of the industry, out of the community, out of the country—to hell, if need be!"[3] The Wobbly eventually did all but go, but the Timber Worker went first (1923), leaving the I. W. W. the only significant alternative to a company union.

With conditions in the logging camps improved—to the accompaniment of ample publicity—the public was in no mood to sympathize with further strikes and demonstrations, especially as the conservative national trade unions renounced the strike at home and as Russians and Germans employed it for revolutionary ends abroad. Local vigilantes followed the lead of agents of the Department of Justice who raided Wobbly halls and arrested members (from September 1917 on), bringing them to trial under the provisions of the Espionage Act. When an

[3]Robert L. Tyler: "The United States Government as Union Organizer: The Loyal Legion of Loggers and Lumbermen," *Mississippi Valley Historical Review,* Vol. XLVII (December 1960), pp. 434–51. Jensen: *Lumber and Labor,* pp. 125–47. *Four L Bulletin,* Vol. I (December 1919), pp. 1, 3.

explosion damaged the back steps of the governor's mansion at Sacramento in 1918, it seemed only natural to arrest Wobblies for the crime—and, without specific evidence, to find forty-six of them guilty of that and of setting various small fires throughout the state. The Seattle general strike of February 6–11, 1919, arose, undramatically enough, from the refusal of the United States Shipbuilding Adjustment Board to authorize wage rates that the local shipbuilders already had agreed to; the government had prepared for strife by granting cost-plus contracts in an area that traditionally had paid high wages. But Mayor Ole Hanson saw proof of conspiracy "to establish bolshevism," and while public interest lasted, he made a career of lecturing on the role he had played in ending the strike and of appealing for selective immigration laws.[4]

The chief critics of radicalism and of organized labor from 1916 through the 1920's were those who had worked for the open shop before the war. The National Civil Liberties Bureau contended (1919) that business interests attacked the I. W. W. not because it opposed the war but because the war was an opportunity for them "to crush their greatest foes at home," pointing out that they similarly opposed the Farmers' Non-Partisan League, which was radical but "aggressively pro-war." In California the Better America Federation, established in May 1920, was essentially a reorganization of the Commercial Federation of California and an auxiliary of the Los Angeles Merchants and Manufacturers Association. It appealed to opponents of municipal utilities and regulatory commissions, which it called "socialistic and bolshevistic in tendency," and to critics of public education, though it concentrated on labor unions and legislation detrimental to business. Claiming credit for passage of the state's criminal syndicalism law and establishment of the "red squad" in the Los Angeles police department, it maintained three paid witnesses for a time, to testify in prosecuting Wobblies. The Law and Order Committee of the San Francisco Chamber of Commerce, founded in 1916, which secured an anti-picketing ordinance that autumn in the midst of the excitement generated by Mooney's trial, became the Industrial Relations Committee the following year and worked for the open shop. There was no essential novelty in the policies of the *Los Angeles Times,* which described strikers in the orange

[4] Ole Hanson: *Americanism versus Bolshevism* (New York: Doubleday, Page & Co.; 1920), p. 39. Obituary in *The New York Times,* July 8, 1940, p. 17, col. 4. Robert L. Friedheim: *The Seattle General Strike* (Seattle: University of Washington Press; 1964).

groves in 1918–9 as "Russians" and "I. W. W.–Russian Bolshevik agitators," though the United States District Attorney said that most of them were Mexicans.[5]

What was new was the spread of ultra-conservatism beyond commercial and industrial lobbies, in communities lately known as progressive. As a member of the legislature in Washington, Mayor Hanson had been instrumental in establishing industrial insurance and the eight-hour day for women and children; in 1914 he had been Progressive candidate for the Senate; but in 1918 he ran for mayor as a businessmen's candidate and antagonist of radical movements and of labor itself. In a more moderate spirit, Hiram Johnson expressed a widespread feeling that progressive reforms left little excuse for radicalism: "In the West we have come nearest democracy," he said in 1919; "and in the West, of all places, where people may suggest and make laws and undo what recalcitrant legislators may attempt . . . there should be neither lodgment nor tolerance of I.W.W.ism."[6] At the beginning of the war the national government singled out treasonable activities of leaders of the I. W. W., but left unrestrained the economic agitation of the rank and file. However, in the emotional excitement of war the distinction was soon lost, especially among local officials. Many people began to associate different kinds of labor organizations and to turn against unionism itself. The open shop came to the maritime trades in 1921 along the coast and in San Francisco itself, long the Western citadel of unionism, where a committee of businessmen and the Industrial Association promoted the "American plan" and made the most of a halfhearted general strike (August 3–27).[7]

As if to answer those who questioned their loyalty, or to atone for the opposition to the war that had been widespread through 1916, the people of the progressive Far Western states had voted by overwhelm-

---

[5] National Civil Liberties Bureau: *Memorandum regarding the Persecution of the Radical Labor Movement in the United States* (1919), p. 3. Norman Hapgood: *Professional Patriots* (New York: Albert & Charles Boni; 1927), pp. 19–20, 32–4, 65–6, 146, 174–5. Edwin Layton: "The Better America Federation . . . ," *Pacific Historical Review,* Vol. XXX (May 1961), pp. 140, 142–3. Nelson Van Valen: "The Bolsheviki and the Orange Growers," *Pacific Historical Review,* Vol. XXII (February 1953), pp. 39, 45–9.

[6] *Sunset,* Vol. XLIII (December 1919), p. 16.

[7] Giles T. Brown: "The West Coast Phase of the Maritime Strike of 1921," *Pacific Historical Review,* Vol. XIX (November 1950), pp. 385–96. Frederick L. Ryan: *Industrial Relations in the San Francisco Building Trades* (Norman: University of Oklahoma Press; 1935), pp. 156–202.

ing majorities for the criminal syndicalism laws of 1917–9 (except in Arizona and in Utah, which had been the least progressive states of the region); and the strongest opposing argument labor legislators could make was that the laws would make it difficult for honest labor to combat the agitation of "Bolshevik martyrs." In California, the sponsor of the bill adopted in 1919 (chairman of the committee that had killed a similar bill in 1917) was a progressive and a spokesman for labor. In later years, the dwindling Wobblies of Seattle cherished a legend that they had stood silent along five blocks of the route President Wilson traveled on his visit in 1919, arms folded, hatbands bearing the words, "Release Political Prisoners," but the contemporary record of dissent is a scanty one; assertive patriotism exceeded provocation against it. In rates of voluntary enlistments in the armed forces and of purchases of war bonds, the Far West ran well ahead of the nation. In Washington, school boards —with the warm commendation of the State Council of Defense, whose chairman was the president of the state university—fired teachers who had been guilty of pacifism.[8] Local committees were no less zealous because they seldom found more seditious influences to expunge than German music in schoolbooks.

As the war passed, the more conservative or conformist spirits of the West sometimes seemed to represent a fundamental change in the people, in the stock itself. Returning from Europe and the East in 1927, Lincoln Steffens saw the "moderately successful, the well-to-do, the respectable people" pouring in and drowning out the old spirit: "California today is not a western, it is a middle western, State." Similarly, Louis Adamic attributed the conservatism of the postwar years to the new immigration, "tired and retired people mostly from the Middle West." As the census showed, the newcomers were in fact from very different backgrounds now, and this had been so long enough to affect those who had achieved influence. Illinois still ranked first among the birthplaces of Californians who were not natives, rather than New York, which had dominated the immigration of the preceding century. But Missouri and Texas had come into second and third place, displacing Massachusetts. In origin the new immigration already resembled that

[8] Dowell: *History of Criminal Syndicalism Legislation*, pp. 67, 88, 90–1. Portland *Oregon Daily Journal*, January 29, 1919, p. 5, cols. 1–2. *Sunset*, Vol. XXXIX (July 1917), p. 30. Louis Adamic: *Laughing in the Jungle . . .* (New York: Harper & Brothers; 1932), pp. 242–54. George R. Leighton: *Five Cities . . .* (New York: Harper & Brothers; 1939), p. 310.

of the 1930's, which Oklahoma led.[9] The typical Far Westerner of the years just after the war, if he was not a native, had come from one of the Mississippi Valley states or one of the Southwestern states whose people never had quite understood labor and the new urban doctrines of reform.

Although the Pacific Northwest tended still to draw more from the northern states of the same latitude than southern California did, its population was changing also. A substantial immigration from the southern Appalachian Mountains into the Northwestern lumber districts had begun in the 1880's, reinforcing the Southern and border-state stock of earlier years. But it was not necessary to go to the lumbering and farming counties to find mores acceptable to Southerners. André Siegfried, to whom racism on the coast (as in anti-miscegenation laws) seemed an imitation of Southern practices, found in Portland and Los Angeles in the mid-twenties "the same bias, the same fears, and the same religious intolerance" as in the Appalachians, and specifically as in Tennessee at the time of the trial of John T. Scopes.[1] The Puritans and the Methodists of the older towns of the Willamette Valley and of the Bible belt of southern California had joined the newcomers in voting for prohibition against the more indulgent inclinations of San Francisco and Seattle, whose seafaring and European immigrant elements reinforced different pioneer traditions.

The brief ascendancy of the Ku Klux Klan in Oregon represented a collaboration of older and newer strains of population, of advocates and enemies of change. Few took it seriously at first in a state that had brought government into public view, that had no significant problems of racial or economic conflict, and in which Roman Catholics had worked with Protestants for progressive reform. Governor Ben Olcott told the New York *World* in September 1921 that it had made "practically no impression on our people."[2] The next year he barely won renomination

[9] *The Autobiography of Lincoln Steffens* (New York: Harcourt, Brace & Co.; 1931), Part II, pp. 846–7. Adamic: *Dynamite; The Story of Class Violence in America* (Gloucester: Peter Smith; 1943), p. 276. Eshref Shevky and Marilyn Williams: *The Social Areas of Los Angeles* . . . (Berkeley: University of California Press; 1949), pp. 21–7.

[1] Woodrow R. Clevinger: "The Appalachian Mountaineers in the Upper Cowlitz Basin," *Pacific Northwest Quarterly,* Vol. XXIX (April 1938), pp. 115–34; and "Southern Appalachian Highlanders in Western Washington," *Pacific Northwest Quarterly,* Vol. XXXIII (January 1942), pp. 3–25. André Siegfried: *America Comes of Age* . . . (New York: Harcourt, Brace & Co., 1927), pp. 64–5, 330.

[2] Eckard V. Toy: "The Ku Klux Klan in Oregon . . ." (unpublished master's thesis, University of Oregon; 1959), pp. 94–109.

in the Republican primary against the Klan's candidate, who thereupon switched his support to the Democrat, Walter Pierce. Crosses burned; local Klans paraded and publicly initiated new members by the hundreds; former nuns and former priests lectured on conspiracy and scandal. "Oregon vies with Texas and Oklahoma as the state in which the Ku Klux nuisance comes nearest being an actual menace," remarked *Survey,* which diagnosed the trouble as a failure in education and the outgrowth of wartime spying and informing.[3] In the general election, the Klan elected Pierce to the governorship and threatened to control the legislature; the new speaker of the House was one of the authors of the state criminal syndicalism act of 1919.

The Oregon legislature of 1923 adopted several nativist measures, including an alien land bill (which Washington and California already had), but the most drastic and significant of all was the compulsory school attendance law passed by initiative in 1922. Its effect would have been to destroy the Roman Catholic and other parochial schools. The religious issue seemed to dominate the election; Pierce himself later said that he had owed the governorship to it. The original sponsors of the school bill were Freemasons, who had supported such legislation nationally since 1920, and who circulated initiative petitions in Oregon in June 1922, "to set the example for the rest of the country." "Oregon First," exulted the national Masonic magazine, *New Age,* in announcing the bill's adoption. But the Masons had divided on the issue and the Klan had quickly taken it up, challenging candidates for office to endorse the bill. The election followed "a campaign of calumny and vilification against the Catholic Church on the part of the suburban, small town, and rural Protestant churches,"[4] said the Reverend Edwin V. O'Hara, Roman Catholic liberal and himself a target of the Klan for his work with students at the state university.

How significant the success of the campaign had been was seriously in doubt by 1925, when the Supreme Court of the United States declared the school bill unconstitutional before it could take effect. No

---

[3] Toy: "The Klu Klux Klan in Tillamook, Oregon," *Pacific Northwest Quarterly,* Vol. LIII (April 1962), pp. 60–4. "Intolerance in Oregon," *Survey,* Vol. XLIX (October 15, 1922), pp. 76–7.

[4] *Oregon Voter,* Vol. XXXI (November 11, 1922), pp. 200–1. Toy: "Ku Klux Klan in Oregon," pp. 100, 108. *New Age Magazine,* Vol. XXVIII (July 1920), p. 322; and Vol. XXX (December 1922), p. 730. Edwin V. O'Hara: "The School Question in Oregon," *Catholic World,* Vol. CXVI (January 1923), p. 487.

one seriously attempted to resume the battle. That fall, less than five years after the first organizers had appeared in the state, the *Oregon Voter* observed that the Klan was about defunct and that the general feeling was that having its support was a distinct disadvantage.[5]

Oregon's brief adventure may have tapped more complex currents than were visible at the time. The religious issue had become confused with Americanization and educational reform: some who favored requiring attendance at public schools emphasized not religion but the preparation of teachers, the danger of snobbery, and the desirability of using the English language in the interests of Americanization. On the other hand, Father O'Hara's concern with rural Protestantism does not square with the distribution of votes, which in general ran strongly in favor of the bill (and of Pierce) in the cities and strongly against in the rural counties.[6] Portland was the center of strength for both the Klan and the Roman Catholic Church. Elsewhere, evangelical Protestantism was most conspicuously associated with ideas congenial to the Klan in the largest of Far Western cities, Los Angeles, which Carey McWilliams had described as "a center of Comstockism and Fundamentalism" when he went there in 1922. It was the Los Angeles police who arrested Upton Sinclair in 1923 when he tried to read the Constitution at a meeting on private property during a strike.[7] And fundamentalism in California politics advanced as Los Angeles and southern California became more nearly able to run away with a state election, as Portland and the Willamette Valley were able to do in Oregon.

The religious basis of the original fundamentalism of southern California was the Eastern and Middle Western Protestantism of the arrivals of the 1880's and 1890's, respectable rather than patrician or plebeian. Methodists were as influential in Los Angeles and its neighbors as Unitarians, Episcopalians, and Roman Catholics were in San Francisco. (Southern Californians were never so Eastern in their antecedents and connections as they liked to talk of being, outside of occasional islands of exiles such as Pomona; and the New York edition of the *Social Register* was correspondingly slow to recognize the existence of Cali-

---

[5] *Oregon Voter,* Vol. XXXVII (April 5, 1924), p. 35; and Vol. XLIII (November 28, 1925), p. 295.

[6] Portland *Oregonian,* November 26, 1922, Sec. IV, p. 11, cols. 2–8.

[7] Carey McWilliams: *Southern California Country, An Island on the Land* (New York: Duell, Sloan & Pearce; 1946), p. 343. *The Autobiography of Upton Sinclair* (New York: Harcourt, Brace & World; 1962), pp. 228–32.

fornia south of the Monterey peninsula.) These early immigrants and their descendants were the strength of the temperance and prohibition movements, which brought local option to Pasadena in 1887, and later of the progressive movement. Before the end of the century a larger immigration was arriving, still more Western and Southwestern in origin than its predecessors. It remained urban rather than rural in background; but it was more likely to be still earning a living than to have retired; it was less likely to live in hotels or mansions on the more fashionable streets than in cottages in the suburbs. Having seen less of labor unions, it was no more tolerant than older residents were of them or of the kinds of political relationships that long had existed in San Francisco among labor, political bosses, and Italian, Irish, and other immigrants. It reinforced the traditional prejudice against liquor drinking and liquor dealers in the southern counties, while shifting the general direction and tone of politics and reform.

These newer southern Californians swelled the congregations of such evangelists as Aimee Semple McPherson (1890–1944), who first arrived in Los Angeles in 1918, and Robert P. (Fighting Bob) Shuler (1880–   ), who arrived in 1920. Daughter of a Salvation Army lassie and widow of a Pentecostal missionary, Mrs. McPherson attracted small shopkeepers and pensioners rather than laborers and derelicts. "I bring spiritual consolation to the middle classes," she once said, "leaving those above to themselves and those below to the Salvation Army."[8] In her autobiographical sketch in *Who's Who in America* she identified herself as a Baptist and a member of the W. C. T. U. and of the Los Angeles Chamber of Commerce. She became a regional celebrity, holding tent revivals along the coast and praying for the sick and crippled early in the twenties, when Couéism, rejuvenation, and assorted panaceas swept the country. Faith-healing was so far from being either lower middle class or peculiarly southern Californian in its appeal that a healing mission ran from 1920 to 1923 at Grace Cathedral (Protestant Episcopal), San Francisco. But at Angelus Temple, a 5,300-seat auditorium that "Sister Aimee" built in 1922, she practiced a species of ecclesiastical theater that featured elaborately staged backdrops for her exhortations to salvation and against cards and cocktails. Her followers contributed lavishly to enable her to do the Lord's work in style and comfort and remained enthusiastically loyal while the local press accused

[8] *The New York Times,* September 28, 1944, p. 19, col. 1.

her of self-indulgence and fraud and dissected the details of her tempestuous personal life, especially after the episode in 1926 that some called a kidnapping and resurrection, others an adulterous escapade.

Shuler remained more within the austere habits of the Methodist Episcopal Church, South, in which he had preached in Virginia, Tennessee, and Texas before going to one of the larger Methodist churches in Los Angeles in 1920, though like Mrs. McPherson he had his own radio station, over which he denounced her worldliness and exhorted against the wicked in business and government and against the temptations of the saloon. His jeremiads moved from misconduct among high-school girls to the involvement of politicians with the Julian Petroleum Corporation swindle; by 1929 he had become, Edmund Wilson wrote, the "real boss of Los Angeles," having helped to elect a mayor who shared his passion for total abstinence.[9]

Los Angeles thus had some of the makings of a vigorous nativist movement, and not alone in Shuler himself, who denounced Rome as well as rum, or in Mayor Porter, a former Klansman. The basis of their strength was the large number of people whose swarming after new cults suggested hunger for community and security, whose preoccupation with scandal suggested the tensions of adjusting to new temptations in a new environment. They were glad, Edmund Wilson said, "to get an intimate peek into the debauched goings-on of their neighbors, and at the same time to be made to feel their own superior righteousness and even . . . to have a hand in bringing the wicked to judgment." Many of the wicked themselves were newcomers, newly come to the means to sin in a community whose rapid growth afforded easy money and freedom from old restraints in spending it as well as the novel standards of cinematic life. A student of police methods who found that the police of Los Angeles (about 1930) expressed "a theory of law enforcement more openly opposed to the Constitution than any I had yet encountered" traced much of the pressure on the "Red Squad" and the "Moral Squad" to the tensions between Puritan and sinner in the new immigration.[1]

Still, the protesters and those protested against were not all recent

---

[9] Edmund Wilson: "The City of Our Lady the Queen of the Angels," *New Republic*, Vol. LXIX (December 9, 1931), pp. 89–91; and *The American Jitters; A Year of the Slump* (New York: Charles Scribner's Sons; 1932), pp. 234–5; *The New York Times*, May 29, 1959, p. 23, col. 2.

[1] Wilson: *American Jitters*, p. 230. Ernest J. Hopkins: *Our Lawless Police; a Study of the Unlawful Enforcement of the Law* (New York: Viking Press; 1931), pp. 152–4.

arrivals; fundamentalism drew on a wide heritage, including the heritage of progressivism itself. Progressives could not easily understand why radicalism in labor and politics should develop shortly after progressive legislatures had adopted programs designed to establish a just equilibrium over the whole community. "Political autocracy has been overthrown and democratic government firmly established," the *California Outlook* had explained in 1918, when it stopped publication. "No general reaction seems at this time possible."[2] Thus to the progressives labor seemed ungrateful for favors received—laws that came to seem as noncontroversial as woman suffrage and the initiative and referendum—and unreasonable in making further demands. The one continuing issue on which the two most clearly agreed was that of restricting Oriental immigration; but by the early 1920's, Western opposition to exclusion had declined, and it was difficult to work up the kind of argument on it within the region that one could in the East. Western capitalists were losing faith in the coolie and so were less inclined to dissent from labor's concern for job unionism and the progressives' concern for social homogeneity. And by 1924 Congress had acted to exclude the Japanese, making American immigration policy for the next generation a question between the United States and Japan rather than between West and East in the United States.[3]

One originally progressive issue remained active after the war, becoming in fact more controversial after enactment than before, and continuing to divide progressives from labor: the liquor question. During the long campaign for prohibition, churchmen and leaders of the Anti-Saloon League had come to see the larger moral and political corollaries of the saloon, and the expediency of working with essentially political reformers. The platforms of the state Prohibition parties broadened accordingly. Progressive leaders accepted the argument of the League that the liquor dealers made corrupt legislatures as surely as they made drunken men; they also accepted the assistance of the League in delivering at the polls large cadres of voters who were both disciplined and enthusiastic.

---

[2] *California Outlook,* Vol. XXI (January 1918), p. 218. "The other night I asked [Franklin] Hichborn [crusading journalist whose exposures had helped to elect Hiram Johnson in 1910] what there was left for him to reform," wrote the secretary of Governor William D. Stephens. "I do not see how Franklin can be happy anymore. It seems to me that everything now is cleaned up." Martin Madsen to Arthur Arlett, Jan. 27, 1919 (Arlett papers).

[3] See Chapter X, pp. 275–6.

Well before national prohibition came into effect, Westerners divided on the question of alcohol more sharply than on the broader question of reform: country against town, immigrant against native American, Roman Catholic against Protestant. The farmers of the Willamette Valley had been among the first to attack the saloon, the workingmen of San Francisco and Seattle among the last to abandon it. Northern California was wet in comparison with the southern counties, perhaps in part because many of its farmers were vintners, but southern California was dry because the rural districts outvoted Los Angeles itself, the "chemically pure city," as Willard Huntington Wright had called it several years earlier.[4] Of the ten largest cities in the six states, only one, Salt Lake City, gave a majority to the eighteenth amendment; and though the Saints prevailed in their capital, the sinners carried Ogden.

The victories of the prohibitionists, in the nation and in the states, may have prepared the way ultimately for a broader kind of reform, as Gilman Ostrander has suggested in his history of prohibition in California, by breaking the stuffy alliance of reformism and moralism. Prohibition made the cause of temperance seem reactionary rather than progressive; but it reacted against the progressives themselves insofar as memories of their associations with prohibitionists persisted. Having succeeded in establishing prohibition, the Anti-Saloon League and its allies turned from agitating for a larger fulfillment of democratic purposes by democratic means to circumventing the Bill of Rights in order to maintain the status quo. The most conspicuous prohibitionists in the twenties and thirties were moral fundamentalists such as "Fighting Bob" Shuler, who also crusaded against the teaching of evolution in the public schools while advocating the cause of the public utility corporations of southern California. And by seeming to concentrate on raiding small cafés or searching motorists and spectators at football games for hip flasks instead of turning to the large manufacturers and importers of liquor, agents of both national and state governments reinforced the impression that personal liberties rather than the sources of political corruption were under attack.[5]

The effects of prohibition on attitudes toward recent immigrant

---

[4] Gilman M. Ostrander: *The Prohibition Movement in California, 1848–1933* (Berkeley: University of California Press; 1957), pp. 105–9, 149 *passim.*

[5] Ostrander: *The Rights of Man in America, 1606–1861* (Columbia: University of Missouri Press; 1960), p. 314. Ostrander: *Prohibition Movement,* pp. 165–8, 183–4.

groups (and thereby on relations between the middle class and labor) were various. Die-hard prohibitionist journals, such as the *California Liberator*, continued to blame "a Church which is yet more Roman than American." "From Rome, from Italy and from France," Clarence True Wilson, the veteran Methodist crusader for temperance, warned at Los Angeles in 1933, "through a vast international organization the word has gone out to 'wipe out Prohibition as a means of wiping out American Protestantism.' "[6] But if the frequent mention of Italian-American names in accounts of raids on bootleggers gave the impression that immigrants were both lawbreakers and drunkards, the eventual disillusionment with prohibition helped to bring older and newer Americans together. They were not so different as they had supposed: the wine-drinking Latin was seldom an alcoholic, the hard-cider-drinking Anglo-Saxon seldom an abstainer. By the later twenties, when the success of the prohibitionists dulled the appeal of prohibition, the establishment of restricted immigration, whose advocates had derived much of their strength from the grievances against the saloon, coincided with a general abatement in the effectiveness of appeals to nativist prejudices as memories of the war and its tensions receded. Complaints that racial and religious minorities were undermining prohibition[7] were an indication of the sentiment for repeal (at a time when the number of the foreign-born was declining) rather than of the general persistence of prejudice.

As prohibition and nativism lost appeal, the Democratic Party gained. Even during the early years of the century, the progressive potential of Democrats in the Far West had run high, higher than in most other parts of the country. Democrat Theodore Bell had been a close rival to Republican Hiram Johnson in California, Democrat Fred T. Dubois to Republican William E. Borah in Idaho. As governor, Democrat Oswald West was probably the most effective heir to the Oregon system. The balance between the two parties was close enough to be affected by the issue of prohibition. In California, Bell's dryness helped to counter the Democratic Party's handicap among prohibitionists as the party of wine- and beer-drinking foreigners and laborers; in Oregon, both Pierce and West (who as governor caused a sensation by sending his secretary, a woman, to close the saloons in a disorderly town) were drier than

---

[6] Ostrander: *Prohibition Movement*, pp. 179, 197.

[7] Norman F. Furniss: *The Fundamentalist Controversy, 1918–1931* (New Haven: Yale University Press; 1954), pp. 67–8.

their party or their party's reputation. By the early thirties, however, to be either a wet or a Democrat was no longer the political liability it had been. In 1932, the Democratic presidential landslide and repeal both swept over the West. The liberals were becoming more friendly to the Democrats, who may have lost much of the bad odor of machine politics as progressive reasures for direct legislation and nonpartisanship weakened the structure of both parties, but who were unmistakably urban and wet.

Sentiment against prohibition had gone so far by the early 1930's that it was Utah, where the Latter-day Saints had long applied stronger sanctions against alcohol than the whole body of Protestantism in other states, that gave the deciding vote for repeal of the eighteenth amendment in 1933. Paradoxically, the very strength of the Mormons' commitment to the principle of abstinence—the Word of Wisdom—had served to subordinate the issue in politics, so great had been the danger that an advocate of prohibition would appear as the instrument of the Church and thus arouse gentile fears of theocratic power. When the Church conference of 1908 asked members to work for laws to close the saloons, the Republican machine, under Mormon leadership, decided that prohibition was inexpedient and killed it in the state senate. In 1915, a Mormon governor vetoed a prohibition bill, and Senator Reed Smoot did not advocate prohibition until 1916,[8] when the movement had become general throughout the West and among members of other churches.

Meanwhile the Republican Party in Utah had become identified with the Mormon Church more completely than with the Protestant churches in any other Western state, although Democrats also carried state elections, again to a greater extent than in any other state.[9] The Mormon commitment to the Republicans represented a substantial change since the days when Republican Congresses had attempted to extirpate poly-

---

[8] M. R. Merrill: *Reed Smoot, Utah Politician* (Logan: Utah State Agricultural College; 1953), pp. 17–27.

[9] Utah's first Democratic and non-Mormon governor, Simon Bamberger, served from 1917 to 1921, and other Democrats followed him: George H. Dern—afterward secretary of war (1925–33), Henry H. Blood (1933–41), and Herbert B. Maw (1944–9). The Republican candidates for the presidency carried the state in 1920, 1924, and 1928, but one Democratic United States senator, William H. King, served from 1917 to 1941—replacing George Sutherland when Wilson won his second term—and a second, Elbert H. Thomas, served from 1933 to 1951, replacing Smoot when Roosevelt won his first term. In the five other states the only Democratic governor in the 1920's was Walter Pierce—no typical Democrat—in Oregon (1923–5), and the only Democratic senators were Clarence Dill of Washington (1923–9) and Key Pittman of Nevada (1913–40).

gamy; it followed, if not, as rumor had it, on understandings between Mark Hanna and the Mormon hierarchy, at least on the interest of a sugar-producing state in the protective tariff and on the tendency for respect for economic success to take precedence over the principle of equal economic opportunity in both church and party. Although political preferences changed, the agrarian ideals of frugality and hard work persisted long after Utah had become an urban rather than a rural state, and the Saints themselves more typically business and professional men than farmers.[1] Although politically liberal Mormons sometimes spoke of the New Deal as a movement of the gentile world in the direction of Mormon ideas of social responsibility, still the fact that church and state came to operate parallel sets of social machinery, as in recreation, welfare, and education, apparently reinforced the aversion to the growth of government that Mormons had felt since the days when Brigham Young opposed levying taxes for free schools.

Utah's conservatism may have followed partly on the personal preferences of the Church's leaders, who in the twentieth century were chiefly elderly businessmen, and whom the membership carefully watched for the slightest indication of preference even though it did not always accept their explicit advice (as when President Heber J. Grant endorsed Herbert Hoover in 1932). Certainly the atmosphere of Mormon society under their guidance seemed consistent with the general political behavior of a state that—alone in the West—voted for Taft in 1912 and that produced Senator Reed Smoot (served from 1903 to 1933) and Governor J. Bracken Lee (1949–57). It is no disproof of the power of the Church and the influence of its members that gentiles frequently won high office: gentile politicians in Utah might more safely seek the support and advice of the Church, and thus might be more useful to the Church, than Mormons, who felt obliged to demonstrate their independence.[2]

---

[1] Lowry Nelson: *The Mormon Village: A Pattern and Technique of Land Settlement* (Salt Lake City: University of Utah Press; 1952), p. 279. Despite the average low density of population, Utah has been approximately as urban as the nation—in 1960, 74% as compared with 69.9%; in 1900, 38.1% as compared with 40%; in 1930, 52.4% as compared with 56.2%. Moreover, as elsewhere, the rural non-farm population has greatly exceeded the urban farm population, despite Utah's farm villages.

[2] Frank H. Jonas: "The Mormon Church and J. Bracken Lee," Utah Academy of Sciences, Arts, and Letters, *Proceedings*, Vol. XXXVI (1959), p. 152. Rose (1938) estimated that Mormons who voted as the leaders of the Church publicly told them numbered from 3 to 6 percent of the total voting population. He also suggested that the high incidence of home ownership

Most of the other rural parts of the West were considerably more complex politically than Utah. The Non-Partisan League extended into Idaho and Washington, where it helped to elect John F. Nugent to the Senate in 1918 and Clarence Dill in 1922 on Democratic tickets—and may have strengthened its opponents by stampeding conservative Democrats into the Republican ranks. The Grange urged the cause of public power and contributed to the adoption of measures to authorize public-utility districts in Washington and Oregon in 1930. In Washington, Oregon, and Idaho, the Grange was both large—as in the Northeast, but not in the Mississippi Valley—and disposed to cooperate with labor; in Washington it cultivated, said William Bouck, State Grange Master, "friendly relations with and between all who toil, particularly through the producer to consumer cooperative system." When the National Grange, which had endorsed the open shop, suspended Bouck in 1921, some of his supporters attempted to establish a rival grange dedicated to more progressive policies.[3] As an investigating committee pointed out in 1938, "instead of growing more conservative as its parent organization in the East has tended to become . . . [the Grange] has all along the Pacific tended to become the refuge of the more discontented farmers, who feel that all is not well with the official agrarian philosophies and activities."[4]

Although the Grange often joined forces with labor and progressive groups in the cities that favored public power, or the income tax rather than the sales tax, in some of the most productive agricultural areas farmers increasingly turned rather toward interests whose principal concern was the open shop, the curtailment of labor unions. The Grange was strongest in those states and counties where small family farmers were most numerous, in the Northwest and in northern California: it did not extend into southern California until the 1930's. (Perhaps it

among Mormons (whether it was a result of their frugality or of the Church's emphasis on the family) may have disposed them to vote Republican. Arnold M. Rose: "The Mormon Church and Utah Politics: An Abstract of a Statistical Study," *American Sociological Review*, Vol. VII (December 1942), pp. 853–4.

[3] Harriet A. Crawford: *The Washington State Grange, 1889–1924 . . .* (Portland: Binfords & Mort; 1924), pp. 269–307. Bouck later became head of the Western Progressive Miners and drifted further to the left, accepting nomination for the vice-presidency on the Communist-controlled Federated Farmer-Labor ticket in 1924. Irving Howe and Lewis Coser: *The American Communist Party, a Critical History, 1919–1957* (Boston: Beacon Press; 1957), pp. 124, 138–40.

[4] Clarke A. Chambers: *California Farm Organizations . . .* (Berkeley: University of California Press; 1952), pp. 13–14, 18–19.

failed to develop in Utah because the social program of the Mormon Church left little opportunity for an organization whose tone was so strongly fraternal.) The American Farm Bureau Federation was strongest where the Grange was weak, among the larger farmers and leaders in agricultural marketing associations, banking, and other non-agricultural businesses. Throughout the six states, most of its members were in southern California, and more were in Utah than in Oregon. Its policies tended to be more conservative than the Grange's; in questions affecting labor, it leaned toward the views of employers. When agricultural labor threatened to organize effectively during the New Deal, the Farm Bureau worked closely with the Associated Farmers, which drew its financial support primarily from urban and industrial interests, and which first organized in California in 1933–4 at the instance of the Chamber of Commerce and the Farm Bureau.

In California, especially in the San Joaquin and Imperial valleys, agriculture had moved rapidly away from the pattern of family farming that the Grangers idealized and that accounted for some of the vitality of the old progressivism. The First World War had stimulated the use of machinery to expand production and to save labor; distributors increasingly dominated production. Even the stockmen, dairymen, and poultry producers learned to mechanize and rationalize as droughts in the twenties curtailed grassland grazing and such processed foods as cottonseed cake and sugar-beet pulp appeared. Although the Kern County Land Company had only begun to develop its resources in 1940 and still considered that its principal business was in cattle, its profits from oil and gas royalties had become over eight times as large as those from cattle raising and general ranching. Many of the new farmers, the La Follette Committee reported in 1941, "operate land in other states, have cable addresses, employ regional and district managers, conduct extensive financing, and have other appurtenances of modern large-scale corporations."[5]

The corporate shape of much of Far Western agriculture was so new

---

[5] *California Agriculture* ed. Claude B. Hutchison (Berkeley: University of California Press; 1946), pp. 78, 408. Kern County Land Company: *Report,* 1940. Stuart M. Jamieson: "Labor Unionism in American Agriculture" (unpublished doctoral thesis, University of California at Berkeley; 1943), pp. 183–4.

For a sociologist's description of social decline under corporate agriculture in the San Joaquin Valley, see Walter Goldschmidt: *As You Sow* (New York: Harcourt, Brace and Company; 1947).

and inconspicuous a fact that the public did not quite comprehend it until the strikes of the thirties, the revelations of the La Follette Committee in 1939–45, and the appearance of books such as John Steinbeck's *The Grapes of Wrath* (1939) and Carey McWilliams's *Factories in the Field* (1939). The signs on fence posts with the names of the biggest corporate ranchers, such as Miller and Lux and French-Glenn, had been there so long that few asked what might have been there instead. Because most Far Westerners lived in cities, and had seen and heard more of farm life to the east of the Rockies than to the west, they knew little of agriculture in the region from their own experience. They could easily assume that farming on the coast was essentially what it had been in Pennsylvania or Iowa. Everyone knew that the great Mexican land grants, or the most valuable of them, had been subdivided—witness the transformation of southern California from ranches into suburbs.

It was convenient to allow the electorate to retain its image of the traditional family-operated farm; the Associated Farmers never advertised that its financial support and leadership came more from railroads, power companies, and processors and distributors than from "dirt farmers." Fearing that New Dealers and the labor organizations the New Deal encouraged would undermine the open shop, the Industrial Association of San Francisco, Southern Californians, Incorporated, and urban employers generally hoped to sell anti-union programs to the public as something the farmers wanted. For several years the Associated Farmers succeeded reasonably well in California: they sent vigilantes when strikes occurred or were threatened; they asked for local anti-picketing ordinances and invoked the state Criminal Syndicalism Act. They succeeded in Oregon to the extent of getting a large popular majority for what the *St. Louis Post-Dispatch* called "the most drastic anti-labor law on the nation's statute books" in 1938, when the voters of Washington and California rejected similar bills.[6] Oregon, *The New Republic* observed, had become "a guinea-pig state for experimentation in breaking labor unions by legislative decree."[7]

[6] Richard L. Neuberger: "Who Are the Associated Farmers?" *Survey Graphic,* Vol. XXVIII (September 1939), p. 556.

[7] *New Republic,* Vol. XCVII (December 28, 1938), p. 228. Neuberger pointed out that in Oregon the electorate had become more conservative than its representatives: the people by initiative adopted the anti-picketing bill after the legislature had failed to pass it, as the people by referendum had repealed the Grange's power bill of 1932, which the legislature had passed. "Liberalism Backfires in Oregon," *Current History,* Vol. L (March 1939), pp. 35–6, 39.

Yet rural conservatism was no invention of urban businessmen and their public-relations counsels. In general the rural Far West supported a stronger Democratic Party than did the rural Middle West, but the small farmer sometimes seemed to sympathize with unions more because his interests opposed those of other farmers who resembled urban capitalists than because he resembled urban workingmen. And even the small farmer who depended heavily on his own labor was likely to need extra help in the field at harvest time, and to fear attempts to unionize it. The Portland *Oregonian* charged that a potato farmer's attack on racketeers with his pitchfork was a publicity stunt, but there was no need to manufacture incidents. Union boycotts of farm products in Oregon constituted what the state president of the Associated Farmers called "a swell break for the farmers . . . just the kind of advertising that will help us most . . ."[8] and he had only to point to the waterfront strikes of 1934 and 1936 to support his prediction that the teamsters and the longshoremen would interrupt shipments of seed and fertilizer. With Dave Beck of the Teamsters and Harry Bridges of the Longshoremen tying up transport while fruit and vegetables accumulated in the fields, farmers could easily believe that the rival C. I. O. and A. F. of L. agricultural unions (organized in 1937), which sometimes made up in vehemence what they lacked in strength, were no more trustworthy than the organizers of the Communist Cannery and Agricultural Workers' Industrial Union (1933–4), who clearly looked for economic collapse as a step to revolution. Even the Grange occasionally wavered in its traditional sympathy for labor and its customary dissent from the conservative policies of the Farm Bureau and the Associated Farmers, asking for an end to state relief payments to unemployed who refused work and denouncing radical and irresponsible unionism.[9] The corporations feared the influx of white migrants from the Dust Bowl of the Great Plains because they seemed likely to be less tractable than the Mexicans and Filipinos who had preceded them; the small farmers and their families often had to live near them and had to contend with the suddenly overcrowded schools that immigration entailed.

However the temper of the farmers varied, the rural and the urban Far West never differed deeply enough or long enough between the

---

[8] Bruce Bliven: "'Hey Rube!' The Associated Farmers and the New Deal," *New Republic*, Vol. XCVIII (February 8, 1939), p. 10. Neuberger in *Survey Graphic*, Vol. XXVIII, p. 555. Portland *Oregonian*, June 22, 1938, p. 5, col. 1.

[9] Chambers: *California Farm Organizations*, pp. 33–8, 67–8, 88–9.

two world wars seriously to affect political alignments and elections. Much as in Populist days, in no Far Western state did the strength of political parties and causes vary as much between rural and metropolitan areas as it did in Illinois and New York: farmers were more Democratic, workingmen more Republican than in the Middle West and the East. Rural counties had more than their share of representation in state legislatures, as in other parts of the country, but many of the most productive farms were in counties with predominantly urban and industrial or commercial constituencies (for instance, Los Angeles and Santa Clara counties in California, Salt Lake County in Utah, King and Pierce counties in Washington, Lane County in Oregon). In such areas, the mingling of rural farm population and rural non-farm population and the growth of part-time farming or part-time industrial work helped to limit the areas of misunderstanding between countryside and metropolis. In the outlying grain and stock-raising counties, crop prices, and the number of farms as well, declined with the national and international markets, but per capita income declined less than in the centers of agricultural discontent farther east. In general the farmers of the Pacific slope clung to their traditional Republicanism and respect for property while demanding the governmental assistance that such Republicans as McNary of Oregon held out to them.

The Far West as a whole, in fact, went along with Harding, Coolidge, and Hoover as long as the rest of the country did. Although in 1924 it supported La Follette well beyond the national average, his strength fell below that of Roosevelt in 1912 in California and Oregon; only in Idaho and Nevada was it significantly larger,[1] and even there it did not approach the levels of the more aggrieved states of the upper Mississippi Valley. The only Democratic victories in elections for major offices seemed attributable to Republican overconfidence and clumsiness. In Washington, where only one Democrat had won a statewide contest since Populist days, Senator Miles Poindexter had drifted away from his old progressive supporters so far as to advocate a bill to prohibit railroad strikes, and lost to Clarence C. Dill in 1922. But in 1924 (and again in 1928) the governorship went to Colonel Roland Hartley, outspoken critic of the state university and of its president,

[1] The Progressives' percentages of total votes in 1912 and 1924 were: California, 42.1% and 33.2%; Idaho, 24.1% and 36.4%; Nevada, 27.9% and 37.0%; Oregon, 27.4% and 24.4%; Utah, 21.5% and 21.0%; Washington, 35.2% and 35.8%.

Henry Suzzallo, who as a special arbitrator during the war had pressed for the eight-hour day in Hartley's lumber mill in Everett. Hartley was the candidate of the Federated Industries of Washington, which campaigned against "the La Follette crowd, with its communistic principles," including municipal electric power.[2] In Utah, where Senator Smoot's Republican organization had broken down and where Democrats and progressives had learned to work together, George H. Dern won the governorship in 1924 on a Progressive-Democratic fusion ticket, with the support of Mormon leaders; William H. King won reelection to the Senate as a Democrat in 1922 and 1928, again with powerful Mormon support and against an unpopular Republican nominee. Elsewhere, Democratic victories were few, and Republicans pointed to special explanations: in Nevada, to the bipartisanship of the dominant mining and financial interests; in Oregon, to the Klan's support of Walter Pierce. Pierce was more in the Republican than in the Democratic pattern in his staunch support of prohibition and of economy in state government and in having been a farmer in eastern Oregon.

Meanwhile Westerners repeatedly returned some of the most ruggedly conservative members of Congress, such as the sponsors of the tariff of 1930, Representative Willis C. Hawley of Oregon (1907–33) and Senator Reed Smoot of Utah (1903–33), and Senator Key Pittman of Nevada (1913–40), whose main interest was in having the government subsidize one of the industries of his state by buying silver at more than the world price. And if Oregon witnessed the decay of progressivism in the Klan's use of the referendum against Roman Catholic schools and the Associated Farmers' use of the initiative against labor, California seemed to witness it in the advancing political sterility of Hiram Johnson, so recently the anointed successor to Theodore Roosevelt. He was probably the best hope of the progressive Republicans for the presidency in 1920, when Warren Harding's supporters offered him the vice-presidential nomination, with the suggestion that Harding had a weak heart; he was President Coolidge's only strong

---

[2] *The New York Times,* November 11, 1922, p. 2, col. 3; November 28, 1922, p. 11, col. 2; September 22, 1946, Sec. I, p. 63, cols. 3–4. Howard W. Allen: "Miles Poindexter and the Progressive Movement," *Pacific Northwest Quarterly,* Vol. LIII (July 1962), pp. 114–22. Charles M. Gates: *The First Century of the University of Washington, 1861–1961* (Seattle: *University of Washington* Press; 1961), pp. 165–71. John M. Beffel: "The Line-up in Washington State," *The Nation,* Vol. CXIX (November 5, 1924), p. 492.

opponent in 1924; but he had already distressed many of his old comrades in arms by associating with his old enemies, such as Hearst, and by turning against progressives who disagreed with him. Reactionaries were so prominent at a gathering of Johnson's supporters in 1919 that Katherine Edson, one of the leading California progressives, felt Johnson was "absolutely in the camp of the men we have been bitterly fighting for years. . . . I was ready to cry all through the luncheon." "Frankly," Arthur Briggs, the veteran reformer and editor, observed in 1921, "I am beginning to feel either that Johnson never had the idealism with which we credited him, or else that he has lost it."[3] As a senator he seemed to have lost the capacity for legislation that he had exercised as governor; in state politics he seemed more effective in frustrating progressives with whom he had quarreled, such as his successor at Sacramento, Governor William D. Stephens (1917–23), than in consenting to progressive alternatives to such rightists as Senator Samuel M. Shortridge (1921–33), whose chief recommendation seemed to be that he also opposed the League of Nations. In Idaho, Borah was above and beyond the battle; he neither built a machine nor regularly involved himself in campaigns. Except for occasional issues such as the direct primary, his energy went largely into matters with which his own state had little concern, and there was no more individualistic or unpredictable progressive in Congress—"our spearless leader," Hiram Johnson had called him. "Borah always shoots until he sees the whites of their eyes," remarked George Norris,[4] who had hoped for more help on farm relief and public power.

In the depression, Republican strength declined, though never so completely in state and Congressional as in presidential elections. Franklin D. Roosevelt swept the West in 1932 and 1936 as completely as the Republican presidential candidates had swept it in 1920, 1924, and 1928. In 1933 Republican senators and representatives from the six states dropped from thirty out of thirty-seven to fourteen out of forty-six; by 1935 five of the six governors were Democrats, as compared with two in 1930. In Washington, the Democratic landslide of 1932

---

[3] Katherine P. Edson to Chester Rowell, Oct. 7, 1919 (Rowell papers, Bancroft Library). Arthur H. Briggs to Arthur Arlett, April 11, 1921 (Arlett papers).

[4] Lawrence H. Chamberlain in *Rocky Mountain Politics,* ed. Thomas C. Donnelly (Albuquerque: University of New Mexico Press; 1940), p. 181. *Dictionary of American Biography,* supplement, Vol. II, p. 52.

was so large and unexpected as to sweep a mass of eccentrics and incompetents into office. "The legislature," Mary McCarthy wrote in *The Nation*, "was crammed with machine politicians and irresponsible ignoramuses"; one of the new legislators was in jail for raping a twelve-year-old girl, and the lieutenant governor was Vic Meyers, the former orchestra leader who had amused Seattle when as a candidate for mayor he had dressed as Mahatma Gandhi, had offered saxophone solos in place of campaign speeches, and had promised a hostess in every streetcar. Roosevelt's popular vote in Washington and California increased thirty percent between 1932 and 1936, as compared with seven percent throughout the country in the same period;[5] in each of the six states in 1936 his vote ran ahead of his national percentage.

But the three most populous states, California, Washington, and Oregon, turned sharply to the right in choosing governors in the middle thirties, at the high tide of the New Deal; and the common saying was that while Far Westerners loved FDR, they distrusted his policies and his associates. Californians had turned from a liberal to a conservative regime in 1930, when they elected Mayor James Rolph, Jr., of San Francisco to succeed Governor C. C. Young. An elderly Western counterpart to Mayor Jimmy Walker of New York, "Sunny Jim" had become so well known through his courtly presence on horseback at festivals and county fairs that he swept the Democratic gubernatorial primary in 1918; but as governor (1931–4) he offered little to meet the depression except a firm preference for a sales tax rather than an income tax, which he vetoed. His successor, Frank F. Merriam (1934–9), who also had strong Democratic support, was if anything more resolutely conservative. ("I'm relieved to hear," the aging Lincoln Steffens remarked, "that . . . the governorship [is] to be left to Mr. Merriam, who works for The Revolution without any cost to Moscow gold.") Meanwhile, in Oregon the liberal Republican-Independent, Julius Meier (1931–5), gave way to a Democrat, Major General Charles H. Martin (1935–9), who denounced labor unions, public power, and the New Deal even while he tried (unsuccesfully) to invoke President Roosevelt's support for his renomination. Martin assigned state police to protect strikebreakers in lumber in 1935 and supported the operators so staunchly as to discourage the new conservative unions and thus turn

[5] Mary McCarthy: Circus Politics in Washington State," *The Nation*, Vol. CXLIII (October 17, 1936), p. 442. "Politics on the West Coast," *Fortune*, Vol. XXI (March 1940), p. 46.

the initiative to more aggressive elements. And in Washington another Democrat, Governor Clarence D. Martin (1937–41), so valued economy that his most noteworthy achievements were to keep the legislature from considering relief and slum clearance in 1938 and to sponsor cuts in appropriations the following year, despite shortages in federal and local relief funds.[6] When the Democrats failed to renominate him in 1940, enough of his admirers crossed party lines to elect another exponent of economy, the Republican candidate, Arthur Langlie.

Yet the Far West was far from firmly committed to conservatism between the wars. Much of Far Western conservatism was a response to substantial social change. The social dynamism (or instability) of much of the area was such, moreover, that movements for some of the most drastic innovations arose among members of the lower middle class whose backgrounds might have promised conservative rather than radical political behavior.

Traces of progressivism remained in the practice of direct legislation and nonpartisanship and in the persistence of some old progressive issues such as public power, if not in the election of progressive candidates. Party discipline never recovered what it had lost in the direct primary: if Johnson could not control Republican nominations and officeholders in California as the elder La Follette had controlled them in Wisconsin, neither could the party control him or Borah and other insurgents. Nonpartisanship in local elections effectively eliminated much of the cement of patronage from the party system. California's system of cross-filing—which permitted candidates in the primaries to file petitions for nomination on the ballots of parties other than their own—further rewarded irregularity and individualism at all levels short of the presidency even while it helped incumbents seeking reelection; its possibilities seemed to grow as time passed. Neither was the primary itself simply an inheritance from earlier times: Idaho reintroduced it in 1931, with Borah's support, and Washington four years later pushed it to the ultimate, enabling voters in the "blanket primary" to vote for candidates of any and all parties in any one election;[7] Utah finally adopted

---

[6] Steffens to Robert Cantwell, Sept. 29, 1934, in *The Letters of Lincoln Steffens,* ed. Ella Winter and Granville Hicks (New York: Harcourt, Brace & Co.; 1938), Vol. II, p. 999. *Newsweek,* Vol. XI (May 2, 1938), p. 14. Jensen: *Labor in Lumber,* pp. 175–6, 182, 185. *The Nation,* Vol. CXLIX (August 19, 1939), p. 208.

[7] Robert J. Pitchell: "The Electoral System and Voting Behavior: The Case of California's Cross-Filing," *Western Political Quarterly,* Vol. XII (June 1959), pp. 459–84.

the primary in 1937. Franklin D. Roosevelt's offer of the Department of Interior to Johnson in 1932 recognized alike Johnson's devotion to conservation and the continuing vitality of Far Western and Johnsonian politics in the independent progressive tradition.

Although Johnson himself preferred his independent role in the Senate to an administrative assignment in the new Democratic administration, the Far West in the 1930's moved both toward the Democratic Party and into insurgency. California still had a Republican governor in 1935—the only one in the six states—but its legislative and Congressional delegations were Democratic. Washington had become as predominantly Democratic as it had been predominantly Republican; and a Mormon New Dealer, Elbert Thomas, had replaced Reed Smoot in the Senate.

For several years the coast promised to exceed the New Deal, as a generation earlier it had promised to exceed the Square Deal and the New Freedom. In Washington—the soviet of Washington, as Postmaster-General James Farley called it—old Wobblies and young Socialists helped to organize the Unemployed Citizens' League of Seattle (1931), the Washington Commonwealth Federation (1935), and the Washington Pension Union (1937), which challenged the more conservative political leadership of the state. Between them the Unemployed Citizens and the Federation claimed to have elected the mayor of Seattle in 1932 and four members of Congress in 1932–6; the Federation controlled the Democratic organization in King County (Seattle), whose delegation to the legislature in 1933 included seven relief workers. They found it easier, however, to invoke discontent with the establishment than to construct a program or to find leaders. Within months after electing its first candidate, Mayor John ("Revolving") Dore, the League regretted its endorsement because of his opposition to strikes and turned against him; Representative Marion Zioncheck went insane gradually enough before his suicide in 1936 to make himself and his ideas appear ridiculous; and although Lieutenant-Governor Victor A. Meyers supported the legislators who wanted to expand the state's social welfare programs, he was far better known for his antics as a candidate. The insurgents grew in numbers and in sheer noise faster than in discipline or political acumen, to the point where leaders of the U. C. L. and W. P. U. concurred with the opposition by denouncing Communism within their own ranks. In 1936, the W. C. F. succeeded in capturing the Democratic state convention, only to arouse the conservative wing of the party (perhaps with Republican assistance) to victory in the primary; the result was the reelection of Clarence Martin, a conservative, as governor. Four years later, when the Federation helped to nominate former Senator Clarence Dill to succeed Martin, the victor was the Republican candidate, Arthur Langlie.[8]

Meanwhile, insurgency flared and failed among the Democrats in California, where in 1930 James Rolph won nearly three fourths of the votes for governor in a campaign in which his opponent, Milton K. Young, a former "wet," had persuaded the Democratic convention to accept the platform of the Anti-Saloon League on national prohibition. "Thank goodness," Will Rogers had remarked, "we won't be reformed during this administration at least." Rolph's death in 1934 left the governorship to Lieutenant-Governor Frank F. Merriam, sixty-eight years old and anathema to progressives both for his ethics and for his policy. The prospects of the Democrats had been good as early as 1932, when Franklin D. Roosevelt's landslide had carried William Gibbs McAdoo to the Senate. Their prospects were so much better, and their purposes apparently had moved so much further to the left, that the veteran Socialist writer Upton Sinclair, who recognized the advantages of belonging to "a party which has grandfathers," sought and won the Democratic nomination for governor. Sinclair's program of "production for use" appealed to many who were not Socialists, more perhaps than the planned scarcity of the New Deal's agricultural policy in a state where surplus fruit and vegetables rotted in sight of the unemployed. Chester Rowell, by then editor of the *San Francisco Chronicle,* protested to his publisher his reluctance to support Merriam, whose principal associates had opposed all the progressive measures of the last generation. "These measures, whether all of them pleased you or not, did please the people," he said, "and were our protection against the I. W. W. menace, by removing its only actual grievances.

---

[8] Vern Countryman: *Un-American Activities in the State of Washington; The Work of the Canwell Committee* (Ithaca: Cornell University Press; 1951), pp. 3–9. George Creel: "The Loudest Radical," *Collier's,* Vol. XCVII (May 30, 1936), pp. 15, 52. McCarthy in *The Nation,* Vol. CXLIII, pp. 442–4. Arthur Hillman: *The Unemployed Citizens' League of Seattle* (Seattle: University of Washington Press; 1934). Kate Archibald: "Why the State of Washington Likes Langlie," *Christian Science Monitor* magazine, February 8, 1941, p. 5.

They are our chief safeguard against the Communist menace now." Hiram Johnson remained grimly silent, but the *Chronicle* and most of the press endorsed the Republican ticket. Facing the choice, as George Creel said, between catalepsy with Merriam and epilepsy with Sinclair, associates of Senator McAdoo (with encouragement from Washington) tried to persuade Sinclair to withdraw after his nomination. Ultimately much of the Democratic leadership of the state quietly abandoned Sinclair for Merriam as the candidate more likely to win than the Progressive, Raymond Haight.[9]

When the Democrats did elect a governor of California in 1938—a bad year for New Deal Democrats nationally—their successes were, at best, muted. Culbert L. Olson suffered throughout his term from poor health, but still more from his relations with his own party. Tactless and hot-tempered, he quarreled with Democrats in the legislature and managed to alienate both sides in the controversy over the Ham-and-Eggs pension plan by first endorsing and then opposing it.[1]

Much of the fundamentalism of the West in the twenties and thirties seemed to be a reaction to extremes on the left, which in turn found their own provocation. The drift to class conflict was greatest in California, where Sinclair harvested the fruits of Los Angeles's cultivated indifference to labor and to poverty, and where Merriam in turn profited by the spectacle of the general strike in San Francisco (July 16–19, 1934), which the press described as the harbinger of revolution that the Industrial Association said it was even while conservatives in the labor movement frustrated the Communists and dominated the General Strike Executive Committee. Neither side satisfied moderates or progressives like the veteran publisher of the *Bee* newspapers, C. K. McClatchy, who asked: "Why save California from Sinclair alone? Why not save it also from the greater menace of Merriam?" And yet Merriam made concessions to a changing world: he declared himself

[9] Ronald E. Chinn: "Democratic Party Politics in California, 1920–1956" (unpublished doctoral thesis, University of California at Berkeley; 1958), pp. 47–51. *The New York Times,* November 9, 1930, Sec. III, p. 6, col. 2; September 28, 1930, Sec. III, p. 8, col. 3. Upton Sinclair: *I, Candidate for Governor: And How I Got Licked* (Pasadena, 1935), pp. 6–7 and *passim.* Chester Rowell to George T. Cameron, Aug. 8, 1934 (Rowell papers, Bancroft Library). George Creel: *Rebel at Large . . .* (New York: G. P. Putnam's Sons; 1947), p. 288. Russel M. Posner: "A. P. Giannini and the 1934 Campaign in California," Historical Society of Southern California, *Quarterly,* Vol. XXXIX (June 1957), pp. 190–201.

[1] Robert E. Burke: *Olson's New Deal for California* (Berkeley: University of California Press; 1953).

"heartily in accord with President Roosevelt's policies," recognized his indebtedness to New Dealers who supported him, and, after election, suggested a state income tax and advocated some elements of Sinclair's plan of production for use.[2]

A large part of the progressive program in California, like Hiram Johnson's seat in the Senate, had become too firmly established for conservative politicians to oppose squarely. Both Rolph and Merriam avoided the clumsiness of Governor Friend Richardson (1923–7), whose animus against progressives inspired them to reorganize and defeat him in 1926. The utilities and their associates were able to defeat the progressives' water and power program in the 1920's, but by the time Rolph became governor, public sentiment was so clear that in supporting the Central Valley Project bill (1933) he simply recognized political reality.[3] Even more fully, progressives and conservatives joined in supporting the projects to bring water and electric power from the Colorado River to southern California, which Dr. John H. Haynes sponsored as water and power commissioner of Los Angeles and Hiram Johnson as co-author of the Swing-Johnson Bill in Congress (adopted 1928), and which the utilities' lobbies denounced as "the instrusion of the Federal Government into the field of private business." Water and power had so clearly become prerequisites to the future of Los Angeles that businessmen demanded their development regardless of the monopoly of the Los Angeles Gas and Electric Company, which finally sold its electrical system in 1936.[4] (Meanwhile, most California progressives were no more sensitive than the real-estate men to the interests of

---

[2] Wilfrid H. Crook: *Communism and the General Strike* (Hamden, Conn.: Shoe String Press; 1960), pp. 107–48. Charles K. McClatchy: *Private Thinks by C. K. and Other Writings . . .* (New York: Scribner Press; 1936), p. 122. Posner in Historical Society of Southern California, *Quarterly,* Vol. XXXIX, pp. 199–200. Sinclair: *I, Candidate for Governor* (1935), pp. 203–4.

[3] Russel M. Posner: "The Progressive Voters League, 1923–26," *California Historical Society Quarterly,* Vol. XXXVI (September 1957), pp. 251–61. Posner: "The Bank of Italy and the 1926 Campaign in California," *California Historical Society Quarterly,* Vol. XXXVII (September, December 1958), pp. 267–75, 347–58. Duncan Aikman: "California's Sun God," *The Nation,* Vol. CXXXII (January 14, 1931), pp. 35–7. Robert de Roos: *The Thirsty Land: The Story of the Central Valley Project* (Stanford: Stanford University Press; 1948), pp. 24–6, 30, and *passim.*

[4] 70 Cong., 1 Sess., Senate Document 92, part 71A (Vol. 53, part 1), p. 332. *The Memoirs of Ray Lyman Wilbur, 1875–1949,* ed. Edgar E. Robinson and Paul C. Edwards (Stanford: Stanford University Press; 1960), p. 444.

Arizona and the other claimants to Colorado River water who contested the "water imperialism" of Los Angeles.)

The cause of public power continued to appeal as well in Oregon, which for the most part avoided the political extremes of its neighbors to north and south, as it also had avoided their more speculative economic development. Senator Charles L. McNary, the most popular political leader in the state between the two world wars, personified the moderate, undoctrinaire quality of Oregon politics. A loyal party man, he was on better terms with Franklin D. Roosevelt than with Herbert Hoover, and he did some of his most effective work as minority leader of the Senate in the thirties by persuading his colleagues to contain their partisanship while the Democrats fell out among themselves. His long fights for public power and for farm relief (the McNary-Haugen Bill) appealed strongly to voters. As the editor of the *Oregon Labor Press* said in 1940: "If McNary were the nominee for President and Willkie the nominee for Vice-President, the Republicans would be a 100 per cent better bet out this way." During the later twenties, sentiment for hydroelectric development grew throughout the state, especially among the Grangers, and also in Portland, where State Senator George W. Joseph challenged the granting of an excessively generous franchise to a new electric company. He led a battle that gave him the Republican nomination for governor in 1930 on a platform pledging public development of power. Joseph's sudden death and the State Central Committee's choice of a leader of the opposition to replace him aroused the reformers to nominate the respected Portland merchant Julius Meier as an independent candidate and to elect him overwhelmingly, at the same time adopting a constitutional amendment for public-utility districts.[5]

In the thirties, "conservative Oregon," as the editor of the *Oregonian* called it, seemed to justify its reputation by persistently opposing spending measures and by adopting the anti-picketing initiative of 1938, but its commitment to the right was never clear. At the time of Meier's landslide in 1930, Major-General Charles H. Martin had won election to

---

[5] John D. Phillips: "Charles L. McNary: Progressive Ideology and Minority Politics during the New Deal" (unpublished master's thesis, University of Oregon; 1961). Richard L. Neuberger: "Where McNary Heads the Ticket," *The Nation*, Vol. CLI (September 28, 1940), pp. 268–9. Virgil MacMickle: "A Jolt for High Light Bills," *The Nation*, Vol. CXXXII (January 28, 1931), pp. 96–8.

Congress as a progressive Democrat advocating public development of hydroelectric power. In 1934, as a candidate for the governorship, he emphasized his support of the President's program, and his election, *The New York Times* commented, placed Oregon more solidly behind the New Deal than in 1932. The Democrats even won control of the state house of representatives for the first time since 1878. It was only later that Martin fell out with President Roosevelt and Secretary Harold Ickes (who helped defeat him in the primary in 1938) and that it was clear that he wanted electric power for large factories rather than for homes and farms. Another apparent switch to the right was that of Rufus Holman, who had supported Meier for governor in 1930, but who won a seat in the Senate in 1938 as a conservative Republican supporter of Martin. Martin's Republican successor, Charles Sprague, editor of the Salem *Oregon Statesman*, opposed the anti-picketing measure earlier and more emphatically than the Democratic candidate, Hess, and in general campaigned far to the left of his party's previous platforms, paying tributes to President Roosevelt and recommending the administration's polices on public power.[6] The Republican sweep in Oregon in 1938 coincided with reverses for the New Deal throughout the nation, but with Sprague heading the state government and McNary the Congressional delegation, it was not a clear sign of reaction.

Oregon's moderation extended into the Oregon Commonwealth Federation (1937–41), which played an important part in defeating Martin in 1938. Howard Costigan of the Washington Federation had helped to organize it, but the O. C. F. and Monroe Sweetland, its executive secretary, were never so controversial or so leftist as their neighbors. The Socialists noted with satisfaction that Sweetland and his board resisted Communist arguments on foreign policy in 1937, but by 1938 the Socialist party of Oregon withdrew from the O. C. F., protesting that it had uncritically accepted the New Deal as its platform and had become "simply a pressure group within the Democratic Party." (In fact it backed some Republicans as well as Democrats.)[7]

---

[6] Charles B. Frisbie: "Exciting News from Oregon," *The Nation*, Vol. CXXI (December 24, 1930), p. 707. *The New York Times*, November 18, 1934, Sec. IV, p. 7, col. 2.

[7] Portland *Oregonian*, November 13, 1938, magazine, p. 2, cols. 1–3. A. Robert Smith: *The Tiger in the Senate* (New York: Doubleday & Co.; 1962), pp. 203–4, 207. "Politics on the West Coast," *Fortune*, Vol. XXI (March 1940), pp. 135, 138, 140. *Socialist Call*, Vol. II (December 18, 1937), p. 8, cols. 4–5; Vol. IV (August 13, 1938), p. 3, cols. 1–3.

In the interior states, political alternations and contrasts were on the whole less dramatic. Idaho made a sensation in 1938 by retiring James Pope, one of the few dependable New Deal senators from the Far West at the time, in favor of Representative D. Worth Clark, a conservative who had endorsed the Townsend old-age pension plan. Utah gave an impressive token of the general shift toward the Democrats in 1932 by electing a New Dealer, Professor Elbert D. Thomas, to the seat that Senator Reed Smoot had held for six terms without benefit of personal charm or oratorical skill; and Democrats prevailed through the decade despite the open preference of Mormon leaders for more conservative Republican candidates. Yet Senator William H. King and Governor Henry H. Blood, both Democrats, stood well to the right of Thomas; and the Democratic state government continued conservative despite the economic strains in a population in which unemployment was well above and income well below the national averages. It even went along with the fiction that Utah had little need for public relief because the Church took care of her own (at a time when the percentage of population on relief in the state was at least half again greater than over the nation.)[8] Nevada's leaders were no more interested in reform under Pat McCarran's leadership in the thirties than they had been in the twenties, except insofar as it was expedient to help the New Deal in exchange for low grazing fees and high prices for silver.

During the great depression, the old idea that the West led the nation in opportunity and in democracy seemed out of date. Johnson, Borah, and McNary were still great names, but none of them, or any other Westerner, was a prospect for the presidency as Johnson had been in 1920 and before. Borah, the *San Francisco Chronicle* observed in 1924, was a "Regressive Progressive," one of those progressives who had "the paradise complex about the past."[9] They became old men (Borah died in 1940, McNary in 1944, Johnson in 1945), and they, and the West itself, seemed to have less to say to the older states than in the days when Oregon and California had been showplaces of popular government. In the prosperous twenties and the depressed thirties, Americans seemed to have outgrown the rural and small-town faith that the Pacific

---

[8] *The New York Times*, August 24, 1938, p. 1, col. 1; August 28, 1938, Sec. IV, p. 7, col. 6. *Western Politics*, ed. Frank H. Jonas (Salt Lake City: University of Utah Press; 1961), pp. 275–79, 296. F. E. Hall: "Poor Little Rich State," *Commonweal*, Vol. XXXI (February 9, 1940), pp. 342–3.

[9] *San Francisco Chronicle*, March 7, 1924, p. 8, cols. 5–6.

slope had represented to the nation even while it lived an urban life. The great opportunities, and then the great problems and their solutions, all seemed to be in the East. On the eve of their greatest growth, Westerners worried about the future of their economy and wondered whether it might in fact be hard to find uses for the water and power the New Deal had given them.

X

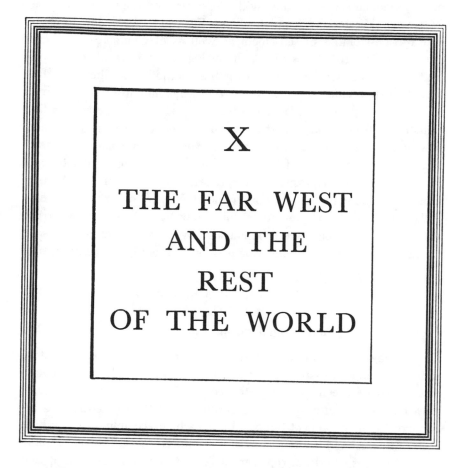

THE FAR WEST AND THE REST OF THE WORLD

War twice transformed the West more than any other part of the United States—in 1917–8 and again in 1941–5. In turn, the West greatly transformed its attitudes toward the rest of the world. In the persons of Johnson, Borah, Key Pittman of Nevada, and Burton K. Wheeler of Montana, the Far West seemed to be one of the most isolationist of sections between the two world wars; and then suddenly it was staging area, training camp, all but battleground, and finally meeting place for the world, when the United Nations came to San Francisco in April 1945.

The Far West had long been or aspired to be gateway for traffiic with the whole Pacific basin. At the beginning it had been little else: traders stopped to pick up furs from China; Jefferson and Benton spoke of "Asiatic commerce" moving by the Missouri and the Columbia. Even later, when Westerners complained that Easterners were slow to recognize the possibilities of settlement as well as of commerce, they concurred in Eastern visions of commercial gain. "I have almost caught a glimpse of the Oriental world over the tranquil and alluring surface of the great ocean," wrote a Missourian who had just returned from Oregon in 1844, and who looked forward to a rising commercial civilization on the Pacific coast.[1] Part of the argument for regular government in Oregon was that a flourishing state would open Asiatic commerce to American capital; the friends and builders of transcontinental railroads held out such prospects from the 1840's on, when Asa Whitney lobbied for a road to the Columbia connecting by train ferry with Siberia. Although the first transcontinental line (1869) found the Orient's trade with Europe moving more economically by Suez, Westerners grasped at the promise of "What the Engines Said" according to Bret Harte:

> You brag of your East! *You* do?
> Why, *I* bring the East to *you*!
> All the Orient—all Cathay—
> Find through me the shortest way.[2]

Dispatching a "silk train" at high speed over a newly completed Western railroad became as standard a ritual as driving the last spike, though apart from its use in publicity, the economic return from such traffic must have been slight: processing continued on the east coast, and because of the high value of the baled silk (which accounted for the high costs of interest and insurance, and thus required that it travel as rapidly as possible), it could not represent a large fraction of the freight that the railroads handled.

Although the riches of Cathay continued to fascinate Westerners in the twentieth century, when the last of the "transcontinental" railroad routes (Milwaukee Road in 1909, Western Pacific in 1910) reached the coast, there was less to divide than their owners had hoped for. James J. Hill had hoped and worked for the Far Eastern trade as much as any

---

[1] Thomas Hart Benton: *Selections of Editorial Articles from the St. Louis Enquirer* [1818–9], *on the Subject of Oregon and Texas* . . . (St. Louis: Missourian Office; 1844). Letter from G. W. from Jefferson City, Missouri, Dec. 28, 1844, in *Littel's Living Age*, Vol. IV (February 8, 1845), p. 383.

[2] J. Quinn Thornton: *Oregon and California in 1848* . . . (New York: Harper & Brothers; 1849), Vol. II, p. 257. *Overland Monthly*, Vol. II (June 1869), p. 577, and cf. pp. 478, 490.

man, believing that China and Japan could supply markets for the westbound freight that his railroad needed; in 1903 and 1904 he launched two huge freighters to run between Seattle and Yokohama and Hong Kong, and he named the Great Northern's new passenger train the "Oriental Limited" in 1905, year of the Lewis and Clark Centennial Exposition and Oriental Fair at Portland. Seattle still emphasized Far Eastern themes at the Alaska-Yukon-Pacific Exposition in 1909, but Hill bluntly pointed out the decline of trade after 1905. "The country needs to rid itself," he said in 1910, "of the illusion that its Oriental trade is to be one of the big elements in its future prosperity—a conception still lingering grotesquely in many minds. . . ."[3]

Hill blamed the weakness of American commerce in the Far East on the failure of the United States to match the subsidies foreign governments gave to their merchant marines. But he and the people of Seattle had raised their hopes just as Japan, victor in the war with Russia in 1904–5, began to tighten her hold on the Asiatic mainland, and shortly before the completion of the Panama Canal (1915) opened a second short route between Pacific and Atlantic markets. By the time American subsidies had increased, during and after the First World War, Japanese influence had increased as well; the effects on trade anticipated the much broader effects of conquests by Japanese and communist forces in the 1930's and after. Total foreign trade dropped off in value relative to the American economy as a whole (the value of exports fell from 7.4 percent of the gross national product just after the Spanish-American War to 4.0 percent in 1940); and though trade with Asia increased more than trade with Europe, it did not keep up with the populations of the Pacific-coast states, through which much of it passed.

Nevertheless, the Orient never fell out of sight and mind in the American West, particularly on the coast. The habit of thinking commercially persisted long after industry and the home market accounted for more of the economy than commerce and foreign markets did. Westerners invested in Asiatic countries and traveled there much more than other Americans did. The great concentrations of population were at the ports where servicemen embarked in wartime to defend the

---

[3] Joseph G. Pyle: *The Life of James J. Hill* (New York: Doubleday, Page & Co.; 1917), Vol. II, pp. 53, 59. George A. Frykman: "The Alaska-Yukon-Pacific Exposition, 1909," *Pacific Northwest Quarterly*, Vol. LIII (July 1962), pp. 89–99. James J. Hill: "A Lost Opportunity on the Pacific," *World's Work*, Vol. XIX (January 1910), p. 12, 503.

American stake in Asia, and where the end of wartime shipbuilding aroused hopes for peacetime uses for the yards. The people of San Francisco and Seattle faced their windows overlooking the water; their pleasure at the scene varied with the count of ships no less than with the sunset. Los Angeles expressed its metropolitan ambitions in its striving for a port to match San Francisco Bay, and the rivalries of Portland and Seattle came to focus in their efforts to improve their channels and harbors and to compete for the sea routes to Alaska and across the north Pacific. Their hopes were more than habit, for major Western industries looked to Far Eastern markets. The Pacific Coast Oil Company (later Standard Oil of California) decided in 1904 to develop facilities at Richmond to supply the Far East with kerosene, and until the First World War kerosene predominated in its foreign sales; petroleum remained a major export, along with lumber, grain, and a few other low-grade commodities, even after the lamps of China became electric and after Westerners used more gasoline and natural gas than California produced. After the First World War, Western as well as Southern cotton planters sold to Asian textile mills. West-coast factories used more tung, soy, sesame, and cocoanut oil than lard or corn oil. About half the foreign trade of the port of San Francisco, 1900–39, was with Far Eastern Asia. Exports of lumber (predominantly trans-Pacific) never accounted for more than a small part of the trade of the Douglas-fir area of the Northwest, but they were highly visible and may have constituted a vital margin.[4] One of the most conspicuous products of Northwestern mills was the "Japanese square," up to twenty-four inches across, trimmed from fir and hemlock logs.

Western awareness of the Pacific beyond fed heavily on contacts with Alaska and Hawaii. Alaska had traded through Monterey and still more through San Francisco when Russia owned both sides of Bering Strait—it did a brisk business in Alaskan ice at $75 a ton in the early 1850's. Hawaii was a regular stopping point for the early traders to the Columbia River, and the Hawaiian trade revived after settlers came to Oregon in the 1830's and 1840's. As Sir George Simpson pointed out

[4] Gerald T. White: *Formative Years in the Far West: A History of Standard Oil Company of California and Predecessors Through 1919* (New York: Appleton-Century-Crofts; 1962), pp. 281–3, 303, 516. Board of State Harbor Commissioners for San Francisco Harbor: *World Trade Center in San Francisco . . .* ([Sacramento: 1946]), pp. 79, 80. *Foreign Trade Interests in the State of Oregon,* 86 Cong., 1 Sess., House Document 232 (1959), pp. 2–3, 24.

after his visit in 1842, the Hawaiian group was a kind of stepping-stone from the American coast to China and also, because of prevailing winds, from Cape Horn and the Atlantic to California and the Northwest coast.[5]

After the middle of the nineteenth century, both Alaska and Hawaii changed, and with them their relationships to the American coast. The primary traders in Alaska had been Russians who remained the year round, because St. Petersburg and Moscow were too far to return to for the winter, and who looked to California and Oregon for provisions. As the harvest in fur seals declined, and still more when the United States bought Alaska (1867) and the salmon fishermen learned to can as well as salt their catch, predominance fell to Americans who moved to and from San Francisco with the seasons. The "San Francisco businessmen," the Sitka *Alaskan* complained in 1890, "do not intend to contribute a cent to the material welfare of the Territory, bringing, as they do, all the supplies they need with them, and engaging the help they require below. . . ." The great gold rush of 1897–8 through Alaska into the Klondike and the Yukon only modified Alaska's essentially dependent condition and extractive economy, although it shifted the principal connection from San Francisco to Seattle, whose newly completed railroads joined in promoting (over the objections of Portland) the idea that she was the natural gateway to the North. Geographical advantages did not operate to the ultimate, however. By the Merchant Marine Act of 1920, sponsored by Senator Wesley Jones of Washington, Congress restricted the Alaskan trade to American ships, eliminating competition out of Vancouver and Prince Rupert, to the north, and thus exposing it to monopoly rates; and both the industry and the fishermen's unions, controlled in Seattle and San Francisco, discriminated against resident fishermen.[6] Meanwhile, population lagged behind production and in fact declined between 1880 and 1890 and between 1900 and 1929. (It was significant of the commercial and exploitative character of Alaska's economy under the domination of the coast that when

[5] E. L. Keithahn: "Alaska Ice, Inc.," *Pacific Northwest Quarterly,* Vol. XXXVI (April 1945), pp. 121–31. *Harper's,* Vol. XIII (June 1856), p. 117. Jones A. Jonasson: "Portland and the Alaska Trade," *Pacific Northwest Quarterly,* Vol. XXX (April 1939), pp. 131–44. George Simpson: *Narrative of a Journey Round the World during the Years 1841 and 1842* (London: Henry Colburn Publishers; 1847), Vol. II, pp. 132–3.

[6] Sitka *Alaskan,* June 14, 1890, quoted in Ernest Gruening: *The State of Alaska* (New York: Random House; 1954), pp. 85, 240–4, 385–91.

the United States government recruited settlers for the Matanuska Valley of southern Alaska in 1934 and 1935, it turned to Michigan, Minnesota, and Wisconsin rather than to the states west of the Rockies, where people were less familiar with a harsh climate and were accustomed to think of Alaska as a place to work or invest in rather than a place to live in.

Hawaii, too, passed under the dominance of San Francisco. Even before American whalers lost most of their fleet in the ice off the northern Alaskan coast in 1871, the industry had declined, and with it New England's trade with the islands, while that of the Pacific coast greatly increased. Although most of the sugar refiners of San Francisco Bay opposed commercial reciprocity, fearing competition of the higher-grade Hawaiian sugars, Claus Spreckels, one of the principal refiners, turned the reciprocity treaty of 1875 to his advantage by obtaining a large concession of plantation land. For a generation, Spreckels and his sons were dominant figures in Hawaiian affairs, economic and political: his California Sugar Refinery in San Francisco refined most Hawaiian sugar; and his Oceanic Steamship Company monopolized traffic with California. By 1890 Hawaiian sugar production was more than ten times what it had been before reciprocity, and San Francisco's trade with Hawaii was second only to its trade with Great Britain, and nearly twice as large as its trade with China. But Spreckels already had begun to develop sugar-beet plantations in the Salinas Valley, south of Monterey. He opposed annexation (1898) because it would end the importation of the cheap contract labor from Asia that he and other planters in Hawaii depended on, and because bringing Hawaiian sugar wholly within the American system of tariffs and subsidies would threaten his interests as a planter in California. On the eve of annexation, Californians owned nearly three fifths of the stock of all the Hawaiian sugar companies,[7] but the balance of control soon shifted. The California and Hawaiian Sugar Refining Corporation (1905) refined its sugar in California, at

[7] Sylvester K. Stevens: *American Expansion in Hawaii, 1842–1898* (Harrisburg: Archives Publishing Company of Pennsylvania; 1945), pp. 87–9, 130–2, 161–2, 283. Jacob Adler: "The Oceanic Steamship Company: A Link in Claus Spreckels' Hawaiian Sugar Empire," *Pacific Historical Review*, Vol. XXIX (August 1960), pp. 257–69. Katharine Coman: "The History of Contract Labor in the Hawaiian Islands," American Economic Association, *Publications*, third series, Vol. IV (August 1903), p. 65. William A. Russ, Jr.: *The Hawaiian Revolution (1893–94)* (Selinsgrove, Pa.: Susquehanna University Press; 1959), pp. 202–3. Russ: *The Hawaiian Republic (1894–98) . . .* (Selinsgrove: Susquehanna University Press; 1961), p. 187.

Crockett, near San Francisco; its owners were Hawaiian sugar agencies, which also acquired stock in the Matson Navigation Company and emulated Spreckels by integrating the related industries while keeping control in the islands. Thereafter the Hawaiian economy was more oligarchical then colonial; Hawaiian commerce accounted for a large fraction of the business of the port of San Francisco, which in turn represented the outside world to the people of Hawaii, but the "Big Five"—the sugar factors who came to control practically all the sugar industry and importantly to influence the rest of the economy—were residents, much as the principal capitalists of California were residents. Hawaii was more important to the prosperity of the port of San Francisco, and in time to that of the port of Los Angeles, than California was in the affairs of Hawaii.

To the North and South, Westerners looked also to British Columbia and its neighbors and to Mexico. The Fraser River gold rush of 1858 was to such a large extent "merely the transplanting of a part of California and the Pacific states to a land under the British flag"—as H. F. Angus has said—that all business was in American currency and the colony itself issued notes in dollars rather than in sterling. The San Francisco merchants established branches at Victoria as they did at the mines of Oregon and Nevada, and the ships of San Francisco were the link between Victoria and Canada and Britain itself. American miners and American promoters of such jumping-off points into British territory as Whatcom (in 1858) and Seattle and Skagway (in 1897) acted as if the boundary settlement of 1846 had never been, as if the whole area still was the old Oregon Country. Confederation and the assimilation of the territories of the Hudson's Bay Company (1867–9) constituted the beginnings of a slow integration north of the border, but the metropolis of the "Inland Empire" in southeastern British Columbia as well as in northern Idaho in the 1880's was Spokane, and for some years American smelters in Washington and Montana handled the ore from the Kootenay mines. "The Kootenay country is peopled altogether by American prospectors," a Canadian customs official observed, "and its development is chiefly in the hands of American capitalists."[8] Americans so predominated in the Klondike gold rush of 1897 that they hardly thought of it as Canadian; Seattle was the San Francisco of the

[8] *British Columbia and the United States* . . . , ed. H. F. Angus (Toronto: The Ryerson Press; 1942), pp. 141–2, 150–1, 171–3, 184–90, 265–6, 280–3, 335–57.

new generation. The great immigration of American wheat farmers into the Canadian West early in the twentieth century came chiefly from the upper Mississippi Valley states, but Mormons moved from Utah into southern Alberta as early as 1887, first to escape political persecution and then to grow sugar beets; Salt Lake City remained their ecclesiastical and social capital, as it did for the Mormons of Idaho.[9] The prospect that western Canada might become American declined; trade across the border increased. Ultimately the trade of the American Far West with western Canada exceeded trade with Latin America, the Orient, and the whole western Pacific basin, and included such lasting connections as pipelines for the transmission of oil and, after 1957, of natural gas from the Peace River region of Alberta. And although Canadian lumber became an offense to the Pacific Northwest, increasingly the major American producers bought into Canada, much as the Middle Western and Southern lumbermen had bought into the virgin stands of the Northwest.

Far Western interests in Mexico in the twentieth century involved fewer persons than Far Western interests in Canada did, and were less coordinate and more colonial. Cattle ranches of southern California operated in Lower California since the 1840's, even after the drought of the 1860's decimated their herds north of the border; they gave an American character to the northern part of the peninsula that persisted in different form after prohibition inspired tourist traffic to the bars of Tijuana. Early in the dictatorship of General Porfirio Díaz (1876–1910), American interests began to become industrial as well as agricultural, and Western capitalists received major concessions along with the Guggenheims, Greenes, and Goulds. George Hearst (later senator from California, 1886–91, and father of the publisher), who made a fortune on the Comstock Lode and thereafter invested still more profitably in Utah, Dakota, and Montana, was one of the first concessionaires; he acquired a rich gold and silver mine in Durango about 1879, and soon afterward extensive timberlands stretching from Vera Cruz into Yucatán, and a baronial ranch in Chihuahua. The Southern Pacific Company controlled two major railroad lines in Mexico, beginning with

[9] Lowry Nelson: *The Mormon Village: A Pattern and Technique of Land Settlement* (Salt Lake City: University of Utah Press; 1952), pp. 215–71. Marcus L. Hansen and John B. Brebner: *The Mingling of the Canadian and American Peoples* (New Haven: Yale University Press; 1940), pp. 200–1.

the Mexican International, which built southwestward from Piedras Negras (Eagle Pass, Texas) to Durango by 1892. When the S. P. sold this line (1903), its chief Mexican outlet became the Southern Pacific of Mexico, which eventually reached Mazatlán and (1927) the mining capital of Guadalajara.[1] Meanwhile the Southern Pacific had built a branch that dipped southward into Lower California, the Inter-California (completed in 1911); and John D. Spreckels built a line that crossed the border to give San Diego a direct connection with the East, the San Diego and Arizona Eastern (completed in 1919), which the S. P. acquired in 1933.[2]

But the most lucrative of Far Western interests in Mexico, and among the politically most significant, were those that concerned oil and water. Edward L. Doheny, whose drilling in Los Angeles in 1892 touched off its first boom in oil, formed the Mexican Petroleum Company of California (1900) to develop fields near Tampico, and thus founded the Mexican petroleum industry as well. The development of irrigation agriculture north of the border inspired southern Californians to explore possibilities in Lower California, particularly in the delta of the Colorado River during the development of the Imperial Valley; General Otis of the *Los Angeles Times,* the California Development Company, and the Southern Pacific Railroad and its affiliates became large landholders. Otis bought over 832,000 acres in 1900; until the 1930's his Colorado River Land Company remained singularly immune to agrarian reforms in Mexico; it leased land to Americans, who used Chinese laborers to grow cotton.[3]

---

[1] In 1951 the Southern Pacific sold this line to the Mexican government for $12,000,000, less than its value as scrap iron. *The New York Times,* December 22, 1951, p. 22, col. 2.

[2] Eugene K. Chamberlin: "United States Interests in Lower California" (unpublished doctoral thesis, University of California at Berkeley; 1949), pp. 402–5. Fremont and Cora M. Older: *The Life of George Hearst, California Pioneer* (San Francisco: John Henry Nash; 1933), pp. 140, 149. David M. Pletcher: *Rails, Mines, and Progress: Seven American Promoters in Mexico, 1867–1911* (Ithaca: Cornell University Press; 1958), pp. 101–4. Cleona Lewis: *America's Stake in International Investments* (Washington: Brookings Institution; 1938), pp. 316–17.

[3] Chamberlin: "United States Interests," pp. 393–400. Edward Bosqui: Memoirs ([San Francisco: 1904]), pp. 240–1. Lowell L. Blaisdell: *The Desert Revolution: Baja California, 1911* (Madison: University of Wisconsin Press; 1962), p. 35. Charles D. Willard: *A History of the Chamber of Commerce of Los Angeles . . .* (Los Angeles: Press of Kingsley-Barnes & Neuer Co.; 1899), pp. 74–6. Chamberlin: "Mexican Colonization versus American Interests in Lower California," *Pacific Historical Review,* Vol. XX (February 1951), pp. 43–7.

Commerce and investment helped to keep Westerners aware of their neighbors around the Pacific basin; the circumstance that Hearst and the Otis-Chandler family controlled both land in Mexico and a significant part of the press on the coast may have led to more than awareness. Western interest in seaborne commerce contributed to pressure for naval installations, such as those on San Francisco Bay (Mare Island, 1854; and Alameda, 1940),[4] Puget Sound (Bremerton, 1891), and San Diego (1916); and these in turn, with their corollaries of ships to be built, supplies to be bought, and personnel to be quartered, drew attention to developments in defense and in international relations. But Westerners at times were most aware of foreign nations because foreigners stood out in the West itself.

The percentage of foreign-born was always high in the Far West; until late in the nineteenth century, it was higher on the Pacific slope than in the middle and northeastern Atlantic states. Moreover, various new stocks, in large enough numbers to constitute distinct groups, came first chiefly to the Pacific and mountain states—most obviously the Chinese and Japanese, most of whom remained there, but also the Italians and Greeks. "As yet we, out here, on the fringe of the continent," Frank Norris wrote in 1897, "are not a people, we are peoples—agglomerate rather than conglomerate. All up and down the coast from Mexico to Oregon are scattered 'little' Italys, 'little' Spains, 'little' Chinas, and even 'little' Russias—settlements, colonies, tiny groups of nationalities flung off from the parent stock, but holding tightly to themselves, unwilling to mix and forever harking back to their native lands." Although the percentage of foreign born on the Pacific slope dropped in the twentieth century well below that in New York and New England, they remained conspicuous by concentrating where they were unusually visible (the Italians and the Chinese in San Francisco, the Swedes in Seattle), or by figuring in controversial events and occupations, or simply by looking unlike the dominant racial stocks. The hills of San Francisco became a tower of Babel when men came from all continents to dig for gold in forty-nine, and much of the early cosmopolitan flavor of the city continued long afterwards to impress newcomers. Lord Bryce found "a population perhaps more mixed

---

[4] Frederic L. Paxson: "The Naval Station at Alameda, 1916–1940 . . . ," *Pacific Historical Review*, Vol. XIII (September 1944), pp. 235–50.

than one finds anywhere else in America, for Frenchmen, Italians, Portuguese, Greeks, and the children of Australian convicts abound there, side by side with negroes, Germans, and Irish."[5]

Yet even at San Francisco and other major crossroads the sound of strange tongues was no simple index to the quality of society. Those most audible and most visible were not necessarily the most numerous, the most influential, or the most controversial. The French were few in California—one of thirty of the foreign born in 1900, when one of five was German—but they were at once influential and detached, many of them a species of resident transient. They came more as speculators than as settlers, maintained their press (which told more of French than of American politics), their church, their theaters, gathered to attend performances of Molière—with ballet—in the great new white-and-gold opera house at San Francisco in 1935, and took over the city for an ecstatic demonstration for President de Gaulle in 1960; yet they established the tradition of French restaurants (of different kinds) and French laundries, transplanted the French wine industry to the hillside vineyards around San Francisco Bay, and taught a whole region to eat sour French bread, artichokes, and green salads. The Italians were poor and tended to go into some of the more menial occupations, as in heavy construction and fishing, but they also went far along other lines, where Italian names came to stand for leadership (Giannini and Bacigalupi in banking, Rosellini and Rossi in politics, Di Giorgio in fruit-packing). By the 1880's the Italians dominated fishing, horticulture, and the fish and vegetable markets in California, and had achieved considerable influence in politics.[6] Italians influenced the politics and the cuisine of the West, among other things, far more than did Mexicans, who greatly outnumbered the Italians. In the twentieth century, Scandinavians were most conspicuous in the Northwest, where the landscape and the climate and the jobs in the woods and at the docks reminded them of their old homes, where a Swedish or Norwegian name (Mag-

---

[5] *Frank Norris of "The Wave": Stories & Sketches from the San Francisco Weekly, 1893 to 1897* (San Francisco: Westgate Press; 1931), pp. 134–5. James Bryce: *The American Commonwealth* (New York: The Macmillan Company; 1910), Vol. II, p. 429.

[6] *California Historical Society Quarterly*, Vol. XLI (June 1962), pp. 157–8. See also William Mulder: *Homeward to Zion: The Mormon Migration from Scandinavia* [to 1905] (Minneapolis: University of Minnesota Press; 1957); and Kenneth O. Bjork: *West of the Great Divide: Norwegian Migration to the Pacific Coast, 1847–1893* (Northfield: Norwegian-American Historical Association; 1958).

nuson, Hanson) carried a bonus at the polls, and the chain grocery stores regularly stocked knäckebröd, sill, and lutfisk; yet the logger was less likely to be from Norway or Sweden than from the American South. At most censuses there were more Swedes than Frenchmen in San Francisco, and nearly as many Danes and children of Danes in Utah as in Washington, which had over three times the population and whose dominant churches frowned not on coffee and alcohol as the Mormons did. Despite Utah's inland location and emphatically American traditions, Mormonism maintained old-country connections through the young people who returned from their missionary years versed in European languages and European genealogies.

One of the largest and most influential immigrant groups on the coast was not a group at all, so easily had it merged with the native stock: the English, Scots, Welsh, and Canadians, with the Irish sometimes with them and sometimes not. It was so large that English visitors often described Westerners as more English in appearance and habit than other Americans, despite the influx from continental Europe in the half century after the Civil War.[7] The new immigration, in fact, affected the East and Middle West much more than it affected the Far West; the percentage of all foreign-born whites of continental origin in the Pacific and Mountain states declined after the late nineteenth century whereas it rose in the rest of the country. Canadians and Americans—and their money—moved easily and almost imperceptibly over the border, seldom distinguished by appearance or accent. Although there was long a higher percentage of American-born in Canada than of Canadian-born in the United States, Canadians in twentieth-century Seattle, Spokane, and Portland far outnumbered any other foreign-born group.

Thus the cosmopolitanism of the Far West was not quite what it seemed to be. In cities where the restaurateurs and tourists bureaus advertised foreign ways most, the European-American or Asiatic-American had resided longer than in most of the East and Middle West; and assimilation went far. It had gone far even in the early days, when immigrants constituted a much larger part of the population, perhaps because so many of them were mercantile people, quick to learn new ways in their own interests. The European element in San Francisco,

[7] John White: *Sketches from America* (London: Sampson Low, Son, & Marston; 1870), pp. 135–6. Charles W. Dilke: *Greater Britain . . .* , fourth edition (London: Macmillan and Co.; 1869), p. 182.

Henry George wrote in 1880, was "more thoroughly Americanized than in the Eastern cities." The Sons of Norway and the bagpipe bands held their annual festivals, but there were few foreign "districts"; whether because the immigrant brought too little with him or found too much, his children forgot his language quickly. His most tangible contributions to culture might be in cuisine. As Josiah Royce pointed out, the cosmopolitan origins of the population did not result in a truly cosmopolitan social life. "No one who has grown up in California," wrote Royce (1886), who had grown up there when it was far more foreign than it was later, "can be under any illusion as to the small extent to which the American character, as there exemplified, has been really altered by foreign intercourse, large as the foreign population has always remained."[8]

Two of the most conspicuously different ethnic elements of pioneer times remained distinct in the recent Far West: the Oriental and the Mexican. The Chinese were conspicuous since the early 1850's both because their appearance and customs seemed strange to Americans who had not yet seen many southern and eastern Europeans, let alone Asiatics, and also because they were in fact numerous, especially in certain districts and certain occupations. Only a scattering had settled outside the Far West in the nineteenth century; within the West, most were in California, where according to the censuses of 1860, 1870, 1880, and 1890 they constituted the largest group of foreign born, ahead of the Irish and the Germans. From the mines, where native Americans tried to exclude them along with other foreigners, but eventually suffered them to glean the tailings and the less rewarding placers,[9] they moved to work that at first no one else wanted, washing clothes, digging in the fields under the hot sun, moving earth in baskets on their heads. They had, in fact, done laundry for Californians before they came to Californa; the forty-niners sent soiled shirts to Canton by clipper ship. They planted the vines at Colonel Agoston Haraszthy's estate at Buena Vista in 1860–1, and received eight dollars a month and board (the wine brought \$1.50 to \$2.00 a gallon at San Francisco); they drained the tule marshes of the San Joaquin. By 1866, ten thousand were grading and laying track along the overland route for the Central

[8] Henry George: "The Kearney Agitation in California," *Popular Science Monthly,* Vol. XVII (August 1880), p. 435. Josiah Royce: *California . . .* (1886), pp. 225–7.

[9] Nearly a third of the population of Trinity County in 1860 was Chinese (over two fifths by 1880).

Pacific. "Sometimes I see these Eastern laborers with their broad hats leisurely working in the fruit-gardens," wrote Charles L. Brace, who saw them in 1867–8, "as if in a tea plantation. . . . Without them," Brace said, "no railroads would be built or manufactures carried on, and half of the grain and fruit production of the State would at once be cut off or never gathered."[1] In 1870 in San Francisco they made 19 percent of the shoes, 64 percent of the woolens, 91 percent of the cigars;[2] all over the Far West they operated laundries and restaurants, peddled vegetables, mended cane-seat chairs, cooked, and kept house.

Westerners divided in their opinions of the Chinese almost from the beginning. Especially after the Chinese were no longer available, employers, shipowners, and the "better elements" considered them trustworthy, skillful, and more reliable than the Irish, and contended that no one else in the West would do the work they did, that the alternative was not to give jobs to native American workmen but to do without or to import goods from the East or Europe. A farmer could forget his labor problem for the season once he had contracted with the foreman of a gang of Chinese laborers, whom the Americans called coolies. The Chinese will "be to California what the African has been to the South," predicted the *California Farmer* (1854), which sought a source of agricultural labor.[3] Householders found them trusted domestic servants (more housekeepers or butlers than charmen, and at once the means and the symbols of domestic comfort)[4] and cultivated merchants whose invitations to holiday dinners conferred social distinction. Friends of the Chinese often observed that their principal critics were themselves

---

[1] Vincent P. Carosso: *The California Wine Industry: A Study of the Formative Years, 1830–1895* (Berkeley: University of California Press; 1951), p. 45. Ellis P. Oberholtzer: *A History of the United States Since the Civil War* (New York: The Macmillan Company; 1917–37), Vol. I, p. 330. Charles L. Brace: *The New West: or, California in 1867–1868* (New York: G. P. Putnam & Son; 1869), pp. 208, 223–4.

[2] Mary R. Coolidge: *Chinese Immigration* (New York: Henry Holt & Co.; 1909), pp. 358–77.

[3] Varden Fuller: "The Supply of Agricultural Labor as a Factor in the Evolution of Farm Organization in California," U. S. Senate, Committee on Education and Labor: *Violations of Free Speech and Rights of Labor,* Hearings before a Subcommittee on S. Res. 266, 76 Cong., 3 Sess., Part. 54, *Agricultural Labor in California* (1941), pp. 19,400, 19,802, and *passim.*

[4] An Englishman remarked of the idleness of housewives who had Chinese servants: "For what good purpose this assistance sets the women free is not easy to guess; rocking the chairs seems the most arduous duty in many California homes, and it is one which is faithfully carried out." W. Shepherd: *Prairie Experiences in Handling Cattle and Sheep* (New York: O. Judd Co.; 1885), pp. 116–7.

recent immigrants—Irish draymen and German cigar-makers—and suggested that they might be trying to prove their Americanism by denying that of others who had better manners. "It pleased the rude element and the noisy politician and saloon-keepers who got nothing out of them," according to the poet Joaquin Miller, "to see the newspapers mock the quiet and solitary Chinaman. . . ."[5]

Criticism of the Chinese mounted in hard times, when the unemployed felt it was wrong that jobs should go to men who lived on handfuls of rice and sent their savings overseas. The first major wave of discriminatory taxes came as the yields in the placers declined in 1854–6; agitation increased during the dislocations following the arrival of the first transcontinental railroads in 1869 and 1883 and during the depressions of 1873 and 1893. The completion of the railroads may have contributed to unemployment more by bringing goods from Eastern factories into the Western market than by releasing construction crews (in California the Southern Pacific set the Chinese to building southward, toward Los Angeles, in the 1870's), but the railroads had brought Oriental labor into the West much more effectively than they opened Oriental markets; their role as large importers and employers of Chinese made the Chinese seem instruments of monopolists in transportation and land rather than comrades in toil. Henry George pointed to the great latifundia of the central valleys in 1871, when agriculture was still predominantly extensive and the use of cheap agricultural labor was just beginning: "What the barbarians enslaved by foreign wars were to the great landlords of ancient Italy, what the blacks of the African coast were to the great landlords of the Southern States, the Chinese coolies may be, in fact already are beginning to be, to the great landlords of our Pacific slope."[6]

Critics of Denis Kearney within the labor movement complained that his slogan, "The Chinese must go," was more relevant to the problems of small-property owners, especially farmers, than to the prob-

[5] Joaquin Miller: "The Chinese and the Exclusion Act," *North American Review,* Vol. CLXXIII (December 1901), p. 734.

[6] John S. Hittell: *The Commerce and Industries of the Pacific Coast . . .* (San Francisco: A. L. Bancroft & Co.; 1882), pp. 117–8. Rodman W. Paul: "The Origin of the Chinese Issue in California," *Mississippi Valley Historical Review,* Vol. XXV (September 1938), pp. 181–96. Elmer C. Sandmeyer: *The Anti-Chinese Movement in California* (Urbana: University of Illinois Press; 1939), pp. 32–3, 67. Henry George: *Our Land and Land Policy . . .* (New York: Doubleday & McClure Co.; 1902), p. 74.

lems of laborers. But in the early years rural protest was slight. The sponsors of the first state anti-Chinese convention, at San Francisco in 1870, were the unions, led by the Mechanics' State Council and the Knights of St. Crispin. In the later 1870's and the 1880's the unions' agitation reached its peak, and the Chinese themselves rapidly ceased to compete in the general labor market. Eventually, the more substantial threat to wages came from the new immigrants from southern and eastern Europe, both in the older states and in parts of the West where the ditchdigger or hod carrier was likely to be a Sicilian, the miner a Pole. The American Federation of Labor, nevertheless, proposed no general restriction affecting Europeans until 1897, perhaps because it was reluctant to offend potential members and relatives of members or to deny the brotherhood of European man. Labor leaders had long made their argument against the Chinese, on the other hand, on economic and social grounds; they contended, as Henry George told John Stuart Mill in a much-quoted correspondence in 1869, that it was impossible to assimilate the Chinese population and raise them to the level of the American, that they were both incurably filthy and immoral and unlikely to understand American institutions or to develop any attachment to the country. The A. F. of L. recommended exclusion in 1881; in 1902 and 1905 it repeated the nativist arguments of the Far West, warned against a "silent and irresistible" racial tide, and argued that labor should not have to meet "the enervating, killing, underselling, and underliving competition of that nerveless, wantless people, the Chinese."[7]

By that time Chinese labor was no longer the major and dynamic economic fact in the West that it had been. Responding to pressure from the Californians, and taking full advantage of the treaty of 1880, by which the United States might undertake a "reasonable" limitation or suspension, but not an absolute prohibition, Congress "suspended" —in effect, terminated—immigration of Chinese laborers in 1882. During the 1880's, as departures exceeded arrivals, the foreign-born

[7] *Frank Roney: Irish Rebel and California Labor Leader; an Autobiography,* ed. Ira B. Cross (Berkeley: University of California Press; 1931), pp. 300–1. Charles A. Barker: *Henry George* (New York: Oxford University Press; 1955), pp. 122–3, 133–4. Henry George, Jr.: *The Life of Henry George* (New York: Doubleday & McClure Co.; 1900), pp. 192–203. American Federation of Labor: *Some Reasons for Chinese Exclusion: Meat vs. Rice. American Manhood Against Asiatic Coolieism. Which Shall Survive?,* 57 Cong., 1 Sess., Senate Document 137 (1902). Philip Taft: *The A. F. of L. in the Time of Gompers* (New York: Harper & Brothers; 1957), pp. 302–5.

Chinese population began to decrease; in the 1890's it dropped more sharply still. Moreover, those who remained tended to move away from factory and farm into the less competitive occupations in the towns, typically in restaurants, laundries, and stores selling Chinese merchandise or serving chiefly Chinese. These were the years of the great growth of San Francisco's Chinatown, the mass of tenements, rooming houses, and shops along Grant Street.[8] It was already a museum piece. Yet to labor and its antagonists, the Chinese long symbolized a continuing struggle. When General Otis took over the *Los Angeles Times* in 1886, it became pro-Chinese, reversing its stand on immigration; exclusion stood for restraint of industrial freedom. "The real contest," an organizer of the Knights of Labor said in 1886, "is between labor and capital. The Chinese question is only a local affair, useful for agitation and education."[9]

Japanese immigrants partly replaced the Chinese. They came chiefly to Hawaii and the coast, and increasingly to California. In 1880 there were 92 in the six states; in 1890, there were 1,638 (1,224 in California); in 1900, 20,507 (10,264 in California; 5,769 in Washington); in 1910, 57,903 (38,214 in California; 12,177 in Washington). Some worked on railroads in Oregon and Idaho in the early 1890's, but more became farm laborers, in sugar beets in eastern Washington and truck crops in California. As on the sugar plantations of Hawaii, they were exemplary workers, having been accustomed in Japan to low incomes and to long hours of stooping in the fields, and they quickly organized in groups that employers found convenient to deal with. By 1910, when they substantially outnumbered the Chinese (67,766 to 56,934 in the United States; 57,903 to 38,377 in the six states), they seemed indispensable to California agriculture.[1]

---

[8] In the six states the foreign-born Chinese population dropped from 97,124 to 89,422 in the 1880's (increasing by 89 in Washington and by 307 in Utah); during the 1890's it dropped from 89,422 to 56,325. The Chinese-born population of San Francisco increased from 7.8 percent of the state's Chinese population in 1860 to 24.4 percent in 1870, 28.9 percent in 1880, 35.7 percent in 1890.

[9] Fred W. Riggs: *Pressures on Congress: A Study of the Repeal of Chinese Exclusion* (New York: King's Crown Press; 1950), p. 2. Coolidge: *Chinese Immigration*, pp. 382, 503. Fuller: "The Supply of Agricultural Labor," p. 19,831. Stimson: *Rise of the Labor Movement in Los Angeles*, pp. 10, 61–3. Robert C. Nesbit: *He Built Seattle: A Biography of Judge Thomas Burke* (Seattle: University of Washington Press; 1961), p. 180.

[1] Majorie R. Stearns: "The Settlement of the Japanese in Oregon," *Oregon Historical Quarterly*, Vol. XXXIX (September 1938), pp. 262–9. John T. Bramhall: "The Orient in California . . . ," *World Today*, Vol. XX (April 1911), pp. 466–7.

The growth of controversy over the Japanese was no less rapid than their advance in agriculture; they inherited the jobs of the Chinese and the old suspicions and hostility as well. American Socialists—perhaps most emphatically Jack London—turned away from their Oriental comrades; and although a Wobbly expressed characteristic scorn for the exclusionist movement as "the fight of the middle class of California, in which they employ the labor faker to back it up" (1907),[2] the I. W. W. was not interested in organizing the Japanese. Following a sharp increase in immigration early in 1900, representatives of labor organizations met in Seattle, San Francisco, and New York to ask that Congress amend the Chinese exclusion act to cover the Japanese as well. The Japanese government promptly restricted the movement of laborers, but it soon increased again, from Japan and from Hawaii, and with it alarms of a new and greater yellow peril. "If Japanese immigration is unchecked," the *San Francisco Chronicle* warned in 1905, "it is only a question of time when our rural population will be Japanese, our rural civilization Japanese, and the white population hard pressed in our cities and towns."[3]

As the editor of the *Chronicle* later pointed out, the opposition to Japanese immigration extended well beyond the labor unions;[4] it had a much broader base than the movement against the Chinese. At first it reflected a feeling that Japanese laborers were abetting monopoly in land, that they were a link in a long chain of cheap farm labor that had begun with the Chinese (or, as some insist, with the Indian) and continued in the middle twentieth century with the Mexican. Operators of large farms in California readily admitted this, insisting that to turn to the higher-priced native white labor would require radical readjustments. The perpetuation and development of "these great and highly specialized forms of agricultural activity," the state labor com-

---

[2] Paul F. Brissenden: *The I. W. W. A Study of American Syndicalism* (New York: Russell & Russell; 1957), pp. 208–9. The quotation is from George Speed, a delegate from California.

[3] Allen McLaughlin: "Chinese and Japanese Immigration," *Popular Science*, Vol. LXVI (December 1904), p. 119. B[ertram] Schrieke: *Alien Americans; a Study of Race Relations* (New York: Viking Press; 1936), p. 26. *The New York Times*, May 8, 1900, p. 1, col. 5. Portland *Oregonian*, May 9, 1900, p. 2, col. 4. Yamato Ichihashi: *Japanese in the United States . . .* (Stanford University: Stanford University Press; 1932), pp. 231, 234. Kiyoshi K. Kawakami: *American-Japanese Relations . . .* (New York: Fleming H. Revell Co.; 1912), pp. 304–6. *Literary Digest*, Vol. XXX (March 25, 1905), p. 420.

[4] John P. Young: "The Support of the Anti-Oriental Movement," *Annals of the American Academy*, Vol. XXXIV (September 1909), p. 238.

missioner reported in 1910 after listening to testimony from bonanza farmers, "must largely depend upon a supply of labor coming from without the United States. . . ."[5] Small farmers as emphatically protested that they could not survive against such competition. The California progressives' program of land settlement was in large part an attempt to maintain the family farm against it.

Actually the Japanese were the successors of the Chinese only in a loose sense. During the middle 1880's, after the Exclusion Act, hard times flooded the labor market with the urban unemployed: white men kept the great ranches together. The small white farmer was selling out long before the Japanese came and in areas they never reached. Their honeymoon with the large operators soon ended. They first antagonized the small farmer by agreeing to low wages and high rents, and then they antagonized the large farmer by competing with him as well. They were not long satisfied to work as laborers at low wages, as tenants at high rents, or indeed at any wages or rents. As the progressive leader, Chester Rowell (then editor of the *Fresno Republican*), pointed out, they fitted less satisfactorily than the Chinese into the status that white Americans preferred for them, "that of biped domestic animals in the white man's service."[6] At the time of the Japanese-American crisis of 1913, Secretary of Agriculture D. F. Houston noted that many Californians made a point of the difference between the Chinese and the Japanese; the Japanese were objectionable because they were "unwilling to remain 'mudsillers.' . . . Many of these same people tell me that they would not object to Chinese, because they are thrifty, will work for little, and are content to remain in humble status."[7]

In the long run the Japanese may have sustained the small farm more than they undermined it. A few Japanese succeeded so well that they moved into the city, as the larger white farmers had done; George Shima, the "Potato King," who began as a laborer in 1889 and became a millionaire, lived in Berkeley. But the average Japanese farm declined in size while other farms increased. By 1942 the Japanese farm averaged forty-five acres as compared with three hundred acres for other farms. And it was small not only because the Japanese produced

[5] Bramhall in *World Today,* Vol. XX, pp. 466–7.

[6] Chester H. Rowell: "Chinese and Japanese Immigrants—A Comparison," *Annals of the American Academy,* Vol. XXXIV (September 1909), pp. 223–5.

[7] David F. Houston: *Eight Years with Wilson's Cabinet, 1913 to 1920* . . . (New York: Doubleday, Page & Co.; 1926), Vol. I, p. 51.

chiefly crops that demanded more hand work than most other farmers cared to give and because at first they were content with a low standard of living, but also because they took full advantage of irrigation and other techniques to make the small unit viable and profitable. Their ascent on the agricultural ladder was unusually fast. Japanese agricultural employment reached its peak about 1909, when 41.9 percent of the labor supply on 2,369 farms in California was Japanese (ranging up to 66.3 percent in sugar beets, 85.5 percent in berries); figures for 1930 range from 7.4 percent down to less than half that. Although the Japanese helped to perpetuate corporate agriculture in the Far West, they soon ceased to be available to it.[8] No other immigrant group realized more rapidly the American dream of opportunity and home on the land.

The very success of the Japanese became their worst offense, an offense more social than economic. The complaint that they could not be assimilated into the American economy because they worked in gangs under the control of boardinghouse keepers in San Francisco changed to the complaint that they were becoming farmers in their own right. The first generation of Japanese immigrants was disturbing enough to Americans simply because they came fresh from the least Westernized sector of society in Japan (most of those who came to America, unlike the Chinese, were peasants) and were conspicuous in their adherence to ancestral ways and speech. But on top of that, their Yankee-like ambition and industry brought them ahead so fast economically that they presented the frightening spectacle of the engulfment of the rural West—the traditional seat of American opportunity—by a totally different culture.

Dissatisfaction with the Japanese developed in an atmosphere of conflicting desires that was bound to breed frustration. By the time the Japanese came, as the *Pacific Rural Press* admitted unhappily in 1909, farmers in California felt that the burden of their investments was so heavy that they must have cheap labor. It must be dependable, but dependability meant that the supply of labor must be permanent, the individual laborer temporary: he must not stay long enough to learn

---

[8] Roger Daniels: *The Politics of Prejudice; The Anti-Japanese Movement in California and the Struggle for Japanese Exclusion,* University of California Publications in History, Vol. LXXI (Berkeley: University of California Press; 1962), p. 10. Adon Poli and Warren M. Engstrand: "Japanese Agriculture on the Pacific Coast," *Journal of Land and Public Utility Economics,* Vol. XXI (November 1945), p. 355. Carey McWilliams: *Brothers under the Skin* (Boston: Little, Brown & Co.; 1943), p. 165.

Mission San Antonio, about 1895.

While building lavish imitations of European hotels and resorts, Westerners neglected the Spanish and Mexican missions of California.

Canal at Venice, California, about 1900.

Although southern California in a state of nature looked more like North Africa than like the marshes of the Adriatic coast, for a generation it tried bravely to be "the Italy of America."

Pacific Electric: first cars at Santa Monica, 1896.

When Henry E. Huntington began his investments in street railways in southern California, he allegedly predicted: "We will join this whole region into one big family." "Before Huntington," wrote Remi Nadeau (1960), "the Southland was a collection of isolated country towns. After Huntington it was a collection of 'bedroom cities,' with an unlimited source of new population."

Yosemite—Valley View, 1902.

Before the era of the automobile, most visitors to the parks saw the sights in conducted parties and stayed at hotels. The policy of the Yosemite commissioners was to "reduce the number of campers in the Valley to a minimum . . ."

Mission Inn, Riverside, California, about 1905.

The frame wing of the Glenwood Hotel that Frank A. Miller replaced in mission style in 1902–3 was, according to his biographer, "guiltless of any Spanish influence whatever." The Mission Inn, which was the

and others were trying to restore; some people supposed it was as authentically Spanish as the San Gabriel Mission, which once owned the site of Riverside, more than forty miles away.

Camping at Wallowa Lake, Oregon, in the 1890's.
The few who camped before the day of the automobile sometimes went prepared to stay.

Las Vegas, Nevada, 1906.

Las Vegas was a construction siding on the Los Angeles–Salt Lake Railroad in 1905, in its first incarnation.

Last Frontier Village, Las Vegas, Nevada, about 1956.

"The old west," observed the Las Vegas News Bureau, "is still alive at the Last Frontier Village, where tourists find a complete 'wild and woolly' western town in actual operation with attractions for the entire family. All of the buildings and their contents have been gathered from old western 'ghost towns' thus making the Last Frontier Village real and authentic."

Steamboat Rock, Green River, Dinosaur National Monument, about 1954.

During the controversy as to whether to obliterate Dinosaur Canyon with a dam, Secretary of the Interior McKay pointed out that only about 500 persons went down the Green River by boat in 1953, whereas 2,200,000 had visited Lake Mead, at Hoover Dam.

Planting trees: technology in the forest.
The helicopter is dropping Douglas fir seeds as a tractor finishes the harvest of logs.

to ask for more wages or to become a competitor.[9] When the laborer did buy his own farm, and at a high price, the white man whose neighbors had sold to him and who himself was considering selling protested that the profits of sale were irrelevant, that the American way of life was disappearing. Elwood Mead, prophet of the progressive attempt to revive rural society through irrigation (head of the California Land Settlement Board, 1917–24), quoted a farmer who answered economic arguments in defense of the Japanese by describing the changes in his own neighborhood (1920): "I live on the farm . . . where my six children were born. They go to the country school. Three years ago all their playmates were white children. Now all the children in that school except mine and those of one other farmer are Japanese. . . . I am living there without neighbors."[1] Such complaints may have reflected nothing more complex than prejudice against an unfamiliar race, but they also may have been an indication that members of the old stock were unhappy because they were abandoning their own heritage, and needed a scapegoat.

The movements to restrict Japanese immigrants and Japanese immigration ran into other difficulties from the beginning. First was the clear fact that the Chinese, many of whom came essentially as transients, had a weak government that could not effectively protect them, whereas the Japanese, who typically came to stay, had a strong government that was in no mood to accept discrimination silently. When mobs attacked and expelled Chinese in Wyoming, Washington, California, and Idaho during the hard times of the 1880's (1885–6), President Cleveland neither intervened nor apologized. Shipping firms and the San Francisco and Portland chambers of commerce occasionally expressed concern about the more extreme official measures, such as the Scott Act (1888),[2] but most Westerners felt little respect for a government that scarcely controlled its own territory. Apparently seeking Western support of his administration in 1904, President Roosevelt recommended that Congress reenact exclusion; and when nationalist feeling against exclusion and

---

[9] Varden Fuller: "The Supply of Agricultural Labor as a Factor in the Evolution of Farm Organization in California," in U. S. Senate, Committee on Education and Labor: *Violation of Free Speech and Rights of Labor,* Hearings, 76 Cong., 3 Sess., on S. Res. 266, January 13, 1940, Pt. 54 (Washington: Government Printing Office; 1940), p. 19,827.

[1] Mead: "The Japanese Land Problem of California," *Annals of the American Academy,* Vol. XCIII (January 1921), p. 52.

[2] The Scott Act refused readmission to Chinese residents temporarily absent from the United States.

against private violence against Chinese in the United States inspired an anti-American boycott (1905), Roosevelt rebuked the Chinese government sternly for the boycott but went no further to protect the Chinese than to order immigration officers to treat them courteously.[3] China's bargaining power was slight.

The movement against the Japanese ran squarely into Japanese national pride and power. Japan's victory over Russia in 1905, which alarmed exclusionists in the West, indicated to the American government that it could not exclude the Japanese as simply as it had excluded the Chinese. The Japanese people, already sensitive because of what they incorrectly imagined to have been unfriendly American intervention in the peace negotiations with Russia, were quick to take offense at suggestions of racial discrimination by law. President Roosevelt suspected that political expediency was back of much of the agitation against attendance of Japanese (a total of 93) in the public schools of San Francisco in 1905–7, when Mayor Schmitz had grasped the opportunity of a conference in the White House to renew his fading prestige—"butted himself in," as the *San Francisco Chronicle* put it, "with the obvious intent to divert public attention from his impending trial for alleged boodling."[4] "I am inclined to think," the President told Governor Gillett, "that many of [the San Franciscans] do not really wish to secure the exclusion of Japanese laborers, because they feel that to do so would be to take away one of their political assets. . . ." But Roosevelt and his successors in the White House had to make substantial concessions to the politicians of San Francisco and the coast and to the Japanese as well. Roosevelt persuaded the San Francisco school board and the California legislature to renounce anti-Japanese measures in return for promises of more effective though less provocative action by the United States government. By the Gentlemen's Agreement of 1908, exclusion rested essentially on the cooperation of the

---

[3] B. P. Wilcox: "Anti-Chinese Riots in Washington," *Washington Historical Quarterly*, Vol. XX (July 1929), pp. 204–12. Jules A. Karlin: "The Anti-Chinese Outbreaks in Seattle, 1885–1886," *Pacific Northwest Quarterly*, Vol. XXXIX (April 1948), pp. 103–30. Lynwood Carranco: "Chinese Expulsion from Humboldt County," *Pacific Historical Review*, Vol. XXX (November 1961), pp. 329–40. Howard K. Beale: *Theodore Roosevelt and the Rise of America to World Power* (Baltimore: Johns Hopkins Press; 1956), pp. 211–38.

[4] Raymond L. Buell: "The Development of Anti-Japanese Agitation in the United States," *Political Science Quarterly*, Vol. XXXVII (December 1922), p. 637.

Japanese government[5] and thus on Japanese rather than American action in a jurisdiction that—whatever its international repercussions—was essentially domestic. Several years later, in 1913, when the California legislature was considering the Webb bill to restrict Japanese land tenure, President Wilson responded immediately to reports of popular reactions in Tokyo by sending Secretary of State William Jennings Bryan to Sacramento.[6]

In the long run, the concern of the national government over relations between America and Japan did not effectively restrain sentiment against the Japanese on the coast or help to solve their problems. Westerners lost faith in presidential guarantees as they learned that the Gentlemen's Agreement did not stop immigration of wives of Japanese laborers already resident, including those married by proxy—the "picture brides"—or the birth of children, who to the exclusionists seemed no more acceptable for being American citizens and having the rights of citizenship. And the Presidents who intervened to help the Japanese drew the fire of partisans in the Western states, where the use of racial prejudice for political advantage went back to the era of Denis Kearney. Thus Democrats in California attacked Roosevelt and Taft as pro-Japanese in the campaigns of 1908, 1910, and 1912; then progressive-Republican legislatures resented appeals from Taft and Wilson, who had inherited their predecessors' problems and policies. Ultimately the Japanese problem came to represent for many Westerners the growing issues of state versus national authority and legislative versus executive authority, and even of postwar unemployment. The states continued to discriminate, some of them—as Governor Johnson pointed out when California adopted the alien land law of 1913—by virtue of measures adopted without controversy years earlier. Alien land bills in Idaho and Oregon failed to pass in 1917 after representations from the Department of State. But Oregon and Washington discriminated against aliens in

---

[5] Previously (March 14, 1907) Roosevelt had issued orders excluding from continental United States Japanese laborers who had received passports authorizing them to travel to Mexico, Canada, and Hawaii.

[6] Theodore Roosevelt to J. N. Gillett, March 9, 1907, in Roosevelt: *Letters,* Vol. V, p. 608, and cf. Vol. IV, p. 1274. Thomas A. Bailey: "California, Japan, and the Alien Land Legislation of 1913," *Pacific Historical Review,* Vol. I (March 1932), pp. 40, 43–4, 55–6. Burton F. Beers: *Vain Endeavor: Robert Lansing's Attempts to End the American-Japanese Rivalry* (Durham: Duke University Press; 1962), pp. 32, 40, 112.

the fishing laws of 1913 and 1915,[7] and California, Washington, and Oregon adopted alien land laws in the early 1920's. Shortly before the California legislature acted, Governor Stephens rebuked a committee of the Oriental Exclusion League, declaring that exclusion was an international problem and ascribing the local movement to political ambition,[8] but he shared the general feeling. "It may be an exquisite refinement," he told Secretary of State Bainbridge Colby in a widely circulated letter (1920), "but we cannot feel contented at our children imbibing their first rudiments of education from the lips of the public school teacher in classrooms crowded with other children of a different race."[9]

Meanwhile pressure built up for halting immigration altogether. Congress considered the Johnson bill (introduced by Representative Albert Johnson of Washington, who had promised restriction when elected to Congress in 1912),[1] which would suspend immigration for a year. It finally adopted total exclusion of the Japanese in the Immigration Act of May 26, 1924.

In stopping Japanese immigration, Congress accepted the Western argument that it was impossible to assimilate Orientals into American society. At the same time, by refusing to let Orientals become American citizens or buy land, the national and state governments retarded assimilation and thus proved themselves right. Although the alien Japanese population declined during the 1920's, as the alien Chinese population had declined after the Exclusion Act of 1882, those Japanese who stayed looked for advice to Japanese consular officials and employees of Japanese banks and business firms. They continued such contacts

---

[7] There was no legal restriction on Japanese fishermen in California, where they made great gains during the First World War, prospering especially in the tuna fisheries of San Pedro. Washington had incorporated a general provision discriminating against alien landholders in the Constitution of 1889.

[8] Daniels: *Politics of Prejudice*, pp. 46–64. Ichihashi: *Japanese in the United States*, pp. 261–71, 277–8. Rodman W. Paul: *Abrogation of the Gentlemen's Agreement* . . . (Cambridge: Phi Beta Kappa Society; 1936), pp. 21–3, 74. *Literary Digest*, Vol. XLVI (May 3, 1913), p. 992; Vol. LIV (February 17, 1917), p. 390. Eliot G. Mears: *Resident Orientals on the American Pacific Coast; Their Legal and Economic Status* (Chicago: University of Chicago Press; 1928), pp. 179–86, 219–25. *San Francisco Chronicle*, February 7, 1921, p. 10, col. 1.

[9] William D. Stephens: "California and the Oriental," *Pacific Review*, Vol. I (December 1920), p. 354.

[1] John Higham: *Strangers in the Land: Patterns of American Nativism, 1860–1925* (New Brunswick: Rutgers University Press; 1955), p. 307.

longer than most immigrants did because as Japanese subjects they had obligations under Japanese law and still more because they needed protection from public and private harassment, which resulted partly from resentment at their continuing foreign attachments. In turn the consuls discouraged them from leaving California and the Far West, where they could easily call on consular offices and on one another in case of trouble. (Whereas the Chinese had tended to disperse throughout the country after the 1850's, the Japanese concentrated more in the coastal states between 1900 and 1940.) Economic success did not always help the alien Japanese to integrate socially as it helped other immigrants, for under the alien land acts they had to remain tenants, and tenancy itself added to the differences between them and their Caucasian neighbors. It was easy to distinguish between Japanese and white farms, wrote Konrad Bercovici, the novelist, in 1925: "The neatness of the field, the straightness of the rows of . . . vegetables, as well as the compactness of the carefully constructed greenhouses, are in direct contrast with the flimsy, improvised condition of the living quarters of the Japanese."[2] Some features of Japanese farming were distinctive enough and suggested indifference to ordinary comforts—for example, the women and children worked in the fields—but the permanent improvements made by the minority who owned their own land suggest that the land laws tended to justify themselves by forcing Japanese aliens, like other tenants, to concentrate on the crop.

The Mexicans, who replaced the Japanese, were at once an older and a newer element in Western agriculture, in the Western labor market, and in Western social consciousness. In the nineteenth century few of them lived outside California, other states and territories along the Mexican border, and Colorado; and the Californians generally ignored or despised them as slothful obstacles to progress. The American settlers, Walter Colton wrote in 1846, "seem to look upon this beautiful

[2] Ichihashi: *Japanese in the United States,* pp. 321–2. Bradford Smith: *Americans from Japan* (Philadelphia: J. B. Lippincott Co.; 1948), pp. 231–2. Carey McWilliams: *Prejudice; Japanese-Americans: Symbol of Racial Intolerance* (Boston: Little, Brown & Co.; 1944), pp. 84–5. Fuller: "Supply of Agricultural Labor," pp. 19,821, 19,829, 19,-837. Poli and Engstrand in *Journal of Land and Public Utility Economics,* Vol. XXI, p. 352, 354–5. Masakazu Iwata: "The Japanese Immigrants in California Agriculture," *Agricultural History,* Vol. XXXVI (January 1962), pp. 32, 35–6. Konrad Bercovici: "The Japanese in the United States: An Old Race in a New Land," *Century Magazine,* Vol. CX (September 1925), p. 608.

land as their own Canaan, and the motley race around them as the Hittites, the Hivites, and Jebusites, whom they are to drive out."[3] The Sonorans, who dominated the mines along the southern Sierra Nevada, were the most unpopular foreigners until feeling rose against the Chinese; there was more contempt than active dislike in the general American attitude toward the native Mexican-California stock, which was seldom competitive. (Immigrants resented Mexican land grants, but most Mexicans had none, and the most desirable land soon passed out of the hands of the original owners.) Traces of Mexico survived longest in the southern counties of California, along with remnants of the old cattle herds, and somewhat to the embarrassment of the newcomers, whose hopes ran to Yankee bustle and enterprise.

The Mexicans indeed were neighbors to the most insistently Protestant settlers of the state rather than to the more cosmopolitan immigrant population of San Francisco. Eventually, after the railroads had safely established a Middle Western Anglo-Saxon hegemony, southern Californians indulged themselves in romantic fancies about their Spanish roots and traits. In the early years they pointedly distinguished the Spanish-speaking inhabitants from white men. "But these clogs to human progress and to the advance of a purer and more rational system of human belief, are passing away," a visitor to San Bernardino rejoiced in 1876.[4] When the forty-niners began to form pioneer societies in the seventies to perpetuate memories of themselves and early times, they rediscovered their Spanish and pre-Columbian antecedents; they even published documents concerning the founding of the missions in the 1770's; but they did not renounce their prejudices. "The advent of the American immigration was the advent of law and order," said an orator of the Territorial Pioneers of California (1876); "the darker races rapidly disappeared before the superior intelligence and energy of the rightful owners of the soil."[5]

Within a few years, newcomers and the promoters of tourist travel began to exploit the romantic possibilities of Spanish color and traditions. When David Starr Jordan moved from Indiana to the campus

[3] Walter Colton: *Three Years in California* (New York: A. S. Barnes & Co.; 1850), p. 118.

[4] David L. Phillips: *Letters from California* (Springfield: Illinois State Journal Co.; 1877), p. 115.

[5] *First Annual of the Territorial Pioneers of California* . . . (San Francisco: W. M. Hinton & Co.; 1877), pp. 6–7, 11–12, 129–30. John J. Powell: *The Golden State and Its Resources* (San Francisco: Bacon & Co. Printers; 1874), p. 218.

of the new Leland Stanford Junior University in 1891, as its president, he lavishly bestowed Spanish names on streets, houses, and even a dormitory, somewhat to the amusement of the natives. "The golden haze through which . . . easterners viewed the early Spanish and Mexican settlers rather surprised and mystified those of us brought up in the golden state," a student at Stanford later recalled, "who certainly at that time had no illusions concerning our Latin American neighbors."[6] ("The Argonauts of '49 in California slaughtered the Spanish names even more recklessly than did the white-wagon immigrants of Oregon the Canadian-French titles of the adjacent state," a writer in *West Shore* remarked [1889].[7]) Likewise the California historian Charles Howard Shinn deplored the romantic inventions of Gertrude Atherton, who passed over "the isolation of early California, the almost entire lack of intellectual activity, and, in brief, the very primitive conditions of the daily life of the people. . . . Mrs. Atherton sets forth their period [1769–1847] in gorgeous colors, sometimes glowing with stately, old-world effects, sometimes passionate with Parisian intrigues, but always too complex and always too modern."[8]

By this time substantial scholarly accounts of the Spanish-speaking Southwest already existed; Hubert Howe Bancroft had published the fullest of them in 1884–90. And Charles F. Lummis, editor of the *Los Angeles Times* and later of the promotional magazine, *Land of Sunshine*, had begun to organize enthusiasm for the restoration of the Franciscan missions and to collect material for the Southwest Museum. The study of Spanish in Western schools advanced; it eclipsed French before the First World War made it eclipse German as well.[9] Artists and architects were turning to Spanish and Indian themes.

Yet wide gaps remained between scholarship and popular interest and understanding, between interest in Mexicans who were dead and in those who remained alive. Although Mrs. Atherton was born in San Francisco (1857), she first wrote of Mexican California while stay-

---

[6] David Starr Jordan: *The Days of a Man* . . . (Yonkers: World Book Co.; 1922), Vol. I, pp. 383–4. Henry D. Sheldon: "Autobiography to 1914" (unpublished ms., University of Oregon Library), ch. 2, p. 13.

[7] H. L. Wells: "Nomenclature of the Pacific Coast," *West Shore*, Vol. XV (May 1889), p. 248.

[8] Charles H. Shinn: "Literature of the Pacific Coast," *Forum*, Vol. XXVIII (October 1899), p. 254.

[9] J. Preston Hoskins: "Statistical Survey of the Effect of the World War on Modern Language Enrollment . . . ," *Modern Language Journal*, Vol. X (November 1925), p. 104.

ing at a convent in France; by her own account, she had never visited the old Spanish towns or even read a history of the state. A reviewer (in *The Nation*) of two volumes of Bancroft's nine on the history of California puzzled over the sudden transformation of the historiography of the state from total neglect to a total recall that seemed to extend to "a careful cataloguing of every bullock whose hide was ever exported from Mexican California," and suggested that it might represent "the late and now fruitless repentance of the American as he remembers the little world of life that his cruel progress in California has destroyed. If there was any purpose strong in our American mind in the early golden days of California, it was to neglect, to despise, or to ignore everything peculiar to the natives of the land that we had so rudely seized. . . . We who came to contemn have remained to study most lovingly and devoutly."[1] But even Bancroft himself deplored recent Latin and Slavic infusions into the stock of the founders of the Republic, "selections from the best strains in Europe, that is to say Anglo-Saxon and Teutonic." Fiestas became commonplace after Los Angeles held the first in 1894, and were no less enthusiastic for being counterfeit, but for a generation they represented most of the heritage of Spain that the visitor could see. The Los Angeleno "built on the ruins of Spain," Willard Huntington Wright wrote in 1913, "but he might as well have built on a virgin desert for all the effect those ruins had upon him."[2] Least of all did he notice the Mexican laborer.

The Mexicans of the states west of the Colorado River were both few and uncontroversial until the First World War. Typically unskilled and unaggressive, they did not compete for jobs with members of labor unions. Many who worked on the tracks of Western railroads lived in boxcar settlements that moved with their jobs. Although the number in California increased threefold between 1900 and 1910 (from 8,086 to 33,694),[3] they attracted little attention until agricultural employers, protesting that they faced a wartime shortage of labor, imported large numbers under temporary waivers of the Immigration Act of 1917, which excluded illiterates and laborers under contract. Meanwhile, cotton had moved into California (by 1910 to the Imperial Valley,

---

[1] Gertrude Atherton: *Adventures of a Novelist* (New York: Liveright, Inc.; 1932), pp. 168, 186. *The Nation,* Vol. XLII (March 11, 1886), p. 220.

[2] Hubert H. Bancroft: *Retrospection, Political and Personal* (New York: The Bancroft Co.; 1912), p. 504. Willard H. Wright in *Smart Set,* Vol. XXXIX (March 1913), p. 113.

[3] By 1920 there were 88,771.

where some of the larger landholders also had interests across the border in Mexico), and with it the Texan and Mexican practice of relying on Mexican field workers. After the war, when the small reservoirs of Oriental labor continued to shrink, values of land and indebtedness capitalized at wartime price levels put pressure on farmers to find cheap labor, especially as prices of crops declined. Seventy-eight percent of the Mexicans of California were still in the ten southern counties in 1920, but the following year farm workers in considerable numbers for the first time found a new mobility in the automobile; by 1922 the migratory fruit-picking families of the whole state were predominantly Mexican.[4]

Outside California and the other border states, Mexicans remained relatively few, though they worked in the sugar-beet fields of Idaho, Oregon, and the Rocky Mountains, and tended railroad tracks throughout most of the West. The census of 1930 recorded 199,359 Mexicans in California, 7,259 in Oregon, Washington, Idaho, Nevada, and Utah combined.[5] In general they were inconspicuous, not only because few others wanted their jobs but also because they seldom disputed the terms of employment and seldom remained as burdens to northern communities after the harvests; instead they retreated to winter across the border or in cities such as Los Angeles, which a reporter in 1928 called "the great Mexican peon capital of the United States."[6]

Social workers and others already were questioning social costs, asking whether it made even economic sense to increase relief rolls each winter to subsidize corporate agriculture in the summer, and whether the cotton, sugar-beet, and melon growers of the West were not creating social problems comparable to those that the cotton, sugar-cane, and tobacco planters of the South had created before the Civil War by insisting that they must have cheap labor. Businessmen pointed to the

---

[4] Otey M. Scruggs: "The First Mexican Farm Labor Program," *Arizona and the West,* Vol. II (Winter 1960), pp. 320–3. James L. Slayden: "Some Observations on Mexican Immigration," *Annals of the American Academy,* Vol. XCIII (January 1921), pp. 121–3. Max S. Handman: "Economic Reasons for the Coming of the Mexican Immigrant," *American Journal of Sociology,* Vol. XXXV (January 1930), p. 606. *Mexicans in California; Report of Governor C. C. Young's Mexican Fact-Finding Committee* (San Francisco, 1930), pp. 46, 47, 49. Fuller: "Supply of Agricultural Labor," pp. 19,862, 19,866, 19,871–2.

[5] The total foreign and naturalized Mexican population in California numbered 368,013 (an increase from 121,176 in 1920); in Idaho, 1,278; in Nevada, 3,090; in Oregon, 1,568; in Utah, 4,012; in Washington, 562.

[6] Kenneth L. Roberts: "The Docile Mexican," *Saturday Evening Post,* Vol. CC (March 10, 1928), pp. 39, 41.

taxes and low purchasing power that followed on cheap labor, and to its effects on competing native producers. But spokesmen for the farmers argued that the wages the Mexican received were well above the national average—that he was not cheap labor, and that in any case he was a transient and showed little disposition to acquire land and make a permanent settlement. "Mexican casual labor fills the requirements of the California farm [for a fluid labor supply] as no other labor has done in the past," President Charles C. Teague of the California Fruit Growers' Exchange wrote in 1928.[7] "We need unskilled labor," said a farmer in the delta of the San Joaquin River, "just as we still need eighty horses, despite our thirty tractors."[8] The case was similar to the case for Oriental labor earlier in the century, but labor applied much less pressure for Mexican exclusion, perhaps because the Mexican was not exotic enough in appearance and culture to arouse strong nativist feeling or because relatively few Mexicans ventured from the fields and railroad tracks into more competitive employment. The leaders of the American Federation of Labor, who tried to maintain some measure of hemispheric unity through the Pan-American Federation of Labor, decided as early as 1925 not to agitate for exclusion, but instead to work with their counterparts in Mexico toward some voluntary restraint of emigration. Ultimately the Department of State quietly instructed American consuls to apply existing regulations at the border more strictly, with the result that immigration dropped off markedly in 1929 without any of the acrimony or loss of face attendant on legislative exclusion.[9]

During the depression of the 1930's, enthusiasm for the Mexican declined further, somewhat as it had earlier for the Japanese, and for the Hindu and the Filipino, whose roles in the labor market had been both smaller and of shorter duration. Opposition might have been greater if the number of immigrants had not greatly declined. The Mexican government itself by this time both restrained emigration and encouraged emigrants to return home. Thus the immediate problem was not that more Oriental immigrants came, as they did in the depression of the

---

[7] Roy L. Garis: "The Mexicanization of American Business," *The Saturday Evening Post,* Vol. CCII (February 8, 1930), p. 46. Charles C. Teague: "A Statement on Mexican Immigration," *The Saturday Evening Post,* Vol. CC (March 10, 1928), pp. 169–70.

[8] Commonwealth Club of California: *Transactions,* Vol. XXI (March 23, 1926), pp. 4–5, 30–1; Vol. XXII (November 22, 1927), p. 607.

[9] Robert A. Divine: *American Immigration Policy, 1924–1952* (New Haven: Yale University Press; 1957), pp. 54–5, 57–8.

1890's, but that some American-European (Mexican) immigrants remained. And the difficulty was not so much that the Mexican who remained became a farm operator, and thus a competitor; it was rather that he became a greater burden on county relief budgets: increasingly he had come to disappear each winter not across the boundary into Mexico, where his old home was probably too far in the interior to make annual trips feasible, but into a collection of shacks near the first crops of the next season. When hard times came, his wages dropped faster than the prices of beans and rice, and his savings ran out soon after harvest. Beginning with Los Angeles County early in 1931, local governments promoted "repatriation," which saved them more in relief payments even in a season than it cost them in train fares. To send a Mexican family back to Mexico in the fall was safer than it had been: now native Americans also were available, especially newcomers to the coast from the South and Middle West. And although the refugees from the dust bowls of Oklahoma, Texas, and Arkansas were quicker than foreigners to ask for higher wages (if only because they had no fear that employers would report them to immigration officers for illegal entry), the Mexican *bracero* also learned to be less docile, more assertive. A Mexican labor union had appeared in southern California in 1927 and 1928; Mexican agricultural workers were on strike in Los Angeles County in June 1933, and by 1936 in Idaho, Washington, and other states. While still uninteresting or unwelcome to most of organized labor, they thus lost much of their appeal to employers.[1]

In the long run, the succession of immigrants who came to the Far West to dig its ditches and harvest its crops may have done well both in improving their economic condition and in establishing themselves in American society. If the Mexican, the Japanese, and the Chinese did not fare so well as the Italian, the Swede, and the German, still they did, on the whole, incomparably better than the African in the South, the Indian in South Africa, the Jew in central and eastern Europe. Although other Americans may not have felt grateful to the newcomers in proportion to the hard work they did and the low wages they received, neither did they feel the sense of guilt that complicated relations with Negroes and with American Indians. Prejudice and discrimination were too widespread and spontaneous to ascribe to any small group,

---

[1] Carey McWilliams: *North from Mexico: The Spanish-Speaking People of the United States* (Philadelphia: J. B. Lippincott Co.; 1948), pp. 190–3, 224–5.

whether to the demagogic politicians whom employers have blamed or to the exploiting employers whom some reformers have blamed instead (and who had a kind of original responsibility in that they encouraged the immigrants to come and profited most directly at their expense); and yet for all its irrationality, prejudice seldom had the religious and the sexual overtones that made intercultural conflicts so ugly in other places. (The brief episode of feeling in the late 1920's and early 1930's against the Filipino, whose offense was less that he worked for low wages than that he spent them on white girls,[2] shows what might have happened, but it left little trace.) The West and the immigrants alike were fortunate in that the region was religiously diverse before the influx of some of the largest and most controversial groups; in that the immigrants moved into occupations that required relatively little adjustment on their part (rural groups moved chiefly onto farms rather than into tenements, as in New York City), and in that in the main the strongest traits of the newcomers were among those that Americans respected, from love of children and family to pride in the job well done.

As historians of American nativism have pointed out, in the long run the restriction of immigration may have had some ameliorative effects, for all the passion that inspired it at home, for all the resentment it aroused abroad. The percentage of the foreign born in the West dropped by nearly half between the two world wars; the depression of the 1890's followed sharp absolute and relative increases; and the depression of the 1930's followed relative decline. In 1870, on the eve of the most notorious agitation against the Chinese, nearly three out of ten Westerners were foreign born; in 1940, less than one out of nine. The West had been much more foreign than the nation; it became much less so. Moreover, the most conspicuous of the Western foreign-born, the Orientals, were old and few. When the depression came, foreign scapegoats were in short supply; it may be more than a coincidence that racial antagonism seemed to have spent itself.[3]

The decline extended to those foreign-born stocks that, perhaps to assert their own Americanism, had contributed some of the chief agitators against foreign influence. The leadership of Far Western nativism had

---

[2] Bruno Lasker: *Filipino Immigration to Continental United States and to Hawaii* (Chicago: University of Chicago Press; 1931), pp. 358–68.

[3] Higham: *Strangers in the Land,* p. 326. Ostrander: *Rights of Man in America,* p. 315.

been conspicuously immigrant in background, from Denis Kearney in the 1870's and the American Party of California in the 1880's to Fred Schwarz in the 1960's. The president of the Building Trades Council of San Francisco, which financed the Japanese and Korean Exclusion League, was Patrick H. McCarthy, a native of Ireland; the first head of the League and secretary of the Council, Olaf A. Tveitmoe, was a native of Norway, as was Haakon J. Langoe, one of the leaders of the Americanization movement in the Northwest after the First World War. Langoe had changed his Norwegian-language magazine, the *Pacific Skandinaven,* ultimately to *The United American: a Magazine of Good Citizenship,* and exhorted members of the Scandinavian community to abandon their native language in school, church, and press.[4] In 1870 the Irish foreign-born of California constituted one in four of the state's foreign-born—one in ten of the total population (more than any other single element); by 1920 they were one in seventeen and one in seventy-one; by 1940, one in twenty-five and one in one hundred ninety-eight. The native Norwegians, who came later, reached their peak in numbers along the coast in 1930 (earlier in the interior), but even in Washington, which had more than the other states together, they had dropped by then to only one in fifty of the total population.

Yet racial conflict returned in the 1940's. After the Japanese attack on Pearl Harbor, feeling against Japanese-Americans mounted, and when the United States government decided in February 1942 to evacuate them to concentration camps in the interior, the chief differences in public opinion concerned not whether they should go, but whether it was necessary to remove them to prevent sabotage and espionage or to protect them from those who believed that they were actively disloyal. Private hostility and public harassments, including the virtual requirement that they sell their property at great loss, went so far that when the army ended the policy of mass exclusion in January 1945 and began to close down the Relocation Centers where most of them had been held, only about two thirds chose at first to return. The census of 1950 showed that the percentage of Japanese and Japanese-American population in the Western states had decreased by about one sixth in

---

[4] John Higham: "The American Party, 1886–1891," *Pacific Historical Review,* Vol. XIX (February 1950), pp. 37–46. Kawakami: *American-Japanese Relations,* pp. 303–5. Daniels: *Politics of Prejudice,* pp. 27–9, 48, 52. *The United American: a Magazine of Good Citizenship* (Portland, 1923–7), succeeding *The Western American* (1922), *The Northman: a Weekly Journal of Progress and Good Citizenship* (1920–2), and *Pacific Skandinaven* (1904–20).

the decade, whereas the percentages of other nonwhite groups had considerably increased.[5]

The outburst against the Japanese-Americans had not spent itself when riots broke out, beginning in Los Angeles (June 1943), against Mexican-Americans, whom the newspapers called "zoot-suiters" and pachucos. Following charges of Mexican delinquency and crime on the one hand and of harsh and discriminatory treatment by the police on the other, the riots in Los Angeles seemed unpleasantly like interracial riots in Middle Western and Eastern cities, as at Detroit in 1942.[6]

The wartime antagonisms against Japanese and Mexicans seemed to represent a new pattern of intolerance in the Far West. They occurred in a time of full employment rather than of depression, in contrast with the early movements against Orientals, which had fluctuated with the labor market; and they were predominantly urban rather than rural, although significant interracial competition was almost entirely on the farm. Except for the produce markets and a few curio shops and restaurants, Mexican- and Japanese-owned stores served chiefly small ethnic clienteles. And Californians recognized Japanese dominance of the truck-garden industry: officials of the state of California proposed (February 1942) moving the Japanese not out of the state, but merely from urban and coastal areas to agricultural areas. They particularly wished to avoid depleting the supply of agricultural labor and having to replace the Japanese with imported Mexicans and Negroes. None of the major farmers' organizations of the coastal states, and only a small minority of the trade associations, recommended evacuation. The authors of an exhaustive study (a project of the University of California) of the Japanese-American evacuation and resettlement found no evidence that pressure groups or politicians exerted decisive influence on the army and the government to move from curfews and individual arrests to general detention; a study of the army's records suggests that

---

[5] *The New York Times,* February 21, 1943, p. 23, cols. 4–5. Dorothy S. Thomas and others: *Japanese American Evacuation and Resettlement* (Berkeley: University of California Press; 1946–54). Leonard Bloom and Ruth Riemer: *Removal and Return; The Socio-Economic Effects of the War on Japanese Americans* (Berkeley: University of California Press; 1949). Davis McEntire: *Residence and Race* (Berkeley: University of California Press; 1960), p. 12 and *passim.*

[6] McWilliams: *North from Mexico,* pp. 228–37, 244–51. Remi Nadeau: *Los Angeles, From Mission to Modern City* (New York: Longmans, Green & Co.; 1960), p. 242–6. *While You Were Gone; a Report on Wartime Life in the United States,* ed. Jack Goodman (New York: Simon & Schuster; 1946), p. 90.

the responsibility lay more in Washington, and particularly with the President, than with General DeWitt and his command on the coast.[7] It was a time of unparalleled stress, when the line between firmness and hysteria wore thin, when the fears of a few in one region spread over the nation, and when it was easier to act on an alarm than to investigate it.

Grim though the experiences of these Western minorities were, in the long run the war only set them back temporarily. In the years of the worst discrimination, assimilation of some groups speeded up, and inequality declined. The movement of Mexicans into cities, where the worst incidents occurred, corresponded to their economic and social advance: they were becoming more visible both because they were in fact more numerous and because they were moving from agricultural to higher-paid urban employment, not merely to urban relief. Their most active antagonists in the central cities were no simple cross-section of the white population, but to a large extent they were newcomers also, including the sailors who started the zoot-suit riots in Los Angeles and the civilians who came from the South and the Southwest to better-paying jobs in aircraft and munitions factories. Perhaps some friction arose because of the fuller citizenship Mexican-Americans found in the armed forces—as happened also among American Negroes in the same years. Mexican-Americans began to find fuller citizenship in politics also, as politicians gradually discovered the resident, registered population and tried to cater to it.

Fundamentally, employers wanted Mexican laborers because they were cheap and docile; agricultural production could not have held up during the war and flourished after the war without a great increase in cheap seasonal field labor. Hourly wages for temporary farm work in southern California, where the availability of Mexicans set the scale, ran significantly below national and Northwestern levels even while factory wages in California continued high. Yet the very increases in the number of Mexican nationals and in the demand for them prompted their government to insist on guarantees of wages and working conditions that for a time, under the Mexican Farm Labor Agreement of 1942, as later under the act of 1951 (Public Law 78), favored Mexican

---

[7] Stetson Conn: "The Decision to Evacuate the Japanese from the Pacific Coast," *Command Decisions*, ed. K. R. Greenfield (Washington: Office of the Chief of Military History; 1960), pp. 136, 140–1, 147–9, and *passim*. Thomas: *Japanese American Evacuation*, Vol. III, pp. 185–208.

over native American agricultural laborers. And if labor unions were slow to organize Mexicans (slow, indeed, to organize all agricultural workers), concentrating rather on asking Congress to reduce the importation of labor to meet artificially established labor shortages, there were signs that Mexican wages would not remain substandard indefinitely. When Congress renewed the program—presumably for the last time—in 1963, the number of *braceros* entering the United States had declined greatly, either because mechanization in the fields was catching up with production or because they somehow commanded a better price and thus were less profitable to employ.[8]

Meanwhile, the antagonism against the Japanese declined rapidly; even during the war, it had depended on a few noisy exponents and on general hysteria rather than on effective organization. "This is our time to get things done that we have been trying to get done for a quarter of a century," an official of one of the exclusionist organizations in California observed (February 1942),[9] but the organization put little force even into its appeal for evacuation and had little to suggest beyond that. The limits of racism appeared in the wartime movement for the repeal of Chinese exclusion (1943), whose chief exponents included labor leaders and which had no substantial opposition on the coast. Enthusiasm for China had mounted, in fact, since the 1930's, along with feeling against Japan and the Japanese, corresponding to the course of aggression in the Far East and to growing esteem for the Chinese of California. In 1944 the Attorney General of California ruled that alien Chinese might own land. Shortly after the war, Far Western state governments eliminated some of the principal remaining legal forms of racial discrimination, and not simply because of prompting from Washington. In 1950 there were almost as many Japanese in Los Angeles as in 1940, more in the San Francisco area, where, moreover, they were less concentrated in Japanese neighborhoods; the Chinese

---

[8] Otey M. Scruggs: "Evolution of the Mexican Farm Labor Agreement of 1942," *Agricultural History*, Vol. XXXIV (July 1960), pp. 140–9. Scruggs: "The Bracero Program under the Farm Security Administration," *Labor History*, Vol. III (Spring 1962), pp. 149–68. Scruggs: "The United States, Mexico, and the Wetbacks, 1942–1947," *Pacific Historical Review*, Vol. XXX (May 1961), pp. 149–64. Ed Cray: "New Fight, Old Issue . . . ," *Frontier*, Vol. XII (July 1961), pp. 9–10. James F. Rooney: "The Effects of Imported Mexican Farm Labor in a California County," *American Journal of Economics and Sociology*, Vol. XX (October 1961), pp. 513–21. *Wall Street Journal*, February 21, 1963, p. 1, col. 4. *The New York Times*, Western ed., May 31, 1963, p. 1, col. 1; p. 8, col. 4.

[9] Thomas: *Japanese American Evacuation*, Vol. III, pp. 78, 195.

population had increased greatly in the same years (in San Francisco by about 40 percent in the 1940's, by about 47 percent in the 1950's; still more in the whole coastal region).[1]

Until the 1930's and 1940's, Westerners in general were more distinctively concerned about resident foreign nationals than about foreign policy. They seemed more interested than other Americans in the purchase of Alaska, the annexation of Hawaii (despite some opposition by beet-sugar farmers), the acquisition of the Canal Zone, and the building of the Panama Canal. Californians (especially opponents of Oriental immigration, such as Senator Phelan) protested at reports that Japanese interests might acquire a fishing port or agricultural lands in Lower California. But Westerners seemed little more interested than other Americans in the remarkable extension of Japanese power over the German holdings in China and the Pacific in 1914. From time to time, between the revolution that began in Mexico in 1910–11 and the expropriation of oil lands in 1938, various Westerners, particularly in California, urged intervention in Mexican affairs. In 1910, American Socialists and Wobblies based in Los Angeles supported two invasions of Lower California, and General Otis of the *Los Angeles Times* appealed for troops to protect his interests; in 1915, a federal grand jury indicted Harry Chandler, Otis's son-in-law, and the manager of one of his ranches for conspiring to foment an insurrection against the governor of Lower California; and in 1927, William Randolph Hearst published documents purporting to show that the Mexican government had bribed four United States senators. On the other hand, the publishers were unable to rally much support in the West or anywhere else or to affect the main course of American policy; and Senator Smoot of Utah, representing the interests of Mormon settlers in Mexico who feared reprisals from the rebels, vigorously opposed American intervention.[2]

---

[1] *The New York Times,* February 14, 1944, p. 7, col. 6. Riggs: *Pressures on Congress,* pp. 31–5, 73, 212–3. McEntire: *Residence and Race,* pp. 12, 45. S. W. Kung: *Chinese in American Life* . . . (Seattle: University of Washington Press; 1962), pp. 31, 41, 43, 104.

[2] Victor J. Farrar: *The Annexation of Russian America to the United States* (Washington: W. F. Roberts Co.; 1937), pp. 26–35. Chamberlain in *Pacific Historical Review,* Vol. XX, p. 47. Lowell L. Blaisdell: *The Desert Revolution: Baja California, 1911* (Madison: University of Wisconsin Press; 1962), pp. 64–5, 67, 84, 175. McWilliams: *North from Mexico,* pp. 203–5. *Independent,* Vol. LXXXI (March 8, 1915), p. 352, cited in Clarence C. Clendenen: *The United States and Pancho Villa* . . . (Ithaca: Cornell University Press; 1961), p. 199. W. A. Swanberg: *Citizen Hearst* (New York: Charles Scribner's Sons; 1961), pp. 394–403. A. F. Cardon: "Senator Reed Smoot and the Mexican Revolution," *Utah Historical Quarterly,* Vol. XXXI (Spring 1963), pp. 154, 158–9.

If there was any distinctively Far Western predisposition in foreign policy in general, it was not clearly and persistently isolationist or anti-European, in the spirit of Asia First or America First. In the 1930's, the most prominent spokesmen on international questions from the coast in Congress were men whose political support had become quite independent of their opinions. "Senators Johnson of California and Borah of Idaho," according to Chester Rowell (1940), "both had their attitudes fixed long ago. . . . What they really were voting on in October 1939 was the League of Nations and the original 1919 controversy, from which they are the surviving champions of isolation." The people of California and Idaho, however, seemed far less interested in those issues than their senators were at either time.[3] Johnson's record on international loans and aid in the 1920's was almost completely opposed to that of his colleague Shortridge, and both won reelection easily until Shortridge lost in the Democratic landslide of 1932. Referring defiantly to a poll indicating that two thirds of the people of California favored changing neutrality legislation (1941), Johnson told the Senate that he would not vote for war even if 99 percent of the people favored it. The third senator from the six states who most conspicuously (but far less consistently than Johnson and Borah) stood for isolation in the middle 1930's was Key Pittman of Nevada, whose constituents clearly enough agreed with him on the importance of high tariffs and of subsidies for silver, whatever they may have thought of his somewhat inscrutable stands on neutrality. Most Far Westerners favored a high tariff in the 1920's, perhaps in part because, as *Sunset* suggested, the restriction of immigration increased the costs of agricultural production,[4] as well as because of traditional Republican doctrine; but the sponsors of the tariff of 1930, Willis C. Hawley of Oregon and Reed Smoot of Utah, both veteran survivors of earlier political upsets, went down to defeat

---

[3] Of the three Republican senators who opposed the League in 1919 and 1920, two were reelected and one was defeated; of the three who supported the League, all were reelected. The complexity of alignments appears in the fact that Senator Charles L. McNary (R., Ore.), who supported Johnson for the presidential nomination in 1920, led the mild reservationists, who favored ratification of the Treaty of Versailles; Pittman supported the League, though he followed Wilson's strategy in voting against the Treaty.

[4] Rowell in *Foreign Affairs,* Vol. XVIII, p. 216. *Congressional Record,* 77 Cong., 1 Sess., November 5, 1941, p. 8514, cited in George L. Grassmuck: *Sectional Biases in Congress on Foreign Policy* (Baltimore: Johns Hopkins Press; 1951), pp. 166–7. *Sunset,* Vol. XLIX (December 1922), pp. 36–7. On Pittman, see Fred L. Israel: *Nevada's Key Pittman* (Lincoln: University of Nebraska Press: 1963).

in the election of 1932; and the delegations from the six states favored the reciprocal trade program in 1934.

That such conspicuous spokesmen as Johnson, Borah, and Pittman may not have represented public opinion on international issues seems evident in a survey of 161 votes in Congress between 1933 and 1950, by which Nevada appeared as one of the most isolationist states in the Senate (sixth) but one of the least isolationist in the House; on the basis of votes by Congressional districts, the whole group of states was less isolationist between 1933 and 1942 than New England, New York, and Pennsylvania, which had the reputation of being relatively internationalist.[5] Idaho was heavily isolationist in Congress, but in public-opinion polls ranked as unusually favorable to the draft in 1940 and to war in 1941. The Far West seemed to resemble the Northeast more than it did the Middle West and the northern plains in popular and Congressional sentiments on international questions. The more rural areas, including Idaho, the most rural state, were most like the Middle West.[6] Alfred de Grazia found (1954) the rural parts of the Pacific-coast states more isolationist than the rest of rural America, the urban parts more internationalist than the rest of urban America; he also found native Californians more internationalist than the immigrants. Other surveys indicated that members of the House of Representatives from the Pacific states were somewhat more internationalist than party loyalties required (1921–41) and that Republican members of Congress from the Pacific states (like those from New England, but unlike those from most other sections) heavily favored international economic aid in 1948–55.[7]

During the Second World War, Far Westerners added to their heritage of contradictions in relations with foreigners and foreign

---

[5] A factor in the difference between the delegations from the two coasts may be the strength of the Republican Party in metropolitan areas in the Pacific states. Most of the Republicans in the House from the Northeast represented nonmetropolitan constituencies, whereas Democrats in any section tended to support the administration out of loyalty to party.

[6] Idahoans traveled abroad much less than other Americans; Californians, much more.

[7] Ralph H. Smuckler: "The Region of Isolationism," *American Political Science Review*, Vol. XLVII (June 1953), pp. 386–401. *Public Opinion, 1935–1946*, eds. Hadley Cantril and Mildred Strunk (Princeton: Princeton University Press; 1951), pp. 461, 972. Alfred de Grazia: *The Western Public, 1952 and Beyond* (Stanford: Stanford University Press; 1954), pp. 130–1, 153, 178–9. Grassmuck: *Sectional Biases in Congress*, pp. 104, 168, and *passim*. Samuel Lubell: *Revolt of the Moderates* (New York: Harper & Brothers; 1956), p. 274.

nations. They renounced the profits of Far Eastern trade (which had been predominantly with Japan rather than with China) and set themselves to rearranging the destinies of Asia; they launched vast fleets across the Pacific and, while so doing, developed industries and population whose demands after the war greatly overshadowed foreign commerce. A new tide of immigration from the older states and from Mexico outnumbered old racial minorities. Westerners revived and forgot old prejudices and found new objects for them. The West became a gateway to the future of America rather than to lands beyond.

XI

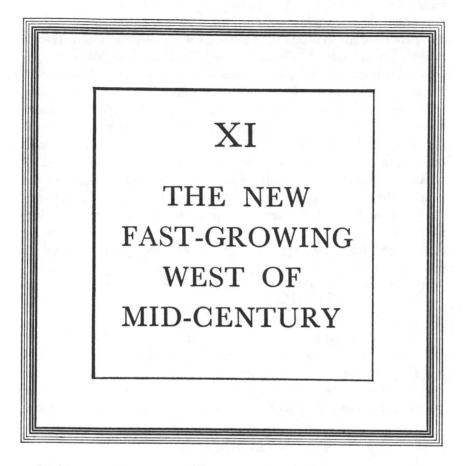

THE NEW FAST-GROWING WEST OF MID-CENTURY

THE WEST FELL on evil days during the depression of the 1930's. Per capita income declined between 1929 and 1933 more than in the rest of the country. The rate of increase in population also declined: Although it was still larger for the six states than for the nation, it was substantially less than it had been.[1] The two declines were significantly related in an area whose economy was heavily speculative and depended, like the boom in stock prices in the 1920's, on expectations of what the market would bring, and particularly on expectations of ever larger

[1] Changes in per capita income, 1929–33, in 1947–9 dollars: United States -28%, California -29%, Idaho -39%, Nevada -28%, Oregon -31%, Utah -33%, Washington -33%. Rates of increase in population for the six states and for the nation: 1920–30, 41.6% and 16.2%; 1930–40, 18% and 7%.

numbers of newcomers with money to spend. "The future growth of population on the Pacific coast," Warren S. Thompson concluded in the Report of the President's Commission on Recent Social Trends (1933), "would seem to depend in large measure upon the extent to which the lure of climate can be made effective through the increase of a leisure or semi-leisure class which can afford to live in the climate of its choice and through the growth of tourism, also upon the increase of commerce with the Far East. It is not a region with large natural advantages for the development of manufacturing." The experts seemed to be right about the industrial future of the coast: the percentage of population engaged in manufacturing in the twelfth federal reserve district always had been low, and it declined substantially between 1925 and 1939. But the alternatives were not much more promising. Migration into California in the 1930's dropped to about two fifths the rate of the 1920's;[2] by 1937, the Japanese movement into the ports of China brought to a climax a series of disillusionments with Asiatic trade. *Fortune* reported in 1940 that the Pacific coast harbored more doubts about the future of the American system than any other section of the country.[3] The frontier had lost its magic.

Some parts of the Far West were in trouble economically well before the depression. Much of the intermountain area had depleted its gold and silver without finding new wealth in agriculture. Before 1920, the mountain states, like those on the coast, had been well above average in personal income; by 1930 they were a sixth below and, as a group,

---

[2] Rates of net migration (per 1,000 average population)

	1900–10	1910–20	1920–30	1930–40	1940–50
CALIFORNIA	418	319	427	172	317
IDAHO	524	117	-131	48	-61
NEVADA	665	-97	97	144	251
OREGON	407	87	124	101	213
UTAH	92	-1	-75	-65	12
WASHINGTON	665	89	63	73	196

Everett S. Lee and others: *Population Redistribution and Economic Growth, United States, 1870–1950,* Vol. I, American Philosophical Society Memoirs, Vol. XLV (Philadelphia, 1957), pp. 114–219.

[3] National Bureau of Economic Research: *Regional Income,* Studies in Income and Wealth, Vol. XXI (Princeton: Princeton University Press; 1957), pp. 248–53. Warren S. Thompson and P. K. Whelpton: *Population Trends in the United States* (New York: McGraw-Hill Book Co.; 1933), p. 36. William A. Spurr: *Forecasts of California's Population and Production, 1950–1960* (Stanford: Graduate School of Business, Stanford University; 1949), p. 9. *Fortune,* Vol. XXI (March 1940), p. 55.

more like their neighbors on the high plains to the east in income and in shifts of population. Utah had not reported more arrivals than departures since the census of 1910; in the twenties she lost nearly 31,000 emigrants, and she lost nearly as many in the thirties as well, when all the states to the west were gaining. The number of families on relief in Utah in 1935 ran almost half above the national rate.[4] In Idaho, the agricultural boom of the early days of railroad and irrigation gave way to deflation and (after Montana) to the heaviest rate of emigration west of the Rockies in the 1920's. Idaho's losses would have been greater but for the movement of farmers into the cutover and other unimproved land of the northern counties, where substantial numbers of refugees from the drought-stricken high-plains states and from urban unemployment found a marginal existence. A survey in 1938 disclosed that most of them lived in rough log or frame buildings of three or four rooms, without inside running water.[5]

In Oregon and Washington, economic growth also slackened after the First World War: the great shipyards of 1917–19 became totally inactive by 1925; the lumber industry suffered from the weakness in construction that anticipated the general depression. But the most striking signs of trouble were in California, which continued to dominate the economy of the Far West. In breaking the maritime unions in 1919–21, the Industrial Association of San Francisco established arrangements for hiring that left the waterfront resentful even when times were good. As unemployment increased in the thirties, the longshoremen accepted radical leadership that, according to a special committee of the Congress of Industrial Organizations some years later, was "directed toward the achievement of the program and policies of the Communist Party rather than the objectives set forth in the constitution of the CIO." The coastwise maritime strike of May to July 1934 and the general strike in San

---

[4] In 1933, Wilson McCarthy of the Reconstruction Finance Corporation told the Utah State Relief Committee that it was embarrassing to have his home state use more RFC relief money per capita than any other state. (Marriner S. Eccles: *Beckoning Frontiers* ... [New York: Alfred A. Knopf; 1951], pp. 119–20). In time the Mormon Church's plan of "no more Mormons on the dole," announced in 1936, gave rise to a legend that no one in Utah had been on relief.

[5] F. E. Hall: "Poor Little Rich State," *Commonweal*, Vol. XXXI (February 9, 1940), pp. 342–3. U. S. Bureau of Agricultural Economics: *Migration and Settlement on the Pacific Coast: Cut-over Land of Northern Idaho* (Berkeley: Bureau of Agricultural Economics; 1941), Report no. 5, pp. 2–5, 25. John B. Appleton: "Migration and Economic Opportunity in the Pacific Northwest," *Geographical Review*, Vol. XXXI (January 1941), pp. 46–62.

Francisco that followed (June 16–19) led to new distrust within labor and between unions and employers, and so to new burdens on shipping, which in the postwar boom remained well below the levels of the thirties.[6] Eventually San Francisco learned that it could prosper with less waterborne commerce—that the coast was shipping out less oil and foodstuffs partly because it was becoming big and busy enough to use them itself, partly because railroads and trucks had become more economic than intercoastal freighters—but the change in marketing and transportation was uncomfortable for a city accustomed to gauge the times by the volume of business at dockside.

Meanwhile Los Angeles, whose growth the San Franciscans regarded as a threat to their prosperity and prestige, was having troubles of its own. Southern Californians were right in expecting much from oil and airplanes, suburban developments and beach resorts, but they borrowed so heavily on the future that they were living on the brink of bankruptcy. The great real-estate boom in the new west-side shopping and business districts collapsed by the beginning of 1925; a vast exodus into residential suburbs seemed to depend on the plans of new householder-landlords to rent units in "courts" to each other. The stock-market crash found much of the economy operating on margin and forced to liquidate. Everything seemed for sale or exchange.[7] By 1936 the city of Los Angeles, which long had solicited the yearly influx of tourists and new residents, had stationed policemen along the border of the state to turn back immigrants likely to become public charges.

Speculation and unessential consumers' services had been so prominent in Los Angeles—the mortuary chapels and pets' beauty parlors were more visible to tourists than the rising aircraft factories—as to support the doubts of those who felt that the whole Western economy was insubstantial, immature. Actually, industrial output in California, sustained by the expanding local market and by the growing availability of electric power and petroleum products, held up remarkably well during the depression, far better than in most other states. But the total industrial structure still was backward by Eastern models. San Francisco, Seattle-Tacoma, and Los Angeles lagged behind all but one of thirty

---

[6] Wytze Gorter and George H. Hildebrand: *The Pacific Coast Maritime Shipping Industry, 1930–1948* (Berkeley: University of California Press, 1952–4), Vol. II, pp. 274, 340.

[7] Remi Nadeau: *Los Angeles: from Mission to Modern City* (New York: Longmans, Green & Co.; 1960), pp. 149–54.

Eastern and Middle Western industrial areas in the proportion of their labor force engaged in manufacturing.[8]

The Second World War brought probably the most drastic changes in the Far West since 1849. "The second gold rush has hit the West Coast," the *San Francisco Chronicle* reported in 1943, when mobilization was near its peak. Some industries grew at revolutionary rates. In January 1940, only one of eight shipyard workers in the country was on the coast (13 percent, or 18,400), but by July 1943, when employment reached its peak both there and nationally, the ratio was one of three (34.5 percent, or 592,900). San Francisco Bay had the largest concentration in the country, and Portland-Vancouver followed with about half as many. Henry J. Kaiser, who laid down his first ships on the Columbia River in May 1941 and built the largest shipyards on the coast, gathered trainloads of workmen from other states, promised them high wages, housing, and medical care, and paid them before he needed them, to be sure they would be there when he was ready. The Western yards paid the highest wages in the country and kept the largest percentages of their employees in the high-wage classifications, and no other yards employed more women. The result was that many thousands of families found far larger incomes than they had ever known, in a region that offered more temptations for permanent residence than most of the places people went to in wartime. Householders on the hills of Berkeley and El Cerrito shuddered at conditions in the jerry-built slums on the mud flats of Richmond, whose population increased over four times in less than three years, 1942–4. "Women in slacks and leather jackets and shiny scalers' helmets wait in long lines to buy food," *Fortune* reported in 1945. "Nobody knows anybody. Children go to overcrowded schools in two shifts. The jail is jammed. Streets crack under heavy traffic. Overloaded sewers back up. . . . The twelve movie houses can't keep everyone amused, even though four of them are open all night. . . . 'There's not much they can spend their money on but booze.' Policemen still walk their beats in pairs." Yet most of the new-

[8] Margaret S. Gordon: *Employment Expansion and Population Growth: The California Experience, 1900–1950* (Berkeley: University of California Press; 1954), pp. 102–4. Frank L. Kidner: *California Business Cycles* (Berkeley: University of California Press; 1946), pp. 54–64. James J. Parsons: "California Manufacturing," *Geographical Review*, Vol. XXXIX (April 1949), pp. 229–30, 241. Harold D. Kube and Ralph H. Danhof: *Changes in Distribution of Manufacturing Wage Earners, 1899–1939* (Washington: Government Printing Office; 1942), pp. 34–5, 36–9.

comers wanted to stay in California, a third of them in Richmond itself, which on that basis might expect to be more than twice as large after the war as before.[9] And though even so optimistic a promoter of the coast's industrial development as Kaiser could foresee no permanent use for more than a fraction of the wartime shipyards,[1] the workers in the yards were a new resource for other industries.

The wartime production of aircraft transformed the Far West even more than shipbuilding, though it demanded somewhat less manpower and though the Far West's share of national production declined rather than increased while the war lasted. As early as 1916, William E. Boeing had made planes in Seattle at Lake Union, Glenn L. Martin at Los Angeles (earlier at Santa Ana), the Lockheed Aircraft Company at Santa Barbara (later at Burbank), but the industry as a whole moved to the coast in the thirties: California was fifth in production in 1929, first in 1937. By February 1940, California and Washington (that is, the metropolitan areas of Los Angeles, San Diego, and Seattle) had 45 percent of the country's total employment in airframe, engine, and propeller plants. During the war, to meet the government's insistence on dispersion outside the range of aerial attack, so much new construction shifted inland that four years later the coast's share of the total employment had declined by more than half (to 21.9 percent). But the total of persons that the industry employed on the coast had increased nearly seven times (from 38,866 to 301,144), and it still included the staffs of the main offices of some of the largest companies and the executives and designers who would affect the industry's location after the war.[2]

The industrial growth of the West in wartime followed on the availability of basic raw materials and energy as well as space and manpower. The war developed some of these apparent prerequisites for industrialization, such as Western sources of steel and aluminum; it merely exploited others that were already available, such as hydroelectric power.

---

[9] The population of Richmond actually increased from 23,642 in 1940 to 71,854 in 1950 and 99,545 in 1960. City officials had estimated that postwar population would be 50,000.

[1] *San Francisco Chronicle*, April 25, 1943, p. 1, col. 1. *Wartime Employment, Production, and Conditions of Work in Shipyards*, Bureau of Labor Statistics, Bulletin no. 824 (Washington, 1945), pp. 3–7, 23. "Richmond Took a Beating," *Fortune*, Vol. XXXI (February 1945), pp. 262, 264–5, 267–9. "Detour Through Purgatory," ibid., pp. 181–4, 234.

[2] William G. Cunningham: *The Aircraft Industry: A Study in Industrial Location* (Los Angeles: Lorrin L. Morrison; 1951), pp. 43–4, 100, 105, 139–40, 169, 206–7, 217.

The great dams that the United States government began to build in the early thirties had started to deliver substantial amounts of power only on the eve of mobilization: Hoover Dam on the Colorado (built 1930–5) had its first generator in operation in 1936; Bonneville and Grand Coulee on the Columbia (built 1933–7 and 1933–42) had theirs only in 1938 and 1941 respectively. By the end of 1945, Nevada and Arizona (Hoover) were producing 309 percent more hydroelectric power than in 1930; Oregon and Washington, 1075 percent more.[3] And the possibility of substantial electrified industrial development in the Northwest seemed at hand, justified by wartime experience. The day seemed far behind when President Franklin D. Roosevelt had thought of sending power primarily to subsistence farmers, many of them refugees from the dust bowl, who would raise what they could of their own food, "canning the surplus for their own use, perhaps even making their own shoes and certain types of clothing. . . ."[4]

Because most Western aluminum had to go to the Middle West for fabrication before returning to the aircraft factories of Seattle and southern California, perhaps the most significant additions to the industrial base at the time were in steel. "Steel is a magnetic industry," Assistant Attorney General Wendell Berge remarked just after the war. "It makes jobs."[5] By 1945 the Far West had nearly three and a half times its prewar capacity in steel ingots. The steel that Kaiser made at Fontana, near Los Angeles, and that United States Steel made at Geneva, near Provo, seemed to violate the old rules for locating mills near raw materials, markets, and deep water; but it was available for the shipyards of the Northwest and San Francisco Bay, which justified making it.[6]

At the end of the war, in 1945, the Pacific slope could point to substantial increases in industrial capacity and to new uses for it. The

---

[3] As indicators of industrial potential, these increases are less impressive alongside increases in residential demand everywhere along the coast. In California, where most of the Colorado River power went, the increase in hydroelectric power (under 3 percent) was much less than the increase in residential demand. Contrary to the hopes of southern Californians that electricity from Hoover Dam would be a cheap industrial fuel, supporting a smokeless Pittsburgh, rates were not lower than for steam-generated power, which exceeded hydroelectric power in California after 1953.

[4] *The Secret Diary of Harold L. Ickes,* Vol. III (New York: Simon and Schuster; 1954), p. 101.

[5] *Fortune,* Vol. XXXI (February 1945), pp. 131, 258. Wendell Berge: *Economic Freedom for the West* (Lincoln: University of Nebraska Press; 1946), p. 30.

[6] E. T. Grether: *The Steel and Steel-Using Industries of California . . .* (Sacramento: State Printing Office; 1946), p. 113.

six states, which had 8.2 percent of the population of the country in 1940, had received 12.4 percent of the contracts for military supplies (1940–5) and 11.3 percent of new military manufacturing facilities (1940–4). Some of the biggest facilities, such as the steel mills at Fontana and Geneva and the magnesium plants at Mead (Washington) and Las Vegas, were located where no one would have planned them as private ventures in peacetime, but lavish subsidies tended to compensate for long hauls. United States Steel paid $47,500,000 for the $200,000,000 plant at Geneva.[7] But the new capital of the West consisted no less of the talents and resources of its inhabitants than of such leavings from government, which varied widely in their convertibility to civilian uses. Between 1940 and 1945 the six states increased in population by nearly a fourth, well over four times the rate for the United States. The labor force and employment and the percentages of labor in highly skilled classifications increased still more. Because wages, overtime pay, and employment of women all were high, the typical Western "tin-hat" worker in 1945 had accumulated substantial savings, well beyond the national rate,[8] which served to keep him where he was and to maintain the momentum of the economy.

Yet much of this basis for economic growth was evident only later. The *San Francisco Chronicle,* surveying the prospects in 1943, found them mixed. Ten or fifteen years would see the end of petroleum in California. Electric power was in the wrong places—Nevada, Arizona, and the Northwest—rather than where the people were. "If the Columbia River would only flow through Los Angeles county," the *Chronicle* commented, "you could give Detroit and Pittsburgh back to the Indians." The aluminum and magnesium industries faced problems of climate and long hauls. Most of the shipyards were sure to go. The commercial airlines planned to expand their operations, but designing and producing large cargo and passenger planes might take as long as four years; the aircraft industry expected two years of reconversion, unemployment, and confusion. In Los Angeles, chief producer of aircraft, there was con-

[7] Glenn McLaughlin in *Economic Reconstruction* ed. Seymour Harris (New York: McGraw-Hill Book Co.; 1945), pp. 166–7, 169. Berge: *Economic Freedom for the West,* pp. 156–7. C. Langdon White: *Is the West Making the Grade in the Steel Industry?* (Stanford: Graduate School of Business, Stanford University; 1956), p. 13.

[8] The Federal Reserve Bank of San Francisco reported early in 1945 that liquid assets had grown 250 percent in the twelfth district, 1939–44, as compared with 149 percent in the nation; demand deposits, 246 percent, as compared with 116 percent; time deposits, 84 percent, as compared with 40 percent.

fusion even over whether the region ought to attract basic industries, which the Chamber of Commerce promoted but the mayor feared would make the land of sunshine into a "smoky Monongahela Valley."[9] (That fall, Los Angeles noted its first smog, a misty mantle of fumes over the city that set people to coughing and wiping their eyes.) As the war ended, two years later, industrial employment declined with military orders, and manufacturers on the coast expected it to decline still further after conversion to peacetime production—to less than half the volume of 1943. Economists cited unusually strong deflationary pressures in the Far West, the problems of industries not suited to quick conversion, of war workers who might find new jobs but not housing, and who, if they did, would have to finance their moves on reduced working weeks at lower rates of pay. "Except for the minority of the workers who go back East, the few who find jobs in expanding service industries, and the very few who turn to farming," the editors of *Fortune* concluded, "unemployment is in the cards."[1]

Unemployment did rise sharply in the six months after the war—at the peak, in March 1946, it was substantially above the national level[2]—but then it declined rapidly. By September 1946, employment was close to what it had been at the time of the Japanese surrender a year before. New jobs replaced the old, not only in residential construction and in the retail and service trades, all of which had dropped off badly during the war from their normally high levels, but also in manufacturing: in California, for instance, employment in manufacturing had increased 62 percent since 1940, as compared with an increase of 37 percent in total employment.[3] The very uncertainty of the postwar economy prompted shipyard and aircraft-plant workers to take the jobs they could get instead of waiting for those they had hoped to find alongside the houses they wanted to live in. People commuted long distances to new jobs, staying on in jerry-built wartime apartments near

---

[9] *San Francisco Chronicle,* May 6, 1943, p. 7, col. 1; May 2, 1943, p. 4, col. 1; May 4, 1943, p. 24, cols. 4–8; May 5, 1943, p. 10, col. 4; April 27, 1943, p. 12, cols. 3–4; May 12, 1943, p. 14, cols. 3–4.

[1] Federal Reserve Bank of San Francisco: *Monthly Review,* February 1945, pp. 16–20. *Fortune,* Vol. XXXI (February 1945), p. 111.

[2] In March 1946, the ratio of claims for unemployment benefits by non-veterans to the number of employees covered in 1945 was 11.6 percent in the twelfth federal reserve district, as compared with 6.8 percent in the United States.

[3] Federal Reserve Bank of San Francisco: *Monthly Review,* June–July 1946, pp. 23–4; September 1946, pp. 39, 42; October–December 1946, p. 49; January 1947, p. 3; August 1947, p. 69–70.

the shipyards or moving into cottages at summer resort towns and motels on the highways and into tents and trailers.

For all the speed and—compared to expectations—the ease of the change from war to peace in the West, the new economy was much more than a larger version of the old. A major factor in the success of its demobilization was that it did not, in fact, fully demobilize. Production of aircraft, which two years after the war still was the largest single industry around Los Angeles, San Diego, and Seattle, with about twice as many employees as its leaders had expected, depended principally on military requirements. Even when total military spending declined, the West's share increased, particularly in California, which had 13.2 percent of all military prime contracts in 1951 and 24 percent in 1959. In 1950, the aircraft industry had only one sixth as many employees as in 1944, but 30.4 percent of them were in California (which had had 18.9 percent in 1944), 8.9 percent in Washington (3.0 percent in 1944). By 1957 there were more employees in both states than there had been in 1944. By 1962 the coast was getting 46 percent of all contracts of the Department of Defense for research and development, and the *Los Angeles Times* estimated that one out of three workers in the area of Los Angeles and Long Beach depended on a defense industry.[4]

The growth of industry extended well beyond defense and beyond southern California. It was most glamorous in the environs of the major universities, Stanford, the University of California at Berkeley and Los Angeles, and the California Institute of Technology, where electronic manufacturers reinvested large parts of their incomes in research and development. Even San Jose produced computers as well as dried prunes and canned cherries. In Washington, by 1956, aircraft manufacturing employed more persons than logging and lumbering, as compared with less than one seventh as many before the war.[5] (By 1962 production at Boeing was divided almost equally between military and commercial contracts; as late as 1956 it had been about 98 percent

[4] Federal Reserve Bank of San Francisco: *Monthly Review*, January 1947, p. 3; August 1947, pp. 69–70. James L. Clayton: "Defense Spending: Key to California's Growth," *Western Political Quarterly*, Vol. XV (June 1962), pp. 280–7. Cunningham: *Aircraft Industry*, pp. 100, 153, 164, 213, 224. *The New York Times*, September 30, 1962, Sec. I, p. 80, cols. 3–5. Wesley Marx: "Sparta in the Southland," *Frontier*, Vol. XIII (April 1962), pp. 5–8.

[5] In 1958, manufacturing of transportation equipment in Seattle accounted for 67,716 of the total 212,049 employed in manufacturing in the state, as compared with 41,568 in lumber and wood products.

military.) At the time of the census of manufacturers in 1958, Portland had almost as many employees as the San Francisco Bay area in electrical machinery in proportion to population. Even Idaho began to move into the new industrial era as the National Reactor Testing Station of the United States Atomic Energy Commission at Arco (1949), the largest concentration of nuclear reactors in the world, built up a permanent force of over 400. And in Utah, where employment in manufacturing surpassed employment in agriculture by the middle fifties and increased by 70 percent over the decade, the economy advanced as it had not since the previous century. By 1961 Utah was first among the states, in proportion to population, in expenditures on research for defense and exploration of space and in the production of missiles. Perhaps the state qualified for these types of production simply by not having qualified for others—that is, by having vast unused expanses—but it grew substantially also in petroleum, steel, copper, phosphates, and machinery, and in distribution for Eastern manufacturers.[6]

As economic opportunity advanced after the war, so did population. Between 1940 and 1950, the six states grew from 8.2 to 10.6 percent of the population of the United States; by 1960, to 12.5 percent. Only Idaho lagged behind the national rate of growth, which California more than tripled in the twenty years.[7]

---

[6] Howard M. Brier: *Sawdust Empire: the Pacific Northwest* (New York: Alfred A. Knopf; 1958), p. 128. *The New York Times,* October 30, 1962, p. 49, cols. 7–8. Federal Reserve Bank of San Francisco: *Monthly Review,* February 1960, pp. 34–5. Leonard Arrington: "From Panning Gold to Nuclear Fission . . . ," *Idaho Yesterdays,* Vol. VI (Summer 1962), p. 10. *Utah Economic and Business Review,* Vol. XX (December 1960), pp. 5, 8. *United States News and World Report,* Vol. LIII (August 20, 1962), p. 62. *Utah Economic and Business Review,* Vol. XX (June 1960), pp. 3–5.

[7] Population and (in parentheses) increase during previous decade

	1940	*1950*	*1960*
United States	131,669,275 (7.3%)	150,697,361 (14.5%)	178,464,236 (18.5%)
California	6,907,387 (21.7%)	10,586,223 (53.3%)	15,506,974 (48.5%)
Idaho	524,873 (17.9%)	588,637 (12.1%)	662,856 (13.3%)
Nevada	110,247 (21.1%)	160,083 (45.2%)	282,137 (78.2%)
Oregon	1,089,684 (14.2%)	1,521,341 (39.6%)	1,757,691 (16.3%)
Utah	550,310 (8.4%)	688,862 (25.2%)	886,926 (29.3%)
Washington	1,736,191 (11.1%)	2,378,963 (37.0%)	2,829,871 (19.9%)

Between 1950 and 1960, net migration (excess of immigrants over emigrants) accounted for 3,145,000 of the increase in California; 86,000 in Nevada; 16,000 in Oregon; 10,000 in Utah; 88,000 in Washington. Idaho lost 40,000 (excess of emigrants).

Economists who surveyed the prospects of Los Angeles at the end of the war learned by 1950 that in their most optimistic predictions they had badly underestimated the growth of both state and county. Why so many came and stayed was a matter for some debate. Throughout much of the Far West, and especially in California and the Southwest, the new immigration seemed less confined to people of working age than before, and much postwar economic expansion apparently followed simply on the presence of people with money to spend, people in sufficient numbers to warrant Western production of goods that previously had had to come from the East. But in the main, migration followed economic opportunity; the states and cities that grew the fastest were those with rapidly expanding industries.[8] Of the six states, only Idaho remained below the national average in both income and growth.

Rapid though change was, it reinforced more than it violated the main trends of years past in the growth and organization of society. In the distribution of occupations and of population, the Pacific slope, overshadowed by California, still greatly resembled the Middle Atlantic area and New England. Only New York had as high a percentage of workers in distribution and in the service trades as California, Margaret S. Gordon pointed out in 1954; the two states were similar in their commercial and financial leadership, in the tourist industry, in levels of income.[9] Los Angeles, which had dreamed of being a Western Miami or Palm Beach, dominated a metropolitan area only slightly behind Chicago and its neighbors in numbers and congestion. San Francisco, Oakland, and Portland, the older urban centers of the West, were all losing population within their city limits (like New York, Chicago, Boston, and Philadelphia), but were gathering fast-growing satellites along the freeways that extended around the Bay and across the Columbia and up the Willamette. Nearly all cities in the coastal states were attracting more Negroes, who had been numerous enough even in 1942 to fill up some former Japanese neighborhoods; the movement of Negroes into declining districts of the largest central cities recalled the

---

[8] Frank L. Kidner and Philip Neff: *Statistical Appendix to an Economic Survey of the Los Angeles Area* (Los Angeles: Haynes Foundation; 1945), p. 663. Federal Reserve Bank of San Francisco: *Monthly Review* (February 1960), p. 24. Gordon: *Employment Expansion.*

[9] Gordon: *Employment Expansion,* pp. 28–31.

experience of major cities elsewhere and also the movement of Chinese into declining Western mining towns in the 1860's and 1870's.[1]

Of the larger urban areas, southern California was the fastest growing, as it had been for many years. Los Angeles had been a long time establishing confidence in a solid economic base of its own apart from the savings of newcomers, "retired elderly people, whose health has broken down, and who have come here to live on their incomes," according to Upton Sinclair, who called the area "a parasite upon the great industrial centers of other parts of America."[2] The success of its first major industry, the production of motion pictures, which was fairly clear by the time Jesse L. Lasky, Samuel Goldwyn, and Cecil B. DeMille produced *The Squaw Man* in 1914, reinforced impressions of an economic façade or gigantic stage set. But the completion of the Los Angeles Aqueduct and the arrival of natural gas from the San Joaquin Valley in 1913 already had contributed to more orthodox industrial development. By the time of the discoveries of oil in 1920–22 at Huntington Beach, Signal Hill, Santa Fe Springs, and Torrance, which made Los Angeles the center of both producing and refining, other industries were immigrating in force. Whether because of fuels and raw materials or, as the *Los Angeles Times* insisted, because of the open shop, by 1923 the port of Los Angeles handled more tonnage than San Francisco; in 1925 Los Angeles had almost as many factory workers as San Francisco and Portland combined. It was easy to miss what was

---

[1] Growth of Negro population, 1930–60

	1930	*1940*	*1950*	*1960*
Berkeley	2.6%	3.9%	11.6%	19.0%
Los Angeles	3.1	4.2	8.7	13.5
Oakland	2.6	2.8	12.2	22.7
Portland	0.5	0.6	2.6	2.5
San Diego	1.8	2.0	4.4	6.0
San Francisco	0.6	0.8	5.6	10.0
Seattle	0.9	1.0	2.7	3.1
Tacoma	0.7	0.6	2.1	2.9
California	1.4	1.8	4.3	5.6
Idaho	.2	.1	.2	.2
Nevada	.6	.6	2.7	4.7
Oregon	.2	.3	.7	1.0
Utah	.2	.2	.4	.5
Washington	.4	.4	1.2	1.7

[2] Upton Sinclair: *The Brass Check . . .* (Long Beach, 1920), p. 197.

happening in an area where cultural community lagged behind economic integration—an area that lacked common attributes of mature metropolitan life, ranging from the legitimate theater and opera to concentrated industrial districts and effective systems of transporting people and garbage—and where immigration was so large that manufacturing declined in proportion to other occupations between the wars, as in most other Western cities, even while it increased absolutely.[3] The promoters themselves had absorbed much of the rhetoric of the entertainment and tourist industries, describing (to quote from a publication of a firm of financial representatives and advisers in 1923) Los Angeles as "the home of monster industries" in "a valley still *retaining* the romantic charm of the Spanish *occupation* . . . *quiet* streets, *mirroring* the splendors of *Rome* and the glories of Greece."[4]

After the war the change was inescapable, though much of the new research-based electronic economy took shape in plants as clean and almost as quiet as the ubiquitous Western college campuses: southern California's smog may have been the price of progress, but apparently came more from automobile exhaust than directly from factories. By 1950 a fourth of the jobs were in manufacturing, more than in San Francisco or Seattle. Between 1945 and 1955, capital expenditures on plants and equipment in the Los Angeles area exceeded six billion dollars, and the rate of growth more than doubled in the second half of the decade. Although defense industries still were prominent, the economy of southern California no longer seemed to depend on airplanes, entertainment, or oranges: motion pictures, television, and radio accounted for only 3 percent of employment in Los Angeles in 1950, and expansion in the clothing trades, steel, and assorted industries serving the Western market tended to make even fluctuations in missile contracts less than decisive. Surveying postwar changes in 1956, the Bank of America

---

[3] Vincent Ostrom: *Water & Politics: A Study of Water Policies and Administration in the Development of Los Angeles* (Los Angeles: Haynes Foundation; 1953), pp. 144–67. *The Forty Year War* . . . (Los Angeles: Times-Mirror Co.; 1929), pp. 1, 26–7. Clarence H. Watson: *Building a World Gateway: The Story of Los Angeles Harbor* (Los Angeles: Pacific Era Publishers; 1945), p. 13. Portland *Oregonian*, December 27, 1926, p. 14, cols. 6–7. Jacqueline R. Kasun: *Some Social Aspects of Business Cycles in the Los Angeles Area, 1920–1950* (Los Angeles: Haynes Foundation; 1954), pp. 17–18. Kidner and Neff: *Economic Survey*, pp. 18, 26, 37.

[4] Sherley Hunter: *Why Los Angeles* WILL *Become the World's Greatest City* (Los Angeles: H. J. Mallen & Co.; [1923]), p. 23.

pointed out that California was no longer a peripheral economy, supplying a few specialties to the national market in return for most of its manufactured goods: it covered its own needs and more.[5] When Kaiser Steel Corporation in 1962 cut steel prices at Fontana approximately to Eastern levels (after having refused to go along with United States Steel's increases earlier in the year), the West and particularly southern California seemed to have come of age.

San Francisco meanwhile had not entirely deferred to its southern rival; it maintained its leading position in finance and (if one compares all the ports of the Bay with all the ports of the area of Los Angeles) in maritime trade. The establishment of the Twelfth Federal Reserve District in 1914 had only recognized the dominance of the San Francisco banks, whose clearings amounted to nearly twice those of Los Angeles, Seattle, and Portland combined, though these cities had about twice the population San Francisco had. Although by 1937 Los Angeles passed San Francisco in volume of bank debits, in 1955 San Francisco ranked third in the United States in amount of non-local loans (Los Angeles was eighteenth) and was a principal source of loans for all major Far Western cities, none of which—not even San Diego, the nearest of them—looked first to Los Angeles. The Bank of America, which, as the Bank of Italy under Amadeo P. Giannini, had begun establishing branches and buying independent banks soon after the earthquake of 1906, by 1945 was the largest bank in the world, with assets of over five billion dollars and subsidiaries in Oregon and Nevada as well as throughout California.[6]

The Northwest also developed enormously, though at a lower and more sharply decelerating rate than California and the Southwest. After growing in population 2.7 times as fast as the nation in the forties—the decade of the shipyards—Oregon dropped behind it in the fifties. Only two standard metropolitan areas in the Northwest, Seattle and Eugene,

---

[5] Southern California Research Council: *The Next 15 Years, 1955–1970, The Los Angeles Metropolitan Area* (Los Angeles, 1955), pp. 20–21. Commonwealth Club of California: *Transactions,* Vol. LI (1956), p. 7.

[6] Portland *Morning Oregonian,* February 3, 1914, p. 1, col. 5; p. 2, col. 3. Otis D. Duncan and others: *Metropolis and Region* (Baltimore: Johns Hopkins Press; 1960), pp. 117, 119. George D. Dowrie: "History of the Bank of Italy in California," *Journal of Economic and Business History,* Vol. II (February 1930), pp. 271–98. Marquis James and Bessie R. James: *Biography of a Bank; the Story of Bank of America* (New York: Harper & Brothers; 1954), pp. 114, 310, 376, 477.

grew at more than the national rate.[7] And the lags in population corresponded to lags in employment and income. Even during the forties, the percentage of production workers increased at much less than half the national rate.[8]

Basically the Northwest's limitations were still what they had been: it depended on selling its resources in other markets, and its marketable resources were few. Electricity became so abundant and cheap—production in Oregon and Washington increased over seven times between 1940 and 1960—that Northwesterners learned to use it lavishly for cooking, heating, and manufacturing, and the woodpile on the residential sidewalk ceased to be a familiar sight. Yet the region continued to use more energy that it produced. By 1962, public utility districts in Washington were planning major development of steam power to supplement hydroelectric production, and the Bonneville system was preparing to distribute power from a nuclear reactor at Hanford. Continuing demand for power and fuel brought oil refineries to Puget Sound in 1954–6[9] and natural-gas pipelines from Canada through Washington and Oregon in 1956–8.

Electricity never did for any Northwestern state what oil had done for southern California. Reduction of aluminum was the only major industry that cheap power attracted, and aluminum was more effective at using power than at providing jobs: production of half the national supply in the later 1940's employed only about 6,000 men, and about half the output went out of the region for processing. Aluminum was conspicuous on the planes Boeing produced, but trivial in amount: in 1949, less than one fourth of one percent of the Northwest's output in new aluminum. Henry Kaiser acquired the aluminum rolling mill at Trentwood, Washington, and the reduction plants at Mead and Tacoma

[7] Growth of major standard metropolitan statistical areas (including all five in the Northwest), 1950–60

United States (212 areas)	26.4%	Salt Lake City	39.3%
Eugene	29.5	San Diego	85.5
Los Angeles–Long Beach	54.4	San Francisco–Oakland	24.2
Ogden	32.9	San Jose	121.0
Portland	16.6	Seattle	31.1
Provo–Orem	30.6	Spokane	25.6
Reno	68.8	Tacoma	16.6
Sacramento	81.4		

[8] Edwin J. Cohn: *Industry in the Pacific Northwest and the Location Theory* (New York: King's Crown Press; 1954), pp. 29–30.

[9] Portland *Oregonian*, July 13, 1962, p. 1, col. 1. *The New York Times*, October 7, 1962, Sec. I, p. 43, col. 2. Brier: *Sawdust Empire*, pp. 111–5.

from the government at bargain prices to furnish metal for the automobile business he went into in 1946, but in the fifties he and other producers built most of their new capacity in the Mississippi and Ohio valleys, near enough to major markets and processing centers to reduce the cost of freight and to expedite deliveries. By the end of the decade the Northwest's share of national capacity in ingots had dropped from 52 to under 29 percent.[1]

The aircraft industry was a much larger employer than aluminum; Boeing reached a postwar peak of 73,000 employees in 1958, before production of B-52 bombers moved to Wichita. It was also the only large growth industry in the Northwest. Although the development of the B-707 and other jet airliners eventually provided a promising commercial market that about matched military demand in the early 1960's,[2] the future of the industry and so of a large fraction of the region remained somewhat speculative. A few military and corporate purchasers accounted for nearly three fifths of employment in manufacturing in Seattle. When a strike seemed imminent at Boeing in 1962–3, some of the people of Washington were not sure how much they had improved themselves when transportation equipment moved past lumber in the state's distribution of employment.

The lumber industry had changed much earlier in the century, and it continued to change. Development of more complex products and more sophisticated techniques followed the exhaustion of stands of virgin timber, the consolidation of the industry, and competition with new building materials. Fir plywood had been on exhibit at the Lewis and Clark Exposition at Portland in 1905, but moisture-resistant types suitable for exterior construction found new markets, especially after the war. Although the whole industry required less labor as efficiency advanced, employment in production of plywood in Oregon increased more than four times between 1947 and 1962. The mechanization of logging itself in the 1920's and 1930's, and the substitution of trucks,

---

[1] Paul B. Simpson: "Factors Which Determine Growth in the Pacific Northwest," *Oregon Business Review*, Vol. XXI (November 1962), pp. 1–5. James N. Tattersall: "River Basin Development Vital for Economic Growth of Northwest," *Oregon Business Review*, Vol. XVI (October 1957), pp. 1–2. Robert Sheehan: "Kaiser Aluminum—Henry J.'s Marvelous Mistake," *Fortune*, Vol. LIV (July 1956), pp. 80–82. J. Granville Jensen: *The Aluminum Industry of the Northwest* (Corvallis: Oregon State College; 1950), pp. 4, 6. Federal Reserve Bank of San Francisco: *Monthly Review*, February 1960, pp. 34–5.

[2] *The New York Times*, October 30, 1962, p. 9, cols. 4–7; p. 10, cols. 1–2.

tractors, and light cables (by the 1950's, even helicopters) for logging railroads, donkey engines, and heavy overhead rigging gave the industry both new mobility and new stability; bulldozers and other rubber-tired equipment went where locomotives could not, and more cheaply. But the new techniques also facilitated selective cutting, reseeding, and other conservationist practices, and the substitution of sustained yield for the old policy of "cut out and get out," and they demanded skilled operators, who typically wanted to live in town with their families instead of carrying their bindles to camp. Even as logging moved from Washington into the hitherto inaccessible mountains and canyons of western and southern Oregon, the greater part of the industry's labor force moved from the woods to huge electrically operated factories that resembled the steel foundries of Pittsburgh more than the old water- and steam-powered sawmills. (The traditional millrace disappeared, except where it was preserved for scenery or recreation; now the chief reason for locating a mill by a stream was to keep the logs wet.) Eventually the industry became more successful in converting raw material to profit than the meat packers of Kansas City and Omaha had been: some of the larger concerns went so far in making sawdust, chips, bark, noxious fumes, and effluvia and dust in the air into composition board, paper, wax, pressed logs for fireplaces, and alcohol that they had to buy the wastes of small independent mills. Oregonians still tended to gauge the strength of their economy by the price of standard sawn lumber. Yet the earnings of some of the larger corporations held up and even increased while employment continued to decline and both industry and labor complained of competition from low-priced products of Japanese, and later of Canadian, mills. The Canadians moved into the markets of the Northeastern states where Northwestern Douglas fir, by virtue of greater mechanization in the mills, long had predominated over Southern pine.[3] Lumber's prob-

[3] Alfred J. Van Tassel and David W. Bluestone: *Mechanization in the Lumber Industry . . .* (Philadelphia, 1940), Works Progress Administration, National Research Project, Report no. M-5, pp. xvii–xviii, 12–17, 42–50, 131. *Timberman,* Vol. L (October 1949), pp. 63–4, 66, 68, 76, 78, 86–91, 168–70. *Forests for the Future; The Story of Sustained Yield as Told in the Diaries and Papers of David T. Mason, 1907–1950,* ed. Rodney C. Loehr (St. Paul: Minnesota Historical Society; 1952). Clark Kerr and Randall Randall: *Crown Zellerbach and the Pacific Coast Pulp and Paper Industry* (Washington: National Planning Association; 1948), pp. 12, 14–15. Wesley C. Ballaine: "Oregon Economic Outlook for 1963," *Oregon Business Review,* Vol. XXI (December 1962), p. 2. Ivan M. Elchibegoff: *United States International Timber Trade in the Pacific Area* (Stanford: Stanford University Press; 1949), pp. 204–6.

lems were not simple: it survived, as it had grown, by substituting machines for men, becoming remarkably sophisticated for a resource-based industry that still depended ultimately on harvesting an essentially wild crop. The larger corporations tended to balance profits in paper and fiberboards against losses in traditional lines, and, like the woodworkers' union itself, they extended across the Canadian border. Advancing technology had not helped the smaller operators, nor had it established a much broader and firmer economic base for Oregon and the adjacent lumbering areas.

But however broad or firm the industrial base, all parts of the Far West seemed to be developing a more urban society. Even in those states that depended heavily on the earth's bounty, employment shifted increasingly to the service trades. This was no less true of areas rich in agriculture than of those dependent chiefly on lumbering and mining. Agricultural production flourished: output in both the mountain and Pacific states rose much beyond the national rate of increase after the Second World War, as it had after the First World War (for the three Pacific states, by 27 percent between 1947–9 and 1957). Between 1946 and 1958, production per man hour on farms in the Twelfth Federal Reserve District nearly doubled. Concurrently, population on farms continued to decline both absolutely and relatively; by 1950, only Idaho of the six states had a larger part of its population on farms than the nation (28.4 percent and 15.5 percent, as against 38.5 percent and 23.2 percent in 1940), and California's agricultural population had dropped from 9.7 to 5.8 percent in the decade.[4]

Much of the bounty and efficiency of Western agriculture followed, as in other sections, on the substitution of machines for men. Airplanes sprayed insecticides over fruit trees and vegetables; on the wheat ranches of the Palouse country, they went to town on routine errands; on the desert, they helped to round up cattle and wild horses, partly replacing the jeep, which already had partly replaced the Model T Ford and the horse. By 1961, 90 percent of the cotton of the San Joaquin Valley was harvested mechanically; the cotton picker was as clearly suited to the flat lands around Bakersfield as the combine harvester had been to the rolling hills of eastern Washington a half century earlier, and it explained much of the more than threefold increase of Cali-

[4] *Changes in Farm Production and Efficiency*, U. S. Department of Agriculture, Statistical Bulletin no. 233 (August 1958), p. 6. Federal Reserve Bank of San Francisco: *Monthly Review*, February 1960, p. 39. *Agricultural Census*, 1950, General Report, Vol. II, p. 66.

fornia's cotton crop between 1940 and 1960 and the displacement of fruit and vegetable crops that were still unmechanized. But the Far West did not economize on wages in agriculture (that is, it did not spend on land, improvements, and machinery rather than on labor) as much as it had in the early days of bonanza farms and chronic shortages of farm hands after the Civil War.[5] The more distinctive trend in mid-twentieth century was the shift to crops of higher value (including cotton), which in the main required such intensive cultivation as to absorb more labor rather than less. The Pacific states had the highest increase in production per acre in the nation in the years 1919–46 and reached the highest level of production per acre; they were the only area where man hours per acre of total crops increased substantially. Acreage under irrigation declined after the war in some of the driest areas, including Nevada and Utah, in part because uncontrolled watering without proper drainage had brought up alkali and made good farmlands into salt-marsh pasture, as in parts of the Jordan Valley; but in California, irrigated land increased (1944–59) by about half; in Washington it nearly doubled. In Oregon, where the net increase was smaller (under 24 percent), much of the new irrigation was in western counties where annual rainfall approximated Middle Western and Eastern levels, but where yields responded gratifyingly to sprinkling during the dry summer months.[6]

Thus agriculture moved along with the rest of the economy into more complex ways. After a fashion, farmers prospered: except in Utah and Oregon, average farm incomes kept well above national levels (in California and Nevada they were two or three times as much); on the Pacific coast as a whole, they exceeded nonfarm incomes. Yet agriculture was in retreat in several senses. Individual incomes remained high in large part because the number of farmers greatly declined.

---

[5] Acres per farm in the Pacific states declined from 420 in 1870 to 204 in 1925, 231 in 1930, 209 in 1935, and rose again to 279 in 1950.

[6] *The New York Times,* November 18, 1962, p. 125, col. 1. Alvin S. Tostlebe: *The Growth of Physical Capital in Agriculture, 1870–1950,* National Bureau of Economic Research, Occasional Paper 44 (New York, 1954), pp. 31, 55, 56, 58. U. S. Census of Agriculture, 1959, *Final Report,* Vol. I, part 46, p. 7. Reuben W. Hecht and Glen T. Barton: *Gains in Productivity of Farm Labor,* U. S. Department of Agriculture, Technical Bulletin no. 1020 (December 1950), pp. 15–18, 46, 48. *Changes in Farm Production and Efficiency,* pp. 11, 12, 23, 27. Richard M. Highsmith, Jr.: "Irrigation in the Willamette Valley," *Geographical Review,* Vol. XLVI (January 1956), pp. 98–110.

After the Second World War, total net income of farmers in the six states fell off badly in relation to production despite the greatly increased consumption of agricultural products in and from the area. Only in California, following on spectacular increases in production and costs, did farmers gain in total realized net farm income between 1949 and 1961 (16.9 percent, as against a loss of 7.2 percent nationally); farmers in the other five states as a group lost 22.9 percent. In no state of the six, in the years 1949–61, did income rise relative to expenses of production as much as it rose throughout the country.[7]

The averages covered great spreads in profits and also in crops and living conditions; there was ever less comfortable middle ground between the older extensive agriculture of farmers who raised mainly livestock and sold it across state boundaries and the newer intensive agriculture of farmers who lived in the shadows of the cities that consumed and processed their fruits, nuts, and vegetables. The livestock states, Nevada and Utah, lost most in realized net farm income in the fifties; the drop coincided with nationwide troubles in livestock, but also with a major regional exodus from the farm that had extended through better years as well. To the casual tourist, Northwesterners seemed more fortunate than most in holding to the family farm, on well-watered land near pleasant communities along the Rogue, Willamette, and Cowlitz; and yet, perhaps, for lack of large metropolitan markets, many farms were more picturesque than prosperous, or their owners kept up appearances through jobs in town. Michael Harrington, describing the forgotten American poor in 1962, located the centers of "property-owning poverty" in the Pacific Northwest as well as in the eroded hillsides of the South and the desert pastures of New Mexico and the northern Rockies.[8] The outsider might shrink at the heat and drab flatness of the irrigated deserts and the Central Valley of Cali-

---

[7] Robert H. Masucci: "Regional Differences in Per Capita Farm and Nonfarm Income," *Agricultural Economic Research*, Vol. XII (January 1960), pp. 2–3. "Farm Income State Estimates, 1949–61," in U. S. Department of Agriculture, Economic Research Service: *Farm Income Situation*, no. 187, supplement (August 1962), pp. 8–9, 36–7, 40–1, 64–5. Harvey S. Perloff: *Regions, Resources, and Economic Growth* (Baltimore: Johns Hopkins Press; 1960), pp. 377, 625.

[8] John R. Evans: "Utah's Changing Agricultural Economy," *Utah Economic and Business Review*, Vol. XXII (May 1962), pp. 5, 8. Richard B. Weed: "Reclamation and Agriculture," ibid., Vol. XVII (June 1957), p. 2. Michael Harrington: *The Other America: Poverty in the United States* (New York: The Macmillan Company; 1962), p. 44.

fornia, where sand and peat-mulch dust sometimes seemed to foul the atmosphere as badly as the smog of the cities; but these were the places where employment and production were holding up best. Agriculture survived by transforming itself: the states where the range seemed to have changed least since pioneer times lost more than states where farmers had rationalized and industrialized; agricultural employment fell sharply in Utah while it rose in California.

As the rural West emptied its population into the cities from mine, farm, and forest, it almost seemed to be reverting to that degree of detachment from urban ways that had obtained when pioneer San Francisco was a piece of the East in exile, having no more in common with the Mexican cattle ranches to the south than a clipper ship had with a school of whales that crossed its wake. Yet the essence of the new Western countryside was its integration into a new urbanism. More efficiently than ever before, the city commanded the hinterland, increasingly performing the services and making the decisions that in a simpler day had been adjuncts of the physical work, and absorbing the yield. The sharp decline in farm population represented both greater efficiency and change in residence of persons ultimately dependent on agriculture for their living.

The new society was far too complex to admit any simple distinction between country and city, between exploiter and exploited. "The individual farmer [in the Santa Clara Valley, around San Jose] is a more or less skilled worker who performs a certain specialized task in the fruit industry," a Dutch visitor wrote even in 1932. "He produces practically nothing for his own consumption and depends for his daily needs on the delivery services which supply the countryside."[9] Proximity to urban markets, employment, and services variously subsidized rural ways. Water sold for agricultural irrigation around Los Angeles at rates so low that it seemed to be essentially a weapon in urban imperialism, a means of establishing artificial shortages. (Los Angeles had set special irrigation rates as early as 1915 to provide water for farms in the San Fernando Valley, which had been desert and soon became part of the metropolis.) And where cities grew slowly, nearby farmers who were ready to retire might sell profitably to subdividers. But suburbs and freeways grew so fast in the forties and fifties that they pushed up taxes on adjacent rural property, and farmers who sold out

[9] Jan O. M. Broek: *The Santa Clara Valley, California; a Study in Landscape Changes* (Utrecht: N. v. A. Oosthoek's Uitg. Mij.; 1932), p. 102.

and still wanted to farm had to pay out their profits to develop desert and hillside land. As San Jose and other cities that formerly had depended on food-processing began to swallow up farmlands to meet the needs of other industries, new problems developed for both townspeople and farmers. Agricultural areas in the paths of the new metropolitan juggernauts incorporated themselves as sixth-class cities in California to protect themselves against capricious annexation. By 1954 the county authorities reserved, on the northern side of San Jose, the state's first agricultural zone.[1] If metropolitan regions did not soon extend continuously from Sacramento to Los Gatos, from Santa Barbara to San Diego and Riverside, apparently it would be because there was not enough water to supply them and their transplanted truck gardens or because of some such steps to divert the cities onto less arable land.

The new distribution of population and occupations in the Far West roughly paralleled changes in the patterns of politics. The newcomers moved chiefly to cities, which in the West, as nearly everywhere outside the South, long had tended to be more Democratic than the rural hinterlands, and most of them came from states that were usually more Democratic than the states west of the Rockies; substantial numbers were Negroes and members of other minority groups. By the fifties, Democrats were congratulating themselves on a new basis of strength apparently more substantial than the reaction against the depression that, with varying degrees of logic, had helped to elect the two Martins in Washington and Oregon, McAdoo and Olson in California, Thomas and Maw in Utah. The transformation seemed especially clear on the coast, where urbanization went furthest. In Oregon, the number of registered Democrats increased beyond the number of registered Republicans in 1950 (it reached 54.3 percent of the major-party registrations in 1960), but as late as 1953, of a total membership of ninety, there were only fifteen Democrats in the legislature, including Richard and Maurine Neuberger, the future United States senators; in 1959 the Democrats organized both houses of the legislature for the first time since 1879. California, which had had a majority of Democratic registrations since 1936, finally overcame the habit of nominating

[1] Jack Hirshleifer: "Water Supply for Southern California—Rationalization or Expansion?" *Proceedings of the Western Economic Association, 35th Annual Conference* (1960), pp. 46–51. Vincent Ostrom: *Water & Politics: A Study of Water Policies and Administration in the Development of Los Angeles* (Los Angeles: Haynes Foundation; 1953), pp. 144–67. Commonwealth Club of California: *Transactions,* Vol. LII (1958), p. 76. Editors of Fortune: *The Exploding Metropolis* (New York: Doubleday & Co.; 1958), pp. 138–9.

Republican candidates in Democratic primaries and in 1958 elected a Democratic governor, the second since the depression of 1893. And in 1955, Oregon had two Democratic senators for the first time since 1917 and an elected Democratic senator for the first time since 1921. By 1959 there were five Democratic senators from the three coastal states, more than ever before, and five more from Idaho, Nevada, and Utah. Between 1951 and 1961, the numbers of Democrats and Republicans in the six state legislatures more than reversed themselves, from a Republican majority of 347–254 to a Democratic majority of 361–252.

Yet the political balance was closer than such shifts in votes and voters may suggest. In 1941, of the six states five had Democratic governors; by 1949, only one governor was a Democrat; in 1959, three were Democrats. Most of the six states' representatives in Congress were Republicans from 1947 to 1959, and the Democratic majorities seated in 1961 and 1963[2] were smaller than the Republican majorities had been, as well as smaller than the Democratic majorities of 1933–43. In the first four postwar presidential elections, 1948–60, the Republican vote ran above the national percentage in most of the states most of the time (seventeen of twenty-four times that the electorates of the six states voted). And whereas only one of the six (Oregon) voted Republican in 1948, all did so in 1952 and 1956; all but one (Nevada) in 1960. Even as Democrats gained offices in California, Republicans gained registrations (from 37.6 percent of major-party registrations in 1940 to 41.2 percent in 1962).

Such Republican strength represented not merely cultural lag, as Democrats liked to believe, but some more fundamental aspects of the new society. Although the rest of the nation was catching up with the Far West in wealth and income, narrowing gaps that had persisted since the mining rushes of the last century, Westerners on the average still were distinctively prosperous.[3] When they were not, they were

[2] The delegations of 1959–61 tied, 23–23.

[3] Per capita income in the Far West was again highest in the country in 1950 (120.4 percent of the national average) and in 1957 (118.7 percent), after dropping to second highest in 1930 (130.8 percent) and 1940 (131.9 percent). Perloff: *Regions, Resources, and Economic Growth*, pp. 137, 27, 38. Cf. Richard A. Easterlin: "Interregional Differences in Per Capita Income, Population, and Total Income, 1840–1950," in National Bureau of Economic Research: *Studies in Income and Wealth*, Vol. XXIV, *Trends in the American Economy in the Nineteenth Century* . . . (Princeton: Princeton University Press; 1960), pp. 137, 139–40.

likely to think that they were or might become so; and though they were often wrong in their beliefs and expectations, statistics tended to understate the material advantages and psychological effects of Western living conditions. Most of the new immigration probably confirmed the existing economic and social profile rather than revised it: retired businessmen constituted a smaller fraction of the population in the six states than in Arizona, but the migrants to California in the thirties and forties maintained or raised the educational level and so were not predominantly the "little people" whom John Steinbeck described in the vineyards and lettuce fields. Substantial numbers of the newcomers from predominantly Democratic Southwestern states such as Arkansas, Mississippi, Oklahoma, and Texas may have been conservative enough by interest or habit so that, however they registered, they behaved more like Republicans than Democrats once they arrived.[4]

Industrialization was especially slow to change the political temper of the fast-growing metropolitan areas. Union membership advanced greatly, especially in the coastal states, and within them especially in southern California, but predominantly in A. F. of L. rather than C. I. O. unions, as before the war.[5] On the whole, labor inclined more to the essential conservatism of the teamsters than to the radicalism of the longshoremen. The I. L. W. U. itself essentially abandoned what one of its own committees called a policy of "intermittent guerrilla warfare," and in 1960 agreed with the Pacific Maritime Association to accept modern mechanized methods in return for financial security. There was relatively little evidence of class consciousness or proletarian political behavior in the suburban developments most Western workingmen lived

---

[4] Davis McEntire: "Characteristics of California's Migrant Population," Institute of Economics and Finance, *Proceedings* (Los Angeles: Occidental College; 1948), pp. 28–9, 33. Warren S. Thompson: *Growth and Changes in California's Population* (Los Angeles: The Haynes Foundation; 1955), pp. 237–50. David Farrelly and Gerald Fox: "Capricious California: A Democratic Dilemma," *Frontier,* Vol. VI (November 1954), p. 7.

[5] Union membership of persons in non-agricultural employment rose between 1939 and 1953 from 41.3% to 53.3% in Washington, 30.1% to 43.1% in Oregon, 23.4% to 35.7% in California, 18.2% to 30.4% in Nevada, 19.3% to 26.3% in Utah, 13.7% to 21.5% in Idaho, as against 21.5% to 32.0% in the United States. Total union membership in the six states in 1939 was 77.8% A. F. L., 13.7% C. I. O., and 8.5% unaffiliated (as against 59.0%, 27.7%, and 13.3% for the United States); in 1953, it was 82.2% A. F. L., 11.8% C. I. O., and 6.0% unaffiliated (as against 61.3%, 28.1%, and 10.6% for the United States). Figures derived from Leo Troy: *Distribution of Union Membership among the States, 1939 and 1953,* National Bureau of Economic Research, Occasional Paper 56 (New York, 1957), pp. 4–5, 18, 21–2.

in. Political scientists pointed out that urban and rural voters behaved more alike in California and the Far West than in other states, that voting in metropolitan areas was less Democratic than in other metropolitan areas outside the South, and that the Far West was the only section where the Republican Party was stronger in cities and large towns than in small towns and the country. Although some parts of the metropolitan areas of San Francisco and Los Angeles were as solidly Democratic as others were solidly Republican, the Third Oregon Congressional District (Portland), which coincided with an entire metropolitan area more nearly than any district in the other states, elected in 1938–52 a Republican representative, who had the support of labor, and turned Democratic only when he lost in the primary. Portland voted for Republican presidential candidates in 1952, 1956, and 1960, and for a Republican governor, Mark Hatfield, in 1958 and 1962. Except for districts that first Republicans and then Democrats skillfully gerrymandered, the clearest Democratic gains in California in the fifties were in the rural counties, which had few industrial laborers and in which Democratic clubs and committees were weak and campaigning conditions seemed to favor Republicans rather than Democrats.[6]

In Utah, where Republicans came back strongly during and after the war, Democrats often pointed to the Mormon Church and to the preponderantly conservative and Republican sentiments of its leaders. After the Church instructed its members to attend district mass meetings to choose delegates to nominating conventions, gentiles all but disappeared from the ballot (95 percent of all candidates in 1956 were Mormons). Many believed that the Church had helped to elect J. Bracken Lee (a gentile) as governor in 1948 and Wallace F. Bennett, recently president of the National Association of Manufacturers, as senator in place of Elbert Thomas in 1950. When Lee lost the primary in

[6] *New York Times,* May 27, 1963, p. 1, cols. 7–8; p. 15, cols. 1–5. V. O. Key, Jr.: *American State Politics: An Introduction* (New York: Alfred A. Knopf; 1956), p. 234. Alfred de Grazia: *The Western Public, 1952 and Beyond* (Stanford: Stanford University Press; 1954), pp. 163–6; James Q. Wilson: *The Amateur Democrat: Club Politics in Three Cities* (Chicago: University of Chicago Press; 1962), pp. 320, 322. Eugene C. Lee: *The Politics of Nonpartisanship: A Study of California City Elections* (Berkeley: University of California Press; 1960), pp. 56–7, 60. Dean R. Cresap (*Party Politics in the Golden State* [Los Angeles: Haynes Foundation; 1954], p. 61) traces nonpartisan voting in the state senate of California to the tendency of rural voters to vote for men rather than parties: candidates (especially Republicans) are easily known and interest groups find it economical to spend money in rural districts.

1956, it was after he had alienated many conservatives by attacking the Eisenhower administration, in which Ezra Taft Benson, one of the Twelve Apostles, served as secretary of agriculture. On the other hand, the Mormon sense of common purpose, or mission, might help liberals and Democrats as well as conservatives, as when Mormon members of labor unions enlisted their wives in campaigning for David S. King for Congress in 1958. And Mormons clearly resented the Church's intervention on behalf of Hoover and Landon in 1932 and 1936 and against Senator (Elbert) Thomas in 1938,[7] and the appeals of Reed A. Benson, coordinator for the John Birch Society in Utah, for the support of his co-religionists in his (unsuccessful) campaign for the Republican nomination for Congress in 1962. Republican margins were not wide enough to suggest that the Church could command votes as it commanded tithes, missionary service, and support for local social activities.

The influence of conservative Mormon leadership was not so inconsistent with main trends in Far Western society as it seemed. Perhaps because most Westerners lived comfortably and because the rich at play, at school, and even at home stood apart from the masses more in degree than in kind, it was no handicap in most of the West to be a member of a well-known family, or well educated, or Protestant: the balanced ticket of Eastern city and state elections did not exist. If being a Roman Catholic or a Jew had taken the bloom off Western opportunity, minorities and the politicians that catered to them might have organized to see that they got more than their share of public office; as it was, often they got less and seemed content. Members of minorities sometimes were impressively successful vote-getters, but more than in other sections, religion and race seemed irrelevant to most voters. Thus the two Jews who went furthest in Far Western politics, Julius Meier, governor of Oregon (1931–5), and Simon Bamberger, governor of Utah (1917–21), may have been stronger at the polls for being well known as heads of large business firms but not for commanding support

[7] *Western Politics,* ed. Frank H. Jonas (Salt Lake City: University of Utah Press; 1961), pp. 278–9, 280–1, 300. Jonas in *Rocky Mountain Politics,* ed. Thomas C. Donnelly (Albuquerque: University of New Mexico Press; 1940), pp. 34–5. E. Larkin Hess: "Mormons and Politics," *Frontier,* Vol. IV (February 1953), pp. 10, 12. Frank H. Jonas: "J. Bracken Lee and the Mormon Church," Utah Academy of Sciences, Arts, and Letters, *Proceedings,* Vol. XXXIV (1957), pp. 110–11, 121–3; Vol. XXXVI (959), p. 152 n. John Herling: "The Mormons and Mormon Utah," *New Leader,* Vol. XLIII (May 2, 1960), p. 15. Ross Thompson (pseud.): "Utah: The Mormon Church and that Amendment Fight," *Frontier,* Vol. VI (January 1955), pp. 10–11.

from their co-religionists, who happened to be unusually few in their states. Their personal strength was of the kind that political sociologists found somewhat less often among Democrats than among Republicans, who as members of the social and economic elite tended to be visible in a wide variety of organizations and civic affairs. That the drift to monopoly in the newspaper press (under Republican leadership primarily, of course) had gone further in the Far West than in most other areas outside the South, and that higher percentages of Republicans than of Democrats seemed to vote,[8] probably was no handicap to leaders in church and marketplace.[9]

Personal visibility was especially useful in the absence of strong party organizations like those that advanced candidates and delivered the vote in other parts of the United States. The weakness of party in the West may have followed chiefly on the progressive tradition and on progressive laws and constitutional amendments that removed party labels from local government and turned control of most other offices to civil service commissions and to the voters. Thus, though no state put all state offices as well on a nonpartisan basis (as the legislature of California proposed to do in 1915), civil service systems and legal nonpartisanship extended far enough, except possibly in Utah, to leave little patronage for party workers; the Far West seemed to illustrate the thesis that where patronage is small, the leaders allocate it so as to improve their own immediate positions rather than to increase the party's vote to a maximum. There were at the same time traditions of looseness in loyalty to party dating back to the days when Westerners cared more about railroads and land than about slavery, and when railroads and great landlords impartially corrupted any who would serve them. And some felt that the new and larger metropolitan areas bred a kind of nonpartisanship among elected officials who might have used, for instance, the office of mayor as a stepping stone to larger influence in the party but who developed independent strength in the electorate around issues that were of little concern to their own statewide or national organization, and even became its enemies. The per-

---

[8] This does not mean that they tended more to vote a straight ticket. De Grazia found (*Western Public*, pp. 20–1) that despite disparities between Democratic registrations and Democratic strength at the polls, Republicans were less likely than Democrats to vote for a candidate of their own party whom they disliked or disagreed with.

[9] Lee: *The Politics of Nonpartisanship*, pp. 139–40, 145–6.

sonal advantages of politicians who came from Republican strata of society and the divergence of metropolitan from state or national politics tended to balance whatever advantage may have accrued to Democrats from the movement of Republican voters from the central cities to the outer suburbs.[1]

The weakness of party machinery invited movements to take it over or to substitute for it, and from both left and right. The Washington Commonwealth Federation and its affiliates and supporters continued to be influential in the state Democratic Party through the mid-1940's; former Representative Jerry O'Connell of Montana (1937–9) became executive secretary of the Democratic State Central Committee (1944–1947) before he and Representative Hugh De Lacy (1945–7) turned to Henry Wallace and the new Progressive Party. (California and Washington stood second and fourth in percentages of votes for Wallace in individual states in 1948.[2]) Monroe Sweetland and the Oregon Commonwealth Federation had never attained such influence or so radical a position, though they were widely accused of both; the OCF itself faded away early in the war. When Sweetland, Howard Morgan, and other liberal Democrats such as Charles O. Porter (representative, fourth district, 1957–61) displaced the older leadership of the party between 1948 and 1954, the party was so moribund that there was no county in Oregon with a Democratic precinct organization.[3]

Chaos reached its extremity in California, which required that the state and county central committees be composed on different bases, and thus contrived conflict between them. Interest groups ranging from the State Federation of Labor to a major oil company and the liquor

---

[1] James Q. Wilson: "The Economy of Patronage," *Journal of Political Economy*, Vol. LXIX (August 1961), p. 372. Scott Greer: *The Emerging City; Myth and Reality* (New York: Free Press of Glencoe; 1962), pp. 156–62.

[2] The order was (1) New York, 8.12%; (2) California, 4.73%; (3) North Dakota, 3.81%; (4) Washington, 3.51%; (5) Montana, 3.27%; (6) Oregon, 2.86%; (7) Nevada, 2.37%; (8) Idaho, 2.32%; (24) Utah, 0.97%. Karl M. Schmidt: *Henry A. Wallace: Quixotic Crusade, 1948* (Syracuse: Syracuse University Press; 1960), p. 331.

[3] Vern Countryman: *Un-American Activities in the State of Washington: The Work of the Canwell Committee* (Ithaca: Cornell University Press; 1951), pp. 5, 35. Richard L. Neuberger in Robert S. Allen: *Our Fair City* (New York: Vanguard Press; 1947), p. 331. Portland *Oregonian*, June 16, 1939, p. 16, col. 1. A. Robert Smith: *The Tiger in the Senate: The Biography of Wayne Morse* (New York: Doubleday & Co.; 1962), pp. 207–8. Jill Hopkins Herzig: "The Oregon Commonwealth Federation . . ." (unpublished master's thesis, University of Oregon; 1963). Lester G. Seligman: "A Prefatory Study of Leadership Selection in Oregon," *Western Political Quarterly*, Vol. XII (March 1959), pp. 153–67.

industry exercised functions ordinarily left to public officials or party organizations. From the late thirties through the forties, the government of the state periodically seemed about to fall under control of the managers of a quixotic pension plan, popularly called Ham and Eggs, who organized support for initiative measures with impressive efficiency and even during the depression received monthly dues from 175,000 members. Major candidates of both parties catered to advocates of competing plans; one of California's senators, Sheridan Downey, recommended as late as 1950 that social security be scrapped in favor of Ham and Eggs as "a short cut out to Utopia." Eventually one superlobbyist rose to power as a kind of broker for competing interests—Arthur H. Samish, who posed for photographers for a national magazine with a ventriloquist's dummy marked "legislature" in his lap and told a reporter: "I can tell if a man wants a baked potato, a girl, or money." (Governor Earl Warren commented: "On matters that affect his clients, Artie unquestionably has more power than the governor.")[4] When stronger and more responsible political leadership came, moreover, it also developed outside the formal structure of party politics and state government. The supporters of Earl Warren (governor, 1943–53) first worked chiefly through the California Republican Assembly, which leaders of the Young Republican Clubs established (1935) to endorse liberal candidates in the primaries, thus recalling the techniques of the progressives of 1910. But the liberals also relied, like the pensioners and like Samish, on new techniques of mass persuasion, and employed a commercial public-relations firm to run Warren's campaign for the governorship.[5]

More than anyone else, Warren came to fit the opportunities peculiar to the elusive, nonpartisan Western political system. For a

---

[4] Wilson: *Amateur Democrat,* pp. 98–100. Elmer R. Rusco: "Machine Politics, California Model: Arthur H. Samish and the Alcoholic Beverage Industry" (unpublished doctoral thesis, University of California at Berkeley; 1960), pp. 479–95. Frank A. Pinner, Paul Jacobs, and Philip Selznick: *Old Age and Political Behavior . . .* (Berkeley: University of California Press; 1959), pp. 4–6, 33–4. Lester Velie: "The Secret Boss of California," *Collier's,* Vol. CXXIV (August 13, 1949), p. 13; (August 20, 1949), p. 63.

[5] Hugh A. Bone: "New Party Associations in the West," *American Political Science Review,* Vol. XLV (December 1951), p. 1115. T. J. Anderson in Jonas: *Western Politics,* pp. 88–9. Robert J. Pitchell: "The Influence of Professional Campaign Management Firms in Partisan Elections in California," *Western Political Quarterly,* Vol. XI (June 1958), pp. 278–300. Irwin Ross: "the supersalesmen of California politics: Whitaker and Baxter," *Harper's Magazine,* Vol. CCXIX (July 1959), p. 61.

time it had seemed that no one in California could. After the twenties, Hiram Johnson and his old friends had little to do with state government or the governorship, which in the thirties passed from Republican reaction and irrelevance to Democratic incompetence while extremists gathered support. Without adopting Johnson's crusading fervor, Warren restored to the governorship a moderate progressivism that aroused suspicions in the most conservative Republicans and the most partisan New Deal Democrats alike, and an independence that appealed strongly to the majorities of both parties. He promised to "conduct a non-partisan administration," and assured his first legislature that "no clique, no faction and no party holds priority on all the rights of helping the common man."[6] Although advanced liberals complained that in picking up an "issue by its four corners" he looked too long at the corner of expediency, California had decent government and programs of social legislation that went far beyond those of other states. Warren never sought or received the backing of his party's state central committee or county committees and ordinarily ran as if other Republican candidates did not exist; he received the Democratic nomination in 1946. Californians quoted President Truman as saying: "He's really a Democrat and doesn't know it."[7] Several years before President Eisenhower appointed Warren chief justice of the United States (1953), strong opposition to him had developed among conservatives of his own party, who hoped to displace him in the governorship with Lieutenant Governor Goodwin Knight and who responded to his candidacy for the presidential nomination in 1951–2 by proposing a delegation instructed to support "anyone" else.[8]

Warren's departure for the Supreme Court was not the end, however, of Warrenism and other appeals across party lines in California and its neighbors. Despite Knight's originally conservative support and his

[6] James R. Bell: "The Executive Office of the California Governor under Earl Warren, 1943–1953" (unpublished doctoral thesis, University of California at Berkeley; 1956), p. 53

[7] Herbert L. Phillips: "Warren of California," *The Nation*, Vol. CLXXIV (May 24, 1952), pp. 496–7.

[8] *The New York Times*, December 2, 1951, p. 40, col. 1. *San Francisco Chronicle*, September 14, 1953, p. 1, col. 3. In 1959, after Earl Mazo (in *Richard Nixon: A Political and Personal Portrait* [New York: Harper & Brothers; 1959] gave Richard Nixon's version of his alleged betrayal of Warren as a member of the delegation from California pledged to Warren for the presidency in 1952, describing Warren's detachment from Nixon's campaigns in 1946 and 1950, Warren publicly called Mazo "a damned liar" and accused him of writing "a dishonest account to promote Nixon." *The New York Times*, July 1, 1959, p. 26, cols. 6–7.

opposition to much of Warren's program (which prompted a reporter to call him not a Hoover Republican but a Garfield Republican), he had the endorsement of Labor's League for Political Education and built up a strong independent following that helped him to keep the governorship by election in 1954. When Knight ran for the Senate in 1958 as a result of complex maneuvers by Senator William F. Knowland and Vice-President Richard Nixon, his Democratic successor, Edmund G. (Pat) Brown, had substantial Republican support against Knowland, who moved far to the right, endorsing a measure to establish the open shop. As the *San Francisco Chronicle* commented in explaining why it had withdrawn its endorsement of Knowland,[9] the managers of Knowland's campaign "could not find time or inclination to point to the progressive Republican record of the past; that field was left to Pat Brown, the Democrat, to claim and to promise to occupy."[1] Brown was a former Republican[2] who had become popular as a reforming district attorney in San Francisco, and whom some reporters had thought Warren might prefer to Knight as his successor in 1953; he announced his nonpartisan approach to appointments in words that might have been Warren's: "I don't care whether they are Democrat or Republican. I want to get the best men I can to assist me in the operation of the State."[3] A moderate in manner as well as in policy, outwardly (as some liberals complained) "the perfect Organization Man," Brown aroused neither great enthusiasm in his party nor the dissension that had followed on the ambitious but ineffective efforts of Governor Culbert Olson (1939–43) to achieve the "millennium in the biennium," and on the struggle between Manchester Boddy and Representative Helen Gahagan Douglas for the senatorial nomination in 1950. In 1962 the election returns seemed to justify Brown's prudent concentration on "responsible liberalism" when Richard Nixon, who won the Republican nomination for the governorship as a moderate ("vote for the man, not the party"),

---

[9] Although in recent years the least orthodox of the major Republican papers, the *Chronicle* traditionally had joined the *Los Angeles Times* and the *Oakland Tribune* (owned by the Knowland family) in influencing Republican policy. Warren had appointed Knowland to the Senate in 1945; Knowland had nominated Warren for the presidency in 1952.

[1] Stanley P. Isaacs: "Knights over California . . . ," *The Nation*, Vol. CLXXVIII (May 29, 1954), p. 464. *San Francisco Chronicle*, November 7, 1958, p. 30, col. 1.

[2] Brown changed his registration to Democratic in 1934. He had run for the state assembly as a Republican in 1927. In 1958 he received 22.5 percent of the vote in the Republican primary.

[3] *Time*, Vol. LXII (September 14, 1953), p. 24. *San Francisco Chronicle*, November 6, 1958, p. 1, col. 8.

failed to persuade the voters with the kinds of charges that, with Democratic help, he had made against Mrs. Douglas so successfully in 1950.[4]

Some old ways continued despite the new Democratic-sponsored requirements, adopted in 1952, that candidates who cross-filed—ran in primary elections of other parties—must indicate their registration on the primary ballots, and despite the abolition of cross-filing itself in 1959. The new procedures at least insured that Republicans would not win both primaries (as nine tenths of the members of the state senate did in 1952). In 1953–4, Democrats tried further to hold themselves together by coordinating their party clubs in a California Democratic Council and by organizing a state convention to make endorsements for nominations before the primary. Yet these steps did not so much eliminate as bring into focus the running differences of the amateurs with the professional politicians and with the representatives of labor. Some of the traditions of the nonpartisan reformers seemed to split, the fervor of political amateurism persisting in the clubs and the Council, whereas the most conspicuous Democratic exponent of the pragmatic approach, after Brown, was Jesse Unruh, whose methods as speaker of the assembly (1961–   ) evoked charges of "Tammanyization." Unruh looked like the leader of a big urban machine, but his rise, like Samish's, followed essentially on political atomism, on the failure of organization. He depended neither on racial and religious minorities, who continued essentially apolitical despite his attempts to invoke their support and labor's against the middle-class reformers of the clubs, nor on the distribution of patronage at the grass roots, which was no more available after the abolition of cross-filing than before. Much of his power followed, in fact, on his command of campaign contributions that would have been less interesting to members of the legislature if there had been more patronage, and less easy for him to control if there had been well-developed party machinery. Outside the areas of Unruh's immediate strength, which was greatest in the assembly and in Los Angeles and among national political leaders who found the looseness of Western political practice puzzling,[5] the older, more liberal nonpartisan appeal

---

[4] Robert E. Fitch: "The Organization Man *vs.* the Hipster," *New Republic*, Vol. CXXXIX (October 13, 1958), p. 8. "Man in the Middle," *Economist*, Vol. CXCVI (July 9, 1960), p. 150. Anderson in Jonas: *Western Politics*, pp. 82–3, 85.

[5] Currin V. Shields: "A Note on Party Organization: The Democrats in California," *Western Political Quarterly*, Vol. VII (December 1954), pp. 675–83. Robert J. Pitchell: "The Electoral System and Voting Behavior: The Case of California's Cross-Filing," *Western Political Quarterly*, Vol. XII (June 1959), pp. 480–4. "California's Non-Par-

continued to work for Brown and for Republicans in the tradition of Warren, like Senator Thomas H. Kuchel, whom Warren had appointed to succeed Nixon in 1952, and who had wide support from labor in 1956 and 1962 ("He serves *all* the people").

The successes of Republican ultraconservatives in 1964 (when Senator Barry Goldwater's victory in the primary anticipated his nomination for the presidency) followed on militant organization that was new in Western politics and that at the same time owed much of its effectiveness to the extreme decentralization that the progressives had brought about: Goldwater's supporters, for example, had taken advantage of the influence of defeated candidates, under state law, in the State Central Committee.

Officeholders and voters continued independent also in the Northwest, where admirers of Arthur Langlie, three times Republican governor of Washington (1941–45, 1949–57), compared him with Warren. As reform mayor of Seattle (1938–41), Langlie had developed a nonpartisan following; in 1944 he had the endorsement of the State Federation of Labor, and in 1948, when Dave Beck supported the Democratic gubernatorial candidate, Mon Wallgren, Langlie was confident enough to appeal vigorously—and successfully—to labor with the slogan, "A vote for Wallgren is a vote for Beck," charging that Beck had "attempted to destroy the free democratic trade unions of this state." His defeat in the senatorial election of 1956 followed a campaign that some Republicans considered overpartisan and a right-to-work measure that conservative Republicans promoted in spite of his opposition (somewhat as in California in 1958). His Democratic successor as governor, Albert D. Rosellini (1957–65, defeated 1964), was a moderate or conservative who had sought the nomination in 1952 on the issue of Communism and who promised a bipartisan administration with no turnover in career employees. In Oregon, where a less spectacular but more consistently liberal Republican, Charles Sprague (1939–43), replaced the conservative Democrat, Brigadier-General Charles H. Martin, as Langlie had re-

tisanship—Extend? Extinguish?" Commonwealth Club, *Transactions*, Vol. XLVI (February 25, 1952), pp. 60, 67–8. Rusco: "Machine Politics," pp. 6–8. Wilson: *Amateur Democrat*, pp. 275, 295–301, 321. Helen Fuller: "The Man to See in California," *Harper's Magazine*, Vol. CCXXVI (January 1963), pp. 70, 72. Ed Cray: "Jesse Unruh, 'Big Daddy' of California," *The Nation*, Vol. CXCVI (March 9, 1963), pp. 199–207. James Q. Wilson: *Negro Politics; The Search for Leadership* (New York: Free Press of Glencoe; 1960), pp. 214, 24, 27, 103, 108.

placed Clarence Martin, Senator Charles McNary (1917–44) maintained an older progressive tradition. McNary's colleague in the Senate, Rufus Holman (1939–45), a political maverick who had supported the independent candidates for governor in 1930 and 1934 and Franklin D. Roosevelt for President in 1932, became so extreme in his isolationist and nativist prejudices that he had little support in the press against Dean Wayne L. Morse of the University of Oregon, who defeated him in the Republican primary in 1944.[6]

Throughout his long service in the Senate, Morse carried to an extreme the extroverted individualism that Far Western politics permitted or produced. Oregonians relished his combativeness as a member of the University faculty when he led the fight against an unpopular administration in 1932–3; as a member of the War Labor Board when he criticized the administration, John L. Lewis, and various employers; as a senator when he challenged the leaders of his own party as well as Secretary of the Interior Harold Ickes and President Truman himself. His "outstanding distinction," the *Oregon Voter* observed in 1950, was "in part due to his independence of republican party leadership, . . . [which was] in line with the opinion of many thousands of Oregon republicans. . . ." The Senate was a sounding board for him as it had been for Borah and Johnson; it may be significant that the House, where to a greater extent individual representatives must work and rise within the party and within more confining procedures, did not develop such well-known and influential Far Westerners. Morse's refusal to support the Republican ticket for the presidency in 1952 and his formal break with the party followed on differences with leaders of the party nationally and in the state rather than on his standing with the voters, who despite ominous and well-financed rumblings on the right easily renominated and reelected him in 1950 over conservative opponents. It was not until 1955 that he registered as a Democrat, after Democratic leaders in Oregon pointed out that otherwise they could not nominate him under state law. In 1954 he had campaigned for a former student, Richard

---

[6] Bone in Jonas: *Western Politics*, p. 304. Kate Archibald: "Why the State of Washington Likes Langlie," *Christian Science Monitor*, February 8, 1941, magazine, p. 5. *The New York Times*, September 19, 1948, Sec. IV, p. 7, col. 4; October 21, 1948, p. 20, col. 3. Joe Miller: "Labor's New Strong Man," *New Republic*, Vol. CXXI (August 1, 1949), p. 17. Daniel M. Ogden, Jr.: "The 1952 Elections in Washington," *Western Political Quarterly*, Vol. VI (March 1953), pp. 132–3. *Oregon Voter*, Vol. CIV (May 20, 1944), pp. 588–9.

L. Neuberger (1912–60),[7] whose election gave Oregon two conspicuously liberal senators and, for a time, a Democratic delegation in Congress that was both larger and more harmonious than the state was accustomed to. Morse's position was all the stronger when, in 1956, national Republican leaders persuaded Secretary of the Interior (former governor) Douglas McKay to seek the nomination, which contributed to a split in the Republican Party and to a landslide vote for Morse. By 1958, however, Morse was openly at odds with Neuberger, who seemed instinctively to reach for his own independent contact with the electorate, and in effect competed with Morse for the same audience, as Neuberger's undramatic, conservative Republican predecessor never had. In 1959, a year before Neuberger's sudden death, Morse announced that he would campaign against him in 1960. By the time of his own reelection in 1962, Morse was differing strongly with the Kennedy administration on major policies,[8] prompting speculation about how long he would remain a Democrat.

Morse's popularity was consistent with that of a man he particularly disliked on the Republican side, Mark O. Hatfield, another former college professor. In contrast with his predecessor as governor, Robert Holmes (1957–9), who managed to throw away the support of many fellow Democrats, Hatfield carefully cultivated the arts of making political friends, establishing a reputation among Republicans as a winner and among independents and Democrats as a liberal. "You are the only future hope for us," Herbert Hoover telegraphed after Hatfield's election as secretary of state in 1956, a year of major Democratic victories in Oregon.[9] Yet even as Republican candidate for the governorship (1958 and 1962) he kept the name of the party out of his campaigns, and he managed to find other business when prominent senatorial spokesmen for the right wing visited Oregon. Commanding wide support in labor

---

[7] An admirer of liberals in both parties, in the Senate Neuberger moved increasingly toward nonpartisan support of the Eisenhower administration, whereas Morse emphasized his new Democratic loyalties.

[8] *Oregon Voter*, Vol. CX (May 13, 1950), p. 462. Ezra Taft Benson: *Cross Fire: The Eight Years with Eisenhower* (New York: Doubleday & Co.; 1962), p. 330. Sherman Adams: *Firsthand Report: The Story of the Eisenhower Administration* (New York: Harper & Brothers; 1961), pp. 235–7. A. Robert Smith: *Tiger in the Senate: The Biography of Wayne Morse* (New York: Doubleday & Co.; 1962), pp. 308–11.

[9] John M. Swarthout: "The 1958 Election in Oregon," *Western Political Quarterly*, Vol. XII (March 1959), pp. 334–5. Milton MacKaye: "Oregon's Golden Boy," *Saturday Evening Post*, Vol. CCXXXI (May 9, 1959), p. 106.

in his own state, he lectured Republicans of Michigan on the virtues of progressive taxation and those of California on the possibilities of attracting unionists to Republican causes.[1]

The interior states failed to develop significant liberal nonpartisan movements, because their progressive antecedents were weaker or because they were less urban than their neighbors on the coast. In Utah, Marriner S. Eccles, as a candidate for nomination for the Senate in 1952, suffered from charges that he had deserted the Republican Party during the early days of the New Deal by accepting appointment on the Federal Reserve Board; he lost to Senator Arthur V. Watkins, whose irreproachable conservatism and isolationism qualified him to preside over the committee of the Senate that heard the charges against Senator Joseph R. McCarthy in 1954. Though as governor (1949–57) and as mayor of Salt Lake City (1960–), J. Bracken Lee presented himself as a champion of lower-income groups, his principal financial supporters in his early and more successful campaigns were wealthy conservative businessmen, who dropped him only when he proposed a third party in opposition to the Eisenhower administration. Although the Democratic victories in Utah in 1956–62 coincided in time with those in Washington, Oregon, and California, the Republican temper gave no encouragement to liberalism; and moderate and conservative Democrats had largely replaced New Dealers in positions of influence in the party. Relying on his own impulses and on the public-relations firms that he employed in his campaign, Lee resembled some leaders on the coast in his independence of party organization, but in little else: he almost systematically alienated one major group after another—educators, the Mormon Church, labor, farmers—and yet managed almost by his sheer irrelevancy to make a comeback in Salt Lake City, center of gentile strength and of labor.[2]

In Nevada the politics of cattle and silver prevailed over rumors of

---

[1] *Wall Street Journal,* October 5, 1962, p. 1, col. 5. *The New York Times,* Western ed., February 12, 1963, p. 7, col. 2.

[2] Garth N. Jones and Frank H. Jonas: "Some Recent Employment Practices in Utah State Government," Utah Academy of Sciences, Arts, and Letters, *Proceedings,* Vol. XXXIII (1956), pp. 156–7. Jonas: "The Mormon Church and J. Bracken Lee." Utah Academy of Sciences, Arts, and Letters, *Proceedings,* Vol. XXXVI (1959), p. 149. Jonas: "The 1958 Election in Utah," *Western Political Quarterly,* Vol. XII (March 1959), pp. 352–3. Jonas: "The Third Man in Utah Politics," Utah Academy of Sciences, Arts, and Letters, *Proceedings,* Vol. XXXVII (1960), pp. 115–21. Jonas: "The 1956 Election in Utah," *Western Political Quarterly,* Vol. X (March 1957), pp. 155–8.

reform and over mere party lines; when a young insurgent, Tom Mechling, introduced grass-roots campaigning and captured the Democratic nomination for the Senate in 1952, Senator Pat McCarran (1933–54) simply supported his Republican colleague, George Malone (1947–59). Thereafter candidates did not dare to neglect new techniques for reaching the voters; neither did they significantly change their policies or their support, which resembled the old "bipartisan machine" of George Wingfield early in the century. Idahoans seemed to like color in their politicians, as in Borah's time, and especially in the person of Glen H. Taylor, who, as senator (1945–51) and as candidate for the Senate in the forties and fifties, attracted wide support in campaigns that featured his family's hillbilly singing. Idaho surpassed its neighbors in developing the negative attributes of the new Western politics: weakness of party organizations (which in consequence frequently had to contend with candidates who generated more embarrassment than enthusiasm), but mild commitment to policy. There was no general support either for Taylor's left-wing associations in the Progressive Party of 1948, which nominated him for the vice-presidency, or for (or, in fact, opposition to) the extreme isolationism and Communist-hunting of Herman Welker, who as senator (1951–7) stood out as a champion of Joseph McCarthy; Welker's Republican colleagues clearly disliked him, as did labor, but his opponent and successor, Frank Church (1957–), was more emphatic in oratorical style than in his commitment to liberal alternatives on such issues as conservation.[3] Perhaps the state's perennial problems of geographical and social disunity kept it from developing consensus on major issues.

The fluidity of politics in the coastal states supported frequent migrations across the lines of parties and doctrines. Stephen F. Chadwick, Republican candidate for governor of Washington in 1940, was a former Democrat, having lost in the Democratic primary of 1932 to Homer T. Bone, a former Republican. Governors Holmes of Oregon and Brown of California both had been Republicans; Richard P. Graves, the Democratic candidate for governor of California in 1954, had been

[3] Don W. Driggs in Jonas: *Western Politics*, pp. 220–1. Tom Mechling: "I Battled McCarran's Machine," *Reporter*, Vol. VIII (June 9, 1953), pp. 21–5. Claude C. Smith: "The 1954 Election in Nevada," *Western Political Quarterly*, Vol. VII (December 1954), pp. 615–6. Austin E. Hutcheson and D. W. Driggs: "The 1956 Election in Nevada," *Western Political Quarterly*, Vol. X (March 1957), p. 133. Boyd A. Martin: "The 1956 Election in Idaho," *Western Political Quarterly*, pp. 122–6. "Upset in Idaho," *Economist*, Vol. CLXXXI November 10, 1956), p. 510.

a Republican only the year before; allegedly, he had changed registration five times. Morse's two Democratic opponents in 1944 and 1950 were both well to the right of him; the second, Howard F. Latourette, changed registration before Morse did. In California, Senator Sheridan Downey (1939–50), originally a Republican, had run for lieutenant governor with Upton Sinclair on the EPIC ticket in 1934, for the House again as a Townsendite (and attorney for Dr. Francis E. Townsend) in 1936, for the Senate as a Democrat, advocating the Ham and Eggs plan, in 1938. Soon he had swung well to the right as a critic of federal control of irrigation and of oil lands, leading Representative Helen Gahagan Douglas to run against him in the primary in 1950; after he withdrew because of ill health, and when she won the nomination, he refused to support her against the Republican candidate, Richard Nixon. Meanwhile the earliest and most persistent and outspoken critics of alleged Communist tendencies in the Democratic Party in California had been not Nixon (who in fact was able to borrow much of the material for his campaign from Democrats), but Samuel W. Yorty and Jack B. Tenney, in their early years both supporters of left-wing movements as Democratic members of the state legislature, who became chairmen of committees to investigate the state relief system and un-American activities generally in 1940 and 1941. In Washington, on the other hand, unexpected support for civil rights came from Harry P. Cain, who as senator (1946–53) had shown little interest in it; in fact he seemed an enthusiastic follower of McCarthy. However, given a position in the Eisenhower administration, which Senator Taft urged him to take "so the President would have at least one conservative near him," he challenged procedures in checking on loyalty ("The Cain Mutiny") and defended "the dreamer and nonconformist." (Actually, his former constituents, knowing his liberal record as mayor of Tacoma and the general fluidity of Washington politics, were less surprised than his senatorial friends.)[4]

---

[4] Thomas S. Barclay: "The 1954 Election in California," *Western Political Quarterly*, Vol. VII (December 1954), p. 601. *The New York Times*, January 10, 1954, p. 53, cols. 1–2; June 6, 1954, p. 59, col. 3. George Creel: *Rebel at Large: Recollections of Fifty Crowded Years* (New York: G. P. Putnam's Sons; 1947), pp. 308–9. Sheridan Downey: *They Would Rule the Valley* (San Francisco, 1947). Mazo: *Nixon*, p. 75. Edward L. Barrett: *The Tenney Committee; Legislative Investigation of Subversive Activities in California* (Ithaca: Cornell University Press; 1951), pp. 7, 9–10, 13, 17. L. Edgar Prina: "The Harry Cain 'Mutiny,'" *Collier's*, Vol. CXXXVI (September 2, 1955), pp. 32–4, 36. "The Road to Damascus," *Reporter*, Vol. XII (February 10, 1955), p. 4.

* * *

Thus the postwar generation in the Far West had seen both remarkable change and remarkable continuity. New industry had drawn new population that in some of the most measurable lines of behavior, those of politics, seemed to accept old habits. "The voters of California, even the new ones, are unconscious followers of Hiram Johnson," a writer in *The Nation* commented nearly a decade after Johnson's death and fourteen years after his last election.[5] Westerners were frightened at how much some of their cities had grown, half persuaded that life had been better before there were so many people in southern California and around San Francisco Bay and Puget Sound, but more confident than before that greater growth and greater wealth were still to come.

---

[5] Grant McConnell: "California Conundrum: Why it Votes G. O. P.," *The Nation,* Vol. CLXXIX (December 4, 1954), p. 478.

XII

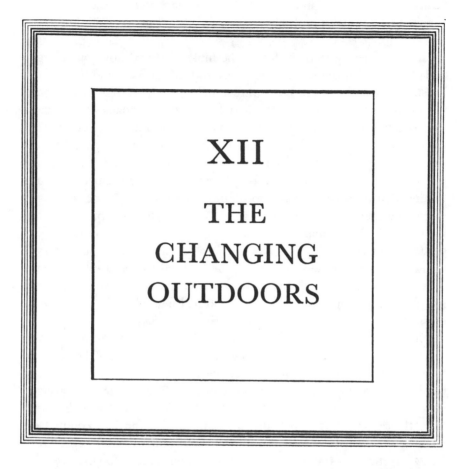

THE CHANGING OUTDOORS

Westerners commonly observed, after the first third of the twentieth century, that the Far West was filling up, that California especially had too many people and so was not what it had been. Yet no section had larger expanses of practically unpopulated land, essentially unchanged from what it had been when man first came there. Although by 1930 California had a denser population than the nation, the average was only about three persons to a square mile in eastern and northeastern California, eastern Oregon, Nevada, and most of Utah; and within a few minutes from most Western metropolitan areas a hiker could easily lose himself in some of the least-spoiled mountains and deserts on earth. From the sky it seemed that men barely had begun to cut the forests, break the sod, spread factories and suburbs and farms over the wild landscape. But the West between the cities had changed much, and with it men's access to it and men's attitude toward it.[1]

If Westerners sometimes forgot the hinterland and how much larger and emptier it remained than the hinterlands of the East and the Middle West, at an earlier time they were much less interested in it. Those who had come overland as children before the railroads might recall the first stages of the trip as a summer-long picnic, but, for most of their elders, following "the accursed Humboldt" or warping wagons through Emigrant Gap was a price to pay only once in a lifetime for the joy of the promised land. Once they were there, they seemed too busy getting rich or poor to return to nature: pioneer San Francisco might match the East in most respects—shops, cuisine, theater—but not in the habit of climbing mountains. "There are no useful avocations rendered necessary by a long spell of hot weather, as on the Eastern coast," an English visitor observed in 1874, "and a man feels under a constant pressure of excitement."[2] Josiah Royce recalled that as a boy he had heard of busy men in San Francisco who had never left the city even to cross the Bay, since the time they arrived in 1849.[3]

Since the building of the first railroads, however, Westerners hoped to sell recreation at a profit to Easterners and foreigners. "The summer pleasure travel over the line will be very large from the outset," Jay Cooke & Company promised of the Northern Pacific (1873).[4] Freight developed so slowly, and the West got so little of the traffic between the Atlantic and Asia that William Chapman Ralston had counted on when he planned the Palace Hotel, that both railroads and hotels were badly overbuilt in the 1870's and 1880's; their agents fought over the tourists who arrived at the Ferry Building—"a crowd of screaming, hustling hotel-touters," said an English traveler, Mrs. Carbutt (1889), "who knocked us down and trampled upon us and tore us to pieces."[5]

In the early years, when southern California was still too poor to offer

---

[1] I have tried not to repeat Earl Pomeroy: *In Search of the Golden West: The Tourist in Western America* (New York: Alfred A. Knopf; 1957).

[2] J. W. Boddam-Whetham: *Western Wanderings: A Record of Travel in the Evening Land* (London: Richard Bentley & Son; 1874), p. 147.

[3] Royce: "The Pacific Coast: A Psychological Study of Influence," *International Monthly*, Vol. II (November 1900), p. 562.

[4] *The Northern Pacific Railroad, Its Land Grant, Resources, Traffic, and Tributary Country . . .* (Philadelphia: Jay Cooke & Co.; 1873).

[5] Mrs. E. H. Carbutt: *Five Months' Fine Weather in Canada, Western U. S., and Mexico* (London: S. Low, Marston, Searle & Rivington, Ltd.; 1889), p. 79.

luxurious hotels, it depended heavily on boarding invalids attracted by reports of the curative powers of dry, warm air. "Men go there," the San Francisco *Alta* remarked, "not to buy land, but to buy lungs."[6] Eventually the promoters feared that the sick would drive away more lucrative visitors, especially as many of them had exhausted their resources on the trip west; but enough recovered enough of their health to contribute to some of the most distinctive traits of the region: willingness to work at less than union wages (thus leading to the open shop) and a fervor of enthusiasm for the climate and new crops that suggested more than ordinary physical comfort, more than ordinary reluctance to admit homesickness. For a generation, the health-seekers outnumbered those who came primarily for diversion, and they were prominent even in the organized tours that the travel agents escorted regularly after trains began to operate from the East through to Los Angeles in 1881. A correspondent of *The New York Times,* who reported a tour of 620 persons (occupying two trains), described how the forty-niners' search for gold had "given place to a pursuit quite as desperate on the part of some of the 'argonauts' of 1886—the pursuit of life, or a prolongation of it by but the briefest period. . . ." Two of that party died en route, in New Mexico.[7]

Most of the early promotion of the scenic and climatic attractions of the West was in some degree an undertaking of the Western railroads. They could advertise with fair confidence of return on their investments because for practical purposes there was no way to see the West except by rail, and each company ruled its special provinces. "Like Roderick Dhu," *The New York Times* observed, "the railway companies, who jealously 'hold every mountain pass and ford,' summon the vassal public to meet on the Missouri for semi-monthly incursions into Southern California."[8] The first of the great resort hotels, the Hotel del Monte (1880), near Monterey, was an enterprise of the Southern Pacific Railroad, whose subsidiary, the Pacific Improvement Company, owned over 7,000 acres nearby, as well as the only practical means of transportation from San Francisco, and which so commanded the economy of California that almost any development increased its earnings. The

---

[6] John E. Baur: *The Health Seekers of Southern California, 1870–1900* (San Marino: Huntington Library; 1959). *Southern California* (n.p.: Atchison, Topeka and Santa Fe Railroad; [1890]), p. 12.

[7] *The New York Times,* January 5, 1887, p. 8, cols. 3–4.

[8] Loc. cit.

owner of the Raymond, the great hotel built at Pasadena in 1886, was a son of the senior member of Raymond and Whitcomb, the Boston travel agency, which established the most popular of the railway tours.

But businessmen hoped that some of the spendings of rich visitors would find their way into everyone's pockets, that those who came for a reason might return and invest their capital. H. H. Bancroft wrote of the prospects of "the overflow from the east, [which] optimists say . . . will make us rich,—tourists, retired capitalists with enterprise all sucked out of them making homes here . . . so may we content ourselves with the crumbs that fall from the tables of progressive industry over the way, and henceforth write ourselves The happy land of Eastern Overflow." *Land of Sunshine,* organ of the Los Angeles Chamber of Commerce, expressed the common view that "the tourist is . . . scout for the business man."[9]

The agencies continued to escort parties of wealthy tourists by Pullman car each winter until the 1930's, but by the 1890's the chambers of commerce were joining the railroads in organized campaigns to attract larger numbers to conventions, expositions, and festivals. At first they chose dates in the winter and early spring when Easterners seemed most likely to come. When Michael H. de Young, publisher of the *San Francisco Chronicle* and custodian of California's exhibits at the World's Fair of 1893 at Chicago, heard that some foreign governments wished to exhibit after the Fair closed and proposed that San Francisco invite them for the following year, his purpose was not to entertain Californians who had not been able to go to Chicago, but to advertise San Francisco and its mild winter climate to Easterners. Hence the Midwinter Fair opened on January 1, at the season when the tourists then came in force, and closed six months later.[1]

The profits from entertaining large numbers of paying guests increased rapidly after the Midwinter Fair, which drew over two and a quarter million visitors in six months. The embarrassment of winter and spring rains forced the Northwest into what proved to be a still

---

[9] Hubert H. Bancroft: *Why a World Centre of Industry at San Francisco Bay?* (New York: The Bancroft Company; 1916), p. 15. *Land of Sunshine,* Vol. IX (October 1898), p. 263.

[1] *Pacific Monthly,* Vol. XXIII (January 1910), p. 112g. Christina W. Mead: "Las Fiestas de Los Angeles . . . ," Historical Society of Southern California, *Quarterly,* Vol. XXI (March–June 1949), pp. 67–9. *Land of Sunshine,* Vol. VI (March 1897), p. 165; Vol. X (February 1899), pp. 158–9. *Overland Monthly,* second series, Vol. XXII (November 1893), pp. 452, 455. Oscar Lewis: *Bay Window Bohemia . . .* (New York: Doubleday & Co.; 1956), pp. 48–9.

more lucrative market. The Lewis and Clark Exposition at Portland (June–October 1905) and the Alaska-Pacific-Yukon Exposition at Seattle (June–October 1909) drew record-making summer crowds to all the West. In view of these successes in what had been the slack season, the Panama Pacific Exposition at San Francisco operated from February to December 1915, and nearly nineteen million attended. The Panama-California Exposition at San Diego (1915–17) continued through two summers and three winters, for all of twenty-seven months. Meanwhile the railroads had set special fares for summer conventions, beginning with the Christian Endeavor Society, which met in San Francisco in July 1897; after 1906, reduced rates applied over the entire summer. Those who took advantage of the bargain rates tended to be younger, less affluent than those who came in winter, and more likely to ride in the cane-seated tourist sleepers that the railroads began to run in the later 1880's than in the lavishly curtained and upholstered palace cars. Yet it was profitable to carry and entertain them.

As the tourists increased, they became most interesting for different reasons: first, as investors and passengers; then, as colonists; finally, simply as spenders on a large scale, patrons of restaurants, gasoline stations, and beach resorts. Businessmen founded new promotional agencies to divert the growing traffic in their direction, and the railroads tended to shift the burden of general advertising to them, to chambers of commerce, and to state governments. (The Southern Pacific, which had founded *Sunset* magazine in 1898 to promote the states that it served, sold it in 1914.) Especially in times of depression, and in states where more orthodox industries failed to rise to early expectations, the spending of transients loomed large; much of the mountain and desert country came, as Carey McWilliams has said, "to improvise economically: that is, to attempt to balance its economy by capitalizing on its myth."[2] The tourist bureaus and the automobile clubs, arguing for larger expenditures for advertising and for highways, calculated the money left behind and the place of tourism among other industries (most important of all in Nevada, where the estimated average daily expenditure by tourists in 1955 was $37.59, the highest in the country.)[3]

---

[2] McWilliams in *Rocky Mountain Cities*, ed. Ray B. West, Jr. (New York: W. W. Norton & Co.; 1949), p. 22.

[3] American Automobile Association: *Americans on the Highway . . .* , sixth edition (Washington, 1956), pp. 11–12. Andrew H. Trice and Samuel E. Wood: "Measurement of Recreation Benefits," *Land Economics*, Vol. XXXIV (August 1958), pp. 199–200.

Tastes and opportunities in Western vacationing changed along with the volume of travel. The early resorts sought the kind of fashionable clientele that had patronized White Sulphur Springs, Saratoga, and other antebellum watering places in the older states. Sam Brannan founded Calistoga, north of San Francisco, and prophesied it would be the Saratoga of California. Despite the heat of the valley, he developed it as a summer resort in the style of the springs of Virginia, each of the small cottages having a classical or historical name, balcony, summer house of latticework, date palm and cypress in front. White Sulphur Springs, nearby, had a reputation for "excellent society" in the early 1870's and the finest summer hotel in the state. For several decades, mineral springs were prominent in tourist itineraries and in the advertising of hotelkeepers, who carefully enumerated the content of "sulphuretted hydrogen," arsenic, alkalines, and iron. "Nature seems to have chosen California as a safety valve for all the nasty tasting water she could not provide for elsewhere," an Englishman complained.[4] Santa Barbara, Elsinore, Arrowhead, and, across the Mexican border, Tijuana all began as spas. Though too far from the railroads and civilization to be fashionable at first, the area of Mount Rainier National Park first became interesting to tourists for the springs that James Longmire discovered in 1883 and shortly developed, building a bathhouse and a rustic hotel. But in the last years of the century, fashion tended to lose interest in therapeutic themes: mineral springs often became adjuncts to baths and sanitaria in the more restricted sense, or they became features of public parks; the rich who wintered at the more luxurious "watering places" made no pretense of early rising, fasting, and purging.

The most celebrated stopping places by the 1880's offered neither cures nor local color, but the conveniences and displays of up-to-date innkeeping. The Palace Hotel (1875) incorporated air-conditioning, pneumatic tubes, and hydraulic elevators in an architectural setting that owed more to Vienna and Paris than to San Francisco despite the bay windows that Californians had come to demand to catch the sunlight. The Hotel del Monte offered an appropriate setting for San Francisco society and for the families of officers in the navy and army who were on maneuvers or encamped nearby. "It seemed queer to see this mod-

---

[4] Frank W. Green: *Notes on New York, San Francisco, and Old Mexico* (Wakefield [England]: E. Carr; 1886), p. 84.

ern, extravagant life," a Danish visitor wrote in 1888, "a few stone's-throws away from the old mission house called El Carmelo, with its small, neglected churchyard and a quiet, black-robed priest praying before the altar in the chapel."[5] The formal landscaping in the 126 acres of the gardens of the hotel seemed to impress the early tourists more than the natural setting of pine, cypress, rock, and surf. In similar spirit, a Pasadenan boasted of the Raymond that "you are taken from a snow storm in Boston, and a few days later find yourself in a Boston hotel, or with all the conveniences and luxuries of one"[6]—an illusion that the management enhanced by importing the servants seasonally from New England.

But even as the Pullman cars of the first of the parties of winter excursionists from the East stopped at the de luxe hotels, Westerners found simpler pleasures and eventually the basis for a larger tourist industry. In the seventies and eighties, campers went out each summer by the thousands, especially to the seacoast. "I recall our hay-rides to Pizmo beach," Horace Vachell wrote of his "lotus life" on a ranch in San Luis Obispo County in 1882, "where we bathed, dug clams to make a chowder over a camp-fire, and then shot ducks till still evening came on, when we danced on the firm sand, returning homealong at midnight."[7] City dwellers and foreigners predominated, rather than rural folk, who were likely to see enough of the outdoors while at work (Vachell's farmer neighbors called him the "picnic king"). But in Oregon the families of farmers passed as many as from three to five weeks in the mountains in late summer or autumn, hunting and fishing, picking berries, and making jam. Permanent resorts appeared as well—the developments on Salt Lake that became Saltair and Lake Park, and several along Monterey Bay and the Oregon coast opposite the Willamette Valley. At Newport, on Yaquina Bay, the campers came to the hotel for folk dances, lectures, and Sunday services. Along the Columbia, even before the railroad to Astoria (1895–8), boardinghouses and private cottages and, according to Frances Fuller Victor, "some quite capacious mansions" were supplementing the tents in which many Portlanders

---

[5] Alexandra Gripenberg: *A Half Year in the New World; Miscellaneous Sketches of Travel in the United States* (1888), ed. E. J. Moyne (Newark: University of Delaware Press; 1954), p. 141.

[6] Charles F. Holder: *All About Pasadena and Its Vicinity* . . . (Boston: Lee and Shepard; 1889), p. 17.

[7] Horace A. Vachell: *Distant Fields, a Writer's Autobiography* (London: Cassell and Co.; 1937), p. 65.

slept on hay that they bought from farmers.[8] But life remained simple; the chief amusements, fishing, hunting, and driving along the beaches. By the eve of the First World War, many families in Seattle had formed a vacationing habit peculiar to that area, cruising the Sound in boats and staking out summer camps on wooded islands.

California developed traditions in vacationing that befitted an area with a larger population, more wealth, easier access to the coast, and milder climate than the Northwest. San Franciscans promenaded Sunday afternoon in Woodward's Gardens, later in Golden Gate Park (1869), or took the cars to the Cliff House to watch the seals, or to the salt-water baths that Adolph Sutro opened in 1894. The railroad along Monterey Bay (1876) opened fifty miles or more of potential resort country; soon Camp Capitola (1869), which at first drew only campers who brought their own tents, had cottages and a hotel, and the old Mexican town of Santa Cruz, according to an English traveler, was "simply a typical American watering-place, with a sandy beach, and a long, broad, bright-looking street, with the inevitable tram-car rails laid down the center."[9] In southern California, projects for harbors and agricultural colonies dominated the propaganda of the early promoters, but residents of Los Angeles and other inland communities picnicked and pitched their tents along the beaches. By the time Mrs. Frank Leslie stopped at Santa Monica in 1877, the railroad, which its developers had built (1875), was carrying enough traffic to justify a hotel above the beach—"two large two-storied buildings," she wrote, "similar to, and quite equal to the same class of accommodations in our best hotels at Long Branch." Excursion steamers began serving Catalina Island as early as 1887.[1]

The great hotels looked to the elite who came by Pullman car from the East, or, at Del Monte, from the four hundred of San Francisco, but some of the less fashionable resorts owed much to organized morality and religion. The first development on the Monterey peninsula for vacationers followed on the incorporation of the Pacific Grove Retreat

---

[8] Frances F. Victor: *Overland*, second series, Vol. XXIII (February 1894), pp. 145–7.

[9] W. Henry Barnaby: *The New Far West and the Old Far East, being Notes of a Tour in North America, Japan, China, Ceylon, Etc.* (London: Edward Stanford; 1889), pp. 145–6.

[1] Mrs. Frank Leslie: *California. A Pleasure Trip from Gotham to the Golden Gate (April, May, June, 1877)* (New York: G. W. Carleton & Co.; 1877), p. 270. Glenn S. Dumke: *The Boom of the Eighties in Southern California* (San Marino: Huntington Library; 1944), p. 74.

Association, whose trustees met at the Howard Street Methodist Church in San Francisco in 1875 to plan a "Christian Seaside Resort and Camp Meeting Ground," following the example of Ocean Grove, New Jersey. Its arrangements, the *California Christian Advocate* promised, were "for those who seek religious recreation, away from the excitements and dissipation of places of usual public resort, as well as for those who desire to spend a week in the worship of God in his 'first temple.' "[2] Larger crowds came for the Chautauqua assemblies that began in 1880, renting tents at from $2 to $9.50 a week; the Southern Pacific carried camping equipment free of charge and promoted "The Grove" as "the great Family Resort of the Pacific Coast within the means of all . . . a home and a haven for the gentle, the refined, the cultured, where carousing and dissipation are unknown."[3] Meanwhile the Chautauqua Association of Southern California scheduled its first assembly, cautiously enough, for one day at Long Beach (1884); soon it drew a large clientele as "an educational watering-place," and the Chautauqua summer school, which began in 1895, ran for four weeks. "No saloons are tolerated," commented an admirer (1888), "and all objectionable elements of society are kept out."[4] Although Long Beach came to call itself, as did Santa Cruz, the "Atlantic City of the West," a tone of Middle Western respectability long remained, making it the natural setting for the Iowa picnics that began in Bixby Park in the 1920's. In Oregon the largest assembly met at Gladstone Park in Oregon City, where the crowds converged by electric car from Portland and the valley. Gearhart corresponded to Pacific Grove, with lots for summer homes and camps as well as an auditorium. The University of Oregon held summer sessions there in the 1890's and later incorporated features of Chautauqua into the session on its own campus, including tents for students to live in. Officials of the Mormon Church, who had gone into the salt-refining business on Great Salt Lake, organized the Saltair Beach Company (1891) to establish Saltair as a resort "for the benefit of the Latter-day Saints," under strict regulations, though their income proved so small that the Church soon turned the resort over to a private concessionaire,

---

[2] Pacific Grove Retreat Association, articles of incorporation, June 1, 1875 (Bancroft Library). *Hand Book of Monterey* (n.p.; 1875), p. 51. *California Christian Advocate,* May 11, 1876, p. 7, col. 1; May 25, 1876, p. 5, col. 2.

[3] Pacific Improvement Company: *The Christian Seaside Resort* ([San Francisco, 1891]).

[4] Dumke: *Boom of the Eighties,* pp. 71–2. Walter Lindley and J. P. Widney: *California of the South . . .* (New York: D. Appleton & Co.; 1888), pp. 138–9.

who operated it on Sundays and opened saloons. Moral and intellectual improvement also extended into the mountains, where the Mount Hermon Association established a resort "on Bible Lines" near Santa Cruz (1905); the sponsors of the Chautauqua Assembly at Shasta Retreat, near Mount Shasta (1896), looked to the model of Pacific Grove and put the property under the control of directors approved by the Methodist Episcopal California Conference: "This insures a moral atmosphere in the resort, as healthful as the bracing air of the mountains . . . and the absence of all objectionable influences."[5]

While recreation outside the cities thus developed at different levels of price and morality, both the rich and the not-so-rich for many years continued to look chiefly to the styles of the older states. Some of the less fashionable resorts ignored the local settings and traditions as bravely as the Raymond and the Del Monte, affecting to be the Western Coney Island, Nantucket, Nice, Naples, or Mentone. Gospel Swamp, southeast of Los Angeles, became Newport Beach; Abbot Kinney, an eccentric and wealthy Pasadenan and a former associate of Helen Hunt Jackson in good works for the mission Indians, dredged canals in the mud flats south of Santa Monica for the Venice of America (1904), which also boasted imported Italian gondoliers and pigeons, a St. Mark's Hotel, a Chautauqua series, and midway concessions from the Lewis and Clark Exposition at Portland.[6]

Even the sportsman was more likely to wear a tailored hunting jacket than jeans; typically he was an Easterner or a foreigner rather than an old resident. Guests at the Raymond rode to hounds (the Valley Hunt Club was probably Pasadena's major social and civic organization); Horace Vachell, who claimed to be the father of polo in California, imported a dogcart and drove tandem on his ranch near San Luis Obispo; Claus Spreckels, the sugar magnate, bought 7,500

---

[5] *Long Beach Chautauqua Assembly* ([n.p.; 1899?]). Carey McWilliams: *Southern California Country: An Island on the Land* (New York: Duell, Sloan & Pearce; 1946), p. 167. Victor: "Northern Seaside Resorts," *Overland*, Vol. XXIII (1894), p. 144. Portland *Oregonian*, August 1, 1912, p. 17, col. 4. Leonard J. Arrington: *Great Basin Kingdom: An Economic History of the Latter-day Saints, 1870–1900* (Cambridge: Harvard University Press; 1958), pp. 392–3. *The Mount Hermon Association . . .* ([n.p., 1907?]). *Camping in the Vicinity of Mt. Shasta and in the Santa Cruz Mountains* ([n.p.: Southern Pacific Co.]; 1896).

[6] Marco R. Newmark: *Jottings in Southern California History* (Los Angeles: The Ward Ritchie Press; 1955), pp. 20, 35–6. Franklin Walker: *A Literary History of Southern California* (Berkeley: University of California Press; 1950), pp. 235–8. Morrow Mayo: *Los Angeles* (New York: Alfred A. Knopf; 1933), pp. 204–10.

acres in Santa Cruz county (1873) for a deer park, laid out a race track and gardens, and planned a hotel and casino.[7] Seabathing had its devotees—who had about the same view from the Pacific beaches westward as they had had from the Atlantic beaches eastward, and who may have gone to the coast to escape nature rather than to seek it out. The Monterey peninsula was the setting for the Hotel del Monte and its gardens, where the trains stopped conveniently on their fast run from San Francisco; although the Southern Pacific laid out the Seventeen-mile Drive at the same time as it built the hotel, apparently —and fortunately for the rocks and trees—there was no thought then of building on the outward-looking sites that became so popular in the 1920's and after. Similarly, the San Franciscans who moved from their hotel suites to "the peninsula" north of San Jose in the 1860's and 1870's developed estates in the style of the Main Line of Philadelphia, on the flat lands near the railroad rather than on the oak-covered hills above.

The native wilderness, particularly the high mountains and desert that dominated the Far West, at first chiefly bored or repelled. "We have been an unaesthetical people," a Californian observed in 1896, "and are only now beginning to visit our Yosemite," let alone the Sierra beyond. "Famous California scenery, it appears, is that part of our finest scenery which is adjacent to hotels."[8] Tourists dutifully inspected the most celebrated natural "curiosities" (the petrified trees near the Geysers seemed to many the most impressive sight), making the circuit so rapidly and with such grim determination that their most durable impressions were likely to be of expense and extreme physical discomfort. "To my dying day," Horace Greeley wrote of his visit to the Yosemite in 1859, "I shall remember that weary, interminable ride up the valley. . . . Gladly could I have thrown myself recklessly from the saddle, and lain where I fell till morning."[9] Elizabeth Cady Stanton arrived on foot (1871) because her horse was too broad for her to ride: "Alternately sliding and walking, catching hold of rocks and twigs, drinking at every rivulet, covered with dust, dripping with perspiration, skirts, gloves, and shoes in tatters, for four long hours I

---

[7] Vachell: *Distant Fields*, p. 69. *San Francisco Chronicle*, April 10, 1926, p. 11, col. 1.

[8] Theodore S. Solomons: "Unexplored Regions of the High Sierra," *Overland Monthly*, second series, Vol. XXVII (May 1896), p. 479; Vol. XXIX (January 1897), p. 68.

[9] Greeley: *An Overland Journey from New York to San Francisco in the Summer of 1859* (New York: C. M. Saxton, Barker & Co.; 1860), pp. 304–5.

struggled down to the end, when I laid myself out on the grass, and fell asleep, perfectly exhausted, having sent the guide . . . [for] a wheelbarrow, or four men with a blanket to transport me to the hotel."[1] Most who accepted such torture stayed only long enough to recover from the trip, remaining on the floor of the valley, where, according to a writer in *Overland* (1886), "all the celebrated features of Yosemite can be enjoyed from a carriage."[2] Greeley left within a day, though he had taken two days for the trip in; he shut his eyes on the descent to keep from becoming dizzy. Visitors commonly found the very scale of the mountains tiresome and oppressive after reviewing the most famous points of interest.

If the few who went to the mountains soon exhausted them and themselves, the dry country usually offended at first glance. California, Hittell observed in 1890, "is marvelously blessed in the combination of her resources and beauties, but in compensation, much of her tributary territory is miserably poor. Nevada, Utah, and Arizona, look as if they had been impoverished for the purpose of enriching her." In Utah no one stopped for the spectacular rock formations that later became Zion and Bryce national parks, though most travelers made the detour from Ogden to Salt Lake City to observe what writers friendly to the Mormons described as a re-creation of the civilization of the Holy Land and others called legalized lascivity. (The appearances of the polygamous wives surprised Helen Hunt Jackson, who remarked that if she had not known she was in Salt Lake City, she would have said they were contented.)[3] There was no interest either in the Indians, who had retreated from the better land before advancing civilization: even when they had ceased to be dangerous as warriors or inconvenient as landowners, most of them were degraded, utterly lacking in picturesqueness or in associations with James Fenimore Cooper's novels.

Interest in the West as it had been when the Americans first came—in Mexican and Indian culture and in the uncultured wilderness itself—nevertheless developed rapidly even while a genteel tradition still dominated the tourist industry. Perhaps the generation of tourists that suffered and complained into and out of the mountains already were

---

[1] Stanton: *Eighty Years and More (1815–1897)* . . . (New York: European Publishing Co.; 1898), pp. 292–3.

[2] Charles A. Bailey: "Unfrequented Paths of Yosemite," *Overland*, second series, Vol. VIII (July 1886), p. 88.

[3] John S. Hittell: "The Boom in Western Washington," *Overland Monthly*, second series, Vol. XVI (September 1890), p. 228. Helen H. Jackson: *Bits of Travel at Home* (Boston: Roberts Brothers; 1878), pp. 21–2.

victims of the change; they did what fashion demanded, but little more than enough to be able to say they had done it. When John Muir began in the 1870's a life's labor of saving the Sierra Nevada from sheep ("hoofed locusts") and lumbermen, he was torn between his conviction that conservation could come only through popular support and his contempt for "the rough vertical animals called men, who occur in and on these mountains like sticks of condensed filth."[4] He at once despised them for staying close to the hotels and rejoiced that they contaminated so little of the wilderness. He had little hope of success when he agreed to write articles (1890) appealing for a Yosemite National Park—a reservation of the high country above the valley, which the state of California controlled until 1906; but Congress acted, and created two other parks in the Sierra as well that year. Muir found that more tourists came to the parks and to the Far Western forest reserves that the government set aside in the 1890's, and they ranged farther beyond the standard curiosities, at first fearfully, but with growing appreciation. "Most travelers here," he wrote in 1897, "are content with what they can see from car windows or the verandas of hotels, and in going from placc to place cling to their precious trains and stages like wrecked sailors to rafts." Yet good might follow on small beginnings—even on excursions by travelers who shrieked so much at the prospect of snakes and Indians in the woods, and made such display of cameras and umbrellas, that the wild game fled before them.[5] These were the years when families learned to go to the woods simply to enjoy the outdoors. "Half a score of years ago," a contributor to *Out West* said in 1904, "the camping habit was confined almost entirely to the bohemian element and the devotees of science, but of late it has infected all classes of society. . . ."[6] Members of the Sierra Club, which Muir had organized in 1892, began their annual summer outings in 1901.

At about the same time, the Westerner and his visitors began to turn sympathetically to the Mexican and Indian heritage of the Southwest and to its surviving representatives. They had been slower to appreciate the human than the natural remains of the pre-American West, as if a

---

[4] Muir to Emily Pelton, April 2, 1872, in William F. Badè: *The Life and Letters of John Muir* (Boston: Houghton Mifflin Co.; 1924), Vol. I, p. 325.

[5] Linnie Marsh Wolfe: *Son of the Wilderness; The Life of John Muir* (New York: Alfred A. Knopf; 1945), pp. 244–6. Muir: "The Wild Parks and Forest Reservations of the West," *Atlantic Monthly,* Vol. LXXXI (January 1898), pp. 15, 16, 25.

[6] Henrietta S. Breck: "Camping in California Redwoods," *Out West,* Vol. XX (May 1904), p. 401.

psychological barrier, more than concern for physical comfort, had made them cling to transported Eastern hotels and styles. They persisted in looking for resemblances to Italian scenery and climate on the coast while ignoring the Latins who were there when the first Americans came; for visions of the Holy Land in the deserts of the interior, but not for the descendants of the cliff dwellers. A generation of tourists at the Hotel del Monte left Monterey and the mission at Carmel to eccentrics like Robert Louis Stevenson. "There is nothing at all remarkable about Monterey," an English traveler wrote in 1883, "except that it is very dirty."[7] The surviving Mexicans, too, turned away from their own heritage, like General Vallejo, who abandoned his old home at Sonoma to build a rococo frame house (1851). Then the Spanish background began to be fashionable, though, at first, fashion recognized literary idealizations of eighteenth-century Castilians rather than living nineteenth-century Mexicans. Soon after Mrs. Jackson published her life of Father Junípero Serra (1883) and H. H. Bancroft issued the first of his ponderous histories of Mexico and the Far West (1883–90), Californians ceased to conceal and destroy their past and began to display and recreate it. In Los Angeles, where the early promoters had nervously directed tourists away from the remnants of Mexican ways that persisted there more than in most of the state, Charles F. Lummis, a New Englander who had gone to southern California just before the boom of 1886, discovered the missions and the Indians. As editor of *Land of Sunshine* (1895–1909), a promotional magazine subsidized by the Los Angeles Chamber of Commerce, he preached and practiced local color in a spirit at once sentimental and commercial. The missions, then nearly all in ruins, were to Lummis and his associates "a greater asset . . . than our oil, our oranges, or even our climate"; the trail that had connected them, potentially "a route of pilgrimage rank[ing] with that to Canterbury. . . ."[8] (When automobile dealers asked the legislature to improve a highway along the coast and designate it as El Camino Real, a pioneer protested [1905] that El Camino was a myth: there had been no roads between the missions when he visited them in 1850, only trails, and he recommended the example of the Bostonians, who had changed King Street to State Street in 1776.[9]) In towns where for decades hardly any-

---

[7] Rose Pender: *A Lady's Experience in the Wild West in 1883* (London: G. Tucker; 1888), p. 25.

[8] Edwin R. Bingham: *Charles F. Lummis: Editor of the Southwest* (San Marino: Huntington Library; 1955); Walker: *Literary History*, pp. 132–44.

[9] Letter by Edwin A. Sherman in Oakland *Enquirer*, Aug. 19, 1905 (clipping in Huntington Library).

one had visited the crumbling walls of mission buildings except to salvage what was movable, committees raised funds for restoration and advertised historic monuments. At Riverside, an imaginative hotelkeeper, Frank Miller (1857–1935), who made up in enterprise what the town lacked in Spanish background, began in 1902 to build the Mission Inn, a fantastically eclectic structure[1] that tourists came to regard as at least as authentic a revival as the missions themselves[2]—which, in view of how little had remained of some of them, perhaps it was.

Spanish, Indian, and pioneering themes appeared increasingly in the displays and entertainments that Westerners already were organizing for visitors, and that they now began to recast as continuations of local customs, whether of the fiestas of the *hacenderos* or of the rodeos of the cowboys. Most of the early celebrations had ignored the past and the setting: thus Pasadena featured Roman chariot races in lieu of football games as late as 1915 at its Tournament of Roses (1890–   )—roses, which grow but hardly thrive in dry, warm weather, rather than cacti. Native themes emerged in the Midwinter Fair at San Francisco and in La Fiesta de Los Angeles (1894). At the fairgrounds in San Francisco, Spanish and Mexican architecture competed with East Indian, classical, and Egyptian architecture: the Santa Barbara building was a pyramid. The southern California building was, according to a guidebook, "Southern in tone and effect, being a happy combination of the French and Spanish, with a touch of the Moorish style so noticeable in the old mission buildings," though the central feature of the exhibit of Los Angeles County was an Oriental mosque with a figure of an elephant constructed of English walnuts.[3] Santa Cruz's Water Carnival the next year, however, was Venetian, complete with gondolas and a representation of St. Mark's, and also with galleys and Japanese lanterns. But ten years later, at the Lewis and Clark Centennial Exposition (1905)

---

[1] Walker: op. cit., pp. 238–42. Zona Gale: *Frank Miller of Mission Inn* (New York: D. Appleton-Century Co.; 1938), pp. 38, 44, 78.

[2] In 1939 a popular writer on Latin-American themes, Carleton Beals, complained that traditions in southern California were "too new, too hastily improvised . . . merely grist in the mill of the booster spirit to be ground out deftly into seasoned hamburgers of pat showmanship. Thus the old Riverside mission has become a swank hotel; the time-worn vaults and corridors have been turned into a curio shop that attempts to retain historical accuracies but merely makes old reverences and beauties a side show for penny post-cards, tiny miniature crates of oranges and owls carved out of redwood." *American Earth* . . . (Philadelphia: J. B. Lippincott Co.; 1939), p. 17.

[3] *The "Monarch" Souvenir of Sunset City and Sunset Scenes; Being Views of California Midwinter Fair* . . . (San Francisco: H. S. Crocker Co.; 1894).

at Portland, six hundred miles beyond effective Spanish power, all the main exhibit buildings were in Spanish stucco and tile excepting the forestry building, a gigantic log cabin; each of the four wings of the California building represented a mission. Other styles in expositions persisted—the Panama-Pacific Exposition (1915) was predominantly classical. Because the California mission style was too simple to appeal so soon after the Gothic and Renaissance revivals, the planners of the Panama California Exposition at San Diego (1915–17) reached back to the more decorative baroque of Mexico proper,[4] which had never reached the borderlands. Still, the West was accepting and advertising its Spanish heritage, if only metaphorically.

Sentimental commitment to the past reached its height in some of the local pageants that became major tourist attractions between about 1910 and 1940. The Mission Play of San Gabriel (1912–23) was a project of Frank Miller, who conceived of it as a Southwestern equivalent of the Passion Play of Oberammergau and at first intended it for the Mission Inn; the author was John Steven McGroarty, feature writer for the *Los Angeles Times*, editor of *West Coast Magazine*, and promoter of a real-estate development and other enterprises. Both it and its successor, the Ramona play, near Hemet (1923–), a project of the local chamber of commerce derived from the popular novel by Mrs. Jackson (1884), were essentially colorful costume pageants that transcended mere history. They were so patently romantic in rhetoric, action, and setting that their popularity may have meant not so much that Westerners had come to understand the old West as that they felt less dependent on the East and looked elsewhere for roots. In the northern and mountain states the most popular events came to be rodeos, which were somewhat closer to reality, but which few Far Westerners had seen on the range or even in the form of the sprees cowboys indulged in in the cattle towns at the end of the season. (According to William Kent, whose family had had a ranch in Nevada since the 1880's, the state law prohibiting gambling [1909], rather than tradition, was responsible for the most spectacular displays: "When the money stuck longer the spree was lengthened and the process of getting rid of surplus funds led to disordered nerves and digestive upsets. . . .")[5] Exhibitions of roping

[4] Carleton M. Winslow: *The Architecture and Gardens of the San Diego Exposition* (San Francisco: Paul Elder & Co.; 1916), p. 12.

[5] Walker: op. cit., pp. 242–5. William Kent: *Reminiscences of Outdoor Life* (San Francisco: A. M. Robertson; 1929), p. 105.

preliminary to baseball games in the ball park at Pendleton, Oregon, in 1908 and 1909, however, were so popular a novelty that local businessmen organized the Pendleton Round-Up (1910), which soon became a major money-maker and stopping point on the circuit of professional Western entertainers and carnival operators. "The fact that the cowboy is making a final stand in Oregon has aroused the desire to perpetuate his past glories," the London *Times* commented, "and to commemorate his sports and the accompanying dare-devilry that have always been associated with him." Eventually it was a poor chamber of commerce and tourist bureau that did not have a festival; the oldest often celebrated local products of the soil, such as Raisin Day at Dinuba (later Fresno, 1911–), the Loggerodeo at Sedro-Woolley, Washington (1900–), the Portland Rose Festival (1907–), and the Florence Rhododendron Festival (1907–); most of the newer, usually the more lucrative, commemorated more or less historical themes: Old Spanish Days at Santa Barbara (1924–), the Jumping Frog Contest at Angels Camp (1928–), the Gold Rush Festival at Auburn (1934–), Helldorado at Las Vegas (1935–), Admission Day at Carson City (1939–), De Anza Days at Riverside (1940–).[6]

Whether they attracted the new traffic or merely fed on it as it came by, the success of the lesser local celebrations corresponded to a new dispersion as well as new volumes of vacationers. From the 1920's on the traveler confined himself less to the major cities and a few other points of interest, perhaps because he could be more mobile by car than by train, or because he had already seen San Francisco and Yosemite, or because he came from other parts of the West rather than from the East and felt that he could see them on the next trip. More and more tourists wanted to go off the main routes to places that were neither modern, crowded, nor famous—even to places that lacked waterfalls, geysers, and inspiration points—and moreover tourists were willing to go there at different seasons.

Attitudes toward the climate or climates in the Far West changed drastically between the 1880's and the 1920's; the result (or was it the cause?) was that habits of travel and residence changed also, over the map and over the calendar. Once Northwesterners had roofs over their heads and turned to farming, they stopped complaining about the rains

---

[6] London *Times*, December 31, 1913, p. 53, col. 6. Robert Meyer, Jr.: *Festivals U.S.A.* (New York: Ives Washburn; 1950).

that had plagued Lewis and Clark in 1805–6 on the Oregon coast (which never became popular for camping in January and February) and praised the mild winters. For decades, however, the weather baffled visitors to California. "From July to November San Francisco and nearly all of California is an excellent place to keep away from," a writer in *Scribner's* advised (1880). "Dust and intense heat in the interior, dust and cold winds and heavy fogs on the coast, make it a most undesirable place of residence."[7] The climate of Santa Barbara was dry and hot, observed a tourist who was there in 1875, when tourists were just beginning to come. "Its admirers must come from some worse place,—probably often from the interior; no one from Puget Sound ever praises it."[8] In the summer, the heat and dust in a railroad car crossing Arizona or Nevada and Utah were unspeakable, so that those who could returned from the coast in April (the month of heaviest eastbound traffic, as of northbound traffic from Florida); the better southern California hotels, like the Raymond, whose season ran from November to May, closed until well along in the fall. As late as 1908, an English traveler who had entered California by the southern route complained of two days of "scenery that might have been expressly designed to drive a man to drink. . . . Although there is here and there a fleeting gleam of beauty, I doubt whether one consecutive mile of the scenery between New Orleans and San Francisco is worth keeping awake for; and the observation car is welcome rather as a cool balcony for evening use, after the sun is down, than as an introduction to landscape better left unseen."[9]

But already a change was underway: the scheduling of conventions and expositions in the summer signified both that there was room in the hotels then and that people seemed likely to come to occupy them. Businessmen in Los Angeles formed the All-Year Club of Southern California (1921) to promote travel in what was still the slack season; by 1935 summer tourists exceeded winter tourists by fifty percent.[1] The sharpest increases in tourist travel in the 1920's and 1930's came in those parts of the West that people had thought uninteresting at any time but

---

[7] George H. Fitch: "Hints for the Yosemite Trip," *Scribner's Monthly*, Vol. XX (May 1880), p. 150.

[8] Caroline C. Leighton: *Life at Pudget Sound, with Sketches of Travel in Washington Territory, British Columbia, Oregon and California, 1865–1881* (Boston: Lee and Shepherd; 1884), p. 196.

[9] F. G. Aflalo: *Sunset Playgrounds* . . . (London: Witherby & Co.; 1909), pp. 66–7.

[1] Pacific Railway Club: *Proceedings*, Vol. XX (May 1936), p. 4.

particularly insufferable in warm weather—Nevada and Utah; among the national parks, Zion and Bryce.

What Westerners and others who visited the West were coming to do in their spare time told much about what they did and thought the rest of the time. The new dimensions of recreation reflected major social changes. More people had vacations and money to spend while they took them. People who lived in cities sought outdoor recreation more than those who lived in small towns and on farms, the literate more than the illiterate; and these were years of rapidly extending urbanization and education. Air-conditioning began to make railroad cars and houses comfortable in the desert country; paving reduced the dust. The West became so much like the East, so approachable, that it no longer frightened its visitors and residents; it even acquired literary sanctions, as novelists and poets began to describe it along with more familiar settings. Discussing "The 'Nature' Revival in Literature," Frank Norris wrote: "The sun has come in and the great winds, and the smell of the baking alkali on the Arizona deserts and the reek of the tar-weed on the Colorado slope, and nature has ceased to exist as a classification of science . . . and has become a thing intimate and familiar and rejuvenating."[2] Now that the Western setting seemed to be losing its uniqueness, Americans wanted to see what was still unique in it. And in their automobiles they could see it conveniently, cheaply, even comfortably.

Prosperity was perhaps the most indispensable condition of the new Western tourist travel. Leisure-time activities everywhere fluctuated with the business cycle, but particularly in the West, where the distances are so great that the price of admission tended to screen out the poor. (There were always exceptions, like the indigent who walked or begged rides or came in their own broken-down automobiles, but most of these marked time where they could live cheaply or wait for work rather than enjoy the mountains or the seacoast; there was no confusing the uses of the trailer camp for sport and relaxation and the trailer park for marginal subsistence, and it was far safer to leave baggage untended in most forest camps than in most hotel lobbies.) In the early years, when Westerners hungered after the capital that rich visitors might invest and the recognition that they might confer, some rejoiced that the lower classes could not easily afford the trip, which ordinarily cost about

---

[2] Frank Norris: *The Responsibilities of the Novelist* . . . (New York: Doubleday, Page & Co.; 1903), pp. 141–2.

as much in the 1870's and 1880's as at the very different price level of the 1960's. The writer of a prize-winning letter on reasons for preferring southern California (1894) cited the high cost of travel as an advantage in that it excluded "the scum of the earth, admitting the 'cream' of the sections from which they come. . . ."[3] Even in the twentieth century, when the cost of going there had become a much less formidable outlay for most Americans, visits to national parks and other places of interest to tourists tended to fluctuate with per capita income—at least to the extent of increasing most in prosperous times.[4]

New tastes developed along with the new capacity to indulge them. The experience of the British, who became sportsmen, hikers, and mountain-climbers in the years when they prospered as merchants, financiers, and manufacturers, suggests that a kind of natural appetite for the outdoors asserts itself when men move from the country to the city. Some Englishmen had satisfied it vicariously, responding more than Americans themselves did to American writers on the wild West of the middle nineteenth century, like Joaquin Miller, who (as he told the story), wearing sombrero and red shirt, "tickled the duchesses" with his "tales of 'My California' [and] of buffalo running wild down Beacon Street, Boston. . . ."[5] Others made the long trek to the West, sometimes dominating the high mountain country. But whether because America on the make could not abandon the energy and excitement with which it threw itself into its work or because it had to reassure itself of its destiny after grappling with the raw frontier, on holiday it sought out not so much solitude and the wilderness as crowds and the accepted attributes of civilization—characteristically at congested and highly organized resorts where vacationing seemed rather a business than a pleasure.[6]

In the second half of the nineteenth century, American taste for nature began to follow British precedent. Frederick Law Olmsted, the distinguished landscape architect and head of the Yosemite Commission,

---

[3] John E. Lester: *The Atlantic to the Pacific* . . . (London: Longmans, Green & Co.; 1873), pp. 224–5. "A Prize Letter," *Land of Sunshine,* Vol. I (October 1894), p. 99.

[4] U. S. Outdoor Recreation Resources Review Commission: *Prospective Demand for Outdoor Recreation* . . . , Study Report no. 26 (Washington: Government Printing Office; 1962), pp. 6, 19.

[5] Julian Hawthorne: *Shapes that Pass* . . . (Boston: Houghton Mifflin Co.; 1928), p. 78.

[6] Baron de Stampenbourg: "Spending a Vacation, Here and Abroad," *Independent,* Vol. LV (June 4, 1903), pp. 1301–2.

traced the change in his own lifetime (1865). Although Californians as yet had shown little interest in the Yosemite Valley, visitors from the Atlantic states had joined foreigners in paying homage to it; Westerners might soon discover the Sierra Nevada as Easterners had discovered the White Mountains. Perhaps those who stayed at a large hotel in the mountains came because of the crowds rather than despite them, or came because it was the thing to do. The tourists who came on a new scale to California in the 1890's were there, the editor of *Overland* suggested, more because writers such as Harte and Mrs. Jackson had created an "idealized halo" over the stories of miners and missionaries than because of all the advertising of railroad and steamship companies.[7] And yet, Olmsted observed in a later address (1880), when his predictions were beginning to come true, the new interest in natural scenery was too widespread for such explanations; it was too general, too spontaneous to be merely a fashion; it seemed to follow on irrepressible human needs, as fundamental as the needs for air and rest. "Considering," he asked, "that it has occurred simultaneously with a great enlargement of towns and development of urban habits, is it not reasonable to regard it as a self-preserving instinct of civilization?"[8]

Both the general growth and the specific directions of interest in the West outside city limits seemed to follow closely on a further factor as elemental in Far Western society as wealth and urbanization, and intimately related to both of them: the development of transportation, especially in the twentieth century. The completion of the first transcontinental railroads (1869–83) transformed Western society more than even their builders foresaw. The locomotive affected ideas no less than settlement, industry, and politics. It drastically changed the psychological and aesthetic impact of the parts of the West beyond the tracks and terminals. Even before the hunters and the homesteaders that the trains carried had destroyed buffalo and buffalo range and with them the livelihood of the Indian tribes, there could be little doubt about the relationship between the traveler, who carried the comforts and reassurances of civilization with him behind the plate-glass windows of his

---

[7] Olmsted: "The Yosemite Valley and the Mariposa Big Trees," *Landscape Architecture,* Vol. XLIII (October 1952), pp. 17, 20, 22. Rounsevelle Wildman: "Well Worn Trails . . . ," *Overland,* Vol. XXVI (July 1895), pp. 50–1.

[8] Olmsted: "The Justifying Value of a Public Park," *Journal of Social Sciences,* Vol. XII (December 1880), pp. 152–3, 162–3.

sleeping car, and the blanketed derelicts lounging at the stations of towns that the railroad had created. Disgust was possible, but seldom fear. Perhaps the "subtle inflowing current of Eastern refinement" that Bret Harte anticipated in the first issue of *Overland Magazine* (1868)[9] was slower than he expected, but from the beginning, the wilderness itself seemed less wild and lonely to the passenger who could be home within the week, with good food and lodging all the way.

For half a century and more, railroads were probably the largest facts in Far Western life. Californians cared more about a railroad than about slavery in the 1850's; they might have been justified if they had cared more about it than about gold, for the new railroads brought more people to Oregon and Washington in the 1880's than there were in California in 1860. Brigham Young cursed both the gamblers and the liquor dealers who followed the Union Pacific to Utah and the officers of the railroad who chose to run it by way of Ogden instead of Salt Lake City; he wasted no time in building a connecting line and in directing one of his sons to build the line further north that, under control of the Union Pacific, reached Butte in 1881.[1]

Westerners might disagree over the policies of the railroad builders, like Hill, whom many respectfully called the "Empire Builder" and others charged, as Brooks Adams did, with exploiting the Northwest "precisely as a Roman proconsul might have plundered a conquered province." But no one could doubt their power. Few ventured to affront those who might either bring new prosperity to their town on main-line tracks or divert all its commerce and prospects to a competitor. Some of the later celebrations of driving the last spike on newly completed lines were as much charged with excitement as the first of them, for Los Angeles, Spokane, Tacoma, and Seattle still had to win the future that was already San Francisco's in 1869. Looking to them and to those the railroad passed by, most civic leaders were glad to be able to pay homage and subsidy. As late as the 1920's, the businessmen of Boise helped pay for rerouting the main line of the Union Pacific through town (1924) so that they would not have to depend on a branch, and celebrated the event by driving a golden spike; the completion of the last of the transcontinental routes, the connection of the Great Northern and the Western Pacific through Bend and Klamath Falls (1931), was

[9] *Overland,* Vol. I (July 1868), p. 99.

[1] Merrill D. Beal: *Intermountain Railroads, Standard and Narrow Gauge* (Caldwell: Caxton Printers; 1962), pp. xix, 4–43, 92, 133.

a climactic event in the country east of the Cascades, where mule- and horse-drawn freighters were contemporaries of the airplane. Whether thousands of people lived, in effect, in the early nineteenth or in the twentieth century depended on the rivalries of railroad tycoons like Harriman and Hill, whose race up the Deschutes Valley in 1910–11 had drawn in its wake the greatest migration into central Oregon—and, after the competitors agreed to compete no longer, left some settlers waiting twenty years for construction to resume.[2]

The effects of railroads on the back country, away from the tracks, were curiously uneven. Ranchers so far away that their stock walked off their profits on the way to the nearest railhead suffered a new disadvantage as soon as cattle cars ran alongside their competitors' herds. Farmers who could divert capital from freighting to irrigation or machinery undersold those who still had to depend on teams or portages. A few tourists enjoyed the range country and the high mountains more when they could leave civilization behind them and arrive in the style of an earlier day, though without bruises or danger: two thousand miles by Pullman, twenty by buckboard. The dude ranches developed in belts parallel to the railroads from the 1880's. Yet the advent of railroads increased still more the numbers of travelers who cherished comfort so much that they spent most of their time in the luxurious hotels that appeared conveniently nearby—some advertised, like the Del Monte or, at Pasadena, the Green, that the trains stopped on their grounds. William Shepherd, an English visitor to California in 1883, found a general and increasing ignorance of the byways: "I was surprised to find how little the people hereabouts seemed to know about the country roads and trails, even within twenty miles of their homes. I could not find anyone who had crossed the desert, or who had any sound information on the subject; whereas in the more newly settled territories, as Wyoming and Montana, the boys seemed to be at home, so far as knowing the roads, over the whole place. Knowledge of the country roads has decreased considerably wherever the railway has supplanted freighting."[3]

---

[2] Brooks Adams: *Railways as Public Agents; a Study in Sovereignty . . .* (Boston, 1910), p. 60. Merrill D. Beal and Merle W. Wells: *History of Idaho* (New York: Lewis Historical Publishing Co.; 1959), Vol. I, p. 535. Beal: *Intermountain Railroads* (Caldwell: Caxton Printers; 1962), pp. 210–11. Bowman: *The Pioneer Fringe*, pp. 96–104.

[3] W. Shepherd: *Prairie Experiences in Handling Cattle and Sheep* (New York: O. Judd Co.; 1885), pp. 163–4.

Soon the railroads built branches that reclaimed and transformed the countryside. Some tapped farming and mining country, like those that radiated from the Hill and Harriman lines in the northern Cascades and Rockies. The first mining railroads, like the Virginia and Truckee (1870), were essentially improvements or adjuncts of the mines themselves; their owners were the mining companies, which sought to cut their costs. But by 1880 two major lines were racing toward Butte. Prospectors in the later rushes of the Inland Empire paused at the Missouri River, not to pack their wagons, but to choose among the lithographed schedules that promised the shortest routes to the mines, and homesteaders loaded their household goods and nursery stock on freight cars. The builders of some of the local lines to the coast (San Pedro, 1869; Santa Cruz, 1876 and 1880; San Diego, 1885 and 1919; Santa Barbara, 1887 and 1901; Yaquina, west of Corvallis, 1889; Astoria, 1895; Tillamook, 1912; Eureka, 1914; Coos Bay, 1916) got less in seaborne cargoes than they hoped for, but they developed seasonal traffic to the beaches and year-round markets for dairy products and lumber from the coast range.

Local and short-line rail service reshaped Western life near the larger cities still more fully, and especially when it substituted electric for steam power. The cable car (1873) had taken the people of San Francisco up its hills, so that they could build houses almost regardless of elevation. The trolley car could mount almost as steep a grade; it was cheaper to install and accelerated quickly to speeds that suited it to interurban as well as downtown traffic. Although oil-burning locomotives still were hauling commuter trains in Oakland in 1912 and southward from San Francisco along the peninsula in 1964, electricity replaced steam and horsepower for most local traffic in the 1890's and early 1900's and became, for a generation, the major conditioning force in the growth of cities and the urbanization of the countryside. In Los Angeles, which was just beginning to grow and was still searching for directions to grow in when it got its first transcontinental railroad service, the trolley found its first and most malleable subject (1887). It established a pattern in the transportation systems of the West of taking people out of the city into the suburbs and the countryside rather than, as in the East, of taking them into the city; it dispersed more than it concentrated, and in so doing it brought urban ways and services so effectively into the rural areas that conventional definitions of city and country lost their meaning.

The electric car found special opportunities in the three coastal states and in Utah. Their cities were growing rapidly around the turn of the century, doubling and tripling in a decade[4] as they absorbed new subdivisions. Most of the people lived in the outskirts of the major central cities or within a hundred miles or so of them: around San Francisco Bay, in the Los Angeles basin, along the Willamette Valley, on Puget Sound, and east of Utah and Great Salt lakes. Only San Francisco had grown in the pattern of Manhattan, its business and its population concentrated within the radius of the horsecar and cable lines on its narrow peninsula; and even San Francisco had its hinterlands, from which people who wanted more space or less fog came to work by ferry or steam train. People in the smaller towns and on the farms were Eastern enough to want to visit the city, Western enough to think nothing of taking time to go there, prosperous enough to be able to make the trip. The Western climate itself favored travel by electric car, for though heat or cold seldom kept people at home, dust during the long dry season and slippery mud the rest of the year limited the pleasures of riding by private carriage or automobile before the roads were paved.

Thus it was only natural that urban and interurban electric lines grew rapidly and figured importantly in Western life. The coastal states soon had much more trackage and more traffic, relative to population, than the rest of the country.[5] Henry E. Huntington's Pacific Electric Railway became the largest system in the country as well as in the West; at its peak it operated about 520 miles of nonduplicating routes ranging about Los Angeles as far as Riverside and Redlands. But perhaps the most ambitious systems and the most generous service were in the Willamette Valley, where the Oregon Electric ran sleeping cars 122 miles from Portland to Eugene (population about 10,000) and competed with the Southern Pacific's electric lines for the patronage of Corvallis (population about 5,000); Portland soon would have, the London *Times* reported in 1913, more extensive systems than any other American city except Indianapolis and Columbus, with 770 miles completed or under construction.[6] Where there had been such overbuilding the social returns to the communities often exceeded the profits of the

[4] Increases in 1890–1900 and 1900–10 in Los Angeles were 103.4% and 211.5%; Seattle, 88.3% and 194.0%; Portland, 94.9% and 129.2%; Spokane, 85.0% and 183.3%; Tacoma, 4.7% and 122.0%; Salt Lake City, 19.4% and 73.3%; San Francisco, 14.6% and 21.6%.

[5] By 1917, with 5.7 percent of the population, the coastal states and Utah had 11.5 percent of the trackage (California, with 2.9 percent of the population, had 6.7 percent).

[6] *Census of Street and Electric Railways, 1902* (Washington, 1905), pp.

companies. The electric cars carried the suburbanite to work and the student to school and college; three of the lines in Utah operated school trains under contract and thus advanced the movement toward consolidated schools. They brought the Chautauquans to Gladstone Park and Long Beach. They affected nearly everyone somehow.

When the first interurban tracks extended alongside rutted county roads and across fields and streams, their principal meaning, to a generation already deeply concerned about the progressive abandonment of rural virtues for urban vices, seemed to be the transformation of country life. William E. Smythe, the prophet of the irrigated family farm, saw Huntington's lines as second only to irrigation in facilitating the breakup of large ranches into small units throughout a large part of California.[7] According to the *Street Railway Journal* (1904), one of the lines out of Portland had awakened farmers who had made little progress since pioneer days: "Fences have been improved, crops that were formerly fed to the hogs are now garnered and marketed, new barns and houses are being built, land is being cleared and new crops planted . . . and a general enlightenment is seen everywhere."[8] The cars stopped where they crossed the farmer's land, taking milk and berries to town, bringing back the empty cans and crates and the morning's newspaper; they brought the farm closer to the grange hall, the church, the school, the department store, and the theater.

They also brought the city dweller out of the city. "The electric car," Smythe said, "is the poor man's carriage. It opens the doors of the country to those hitherto housed up in the town."[9] To develop traffic between commuting hours, the companies solicited picnickers, cyclists, campers, and fishermen; they served cemeteries, beaches, and parks. They ran special trains for outings of lodges, churches, schools, and real-estate promoters. They advertised excursions to see the prune blossoms or simply to cool off on a hot day. Some lines existed primarily to

---

17, 24. Ibid., 1907 (1910), p. 83. *Census of Electrical Industries: 1917; Electric Railways* (Washington, 1920), p. 30. George W. Hilton and John F. Due: *The Electric Interurban Railways in America* (Stanford: Stanford University Press; 1960), pp. 116–7, 383–7, 389–413. Walker: *Literary History*, pp. 231–5. Randall V. Mills: *Railroads down the Valleys* . . . (Palo Alto: Pacific Books; 1950), pp. 71–97. London *Times*, December 31, 1913, p. 44, col. 5.

[7] William E. Smythe: "Social Influence of Electric Lines," *Out West*, Vol. XIX (December 1903), pp. 694–5.

[8] London *Times*, December 31, 1914, pp. 44, col. 5. *Street Railway Journal* in Frank J. Rowsome, Jr.: *Trolley Car Treasury* . . . (New York: McGraw-Hill Book Co.; 1956), pp. 123–4.

[9] Smythe in *Out West*, Vol. XIX, p. 695.

serve the railroads' own resorts or points of interest, such as Saltair Resort (which the Salt Lake and Garfield bought in 1918) and the Alpine Tavern (1895), north of Pasadena on Mount Lowe. All of them greatly expanded the horizons that the steam trains had penetrated a generation earlier.

In so doing, the electric lines may have helped to destroy themselves. Some transformed rural life simply because their patrons never had been numerous or prosperous enough to support any other system of transportation; and the gap between what would attract steam service and what electric service could survive on proved embarrassingly narrow. Lines like the Willamette Valley Southern (thirty-two miles to Mount Angel, population about 700) and the Utah-Idaho Central's line to Preston, Idaho (twenty-six miles, population about 2700) had little to draw on from the start. Others paralleled the steam lines and could not maintain an adequate advantage in cost over them as the wages of trainmen rose. By 1917 the Pacific area was the only part of the country where patronage of electric railways was declining; the decline was greatest in Oregon, where building programs, by virtue of competition between the Hill and Harriman lines, had been most reckless.[1] Their worst problem was the automobile, which drew away the traffic that the electric car had developed. Some of the cars continued to run—the Oregon City line, longest in service of all interurbans in the country, until 1958—but in flexibility of service and often even in cost, the case for gasoline over electricity proved as good as the case for electricity over steam.

By the time of the First World War, Westerners were accepting the automobile as a routine convenience rather than a luxury or a toy. From the beginning, some of them were interested in it far beyond other Americans. The coastal states anticipated the general tendency of the West to use more motor vehicles, in proportion to population, than the East did,[2] and led in building highways: California began work in

[1] *Census of Electric Industries: 1917; Electric Railways*, pp. 44, 46.

[2] Ratios of population per motor vehicle

	1910	*1915*	*1920*	*1930*	*1940*	*1950*
California	54.5	18.4	6.1	2.8	2.5	2.3
Idaho	700.5	55.8	8.5	3.8	3.2	2.2
Nevada	178.0	41.0	7.5	3.1	2.5	2.1
Oregon	127.5	31.6	6.8	3.8	2.8	2.2
Utah	278.9	46.9	10.6	4.5	4.0	2.8
Washington	157.1	31.9	7.9	3.5	3.1	2.6
United States	197.2	40.4	11.5	4.6	4.1	3.1

1912 on a state highway program second only to New York's, and Oregon adopted the first gasoline tax for highway-building, in 1919.[3]

The early automobilists in the West, as elsewhere, were chiefly well-to-do city dwellers; the leaders in the movement for good roads that developed after about 1910 seemed to be sportsmen and automobile dealers rather than farmers. Californians hoped that their state highway system would attract crowds to the expositions of 1915–6, which were also the goals of the organizers of the Lincoln Highway Association (1912). "We shall do all we can," one of the state highway commissioners promised, "to send the automobilist from the Panama-Pacific down the six hundred miles of marvelous coast line to the Panama-California without his realizing that he has left the polished surface of Van Ness avenue behind."[4] Most of the promotional organizations, like the Pacific Highway Association (1910), emphasized the routes between major cities, and parties of their leaders set out on them with great show of valor. Typically automobile tourists, the president of the Lincoln Highway Association said in 1917, were pioneers, adventurers, "willing to put up with trouble, disagreeable situations of all kinds, and mediocre accommodations," to challenge the "barriers of mud and alkali and sand" between the bulk of the population and "our native wonders, the outdoor play spots of our great West."[5]

Some of the parts of the Far West that were slowest to shift to rubber tires had once been its leaders. Utah lagged for a time behind even Idaho, perhaps because until the middle twenties the roads across the desert west of Salt Lake City were so poor that many transcontinental travelers sent their cars across by train. San Franciscans had little use for automobiles within the compact area of the city, and if they wanted to drive anywhere else they faced the problem of getting out of town: the first project of the California state highway system was to cut through the hills across the peninsula, and adequate auto ferry service across the Bay was not available until 1921–7.[6] Even then the

---

[3] U. S. Bureau of Public Roads: *Highway Statistics, Summary to 1955* (Washington: Government Printing Office; 1957), pp. 18–29. *Good Roads Year Book, 1917* (Washington: American Highway Association; 1917), pp. 64–5, 473. *San Francisco Chronicle*, December 31, 1920, p. 7, col. 4. John C. Burnham: "The Gasoline Tax and the Automobile Revolution," *Mississippi Valley Historical Review*, Vol. XLVIII (December 1961), pp. 437–40.

[4] Rufus Steele: "The Road to Tomorrow . . . ," *Sunset*, Vol. XXXII (May 1914), pp. 1037–9.

[5] Henry B. Joy: "The Traveler and the Automobile," *Outlook*, Vol. CXV (April 25, 1917), pp. 740–1.

[6] Service to Oakland Pier (as well as the slower service to the foot of Broadway) began in 1921; to Alameda, in 1926; to Berkeley, in 1927.

ferries could carry only a fraction of the traffic that developed with the bridges at Dumbarton, Carquinez (1927), San Mateo (1929), and still more with the bridges across the main part of the Bay (1936) and the Golden Gate (1937), which by 1940 and 1941 were carrying enough cars to eliminate three systems of electric trains.

The newer cities changed much earlier, taking both to the automobile and to the patterns of urban growth that it made possible. In southern California, which as early as 1913 had boasted of more automobiles than the northern counties (considering the population, nearly two and a half times as many), the suburbs moved boldly beyond public transportation; the businessmen of Wilshire Boulevard and Westwood made much, in fact, of freedom from the clutter of tracks and trolley wires. The dispersion of residential developments and attendant shopping districts that the electric car facilitated meant increasingly that people wanted to go where rails did not—from one suburb to another instead of to and from the central business district. By 1925 Los Angeles had the first subway in the Far West. However, the reason for putting tracks underground was not, as in the East, to serve a high density of working population developed in the day of the horsecar, but to avoid a congestion of automobiles blocking the suburban trains at their terminal. And though traffic eventually was congested everywhere, for a long time the low density of urban development in Los Angeles County meant that people could find parking places for automobiles almost everywhere they wanted to go and also that the transit companies could not easily run cars often enough to hold a profitable level of patronage.[7]

Once begun, the shift from public to private transportation was rapid. The more successful lines already had served the purposes of those who had built them in order to sell real estate; the retirement of Henry E. Huntington in 1910 put the largest of the electric systems into the control of the Southern Pacific, which by the twenties took a more pessimistic view of its electric and short-line passenger traffic. The number of persons entering downtown Los Angeles (where access by public transportation still was reasonably efficient) by car increased from 35 percent in 1924 to 56 percent in 1940.[8] By the twenties and early thirties, the new styles of buildings and types of businesses de-

[7] Sunset, Vol. XXXI (November 1913), p. 1026. Arthur L. Grey, Jr.: "Los Angeles: Urban Prototype," *Land Economics,* Vol. XXXV (August 1959), p. 232–3.

[8] In 1960, 75 percent by car.

veloping throughout much of the West, and particularly in southern California, corresponded to the new reliance on the motorcar: the single-family subdivision with two-car garages, the one-story factory, the motel, the drive-in restaurant (perhaps shaped like a hat or an igloo, to catch the motorist's eye).[9] Not everyone welcomed the new ways, but the time came when one had to go along with them and live by car with the rest of the region—when the neighborhood stores had lost so much business to the shopping centers that their produce and meat no longer were fresh, when the job itself moved into the suburbs or onto the road, when the electric cars reduced service and finally stopped running.[1]

The automobile seemed first to move more people into the city, extending its radius of effective control much as the steam and electric car had extended it a few years before. A study of farmers' trading centers in Washington shows that most of them disappeared as highways expanded between 1910 and 1920. The farmer could drive to better markets and more varied services, or he could live in town while field laborers (whether highly trained technicians or wetback pickers) came to work by car.[2] States with many automobiles were also states of rapidly advancing urbanization. The boarded-up rural church and schoolhouse indicated the drift of life to the city—perhaps by stages, as young people who went there to attend college stayed to work. Even summer resorts that had welcomed the new highways from the city found that although the crowds were larger, they came for shorter periods by car than they did by railroad, for a weekend or even a day at a time rather than for the season; the seaside family hotels and boardinghouses decayed, and in the twenties and thirties people seemed less interested in committing themselves to maintaining summer homes. (A few years later, when incomes caught up with the capacities of automobile transportation, some formerly depressed vacation places found that city people were willing to pay city prices for almost anything with a roof; some nailed insulating board over the termites

---

[9] Wilbur Smith and Associates: *Future Highways and Urban Growth* (New Haven: [for Automobile Manufacturers Association;] 1961), pp. 101, 38.

[1] In San Francisco, where 30 percent came by car in 1924, the shift was much slower—to only 51 percent in 1954, perhaps because of the efficiency and cheapness of public transportation and the congestion of automobile traffic and parking.

[2] Paul H. Landis: *Washington Farm Trade Centers, 1900–1935*, Washington Agricultural Extension Bulletin no. 360 (Pullman, July 1938), pp. 35, 39. Broek: *Santa Clara Valley*, p. 125.

and stayed the year around, commuting to the city by the new freeway.)

Meanwhile the city declined even while it increased; the automobile carried vitality from its center to its peripheries, which extended in ribbon developments along highway approaches where city lots abutted farmlands. So many people could go downtown, and did, that soon fewer wanted to, except to go somewhere else. A reporter for *The New York Times* who in 1955 visited Los Angeles paraphrased Lincoln Steffens on the Soviet Union—"I have seen the Future—and it doesn't work"—and went on to describe the whole area as an extreme case of urban sprawl, the center of the city as more and more resembling "a Swiss cheese, tunneled at the core and gnawed at the edges." Two thirds of downtown Los Angeles consisted of streets, freeways, and parking and loading facilities; the maximum number of persons accumulated there during working hours had declined by nearly 14 percent in fourteen years—a change not immediately evident because the number of persons who came by car had increased still more.[3] The population of the central city—the area within the city limits—continued to increase, but the fringes increased at a higher rate, so that relative to the whole metropolitan area the Far Western central city declined to a greater extent and more rapidly than central cities elsewhere.[4] As far back as 1930, moreover, rural Californians were edging above the statewide rate of automobile ownership; and this seemed to be so both because farmers had to go to market and because automotive and other urban ways were increasingly establishing themselves in the countryside.[5] "It is evident," *Country Life* reported as early as 1923, "that we are . . . becoming a nation of squires, and the chief vehicle of our departure is the motor car."[6] There were various reasons besides farming for living beyond city limits: some people still went there to save on land and taxes, but more and more expected to take the conveniences of

---

[3] Harrison Salisbury in *The New York Times,* March 3, 1959, p. 1, cols. 4–5; p. 26, cols. 1–8.

[4] According to Warren Thompson, the populations of central cities declined nationally, in 1900–50, from 77.3 percent of their metropolitan areas to 59.1 percent; in San Francisco and Los Angeles, from 85.5 percent to 47.4 percent.

[5] Smith and Associates: *Future Highways,* p. 101. U. S. Bureau of Public Roads: *Report of a Survey of Traffic on the Federal-Aid Highway Systems of Eleven Western States, 1930* (Washington: Government Printing Office; 1932), p. 36.

[6] J. C. Long: "The Motor Car as the Missing Link between Country and Town," *Country Life,* Vol. XLIII (February 1923), p. 112.

the city itself. The people outside the city lived so much like those in it that the new definition of urban population that the Bureau of the Census introduced in 1950—including persons in densely populated urban fringes around cities of 50,000 or more—probably understated the fact.[7] More in the West than elsewhere, urbanhood triumphed while *urbs* declined, and urban and rural elements fused in a new form.

Whatever primarily caused or inspired the new highway society that had succeeded the post-road and railroad societies of earlier times and of older sections[8]—whether it denoted new values or merely new affluence and technique—its development coincided with a further dispersion of activities beyond the definitions of any census. Outside of working and sleeping hours, life was becoming as hard to plot on a map as the automobiles in which it chiefly moved.

The new dimensions of leisure were especially evident in the national parks, whose visitors (in parks wholly within the six states) already were approaching a quarter of a million in 1921; twenty years later, just before the Second World War curtailed travel and vacationing, they were nearly two and a quarter million; twenty years after that, nearly seven and a half million. As visitors to the parks increased, moreover, they moved from trains to automobiles and from the hotels into the campgrounds, from the more accessible areas toward unimproved nature. The greatest increases were in the parks that offered extensive wilderness rather than specific points of interest where crowds gathered—Olympic, for instance, and Kings Canyon, which was established (1940) as a wilderness park, with only one road, rather than Yosemite. It was true that some of the older parks had no more room: cars sometimes waited in line at El Portal, gateway to Yosemite, for others to leave before they could enter. But interest in the outdoors widened in

---

[7] Rural nonfarm population as percentage of total rural population, 1930–60

	1930	*1940*	*1950*	*1960*
California	61.8%	68.3%	72.2%	84.4%
Idaho	41.0	42.6	50.9	62.1
Nevada	71.2	76.7	80.3	88.1
Oregon	52.3	53.9	67.5	79.3
Utah	55.9	61.5	66.3	80.6
Washington	55.8	58.8	68.7	82.1
Six States	56.9	61.9	68.9	81.2
	[1,862,953]	[2,500,126]	[2,938,888]	[3,558,605]
United States	44.0	47.2	57.5	71.8

[8] *Highways in our National Life; A Symposium*, eds. Jean Labatut and Wheaton J. Lane (Princeton: Princeton University Press; 1950), pp. 129–34, 154–63.

various directions: in the tremendous expansion of boating, hunting, fishing, and the attendant industries; in the rediscovery of the Mother Lode country; in the rise of winter sports after all-year roads tapped the mountain resorts (into the Yosemite, 1926); in the vogue of river excursions after the first commercial passenger trip down the canyons of Utah in 1934; in the sharp criticism of projects for dams that threatened scenic and recreational resources in remote mountain areas. The defenders of Dinosaur Canyon in the 1950's were much more numerous and influential than the defenders of the Hetch Hetchy Valley (in the Sierra Nevada) had been in a comparable controversy forty years before.[9]

Part of the increase in tourist travel represented the new ability of families from distant states to explore the West. The newspapers and popular magazines of the 1920's described the speed and low cost of transcontinental travel on the new highways—"cheaper than staying home"—and promoted still more of them, such as a national park-to-park highway, six thousand miles long, that would speed tourists through twelve parks in a summer. Drivers felt challenged to see how far they could go over Western grades in a two-week vacation. Campers in the West were likely to be Easterners or Southerners, according to a reporter on "The Dude Invasion of the Once Old West" in *Touring Topics* (1926); they found an aura of romance in mountains that to the natives were only part of the workaday world.[1] R. L. Duffus explained that the perpetual open spaces of the Far West symbolized the nation's youth, the adventurousness of the frontier, and that the automobile tourist turned to them from the crowded cities of the older states "in a kind of nostalgia. . . . To the casual observer he may be a vulgar Babbitt, defacing the landscape with his very presence. But to himself, unconfessed, he is Daniel Boone, he is Kit Carson, he is Frémont, hunting for the road to India."[2]

---

[9] John Ise: *Our National Park Policy* . . . (Baltimore: Johns Hopkins Press; 1961), pp. 85–96, 403, 476–80, 558–9, and *passim*. Weldon D. Woodson: "River Rats in Utah," *American Forests*, Vol. LXI (September 1955), pp. 28–9, 59–60. Joseph T. Hazard: "Winter Sports in the Western Mountains," *Pacific Northwest Quarterly*, Vol. XLIV (January 1953), pp. 7–14.

[1] Myron M. Stearns: "From coast to coast—cheaper than staying home," *Collier's*, Vol. LXXVI (October 17, 1925), pp. 8–9. H. O. Bishop: "The National Park-to-Park Highway," *Outdoors Pictorial*, Vol. II (July 1925), p. 13. Chauncey H. Vivian: "The Dude Invasion of the Once Old West," *Touring Topics*, Vol. XVIII (February 1926), pp. 14–15, 32.

[2] Duffus in *America as Americans See it*, ed. Fred J. Ringel (New York: Harcourt, Brace & Co.; 1932), pp. 2–4.

Some of the tallies of tourist traffic supported such arguments of escape from other ways of life. Over one fifth of out-of-state cars in California in 1929–30 came from Northeastern states. Vacationers in the High Sierra (1960) were significantly more urban, prosperous, and well educated than the general population—49 percent with college educations, 48 percent in professional and semi-professional occupations.[3] The vacationer in the Western wilderness in the twentieth century tended to come from the same general sections of society as his ancestor who had crossed the mountains by Pullman car to stay in a hotel in the 1880's or had come by ship to dig gold in 1849.

Yet the traveler and outdoorsman in the West tended even more clearly to be a Westerner, either because Westerners had as much to escape from as anyone else or simply because they were well off and on the scene. In general, most of the tourists in a Western state were from that state; most of the visitors from out of state were from nearby states; and the rate at which Westerners traveled increased faster than Western population, whereas the percentage of tourists from the East declined sharply. In Oregon, where visits to recreational areas of all kinds had increased nearly four and a half times between 1950 and 1960, over three fourths of the visitors to the parks in 1961 came from within the state; over three fourths of the rest came from Washington and California. Californians seemed to take vacations more than other Westerners; as early as 1929–30, they outnumbered all others in national parks except residents of the states in which the parks were located.[4] Despite the proximity of the various nationally controlled sites for recreation, the people of the Pacific states exceeded the rest of the country in establishing and using municipal and county parks, many of them essentially similar to the camps of the Forest Service. At Sun Valley,

---

[3] Bureau of Public Roads: *Report of a Survey of Traffic on the Federal-aid Highway Systems of Eleven Western States, 1930* (Washington, 1932), p. 40. Outdoor Recreation Resources Review Commission: *Wilderness and Recreation . . .*, Study Report 3 (Washington, 1962), pp. 131–3.

[4] *The Washington Tourist Survey, 1952*, Bureau of Economic and Business Research, State College of Washington, Bulletin no. 23 (Pullman, 1953), p. 9. Oregon State Highway Department, Parks and Recreation Division: *Oregon Outdoor Recreation* (Salem, 1962), pp. 122–4. *San Francisco Chronicle*, February 24, 1924, p. 4A, col. 1. Outdoor Recreation Resources Review Commission: *Participation in Outdoor Recreation . . .*, Study Report 20 (Washington, 1962), p. 67. Forty-five percent of the Westerners who took trips camped (1959–60), as against less than half that many from other sections.

Idaho, which the Union Pacific Railroad developed (1936) to bring traffic over its tracks during the slack winter months, the skiers who arrived in their own cars from adjacent Western states soon outnumbered the Easterners who came by Pullman. People returned again and again to the mountains—some every Saturday for family outings when the roads permitted—instead of making the grand tour once in a lifetime.

Yet although Westerners and other Americans spent more of their leisure time over wider stretches of the West, what they sought and what they found varied tremendously. Skiing could be just that, with classes for beginners sponsored by the Y.M.C.A. in the next town, and the simplest rope tow and warming shed, or it could be an elaborate setting for fashion, as in Squaw Valley, whose promoters called it a "Sierra Shangri-La" (1950), strategically located near the highway to Reno. Improvement came almost inevitably, and through public as well as private agencies: there came a stage at every beach within range of rubber tires when those who had shared it with the wild seabirds had to welcome the crews that gathered broken liquor bottles and debris from picnic lunches, installed latrines, and bulldozed away the mounds of bleached driftwood (lest they tempt someone to build a fire, or simply in order to leave room for the machines to give a manageable smoothness and symmetry to the sand, free from the disorderly little cliffs and coves that the waves might carve out). The municipal camps, which the Forest Service had permitted for the sake of poor children, soon acquired professional staffs skilled in the arts of organizing intramural games and drawing everyone in—and everyone became primarily the salaried and professional classes.[5]

Sometimes the loneliest and simplest of places seemed to become the most congested and transformed, as at Yosemite, which John Muir saved from hoofed locusts only to deliver it to those with trailers; or Lake Tahoe, where Mark Twain had taken refuge from the bustle of Virginia City, but which before the end of the century was already an outpost of San Francisco society; or the mining towns themselves, which were almost forgotten before the automobile tourists rediscovered them in

---

[5] "California's Snow Boom," *Holiday*, Vol. XV (February 1954), p. 64. Tyler Micoleau: *The Story of Squaw Valley* . . . (New York: A. S. Barnes & Co.; 1953), p. 5. Ralfe D. Miller: "Municipal Family Vacation Camps in California . . ." (unpublished master's thesis, University of California at Berkeley; 1939), pp. 16–17, 72–4.

the 1920's, and some of which eventually had all the trappings of promotion, including a New York City society columnist who revived Nevada's oldest newspaper. (A couple from Seattle said they loved the gold-rush country; it made television mean so much to them.) On the Monterey Peninsula, where since the 1880's society at Del Monte, morality at Pacific Grove, and the half-forgotten remnants of an older culture at Monterey had gone their separate ways, early in the century some of the regional literati made their retreats at the village of Carmel and along the shore beyond; then fashion and enterprise began to move in. In the 1920's the millionaires came to build villas in the Del Monte Forest, and Carmel became their shopping center and that of the tourists who followed them, an exhibit of their commitment to nature and to art. Returning after seventeen years in 1927, Sinclair Lewis found "where once the main street had just simple ordinary grocery stores and so on, now it has arty shops selling English poetry and French lamp shades and that sort of junk . . . where once we went picknicking on the rocks, carrying our grub in baskets, now they go over to the Del Monte Grill to dine and dance . . . and those same once wild rocky shores, so free and uninhabited then, are covered with expensive houses."[6] After the Second World War, the traffic was so dense among the pine-covered hills that the State Highway Department removed some of them to make room for a freeway, and residents of the rugged coast to the south developed a plan to establish a "scenic reserve" over an area whose wild beauty so many people had come to enjoy that it was already too expensive to be a park but seemed on its way, eighty miles from the nearest metropolitan area, to becoming a conventional subdivision.[7]

Yet a simple two-lane road was enough along the Big Sur, even in the 1960's; still more vacationers came in the era of the automobile to those parts of the West in which there was never much pretense of preserving natural settings. At Los Angeles the great boast long had been that where nature had done no better than cactus, oaks, and chaparral, a good flow of water would support citrus trees and lawns. The mountains were large enough so that, on those days when one could

[6] Mark Schorer: *Sinclair Lewis, an American Life* (New York: McGraw-Hill Book Co.; 1961), pp. 442–3. The story about the couple from Seattle comes from James McC. Truitt (1958).

[7] Outdoor Recreation Resources Review Commission: *Open Space Action . . . ,* Study no. 15 (Washington, 1962), pp. 93–7.

see them, the advancing residential developments seemed not to have trespassed beyond their lower slopes, but the most visible features of the landscape were man-made. The ocean itself, beyond barriers of traffic and filled parking spaces and fenced-off shoreline, seemed less important than public and private swimming pools. The motion-picture industry found its environment here, as much in extravagance and fantasy as in desert sunlight and a wide choice of scenery. If the national parks offered a return to nature and the primeval past, Hollywood offered at least a glimpse of the most-advertised and most-admired indulgences of the present.

Probably the most lucrative resort developments were in the desert country east of the mountains, which once had offered something like the serenity of the sea; Mary Austin had alternated between the two and finally settled in New Mexico when Carmel had lost its charm for her. Nevada had built up a profitable traffic in divorces in the 1920's, despite competition from Europe and Mexico and the threat of easier requirements for residence in Idaho and other states. After the hotelkeepers lobbied through a reduction of the requirement from six months to three in 1927, the number of divorces increased gratifyingly (from 770 in 1926 to 2,500 in 1928). Divorces increased still further when residence dropped to six weeks in 1931 (to 5,260 that year, despite the depression). But the larger profits were in marriages and in gambling, which the legislature also sanctioned in 1931;[8] the demand for divorce was less elastic, and many of the candidates were persons of moderate means who took advantage of excursion rates on the railroads. The typical dude ranch before the Second World War was an old-fashioned boardinghouse on the edge of Reno, with a few rented horses. Soon the gambling houses increased and prospered, most of them at first in frontier décor. The more elaborate establishments developed at Las Vegas, which had been little more promising than the other townsites along the Union Pacific tracks to Salt Lake but which picked up business during the construction of Hoover Dam (1930–6), nearby. It had the first of its luxury hotels by the time of a new influx of patrons came during the war, which put more money into circulation and, by cutting supplies of tires and gasoline, helped resorts with good railroad transportation from metropolitan areas. Some of their patrons came for boating at Lake Mead, some for the desert sun, most for gambling and

[8] The ban on gambling adopted in 1909 had lasted only three years.

the kinds of entertainment, fresh from Los Angeles, that might not pass censorship in Los Angeles itself.[9]

Thus, near the end of the first century of Far Western tourist travel, as at its beginning, travel and vacationing seemed to demand more of the artifices of civilization and at the same time more escape from civilization. Nature-lovers continued to scorn those who were less in tune with the wilderness but were not sure how much they wished them to be otherwise. It was well for everyone to learn not to destroy trees and dam streams and even perhaps to want to visit the wilderness. Yet the fragile soils of the high mountains could not support a much higher ratio of back-packing members of the Sierra Club per acre than of grazing sheep; and part of the charm of the mountains lay in the absence of the improvements that eventually became necessary simply to protect the hikers from each other and the land from the hikers—and in the loneliness.

As recreation developed, it became both a larger business and a less dynamic part of the Western economy. The typical vacationer in a Pullman-car excursion party in the 1880's was a generation or two older than the prospector of 1849 had been, but often he also was a pioneer and planned whole communities from the veranda of his hotel in Pasadena. As an outsider less concerned than residents were with whether the West had succeeded in transplanting the East, he might be more interested than they were in the most distinctive features of the region, in its pioneers and in nature itself. Then, when nearly everyone had time and money for a vacation, the vacationer became only a unit of buying power in a mass market, no more independent a force than the man down the block, which he was quite likely to be. Blowing up his air mattress in the bulldozed slot alongside his car in a state park, he represented a major industry and major trends in American life, but if he was an innovator, appearances were against him; the campfire might be the ancestor of the electrically ignited charcoal grill in his back yard, or it might be its descendant.

Tourism became a Western growth industry ranking with the manufacture of aircraft, and a good deal more consistent in its advance,

[9] Nelson M. Blake: *The Road to Reno: A History of Divorce in the United States* (New York: The Macmillan Company; 1962), pp. 155–9, 165–6. Oscar Lewis: *Sagebrush Casinos: The Story of Legal Gambling in Nevada* (New York: Doubleday & Co.; 1953), pp. 55–8, 191–6. Max Miller: *Reno* (New York: Dodd, Mead & Co.; 1941), pp. 52–3.

whatever the trend of the economy or (short of war) of politics. The chain drug stores took out their soda fountains to make room for racks of mess kits and sleeping bags. Government could not keep up with the demand for camp sites. Yet, except for those who operated airlines and motels, there was less interest on the whole than there had been in importing tourists from out of state. In the thirties San Franciscans were still justifying efforts to promote tourist travel by describing tourists as prospective settlers, whose qualifications were verified in a survey by Dun and Bradstreet; they blamed San Francisco's lag in growth on the diversion of tourist travel to southern California as well as on Harry Bridges and the longshoremen. But after the war, when the more imminent problem seemed to be rather the "Los Angelization of San Francisco," the treasurer of the Golden Gate Exposition of 1939 reported a general lack of enthusiasm: "The business interests of San Francisco are not eagerly tourist-minded."[1] Travel still had the reputation of being one of the three most important industries in Nevada (where it had exceeded all others), Utah, and Washington,[2] but its clientele and its justification had changed. Members of industrial and professional organizations who succeeded, after many years, in persuading their colleagues to consider holding their national conventions on the coast sometimes found, to their embarrassment, that hotel managers and chambers of commerce were less interested in quoting convention rates than were their counterparts in Miami Beach and Atlantic City.

By the middle of the twentieth century, if not before, tourist travel perhaps told most about the Far West as the most visible sign of its essential mobility. It was less the key to the westward movement of population from the East than it had been, though increasingly Americans could afford to live where they chose to live because of climate and other amenities that attracted vacationers, as well as because of jobs. In a suburban society, Americans who customarily divided their lives between the different communities where they worked and lived and the automobiles that took them from one to the other could afford also to ride to their recreation. Rails and highways bridged West and East and assured the one that it had not wholly divorced itself from the other. And in carrying Westerners around the West, in time they also carried the newest part of the new American society.

---

[1] John Cuddy: unpublished address, October 27, 1937. *The New York Times*, February 21, 1954, p. 41, cols. 1–5.

[2] American Automobile Association: *Americans on the Highway . . .*, sixth edition (Washington, 1956), p. 11.

XIII

THE TREND OF THE FAR WEST

IF ANY LARGE GENERALIZATION about Western history is possible in the face of the vast amount of it that historians have yet to explore, it is that the West itself as an area separate and different from the rest of the United States is disappearing. Each census records approximation to national averages. Sociologists long had contended that most of the distinguishing features of Far Western society followed on deviations from national norms in wealth and age; in the middle decades of the twentieth century, these were narrowing, and with them, others.[1] In 1960, three of the six states were more urban than the nation; California tied for second place with Rhode Island, after New Jersey; and Utah, whose people had left the Middle West to live

[1] William F. Ogburn: "Social Characteristics of Cities," *Public Management*, Vol. XVIII (June, July 1936), pp. 202–3.

like the Biblical patriarchs, was more urban than Ohio and Missouri. Increases in wages, salaries, and personal incomes fell behind national rates, so that even in California, site of the greatest economic expansion at mid-century, per capita personal income, 1929–60, rose nearly a fifth less than throughout the United States. In the years when more Americans than ever before were moving to the Far West to take better jobs, the differences between Western and other wages, prices, and costs of living were less than they had been, and were still declining.[2] In distribution of ages, races, sexes, health, educational attainment, occupations, and atmospheric pollution, Westerners were becoming as representative of the nation as they were in speech.

Approximation to the older states extended well beyond statistics and what statistics could represent. When Far Western institutions were taking shape most decisively—as in the era of the gold rushes and in the great expansion following the Second World War—the heaviest immigration came from areas and social classes that were already firmly committed to social values commonly accepted throughout the whole nation. Most of the new settlers of the 1940's and 1950's, for instance, were very different from the immigrants who had brought variants from Europe to metropolitan New York City, Boston, Chicago, and Milwaukee when the East and the Middle West were developing their characteristic industries and educational and political systems in the late nineteenth and early twentieth centuries.[3] Most of the urban growth of the Far West, moreover, occurred within the years when streetcars, automobiles, airplanes, nationwide advertising, and chain stores made

---

[2] Rates of urban population in 1960 were: the United States, 69.9%; California, 86.4%; Idaho, 47.5%; Nevada, 70.4%; Oregon, 62.2%; Utah, 74.9%; Washington, 68.1%.

Personal income per capita

	1880	*1900*	*1919–21*	*1949–51*	*1960*
UNITED STATES	$175	$203	$658	$1355	$2223
CALIFORNIA	392	365	998	1663	2741
IDAHO	281	221	597	1200	1796
NEVADA	606	395	939	1824	2844
OREGON	234	248	774	1437	2259
UTAH	134	183	556	1225	1910
WASHINGTON	234	296	770	1502	2317

Everett S. Lee: *Population Redistribution and Economic Growth in the United States, 1870–1950*, Vol. I, American Philosophical Society Memoirs, Vol. XLV (Philadelphia, 1957), p. 753. *Statistical Abstract*, 1962, p. 319.

[3] Carle C. Zimmerman and Richard Du Wors: *Graphic Regional Sociology* (Cambridge: The Phillips Book Store; 1952), pp. 127–9.

the rise of a city, even in an area with a long cultural tradition of its own, less the expression of a regional personality than the application of a standard format. The process of moving across the continent no longer screened and transformed men and institutions as it once had. The Easterner on the West coast might bring, among other habits, even his brands of bread and beer, his clubs, his subscription to his daily newspaper.

Much more than earlier frontiers that were closer in miles to the East, the Far West from the beginning of substantial American settlement resembled the most dynamic part of the nation—the eastern Middle West, New England, and the Middle Atlantic area. The coast had long insisted that it was Eastern, most loudly when it had little to show beyond origins and aspirations; first Portland, then San Francisco, then Los Angeles and its neighbors, and then again San Francisco claimed the closest resemblances. The claim was no less substantial for sometimes seeming preposterous: it stood up under both impressionistic and statistical tests. When Charles Angoff and H. L. Mencken looked for "The Worst American State" in the series of articles that they published in *The American Mercury* in 1931, they set up tables in which the names of the states appeared in order of rates of literacy, reading, income, alcoholism, suicide, and a hundred other random categories, in most of which Mississippi and her neighbors stood at one end and the states of the Northeast, the Pacific coast, and the northern Middle West at the other.[4] Essentially the same pattern appeared in later data concerning attributes as varied as churchgoing (frequency and denominations), tastes in food and drink (particularly "foreign" items: wine versus whiskey, artichokes versus creamed corn), reading *The New York Times* and *The Wall Street Journal,* driving foreign cars. The large and increasing numbers of Western students at Ivy League colleges, despite the growing stature of Western universities and the still larger numbers of Eastern alumni who moved west, suggested that it was no accident that the young businessmen of San Francisco looked so much like their counterparts in Manhattan.

Much that reminded the newcomer of what he had read of the pioneer past of the Far West actually represented trends common to both coasts. Most of the large Spanish-speaking population of the states west of New Mexico and Colorado came during and after the Second

[4] Angoff and Mencken: "The Worst American State," *The American Mercury,* Vol. XXIV (September, October, November 1931), pp. 1–16, 175–88, 355–71. Cf. Wilson: *Geography of Reading.*

World War; these people had little more connection with the region than the Puerto Ricans had with New York City, except that their ancestors once had owned much of it and that the climate and some of the available occupations were familiar to them. Like the Puerto Ricans, they moved to economic opportunity in an economically dynamic area, rather than to their cultural heritage. Likewise, twentieth-century patterns of political nonpartisanship probably owed little or nothing to the mines and much to the metropolis: the forty-niner had been politically independent first because as a transient and an exile he had only the most limited concern with politics, and then, when he became a resident, because geography made national issues seem distant and irrelevant to men concerned above all else with getting a railroad, free land, and mineral rights. But independent voting eventually developed in response to the complexity of urban living in a technological age—on the one hand, to the centrifugal tendency of municipal politics, in which efficiency and personality transcended loyalty to party; on the other hand, to the attractiveness of nationally advocated reforms that the state party organizations and state and local governments were slow to take up.[5] And though the suburbanite might be a commuter, he was a homeowner rather than a transient.

Not only was the West much like the dominant parts of the nation, but the most dynamic parts of the West were those where national trends were strongest. California continued to lead, as in the 1850's: as if by a series of new discoveries of gold, it throve in turn on agriculture, climate, oil, motion pictures, aeronautics, and electronics, and simply on supplying its own needs and its neighbors'. After the first decade of the twentieth century, no state of the six closely approached California's rate of growth in population for even a short period except Nevada,[6]

[5] A contrary argument, to the effect that independent voting was evidence of regionalism, appears in Lancaster Pollard: "The New Northwest," in *Regionalism in America*, ed. Merrill Jensen (Madison: University of Wisconsin Press; 1951), p. 201.

[6] Rates of increase in population

	1900–10	*1910–20*	*1920–30*	*1930–40*	*1940–50*	*1950–60*
California	60.1%	44.1%	65.7%	21.7%	53.3%	48.5%
Idaho	101.3	32.6	3.0	17.9	12.1	13.3
Nevada	93.4	-5.5	17.6	21.1	45.2	78.2
Oregon	62.7	16.4	21.8	14.2	39.6	16.3
Utah	34.9	20.4	13.0	8.4	25.2	29.3
Washington	120.4	18.8	15.2	11.1	37.0	19.9
United States	21.0	15.0	16.2	7.3	14.5	18.5

In 1860, California had 77.3 percent of the population of the six states. By 1900 it had only 51.3 percent, but in 1960 it had 70.8 percent.

which moved from an absurdly small base and still was about as much of an adjunct to its neighbors as it had been in the days of the Comstock, and with on the whole a more profitable traffic across the state line in sin than it had had in silver. Idaho still lived apart from the others in that it lagged while they grew and in that it remained heavily committed to agriculture—beyond any other state west of the Rockies. In general the inland states, like their neighbors in the mountains and plains just beyond, were more conservative politically and less creative culturally than California, Oregon, and Washington, though Nevada had whatever advantages or opportunities might come from easy money; Utah, those from morals and literacy.

The speed with which some parts of the West grew and changed did not mean that they welcomed new and liberal ideas. When residents of new Western communities boasted of being "progressive," they usually meant that their stores were as well stocked, their businessmen as enterprising, their houses and city halls as expensive as anyone else's, not that they were advanced or liberal in their social polity. From the gold miners of 1849 to the shipyard workers of 1942, men were so ambitious to get ahead individually that they tended to brush aside claims on time and conscience for causes that did not affect them directly and urgently. The experience of having come where they were made them feel free to go when and where they chose. And since they had social mobility, why should they reform society? Political parties had no strong claims on their members, therefore, even before the progressives institutionalized their weakness. Indifference to the possibilities of collective action seemed to extend, at least until the early 1960's, even among Negroes in Western cities, though most Negroes lived in communities that had more people of all races who had improved themselves economically so recently that they could not feel certain of themselves socially, and who expressed their insecurity in their prejudices. Under such circumstances, part of the new social mobility of minorities consisted of only a wider choice among various areas of segregation, in homes and in jobs.

The looseness of political parties often was less clearly an opportunity for their members to deviate from orthodox political principles than it was an opportunity for them to advance themselves personally. It sometimes invited the politician to take an independent stand not merely to appeal to the opposition on issues, but also to establish his individuality, demonstrate his freedom from the organization; independence was a virtue in itself. Perhaps Nixon's rise and fall in California politics illustrates this atmosphere: he appealed as a candidate for the Senate in 1950 both by riding the wave of national excitement over Korea and subversion and by seeming to have stepped out of line, as a young representative, in challenging respectability and seniority. When he ran for governor of California in 1962, his indictment of the opposition had lost the drama of the new and the specific, and though he failed (as politicians on the coast often had failed) to unite his party behind him, his attempts to find a middle way in the party made him less interesting as well as more vulnerable to charges that he had betrayed those on both the liberal and the conservative wings—the individualists.

The fate of education in the West was very different from that of politics, but it illustrates essentially the same preoccupation with getting ahead individually, the same tendency to accept society rather than change it. The beginnings were slow, sometimes because expectations were high as well as because means and commitments to the new country were limited: in pioneer times, many families on the coast, like the missionaries of Hawaii, sent their sons to the older Eastern colleges, whose resources far exceeded any others that they could command. Some of the states with the highest levels of literacy and wealth therefore lagged most behind their contemporaries of the Mississippi Valley in authorizing state support for higher education.[7] The pioneer colleges and universities testified rather to religious zeal, local pride, and good intentions than to substantial academic achievement: Willamette University (1842), Pacific University (1849), and the University of the Pacific (1851), despite their impressive names, were actually secondary or preparatory schools, and the University of Deseret [Utah] (1850), which at first amounted to a normal school serving the territory's elementary schools, closed from 1852 to 1869 and awarded its first degrees (to a class of two) in 1886.[8]

---

[7] Iowa (a territory in 1838, a state in 1846) established its university in 1847, Wisconsin (1836 and 1848) in 1849, Minnesota (1849 and 1858) in 1851. When California, the richest of all, opened the state university nineteen years after statehood, and the state normal school two years later, it was from two to ten times as populous as any of them at the corresponding times.

[8] Nash: *Oregon,* p. 50. Ralph V. Chamberlain: *The University of Utah; a History of Its First Hundred Years, 1850 to 1950* (Salt Lake City: University of Utah Press; 1960), pp. 11–134. Brigham Young, on whose motion the regents of the University of Deseret discontinued the part-time services of the professor of Greek and Latin in 1871, "thought the classics had been used by the learned to keep the unlearned in subjection and ignorance." Ibid., p. 95.

Once Westerners thought of themselves as residents, they made substantial and widening commitments to education by various channels: academies that gave way to public high schools, normal schools that became teachers' colleges and state colleges (or even affiliates of state universities), Chautauqua assemblies that merged into summer sessions and extension divisions of more formal institutions. Ultimately the West's schools and colleges became its most efficient agencies of social mobility, its most powerful engines of assimilation. The junior college appeared in the Pacific states, not as a frank admission by a struggling private liberal-arts college that it could not offer what it had proposed, but as a commitment by a school district and the state to extend free public education two years beyond the high school. What it extended covered much ground, from a good imitation of the first two years at the state university to instruction in the trades and programs of personal development and rehabilitation, but the statistics were impressive. When President Truman's Commission on Higher Education recommended universal free education at the thirteenth and fourteenth years, it showed that the six states, with less than 8 percent of the population, had had nearly 46 percent of the country's students in public junior colleges (1940).[9] Although Stanford University could not long continue to offer a free college education (by the 1920's not much remained of the early idea of the poor boys' university except a tradition of expensive informality in dress), publicly supported institutions were open, at nominal cost, to most high-school graduates interested in beginning some kind of college work.

The limits of the system seemed obvious enough. The Far West was more successful in legislating a high average of educational attainment as measured by years in the classroom than in raising the intellectual level of society outside the more formal channels. From the time that the Census Bureau counted years of schooling completed, the six states were among the nine with the best records in the country, but Utah, which repeatedly ranked first, was (with Idaho) below the national average in teachers' salaries and—in a series of surveys in the 1930's—in sales of books and circulation of magazines and of learned journals; Idaho was below average in several categories. Even during the prosperous years after the Second World War, when college

[9] President's Commission on Higher Education: *Higher Education for American Democracy* (Washington: Government Printing Office; [1947]), Vol. VI, pp. 20, 24–5.

faculties were large and on the average well paid by national standards, memberships in scholarly organizations were low. Especially in the 1920's and 1930's, many Western colleges seemed to prize athletic more than academic excellence, whether because it was comprehensible to their administrators (who in the teachers' and junior colleges almost never had liberal-arts backgrounds and, like Western school superintendents, often had been football coaches), or because the entertainment appealed to taxpayers and alumni, or because students found the teaching uninspiring. As Dean C. H. Parker of the University of Washington suggested (1917), athletics was "a sort of psychic cure for the illness of experiencing a university education"; and the illness may have afflicted the promoters who became college presidents as grieviously as the undergraduates. Surveys of the distribution of fields of study in Western graduate schools seemed to confirm Eastern aspersions to the effect that the great forte of the West was in copying rather than creating: engineering and especially education ran high, the humanities low. Announcing in 1963 that, for lack of an appropriately stimulating atmosphere, The Institute for Philosophical Research would move from San Francisco to Chicago, Mortimer Adler warned against the danger in California of succumbing to the temptations of a "mellifluous climate" and of thinking about quantity almost exclusively.[1] Westerners who liked to boast that they were the most American part of America had to listen to Middle Westerners and Easterners make the same kinds of indictments of them for materialism and spiritual shallowness that Europeans made of the whole country.

Complaints of intellectual isolation and lassitude were far from new. For years visitors to the coast had deplored disparities between artistic creativity and ability to support it (or pretense of it). Among the Californians, Clarence King said (1872), "aspirations for wealth and ease rise conspicuously above any thirst for intellectual, cultural and moral peace." They told how men in evening clothes had pulled Luisa Tetrazzini's carriage through the streets of San Francisco, but

[1] Louis R. Wilson: *The Geography of Reading . . .* (Chicago: University of Chicago Press; 1938), pp. 201, 207, 230, 307, 311, and *passim*. President's Commission on Higher Education: *Higher Education*, Vol. IV, pp. 30–1. Parker: *The Casual Laborer*, p. 51. National Research Council and National Academy of Sciences: *Doctorate Production in United States Universities, 1936–1956*, Publication 582 (Washington, 1958), pp. 9–13. *The New York Times*, Western edition, May 6, 1963, p. 9, cols. 7–8.

in a community suddenly come into money there was a question, the editor of *The Californian* had observed (1881), "'how much of what is genuine there is behind the show." Such stories might reveal more of gallantry than of art. The San Francisco Opera Association gave its first performance in 1923; the San Francisco Symphony Orchestra, in 1911. Then both did missionary work along the coast in other cities that (as San Franciscans liked to recall) had still less, while for years their home seasons were short and their settings inadequate. The new San Francisco War Memorial Opera House (1932), an economic and a cultural success from its opening at the bottom of the great depression, showed that there was substantial interest and demand, but the late date at which it was built suggested again the gap between claim and realization. Likewise Westerners had spent much money on building without achieving architectural distinction or even good taste. Henry Adams, even though he regarded San Francisco before the fire of 1906 as the most interesting city west of the Mississippi, did not believe it contained one object that could not be replaced better in six months.[2] The coast, in fact, already had its outstanding architects, but it was slow to recognize them: thus Bernard Maybeck (1862–1957) did not even keep his position as professor of architecture at the University of California, which adopted plans for its campus at Berkeley straight out of the Beaux-Arts school, plans that were considerably less suited to its setting than the Romanesque colonnades at Stanford were to theirs.

The West may have been slow to create and to recognize creativity in the first century of American settlement in part because it had so many immediate and urgent tasks in taming the wilderness and because, until it had shown that it could be like the East, it feared that differences would suggest inferiority. But by the 1950's and 1960's, when there could be no doubt of wealth and power and technique, much energy was going into movements to suppress novelty and dissent, to enforce a conformity that was no less demanding for failing to define precisely what it proposed. There had been antecedents enough: the anxiety over pro-German and pro-Bolshevik dis-

---

[2] Clarence King: *Mountaineering in the Sierra Nevada* (Boston: James R. Osgood & Co.; 1872), p. 291. *Californian . . .*, Vol. III (June 1881), pp. 571–2. Henry Adams to C. M. Gaskell, April 23, 1906, in *The Selected Letters of Henry Adams,* ed. Newton Arvin (New York: Farrar, Straus, & Young; 1951), p. 247.

loyalty during the First World War; the Ku Klux Klan and persecutions under criminal syndicalism laws in the 1920's; the anti-labor agitation of various industrial groups in California; recurrent outbursts of racism, which, as an Englishman commented (1884), represented essentially intolerance of the crime of deviation from prevailing ways, of daring "to appear or behave differently to the accredited type, not to care for local topics or the politics of the saloon. . . ."[3] Nevertheless, the spirit and direction of criticism seemed new when citizens of states that had been outstanding for their support of education and of political reform began to level wholesale charges of disloyalty against teachers in the schools and colleges and against public officials who supported proposals as assorted as fluoridation of water supplies and the enforcement of the first and fourteenth amendments to the Constitution of the United States.

The most striking incidents affecting higher education preceded Senator Joseph R. McCarthy's charges of subversion in the national government. In Washington the Canwell Committee, which inquired into reports of Communism on the faculty of the state university (1948–9), was heir to a long tradition of political interference, and when the president and the regents of the university hastened to anticipate the suggestions of the Committee, they were least surprising to those best acquainted with them and with the local setting. But the University of California commanded respect among educational leaders and among the people that corresponded to its position under the state constitution, which established it as an independent organ coordinate with the legislature and not responsible to it except for financial support. Stanford University had preempted the name of "Harvard of the West" before it became a serious rival, but its larger neighbor, the senior unit of the state university, at Berkeley, was by general ackowledgment the academic and scientific center of the Western half of the country; the two together, as David Riesman has observed, did much to give the San Francisco Bay area the relationship to Los Angeles that Boston traditionally had had to New York. Thus there was a general sense of shock in the spring of 1949 when the regents of the university, following the suggestion of the president, required as a condition of all appointments an oath repudiating revolutionary

[3] W. Shepherd: *Prairie Experiences in Handling Cattle and Sheep* (New York: O. Judd Co.; 1885), p. 123.

ideas and affiliations. "I want to organize 20th Century vigilantes," said Regent Giannini. "If we rescind the oath . . . the flag will fly in the Kremlin." By the time, two and a half years later, when the regents accepted a judicial decision upholding members of the faculty who refused to sign, the university had lost much in personnel, morale, and energy diverted from normal pursuits; it had discovered and discharged one alleged Communist, a pianist in the Department of Physical Education for Women at Los Angeles;[4] and the controversy had deepened misunderstanding between educators and others who could not comprehend what was at stake.[5] (Most laymen were no less confused when protesting members of the faculty took an oath that was required [1950] of all state employees and that thus did not single out educators for suspicion.)

Although within a few years, by all outward appearances, the two universities had resumed and accelerated their advance, suspicion of intellectuals continued in channels more subject to popular and political pressure, particularly affecting the public schools. Conformism was especially insistent in southern California, where the regents of the University of California had been (to use the terminology of the university community) predominantly anti-faculty while the northern regents had been predominantly pro-faculty; and where the press traditionally had frowned on most kinds of heterodoxy apart from dress and manners. It was a long time since Job Harriman had nearly become Socialist mayor of Los Angeles and since the southern counties had had so many utopian communities as to recall western New York in the day of the Oneida Community and the early Mormons. In response to a barrage of protests, the Los Angeles School Board in 1952 ordered the schools to discontinue using a teachers'

---

[4] It was not until December 1954 that the regents paid the salaries of five nonsigners. The regents of the University of Washington had discharged (1949) three members of the faculty on the recommendation of President R. B. Allen, who identified two of them as Communists.

[5] Vern Countryman: *Un-American Activities in the State of Washington* (Ithaca: Cornell University Press; 1951), pp. 72–276 and *passim.* David Riesman and Christopher Jencks in *The American College: A Psychological and Social Interpretation of the Higher Learning,* ed. Nevitt Sanford (New York: John Wiley & Sons; 1962), p. 171. George R. Stewart and others: *The Year of the Oath: The Fight for Academic Freedom at the University of California* (New York: Doubleday & Co.; 1950), pp. 94–5 and *passim. The New York Times,* April 22, 1950, p. 1, cols. 6–7.

manual concerning the United Nations Educational, Scientific, and Cultural Organization and, according to one critic, purged "everything 'international' from the curriculum."[6] The next year it refused a grant from the Ford Foundation after hearing charges that Ford was "UNESCO-tainted." Crusading political fundamentalism seemed to be more conspicuous than in the Mississippi Valley: when Dr. Fred C. Schwarz, the Australian physician who incorporated the Christian Anti-Communist Crusade in Iowa in 1953, moved his headquarters to Long Beach, he collected enormously larger revenues. The headquarters of the John Birch Society for six Far Western states was in San Marino. Southern California industrialists contributed lavishly to rallies and television programs during which speakers denounced treason, reaching from the classroom to the White House, and called for the impeachment and hanging of Chief Justice Warren.[7] By 1964 the right wing of the Republican Party of California, based in the southern counties, seemed to have come into its own by capturing the state organization and by delivering California's delegation at the Republican National Convention to Senator Goldwater.

Some of the strongest pressures for conformity in thought occurred in the newest and most rapidly changing parts of the West (Los Angeles and Seattle more than San Francisco); their principal vehicles were the most modern media of communication. Westerners had a prodigious appetite for newspapers, which contrasted with a more-than-national and earlier-than-national tendency for Western cities to support no more than one newspaper (Because costs were high? Because political nonpartisanship made an opposition press seem unimportant? Certainly not because of universal affection for the *Los Angeles Times* and the *Oregonian,* whose editorial policies aroused deep and widespread opposition even in the 1890's). And that newspaper was likely to be both politically conservative and journalistically regressive, singularly lacking in editorial initiative and even in news. Westerners subscribed to more than their share of magazines,

---

[6] Robert V. Hine: *California's Utopian Colonies* (San Marino: Huntington Library; 1953), pp. 6–7, 9. *The New York Times,* March 20, 1953, p. 10, col. 3. Gloria Farquar: "Retreat from Reason: the Attack on UNESCO," *Frontier,* Vol. IV (November 1952), pp. 5–7.

[7] *The New York Times,* July 19, 1953, p. 18, col. 1; October 29, 1961, p. 43, cols. 1–5; June 24, 1962, p. 9, cols. 1–7; Western edition, March 16, 1963, p. 4, col. 5; December 17, 1961, p. 58, col. 1.

nearly all published in the East, and also of Eastern newspapers;[8] the one general magazine published on the Pacific slope that survived for more than a few years was *Sunset,* which after adopting a new editorial policy in 1928 became both an impressive commercial and journalistic success and a formidable force in indoctrinating Westerners in the regional mores of tossed salads, homemade patios, and automobile recreation.

Despite the prominence of printed and electronic channels that relayed nationally syndicated news and entertainment, old residents and their ways long maintained prestige and power on the Pacific slope, all the more impressively because the process of indoctrination was so elusive. Those who relegated the Mexican ranchers of California and the Hudson's Bay men of Oregon to the status of spear-carriers in pageants never had to face the inundations of politically aggressive immigrants from abroad that elbowed aside the colonial stock of New York and New England; rather they were so secure that they tended to defend foreigners during the West's occasional outbursts of nativism. They never had the automatic bonus at the polls that the mere fact of being a native son gave a Southern politician over an opponent from the North, and they had no need for it. From the time of the pioneers, who seemed preoccupied simultaneously with thoughts of returning to the East and of civilizing neighbors who had arrived more recently still—the mountain men in Oregon and California, the gentiles in Utah—a kind of continuing reinforcement of original traits seemed to prevail, a species of cultural imprinting almost as effective as the imprinting that behavorial psychologists observed in their animal laboratories. The Okies and Arkies of the 1930's caused brief alarm for what they might add to the cost of harvesting fruit and to local taxes for schools and relief or what they might take from rural clotheslines and garden patches, but when they stayed long enough in one place to register as voters, they soon began to conform to the mores of the community, the unchurched becoming churched, the Pentecostals becoming Presbyterians,[9] Democrats voting Republican

[8] In 1962 the Sunday *Times* went to one of 1,429 residents of the six states, to one of 1,316 of California, as against one of 1,731 of the West North Central states, which received it one or two days earlier. In 1963, *The Wall Street Journal* went to one of 181 residents of the six states, one of 165 of California, one of 213 of the United States.

[9] Walter R. Goldschmidt: "Class Denominationalism in Rural California Churches," *American Journal of Sociology,* Vol. XLIX (January 1944), pp. 348–55.

and perhaps joining the John Birch Society; they had not, in fact, been so different as they seemed. Imprinting was probably most complete in Utah, where the Mormon Church was an educational and integrating force with few rivals in American society; imprinting was even more striking on the coast, where immigration sometimes seemed to reinforce regional traits rather than dilute them. Either the immigrants sorted themselves out, so that those with a taste for shorts, dark glasses, freeways, and the open shop went to Los Angeles; for opera, fog, scandal, and sour French bread, to San Francisco; for hiking, respectability, soundness at five percent, and complaining and boasting about Reed College, to Portland; or they soon learned their proper roles from their neighbors and the appropriate editions of *Sunset* and its supplements, not submissively but with the zeal of the convert.

The stubborn persistence of Far Western ways was especially remarkable in view of the high rates of immigration and the low rates of natural increase. Except in Utah and Idaho, where Mormon or rural doctrines of fruitfulness prevailed, families were unusually small. In California, where they were smallest of all, visitors in early days had variously attributed the fact to the transience of the population, the chill temperatures of the evenings, and the high cost of coal (which confirmed the habit of living in hotels and also led husband and wife to go out because their homes were cold, and so to divorce); but the birth rate fell even lower when fuel became cheap,[1] and families were small on farms as well as in the cities. Thus the prevailing tendency, outside of Utah and Idaho, was for increases in population to follow overwhelmingly on immigration (the percentage of net gain per decade attributable to immigration ranged in California between 83.8 and 87.1 percent, 1900–40) and for the native born to be a minority. Moreover, most immigrants to the Far West, like most migrants throughout the country, had more education than the populations of the states they moved to, even during the influx of refugees from the drought-stricken Southwest in the 1930's. Countervailing tendencies were for the Pacific area to hold the leaders that it produced more than other areas held theirs, and for immigrants long after the gold rush to

[1] By 1910, when there were 670.6 children aged 0 to 4 to each 1,000 women aged 20 to 44 in the United States, there were only 456.9 in California. Warren S. Thompson: *Growth and Change in California's Population* (Los Angeles: The Haynes Foundation; 1955), p. 22, and cf. 25.

be slow to take root, backward even in voting in the 1950's.[2] Chancellor Franklin Murphy of the University of California at Los Angeles, himself an immigrant, suggested that the new migration of later years would commit itself as the old had not: "In largest measure [he said in 1963], the people who came to Southern California after the turn of the century were fleeing drought, arthritis, sleet, snow, rheumatism. . . . That wave thought of California as a semi-permanent vacation. Home was not California. Home was Iowa. They were the rootless ones." In contrast, those who came after getting acquainted in the 1940's, perhaps in the course of a wartime assignment, were "going toward something—toward jobs in the space industry, architecture, the universities. . . . They came back after the war. They had already broken the umbilical tie. . . . They were ready to marry, settle down and make their futures here."[3] If Murphy was right, the result might be much the same: in place of exiles who lived in a Middle Western past and contributed little more than buying power, there was a more dynamic group who brought more energy but less divergence of purpose and values. After exploring alternatives (often, returning temporarily to their old homes, purging themselves of homesickness), they made a more positive commitment to the new country and its opportunities. Perhaps they reinforced more than they transplanted even while they exercised more influence than their predecessors in immigration.

Actually even to increase buying power, as any additions to population do, may have helped to maintain the distinctiveness of Western ways, which depended heavily on continuing economic growth. In the first years of American settlement, the gold rushes had taken the Far West beyond the usual agricultural frontiers, to which it might have lapsed if the gold seekers had not stayed to spend what they brought and what they dug. San Francisco was metropolis of what the editor

---

[2] Lee Meriwether: *The Tramp at Home* (New York: Harper & Brothers; 1889), p. 170. John S. Hittell: *A History of the City of San Francisco . . .* (San Francisco: A. L. Bancroft & Co.; 1878), p. 443. Vernon Davies: *Farm Population Trends in Washington*, Washington Agricultural Experiment Bulletin, no. 501 (Pullman: Washington State College; 1949), p. 1. McEntire in Occidental College, Institute of Economics and Finance: *Proceedings* (1948), pp. 33–5. W. Lloyd Warner and James C. Abbeglen: *Occupational Mobility in American Business and Industry* (Minneapolis: University of Minnesota Press; 1955), pp. 70, 72–3. Douglas E. Scates and others: *The Production of Doctorates in the Sciences, 1936–1948* (Washington: American Council on Education; 1951), p. 174.

[3] *The New York Times*, Western edition, May 22, 1963, p. 6, col. 5.

of *Overland* called (1883) "the most completely realized embodiment of the purely commercial civilization on the face of the earth," but it never consolidated the imperium over the Pacific that its leaders dreamed of. It sustained itself importantly on the remittances of those who came in hope of further bonanzas and the charges it levied for its services as shipper, broker, and administrator for the hinterland. The immigration of workingmen attracted by the inflated wages of early years[4] was not enough; by itself it would soon have dropped off as the profits of mining declined and became inaccessible to the average man, as supply met demand. The legendary retired farmers from Iowa (most of them neither farmers nor Iowans) helped to maintain the high level of urbanization in an economy that was still extractive and agricultural rather than industrial; ultimately they helped to tide the West over to the time when it had built up the power, the skills, and the steady buying power to support industries of its own.

As the Far West maintained and transformed its urbanism, making its bridgeheads into its capitals, it also cultivated images of a past, ranging from the pious and idyllic to the boisterous and extravagant, that reinforced impressions of its uniqueness. Regionalism happened to become fashionable in American literature at about the time that Westerners could afford to indulge themselves in it, in the 1880's and 1890's, and despite the handicap of lacking both a colorful dialect (the English language west of the Rockies is notoriously undialectical, hard to identify) and the sense of defeat that inspired the South, they took up regionalism with enthusiasm. They had help from surviving pioneers, some of whom spent their declining years in rituals at Pioneers' Hall, spinning tales about themselves, comparing (one of their critics said in 1876) "their achievements to those of Cortez and Pizarro—to the disadvantage of Pizarro and Cortez."[5] But some of the most enthusiastic exponents of the cult of the pioneer were newcomers, prone as newcomers often are to seek simple explanations of the present in the remote past.[6] Much of the resulting mass of legend was boldly

[4] *Overland,* second series, Vol. II (December 1883), pp. 657–8. Kingsley Davis in *The Changing American Population,* ed. Hoke C. Simpson (New York: Institute of Life Insurance; 1962), pp. 60–1.

[5] Walter M. Fisher: *The Californians* (London: Macmillan & Co.; 1876), pp. 36–9.

[6] Clarence King complained (1871): "It is very much the habit of newly arrived people to link the past and present too closely in their estimate of the existing status." King: *Mountaineering* (1935 ed.), p. 314.

innocent of historical foundations, as Frank Norris protested when he called for a Western epic distinct from the conventional setting of the dime novel. Frederick Bracher has pointed out that even the best of the California writers passed by the urban themes that interested Norris: "The lower one looks in the literary scale, the easier it is to find references to palm trees, Palm Springs, bearded miners, crumbling missions, orange groves, and old Spanish ranchos."[7]

In later years, romantic stories of pioneer times came to serve assorted economic and psychological needs. Real-estate promoters cultivated the illusion that the subdivisions they had carved out of pastures and desert had the color of history behind them, if not established local institutions; and immigrants were willing and even eager to accept new ancestors, to establish some connection with the land. The Indian and Spanish-speaking owners of the land were so unlikely to reappear to reproach their successors that there was no embarrassment in recalling and celebrating them. The eras of the Hudson's Bay Company and the missions and ranches appealed, as idyllic refuges from the tensions of a complex industrial and commercial society, both to those who deplored modern regulation and taxation of capital and to those who deplored capital itself. In his socialist editorials, Gaylord Wilshire looked back to the missions as "a chain of semi-socialistic communities. . . . There was no fear of starvation on account of overproduction in those silly, primitive days. They produced for use and not for profit."[8] Those who employed *braceros* at low wages or enforced racial covenants in good neighborhoods felt no inconsistency, for the figures in the pageants were always noble Castilians, never Mexicans. Thus the idea of difference between West and East, at least in origins and traditions, developed almost as a consequence of the region's assimilation to standardized, nationalized ways.

Yet tradition did not rise simply from ignorance. It owed much to writers of the early history of the West, such as H. H. Bancroft, who, according to a reviewer, had taken Mexico from oblivion and made it heroic. Scholars in the new Western universities, anthropologists,

---

[7] Frank Norris: "A Neglected Epic," *World's Work*, Vol. V (December 1902), pp. 2904–6. Frank Norris to I. F. Marcosson [Dec. 1898], in Isaac F. Marcosson: *Before I Forget . . .* (New York: Dodd, Mead & Co.; 1959), p. 502. Frederick Bracher: "California's Literary Regionalism," *American Quarterly*, Vol. VII (fall 1955), pp. 276, 279.

[8] "A Talk with Rockefeller," *The Challenge* (May 1903), in *Wilshire Editorials* (New York: Wilshire Book Co.; 1906), p. 55.

archaeologists, and historians, searched the remains of the past with rising enthusiasm, rejoicing to find in the archives of Mexico City and Seville records of European beginnings in the northwestern reaches of the Viceroyalty of New Spain older and fuller than those of English plantations on the Atlantic coast. At the University of California, which in 1894 offered the first course in Latin American history and institutions in the country, the regents acquired the Bancroft Library in 1905 and thus supported major expansion in Latin American studies, which for many years overshadowed the university's teaching and research in the history and literature of the United States. In Oregon, the study of regional history sprang in large part from the efforts of Dean F. G. Young of the state university, founder of the state historical society and editor of its quarterly, who brought to it some of the perspective of his teachers at the early Johns Hopkins. The study of regional anthropology and local history began early also in Washington, where the University gave substantial scholarly support to another local tradition, the link of the West with the Far East, projecting a program of Oriental studies in 1909, year of the Alaska-Pacific-Yukon Exposition, to encourage broader knowledge of countries with which the Pacific Coast states should share commercial and cultural interests.[9] And in Utah the pride of Mormons in the saga of their pioneers and their preoccupation, on religious grounds, with genealogy naturally turned their historians and social scientists to the study of early local history. Local and regional studies in some respects gained rather than lost with the passage of time, as Western scholars came to feel less isolated and less fearful of seeming provincial. There was little undergraduate instruction in state history before the 1930's, when the authorities began to require such courses for certification of teachers in public schools, which served both as a kind of tariff to exclude foreign teachers, and to support the teaching of the units on Indians, missionaries, and pioneers that had become standard in the grade schools.

Whatever it might be in its lowest or most naïve forms, the heritage of the pioneer past had substantial meaning. The fact was both that

---

[9] *American Antiquarian,* Vol. XIV (July 1892), p. 231. James E. Watson: "Bernard Moses' Contribution to Scholarship," *California Historical Society Quarterly,* Vol. XLII (June 1963), pp. 111–2. John W. Caughey: *Hubert Howe Bancroft: Historian of the West* (Berkeley: University of California Press; 1946), pp. 359–65. Charles M. Gates: *The First Century of the University of Washington, 1861–1961* (Seattle: University of Washington Press; 1961), p. 121.

it was more pleasant to recount conventional episodes of riches, adventure, and picaresque lawlessness than to ponder on the somber lessons of social irresponsibility that Josiah Royce drew from the same period, and that the discovery of gold and the ensuing occupation of the Far West were events of such force and magnitude that no one could live in the area for generations after without responding to them. The Sierra Nevada in 1848 and 1849 saw the fulfillment of three centuries' search for El Dorado under circumstances as appropriate, in the early stages, to the democratic society of the nineteenth century as Mexico and Peru had been to the aristocratic and monarchical society of the sixteenth—and all of this, like the fulfillment of prophecy on the shores of Great Salt Lake, in the modern scientific world of steamships and photography. The dramatic impact of Everyman suddenly lifted from routine to great events, to fellowship with Jason and Cortés, was like that of the Civil War, when farm boys walked with the ghosts of Cromwell and Napoleon.

But the Sierra also was the setting of one of a series of Western parallels to major economic and social events extending over much of the contemporary world. Like Henry George's *Progress and Poverty*, which was intelligible wherever the few were profiting by the scarcity of what had once been open to the many, the story of gold and silver had a quality of universality that made it easy for the hopes of young Bostonians and New Yorkers to come to focus on the American River or at the Comstock. It was no less interesting in later years, when the placer miner had become a factory hand and his hopes had been transmuted into types of Western speculation more like those of the East. The dealer in city lots and the builder of irrigation canals found themselves in the tales of the mining camps. Correspondingly, the contrast between the apparent fulfillment of democratic hopes in the mines and the actuality of closed opportunity on either coast catalyzed men into thought; George himself later told an audience in San Francisco how what he had seen on going to New York had shocked him as a Westerner.[1]

The early years fairly well anticipated the varied shapes of the later West. The speculative spirit of twentieth-century promoters followed legitimately on the "gambling tendency" that Josiah Royce saw vitiating the "social value" (that is, the democratic order) of early Western mining and also agriculture, in which the mildness and general predictability of climate sometimes tempted farmers to take undue risks.

[1] Anna George de Mille: *Henry George: Citizen of the World* (Chapel Hill: University of North Carolina Press; 1950), p. 175.

The stabilization of nature through irrigation sometimes had a similar tendency; but heavy commitments in "vast irrigation enterprises," as in the elaborate flumes, tunnels, and mills of industrialized mining, also "introduced once more a conservative tendency," in Royce's words, like that of the highly capitalized agricultural assembly lines of the next century. Antagonists of organized labor and of social reform had their precursors in self-made men of pioneer days who despised the unlucky and invoked lynch law for infractions of property rights. "In reality," an English traveler wrote, "there is no more merit in having been a 'California Pioneer' than in drawing a prize in a lottery," but the pioneers assumed that the riches of the state were "all creations of their own."[2] "The dollar jingles, the bill rustles, with every movement of the tongue," said another, who saw economic man walking the streets of San Francisco in the 1870's; "people speak as if they chewed wheat and mouthed nuggets"; their very coins bore—or should have borne—the maxim, "In Gold We Trust."[3] The most zealous critics of capital and monopoly were no exception, but rather were likely to reveal themselves as holding a water right or presiding over a toll road or fencing in some natural curiosity in hope of great profit. These were, perhaps, the ancestors of workingmen who supported the far right in San Francisco in Abe Ruef's time, or in Seattle in Dave Beck's or in Salt Lake City in Bracken Lee's.

On the other hand, some students of the West emphasized the heritage of forces conducive to change, including innovations in institutions as well as various kinds of mobility for individuals. Frederick Jackson Turner saw them on the coast, where he spent his later years: "The daring initiative and community spirit of the Pacific coast cities, notably Los Angeles and Seattle," he wrote in 1926, "in developing harbours and water fronts, in bringing mountain water supplies and power by long distance electric transmission, and of the Los Angeles suburbs in becoming the center of the moving picture production, are indications of the Western spirit in municipal life." He found the old spirits of self-reliance, idealism, and optimism taking new forms in new associational activities, through government and by cooperation, especially in the arid Far West, where climate, geography, and the demands of irrigation agriculture and of mining "decreed that the destiny of this new

---

[2] Royce in *International Monthly*, Vol. II, pp. 575–6. W. F. Rae: *Westward by Rail: The New Route to the East* (London: Longmans, Green; 1870), pp. 310, 323.

[3] Fisher: *The Californians*, pp. 109, 199–200.

frontier should be social rather than individual." At the time of the Lewis and Clark Centennial Exposition in 1905, Dean F. G. Young hopefully traced a line from the time of Lewis and Clark to the reformers of his day, seeing in "the present rise of the civic spirit in Oregon . . . but an intimation from her glorious past. . . ." Even Josiah Royce, who, in his *California: A Study of American Character,* outlined the antecedents of the immorality of the 1880's in the immorality of the 1840's and 1850's, found qualities of independence of judgment in the Californians, including the looseness of party ties, that recalled the Homeric Greeks and that he attributed to their relation to nature and the newness and isolation of the community (that is, to the fact and circumstances of pioneering).[4]

In the middle years of the twentieth century, then, the Pacific slope still owed much to its past and to geography; in many respects it was still a distinct region, with significant intraregional ties and resemblances. Despite the conveniences of air-conditioning, Americans still responded to the amenities of natural climate in which the more settled parts of five of the six states (excepting Nevada) excelled.[5] Some of the most striking intraregional economic and social deviations of earlier days had greatly diminished, probably nowhere more than in Utah, once the great deviant. Much apparent deviation corresponded to specialization to serve the growing regional market, increases in the exchange of goods and services across state lines; and the improvements in transportation that enabled the whole region to get potatoes from Idaho, airplanes and apples from Washington, sporting goods and wood products from Oregon, steel and copper from Utah, and marriages and divorces from Nevada also enabled fruit pickers, salesmen, and schoolteachers to move about within the region more than they moved outside it. Far more than in the days when open-shop Los Angeles and closed-shop San Francisco watched each other suspiciously, the labor market

---

[4] Turner: "The West—1876 and 1926," *World's Work,* Vol. LII (July 1926), p. 327. Turner: "Contributions of the West to American Democracy," *Atlantic Monthly,* Vol. XCI (January 1903), p. 90. Young: "Oregon History and the Oregon Spirit," *Pacific Monthly,* Vol. IV (September 1900), p. 220. Young: "The Higher Significance in the Lewis and Clark Exploration," *Oregon Historical Quarterly* Vol. VI (March 1905), p. 25. Young: "The Spirit of the West," *Pacific Monthly,* Vol. XVI (July 1906), p. 34. Royce in *International Monthly,* Vol. II, pp. 571–5, 577–81, 583.

[5] Markham describes a favored area in which the hottest weather averages below 75 degrees and the coldest above 10 degrees Fahrenheit, including coastal California, Oregon, Washington, Idaho, and the Salt Lake area. S. F. Markham: *Climate and the Energy of Nations* (London: Oxford University Press; 1944), p. 173.

of the Pacific slope was essentially one, much as when the returns at the placers of the Sierra Nevada dictated wages throughout the Pacific slope; California's neighbors differed in distribution of occupations more than at some earlier times, but much less in standards of living and general social behavior.

As the region matured, moreover, it still exercised the power to innovate for which it had been known in pioneer times and in the progressive period, showing much of its old carelessness of precedent and convention. If its commitments to conformity were conspicuous, they also were brief, often so insubstantial as to suggest rearguard action or accident. The *Los Angeles Times* itself, by the late 1950's and early 1960's, was significantly warm to higher education and cool to the Birch Society, and showed no interest in reviving the long siege against the labor unions that it had lost in the 1940's; energetic newspaper reporting showed some of the noisiest right-wing groups, as in Santa Barbara (1961), to be absurdly weak,[6] though militant tactics sometimes took them far in California's chaotic party system. The California state senate forced Jack B. Tenney to withdraw as chairman of the Committee on Un-American Activities in June 1949, just after he introduced the bill (never brought up for hearing) that inspired the president of the university to propose an oath and the regents to require it.[7] In Washington, Al Canwell, chairman of the corresponding committee and leader of the investigation of the university, failed as a Republican candidate at large for the House of Representatives in 1952, when his party swept the state.[8] In Oregon, where cancelation of plans to install a nude bronze statue of Venus by Renoir on the courthouse grounds at the capital city gave an impression of unusual deference to private censors, the commander of the American Legion issued a statement opposing negative oaths for teachers and declaring that school officials and boards of education should be permitted, if necessary, to "clean their own house without being harassed by other organizations."[9] And in Nevada a legislative inquiry into the state university led to the dis-

---

[6] *The New York Times*, December 10, 1961, Sec. VI, p. 9.

[7] Barrett: *Tenney Committee* pp. 323–6.

[8] Beside Canwell, the only other Republican candidate for major office defeated in Washington in 1952 was Senator Harry P. Cain, then in his rightist phase.

[9] Portland *Oregonian*, June 21, 1953, p. 1, col. 1; January 15, 1953, p. 8, cols. 2–3. The Legion concurred with the stand of a committee of the major veterans' organizations in Oregon, which corresponded to resolutions adopted previously by other groups. The *Oregonian* had commented (June 16, 1952): "The climate of Oregon public opinion is not favorable to the questioning of the integrity of its teachers."

missal of the president for overriding the rights of faculty members.[1]

The quality of the intellectual climate appeared most dramatically in the incidence of talent at Western universities, some of whose faculties after the Second World War repeatedly gathered high distinctions quite out of proportion to their numbers: in 1963 eleven of thirty-four new members of the National Academy of Sciences,[2] and more than one of five Guggenheim fellows,[3] were from California. By the 1950's and 1960's the major Eastern universities were becoming uncomfortably aware that bright young scholars on the coast no longer regarded an invitation to serve even temporarily on their faculties as a command from the throne; they were losing some of their own senior professors to the University of California, Stanford, and the California Institute of Technology. The change was recent and rapid enough so that it caught the Westerners themselves by surprise; they showed it in the triumphant tallies of their acquisitions that they published—at Berkeley, a tabulation of Nobel Prize winners, along with details of the advantages of the system of sabbatical leaves and retirement and the climate, in a pamphlet for prospective members of the faculty. Yet it was clear that the West was producing as well as buying prize winners and that most of the émigrés had moved not to retire in the sun but to work in the libraries and laboratories they had come to know as, perhaps, visiting scholars at San Marino or Livermore.

The record of the educational system—in reaching out for the newest and best even while it wrestled with the tasks of assimilating enormous numbers—illustrates the tendency of the Pacific slope to be at once the most imitative and the most innovative part of America. Innovation, in fact, increased as statistics suggested assimilation to the nation. There had always been some innovation in the West; it was open for newcomers to apply ideas they had developed in the East. It was thus a kind of proving ground for older sections, though always on a limited

---

1 "Academic Freedom and Tenure: The University of Nevada," American Association of University Professors, *Bulletin*, Vol. XLII (Autumn 1956), pp. 530–62.

2 *The New York Times*, April 24, 1963, p. 14, col. 3.

3 Typically, the ratio of Guggenheim fellowships increased faster than the population: in 1930, 5 of 78; in 1940, 4 of 67; in 1962, 57 of 263. In 1940, California had 5.2 percent of the population and 5.9 percent of the fellowships; in 1960, 8.7 percent and 18.2 percent. Representation from other Far-Western states was scattering: in 1930, one from Washington; in 1940, one from Oregon; in 1960, two from Oregon, one from Utah, three from Washington; in 1961, seven from Washington; in 1962, two from Oregon, four from Washington.

scale, because it was easier to transport familiar institutions over rough terrain than to break the instinct to cling to custom in a strange land, far from home, and because the purpose of the immigrant was not so much to try new social inventions (which might consume precious time before they worked) as to establish individual fortune. Willingness to try the new was almost proportionate to the amount of the old that it was possible to bring: thus, with few exceptions,[4] Western styles of architecture developed only after the steam railroad train replaced the stagecoach, though in time they invaded the East. But the family that moved west by automobile or plane after the Second World War not only saw its favorite television programs (originating perhaps in Los Angeles), but also became aware of the more fundamental novelties that gave the West some of the relationship to the East that America as a whole had had to Europe more than a century earlier, when Tocqueville advised his countrymen to look across the Atlantic for their future.

Much of the Pacific slope, as in gold-rush days, changed so fast that it skipped entire stages of normal social evolution and thus seemed less advanced than it was. Some of the conventional earmarks of sound development became as obsolete as the consumption of candles as a test of adequate interior lighting after the invention of the incandescent electric bulb. California had skipped the predominantly agrarian phase when it moved directly into a commercial and urbanized economy in the nineteenth century. In the twentieth century, even the other states seemed to have skipped the phase in which industries demand large amounts of hand labor; rather, they went directly into industries with highly sophisticated technology. Some jumped from strongly resource-oriented economies to foot-loose industries like Boeing in Washington. They even skipped the phase in which the economy of a region could get along without much government, so that the high percentage of officials sent out, in effect, to preside over the liquidation of the federal government's colonial responsibilities merged into the high percentage necessary to provide the kinds of services (including higher education and the production of energy) that private initiative had provided to a greater extent in the older states.

Los Angeles might have the worst as well as the best features of the new, but there was no doubt of its newness. It lacked through

[4] Exceptions include the bay window of San Francisco (well known in Britain) and the colonial style (also an importation, though adapted to local materials) of Monterey.

passenger railroad connections with many cities of the six states (so that, for instance, one had to change cars two or three times and stop overnight in going from San Diego to Seattle), in large part because people had shifted to automobiles and airplanes before there was enough railroad traffic to warrant better service on the single-track lines that served most of the West. It might still seem a collection of suburbs in search of a city, but that was because it had stopped looking: it had built Long Island (though in more interesting style than most of the Eastern tract suburbs) without bothering to build Manhattan. Achievements in architecture and in other arts as well may have exceeded awareness of them simply because they occurred in forms that corresponded to the coming orientation of Western and American society: in a region at once urban and decentralized, some of the most creative possibilities were in small-scale domestic rather than in public architecture, in suburban and semi-amateur rather than in metropolitan musical performance. In turn, Los Angeles lacked the normal urban focus and structure of skyscrapers and rapid transit not only because it had thrown away the opportunity to maintain and develop its interurban railway system, but also because it had been a pioneer in urban planning, restricting the height of office buildings and the development of industry by zones as early as 1909.[5] It and other cities on the coast were less throwbacks to rural Iowa than precursors of what New York and Boston might more painfully become when the Long Island and the New Haven railroads went the way of the Oregon Electric, the Pacific Electric, and the Key System. Only a few need have subways, but nearly everyone could have smog and traffic jams on freeways.

As the rate of growth on the Pacific slope accelerated in the 1940's and 1950's, people first doubted that the new arrivals were, in fact, residents rather than visitors, and then wished that they would stop coming, that the region could learn how to assimilate them before many more arrived. But short of exhaustion of potable water, which people

[5] Roy Lubove: *The Progressives and the Slums* . . . (Pittsburgh: University of Pittsburgh Press; 1962), p. 237. The impression of an agglomeration of unrelated communities prompted the common assumption that southern Californians had to resort to the Iowa picnic as a substitute for the kin associations of older states; yet sociologists found that families in Los Angeles visited their relatives as much as families in other American cities, despite the freeway traffic or perhaps as causes of the freeway traffic. Scott Greer: "Individual Participation in Mass Society," in *Approaches to the Study of Politics* . . . , ed. Roland Young (Evanston: Northwestern University Press; 1958), pp. 331–3; and Greer: *Emerging City*, pp. 90, 96–7.

were using lavishly beyond genuine household, agricultural, and industrial needs, nothing seemed to check the Southwest; water was still abundant in and near the Columbia basin. Moreover, though the new Westerners talked of the glory of the outdoors and even made forays into it, they were content to live in cities, like their ancestors of the early years of settlement.

When the West did stop growing, as presumably it would some day, it might have an opportunity to make a better guess about what had been the essential conditions of Westernness—whether climate or the confrontation of space in one form or another, the memory of the past, or simply the possibility and expectation of immigration and growth in the future. Perhaps by that time it would have imported so much of the East, or the East so much of the West, that the question itself would have receded into the past with its answers. The prospect in the second century of American settlement was that the process of growth and change in any event would continue for some time to keep ahead of its historians.

Notes on Further Reading (1991)

These books are some that seem especially attractive for general reading. For the most part, they do not include the more specialized works cited in footnotes. Other titles appear in library catalogs, including the published catalogs of the Bancroft Library, the Giannini Library, and other major research libraries, and in published bibliographies, including those in some of these books.

I. INTRODUCTION

Although there are no histories of the six states of this book on the scale of those that Hubert Howe Bancroft published in seventeen volumes in 1884–90, textbook and other surveys of state and regional history are useful for reference; some are substantial interpretations. Among the most recent are Walton E. Bean and James J. Rawls, *California: An Interpretive History,* 5th ed. (New York: McGraw-Hill Book Company, 1988); Russell R. Elliott and William D. Rawley, *History of Nevada* (Lincoln: University of Nebraska Press, 1987); Michael P. Malone and Richard W. Etulain, *The American West: A Twentieth-Century History* (Lincoln: University of Nebraska Press, 1989); and Carlos A. Schwantes, *The Pacific Northwest, An Interpretive History* (Lincoln: University of Nebraska Press, 1989). Three volumes by Kevin Starr amount to a selective cultural history of American California: *Americans and the California Dream, 1850–1915* (New York: Oxford University Press, 1973); *Inventing the Dream: California through the Progressive Era* (New York: Oxford University Press, 1985); and *Material Dreams: Southern California through the 1920's* (New York: Oxford University Press, 1990). Ray Allen Billington: *The Far Western Frontier, 1830–1860* (New York: Harper & Brothers, 1956) emphasizes initial American penetration and occupation of the Southwest and the Pacific Northwest; Rodman W. Paul: *The Far West and the Great Plains in Transition, 1859–1900* (New York: Harper & Row, 1988) miners, stockraisers, and members of ethnic groups (especially attitudes toward ethnic minorities). Most textbook surveys of the American West have done little with the twentieth century. The most detailed of them, Ray Allen Billington and Martin Ridge: *Westward Expansion: A History of the American Frontier,* 5th ed. (New York: Macmillan Company, 1982), which extends only to 1896 and concerns physical far more than cultural change, has unusually full bibliographical notes, 159 pages in small type, extending into articles in periodicals.

II. THE FAR FAR WEST OF THE 1830s AND 1840s

John Francis Bannon: *The Spanish Borderlands Frontier, 1513–1821* (New York: Holt, Rinehart and Winston, 1970) describes Spanish outposts from the Floridas to California. In the same series, David J. Weber, *The Mexican Frontier, 1821–1846: The American Southwest under Mexico* (Albuquerque: University of New Mexico Press, 1982), while emphasizing political organization and change, says more of economic development. Warren L. Cook: *Flood Tide of Empire: Spain and the Pacific Northwest, 1543–1819* (New Haven: Yale University Press, 1973) relates exploration and diplomacy. James D. Hart, *The Plate of Brass Reconsidered: A Report Issued by the Bancroft Library* (Berkeley: University of California Press, 1977) surveys controversy over alleged evidence of a visit by Francis Drake, a later contribution to which is Harry Kelsey: "Did Francis Drake Really Visit California?" *Western Historical Quarterly,* XXI (November 1990), 444–62. John Bakeless, *Lewis and Clark, Partners in Discovery* (New York: William Morrow & Co., 1947), and David Lavender: *The Way to the Western Sea: Lewis and Clark across the Continent* (New York: Harper & Row, 1988) are well-written narratives. Kenneth W. Porter: *John Jacob Astor: Businessman,* 2 vols. (Cambridge: Harvard University Press, 1931) remains definitive. James P. Ronda: *Astoria & Empire* (Lincoln: University of Nebraska Press, 1990) sees Astor's enterprise as a phase of a struggle for sovereignty in the Pacific. The large settings of the fur trade appear in Frederick Merk's introduction to *Fur Trade and Empire: George Simpson's Journal, 1824–1825* (Cambridge: Harvard University Press, 1931); John S. Galbraith: *The Hudson's Bay Company as an Imperial Factor, 1821–1869* (Berkeley: University of California Press, 1957); and E. E. Rich: *The History of the Hudson's Bay Company, 1670–1870,* 2 vols. (London: Hudson's Bay Record Society, 1958). On the southwestern fur trade, Robert G. Cleland: *This Reckless Breed of Men: The Trappers and Fur Traders of the Southwest* (New York: Alfred A. Knopf, 1950) covers more territory than David J. Weber: *The Taos Trappers: The Fur Trade in the Far Southwest, 1540–1846* (Norman: University of Oklahoma Press, 1971). David Lavender: *The Fist in the Wilderness* (Garden

City: Doubleday & Company, 1964) treats Astor's American Fur Company to 1834.

William H. Goetzmann: *Army Exploration in the American West, 1803–1863* (New Haven: Yale University Press, 1959); *Exploration and Empire: The Explorer and the Scientist in the Winning of the American West* (New York: Alfred A. Knopf, 1966); and *New Winds, New Men: America and the Second Great Age of Discovery* (New York: Viking Press, 1986) put western explorations in the context of science, eastern expectations, and government's contributions to development. William H. Goetzmann and William N. Goetzmann: *The West of the Imagination* (New York: Norton, 1986) parallels a series on television.

Frederick Merk analyzes national policy and popular attitudes searchingly in *Manifest Destiny and Mission in American History: A Reinterpretation* (New York: Alfred A. Knopf, 1963) and (with Lois Bannister Merk) *The Monroe Doctrine and American Expansionism, 1843–1849* (New York: Alfred A. Knopf, 1966). Henry Nash Smith: *Virgin Land: The American West as Symbol and Myth* (Cambridge: Harvard University Press, 1950) traces their literary images. Donald W. Meinig: *The Great Columbia Plain: A Historical Geography, 1805–1910* (Seattle: University of Washington Press, 1968) describes the strategy of organizing and developing a region. Neal Harlow: *California Conquered: War and Peace on the Pacific, 1846–1850* (Berkeley: University of California Press, 1982) narrates the American occupation; Harlan Hague and David J. Langun, *Thomas O. Larkin: A Life of Patriotism and Profit in Old California* (Norman: University of Oklahoma Press, 1990) is a biography of the trader and consul who prepared for it. Iris Higbie Wilson: *William Wolfskill, 1798–1866: Frontier Trapper to California Ranchero* (Glendale, Calif.: Arthur H. Clark Company, 1965) describes a pioneer who went to Los Angeles in 1830. John D. Unruh: *The Plains Across: The Overland Emigrants and the Trans-Mississippi West, 1840–60* (Urbana: University of Illinois Press, 1979) analyzes social processes. George R. Stewart: *The California Trail: An Epic with Many Heroes* (New York: McGraw-Hill Book Company, Inc., 1962) more briefly chronicles changes in migration year by year. Dale L. Morgan, ed., *Overland in 1846: Diaries and Letters of the California-Oregon Trail* (Georgetown, Calif.: Talisman Press, 1963) is useful for tracing parties of emigrants. Julie Roy Jeffrey: *Frontier Women: The Trans-Mississippi West, 1840–1880* (New York: Hill and Wang, 1979) stands out in its genre. Harold Kirker: *California's Architectural Frontier: Style and Tradition in the Ninteenth Century* (San Marino: Huntington Library, 1960) describes cultural confluence. Robert J. Loewenberg: *Equality on the Oregon Frontier: Jason Lee and the Methodist Mission, 1834–43* (Seattle: University of Washington Press, 1976) analyzes purposes and strategies of missionaries. David Lavender: *Westward Vision: The Story of the Oregon Trail* (New

York: McGraw-Hill Book Company, Inc., 1963) emphasizes the early years of migration, to 1840. Wallace Stegner: *The Gathering of Zion: The Story of the Mormon Trail* (New York: McGraw-Hill Book Company, Inc., 1964) extends from Mormon beginnings to 1856. Leonard J. Arrington and Davis Bitton: *The Mormon Experience: A History of the Latter-day Saints* (New York: Alfred A. Knopf, 1979) is an institutional as well as narrative history.

Among accounts that focus more on Indians than on policies toward them and conflicts with them, Albert L. Hurtado: *Indian Survival on the California Frontier* (New Haven: Yale University Press, 1988) concentrates on the 1840s and 1850s. Douglas Monroy: *Thrown among Strangers: The Making of Mexican Culture in Frontier California* (Berkeley: University of California Press, 1990) treats natives and Iberians through the nineteenth century. Stephen Dow Beckham: *Requiem for a People: The Rogue Indians and the Frontiersmen* (Norman: University of Oklahoma Press, 1959); Alvin M. Josephy, Jr.: *The Nez Perce Indians and the Opening of the Northwest* (New Haven: Yale University Press, 1965); and Robert I. Burns: *The Jesuits and the Indian Wars of the Northwest* (New Haven: Yale University Press, 1965) describe some of the last of the wars.

For general narrative, Bernard De Voto: *The Course of Empire* (Boston: Houghton Mifflin Company, 1952), *Across the Wide Missouri* (Boston: Houghton Mifflin, 1947), and *The Year of Decision, 1846* (Boston: Houghton Mifflin, 1943) are vivid. David Lavender: *Land of Giants: The Drive to the Northwest, 1750–1950* (New York: Doubleday & Company, 1958) emphasizes adventure.

III. POT OF GOLD

Rodman W. Paul: *California Gold: The Beginning of Mining in the Far West* (Cambridge: Harvard University Press, 1947) analyzes the technology and social dimensions of mining. Richard H. Dillon: *Fool's Gold: The Decline and Fall of Captain John Sutter of California* (New York: Coward-McCann, Inc., 1967) does not supersede James P. Zollinger: *Sutter: The Man and His Empire* (New York: Oxford University Press, 1939). David M. Potter's prefaces and introduction to *Trail to California: The Overland Journal of Vincent Geiger and Wakeman Bryarly* (New Haven: Yale University Press; 1945, 1962) put the record of a company of goldseekers in a setting of general experience on the trails and of scholarly interpretation. J. S. Holliday: *The World Rushed In: The California Gold Rush Experience* (New York: Simon and Schuster, 1981) draws on a miner's diary and letters to illustrate a general experience. Robert L. Kelley: *Gold vs. Grain: The Hydraulic Mining Controversy in California's Sacramento Valley* (Glendale, Calif.: Arthur H. Clark Company, 1959) treats the problem of debris in streams.

Beyond California, Rodman W. Paul: *Mining Frontiers of the Far West, 1848–1880* (New York: Holt, Rinehart and Winston: 1963) emphasizes institutional development more than the longer narrative of William S. Greever: *The Bonanza West: The Story of the Western Mining Rushes, 1848–1900* (Norman: University of Oklahoma Press, 1963). Clark C. Spence: *Mining Engineers and the American West: The Lace-Boot Brigade, 1849–1933* (New Haven: Yale University Press, 1970) describes a social element as well as advancing technology. Spence: *British Investments and the American Mining Frontier, 1860–1901* (Ithaca: Cornell University Press, 1958) and W. Turrentine Jackson: *The Enterprising Scot: Investors in the American West after 1973* (Edinburgh: Edinburgh University Press, 1968) treat both capital and capitalists; Jackson in cattle, railroads, and other enterprises as well as in mining. William J. Trimble: *The Mining Advance into the Inland Empire: A Comparative Study of the Beginnings of the Mining Industry in Idaho and Montana, Eastern Washington and Oregon, and the Southern Interior of British Columbia; and of Institutions and Laws Based upon That Industry* (Madison: University of Wisconsin, 1914) offers another kind of international perspective. Duane S. Smith: *Rocky Mountain Mining Camps: The Urban Frontier* (Bloomington: Indiana University Press, 1967) reaches as far west as Idaho, although not Nevada. Eliot Lord: *Comstock Mining and Miners,* U.S. Geological Survey Monographs, Vol. 4 (Washington: Government Printing Office, 1883; Berkeley, Calif.: Howell-North, 1959) is so colorful that local historians have borrowed heavily from it. It and Mark Twain: *Roughing It* (Hartford: American Publishing Company, 1872) are the most readable of contemporary accounts of pioneer Nevada. W. Turrentine Jackson: *Treasure Hill: Portrait of a Silver Mining Camp* (Tucson: University of Arizona Press, 1963); describes a mining district in eastern Nevada whose boom lasted from 1867 to 1869. Russell R. Elliott: *Nevada's Twentieth-Century Mining Boom: Tonopah, Goldfield, Ely* (Reno: University of Nevada Press, 1966) describes strikes in a setting of townsite and railroad promotion. John Fahey: *The Ballyhoo Bonanza: Charles Sweeny and the Idaho Mines* (Seattle: University of Washington Press, 1971) is the biography of an entrepreneur in the lead and silver mines of the Coeur d'Alene.

IV. POLITICAL TIES

On plans for American title, Norman A. Graebner: *Empire on the Pacific: A Study in American Continental Expansion* (New York: Ronald Press Company, 1955) emphasizes the object of controlling coastal harbors.

See also David M. Pletcher: *The Diplomacy of Annexation: Texas, Oregon, and the Mexican War* (Columbia: University of Missouri Press, 1973). Charles Howard Shinn: *Mining Camps: A Study in American Frontier Government* (New York: Charles Scribner's Sons, 1885; New York: Harper & Row, 1965) is still useful despite strained attempts to find European roots. Josiah Royce: *California, from the Conquest in 1846 to the Second Vigilance Committee in San Francisco: A Study of American Character* (Boston: Houghton, Mifflin and Co., 1886; New York: Alfred A. Knopf, 1948; Santa Barbara: Peregrine Publishers, Inc., 1970) exposes the frailty of early political ties and social morality. William H. Ellison: *A Self-Governing Dominion: California, 1849–1860* (Berkeley: University of California Press, 1950) traces political assimilation.

Howard R. Lamar: *The Far Southwest, 1846–1912: A Territorial History* (New Haven: Yale University Press, 1966) puts territorial government in a large setting, going much more into its economic dimensions and into local politics than earlier accounts; it also is the best general political history of Utah, Colorado, and Arizona. For the Oregon country, John A. Hussey: *Champoeg: Place of Transition, A Disputed History* (Portland, Oregon Historical Society, 1967) expertly reconstructs the vanished site of pioneer government. James E. Hendrickson: *Joe Lane of Oregon: Machine Politics and the Sectional Crisis, 1849–1861* (New Haven: Yale University Press, 1967) extends the picture of Robert W. Johannsen: *Frontier Politics and the Sectional Conflict: The Pacific Northwest on the Eve of the Civil War* (Seattle: University of Washington Press, 1955). Norman F. Furniss: *The Mormon Conflict, 1850–1859* (New Haven: Yale University Press, 1960) and Gustive O. Larson: *The "Americanization" of Utah for Statehood* (San Marino: The Huntington Library, 1971) relate political conflict and assimilation; Larson to statehood in 1896. Gilman M. Ostrander: *Nevada: The Great Rotten Borough, 1859–1864* (New York: Alfred A. Knopf, 1966) traces the stakes and structure of politics.

V. A BROADER ECONOMIC BASIS

The best economic histories of Far-Western states are Leonard J. Arrington: *Great Basin Kingdom: An Economic History of the Latter-day Saints, 1830–1900* (Cambridge: Harvard University Press, 1958) and Gerald D. Nash: *State Government and Economic Development: A History of Administrative Policies in California, 1849–1933* (Berkeley: University of California Press, 1964); Arrington's book in the context of social and religious institutions. Arthur L. Throckmorton: *Oregon Argonauts: Merchant Adventurers on the Western Frontier* (Portland: Oregon Historical Society, 1961) shows how mining supported development of a capital base.

On land, Paul W. Gates: *History of Public Land Law Development* (Washington: U.S. Government Printing Office, 1968) is indispensable, on disposition as on legislation. Gates, ed.: *California Ranches and Farms, 1846–1862. Including the Letters of John Quincy Adams Warren of 1861* . . . (Madison: State Historical Society of Wisconsin, 1967) surveys land grants, stockraising, crop farming, and irrigation. Gates: *Agriculture and the Civil War* (New York: Alfred A. Knopf, 1965) surveys development in the 1860s. Clarence H. Danhof: *Changes in Agriculture: The Northern United States, 1820–1870* (Cambridge: Harvard University Press, 1969) surveys technology, management, and marketing. Gilbert C. Fite: *The Farmers' Frontier, 1865–1900* (New York: Holt, Rinehart and Winston, 1966) describes both settlement and technology. J. Orin Oliphant: *On the Cattle Ranges of the Oregon Country* (Seattle: University of Washington Press, 1968) extends to 1890. E. Louise Peffer: *The Closing of the Public Domain: Disposal and Reservation Policies, 1900–50* (Stanford: Stanford University Press, 1951) emphasizes grazing lands. Reynold M. Wik: *Steam Power on the American Farm* (Philadelphia: University of Pennsylvania Press, 1954) describes early mechanization.

The role of government in transportation appears in W. Turrentine Jackson: *Wagon Roads West: A Study of Federal Road Surveys and Construction in the Trans-Mississippi West, 1846–1869* (Berkeley: University of California Press, 1952; New Haven: Yale University Press, 1965). Raymond W. Settle and Mary Lund Settle: *War Drums and Wagon Wheels: The Story of Russell, Majors, and Waddell* (Lincoln: University of Nebraska Press, 1966) describes wagon-freighting, stagecoach, and mail-carrying operations, 1854–61. Henry P. Walker: *Wagonmasters: High Plains Freighting from the Earliest Days of the Santa Fe Trail to 1880* (Norman: University of Oklahoma Press, 1966) extends as far west as Salt Lake City. Oscar O. Winther: *Express and Stagecoach Days in California* (Stanford: Stanford University Press, 1936) and Edward Hungerford: *Wells Fargo: Advancing the American Frontier* (New York: Random House, 1949) emphasize local color. On railroads, David Lavender: *The Great Persuader* (Garden City: Doubleday & Company, 1970) describes the promotional and financial maneuverings of Collis P. Huntington; Norman E. Tutorow: *Leland Stanford, Man of Many Careers* (Menlo Park: Pacific Coast Publishers, 1971) the enterprises of a more conspicuous associate. Don L. Hofsommer: *The Southern Pacific, 1901–1985* (College Station: Texas A & M University Press, 1986) is thorough, the best of the twentieth-century railroad histories. In Ralph W. Hidy, Muriel E. Hidy, and Roy V. Scott, with Don L. Hofsommer: *The Great Northern Railway: A History* (Boston: Harvard Business School Press, 1988), Hofsommer drew on unpublishable annals of finance and construction to write a model account. O. Meredith Wilson: *The Denver and Rio Grande Project, 1870–1901: A History of the First Thirty Years of the Denver and Rio Grande Railroad* (Salt Lake City: Howe Brothers, 1982) and Robert G. Athearn: *Union Pacific Country* (Chicago: Rand McNally & Company, 1971) treat two major systems in the nineteenth century. Athearn. *Rebel of the Rockies: A History of the Denver and Rio Grande Western Railroad* (New Haven: Yale University Press, 1962) continues with the D. & R. G. on a reduced scale to 1961. George W. Hilton: *American Narrow Gauge Railroads* (Stanford: Stanford University Press, 1990) is a detailed description and analysis, by an economist.

Among the more substantial studies of individual industries are Vincent P. Carosso: *The California Wine Industry: A Study of the Formative Years, 1830–1895* (Berkeley: University of California Press, 1951); Gerald T. White: *Scientists in Conflict: The Beginnings of the Oil Industry in California* (San Marino: Huntington Library, 1968); White: *Formative Years in the Far West: A History of Stanford Oil Company of California and Predecessors through 1919* (New York: Appleton-Century-Crofts, 1962); Thomas R. Cox: *Mills and Markets: The Pacific Lumber Trade to 1900* (Seattle: University of Washington Press, 1974); and Ralph W. Hidy, Frank E. Hill, and Allan Nevins: *Timber and Men: The Weyerhaeuser Story* (New York: Macmillan Company, 1963). Cox *et al.*: *This Well-Wooded Land: Americans and Their Forests from Colonial Times to the Present* (Lincoln: University of Nebraska Press, 1985) puts the resource of forests in a broad setting. John G. Clark, ed.: *The Frontier Challenge: Response to the Trans-Mississippi West* (Lawrence: University Press of Kansas, 1971) includes an essay by Vernon Carstensen on salmon canning.

VI. THE POWER OF THE METROPOLIS

The closest to a substantial general history of a city in the six states is the trilogy by Kevin Starr, which spans about eighty years of the histories of San Francisco and Los Angeles, 1850–1930, but only in selective views of cultural development. Other accounts concentrate on other dimensions and shorter periods. Roger W. Lotchin: *San Francisco, 1846–1856: From Hamlet to City* (New York: Oxford University Press, 1974) treats the economy, population, government, and social institutions. William Issel and Robert W. Cherny: *San Francisco, 1865–1932: Politics, Power, and Urban Development* (Berkeley: University of California Press, 1986) analyzes politics and processes of urban development in their social contexts. Judd Kahn: *Imperial San Francisco: Politics and Planning in an American City, 1897–1906* (Lincoln: University of Nebraska Press, 1979) makes the rejection of programs of civic improvement represented in the plans of Daniel P. Burnham a case study in progressive urban reform. Franklin Walker: *San Francisco's Literary Frontier* (New York: Alfred A. Knopf,

1939; Seattle: University of Washington Press, 1969) both develops cultural themes that Starr later treated at greater length and gives them social context. Oscar Lewis: *San Francisco: Mission to Metropolis* (Berkeley: Howell-North Books, 1966) is a popular survey. Robert L. Duffus: *The Tower of Jewels: Memories of San Francisco* (New York: W. W. Norton & Company, 1960) stands out among impressionistic memoirs.

On Los Angeles and its neighbors, Robert M. Fogelson: *The Fragmented Metropolis: Los Angeles, 1850–1930* (Cambridge: Harvard University Press, 1967) emphasizes consequences of real-estate and transit-company promotions. Franklin Walker: *A Literary History of Southern California* (Berkeley: University of California Press, 1950) is less literary than Walker's other books, with chapters on Americanization, the real-estate boom, irrigation, and interurban transit. Glenn S. Dumke: *The Boom of the Eighties in Southern California* (San Marino: Huntington Library, 1944) describes the first major influx. Carey McWilliams: *Southern California Country: An Island on the Land* (New York: Duell, Sloan & Pearce, 1946) is both sprightly and insightful social history, by an attorney, literary critic, administrator (chief, California Division of Immigration and Housing, 1939–42), and editor.

On other cities, the volumes published in the American Guide series in the 1930s and 1940s are still useful. Thomas G. Alexander and James B. Allen: *Mormons and Gentiles: A History of Salt Lake City* (Boulder, Colorado: Pruett Publishing Company, 1984) is indispensable, but interpretations of the larger Mormon community also explain much of Salt Lake City, including Thomas F. O'Dea: *The Mormons* (Chicago: University of Chicago Press, 1957), Leonard J. Arrington, Feramorz Y. Fox, and Dean L. May: *Building the City of God: Community & Cooperation among the Mormons* (Salt Lake City: Deseret Book Co., 1976), and other accounts cited above. George H. Hildebrand: *Borax Pioneer: Francis Marion Smith* (San Diego: Howell-North Books, 1982) is the biography of a mining entrepreneur who tried to build an empire of interurban railroads and real-estate developments in northern California as Henry E. Huntington did in southern California. Architectural approaches to the social history of cities include Harold Kirker: *California's Architectural Frontier: Style and Tradition in the Nineteenth Century* (San Marino: Henry E. Huntington Library; 1960); Joseph Armstrong Baird: *Time's Wondrous Changes: San Francisco Architecture, 1776–1915* (San Francisco: California Historical Society, 1962); and Victor Steinbrueck: *Seattle Cityscape* (Seattle: University of Washington Press, 1962). Gunther Barth surveys types of nineteenth-century western urban experience in *Instant Cities: Urbanization and the Rise of San Francisco and Denver* (New York: Oxford University Press, 1975), including a chapter on Salt Lake City.

VII. LIMITS OF WESTERN OPPORTUNITY

On miners, Vernon H. Jensen: *Heritage of Conflict: Labor Relations in the Nonferrous Metals Industry up to 1930* (Ithaca: Cornell University Press, 1950) remains useful. Mark Wyman: *Hard Rock Epic: Western Miners and the Industrial Revolution, 1860–1910* (Berkeley: University of California Press, 1979); Alan Derickson: *Workers' Health, Workers' Democracy: The Western Miners' Struggle, 1891–1925* (Ithaca: Cornell University Press, 1988), and Richard E. Lingenfelter: *The Hardrock Miners: A History of the Mining Labor Movement in the American West, 1860–1893* (Berkeley: University of California Press, 1974) describe conditions in which miners worked and how they responded.

Extending beyond mining, Martin F. Dubofsky: *We Shall Be All: A History of the Industrial Workers of the World* (Chicago: Quadrangle Books, 1969. 2nd ed.; Urbana: University of Illinois Press, 1988) is the most substantial in a large genre. See also Dubofsky, *"Big Bill" Haywood* (New York: St. Martin's Press, 1987). Patrick Renshaw: *The Wobblies: The Story of Syndicalism in the United States* (Garden City: Doubleday, 1967) is more popular. Joseph Robert Conlin: *Bread and Roses Too: Studies of the Wobblies* (Westport, Conn.: Greenwood Publishing Corp.) contrasts images with reality in essays placing the IWW in the larger labor movement. Robert L. Tyler: *Rebels of the Woods: The I.W.W. in the Pacific Northwest* (Eugene: University of Oregon Books, 1967) also treats images. Gibbs M. Smith: *Joe Hill* (Salt Lake City: University of Utah Press, 1969) explores a legend. Norman H. Clark: *Mill Town: A Social History of Everett, Washington, from Its Earliest Beginnings . . . to . . . the Everett Massacre* (Seattle: University of Washington Press, 1970) delineates an industrial baronage and its challengers.

VIII. THE PROGRESSIVE MOVEMENT

Michael Paul Rogin and John L. Shover, *Political Change in California: Critical Elections and Social Movements, 1890–1966* (Westport, Conn.: Greenwood Publishing Corp., 1970) and Spencer C. Olin, Jr.: *California's Prodigal Sons* (Berkeley: University of California Press, 1968) revise but do not supplant George E. Mowry: *The California Progressives* (Berkeley: University of California Press, 1951); both say more of working-class support. Robert V. Hine: *California's Utopian Colonies* (San Marino: Henry E. Huntington Library, 1953; New Haven: Yale University Press, 1966) describes Socialist and other communitarian movements that preceded the progressives. Claudius O. Johnson: *Borah of Idaho* (New York:

Longmans, Green & Co., 1936; Seattle: University of Washington Press, 1967) stands out still among political biographies partly because the subject cooperated with the author. Lincoln Steffens: *Upbuilders* (New York: Doubleday, Page & Company, 1909; Seattle: University of Washington Press, 1968) reprints articles on William S. U'Ren and Rudolph Spreckels of lasting value. Elmo R. Richardson: *The Politics of Conservation: Crusades and Controversies, 1897–1913* (Berkeley: University of California Press, 1962) relates a national movement to western politics.

IX. FUNDAMENTALISM: POLITICS BETWEEN THE WARS

Richard H. Frost: *The Mooney Case* (Stanford, Calif.: Stanford University Press, 1962) sifts the evidence carefully. Robert L. Friedheim: *The Seattle General Strike* (Seattle: University of Washington Press, 1964) is a careful reconstruction. Harvey O'Connor: *Revolution in Seattle: A Memoir* (New York: Monthly Review Press, 1964) presents a Socialist view. Tracy B. Strong and Helene Keyssar: *Right in Her Soul: The Life of Anna Louise Strong* (New York: Random House, 1983) is useful on the same events. Harold M. Hyman: *Soldiers and Spruce: Origins of the Loyal Legion of Loggers and Lumbermen* (Los Angeles: Institute of Industrial Relations, University of California, 1963) describes the Army's intervention and the decline of the I.W.W. Donald Garnel: *The Rise of Teamster Power in the West* (Berkeley: University of California Press, 1972) relates the ascendancy of Dave Beck in the 1930s to technological change. Charles P. Larrowe: *Harry Bridges: The Rise and Fall of Radical Labor in the United States,* 2d ed. (Westport, Conn.: Lawrence Hill & Co., 1977) is a substantial biography. Beverly Bowen Moeller: *Phil Swing and Boulder Dam* (Berkeley: University of California Press, 1971) recounts the battle for water for southern California in the 1920s. Norris Hundley: *Water and the West: The Colorado River Compact and the Politics of Water in the American West* (Berkeley: University of California Press, 1975) dissects the processes of agreement on complex legal and political questions. Jackson K. Putnam: *Old-Age Politics in California, From Richardson to Reagan* (Stanford: Stanford University Press, 1970) treats movements for the Townsend Plan and Ham and Eggs. Robert E. Burton: *Democrats of Oregon: The Pattern of Minority Politics, 1900–1956* (Eugene: University of Oregon Books, 1970) is the best political history of a Far-Western state for its period. Michael P. Malone: *C. Ben Ross and the New Deal in Idaho* (Seattle: University of Washington Press, 1970) describes an individualistic Democratic governor, 1931–37.

X. THE FAR WEST AND THE REST OF THE WORLD

The literature of immigrant history is belatedly extending beyond chronicles of discrimination. Roger Daniels gives useful overviews in *Coming to America: A History of Immigration and Ethnicity in American Life* (New York: HarperCollins, 1990) and *Asian America: Chinese and Japanese in the United States Since 1850* (Seattle: University of Washington Press, 1988). Shih-shan Henry Tsai: *The Chinese Experience in America* (Bloomington: Indiana University Press, 1986) relates the social organization of Chinese-Americans to the history of China. Gunther Barth: *Bitter Strength: A History of the Chinese in the United States, 1850–1870* (Cambridge: Harvard University Press, 1964) describes the operations of the merchants who financed immigration, the organization of immigrant communities, and processes of acculturation. Ping Chiu: *Chinese Labor in California, 1850–1880: An Economic Study* (Madison: State Historical Society of Wisconsin, 1963) analyzes roles in different fields of employment. Sucheng Chan: *This Bittersweet Soil: The Chinese in California Agriculture, 1860–1910* (Berkeley: University of California Press, 1986) describes a long-forgotten minority. Stuart C. Miller: *The Unwelcome Immigrant: The American Image of the Chinese, 1785–1882* (Berkeley: University of California Press, 1969) gives a wide setting to Sinophobia. Alexander Saxton: *The Indispensable Enemy: Labor and the Anti-Chinese Movement in California* (Berkeley: University of California Press, 1971) traces it to prejudice against Negroes.

On the Japanese: *East across the Pacific: Historical and Sociological Studies of Japanese Immigration and Assmilation*, Hilary Conroy and T. Scott Miyakawa, eds. (Santa Barbara: American Bibliographical Center–Clio Press, 1972) presents assorted case studies, 1850s to 1940s. Roger Daniels: *Concentration Camps USA: Japanese-Americans and World War II* (New York: Holt, Rinehart and Winston, 1971) surveys the experience of immigrants from the 1890s and describes events of 1942–45 from archival sources. Audrie Girdner and Anne Loftis: *The Great Betrayal: The Evacuation of the Japanese-Americans during World War II* (New York: Macmillan Company, 1969) draws on memoirs of opponents of removal; Bill Hosokawa: *Nisei: The Quiet Americans* (New York: William Morrow and Company, 1969) on interviews with evacuees in surveying the history of Japanese-Americans. Peter Irons documents violations of law and judicial process in *Justice at War* (New York: Oxford University Press, 1983) and *Justice Delayed: The Record of the Japanese American Internment Cases* (Middletown, Conn.: Wesleyan University Press, 1989).

On other minorities, Robert F. Heizer and Alan F. Almquist: *The Other Californians: Prejudice and Discrimination under Spain, Mexico, and the United States to 1920* (Berkeley: University of California Press, 1971) describes discriminatory acts and attitudes. Although Francis Paul Prucha focuses on Native Americans as acted on rather than actors in his masterly *The Great Father: The United States Government and the American Indians,* 2 vols. (Lincoln: University of Nebraska Press, 1984) he incidentally surveys wider developments and their literature. Leonard Pitt: *The Decline of the Californios: A Social History of the Spanish-Speaking Californians, 1846–1890* (Berkeley: University of California Press, 1966) surveys the break-up of Mexican and Spanish ranches. Richard Griswold del Castillo: *The Los Angeles Barrio, 1850–1890: A Social History* (Berkeley: University of California Press, 1979); Ricardo Romo: *East Los Angeles: History of a Barrio* (Austin: University of Texas Press, 1983); and Albert Camarillo: *Chicanos in a Changing Society: From Mexican Pueblos to American Barrios in Santa Barbara and Southern California, 1848–1930* (Cambridge: Harvard University Press, 1979) are case studies in quantified urban social history. Dino Cinel incorporates the European background of an emigrant-immigrant community in the style of the new immigrant history in *From Italy to San Francisco: The Immigrant Experience* (Stanford: Stanford University Press, 1982). Andrew F. Rolle: *The Immigrant Upraised: Italian Adventures and Colonists in an Expanding America* (Norman: University of Oklahoma Press, 1968) includes chapters on Italian-Americans in the Far West, emphasizing achievement rather than discrimination and alienation in response to the approach of Oscar Handlin in *The Uprooted* (Boston: Little, Brown, 1951).

XI. THE NEW FAST-GROWING WEST OF MIDCENTURY

Gerald D. Nash: *The American West Transformed: The Impact of the Second World War* (Bloomington: Indiana University Press, 1985) and *World War II and the West: Reshaping the Economy* (Lincoln: University of Nebraska Press, 1990) are indispensable. Walter J. Stein: *California and the Dust Bowl Migration* (Westport, Conn.: Greenwood Publishing Corp., 1973) describes migration from the south-central states in the 1930s. James N. Gregory: *American Exodus: The Dust Bowl Migration and Okie Culture in California* (New York: Oxford University Press, 1989) also analyzes social and economic roles of migrants during and after the Second World War. *Politics in the American West,* Frank H. Jonas, ed. (Salt Lake City: University of Utah Press, 1969) surveys the states in the style of articles on elections in the *Western Political Quarterly*. On California, G. Edward White: *Earl Warren: A Public Life* (New York: Oxford University Press, 1982) supersedes earlier accounts published during Warren's lifetime by Leo Katcher (*Earl Warren: A Political Biography* [New York: McGraw-Hill Book Company, 1967] and Richard B. Harvey: *Earl Warren: Governor of*

California [New York: Exposition Press, 1969]). See also *The Memoirs of Earl Warren* (Garden City: Doubleday and Company, 1977). Arthur H. Samish and Bob Thomas: *The Secret Boss of California: The Life and High Times of Art Samish* (New York: Crown Publishers, 1971) is the recollections of the lobbyist. Bill Boyarsky: *The Rise of Ronald Reagan* (New York: Random House, 1968) is by a journalist who saw it. Royce Delmatier, Clarence F. McIntosh, and Earl G. Waters, eds.: *The Rumble of California Politics, 1848–1970* (New York: Wiley, 1970) is a convenient collection of narratives. Robert C. Fellmeth, ed.: *Power and Land in California: The Ralph Nader Task Force Report on Land Use in the State of California* (Washington: Center for the Study of Responsive Law, 1971) is a useful brief. William L. Kahrl, ed.: *California Water Atlas* (Sacramento: California Office of Planning and Research, 1979) includes essays on the Hetch Hetchy Project and the Owens Valley Aqueduct. Nathan Cohen, ed.: *The Los Angeles Riots: A Socio-psychological Study* (New York: Praeger, 1970) and Robert Conot: *Rivers of Blood, Years of Darkness* (New York: Bantam, 1967) treat the riots at Watts in 1965. Essays in Rob Kling, Spencer Olin, and Mark Poster, eds.: *Postsuburban California: The Transformation of Orange County Since World War II* (Berkeley: University of California Press, 1991) analyze the social, economic, and political changes that developed with traffic on freeways from the 1950s.

XII. THE CHANGING OUTDOORS

Hans Huth: *Nature and the American: Three Centuries of Changing Attitudes* (Berkeley: University of California Press, 1957; Lincoln: University of Nebraska Press, 1990) traces in pictorial art the expectations that artists among others brought to the West and looks beyond them to plot expanding approaches to conservation. Robert Taft: *Artists and Illustrators of the Old West, 1850–1900* (New York: Charles Scribner's Sons, 1953), by a chemist who came into history as a student of photography, includes social history in accounts of artists. Roderick W. Nash: *Wilderness and the American Mind* (New Haven: Yale University Press, 1953, 1973, 1982) emphasizes preservationist approaches, extending to animal rights; it includes chapters on John Muir, Hetch Hetchy (which Holway R. Jones treats in *John Muir and the Sierra Club: The Battle for Yosemite* [San Francisco: Sierra Club; 1965]), and Aldo Leopold. More specialized explorations in intellectual and social history and biography include Susan Flader: *Thinking Like a Mountain: Aldo Leopold and the Evolution of an Ecological Attitude toward Deer, Wolves, and Forests* (Columbia: University of Missouri Press, 1974); Lee Clark Mitchell: *Witnesses to a Vanishing America: The Nineteenth-Century Response* (Princeton: Princeton University

Press, 1981); Stephen R. Fox: *John Muir and His Legacy: The American Conservation Movement* (Boston: Little, Brown, 1981); Michael P. Cohen: *The Pathless Way: John Muir and the American Wilderness* (Madison: University of Wisconsin Press, 1984); Frederick Turner: *Rediscovering America: John Muir in His Time and Ours* (New York: Viking, 1985); and Anne Farrar Hyde: *An American Vision: Far Western Landscape and National Culture, 1820–1920* (New York: New York University Press, 1990). Patricia Nelson Limerick draws on eight writers from John C. Frémont to Edward Abbey in *Desert Passages: Encounters with the American Deserts* (Albuquerque: University of New Mexico Press, 1985). Although Robert G. Athearn excluded the coastal states from his authentic West, he considers responses of tourists and their hosts, writers, and other buyers and sellers of images of parts of them in *The Mythic West in Twentieth-Century America* (Lawrence: University Press of Kansas, 1986). Gunther Barth: *Fleeting Moments: Nature and Culture in American History* (New York: Oxford University Press, 1990) treats responses of "people who . . . lived on the edge of nature or on the edge of culture" in the nineteenth century. On parks and movements to establish them and otherwise to protect wilderness, John F. Reiger: *American Sportsmen and the Origins of Conservation* (New York: Winchester Press, 1975); Alfred Runte: *National Parks: The American Experience* (Lincoln: University of Nebraska Press, 1979); Aubrey L. Haines: *The Yellowstone Story: A History of Our First National Park* (Yellowstone National Park, Wyo.: Yellowstone Library and Museum Associaton, 1977); Richard A. Bartlett: *Nature's Yellowstone* [to 1872] (Albuquerque: University of New Mexico Press, 1974), and *Yellowstone: A Wilderness Besieged* [chiefly 1872–1929] (Tucson: University of Arizona Press, 1985); Donald C. Swain: *Wilderness Defender: Horace M. Albright and Conservation* (Chicago: University of Chicago Press, 1970); and Thomas R. Cox: *The Park Builders: A History of State Parks in the Pacific Northwest* (Seattle: University of Washington Press, 1988).

In accounts of travelers and vacationers extending beyond the West, John A. Jakle: *The Tourist: Travel in Twentieth-Century America* (Lincoln: University of Nebraska Press, 1985) emphasizes quotations from published accounts of impressions and experiences; Warren James Belasco: *Americans on the Road: From Autocamp to Motel, 1910–1945* (Cambridge, Massachusetts: MIT Press, 1979) treats travel and travelers by automobile. Still broader surveys of the social history of automobiles include John B. Rae: *The Road and the Car in American Life* (Cambridge, Mass.: MIT Press, 1971), James J. Flink: *The Car Culture* (Cambridge, Mass.: MIT Press, 1975), and Virginia Scharff: *Women and the Coming of the Motor Age* (New York: Free Press, 1991).

Franklin Walker: *The Seacost of Bohemia: An Account of Early Carmel* (San Francisco: Book Club of California, 1966; Santa Barbara: Peregrine

Publishers, 1973) is a sketch of a literary colony that became a resort for the rich, in the vein of Walker's books on San Francisco and southern California. John M. Findlay: *People of Chance: Gambling in American Society from Jamestown to Las Vegas* (New York: Oxford University Press, 1986) and Eugene P. Moehring: *Resort City in the Sunbelt: Las Vegas, 1930–1970* (Reno: University of Nevada Press, 1990) treat a town that briefly tried to sell itself as the Wild West but built a metropolis on gambling tables.

INDEX

INDEX

Index

INDEX

Index